## DATE DUE

| | | | |
|---|---|---|---|
| | | | |
| | | | |
| | | | |
| | | | |
| | | | |
| | | | |
| | | | |
| | | | |
| | | | |
| | | | |
| | | | |
| | | | |
| | | | |
| | | | |
| | | | |
| | | | |
| | | | |
| | | | |
| | | | |
| | | | |
| | | | |

GAYLORD                                    PRINTED IN U.S.A.

# THE HANDBOOK
# OF MASS MEDIA ETHICS

*The Handbook of Mass Media Ethics* brings together the intellectual history of mass media ethics over the past 25 years. The chapters included summarize existing research and thinking in the field, as well as setting agenda items for future research that is grounded in both philosophy and the social sciences. Each chapter includes a section that summarizes current understanding and research, and contributions come from many of the best minds in the field, including international scholars. Many have worked as journalists, public relations professionals, or advertising practitioners.

The volume's coverage provides:

- Foundations set out to define the boundaries of the intellectual work that follows
- Professional practices that cross many professional boundaries
- Concrete issues, such as privacy and justice
- Institutional perspectives

Key features of the *Handbook* include:

- Up-to-date and comprehensive coverage of media ethics, one of the hottest topics in the media community
- "One-stop shopping" for historical and current research in media ethics
- Experienced, top-tier editors, advisory board, and contributors

Taken in total, *The Handbook of Mass Media Ethics* provides an examination of the depth and the breadth of current thinking on media ethics. For students and professionals who seek to understand and do the best work possible, this book will provide both insight and direction. Readers wanting to learn what scholars believe they know will find in this book a good grounding from which to begin more in-depth and individualized explorations, and the extensive bibliographies for each chapter will aid that process. Standing apart in its comprehensive coverage, the *Handbook* is required reading for scholars, graduate students, and researchers in media, mass communication, journalism, ethics, and related areas.

**Lee Wilkins** is the editor of the *Journal of Mass Media Ethics* and a member of the radio-television faculty at the University of Missouri School of Journalism. She holds a joint appointment in the Harry S. Truman School of Public Affairs.

**Clifford G. Christians** is the Charles H. Sandage Distinguished Professor and a Research Professor of Communications at the University of Illinois, Urbana-Champaign. He holds joint appointments as a Professor of Journalism and a Professor of Media Studies.

# THE HANDBOOK
# OF MASS MEDIA ETHICS

Edited by

Lee Wilkins
*University of Missouri*

and

Clifford G. Christians
*University of Illinois*

Routledge
Taylor & Francis Group

NEW YORK AND LONDON

First published 2009
by Routledge
270 Madison Ave, New York, NY 10016

Simultaneously published in the UK
by Routledge
2 Park Square, Milton Park, Abingdon, Oxon OX14 4RN

*Routledge is an imprint of the Taylor & Francis Group, an informa business*

Transferred to Digital Printing 2009

© 2009 Taylor & Francis

Typeset in Times and Helvetica by EvS Communication Networx, Inc.

*Library of Congress Cataloging in Publication Data*
The handbook of mass media ethics / [edited] by Lee Wilkins and Clifford G. Christians.
p. cm.
ISBN 978-0-8058-6191-4 — ISBN 978-0-8058-6192-1 — ISBN 978-1-4106-1548-0 1. Mass media—Moral and ethical aspects. I. Wilkins, Lee. II. Christians, Clifford G.
P94.H355 2008
175—dc22
2007045403


ISBN10 HB: 0-8058-6191-2
ISBN10 PB: 0-8058-6192-0
ISBN10 EB: 0-203-89304-2

ISBN13 HB: 978-0-8058-6191-4
ISBN13 PB: 978-0-8058-6192-1
ISBN13 EB: 978-0-203-89304-3

# CONTENTS

## PART III: CONCRETE ISSUES

## PART IV: INSTITUTIONAL CONSIDERATIONS

# CONTRIBUTORS

**G. Stuart Adam**
Carleton University
Ottawa, Ontario, Canada

**Mark D. Alleyne**
Georgia State University
Atlanta, Georgia

**Sherry Baker**
Brigham Young University
Provo, Utah

**Jay Black**
University of South Florida
St. Petersberg, Florida

**Sandra L. Borden**
Western Michigan University
Kalamazoo, Michigan

**Peggy Bowers**
Clemson University
Clemson, South Carolina

**Michael Bugeja**
Iowa State University
Ames, Iowa

**Kris E. Bunton**
University of St. Thomas
Minneapolis, Minnesota

**Michael X. Delli Carpini**
Annenberg School for Communication
University of Pennsylvania
Philadelphia, Pennsylvania

**Clifford G. Christians**
University of Illinois
Champagne, Illinois

**Renita Coleman**
University of Texas
Austin, Texas

**Thomas W. Cooper**
Emerson College
Boston, Massachusetts

**Stephanie Craft**
University of Missouri
Columbia, Missouri

**David A. Craig**
University of Oklahoma
Norman, Oklahoma

**Deni Elliott**
University of South Florida
St. Petersberg, Florida

**Mark Fackler**
Calvin College
Grand Rapids, Michigan

**John P. Ferré**
University of Louisville
Louisville, Kentucky

**Robert S. Fortner**
Calvin College
Grand Rapids, Michigan

**Kyle Heim**
University of Missouri
Columbia, Missouri

**Lou Hodges**
Washington and Lee University
Lexington, Virginia

*Seow Ting Lee*
Illinois State University
Bloomington, Illinois

*Matthew P. McAllister*
Pennsylvania State University
College Station, Pennsylvania

*Julianne H. Newton*
University of Oregon
Eugene, Oregon

*Patrick Lee Plaisance*
Colorado St. University
Ft. Collins, Colorado

*Jennifer M. Proffitt*
Florida State University
Tallahassee, Florida

*Linda Steiner*
Rutgers University
New Brunswick, New Jersey

*S. Holly Stocking*
Indiana University
Bloomington, Indiana

*Angharad N. Valdivia*
University of Illinois
Champagne, Illinois

*Stephen J. A. Ward*
University of Wisconsin
Madison, Wisconsin

*Edward Wasserman*
Washington and Lee University
Lexington, Virginia

*Ginny Whitehouse*
Whitworth University
Spokane, Washington

*Lee Wilkins*
University of Missouri
Columbia, Missouri

*Bruce A. Williams*
University of Virginia
Charlottesville, Virginia

*Wayne Woodward*
University of Michigan-Dearborn
Dearborn, Michigan

*Wendy Wyatt*
University of St. Thomas
Minneapolis, MN

# INTRODUCTION

## Lee Wilkins and Clifford G. Christians

This handbook is designed to fulfill five purposes,

First, as is noted in the chapter on the history of US media ethics, scholarly and professional attention to this broad topic has intensified since 1980. This work is scattered through a variety of academic journals, college-level texts, scholarly books and what academics refer to as the trade press—or the popular media of the day. It is time to bring the major insights in the field together—under a single roof. This book is intended to do that, in a thorough but not exhaustive, manner.

Second, the volume is intended to chart the progress in thinking about media ethics. What began as a largely professional quest to improve professional journalistic performance is now able, in a modest way, to contribute to that effort as well as academic efforts to further the insights of moral philosophy. The editors as well as the authors contend that mediated communication is essential to democratic functioning at the institutional level and to flourishing communities and individuals at other levels. Along the way, media ethics allows scholars to ask big questions: is technology morally neutral, is dialogue truly the best way to capture a world-wide conversation, are the understandings of classical ethical philosophy the best lens through which to make ethically based decisions involving entities as disparate as corporations, nation states, communities, and individuals. Readers will not find complete answers to any of these questions in this book; what they will discover is the state of intellectual progress that foregrounds ethical thinking in examining questions where mediated communication play a central role.

Third, the volume's authors attempt to set a research agenda for the field. Further, this agenda is grounded in both philosophy and in some of the social sciences. We believe this blend is unique and important. The facts of social science can inform ethical decision making; they cannot replace the central role of philosophy in that process. The chapters in this book model the effort to allow these often too separate areas of academic work to inform one another. The research questions posed here have both range and vision; the answers to them have the capacity to inform contemporary philosophical understandings as well as to change professional performance.

Fourth, the editors hope that students and citizens with some curiosity about particular issues will find individual chapters in this book a good place to start. Each chapter includes a section that summarizes current understandings and research in the field. In this way, each chapter has a bit of an encyclopedic feel. Readers curious about what scholars believe they know will find in this book a good grounding with which to begin more in-depth and individualized explorations. The extensive bibliographies for each chapter will aid that process. The editors hope that reading one chapter will lead to explorations in others.

Fifth, this book introduces students and their teachers to some of the best minds in the field. Contributors are an international group, and while most of them are Americans, their collective vision extends beyond that country. Many have worked as journalists, public relations professionals, advertising practitioners. Their efforts reflect the sort of understanding and respect for the field that is generated from doing daily work and then, as academics, having the luxury to think deeply about it. All are continuing to grow intellectually. Students who read (or access online) this book in years to come would do well to look and see what the authors writing here have produced since this volume was copyrighted.

Now to a preview of what is between these covers.

Part I: Foundations, sets out to define the boundaries of the intellectual work that follows. It begins with a discussion of the nature of the communicating human being, from biological organism to tool-using community member. Based in the intellectual work of the philosopher Hans Jonas, Wayne Woodward's chapter reviews the way that philosophers have analyzed the nature of the human animal and its vast symbolic capacity. It is through symbols that people build community, understand and confuse one another, and form political and social networks. Next, John Ferré examines the history of the intellectual field of mass media ethics from the American point of view. This view, linked as it is to democratic functioning, has come to dominate much thinking beyond the United States. Ferré traces four periods of intellectual inquiry, concluding with a search for universal ethical principles that has meaning for professionals regardless of geographic circumstance. Next, ethicist Deni Elliott argues that relativism impoverishes both professional performance and intellectual critique. Elliott's work demonstrates that journalists the world over share an emerging set of professional obligations. These obligations, although they are evolving thanks to the interactive medium of the Internet, still hold duties in common with the journalism of previous centuries. That commonality of journalistic ethical thinking is explored by Renita Coleman and Lee Wilkins. Their work begins with the insights of the first chapter of this book—that part of being human is the capacity to think ethically. They then explore the influences on that thinking and link it to moral development. Finally, Clifford Christians and Tom Cooper outline the need for universal ethical principles to guide professional performance. In the process, they link those principles to the larger world of all human activity and demonstrate why understanding the moral source of symbolic activity is the key to philosophy as well as professional work. In addition, they provide a review of why universal standards allow media consumers, as individuals who know themselves through their participation in political community, to evaluate and hold professionals accountable for the work they do.

Part II focuses on issues of professional practice that cross many professional boundaries, such as advertising compared to news, plus many intellectual ones, such as applied philosophy, linguistics, psychology and politics. Collectively, these chapters outline the gestalt contemporary professionals inhabit and focus on the range of issues they navigate. Stephen Ward begins the section with a chapter on truth and objectivity, placing these two concepts in an epistemic as well as professional domain. Ward's chapter must be considered in conjunction with the chapter that follows. Here, Julie Newton asks many of the same sorts of questions raised by Ward, applying then to the visual nature of truth and how that quality of truth influences the work of photojournalists and readers and viewers. The discussion of the nature of truth concludes in the chapter by Ginny Whitehouse who describes what the concepts of diversity, of sociotyping and of stereotyping, have to do with the way mediated messages in news and entertainment are produced and understood. Together, this trio of authors clearly articulates the complex nature of truth, one that is philosophically informed but which also is central to professional performance.

Next, this segment of the volume moves to two separable but related concepts—advocacy, specifically its role in public relations, and propaganda. Authors Sherry Baker and Jay Black develop integrative tools, informed by the fields of philosophy and linguistics, to allow professionals to measure their own performance. Baker is particularly concerned with the connection between public relations professionals and the larger society they serve through client-centered work. Black pays particular attention to the role of the public, and of individuals, in the persistence of propaganda, particularly the sort produced by democratic governments.

With the focus of the volume now moving concretely into the public sphere, the next two chapters tackle two thorny contemporary questions: pornography and violence. Wendy Wyatt and Kris Bunton demonstrate how emerging concepts of feminism have influenced both the law and production of mediated messages considered by some segments of society, but not by others, to be pornographic. They link their analysis to an ethic that places harm to viewers as the central problem of pornography. Patrick Plaisance also focuses on the ethics of harm in his discussion of violence. This chapter is noteworthy for the commonalities it finds between news and entertainment. Both of these chapters also pay serious attention to the larger cultural system in which these mediated messages flourish.

Bruce Williams and Michael Carpini also examine the role of mass media institutions in the political system. Eschewing previously established boundaries—in fact, insisting as does Deni Elliott in the foundations section, that journalism is entering a new paradigm—they develop a four-part, philosophically based, mechanism to evaluate political communication wherever viewers and readers find it. Their goal is the promotion of civic engagement and the authors demonstrate that non-traditional political communication—for example, *The Daily Show* or Internet blogs—can contribute as much as traditional news.

In the concluding chapter in this section, Angharad Valdivia demonstrates why the fungible nature of art and entertainment marketed worldwide by corporate conglomerates demands a universal ethical standard. Her chapter explores how evaluating art and entertainment through the lens of the protonorm of humanness can help both the producers and consumers of this symbolic media content better understand its impact on audiences and artists alike.

Part III turns to concrete issues, and just as in the previous section, the first three chapters are intellectual first cousins and hence have much to say to one another. David Craig's chapter on justice as a journalistic value opens this section with a discussion of how incorporating a concept of justice as one element in a definition of news as well as a role for the news media in general could and sometimes does inform news coverage. Justice is not traditionally considered an ethical imperative in news coverage. Just how those imperatives work, and whether journalists and news organizations should be transparent about them, is the focus of Stephanie Craft and Karl Heim's contribution. Craft and Heim note that transparency should not be considered a "fix" for the ailing credibility of the traditional news media; it has its downsides as well. Some of those downsides the structural routines of reporting and editing—give rise to difficult conflict of interest questions, the focus of Ed Wasserman's contribution. Wasserman points out that some conflicts are embedded in the act of reporting itself, while others are exacerbated by the profit-seeking nature of news organizations owned by corporate behemoths. Wasserman's chapter outlines why the classical remedies for conflict of interest, including the sort of disclosure that transparency would seem to demand, will improve journalistic performance in only a limited number of instances.

All three of these opening chapters make references to the Internet, the focus of Michael Bugeja's piece. Bugeja notes that many have suggested the Internet is the solution to what ails the media, but his nuanced analysis raises important questions, chief among them whether ethical values are easily exportable to the world of electrons. Bugeja's effort also provides a counterpoint to Newton's chapter in Part II of this book, for Bugeja questions whether any technology, but specifically the technology of the Internet, should be considered inherently positive or even ethically neutral. Based in part of the work of French philosopher/theologian Jacques Ellul, the questions raised here should inform discussion about the role of the Internet and the ethical implications of its content.

Chapters on peace journalism and privacy conclude this segment of the volume. While they are indeed concrete issues, Seow Ting Lee's exploration of peace journalism demonstrates that, in a world of conflict, peace journalism also has an international toehold. Privacy, too, has an international footprint. Lou Hodges provides a philosophic definition of the term and explains how a concept that emphasizes human dignity has implications for government as well as media professionals. Work on privacy has focused most extensively on journalism, but Hodges extends that analysis to advertising practitioners as well as entertainment coverage of celebrities.

The volume concludes with an institutional focus. Three theoretically oriented chapters open this section: S. Holly Stocking's chapter on Buddhist ethics, Mark Fackler's effort on communitarianism, and Stuart Adam's review of contractualism. These three chapters speak to each other. Stocking first defines the tenets of Buddhism and then demonstrates how they may be applied to journalism. In so doing, she opens the door to aspirations of "doing well by doing good," a theme that Fackler's contribution also emphasizes. Communitarianism may be more familiar than Buddhism to contemporary students, but Fackler's review suggests that, in these difficult times, communitarianism, too, faces obstacles, particularly as journalists struggle to define community and to understand themselves within it. Although communitarianism rejects a contractualist approach to ethics, Adam's chapter demonstrates the deep roots, and sometime effective outcomes, of contractualism in western intellectual history as it has been applied to speech, to democracy and hence to journalism.

The segment of the volume then turns to Matt McAllister and Jenn Proffitt's analysis of structure: specifically the impact of ownership on media content, ranging from news to comic books, and to why ownership matters in terms of the philosophical construct of autonomy and the relationship between the individual, the culture and the democratic political system.

Next, the volume moves from aspirations to their opposite: evil. Robert Fortner explores the role of media in evil circumstances. His chapter echoes the work on propaganda by Jay Black earlier in the volume and provides multiple examples of how the producers of news and entertainment have been corrupted for despicable ends. Journalism as a profession, and the ethical issues it shares with other professions, is the focus of Sandra Borden and Peggy Bowers' contribution. Your doctor, your city administrator, and your local newscaster share similar ethical concerns, and Borden and Bowers demonstrate how the understandings of one profession can inform others. Linda Steiner reviews the contributions of feminist ethics to understanding and improving media performance. Her chapter speaks not only to what media professionals produce but also their methods of information collection and the points of view that emerge from their work. The volume concludes with counterpoint chapter from Mark Alleyne about the difficulty of arriving at universals in the current context.

Taken in its totality, the book provides an introduction to both the depth and the breadth of current thinking on media ethics. At a time in the academy when applied ethics is attempting to regain a more equal footing with meta-ethics as it is traditionally taught, media ethics has much to contribute to the larger discussion. For students and for professionals who seek to understand their work, and to do the best work of which they are capable, this book will provide both insight and direction. And, for scholars whose life's work is adding, however incrementally, to the base of knowledge on which we all stand, this volume has suggestions aplenty. The editors hope that you learn as much from reading it as we have from editing it.

Enjoy.

# I
# FOUNDATIONS

# 1

# A Philosophically Based Inquiry into the Nature of Communicating Humans

## Wayne Woodward

Inquiry into the 'nature' of communicating humans is certain to strike some readers as misdirected, a step backwards towards a way of thinking that was surpassed through awareness of the discursive, culturally-based (i.e., distinctly 'non-natural') character of human communicative activities. Accordingly, the topic of this chapter requires preliminary justification and an orienting perspective with regard to its central concepts.

The writings of philosopher Hans Jonas (1966, 1974, 1984, 1996) provide the basic framework adopted here for addressing the question of how ideas associated with 'natural' processes can, and should be appropriately employed to examine cultural practices such as communication. Jonas may appear to be an idiosyncratic choice, since he is not widely regarded as a central contributor to a philosophy of communication, nor to communication theory, per se. He should be. The relevance of Jonas' perspective is his consistent adherence, during a long and accomplished philosophical career, to certain foundational premises meant to guide the study of human practices, premises that are basic to comprehending the activities and actions of humans communicating.

The first is that interdependencies between inward experience (i.e., consciousness, the psychological dimensions of meaning-making) and outward experience (i.e., the externalization of consciousness in the form of material productions and observable behaviors) need to be taken into account, theoretically and empirically, in comprehending how humans exercise meaning-making capacities. The aim is to "restore life's psychophysical unity to its place in the theoretical totality, lost on account of the divorce of the mental and the material since the time of Descartes" (Jonas, 1996, p. 59). Analysis considers how "symbolic forms" (Thompson, 1995, p. 18), i.e., diverse formats and genres of communication, develop interdependently with the "*technical medium*" or "material substratum" employed in any instance of communication. Significant attributes associated with technical media include the ability to provide for durable "fixation" (p. 19) of content; ease of reproduction (p. 20); and "*space-time distanciation*" (p. 21), i.e., the spatial/temporal "detachment of a symbolic form from its context of production." In line with these capacities, changes in technical media become interlinked with the development of particular formats and concentrations of content while providing resources for "the exercise of different forms of power" (p. 19).

Thus, social roles and the attainment of status and authority should be considered historically as significantly a matter of how information and knowledge are produced, collected, stored,

augmented, transformed, and retrieved (see Carey, 1989, p. 23), along with how content is transmitted and exchanged through institutional practices. For example, the earliest forms of writing
developed by Sumerians and ancient Egyptians were put to economic uses, such as supporting
property ownership and facilitating trade (Thompson, 1995, p. 19). Today, these interests are
carried forward into a globalizing, digital age, as high-powered computers allow for vast flows
of financial information while diminishing the historically-perceived "tyranny of geography"
(Gillespie & Robins, 1989, p. 7) and turning transactional time into nanoseconds. The analytical
insight is that dramatic transformations take place within broader patterns of continuities. These
patterns are constituted through communication as "a symbolic process whereby reality is produced, maintained, repaired, and transformed" (Carey, 1989, p. 23).

Jonas' second premise is that this demand to integrate analysis of the inner and outer, and the
semantic and the material, can be best met by elaborating how a "philosophy of life comprises
the philosophy of organism and the philosophy of mind" (Jonas, 1974, p. xvii). Humans, along
with other life forms, must derive ways to thrive as organisms in their environments; yet, our
species is distinguished by the particular capabilities of mind that inform the human response to
this fundamental challenge. Since communication is a way of extending mind (see Carey, 1969,
p. 273), understanding the role of communication becomes central to a philosophical understanding of life. Furthermore, as Jonas (1966) notes, "a philosophy of mind comprises ethics—and
through the continuity of mind with organism and organism with nature, ethics becomes part of
the philosophy of nature" (p. 282).

This trajectory of thought allows for distinctive dimensions of human experience, notably
symbolic meaning-making and ethical directedness in actions and relations, to be considered as
part of an integrative picture of human life. From this vantage point, scholars can address the
widest spectrum of contributing factors in human activity—"metabolism, moving and desiring,
sensing and perceiving, imagining and thinking" (Vogel, 1996, p. 10). Basic modes of organismic contact with the environment, as well as advanced socio-cultural and technological ways
of impressing individual and collective intentions and projects on shared worlds of experience,
should be seen as orders of complexity and meaningfulness. These biological elements spring
from a primeval, natural drama that becomes historically conditioned within "an ascending scale
in which are placed the sophistications of form, the lure of sense and the spur of desire, the command of limb and powers to act, the reflection of consciousness and the reach for truth" (Jonas,
1966, p. 2). Communication is, arguably, the key element within repertoires of instinctual, programmable, and creative functions and faculties that undergird this pageant.

Third, special consideration should be directed towards technological practices, since these
have come to be regarded, in modern and postmodern societies especially, as humankind's

> most significant enterprise, in whose permanent, self-transcending advance to ever greater things
> the vocation of man [sic] tends to be seen, and whose success of maximal control over things and
> himself appears as the consummation of his destiny. (Jonas, 1984, p. 9)

Technological augmentation of communication has been a constitutive feature of social interaction in nearly all societies and in so-called advanced societies in particular (see Couch,
1990, 1996). Jonas contends that the modern results of this general path of development should
be critically examined, with particular attention to ethical implications. The "technologizing of
the word" (Ong, 2002) merits special attention as the transformations from oral culture, to manu-
scripts, print, and electronic-digital communications play out in the psyches and the social relations that characterize different eras and societies.

To summarize this set of points derived from Jonas: (1) Communication should be addressed
as human consciousness in vital action, including attention to the material, or physical-artifactual

(see Woodward, 1996) contexts for action. (2) Consciousness and action, with their basis in "the state of being affected and spontaneity" (Jonas, 1996, p. 69), need to be approached with an analytical lens focused on the continuity of human life with other life forms. These range from the simplest organisms, to complex hybrid systems that combine human agency with cybernetic programming. (3) Particular emphasis should be placed on the role of technology as a set of developments that conditions the direction and destiny—for better or worse—that humans embrace through consciousness and set out to realize through communicative action.

These commitments lead to a substantive concept of nature focused on the "omnipresence of life" (Jonas, 1966, p. 8) of which humans and human communication form a part. Nature is "continuity of life forms" (pp. 59 ff.), a phrase that describes and is a "logical complement to the scientific genealogy of life" (p. 63); and the continuity of life forms is significantly a matter of their capacities for organization of information, ultimately of meaning.

> [I]nformation flow, not energy per se, is the prime mover of life…molecular information flowing in circles brings forth the organization we call "organism" and maintains it against the ever-present disorganizing pressures in the physics universe. So viewed, the information circle becomes the unit of life. (Loewenstein, 1999, pp. xv–xvi)

Human communicators have played an obvious, distinctive role within this genealogy of life. Persons develop and exercise unique "potencies" (Buber, 1965a, p. 163) for "knowledge, love, art, and faith." Institutionalized practices result from the exercise of these potencies, as collectivities construct modes of education, norms for family life and community, artistic traditions, and religions. These institutional forms emerge within specific, historically- and culturally-situated contexts. Social roles and identities, along with the person's most basic sense of self, undergo transformations as social actors respond—individually and in collectivities, in conformity with and in opposition to institutional conventions—by shaping perceptions, consciousness, agency, and interactions into "forms of relation" (Jonas, 1966, p. 4). These relations constitute the basis for human, personal identity and provide templates for social cooperation, competition, and conflict.

## THE ANIMAL THAT COMMUNICATES TO DEFINE THE SELF

From this foundational position, Jonas went on to investigate a wide variety of concerns relevant to communication studies: How the "irritability" (Jonas, 1966, p. 99) of the simple cell might be usefully considered as the "germ" of "having a world," which then develops through the experiences of human consciousness into a "world relationship"; the interventions into human purposefulness and behavior of "servomechanisms" (p. 109), such as target-seeking torpedoes, electronic computers, telephone exchanges, and how these may call for reexamination of theories of the human, society, and the nature of the good, the *summum bonum*; investigations of the philosophical dimensions of public policy debates including critical-interpretive, ethical, and phenomenological inquiries into biomedical practices, genetic engineering, euthanasia.

Stepping back again from the appreciation Jonas often expressed for the evolved quality of human capabilities, in order to continue concentrating for a moment more on their organic foundations, one observes with all live entities and systems that "life is essentially relationship; and relation as such implies 'transcendence,' a going-beyond-itself on the part of that which enters the relation" (Jonas, 1966, pp. 4–5). Such "going beyond" entails a degree of freedom that operates even deep within the genealogical substratum of life, in "the dark stirrings of primeval organic substance" (p. 3), since "metabolism, the basic level of all organic existence…is itself the first form of freedom...[one that]...shines forth...within the vast necessity of the physical universe." When living entities develop beyond "mere dynamism" (Jonas, 1996, p. 70) to become "selective and 'informed'" in their metabolic directedness, a natural 'prototype' of "inner identity" has appeared. For all life forms, "being open to what is outside, becomes the subject-pole of a communication with things which is more intimate than that between merely physical units." The movement is from causal patterns of determination and control to forms of agency and responsibility that herald a human capacity to develop towards intellectual and moral freedom.

Jonas shares his insistence on the continuity of life with other phenomenological philosophers who have emphasized "the interrelationship of matter, life, and consciousness" (Cooper, 1991, p. 15). The common premise is that life involves participation; in the case of humans, the processes entail "consciousness transcending itself into the lived body, into the community, history and the divine ground of being" (p. 15). But all life processes, "even the 'simplicities' of metabolism," involve a degree of distinctiveness to be achieved by the life form in question, a particularity that can be considered as "the measure of its independence from its own material contents." This "differentiation of the modes of participation, from inanimate material to animate nature, to the specific modes of human existence" (p. 14), is inherently communicative: The preservation of distinctive forms occurs as activity patterns are traced through time and etched across space, within one or another common medium for behavior or experience that constitutes an organismic environment or a human world. Thus, communication is adaptive in its origins, creative in its human expressions, and complexly combines programmable logic with active agency in its more intricate technological manifestations.

Attending briefly to the elementary case of plant life, one observes that inner need extends towards outer resources through limited relations grounded in physical contiguity and immediacy of exchange. The defining characteristic of a plant's existence is "openness for encountering external reality" (Jonas, 1996, p. 69), based on the condition that "living form must have matter at its disposal, which it finds outside itself in the alien 'world'" (p. 68). Plant life exhibits "outward *exposure*" (p. 69) and "the state of being affected." Communication takes the limited form here of material exchange.

Animal life operates with an expanded repertoire of organic potencies, achieving a further "horizon of freedom" (Jonas, 1996, p. 67). The mobile animal, guided by often highly proficient, instinctually-directed senses of sight, sound, smell, taste, and touch, manifests more dynamic relations within space and time. Concerning "*space*, as the dimension of dependence" (p. 71), the animal's capacity for more active control allows its spatial environment to be "progressively transformed into a dimension of freedom, specifically by the parallel development of the following two abilities: to move about and to perceive at a distance." Similarly, "*time*...is opened up by the parallel development of a third ability, namely emotion...." The animal's capabilities to extend the imperatives of instinctual need across physical space and to preserve the stirrings of need through 'temporal distance' or duration, make the communication of a still-nascent, inner identity with external objects and living things a more actively motivated process than with plant life. Two "distinguishing characteristics" (Carey, 1989, p. 27) of symbolic action, even in its rudimentary forms, are "displacement and productivity": The first reconfigures action from a situation of required, physical co-presence with its stimulus, to a situation in which the stimulating factor can be 'indicated' through some form of representation (see Millikan, 2004, p. 17); the second characteristic allows for multiple representations to accompany an action and for these to play a role in constituting the situation as well as symbolizing it. One might be inclined to consider these as traits solely of human communication, but current research suggests that many animals also employ a "'functional semantics'" (Oller & Griebel, 2004, p. 5), involving a "primitive representational form wherein both 'what is the case'"—i.e., symbolic, or representational displacement of an environmental circumstance—"and 'what to do about it'"—i.e., productivity in the form of instructions about how to act in the case in question—"are transmitted simultaneously." Communicative processes "can be used either to reflect states of affairs or to produce them" (Millikan, 2004, p. 17); thus, they face in two directions at once.

> Does the dance of the honeybee tell where the nectar is, or does it tell worker bees where to go? Clearly, it does both.... Similarly, alarm calls of the various species do not just represent present danger but are also signs directing conspecifics to run or to take cover.

Approaching the domain of human potencies, one observes (1) how an ever-emergent, increasingly complex 'self' not only *exists* in a situation of dependence or interdependence with other entities, a feature shared even with plant life; (2) how the ability of the self to *act* on this situation involves expanded levels of flexibility beyond those of animals; additionally (3) the human self advances towards a continuously redefined quality of ontological, active, and expressive freedom, constructed in circumstances of mutual-personal *relation* (Kirkpatrick, 1986; Macmurray, 1991).

The common element—manifested as a trait in the case of plants and animals, as a vital faculty within human existence—can be usefully thought of as "impressibility" (Woodward, 2000, p. 355). In forms of life that are basically reactive in their responses to environment, impressibility consists of metabolic processes and instinctually-guided behaviors. In humans, impressibility becomes the basis for enactment, the ability of agents to impress their meanings, values, and projects on the world through communication. Impressibility, as communication, is both receptive and productive: Agents are simultaneously responding to the world, while also acting in relation to the world.

The distinctively human form of transactional response and initiative is *"situated creativity"* (Joas, 1996, p. 133), wherein human innovativeness transforms "unreflected routine" (p. 129) into "acts of creativity." Based on the premise that "[a]ll action is embedded in anthropological structures of communication" (p. 133), this view asserts that "creativity is more than merely one of the necessities for the survival of an organism." It is, in human life, "the liberation of the capacity for new actions." John Dewey (1958) famously summarized the indissoluble linkages at play. "Experience is the result, the sign, and the reward of that interaction of organism and environment which, when it is carried to the full, is a transformation of interaction into participation and communication" (p. 22). In short, "[c]ommunication is the process of creating participation, of making common what had been isolated and singular...." (p. 244). Being is always and inevitably co-being (Holquist, 2002, p. 25); and for human communicators, being as co-being develops as both a conscious, reflective theme of living and as a source of desires and bodily repertoires that impress unconscious demands on action and experience.

Human communication marks a distinctive threshold of ontological advance in the development of impressibility as perception, knowledge, action, and relation. Simple and complex forms of "inter-personal and inter-group coordination" (Garnham, 2000, p. 3) derive from innate, communicative capacities connected with the "human species'" (p. 2) large brain and the organic requirements for sociality imposed by this endowment.

> This brain has enabled it [the human species] to develop culture...patterns of behaviour which are not merely instinctual, but are endowed with meanings which can be transmitted through space and time beyond the immediate stimulus/response site of action, and a learning process the lessons of which are cumulative and open to criticism and modification in the light of experience. (p. 2)

As humans develop, their coordination of environmentally relevant activities occurs in, and reciprocally gives continuous rise to, historically situated configurations of "what we might call institutions as well as structures" (p. 23). Human life has then achieved a level at which "a life informed by convention is natural for human beings in much the way that perception, nutrition, growth, and reproduction are natural" (Wallace, 1978, p. 34). The "potencies" that Buber identified find their appropriate expression in institutions that both fund and result from human inventiveness and creativity. On this basis, persons can make legitimate normative claims to have access and to participate in—and to make their own 'impress' on—social, cultural, political, and economic life as it develops through institutional activities.

## COMMUNICATION GIVES RISE TO SOCIAL INSTITUTIONS

Human communicators, as social beings, are active inventors of meaning, situated in environmental fields (Bourdieu, 1985) that are also human worlds (Schutz, 1967). Worldly, environmental fields can also be considered as 'active' in the sense that they condition human activities. "Human expressivity is capable of objectification, that is, it manifests itself in products of human activity that are available both to their producers and to other men as elements of a common world" (Berger & Luckmann, 1966, p. 34). The patterning of environmental elements follows spatial and temporal logics that can tend to become self-organizing—"autopoietic" (Luhmann, 1989, p. 143)—and these environmental logics enter into the acts of communicators and the shaping of communications. In the process, a "duality of structure" (Giddens, 1979, p. 5) is seen to operate, enabling and constraining human action; this duality also applies to human institutions in their historical role of expanding the boundaries of human accomplishment and aspiration while resetting limits on these boundaries.

"The kinds of spaces created by media, and the effects that existing spatial arrangements have on media forms as they materialize in everyday life," are particularly pertinent to understanding communication. Technological invention allows for dramatic expansion of the human capability to extend motivations and meanings across space and to preserve them through time. Technological augmentation of human experience intensifies a committed sense not only of what *does* and *can* occur within a life situation, but what also *must* occur in order for personal identity to express its felt dynamism, and ultimately to achieve an increasingly sought-after sense of creative inspiration and expression that emerges as an ideal (see Taylor, 1985, p. 22). Thus, technological power and expressivity, as fundamental dimensions of vital action, raise moral and ethical questions for the human, social actor.

Sophocles' *Antigone* (see Jonas, 1974, p. 4) conveys dramatically how the technological expansion of human powers can heighten questions concerning their appropriate use. Sophocles' Chorus tells how man "crosses the sea in the winter's storm"; "ensnares…the races of all the wild beasts and the salty brood of the sea"; constructs "shelter against the cold, refuge from rain"; and teaches himself speech and thought and educates his feelings in ways required to build and dwell within what is, arguably, the supreme human artifact, the city. The Chorus concludes,

> Clever beyond all dreams
> the inventive craft that he has
> which may drive him one time or another to well or ill
> When he honors the laws of the land and the gods' sworn right
> high indeed is his city; but stateless the man
> who dares to do what is shameful. (lines 335–370)

These commanding lines convey how inventiveness extends human responsibility across multiple levels of worldly experience—natural (physical environment), ontological (fellow humans and one's own self), and artifactual (human creations, including symbolic and technological worlds).

## THE TECHNOLOGICAL CONNECTION

The technologizing of communication has meant that the natural environment, as a medium of expression (see Douglas, 1973), progressively gave way to emergence of an artificial, constructed, environment. Constructed environmental elements—technological and cultural artifacts as resources for social action—came to displace unconstructed—natural—elements (see Couch, 1990, p. 11), and the constructed, human environment—experienced phenomenologically as 'world' (see Merleau-Ponty, 1962; Schutz, 1967)—started to progress through stages of structural and institutional development. Today, the world's peoples observe and act and feel within a time/space in which technologies, the built environment, the artificial resources and accouterments of post-industrial busyness predominate over natural elements.

With the emergence of "extended availability" (Thompson, 1995, p. 30) of human communications, "[i]nformation and symbolic content are made available to more individuals across larger expanses of space and at greater speeds." Collective life becomes freed, or unmoored, from locale and from shared presence at a point in time. The monuments, memorials, and rituals of our era tend to seek us out, as coveted viewers/consumers of screens and monitors, rather than requiring what was historically the reverse, that we, as pilgrims should trek across space as a labor of holy devotion to the authority of a time-honored shrine or commemoration. A historically-momentous example of how these relations emerged is the appearance of "a *reading public*" (p. 126). This development reflected novel communicative circumstances, since this

> was a public without a place and it was defined, not by the existence or possibility of face-to-face interaction among its members, but rather by the fact that its members had access to the kind of publicness made possible by the printed word. (pp. 126–127)

Ongoing technological developments have comparable impacts on the conditions and consequences of interaction and communicative exchange. As contemporary communications now extend across vast geographical space, they are also technologically "sequenced" (see Couch, 1990, pp. 29ff.) effectively and efficiently within micro-units of programmable time. But whatever technological and social achievements can be ascribed to this contemporary moment in the centuries-long 'communications revolution,' one should not overlook that everyday communication is still enacted from the foundational situation "wherein people align their actions with one another as they confront and are confronted by an environment" (Couch, 1996, p. 2). These environments may increasingly take the form of hyper-real landscapes that invite viewers and players-participants into imagined worlds within the depth of computer screens, but the challenge to subsist environmentally remains basic and compelling.

In aligning their actions while also addressing environmental challenges and opportunities, human social actors engage in *purposive-rational message-sending* directed towards control, on one hand, and in *communicative action* directed towards reaching understanding, on the other (see Habermas, 1984/1987). Communicative partners attempting to exercise cooperative agency, must "harmonize their plans of action on the basis of common situation definitions" (Habermas, 1984, p. 286). This begins with the exercise of communicators' abilities to "distinguish situations in which they are causally exerting an influence *upon* others from those in which they are coming to an understanding *with* them." In the latter instance, communication proceeds in the direction of dialogue.

Contrastingly, "instrumental" (Habermas, 1984, p. 285), or "strategic" message-sending, as a predominant focus, occurs in the context of "following technical rules of action" or "rules of rational choice." The standard of judgment is success or efficiency, either of an "intervention into a complex of circumstances and events," or an attempt at "influencing the decisions of a rational opponent." Reflexivity then takes on a different character, since the achievement of objective outcomes based on an optimal deployment of means is intended. Communication—or, more precisely, information exchange—then becomes an element in control procedures, and the logic of control inclines towards input-output logics that can be programmed into operational sequences. This occurs through standardized procedures and routines—i.e., as techniques—or as part of "the physical structure of a purposive mechanism" (Beniger, 1986, p. 40)—i.e., as programmed technologies, per se, such as computers that guide, and may even dictate, decision-making on a stock exchange.

## THE DIALOGIC VIEW

These modes of contact, and exchange—the communicative and the instrumental, or strategic (Habermas, 1984, p. 285)—both play a part, and often compete with each other, in determining the character of our ways of living and working, particularly in "knowledge societies" (Mansell & Wehn, 1998), where informational and communicative activities become intricately tied up with creating, utilizing, and communicating knowledge. In socio-cultural contexts in which technological mastery is over-valued as the basis for communication—as Jonas and other critics of modern technology suggest it is in modern and postmodern societies—an established set of ideological attitudes and practical assumptions takes precedence: Information exchange in the interests of achieving strategic goals prevails over relation-building. An alternative, dialogical position begins with the norm of communicative coorientation, and the potential mutuality of social interests this implies, and then attempts to recapture instrumentality as a subordinate, supporting principle, thus, "bringing instrumental rationality under the control of communicative rationality" (Dryzek, 1995, p. 114).

A philosophically supportable, dialogical (see Anderson, Baxter, & Cissna, 2004; Nikula, 2006) vision of communication has yet to be realized in empirically-observable instances. Accordingly, normative formulations such as Habermas' theory of communicative action are appropriately criticized for relying on counterfactual ideals, and failing to specify how "democratic discourse and human agency can combine to change the social structure in more desirable directions" (Tehranian, 1999, p. 90). Also, the notion of an "ideal speech situation" (see Benhabib, 1992), based on dialogue has most often predicated a "generalized other" (see Haas, 2001) as the partner in dialogue, thus avoiding the many perplexities associated with conducting dialogue with a historically and culturally specifiable 'concrete other' in his or her many manifestations. Any generalized, philosophical conception that sets out from a supposedly stable, theoretical positioning of 'self' and 'other' will tend to formalize what are actually specific, socio-historical contexts which ground people and their projects. Such generalizations about dialogue also tend to privilege interpersonal communication at a time when communications are increasingly founded on "time-space distanciation" (Giddens, 1981, pp. 4–5; Thompson, 1995, pp. 21–23), a communicative situation "beyond the control of any individual actor[s]" (Giddens, 1984, p. 25).

Notwithstanding these limitations, the theory of communicative action, as an exemplar of emergent dialogic approaches to communication, provides an important precedent for conceptualizing the differences and interconnections between (1) communications directed towards reaching understanding, and (2) forms of informational, purposive-rational message-sending aimed at mastering practical situations. The ability to combine these modes of communication is central to present and future prospects for equitable communication and egalitarian social visions. Scholars must be careful not to over-estimate the capacity of communicative advances to support social well-being nor to devalue the essential role communication plays in human affairs.

The work of Emmanuel Levinas provides the basis of a third position from those that would valorize mainly *system* or *action*, a stance that makes *relation* a central, normative value. From a relational standpoint, human communication is not determined by system requirements, nor is it unconstrained in its capacity to embody human intentions in the form of actions. Rather, communication is ethically oriented by relational "proximity" (Levinas, 1981, pp. 81 ff.) when the human face of the 'other' "shows itself simultaneously in its poverty and height" (Colledge, 2002, p. 179). Communicative partners in face-to-face proximity, encounter in the other these dual aspects of humanity—the 'height' of the commanding presence, and the 'destitution' of the vulnerable sufferer (Levinas, 1969, pp. 197 ff). The tension between these aspects of human face and its authority to impress can guide thinking about the more general prospects for communication as a basis for ethical life.

Levinas detects "a commandment in the appearance of the face, as if a master spoke to me. However, at the same time, the face of the other is destitute; it is the poor for whom I can do all and to whom I owe all" (Levinas, 1985, p. 89). The call to responsibility in proximity to this doubled face introduces the "proto-norm" (Christians, 1997) of providing response, i.e., an ontological call to become "*response-able*" (Booth, 1988, p. 126; see also, Woodward, 2000). "And me, whoever I may be, but as a 'first person,' I am he who finds the resources to respond to the call" (Levinas, 1985, p. 89). Fundamental to this understanding is that the "I" who provides the response from a mature store of resources is also, from another vantage point, a "me" who occupies a position of destitution, one whose face pleads for an ethical response from the corresponding other.

This notion of communicative responsibility can be tracked through six related levels of response-giving. The first three represent technical responses rather than ethical imperatives. These are (1) *control*, (2) *instruction*, and (3) *discussion*; and they are based, respectively, on (a) I-it relations of causation/force; (b) I-it relations of output/programming; and (c) I-you relations of knowledge exchange/persuasion (see Krippendorff, 1996). Examples are how the candy machine delivers up the selected treat; the thermostat regulates the temperature of the room; and the professional, technical expert delivers the service as the knowledge conveyed in the contract specifies. Three additional forms of ethical, dialogic relations can be distinguished as (4) ethics of *care*, based on the ideal of authentic being, e.g., the spousal or parent–child or sibling relations; (5) ethics of *responsibility*, based on ethical community, e.g., the assembly of colleagues, the religious fellowship, the literary 'conversation' among authors, artists, philosophers, and other truth-seekers; and (6) ethics of "*addressability*" (Ediger, 1994), based on intercultural or multicultural community, e.g., the prophetic partnership between the activist and those she engages in a spirit and vision of solidarity. In line with the arguments developed in this essay, I propose an ethics of *impressibility* for communication as appropriate to the challenges and opportunities of an emergent, global, participatory pluri-culture (Ihde, 1993, p. 56).

A communicative ethics of *impressibility* highlights how humans act, interact, and shape their practical and moral identities by receiving impressions from, and making impressions on their "triadic" (Woodward, 1996) fields of experience. The triadic field of human communication/participation is (1) material (physical-artifactual), (2) symbolic, (socio-cultural), and (3) relational (mutual-personal). An ethics of impressibility would make possible an understanding of the multiple levels at which moral agents provide responses to others and, at the same time, enact relations to the shared environments in which communicative action unfolds. Accordingly, responsibility should be seen in terms of how the agent is qualitatively, morally *impressed* by the call of the other, as it is communicated within the three dimensions of the field of experience—i.e., the other as nature and humanly-created artifacts; the other as language and cultural creations; the other as communicative partners in mutual-personal relation. At the same time, the moral agent *impresses* a response on, or within, the triadic field of experience, affecting the world of things, other selves, and the languages of interpersonal contact.

An ethics of impressibility helps to elaborate Buber's (1965a) "four potencies" (p. 163) of the human agent, namely, "knowledge, love, art, and faith." This final attribute of faith extends the tripled context of triadic theory—physical, cultural, and human relational—into a "four-fold field of relations" (Buber, 1965b). This perspective would predicate impressibility occurring in two directions—productive and receptive—and at four levels, including the self, others, and things, but also the mystery of being.

The concern to call into play Buber's four potencies returns the discussion to themes Jonas (1984) places at the heart of ethical consideration: (1) knowledge of the facts—a "scientific futurology" (p. x)—concerning the fate of nature, technological consequence, and the sustainable limits of human power; (2) love for the intimate other, including the "metaphysical other" (Levinas, 1969, p. 38), as envisioned in the possible 'being' of a human future; (3) the art required to transform destructive artifice into responsible social productivity; and (4) the faith to restore balance by expanding the reach of ontology to include recognition of what has not yet appeared. This final sphere of experience is what Levinas (1981) describes as beyond being, or "otherwise than being." Levinas' ethics of proximity connects with Jonas' imperative of responsibility by fostering the ethical potency of faith: through faith, persons impress, and are impressed by, human responsibility to what does not yet appear; through communication as impressibility, persons acknowledge responsibility for the consequential ways in which we impress human projects—practical and ethical—on the triadic worlds of our experience and participation.

## REFERENCES

Anderson, R., Baxter, L., & Cissna, K. (2004). *Dialogue*. Thousand Oaks, CA: Sage.

Benhabib, S. (1992). *Situating the self*. New York: Routledge.

Beniger, J. (1986). *The control revolution*. Cambridge, MA: Harvard University Press.

Berger P., & Luckmann, T. (1966). *The social construction of reality*. Garden City, NY: Doubleday.

Booth, W. (1988). *The company we keep*. Berkeley: University of California Press.

Bourdieu, P. (1985). *The genesis of the concepts of "habitus" and "field." Sociocriticism, 2*(2), 11–24.

Buber, M. (1965a). *The knowledge of man*. New York: Harper Torchbooks.

Buber, M. (1965b). *Between man and man*. New York. Macmillan.

Carey, J. W. (1969). Harold Adams Innis and Marhall McLuhan. In R. Rosenthal (Ed.), *McLuhan: Pro and con* (pp. 270–308). Baltimore: Penguin.

Carey, J. W. (1989). *Communication as culture*. Boston: Unwin Hyman.

Christians, C. (1997). The ethics of being. In C. Christians & M. Traber (Eds.), *Communication ethics and universal values* (pp. 3–23). Thousand Oaks, CA: Sage.

Colledge, R. (2002). Ernest Becker and Emmanuel Levinas: Surprising convergences. In D. Liechty (Ed.), *Death and denial: Interdisciplinary perspectives on the legacy of Ernest Becker* (pp. 175–184). Westport, CT: Praeger.

Cooper, B. (1991). *Action into nature*. Notre Dame: University of Notre Dame Press.

Couch, C. (1990). *Constructing civilizations*. Greenwich, CT: JAI.

Couch, C. (1996). *Information technologies and social order*. New York: Aldine de Gruyter.

Couldry N., & McCarthy, A. (2004). *Mediaspace*. New York: Routledge.

Dewey, J. (1958). *Art as experience*. New York: Capricorn.

Douglas, M. (1973). *Natural symbols*. New York: Pantheon.

Dryzek, J. (1995). Critical theory as a research program. In S. White (Ed.), *The Cambridge companion to Habermas* (pp. 97–119). Cambridge, UK: Cambridge University Press.

Ediger, J. (1994). *The ethics of addressability in Emmanuel Levinas*. Presented at Third National Conference on Ethics, Gull Lake, Michigan, May.

Garnham, N. (2000). *Emancipation, media and modernity*. Oxford: Oxford University Press.

Giddens, A. (1979). *Central problems in social theory*. Berkeley: University of California Press.

Giddens, A. (1981). *A contemporary critique of historical materialism*. Berkeley: University of California Press.

Giddens, A. (1984). *The constitution of society*. Berkeley: University of California Press.

Gillespie, R., & Robins, K. (1989). Geographical inequalities: The spatial bias of the new communications technologies. *Journal of Communication 39*(3), 7–18.

Haas, T. (2001). Public relations between universality and particularity. In R. Heath (Ed.), *Handbook of public relations* (pp. 423–433). Thousand Oaks, CA: Sage.

Habermas, J. (1984/1987). *The theory of communicative action. Volumes 1 and 2*. Boston: Beacon Press.

Holquist, M. (2002). *Dialogism* (2nd ed.). New York: Routledge.

Ihde, D. (1993). *Postphenomenology*. Evanston, IL: Northwestern University Press.

Joas, H. (1996). *The creativity of action*. Chicago: University of Chicago Press.

Jonas, H. (1966). *The phenomenon of life*. Chicago: University of Chicago Press.

Jonas, H. (1974). *Philosophical essays*. Chicago: University of Chicago Press.

Jonas, H. (1984). *The imperative of responsibility*. Chicago: University of Chicago Press.

Jonas, H. (1996). *Mortality and morality*. Evanston, IL: Northwestern University Press.

Kirkpatrick, F. (1986). *Community*. Washington, D.C.: Georgetown University Press.

Krippendorff, K. (1996). A second-order cybernetics of otherness. *Systems Research, 13*(3), 311–328.

Levinas, E. (1969). *Totality and infinity*. Pittsburgh: Duquesne University Press.

Levinas, E. (1981). *Otherwise than being*. The Hague: Martinus Nijhoff.

Levinas, E. (1985). *Ethics and infinity: Conversations with Philippe Nemo*. Pittsburgh: Duquesne University Press.

Loewenstein, W. (1999). *The touchstone of life*. New York: Oxford University Press.

Luhmann, N. (1989).*Ecological communication*. Chicago: University of Chicago Press.

Macmurray, J. (1991). *Persons in relation*. Atlantic Highlands, NJ: Humanities.

Mansell, R., & Wehn, U. (1998). *Knowledge societies*. New York: Oxford University Press.

Merleau-Ponty, M. (1962). *Phenomenology of perception*. London: Routledge & Kegan Paul.

Millikan, R. (2004). On reading signs: Some differences between us and the others. In Oller, D. K. & Griebel, U. (Eds.), *Evolution of communication systems* (pp. 15–30). Cambridge, MA: MIT Press.

Nikula, D. (2006). *On dialogue*. Lanham, MD: Lexington.

Oller D. K. & Griebel, U. (2004). Theoretical and methodological tools for comparison and evolutionary modeling of communication systems. In D. K. Oller & U. Griebel (Eds.), *Evolution of communication systems* (pp. 3–11). Cambridge, MA: MIT Press.

Ong, W. (2002). *Orality and literacy: The technologizing of the word* (2nd ed.). New York: Routledge.

Schutz, A. (1967). *The phenomenology of the social world*. Evanston, IL: Northwestern University Press.

Taylor, C. (1985). *Human agency and language. Philosophical papers. Volume 1*.Cambridge, UK: Cambridge University Press.

Tehranian, M. (1999). *Global communication and world politics*. London: Lynne Rienner.

Thompson, J. (1995). *The media and modernity*. Stanford, CA: Stanford University Press.

Vogel, L. (1996). Hans Jonas' Exodus: From German existentialism to post-holocaust theology. In L. Vogel (Ed.), H. Jonas (1996). *Mortality and morality* (pp. 1–40). Evanston, IL: Northwestern University Press.

Wallace, J. (1978). *Virtues and vices*. Ithaca, NY: Cornell University Press.

Woodward, W. (1996). Triadic communication as transactional-participation. *Critical Studies in Mass Communication, 13*(2), 155–174.

Woodward, W. (2000). Design/communication as mutual-personal creative action. *Cultural Studies: A Research Annual, 5*, 337-362.

# 2

# A Short History of Media Ethics in the United States

John P. Ferré

Few treatments of media ethics are historical, and what history they do include tends to be anecdotal and not to stretch further back than a generation. This paucity is sometimes due to the urgency in media ethics. There are so many pressing issues to cover and so little time to examine them—one ethics course in college, perhaps, or part of a reporting course, a professional seminar, maybe one book. The stakes are large and there are so many pitfalls that taking time to consider the history of media ethics can seem like an academic indulgence. There is also a sense of outrage in media ethics. Information that the public needs is hidden or corrupted; reputations that have taken a lifetime to build are destroyed with a few keystrokes. Much that falls under the rubric of media ethics is written in the white heat of the moment. Media ethics seems to call for passion and incisiveness, not history.

Nevertheless, an accurate understanding of the moral dimensions of media requires history. By showing the challenges that others have faced, the responses that others have considered, and the choices that others have made, history can help media ethics to evaluate possible actions and policies. A history of media ethics can provide a comprehensive view of moral victories and defeats and the circumstances that led to them. Like cross-cultural studies, history provides comparisons with other situations that can illuminate our own.

How American media behave has been a concern since 1638 when the first printing press arrived in the colonies. The press carried with it both promise and threat. Its primary purpose was religious enlightenment and edification for colonists as well as Native Americans—in just 25 years the Bible was available not only in English but also in the native Algonquin language—but the press also facilitated legal and business transactions, supported education, and provided colonists with news from Europe and other colonies. Because it could generate discussion and settle disputes, the colonists understood the press to be an agent of truth, both in the narrow sense of factuality and in the wider sense of ultimate and eternal reality.

The colonists also understood that circulating misstatements of fact and faith could cause religious doubt, moral waywardness, and political dissent, so they kept careful watch over the press. In 1689, the governor of Massachusetts complained that "many papers have beene lately printed and dispersed tending to the disturbance of the peace and subversion of the government" (Williams, 2005, p. 24). And a year later, the first colonial newspaper, *Publick Occurrences, Both Forreign and Domestick*, was shut down after one issue because its report that Indian allies of the British had abused French prisoners was considered seditious and its report that the king of

France had seduced his daughter-in-law was considered vulgar. Few printing presses were in the colonies by 1690, but already disagreements had emerged over their relationship with religious and political authorities and over standards of decorum and privacy. How much latitude the media should have has been the subject of media criticism, and by implication media ethics, ever since.

Moral practices and standards evolved through the eighteenth and nineteenth centuries as journalism very slowly took on the characteristics of a profession. As Hazel Dicken-Garcia (1989) explains, until the 1830s the American press operated according to a political model. This era was one of political experimentation, when the party system was taking shape. Oriented to political parties and elites, the press during this era was idea-centered. Critics of the press focused on issues of impartiality, questioning whether equal treatment of opposing parties was desirable.

After the introduction of the penny press and the telegraph in the middle years of the century, the press shifted to an information model, becoming event-centered and oriented more to ordinary individuals than to elites and political parties. The United States experienced advances in transportation and manufacturing as well as commercial and political reforms in its cities. Critics became concerned with the press's watchdog function and what the public had a right to know; they worried that newspaper space was a scarce resource too often squandered on the trivialities of gossip and personal information.

Toward the end of the nineteenth century, as the nation's economy shifted from agriculture to industry and Americans became preoccupied with science and business, the press began to adopt a business model. Oriented to consumers of news, the press added drama to what had become its traditional role of presenting ideas and reporting events. Critics after the Civil War increasingly assumed that news was separate from opinion, public service superseded profit, poor taste had no place in newspapers, and privacy deserved protection. The business-oriented press came to believe that there was no market for controversial ideas, but that their customers had boundless desire for sensationalism.

Although Americans have voiced concern about media conduct and content ever since colonial times, critics did not begin to think of what they were doing in terms of ethics until the 1890s. In this sense, media ethics began in the Progressive Era. The sustained ethical evaluation of the Progressive Era was followed by three periods of ferment: demonstrations of professionalism in the 1920s; the forceful definition of the long-used, but ambiguous concept of social responsibility after 1947; and growing interest in normative theory and ethical universals since the 1970s. Taken together, these four periods of media ethics history—Progressive Era, professionalism, social responsibility, and global humanitarianism—have transformed public concerns about journalism into systematic reflection and practical applications.

## PROGRESSIVE ERA CRITICISM

Press criticism began to be conceived in terms of ethics at the end of the nineteenth century. Ethics as a term appeared occasionally in discussions about journalism in the 1850s, but the first article to use the word "ethics" in its title was "The Ethics of Journalism" by Catholic writer William Samuel Lilly, whose 1889 article in *The Forum* became a chapter in his book *On Right and Wrong* along with other chapters on the ethics of art, marriage, politics, property, and punishment. Lilly argued that journalists were granted freedom of the press in order "to state facts, to argue upon them, to denounce abuses, to advocate reforms," but that "truth is the last thing the average journalist thinks about" (Lilly, 1892, pp. 165, 167). Including journalism in discussions of ethics signaled journalism's increasing importance. In the context of the 1890s, it also meant that journalism was considered a deeply flawed institution and set of practices that required serious analysis.

Critics of the press in the 1890s complained about two major problems: sensationalism and dishonesty. Critics denounced newspapers that pandered to mass readership by filling their columns with personal scandals and gruesome accounts of prizefights, murders, arsons, and suicides. Joseph Pulitzer's *New York World* published grizzly accounts of executions and obsessed about prostitution. The *World*'s chief rival, William Randolph Hearst's *New York Journal,* conducted a jailbreak in Havana and even advocated the assassination of President William McKinley by editorializing, "Institutions, like men, will last until they die; and if bad institutions and bad men can be got rid of only by killing, then the killing must be done" (Mott, 1941, p. 541). A Philadelphia rabbi complained, "Judging from the daily amount of social sewage that is allowed to stream in open sight, through the newspaper, one is often tempted to believe that newspaper proprietors must think that people commit crime solely for the purpose of filling the columns of the press" ("Mission," 1897, p. 24).

Besides sensationalism, the greatest problem that critics addressed was dishonesty. The *New York Times* complained that Hearst correspondents covering the Spanish-American War falsely reported that Cubans decapitated Spanish prisoners. *Gunton's Magazine* exposed *The Boston Herald*'s report of big business laying to waste ten industries in Kearney, Nebraska, as a fabrication designed to promote the newspaper's anti-trust cause. *The Nation* illustrated the unreliability of newspaper reports by comparing three reviews of a theater performance: One reported nearly every seat in the orchestra and the balcony full, another had the lower floor full along with three or four rows in the first balcony, and the third review described the theater as only one-third full. Indeed, making up information or exaggerating stories for effect was so common that Edwin L. Shuman's 1894 journalism textbook devoted a chapter to proper faking. "Truth in essentials, imagination in non-essentials, is considered a legitimate rule of action in every office," Shuman explained. "The paramount object is to make an interesting story" (p. 123).

Observers pinned the blame for the sensationalism and the untruths common to the press on greed and public prurience. Whether true or false, scandal sold. "The mercantile spirit of the day is to blame for what is actually pernicious in our newspapers," said a Universalist minister ("Two sorts," 1897, p. 2). A variant on this theme was the idea that the problem was keen competition, not profit as such. Although competition for circulation did lead to lower prices and more print, it also fostered sensationalism. Journalist Will Irwin said that yellow journalism spread like "a prairie fire" to "nineteen out of twenty metropolitan newspapers" (Campbell, 2001, p. 51).

Closely related to profit-mongering was the prurience of the public. After all, it was the public that was making yellow journalism profitable. "It is because the people love sensationalism that so much of it is furnished," said one critic. "The demand regulates the supply" (Wright, 1898, p. 272). Yellow journalism was a problem of more than just the poor and uncultivated, or as one writer said, "the lower order of mankind," because the middle classes also indulged themselves ("Pernicious," 1898, p. 5). According to historian Joseph Campbell, "The yellow press was doubtless read across the urban social strata in the United States at the turn of the twentieth century" (2001, p. 55). The public hunger for daily newspapers—both sensational and staid—is illustrated by penetration figures from the time. In 1890, two daily newspapers were printed for every three households in the country; ten years later there was one per household. Critics understood press reform to be more than social work among the poor; it was a process of fighting the deterioration of the entire culture.

Journalism of the 1890s was criticized for the negative effects it seemed to have on readers' attitudes, beliefs, and behaviors. Rollo Ogden, who would eventually edit the *New York Times*, wrote that daily contemplation of crime deadened the sense of revulsion to criminal activity, provided the dull-witted with ideas that they could not have conceived on their own, and nudged into action those with criminal tendencies. An article entitled "The Psychology of Crime" argued similarly, saying that regular reading of unwholesome material, especially by impressionable young people, could lead to "murders, suicides, sexual immoralities, thefts, and numberless other disorders" (Wood, 1893, p. 530). Indeed, everyone was vulnerable: details of sensualities and crimes impressed people's minds, corrupted wholesome thinking and, inevitably, character.

Such claims seemed to be confirmed by suicides that followed the publication of "Is Suicide a Sin?" by the famous agnostic Robert G. Ingersoll in Pulitzer's *New York World*. Ingersoll's attack on laws that punished would-be suicides asked, "When life is of no value to him, when he can be of no real assistance to others, why should a man continue?" (1908, p. 376). Some readers apparently took Ingersoll at his word, including Julius Marcus and Juliette Fournier, who ended their three-month extramarital affair in Central Park with a double suicide. A public outcry followed the revelation that police had found Ingersoll's column on suicide in Marcus's pocket, including a condemnation from the New York Minister's Association: "Detailed accounts of suicides are not only obnoxious to all but the morbid, but are among the potent causes of the alarming increase of self-murder, especially when communications extenuating and even advocating it are sought and exploited as a means of increasing circulation" ("The duty," 1897, p. 12).

If immoralities and crimes resulted from the press's profit motive and the public's prurience, then the correctives seemed clear: Limit the profits that newspapers could make from sensationalism and dampen the public's appetite for titillation by changing the basis on which newspapers operated. One common proposal for diminishing the profit motive was to fund newspapers through endowments. Unlike profit-motivated newspapers tempted to pander for circulation by resorting to sex and crime reporting, endowed newspapers could afford to publish solely from conscience. Indeed, steel magnate and philanthropist Andrew Carnegie announced that he would be willing to endow a newspaper if nine other volunteers helped him, but none was forthcoming. Nobody endowed a newspaper.

Others advocated moral and economic pressure. A letter to the editor of the *New York Times* proposed having thousands of people "wear for a period of thirty days some distinguishing badge, ribbon or button as a silent protest against new journalism, which would so shame the readers of yellow newspapers ... that they would as lief fondle a mad dog as they would be seen reading these papers" ("Yellow journalism," 1898, p. 6). But no such public protest ever materialized. Other writers declared that the yellow press would be crippled if moral businesspeople ended their patronage of offensive newspapers and advertised only in respectable publications. No such strategic advertising was ever coordinated. In 1896 reformers called for a boycott of *The New York Journal* and *World* because of their sex and crime stories, but the boycott fizzled.

These solutions failed because consumers enjoyed yellow journalism. Said one contemporary, "The newspaper is just what the public wants it to be" ("Ethics," 1897, p. 2). Recognizing that yellow journalism flourished because people wanted to read it, some critics recommended measures to refine the public's taste. Shifting the focus of media reform from production to consumption, they suggested educating the public through essays, lectures, and college courses. But as hard as changing the press proved to be, it was even harder to convince the public that its taste in newspapers was poor. No media literacy movement emerged.

Although press criticism in the Progressive Era was piecemeal rather than systematic, taken as a whole it comprised a common-sense utilitarianism. Not that the criticism was expressed in terms of the greatest good for the greatest number—but evaluating the press according to the effects that it had upon its consumers, rather than according to its character or its intentions or the nature of its actions, was a sort of utilitarian measurement. Needless to say, the effects were always posited rather than proven, so however thought-provoking such consequentialism may have been, it failed to stimulate any serious improvements in the press. Reform would come from within journalism in the form of professional codes of ethics and higher education.

## PROFESSIONALISM

Daily newspapers were wildly popular in the early decades of the twentieth century. Increases in circulation dwarfed population growth from 1900 to 1930, daily newspaper circulation growing 260% as the population grew only 62%. Daily newspapers reported information faster, more factually, and more comprehensively than ever before, and the tabloids attracted readers with breezy prose, abundant photographs, and titillating stories of sex and crime. But the press's popularity was accompanied by complaints that news was too often false, suppressed, biased, or indecent. Acknowledging its moral lapses, the press moved to show the public that it was serious about improving practices by bolstering professional training and enacting codes of ethics.

In 1900, *The Journalist* declared that college-educated journalists wrote better, thought more broadly, and were more ethical than their colleagues from the school of hard knocks. The trade journal's observations reflected the era's professionalization. Joseph Pulitzer, the publisher of *The St. Louis Post-Dispatch* and *New York World* who donated $2 million to endow the Graduate School of Journalism at Columbia University in 1910, believed that ethics was central to journalism education. "I desire to assist in attracting to this profession young men of character and ability, also to help those already engaged in the profession to acquire the highest moral and intellectual training," he explained. "There will naturally be a course in ethics, but training in ethical principles must not be confined to that. It must pervade all the courses" (O'Dell, 1935, p. 107). By 1915, journalism ethics courses were being taught at Indiana, Kansas, Kansas State, Missouri, Montana, Oklahoma, Oregon, and Washington, and other universities were incorporating ethics in their courses on journalism history and law. This focus on ethics in journalism education continued through the 1920s. In his pioneering 1924 textbook, *The Ethics of Journalism*, Nelson Crawford noted that twenty U.S. institutions offered journalism degrees and that 200 others offered some journalism instruction in an effort to foster "integrity, intelligence and objective-mindedness" (p. 170).

To meet the growing demand for reporters who were ethically sensitive as well as technically proficient, significant works on journalistic ethics were published during this era. Exhibiting what Clifford Christians calls "a dogged preoccupation with public obligation" (2000, p. 22), these works expounded upon what individual newspapers and professional associations had codified. Privileges were no longer taken for granted, sensationalism was dismissed as an excess from the past, and accuracy became the *sine qua non* of journalistic professionalism. The first books on journalism ethics in the United States were *The Ethics of Journalism* by Nelson Crawford of Kansas State University (1924) and *The Morals of Newspaper Making* by Thomas A. Lahey of the University of Notre Dame (1924). These books appeared at the same time the first journalism textbook to include a chapter on ethics appeared: *The Principles of Journalism* by Casper S. Yost, editor of *The St. Louis Globe-Democrat* (1924). Other books appeared in rapid succession: *The Conscience of the Newspaper* by Leon Flint of the University of Kansas (1925), *Newspaper Ethics* by William Gibbons of Pennsylvania State University (1926), and *The Newspaper and Responsibility* by Paul F. Douglass of the University of Cincinnati (1929). After *Ethics and Practices in Journalism* by Albert Henning of Southern Methodist University was published in 1932, the word "ethics" disappeared from titles of books about the media until 1975, when John Merrill of the University of Missouri and Ralph Barney of Brigham Young University published a book of readings entitled *Ethics and the Press*.

Codes of ethics were a primary means that journalists in the early twentieth century used to answer their critics and to articulate their best practices. The first code of ethics for journalists was adopted in 1910 by the Kansas Editorial Association. Written by William E. Miller, the Kansas code called for advertising policies that were forthright and fair and for news that was honest, just, and decent. The admonishments were specific, advising that "all advertising should be paid for in cash," for instance, and that "no reporter should be retained who accepts any courtesies, unusual favors, opportunities for self-gain, or side employment from any factors whose interests would be affected by the manner in which his reports are made" (Miller, 1922, pp. 287, 293–294). Following the lead of the Kansas Editorial Association, numerous state press associations as well as individual newspapers adopted codes of ethics during the 1910s and 1920s.

The codes and creeds would not be limited to newspapers and state press associations. In 1923, the Canons of Journalism were adopted at the inaugural meeting of the American Society of Newspaper Editors, the culmination of Casper Yost's decade-long dream of an ethical organization of newspaper editors. The virtues of responsibility, freedom, independence, honesty, accuracy, impartiality, fair play, and decency that the Canons of Journalism championed summarized the ideals of journalism so well that the Society of Professional Journalists adopted the Canons in 1926, and other newspapers and press associations used the Canons as a model for the codes they would write.

Just as public criticism motivated journalists to write codes of ethics, government regulation motivated the National Association of Broadcasters (NAB) to create one of its own. Written in 1928, the Radio Code was created to minimize the involvement of the Federal Radio Commission, established by Congress the year before to ensure that broadcasting took place in the "public interest, convenience, and necessity." Originally consisting of unenforceable platitudes, the Radio Code grew more specific with every revision, so that the 22nd edition in 1980 was a booklet 31 pages long. The Radio and Television Codes related to advertising and program content, but adherence was voluntary and noncompliance went unpunished. In 1963, for instance, the Federal Communications Commission discovered that 40% of television stations exceeded the time limits for advertising set forth in the Television Code. The codes did have some impact, though, because the advertisements that television and radio stations broadcast were usually designed with NAB Code standards in mind.

Although usually written with good intentions, ethics codes have been neither universally welcome nor effective. Stanley Walker, city editor of *The New York Herald Tribune*, dismissed ethics codes as unrealistic. "Not a bad thing, this eternal seeking for sanctification," he wrote. "There is, it may be, some hope for any reprobate who is capable of turning his head on his pillow and asking: 'Why do I have to be so rotten?' But the next day comes the avalanche of reality. There are compromises. It was always so. The saving law is: We do the best we can—in the circumstances" (1934, p. 176). Walker's dismissal of codes as impractical and unenforceable seemed to be borne out shortly after ASNE adopted the Canons of Journalism. Several ASNE members recommended expelling Fred Bonfils, co-owner of *The Denver Post*, for violating the Canons by accepting bribes to suppress information about the Teapot Dome scandal, but in 1929 the membership voted that following the Canons was strictly voluntary. Blackmail may have been wrong, but violators could not be punished by the ASNE or any other journalism society's code. Their codes of ethics were hortatory only.

The viability of media codes would become questionable toward the end of the century. In 1979, the U.S. Justice Department claimed that the NAB's Television Code violated antitrust laws, saying that limits on the amount of time for commercials per hour, on the number of commercial interruptions per hour, and on the number of products per commercial harmed both advertisers and consumers by raising the price of broadcasting time unnecessarily. The NAB responded by eliminating its codes. Code enforcement would arise again as an issue in the mid-1980s, when news organizations began to fear that written codes of ethics could be used against them by libel plaintiffs claiming that reporters recklessly disregarded journalistic standards. This fear had a chilling effect on journalistic codes of ethics. After 1987, when the Society of Professional Journalists stopped asking its members to censure reporters who violated the SPJ code, most code activity in journalism moved quietly to the privacy of individual newsrooms.

After all of the codes and the chapters and the books of journalism ethics were written in the 1920s, concern for ethics was replaced by a concern for objectivity. In the minds of many at the time, ethics books and journalistic canons were seen as means of ridding journalism of its more outrageous practices. Journalism ethics became synonymous with culling values from the facts of human experience so that reporters could produce news that was neutral, unbiased, factual. Journalistic objectivity became a set of skills that could be learned and practiced. Failure to report objectively was the result of poor training or of clever public relations or propaganda. But this faith in scientific objectivity began to be shaken in the 1960s, when science itself was beginning to be explained in terms of paradigms rather than simple progress. Although the term would continue to be used, "objectivity" came to mean accuracy and fairness. *Time* publisher James Shepley explained the difference:

> We know that the truth is based on an interplay between fact and opinion, and that the two are inextricable. We always try to see to it that our facts are selected through balanced judgment, that our judgments are supported by reliable facts.... It is a fallible process; but it is open, and always subject to inspection, correction and improvement. We think it is the best process available not only for describing events but for making clear their meaning. (1968, p. 17)

As the doctrine of objectivity waned, the study of media ethics reappeared.


## SOCIAL RESPONSIBILITY

Concern for freedom of the press was on the mind of Henry Luce, publisher of *Time* magazine, after World War II. The experience of wartime censorship was fresh. Shortly after Japan bombed Pearl Harbor, President Franklin D. Roosevelt created the Office of Censorship, which issued a code of wartime practices for the press at home to follow and required correspondents abroad to submit their articles and photographs to military censors. Under the Espionage Act, some publishers lost their second-class mailing permits and a few others were indicted, but the press was mostly compliant, censoring itself as it did when it withheld news of plans for the Allied invasion of North Africa in 1942 and the development of the atomic bomb. For Henry Luce, wartime censorship became personal when British Customs detained his wife, Clare Booth Luce, in Trinidad for reporting about Allied weaknesses in Libya.

There were other pressing concerns for media owners such as Luce. Worried about the power of the increasingly concentrated media, the federal government had begun to break up large media companies in an effort to diversify ownership and perspective. In 1940, the Justice Department issued a consent decree to major movie studios to increase competition within a tightly controlled film and theater industry. Three years later, the courts backed the Federal Communications Commission's order for RCA to sell one of its two NBC networks. Not only did Luce own a 12.5% interest in NBC's Blue Network, but he also owned *Time*, *Life*, and *Fortune* magazines, Radio March of Time, Cinema March of Time, and Time Views the News. Because Time, Inc. could easily reach a third of all Americans, Luce's empire was the type of powerful media corporation that the government had begun to investigate. As Luce's friend Robert M. Hutchins would later say, "Mr. Luce and his magazines have more effect on the American character than the whole educational system put together" (Swanberg, 1972, p. 479).

Worried that press freedoms were in jeopardy, Luce turned to Hutchins, then the chancellor of the University of Chicago, who invited a dozen renowned intellectuals including Zechariah Chafee, Harold Lasswell, Archibald MacLeish, Reinhold Niebuhr, and Arthur Schlesinger to form a Commission on the Freedom of the Press. The Hutchins Commission heard testimony from 58 representatives from the press, interviewed 225 people from government and industry, held 17 two- and three-day meetings, and studied 176 documents prepared by its staff before issuing its report, *A Free and Responsible Press*, in 1947. But rather than defend media practices, the report sounded an alarm. If the media failed to act responsibly, the commission prophesied, the government would have no choice but to regulate them. "Those who direct the machinery of the press have engaged from time to time in practices which the society condemns and which, if continued, it will inevitably undertake to regulate or control," the Commission said, adding that "freedom of the press can remain a right of those who publish only if it incorporates into itself the right of the citizen and the public interest" (Leigh, 1947, pp. 1, 18). The Hutchins Commission said that the press was responsible for providing (1) daily news that is trustworthy; (2) a forum for public expression; (3) inclusive reporting, free of stereotypes; (4) stories that pursue and probe democratic life; and (5) universal access to daily news. Anything less was unworthy of a press that had Constitutional protections so that it could help democracy work, not in order to make money.

These were words that Luce and other lords of the press did not want to hear. They denounced the Hutchins Commission report and tried to ignore its fundamental claim that freedom from government interference did not negate the media's public service obligations, that indeed *freedom for* public service was the very premise for *freedom from* government interference. The media clung to their laissez-faire outlook as if newspaper chains and one-city dailies were not sweeping away traditional free market conditions. Dismissing the Commission's concerns, the media provided less and less news and opinion for an informed citizenry. They were increasingly in the business of selling audiences to advertisers.

But while the press was ignoring the Hutchins Commission report, journalism schools started to take it seriously. In 1956, social responsibility was being explained along with authoritarianism, libertarianism, and communism as one of the *Four Theories of the Press* (Siebert, Peterson, & Schramm). The following year Wilbur Schramm published *Responsibility in Mass Communication*. And in 1962, J. Edward Gerald's *Social Responsibility of the Press*, which complained that the media's Jeffersonian idealism had been corrupted by their rapacious quest for profit, called the Hutchins Commission's report "timeless" (p. 103). Generations of journalists would begin their professional lives having considered that their skills were best used for public rather than corporate good.

Social responsibility may not have been a developed theory, but it was a persuasive, other-oriented perspective that valued both freedom from government interference and commitment to the public good. Rejecting government regulation, social responsibility advocated cooperation between the media and citizenry in concrete efforts that would limit market excesses and pressure the media to serve society rather than narrow self-interest. These efforts resulted in the creation of news councils, ombudsmen, and journalism reviews.

The most active news council in the United States was organized in 1970 by the Minnesota Newspaper Association to emulate the British Press Council, which helped maintain public confidence in the press by hearing complaints about news media. The Minnesota News Council, composed of journalists and public volunteers, heard its first case in 1971, when it upheld the complaint about a *St. Paul Union Advocate* story asserting that a legislator was being paid off by the liquor lobby. (The editor confessed that the story was so good that he failed to find out whether it was true.) Since then the Council has conducted about four public hearings a year, upholding half of the complaints it has received. Other state and city councils still operating are the Washington News Council, which held its first hearing in 1999, and the Honolulu Community-Media Council, which began in 1970. In 2006, the John S. and James L. Knight Foundation provided two $75,000 grants to establish The Southern California News Council and The New England News Council.

The only nationwide news council was founded in 1973 with a grant from the Twentieth Century Fund. The National News Council investigated more than 1,000 complaints about media misconduct and published its conclusions in the *Columbia Journalism Review* and later in *Quill*. But major news organizations, including the *New York Times*, Associated Press, and CBS, opposed news councils, claiming that they opened the door to government regulation of the media. The National News Council could not continue without their support, so it ceased operating in 1983.

A more immediate approach to media accountability has been the appointment of ombudsmen, in-house critics who respond to public criticisms of media content. Harkening back to the Bureau of Accuracy and Fair Play that Joseph Pulitzer started in 1913 to handle complaints about his *New York World*, media ombudsmen were first proposed formally in 1967 by media critic Ben Bagdikian as a sort of institutional conscience to help maintain public accountability as family newspapers were absorbed into newspaper chains. Three months later, John Herchenroeder of *The Courier-Journal* and *Times* of Louisville, Kentucky became the first newspaper ombudsman in the United States. Sometimes called readers' representatives, readers' advocates, or public editors, they are usually seasoned and highly respected reporters who criticize newspapers from within. Alfred JaCoby, who served for seven years as readers' representative for *The San Diego Union*, recalls the paper's owner confessing that his criticism sometimes angered her. "But you must go on because it's good for the newspaper" (2003, p. 188), she told him. However valuable to those media who have them, ombudsmen have been appointed by only a few dozen newspapers and broadcast newsrooms.

A third outcome of social responsibility are journalism reviews, periodicals that criticize the news media. Early journalism reviews include the *Nieman Reports*, begun in 1947 as part of Harvard University's Nieman Fellowships for mid-career journalists, which the widow of the founder and publisher of the *Milwaukee Journal* endowed "to promote and elevate the standards of journalism in the United States" ("About the Nieman Foundation," 2006). Veteran reporter George Seldes published a more acerbic review, *In fact*, from 1940 to 1950. The years 1968 to 1975 were a period of ferment for journalism reviews. More than two dozen reviews appeared during this period, ranging from the commercial (*MORE*, 1971–1978) to the militant (*The Unsatisfied Man*, 1970–1975). They represented various groups including African-Americans (*Ball and Chain Review*, 1969–1970), feminists (*Media Report to Women*, 1972 to date), journalists (*St. Louis Journalism Review*, 1970 to date), and students (*feed/back*, 1974–1986). Although most journalism reviews from this period lasted no more than 18 months, their legacy was permanent. Today media criticism is part and parcel of the mainstream media as well as professional organizations such as the Society of Professional Journalists. The university-based *Columbia Journalism Review* (1961 to date) and *American Journalism Review* (originally *Washington Journalism Review*, 1977 to date) are still going strong, as are partisan reviews such as the *AIM Report* (1972 to date) on the right and *Extra!* (1987 to date) on the left of the American political spectrum.

## GLOBAL HUMANITARIANISM

The 1980s brought a new sense of urgency to media ethics. For one thing, the stakes were higher. There were more media than ever before and media audiences seemed insatiable. And the promise of Marshall McLuhan's global village seemed to be momentarily fulfilled in the summer of 1985 with the charity rock concert Live Aid, which simultaneously reached an estimated 1.5 billion viewers in 100 countries and raised more than $250 million for famine relief in Ethiopia. Media continued to multiply in the 1990s, with direct broadcast satellites and cell phones, not to mention the Internet, which by 2007 had an estimated 1.1 billion users across the world.

However impressive the diversity and the reach of the media had become, the 85% of the world's 6.5 billion citizens without Internet access demonstrated the underside of the exponential growth in communications. Penetration was lopsided. Most North Americans (69%) were connected to the Internet, as were most residents of Oceania/Australia (54%) and the European Union (52%), but few Africans (4%), Middle Easterners (10%), or Asians (11%) were online. The stark contrast between communication haves and have nots illustrated one cause for the replication of patterns of wealth and poverty in the world.

This incongruity of media access and media power was the focus of *Many Voices, One World*, the influential report that UNESCO's International Commission for the Study of Communication Problems issued in 1980. The so-called MacBride report, named after the commission's Nobel Peace Prize-winning chair Sean MacBride, proposed a New World Information and Communication Order (NWICO) that advocated "a free and balanced flow" of information internationally. Among its recommendations were measures to help protect journalists, who were increasingly the targets of violence. (According to the Committee to Protect Journalists, an average of 40 journalists were killed every year from 1992–2006 for attempting to report their observations truthfully, and few of the perpetrators were brought to justice.) And bemoaning the predominance of Northern Hemisphere news agencies such as the Associated Press, Reuters, and Agence France-Presse, NWICO called for a UNESCO-funded Southern Hemisphere news agency to help right the imbalance. "Unless some basic structural changes are introduced," the MacBride report said, "the potential benefits of technological and communication development will hardly be put at the disposal of the majority of mankind" (International Commission, 1980, p. 3).

NWICO's insistence on the right to communicate transformed into a broader notion of communication rights that empower people in their own particular circumstances. The handbook *Assessing Communication Rights* (Siochrú, 2005) conceives communication rights as four pillars: (a) communicating in the public sphere, (b) communicating knowledge, (c) civil rights in communication, and (d) cultural rights in communication. According to this framework, communication rights flourish to the extent that media stimulate truly open debate and interaction; that knowledge is generated for the good of all; that citizens are ensured privacy of communication, control over their own personal information, and freedom from surveillance; and that individuals are free to communicate in their indigenous languages and to express their indigenous cultures.

As NWICO promoted just information flows internationally, academic media ethics came into its own organizationally. The first academic center for the study of media ethics, University of Minnesota's Silha Center for the Study of Media Ethics and Law, was established in 1984. That same year, the non-profit Poynter Institute for Media Studies instituted a seminar in applied ethics for reporters and editors. In 1985, the *Journal of Mass Media Ethics* began publication as a semiannual refereed journal; it became a quarterly journal in its fifth year. The semiannual *Media Ethics Update*, now *Media Ethics*, followed in 1988. Courses in media ethics proliferated. A 1980 survey identified 68 colleges and universities with freestanding courses in media ethics; by 1995, more than 158 colleges and universities were teaching courses in media ethics. The Media Ethics Division of the Association for Education in Journalism and Mass Communication was established in 1999 with a membership of nearly 200 scholars, and media ethics has had a presence in the Association for Practical and Professional Ethics from its inception in 1991. Chairs of media ethics were endowed at McGill University, the University of South Florida, and the University of Oregon (which began a graduate certificate program in media ethics in 2006). Since 1990, the Library of Congress has added one book every month under the subject heading of "journalistic ethics—United States," "communication—moral and ethical aspects," or "mass media—moral and ethical aspects."

As media ethics became incorporated into North American academics, international concerns were squarely on the agenda. In 1980, under the auspices of the International Association for Mass Communication Research, Anne van der Meiden of the State University of Utrecht (the Netherlands) published *Ethics and Mass Communication*, a collection of papers from Europe, North America, and Asia that addressed ethical issues cross-culturally. At the end of the decade, Thomas Cooper of Emerson College edited another cross-cultural anthology, *Communication Ethics and Global Change* (1989), which showed that concepts of truth, responsibility, and free expression permeate codes of media ethics across the world. Another set of cross-cultural studies followed in 1997 with *Communication Ethics and Universal Values* edited by Clifford Christians and Michael Traber. This book advanced the thesis that the sacredness of life is a universal belief that yields the moral universals of human dignity, honesty, and non-violence. Articles in the 2002 special issue of the *Journal of Mass Media Ethics* on the "search for a global media ethic" explored the possibility of universal ethical standards and an international code of journalism ethics, and showed that universal standards and principles have continued to preoccupy media ethics scholars.

Attempts to articulate ethical theories with cross-cultural appeal multiplied. Some turned to the discourse ethics of German philosopher Jürgen Habermas (1990), who attempted to describe rational and universal "ideal speech situations." Habermas described democratic life as a state in which the media fostered public conversation and debate based on equality, respect, and empathy. Clifford Christians and two colleagues proposed a theory of communitarianism as an alternative to the dominant individualism and its counterpart collectivism. As articulated in *Good News: Social Ethics and the Press*, communitarianism understood human beings as relational and on this basis proposed democratic transformations of media practices and organizations (Christians, Ferré, & Fackler, 1993). Another theoretical avenue was virtue ethics, which emphasizes what Klaidman and Beauchamp in *The Virtuous Journalist* called "a fixed disposition to do what is morally commendable" (1987, p. 18). Often applied to individuals, virtue ethics also informed discussions of corporations, as Nick Couldry did in *Listening Beyond the Echoes* (2006), which argues that as moral agents that bear essential information, the media need to be accurate, sincere, reflective, open, and accountable. Others drew on Carol Gilligan's *In a Different Voice* (1982) and Nell Noddings' *Caring* (1984) for feminist media ethics, which stressed equality, respect, and attachment as experienced in actual relationships, values that contrasted with the distance of journalistic objectivity and abstracted rules of professional codes.

For leading scholars, international communication had become more than an area of academic interest. Global, multimedia journalism had become the starting point for media ethics. Stephen J. A. Ward, author of *The Invention of Journalism Ethics* (2004), argued that the development of global news media and online journalism necessitated new approaches to journalism ethics. He contrasted parochial perspectives with more ethical, cosmopolitan perspectives. Parochial perspectives settled for a national context, neglecting cross-cultural comparisons of media traditions and practices. They acknowledged international reporting, but as a foreign activity disconnected from local practices. Cosmopolitan perspectives, on the other hand, situated practices and principles in a global context. Thinking of media serving a global human good, they define ethical journalism as helping address the staggering problems of humanity (Ward, 2006).

## CONCLUSION

The four periods of ferment in American media ethics history—the Progressive Era, professionalism in the 1920s, social responsibility after 1947, and global humanitarianism after 1980—signify a century of concern about media ethics on the parts of citizens, practitioners, and academics. The fact that the public has been involved in media ethics from the beginning and that professionals and academics have taken public concerns seriously shows that media ethics is a democratic enterprise. Issues such as fairness, privacy, and truth-telling have been debated in public forums, seminars, and newsrooms to various effects. Assumptions underlying these debates have changed from the caveat emptor of libertarianism to the obligations of social responsibility and global humanitarianism. Sometimes media ethics changes media behavior, sometimes not. Whatever the outcome, citizens in a democracy usually get the media they deserve.

Historical investigations of media ethics tend to be topical. They have traced the histories of ideas such as objectivity or privacy. The most useful of these histories have asked questions that have a bearing on current practice: How have issues in media ethics been framed? What assumptions did various sides of arguments make? What kinds of evidence were employed in the arguments? Were answers to questions translated into policies and practices? How has the enculturation of media ethics changed over time? Who has been revered in media history, and what does such reverence say about the generation that held these individuals in high esteem? What people, institutions, policies, and practices have exemplified key changes in media ethics? What lessons can be learned from the past, and does our present vantage point allow us to render judgments on previous practices? *Is* may not imply *ought*, but the more we know about how media ethics has been conducted in the past, the more perceptively we can address the important issues in media ethics today.

## REFERENCES

*About the Nieman foundation: History.* (2006). Retrieved April 10, 2007, from http://www.nieman.harvard. edu.

Campbell, W. (2001). *Yellow journalism: Puncturing the myths, defining the legacies.* Westport, CT: Praeger.

Christians, C. (2000). An intellectual history of media ethics. In B. Pattyn (Ed.), *Media ethics: Opening social dialogue* (pp. 15–46). Leuven, Belgium: Peeters.

Christians, C., Ferré, J., & Fackler, M. (1993). *Good news: Social ethics and the press.* New York: Oxford University Press.

Christians, C. & Traber, M. (Eds.). (1997). *Communication ethics and universal values.* Thousand Oaks, CA: Sage.

Cooper, T. (Ed.). (1989). *Communication ethics and global change.* White Plains, NY: Longman.

Coultry, N. (2006). *Listening beyond the echoes: Media, ethics, and agency in an uncertain world.* Boulder, CO: Paradigm.

Crawford, N. (1924). *The ethics of journalism.* New York: Alfred A. Knopf.

Dicken-Garcia, H. (1989). *Journalistic standards in nineteenth-century America.* Madison: University of Wisconsin Press.

Douglass, P. (1929). *The newspaper and responsibility.* Cincinnati: Caxton.

The duty of the press. (1897, January 26). *New York Times,* p. 12.

Ethics of newspapers. (1897, March 25). *New York Times,* p. 2.

Flint, L. (1925). *The conscience of the newspaper: A case book in principles and problems of journalism.* New York: D. Appleton.

Gerald, J. (1962). *Social responsibility of the press.* Minneapolis: University of Minnesota Press.

Gibbons, W. (1926). *Newspaper ethics: A discussion of good practice for journalists.* Ann Arbor, MI: Edwards Brothers.

Gilligan, C. (1982). *In a different voice: Psychological theory and women's development.* Cambridge, MA: Harvard University Press.

Habermas, J. (1990). *Moral consciousness and communicative action.* C. Lenhardt & S. Nicholsen (Trans.). Cambridge, MA: MIT Press.

Henning, A. (1932). *Ethics and practices in journalism.* New York: R. Long & R. R. Smith.

Ingersoll, R. (1908). *The works of Robert G. Ingersoll* (Vol. 7). New York: Dresden.

International Commission for the Study of Communication Problems. (1980). *Many voices, one world: Towards a new more just and more efficient world information and communication order.* New York: Unipub.

JaCoby, A. (2003). The newspaper ombudsman: A personal memoir of the early days. In C-J Bertrand (Ed.), *An arsenal for democracy: Media accountability systems* (pp. 185–90). Cresskill, NJ: Hampton.

Klaidman, S., & Beauchamp, T. (1987). *The virtuous journalist.* New York: Oxford University Press.

Lahey, T. (1924). *The morals of newspaper making.* Notre Dame, IN: University of Notre Dame Press.

Leigh, R. (Ed.). (1947). *A free and responsible press.* Chicago: University of Chicago Press.

Lilly, W. (1892). *On right and wrong* (3rd ed.). London: Chapman and Hall.

Merrill, J. & Barney, R. (Eds.). (1975). *Ethics and the press: Readings in mass media morality.* New York: Hastings House.

Miller, W. (1922). Code of ethics for newspapers. *The Annals of the American Academy of Political and Social Science, 101,* 286–94.

Mission of newspapers. (1897, February 7). *New York Times,* p. 24.

Mott, F. (1941). *American journalism: A history of newspapers in the United States through 250 years, 1690–1940.* New York: Macmillan.

Noddings, N. (1984). *Caring, a feminine approach to ethics & moral education.* Berkeley: University of California Press.

O'Dell, D. (1935). *The history of journalism education in the United States.* New York: Columbia Teachers College.

Pernicious yellow newspapers. (1898, March 28). *New York Times,* p. 5.

Shepley, J. (1968, September 20). A letter from the publisher. *Time,* p. 17.

Shuman, E. (1894). *Steps into journalism: Helps and hints for young writers.* Evanston, IL: Correspondence School of Journalism.

Siochrú, S. (2005). *Assessing communication rights: A handbook.* Retrieved April 10, 2007, from http://www.crisinfo.org/pdf/ggpen.pdf.

Siebert, F., Peterson, T., & Schramm, W. (1956). *Four theories of the press: The authoritarian, libertarian, and social responsibility and Soviet communist concepts of what the press should be and do.* Urbana: University of Illinois Press.

Swanberg, W. (1972). *Luce and his empire.* New York: Charles Scribner's Sons.

Two sorts of journalism. (1897, February 8). *New York Times,* p. 2.

van der Meiden, A. (Ed.). (1980). *Ethics and mass communication.* Utrecht, Netherlands: Department of Mass Communications, State University of Utrecht.

Walker, S. (1934). *City editor.* New York: Frederick A. Stokes.

Ward, S. (2006). Ethics for a revolutionary age: A global approach? *Journal of Mass Media Ethics, 21,* 363–71.

Ward, S. (2004). *The invention of journalism ethics: The path to objectivity and beyond.* Montreal: McGill-Queen's University Press.

Williams, J. (2005). Printing in America, 1600–1690. In W. Sloan (Ed.), *The media in America: A history* (6th ed.), pp. 17–34. Northport, AL: Vision.

Wood, H. (1893, October). The psychology of crime. *The Arena,* pp. 529–35.

Wright, T. (1898, April). The secular press. *New Church Review, 5,* 270–73.

Yellow journalism nuisances. (1898, March 23). *New York Times,* p. 6.

Yost, C. (1924). *The principles of journalism.* New York: D. Appleton.

# 3

# Essential Shared Values
# and 21st Century Journalism

## Deni Elliott

If anyone can be a publisher, then who is a journalist? The town square of the past is global today. Individuals and groups have unparalleled ability to capture and broadcast images and events. The Web allows unprecedented access to the opinions of others and to information from credible (and incredible) sources. The start of the 21st century has found American consumers adrift in a flood of visual and textual messages.

Here I argue that technology has, once again, caused a paradigm shift for journalism. While some suggest that the accessibility of information has made journalists unnecessary, I argue that professional journalists, with commitment to the essential shared values of the practice, are necessary to the development and sustenance of democratic process. Commitment to essential shared values allows for journalism to fulfill its social responsibility despite paradigm shift.

Paradigm shifts create confusion. One hallmark of paradigm shift, as described by scholar Thomas Kuhn (1962) who first coined the term, is that a significant number of relevant parties realize that old assumptions for content and process in the social institution under examination no longer hold. Yet, even as the new paradigm is clashing with the old, practitioners in the field need to keep functioning. The "pre-paradigm" period—the time in which new understandings and conventions are in development—is notable for its lack of consensus. During this time, "competing schools of thought possess differing procedures, theories, even metaphysical presuppositions" (Stanford University, 2007).

Yet, some things within the social institution endure, even during paradigm shift. For example, scientific revolutions shake basic assumptions about what citizens and practitioners believe. But, the need for scientists to develop and test new knowledge for the good of society continues. The social responsibility of journalists, at least in democracies, is to notice and report the important events and issues that citizens need to know so that they can effectively govern themselves (Kovach and Rosenstiel, 2001; Elliott, 1986). That remains true despite paradigm shifts. Essential shared values are those values that directly support journalists fulfilling their unique social responsibility (Elliott, 1988, pp. 29–30).

## FORCES OPPOSING TRADITIONAL JOURNALISM IN THE EARLY 21ST CENTURY

Four forces rise to the top as opposing the traditional journalistic practices that developed in the early 20th century:

1. Affordable satellite technology allows for instant transmission of messages by anyone;
2. The Web allows for instant access to information, as well as providing an instant podium and microphone in the virtual, global town-square;
3. Cable and satellite television, along with the Web, has created a 24-hour expectation for information flow, with the destruction of a space- and time-limited news hole; and
4. A lack of hard borders between types of mass communication—news, entertainment, advertising, and opinion—has resulted in a mixed bag of messages that defy easy classification.

Traditional journalism required that visual and text reporters recognize newsworthy events and record details to share with a mass audience. Now, breaking news is as likely to come from the cell phone camera of a participant or an accidental observer as it is from a journalist employed by a news organization. This input has given rise to the term *citizen journalist* as a label for those who are gathering information for news stories without the sanction of a recognized news organization. The collection of information for journalistic products from a large pool of information and information givers is called open sourcing. Citizens at large have gained greater credibility as sources of information.

But, according to long-time editor Robert Giles, "[M]astery of [new technology] is not a substitute for journalistic skills and values" (2001, p. 5). The ability to witness and collect data does not make one a journalist.

Traditional journalism took time. It took time to fact check a story. It took time for editors to review stories and determine placement in newspapers and broadcast news programs. But, every technological advance, from the Guttenberg press to computer to satellite, has cut down the time that journalists thought that they needed to do their work.

For generations, there was more information that a news organization had print or broadcast space to use. In addition, journalists had facts that they believed to be true, but that they could not report (yet) due to a lack of hard evidence or verification.

But, that has changed. According to Bryon Calame, *Times* Public Editor,

> For more than a century, *New York Times* reporters covering the newsworthy developments of the day typically focused on having the stories ready by the evening deadlines for the next morning's paper.... More and more, *Times* staffers are expected to deliver breaking news stories to the Web version of the paper 24 hours a day—as soon as the articles are ready. That means more editors are constantly balancing speed against completeness to decide when an article is good enough to carry *The Times'* respected brand. (Calame, 2006a, November 19)

Calame notes that the result is a different mindset for journalists along with an explosion of "multimedia and video presentations, audio, blogs and interactive graphics" (2006a, November 19). The ability to transmit instantly has created the expectation of instant transmission. The concept of a limited news hole has dissolved.

Traditionally, journalism involved a group of like-minded practitioners, choosing among topics and details, gate keeping and fact checking their way to the creation of a news story.

Reporters and photographers, designers and editors, producers and news directors huddled in separate newsrooms, adhering to common values, each seeking to develop similar news products first.

Now, instead of information givers all being journalists, who operate with similar conventions of practice, print and broadcast tabloids have become players. Bloggers are claiming turf as are citizens. These information givers do not respect the same rules as traditional journalists, but they influence traditional reporting.

Today "Internet journalism, according to those who produce manifestos on its behalf, represents a world historical development—not so much because of the expressive power of the new medium as because of its accessibility to producers and consumers" (Lemann, 2006, 44). Everyone, in turn, can be a producer and consumer of news.

K. Daniel Glover, editor of National Journal's *Technology Daily* and graphic designer Mike Essl call bloggers, "the pamphleteers of the 21st century, revolutionary 'citizen journalists' motivated by personal idealism and an unwavering confidence that they can reform American politics" (Glover and Essl, 2006, p. 13).

But, bloggers have a different role to play from journalists. "They exist to engage citizens in the obligations and magic of politics. They draw people into the fight. They have made millions of people feel that their voices will be heard somewhere and, when aggregated together, can have a real influence on the outcome of policy debates and elections" (Dionne, 2006, p. 34).

The capability of audience members to control collection and dissemination of news, collectively and individually, has led some to conclude that consumer judgment can substitute for news judgment.

> Disintermediated news is…not selected by editors. [It is news based on the assumption that] markets are capable of making better decisions about news than editors. We're getting this from two sides. First, there are the Web people, who have ingeniously figured out how to decide what's important by tabulating the collective wisdom of online readers. How galling for us—to be replaced by algorithm. Second, we're getting it from our own corporate leaders, who believe in market research. Why not just edit by referendum? They wonder. Why not just ask people what they want and give it to them? (Carroll, 2006, p. 5)

The short answer to that rhetorical question is that what is in the public interest and what the public is interested in are very different concepts. Essentially, journalists have the responsibility to seek the former.

Journalism, in the early 21st century, is a practice seeking definition,

> [I]t appears that there are two contrasting theories of journalism…. One consists of established standards and practices that emanate from print and broadcast journalism and the belief that journalism has a social responsibility to inform citizens and nurture democracy, while the other is informed by suspicion of centrally managed, traditional media conglomerates and a belief, inspired by the open architecture of the Internet and flexibility of Web publishing, that citizens can participate in democracy by creating their own journalism. (Berkman and Shumway, 2003, p. 67)

Traditional news was once easy to distinguish from other forms of mass communication. The boundaries between news and opinion, news and entertainment, news and advertising have softened for a variety of reasons, but just whether a particular informational product ought to count as news, reality, analysis, opinion, or parody is sometimes difficult to judge.

Consider two fake news shows that have been shown to be "just as substantive as network television news during the 2004 election" (Dowd, 2006). John Stewart, host of Comedy Central's

"The Daily Show" (TDS), and Stephen Colbert, of "The Colbert Report" (TCR), are 21st century cultural icons that deconstruct the idea of traditional news.

Yet, as ethics scholars Sandra Borden and Chad Tew point out, real news and the 'fake' news of the two comedy shows are deeply intertwined.

> [B ]y relying on raw material that has been "vetted" by journalists, TDS and TCR implicitly buy into factuality—and its associated rules of evidence—as a key norm for good journalism.... At the same time, "fake" news demonstrates how the same set of "facts" can be interpreted differently and contextualized more thoroughly. (Borden and Tew, 2007, pp. 10–11)

Rather than concluding that such shows make it difficult for audience members to differentiate news from other products, Borden and Tew argue that TDS provides a critical perspective, by which true news can be judged.

> Journalists can learn some valuable lessons from their encounter and interaction with 'fake' news, especially since the traditional values serve as the basis behind the critique of journalism. Both mainstream journalists and media critics from entertainment who perform news work within the system. Yet Stewart is ultimately an idealist in the sense that he uses traditional values to make judgments about whether the system can work better. (2007, p. 28)

This easily understood press criticism lets citizens in on the humorous, but value-based, analysis of news coverage.

## MOVING FROM THE 20TH CENTURY TRADITIONAL PARADIGM
## TO THE NEW PARADIGM

Under the traditional paradigm of news reporting, journalists should:

1. Seek external discoverable truth or, if there is no clear single truth, present two opposing sides of the story;
2. Use sources with recognized expertise or authority;
3. Present that material objectively;
4. For consumption by a general mass audience;
5. Through one-way communication.

The new paradigm of journalism, in contrast, looks like this:

1. Notice issue and events;
2. Use own reporting as well as open sourcing;
3. Filter that through journalistic perspective;
4. For consumption by targeted audiences;
5. Who then provide feedback.

This section explores clashes between these two paradigms. However, it important to remember that what is here called the "traditional" paradigm developed through a clash with a paradigm based on the partisan press.

According to Dionne,

> From the beginning of our republic in the 1790s until the turn of the [20th] century, American newspapers were, for the most part, the organs of political parties. There was no ideal of objectivity.... [But, then r]eformers who looked for professionalism, as against bossism, in politics eventually turned to seeking professionalism in journalism.
>
> Walter Lippmann...led the way to a redefinition of journalism's role and the journalist's responsibilities. The notion that newspapers should be objective rather than partisan was the product of Lippman's admiration for the scientific method, his skepticism of ideology, and, some of his critics would argue, his less than full-hearted faith in democracy. (2006, p. 34)

History shows us that new technology loosens old conventions and transforms the way that big stories are covered. In the 19th century, telegraph, the wire service, and the other technological developments created the ability to move a single story or picture to thousands of news outlets at a time. At the same time that these technologies were in development, the industrial revolution and an unending series of scientific discoveries were giving people a new sense of control over their environment. Causes and effects, and solutions to problems could all be discovered if only enough talent and resources were dedicated to the problem. Philosophers and scientists and the lay public agreed: the truth could be known.

These beliefs about human ability to know and control the world reverberated in the 20th century journalistic paradigm. Information could come from a common source, such as the team of Associated Press reporters at the scene of a catastrophe. Text and visual journalistic accounts that resulted were distributed to the thousands of news outlets that subscribed to wire services. News, produced to provide the truth to a broad audience of Americans seemed to exist independent of the age, ethnicity, politics, or geography of its consumer.

An early U.S. journalistic code of ethics adopted by the American Society of Newspaper Editors (ASNE) in 1923 (Illinois Institute of Technology, 2007) reflected the technological, political, and scientific understandings of the new century. For example, journalists were told to exhibit "natural and trained powers of observation and reasoning."

But, technology threatened the status quo.

> Two hundred years ago, James Gorden Bennett of the *New York Herald* was one of many who thought the telegraph would put newspapers out of business. It was a logical conclusion, he said, because "it would eliminate the competitive advantage he had over his rivals. All that would be left to newspapers was commentary and analysis." (Giles, 2001, p. 3)

"In newsrooms of the early 19th century, timeliness was not a priority. Newspapers were almost exclusively local" (Giles, 2001, p. 2). The telegraph changed all of that. Newspapers survived and the journalistic value of timeliness was born. Marketing values had a hand in the development of the non-partisan paradigm as well. Dionne notes: "By being nonpartisan and objective, newspapers did not offend half or more of their potential audience" (2006, p. 36).

But objective reporting was often that which didn't threaten the commonly held values of the audience. American journalism's coverage of World War II provides a good example. This was a non-controversial war from the point of view of most U.S. news consumers. Emerging technology, in the form of radio coverage, seemed to reinforce the notion that objective truth consisted of external reality that journalism helped citizens to experience.

From the time that Pearl Harbor was attacked on December 7, 1941, journalists rallied to give American audiences the American truth and show off new technology. The war was a radio news exclusive from the 2:22 p.m. Eastern Standard Time wire service report the day of the attack until the morning newspapers hit the stands at daybreak Monday.

CBS correspondent Edward R. Murrow gave listeners minute-by-minute descriptions of life in the war zone and experimented with new reporting techniques. For the first time ever, listeners had what we now call "natural sound"—they could hear for themselves what was going on at the scene while it was being reported (Edwards, 2004, pp. 51–52).

Purported objectivity was easy to achieve when it was believed by the audience that there was only one right side. In reality, there were other stories that were barely told or not told at all. For example, information that the U.S. government consistently denied assistance to Jewish families seeking escape from German genocide did not make its way into mainstream coverage of the day (*Jewish Virtual Library*, January 13, 1944). Nationalistic coverage was mistakenly believed to be objective coverage.

Within a decade of the war's end, however, objectivity and the understanding of what counted as news came under serious attack. The United States returned to peacetime comfortable in its military strength, but not as sure of the country's ability to withstand the more subtle threat of anti-democratic politics.

According to contemporary journalist Bob Edwards (2004), U.S. Senator Joe McCarthy, who fanned the fear of Communists in our midst, was a careful student of objective reporting in the early 1950s. Day after day, the Senator waved his new set of allegations too close to the conventional late-afternoon deadline for journalists to find an equally believable source who could give the other side of the story. The news convention of the day dictated that journalists report only what they were told. The Senator, as named source, provided an illusion of expertise. Denials, if published at all, came too late to gain the attention given to the initial claims.

Thoughtful journalists at the time were troubled that their objective, verifiable, named source reporting of external events did not reflect *truth*. But, it took the maverick television reporting of Edward R. Murrow to provide context for McCarthy's allegations. The just-born television documentary had not yet developed norms of conduct. It was different enough from the printed news story that it didn't follow the same rules. The content was controlled by its producer, not its sources. Producers sought to give complete stories rather than simply echo the pronouncements of authoritative sources. The "See It Now" piece, so devastating to Senator McCarthy, was aired in early March, 1954.

Bound by the Federal Communication Commission's requirement of fairness, Senator McCarthy was given an opportunity to produce a response that was later broadcast in the same time slot. But, in the end, McCarthy fell victim to the process that he had himself exploited. The "See It Now" television documentary provoked public disgust over McCarthy's misuse of his power and of news media. McCarthy's denial and explanations, four weeks later, could not rally equal attention or belief (Edwards, 2004, pp. 105–123).

On the face of it, it seemed that 20th-century technology conformed to the traditional paradigm technique of journalists channeling objective information. During that century, technology first, provided still images in addition to text so that citizens could see how something really looked; then audio let people know how events sounded, then video showed them how the event happened, and finally satellite technology put audiences in events as the story was still developing. And, from the beginning of that century, journalists worked to transmit the accounts of sources and story subjects with dispassionate accuracy. But, rather than reinforce the belief of a single Enlightenment-style truth, slice-of-life journalistic reporting ultimately revealed that stories have multiple perspectives rather than a single infallible truth.

Reporting on later 20th century stories such as the U.S. civil rights movement, the Vietnam War, and Watergate could not have happened through exclusive reliance on authoritative sources contributing in traditional ways.

Consider, for example, the reporting on Watergate. Then veteran *Washington Post* reporter Bob Woodward and novice reporter Carl Bernstein did not wait for official pronouncements or for on-the-record credible sources to tell the nation what was happening and why. Woodward and Bernstein obtained information however they could, tricking telephone company clerks and pressuring witnesses called before the grand jury into the disclosure of information. Rather than searching for, finding, and then reporting some indisputable truth, the Watergate reporting included a confluence of perspectives emerging from White House statements, leaked tapes, leaked grand jury testimony, Congressional testimony, stolen files, insiders seeking to expose corruption, those seeking to cover it up, and those changing sides. Woodward and Bernstein drew conclusions from a conglomerate of sources "close to the matter" and provided a narrative that best fit the pieces they were able to collect (Woodward and Bernstein, 1974).

However, the myth of objective reporting continued in the public mind and in journalism schools until the reporting on a new Presidential scandal 14 years later. The coverage of President Bill Clinton and his affair with a White House intern illustrates even more clearly the clash between paradigms.

From the beginning of this scandal, Web communication competed with traditional journalistic process. When Matt Drudge, publisher of the Web-based Drudge Report, told his e-mail recipients and Web-browser audience in January 1998 that *Newsweek* had decided to sit on a story about allegations of a Presidential sex scandal (McClintick, 1998, p. 113) the newsmagazine's editors responded by dumping the story onto online publication immediately rather than waiting additional days to first publish the story in the hard copy magazine.

Here was a story developed by traditional journalists that was force-fed to the public by a Web-based gossip columnist. According to McClintick (1998), that act of Matt Drudge foreshadowed

> the role of the Internet as a new and different journalism medium—and as a catalyst of broader trends in America toward democratization and devolution of the power of big institutions, especially in the media worlds of New York and Washington. In that sense, Drudge can be seen as a modern Tom Paine, a possible precursor to millions of town criers using the Internet to invade the turf of bigfoot journalists. (p. 114)

The reporting on Clinton-Lewinsky also provided an early example of how political leaders could bypass news media. Independent Prosecutor Kenneth Starr released his report simultaneously to journalists in hard copy and to citizens by posting it on the Web. In 2006, it is not surprising that candidates for the 2008 U.S. Presidential run would hold their own Web-based voter communications and, thus, bypass journalistic gatekeepers. But, in 1998, going around the journalistic gatekeepers was highly unusual.

Giles says,

> Posting the Starr Report gave the public an unfiltered version. It did not need a journalist to sort out the lead, to provide the context, to interpret the independent counsel's conclusions. To some it was a splendid example of democracy. For journalists, it was a revealing moment. The capacity to post documents and reports on the Web gave the public a vital point of comparison.... As documents and transcripts on the Web became a potential check against truthful reporting, they raise the bar in newsrooms everywhere for accuracy, balance and fairness. (2006, p. 9)

A final example from the Clinton-Lewinsky coverage illustrates how journalists staying wedded to the traditional paradigm of dutifully reporting what sources say failed to meet the journalistic responsibility of telling citizens what they need to know for self-governance. The faulty adherence to the old paradigm was more noticeable because so many of the old paradigm conventions had been violated in the reporting of the story.

On March 5, 1998, *The Washington Post* published a detailed account of President Clinton's deposition in the Paula Jones case. At the time, the deposition was sealed by court order. The *Post's* report was not attributed, but the ultimate sources for the leak were few. The sealed deposition could have been leaked by Clinton's defense team, by Jones's lawyers, or by Ken Starr's office (Baker, 1998). *Post* reporter Peter Baker, who received and published the information, knew the source of the report. If traditional paradigm holds, at least one *Post* editor also knew the source as well or knew enough about the source to agree that the information supplied was likely to be accurate.

In the published story, the *Post* allowed each potential source to deny the leak. Clinton attorneys called the leak illegal, reprehensible, and unethical. They promised to track down the leaker's identity. Jones' lawyers said that any suggestion that they were responsible for the leak was "erroneous, reprehensible and fallacious." Independent Counsel Kenneth Starr categorically denied that his office was the direct or indirect source of the story (Baker, 1998).

However, logically, someone in the Clinton, Jones, or Starr camps was indeed responsible for the leaked information, and the *Post* reporter and editor knew the identity of that person. The printed denials were probably accurate presentations of these named source's denials, but at least one of them was false. While it was certainly important for readers to know that the various players in the case denied having leaked the information, they also needed to know who was being truthful and why *The Washington Post* knowingly allowed one or more of these sources to lie in the news columns. The citizens were not told. "[P]ure nonpartisanship, in the sense of bending over too far to seem to be fair, can mislead reporters" (Dionne, 2006, p. 37).

As late as journalistic disclosures at the perjury and obstruction of justice trial of White House official Lewis "Scooter" Libby in March 2007, journalists were being exposed for aiding governmental manipulators at the expense of serving them rather than the public. According to media columnist Tim Rutten, most of the 10 journalists who testified a the Libby trial, "had made themselves willing tools of an administration bent on discrediting a guy whose offense was to inform people about how the White House had misled the country about its reasons for invading Iraq" (Rutten, 2007, p. E16).

## PROBLEMS WITH THE OLD PARADIGM AND PROBLEMS WITH THE NEW

Adherence to the traditional paradigm of news reporting can fail to help journalists fulfill their social responsibility to citizens. An objective press is a powerless press that can be exploited by sources. McCarthy's manipulation of journalistic process, which horrified journalists and citizens in the 1950s, had morphed into an accepted method of political survival by the 1990s called *spin*. News organizations should not knowingly report falsehoods or trial balloons without labeling them as such for their readers. Allowing those with power to "spin" a story in the name of objectivity may meet the needs of sources but fails to meet the needs of citizens.

Next, under the old paradigm, students are taught to get "both sides of a story." Most stories have one side or many sides. Natural disasters and house fires generally have one side. Earthquakes have no "side" of the story to tell. The story is what happens to people affected by the disaster. If the story becomes one of how well individuals and social institutions are coping with the disaster, the story becomes one of multiple perspectives. Journalists must choose among the many sides to provide focus for their stories, but when they choose only two, to give a polarized either/or perspective, they lose the nuances that citizens need to understand before they can make educated decisions for self-governance.

Last of all, the old paradigm was built on the idea that journalists were expected to find external news. But, discoverable news is a myth. News is what happens when journalists choose to pay attention to some event or issue, always at the expense of others. Visual journalists have always known that a photograph doesn't mirror what is out there, but shows pieces of reality, selected by the brain and its filters functioning in the photographer behind the camera. Images are given meaning by singling them out, choosing angle, composition, and frame.

Although these pillars of objectivity, two sides to the story, and external news were standards of 20th century American journalism, they more strongly reflect marketing strategies rather than ethical principles. They reflected the technological possibilities of the time and reflected news consortiums' development of an audience and advertising base larger than a community limited by geography or politics. Ultimately, they reflected news organizations' interest in cheap purchase of news products that fit the needs of every person.

But, the new paradigm has its problems as well. The pillars upon which it rests in this development phase are interactivity, multiple source perspectives, and targeted audiences.

Interactivity and multiple perspectives have resulted in Wikiality—the mistaken belief that open participation in providing and editing information results in truth. "The millions of bloggers who are constantly watching, fact-checking and exposing mistakes are a powerful example of 'the wisdom of crowds' being assisted by a technology that is as open and omnipresent as we are" (Naim, 2006, p. 31). Unfortunately, inter-subjective agreement does not equal truth. The crowd can be wrong.

Suspicion of corporate control of traditional news media has led some to bestow greater credibility on the independent blogger. According to journalist Hope Crystal (2002), "Readers may find blogs more credible than traditional media because blogs have no corporate interest to serve" (p. 8).

However, advertisers have infiltrated blogs, paying bloggers to build buzz for their clients' products (Friedman, 2007, p. C1). No reader can be sure if what they are reading is the "true" blogger opinion regarding a movie, book, or restaurant, or whether it is a blog-ad, inserted into the script for a fee.

Careful targeting of audiences and the shaping of news product to fit the individual consumer can lead to less-informed citizens. Individuals who take in information because it fits their comfort zone or because what they are interested in was determined by previous purchasing or online searching, experience life with blinders. Nineteenth century British philosopher John Stuart Mill contended that very few people really know what they think because of what we would call today "selective exposure." He says that most people "…have never thrown themselves into the mental position of those who think differently from them, and consider what such persons may have to say; and consequently they do not, in any proper sense of the word, know the doctrine which they themselves profess" (1859, pp. 42–43).

## ESSENTIAL SHARED VALUES

Journalism, like other important social institutions draws on essential shared values for its identification. It would be easy to draw the erroneous conclusion that journalists are relativists—adherents to a philosophical theory that holds that there is no objective standard for judging right and wrong. However, I will argue here that journalists do hold moral standards by which they judge professional behavior. Indeed, without such standards, journalism would not be recognizable as a discrete industry (Elliott, 1988, p. 28).

This author identified three shared values that are sustained across culture and time, and paradigm shifts as well:

1. Journalists should strive to publish news accounts that are balanced, accurate, relevant and complete (BARC).
2. Journalists should strive to publish news accounts that are BARC without causing harm that could be prevented.
3. Journalists should strive to give citizens information that they need for self-governance. This principle is the defining principle for the practice of journalism and the one that justifies causing harm in the production of news stories. If citizens need to have that information, it is justified to publish it, even if the information causes harm to some individual or group. (pp. 29–30)

"The essential shared values of journalism provide the criteria by which reporters and editors judge the adequacy of their actions and the adequacy of their peers' actions" (p. 30): Ultimately, the essential shared values of journalism are those that support the development and maintenance of democracy: "When news meets journalistic standards of excellence, it empowers citizens to perform…civic functions necessary for full participation in community life" (Borden, 2006, pp. 14–15).

According to Lemann (2006),

Reporting—meaning the tradition by which a member of a distinct occupational category gets to cross the usual bounds of geography and class, to go where important things are happening, to ask powerful people blunt and impertinent questions, and to report back, reliably and in plain language, to a general audience—is a distinctive, fairly recent invention…. It has spread—and it continues to spread—around the world. It is a powerful social tool, because it provides citizens with an independent source of information about the state and other holders of power. (p. 49)

The Internet reinforces the journalistic role in bringing up and sustaining citizen self-governance,

1. The Internet has become a powerful weapon in the fight for freedom. 2. In many countries, where dictatorships or totalitarian governments want to control the flow of information, courageous journalists are getting their stories out on the Web in ways that are not possible over government-controlled radio and television or in some newspapers whose owners are friendly to the government. (Giles, 2006, pp. 6–7)

Essential shared values are the ethical principles that support journalists fulfilling their special social responsibility. The current paradigm of journalism describes the conventions of practice, determined by technology and influenced by marketing considerations.

## THE NEW PARADIGM CAN REINFORCE ESSENTIAL SHARED VALUES OF THE PRESS

Technology allows for the development of a more active and engaged citizenry, so the new paradigm holds the promise of better journalism than ever. For example, the input of citizen journalists and satellite technology has expanded the coverage of newsworthy events. News has to be noticed before it can exist.

The presence of multiple sources and the ability of citizens to seek a variety of information provide a justification for journalistic perspective. Journalists need to maintain voices that are separate from the powerful individuals and groups that would manipulate them and the pull of public opinion as well. Only journalists have the special responsibility of providing information to citizens for self-governance. Journalists are those who are motivated to sift through the mountains of information to provide citizens what they need.

Bloggers, as the new partisan media, play an important role in stimulating active citizenry, but do not substitute for independent journalism.

> There is an enormous need for information that is developed outside the confines of political struggles. Honest debate requires at least some consensus on what the facts are, and honesty, not obfuscation, where there is genuine confusion over the nature of the facts.... What we need, in other words, is to welcome the new partisan and participatory outlets while finding ways to nurture and improve independent journalism. (Dionne, 2006, p. 41)

The Web offers a powerful new tool for good journalism. Newsassignments.net, administered by New York University professor and journalism critic, Jay Rosen (2007) is an impressive hybrid of new and old paradigm journalism. The site "tries to spark innovation in journalism by showing that open collaboration over the Internet among reporters, editors, and large groups of users can produce high-quality work that serves the public interest, holds up under scrutiny, and builds trust."

> The site uses open source methods to develop good assignments and help bring them to completion. It pays professional journalists to carry the project home and set high standards; they work closely with users who have something to contribute.... It does stories that the regular news media doesn't do, can't do, wouldn't do, or already screwed up. (Rosen, 2006)

But the Web is improving journalism in less ambitious ways as well:

> In their Internet versions, most traditional news organizations make their reporters available to answer readers' questions and, often, permit readers to post their own material. Being able to see this as the advent of true democracy in what had been a media oligarchy makes it much easier to argue that Internet journalism has already achieved great things. (Lehman, 2006, p. 48)

A sign that the new paradigm is moving past its infancy is that practitioners of the "new" journalism are working to articulate standards. Professional groups, such as the *Media Bloggers Association*, are establishing ethical standards, correction policies, and professional identity. These bloggers are moving closer to their traditional print and electronic journalism counterparts and are gaining access to coverage of newsworthy events in the process. For the first time in Federal Court, two of the press seats reserved at the January 2007 trial of White House advisor Lewis Libby were held for bloggers (Sipress, 2007, p. D1).

Good journalistic practice, whatever the paradigm of the moment, is that which upholds the essential shared values of the profession.

## REFERENCES

American Society of Newspaper Editors (ASNE ).(1923) Code of Ethics. Retrieved March 10, 2007 from http://ethics.iit.edu/codes/coe/amer.soc.newspaper.editors.1923.html

Baker, P. (1998). "New Details of Clinton's Jones Deposition Leaked," *The Washington Post*. Retrieved March 10, 2007 from http://www.cnn.com/ALLPOLITICS/1998/03/05/clinton.deposition/

Berkman, R. I. and Shumway, C. A. (2003). *Digital Dilemmas, Ethical Issues for Online Media Professionals*. Ames, Iowa: Iowa State Press.

Borden, S. (2006, August). "A Theory of Journalism." Paper presented to the Media Ethics Division of the

Annual Convention of the Association for Education in Journalism and Mass Communication, San Francisco, CA.

Borden, S. and Tew, C. (2007). "The Role of Journalist and the Performance of Journalism, Lessons From 'Fake' News (Seriously)." *Journal of Mass Media Ethics.*

Calame, B. (2006a, November 19). "Breaking News: Can Times Quality Be Preserved Online?" *The New York Times.* Retrieved December 30, 2006 from http://www.nytimes.com/2006/11/19/opinion/19pubed.html?ei=50

Calame, B. (2006b, December 10). "Other Voices: Are Reporters' Aspirations that Noble?" *The New York Times,* p. 12.

Carroll, J. S. (2006, April 26). *What Will Become of Newspapers?* Cambridge, MA: Joan Shorenstein Center on Press, Politics and Public Policy. (Speech delivered at the annual meeting of the American Society of Newspaper Editors under the title, "Last Call at the ASNE Saloon")

Cristol, H. (2002, Sept./Oct.). News in the digital age. *The Futurist,* p. 8.

Dionne, E. J. (2006, November 16). *The Making of Democracy: How the New Media and the Old Media Could Live Together Happily and Enhance Public Life.* Cambridge MA: Joan Shorenstein Center of Press, Politics and Public Policy. (Speech delivered as the Theodore H. White Lecture at the Joan Shorenstein Center of Press, Politics and Public Policy, Kennedy School of Government, Harvard University)

Edwards, B. (2004). *Edward R. Murrow and the Birth of Broadcast Journalism.* New York: John Wiley.

Elliott, D. (1986). "Foundations of Press Responsibility," in D. Elliott (Ed.), *Responsible Journalism.* Thousand Oaks, CA: Sage, pp. 32–44.

Elliott, D. (1988). "All is not relative: Essential Shared Values and the Press." *Journal of Mass Media Ethics, 3*(1), 28–32.

Friedman, J. (2007, March 9). "Blogging for dollars raises questions of online ethics." *The Los Angeles Times,* pp. C1, C6.

Giles, R. (2001). "Bringing News Standards to the Web," in Louis W. Hodges (Ed.), *Ethics in Journalism,* (Vol. 4, pp. 1–21). Lexington, VA: Washington and Lee University Press.

Glover, K. D. and Essl, M. (2006, December 3). "New on the Web: Politics as Usual." *The New York Times.* 13.

Jewish Virtual Library. (1944). *Report to the Secretary on the Acquiescence of this Government in the Murder of the Jews.* Retrieved March 10, 2007 from http://www.jewishvirtuallibrary.org/jsource/Holocaust/treasrep.html.

Kovach, B. and Rosenstiel, T. (2001). *The Elements of Journalism: What Newspeople Should Know and the Public Should Expect.* New York: Three Rivers Press..

Kuhn, T. (1962). *The Structure of Scientific Revolutions.* Chicago: University of Chicago Press.

Lemann, N. (2006, August 7 & 14). "Amateur Hour." *The New Yorker,* pp. 44–49.

McClintick, D. (1998, November). "Towncrier for the New Age." *Brill's Content,* pp. 113–127.

Mill, J. S. (1859/1991). Utilitarianism. In J. Gray (Ed.), *On liberty and other essays.* New York: Oxford University Press.

Naim, M. (2006, December 20). "The YouTube Effect." *Los Angeles Times,* p. 31.

Rosen, J. (2006, August 19). *Welcome to NewAssignment.net.* Retrieved March 10, 2007 from http://www.newassignment.net/blog/jay_rosen/

Rosen, J. (2007, March 9). *PressThink, Ghost of Democracy in the Media Machine.* Retrieved March 10, 2007 from http://journalism.nyu.edu/pubzone/weblogs/pressthink/

Rutten, T. (2007, March 10). "Let's Keep Reporters from being G-Men," *Los Angeles Times,* p. E1, 16.

Sipress, A. (2007, January 11). "Too Casual To Sit on Press Row? Bloggers Credentials Boosted With Seats at the Libby Trial." *The Washington Post,* p. D1.

Stanford University. (2007). Retrieved March 29, 2007 from http://plato.stanford.edu/entries/thomas-kuhn/#3.

Woodward, B. and Bernstein, C. (1974). *All the President's Men.* New York: Simon and Schuster.

# 4

# Moral Development: A Psychological Approach to Understanding Ethical Judgment

## Renita Coleman and Lee Wilkins

## INTRODUCTION

Research on moral development attempts to respond to the following question: how is it that people grow morally, and what influences the development of a moral life? Moral development research makes some important assumptions that are seldom addressed in the literature but which are nonetheless central to it:

- All human beings have the capacity for moral thinking.
- Moral thinking is linked to experience. While philosophers have contributed enormously to a thoroughgoing analysis of the implications of choice within experience, no legitimate ethical theory divorces human action, and hence experience, from moral thinking, learning and growth.
- Moral thinking can be both general and particular. There are general moral questions—is it right to lie or to kill—to which all human beings have a response. But, there are particular elaborations of moral questions—is it ever appropriate for a journalist to deceive a source who is attempting to deceive the journalist—to which professionals must respond within a particular context.

This chapter will briefly review the general understandings of the field, place our research within that context, and then suggest potential paths for additional empirical and theoretical work.

## THEORETICAL BUILDING BLOCKS

The Swiss psychologist Jean Piaget is considered the field's founder in terms of both research results and approach. Piaget was particularly interested in how children put their cognitive worlds in order. He researched and wrote the book *The Moral Judgment of the Child* (Piaget, 1965) just after he had written a book on how children understand causality. In the subsequent work, Piaget was particularly concerned with the following questions:

1. How is it that children understand the moral "rules" of behavior with their peers;
2. Where do the "rules" come from;
3. How, and under what circumstances, can the rules be changed.

Piaget answered these questions with a qualitative study of children playing in their natural environment. He watched and interviewed young boys as they played marbles. The interviews were designed to elicit the boys' understanding of the moral rules as well as their "consciousness" of the rules themselves. The use of the concept of autonomy in Piaget's work is significant for philosophy as well as psychology. Philosophers assert that ethical thinking and action begins with the ability to make an autonomous choice. How such autonomy develops, and how it is bounded by life experience as well as cultural constraint, has significant implications for the fields of both psychology and philosophy.

The boys who played marbles ranged in age from 5 to 12, and Piaget found that their understanding of the moral rules changed according to a predictable, and predictably more sophisticated, pattern—hence, the term moral "development." The very youngest children, age 2, put the marbles in their mouths, a kind of motor exploration every parent will recognize but with little moral import. Piaget called it *motor and individual.* As the children aged, this highly idiosyncratic play became both routinized and ritualized. By age 5, the children moved into the egocentric stage, where the rules were regarded as immutable and originating from authority figures. Boys in the 5- to 6-year-old-range didn't really play together; they engaged in what psychologists today call parallel play. By ages 7 to 8, two important changes occurred. First, the boys actually played together and they moved into what Piaget called *the stage of incipient cooperation.* At this stage, the boys, in separate interviews, would give very different accounts of the actual rules, but they regarded these disparate rules as immutable, emanating from authority figures, and applicable to everyone in all instances—no exceptions. Finally, at about age 9 to 10, the boys entered the stage of the *codification of the rules.* At this stage, the boys gave the same account of the rules. These boys had internalized the rules and understood that they could change them—providing those changes were consistent with the reasons behind the rules themselves. Changing the rules summoned both moral autonomy and moral imagination. Philosophers would recognize some of the changes the boys instituted as reflecting an understanding of distributive justice (Rawls, 1971), and a grasp of the need for universal application of principle.

While Piaget (1965) did his work on children, the applicability of his insights to adult moral behavior is straightforward. Adults sometimes do ethically questionable things (driving a car very fast just for the experience of speed) to see "what it would feel like." Cooperation is the work of adult life—in families and on the job. Adults placed in novel situations—first-time parents, college graduates at the start of a career—often search for the "rule book" as a way of guiding themselves through a bewildering set of options and unanticipated need for decisions. Comfort, experience, and good cognitive skills ultimately allow most adults to internalize some universal understandings—even if those understandings are unevenly and irregularly applied. Adult life mirrors the moral judgments of the child in often uncanny and insightful ways.

Piaget's work stood for more than two decades before psychoanalyst Erik Erikson (1963) expanded on it. Erikson's work will be dealt with in more depth later in this chapter, but it is important to note that Erikson focused on the entire adult life cycle, not just childhood. Furthermore, Erikson postulated that each stage of moral development depended to an important degree on how the issues raised in previous stages had been resolved. Based on the work of these two psycholgists, scholars accepted that moral development was both sequential and hierarchical.

While many scholars have contributed to the theory of moral development, it is Harvard psychologist Lawrence Kohlberg's six stages of moral development that are most widely used today. Kohlberg (1981, 1984), who tested Piaget's framework on undergraduate men at Harvard, proposed that these stages reflect progressively higher quality ethical reasoning, based on principles of ethical philosophy, with the higher the stage the better the reasoning. His theory rests on the assumption that some reasons used to decide ethical quandaries are better than others; good ethical thinking is not relativistic. He said that some reasons for choosing a course of action represent more comprehensive, coherent, elaborated or developed, ideas, and described the course of moral development as evolving from simpler ideas to more complex ones (Rest, Narvaez, Bebeau, & Thoma, 1999).

Kohlberg also intended for his theory to be applied to society, that is, to laws, roles, institutions, and general practices, rather than to personal, face-to-face relationships (Rest, Narvaez, Bebeau, & Thoma, 1999). This type of macro-morality addresses relations between strangers, competitors, diverse ethnic groups and religions, not just the micro-morality of family, friends, neighbors, and acquaintances. His is a psychologically-based theory of social justice—a society-wide system of cooperation among strangers, not only friends.

Kohlberg theorized that people progress through the six stages in hierarchical linear fashion with no slipping backward. People are fully "in" one stage or another, and move up the staircase one step at a time. These hard stages based on a staircase metaphor have since been modified to reflect a softer model based on the concept of schematic thinking. Schemas, which are expectations about the ways events usually unfold, are developed through previous interactions (Fiske & Taylor, 1984). People hold schemas for ethical problems that they use when making decisions about new dilemmas (Rest, Narvaez, Bebeau, & Thoma, 1999). Schemas activate understandings from long-term memory to help people process new information; moral schemas are activated from long-term memory to help people understand and process information that arises from new ethical problems. That is, if a person has acquired the highest quality schema, it will be activated; otherwise, less developed schemas are used. In this model, people can reason using multiple stages at one time. They can regress and use lower stages at the same time they use the higher ones; however, generally, people will show more propensity to use the higher stages more often as they grow and develop.

Kohlberg's six stages were divided into three broad categories—Preconventional, Conventional, and Postconventional, which correspond to the new model of three schemas, but with slightly different names.

The **Preconventional** stage, now called the *Personal Interest schema*, is defined by rules that are delivered by authority and are inviolable; breaking rules results in punishment, and adherence to rules is either to avoid punishment or gain rewards. In this stage, people are concerned with their own welfare. Acts that provide satisfaction to the self and others are "right," but others are considered only when their needs are in line with one's own. This level of moral development is defined by simple, self-interested obedience to the rules—following the rules primarily when it is in one's own interest to do so. People who use the personal interest schema make moral decisions based on reasons that emphasize self-interest and punishment for wrongdoing. In the latter half of this stage or schema, reciprocity and fairness begin to emerge in a self-serving way, for example, children would agree to give others a birthday present because they believe that others will reciprocate on their birthday.

The second stage of **Conventional** reasoning, now renamed the *Maintaining Norms* schema, is where rules begin to be respected for their own sake and are eventually seen as serving society. Rules are necessary for maintaining social order and can be changed if all agree. This category is defined by conformity to the expectations of society. Helping others and gaining their approval drives an individual's actions. At this level, one's moral reasoning is dominated by "doing one's duty" and maintaining social order for its own sake. Authority here is vested in the social group(s) to which the individual belongs. The notion of social systems, or doing what is expected to maintain social order, is paramount. Conformity, or doing what other people expect, is important. Thinking at this stage acknowledges the role of duty. Research suggests that most people operate at this level of moral development most of the time (Kohlberg, 1981, 1984).

Kohlberg's highest stage, the **Postconventional**, is still called *Postconventional* in the schema model. In this stage, Kohlberg relied heavily on Rawls' (1971) concept of justice from an original position behind a "veil of ignorance." When decision-makers do their reasoning behind a veil where they are ignorant of their own station in life as well as that of others, all people will be treated equally and as ends in themselves. This ensures the use of universal principles that all would agree to uphold, even if they did not benefit the person making the decision. Kohlberg referred to this as "moral musical chairs."

In the Postconventional stage or schema, laws and rules are respected only so far as they appeal to universal ethical principles; rules are the result of intellectual reasoning and they should achieve full reciprocity; that is, the rules themselves should not favor one group over another. Right and wrong, and the value of rules and law, are determined by their appeal to mutuality and universality. Individual principles of conscience define morality at this level. People who use this schema are concerned about the reason for the rules and are willing to challenge both social norms and self-interest for a more universal understanding. For example, a journalist operating at this stage of moral development would agree to withhold the name of a rape victim from the public in order to protect that person's privacy even though the professional norm is to name crime victims to enhance journalistic credibility. At this level, there is an awareness of the process by which rules are arrived at as well as the content of the rules. People are aware of concepts such as a social contract that demands citizens uphold laws even if they are not in an individual's best interest, and it includes an understanding that some rights are beyond debate, for example, life and liberty. Those at this stage internalize such principles and apply them evenhandedly.

The following example distinguishes between thinking at the *Conventional* level and the *Postconventional* level: In the 1960s, Martin Luther King, Jr., deliberately marched, sat, and ate in places that were illegal for African Americans to be in during that time. George Wallace, the governor of Alabama, had King jailed for breaking these laws. According to Conventional or Maintaining Norms reasoning, King would be ethically wrong and Wallace right. But Postconventional reasoning would determine that King was in the right because the laws he was defying were unjust; they singled out specific people rather than treating all people equally, thus they did not represent universal principles.

Kohlberg's concept of moral development was challenged by Carol Gilligan (1982), a former student of Kohlberg's who argued that women develop differently from men, placing more emphasis on caring for others. Kohlberg's formulation focused on rights and justice, and was criticized by Gilligan (1982) because women systematically scored lower than men on Kohlberg's test. Her study of women making moral choices about abortion uncovered the idea that moral weight should be given to caring for others. She suggested the moral adult was the person who could reason about both rights and connections or relationships to others. Although Kohlberg had specified his theory was to be applied to macro issues rather than micro ones, he revised his framework to include an ethic of care along with his rights-based reasoning; since then, women and men have done about the same on tests of this theory such as the Defining Issues Test (Thoma, 1986).

TABLE 4.1
Stages/Schemas of Moral Development

| Stage | Description | Sample statements from PR and journalism dilemmas |
| --- | --- | --- |
| **Preconventional/ personal interest** | Avoid punishment, gain rewards. Doesn't consider the interests of others. | Keeping quiet would help my firm's bottom line. Would it advance my career? |
| **Conventional/ maintaining norms** | Belief in the Golden Rule. Living up to what is expected by others. Desire to maintain rules and authority, uphold laws. Right is contributing to society, group, or institution. | Whether a community's laws are going to be upheld. There is nothing illegal about not telling everything we know. What my client wants. |
| **Postconventional** | Concern that laws be based on rational calculation of overall good. Recognizes moral and legal points of view sometimes conflict. Laws are valid when they rest on universal principles of justice. People are ends in themselves and must be treated as such. | What would best serve society? If I would want everyone else who is ever in a similar situation to do the same thing. |

## THE DEFINING ISSUES TEST—HOW IT WORKS

Another student of Kohlberg's who extended his work in important ways was James Rest. He applied the concept of moral development specifically to the professions, starting with nurses and including veterinarians, doctors, dentists, and social workers, among others. Most importantly, Rest and his colleagues devised a paper-and-pencil instrument that was faster and easier to administer and score than Kohlberg's Moral Judgment Inventory, which used in-depth interviews and an 800-page code book to score each thought's stage (Rest & Narvaez, 1998; Rest, Narvaez, Bebeau, & Thoma, 1999).

We take a moment here to note that it is not our intention to suggest that the DIT is the only legitimate way to conduct morality research. There are many good instruments and approaches. However, the DIT has been in use since the 1970s and more than 1,000 studies of literally hundreds of thousands of people in more than 40 countries allow us much comparative data and confidence. It is important to note that the DIT is copyrighted; while we refer to the instrument, for reasons of academic integrity we do not quote directly from it but only from our modifications to it.

Basically, the DIT poses six ethical dilemmas and asks respondents to make a decision about what they would do, for example, would you report to police a neighbor who has been a model citizen for 10 years but turns out to have escaped from prison a decade ago? The answers participants can choose from are rather limited—turn him in, don't turn him in, or can't decide. In reality, there may be tremendous middle ground and alternatives that would go into making a good ethical decision; however, for the purposes of assessing one's level of moral development, this behavioral choice is less important than the other tasks on the DIT (Rest, Narvaez, Bebeau, & Thoma, 1999).[1]

More than 400 published studies using the DIT have established its validity and generalizability. It correlates highly (up to $r = .78$) with other tests of ethical reasoning and developmental measures, and has been shown to measure moral development, not intelligence, education, verbal ability, or some other construct. Test-retest reliability is in the .80s using Cronbach's *alpha* for internal reliability. It contains built-in checks to assure that participants are not randomly giving high ratings to statements that sound important but which have little meaning for them; in other words, trying to fake high. There also is a consistency check that ensures the statements ranked highest also are rated highest. The DIT is a projective instrument; that is, participants know they are taking an "ethics test," but they cannot tell which answers are better than others. Finally, the DIT has been linked to measures of ethical behavior such as cheating on tests, prosocial behavior, professional decision-making, and job performance (Rest, Narvaez, Bebeau, & Thoma, 1999); in other words, it doesn't just measure what people *say* they would do, but correlates with what they would be likely to *actually* do.

Of course, there are limitations to the DIT, only one of which will be discussed here; for more information see Rest, Narvaez, Bebeau, and Thoma (1999). First, in scoring the level of moral development, the original DIT gives "credit" only for statements at the highest stage of ethical reasoning, not for reasoning at the Conventional stage. This is because the DIT is designed to measure the relative importance that a person gives to principled moral thinking, and is not interested in lower stage thinking.[2]

While the DIT measures ways of thinking, its connection to philosophy is clear. Universal principles and their application result in higher scores. In addition, because the DIT was based on Kohlberg's work initially, universal principles which emphasize "rights" constitute the original conception of the postconventional schema.

## MAJOR PREDICTORS

Much research on moral development is concerned with discovering the differences among individuals that are the major predictors of higher levels of ethical reasoning. In this section, we focus on four of the most consistent predictors correlated with higher moral development, and one individual characteristic that is *not* a predictor but is connected to this topic anyway.

Any theory that claims to be "developmental" implies that people change as they age. In the case of moral development theory, the higher the age, the higher the quality of moral reasoning used. Thus, age and education are the primary determinants of moral development (Rest, 1993). Longitudinal studies have found stage progression as predicted by the theory from high school into adulthood (White, Bushnell, & Regnemer, 1978) and moral development levels off when formal education stops (Rest, 1979). The two are obviously correlated—one cannot usually achieve high levels of education at an early age—yet age and education are not the same thing. Advanced age alone does not guarantee high levels of education, and education is a more powerful predictor of moral development. One scholar who focused on delineating what it is about age that fostered moral development found the best predictors were when people's life experiences involved intellectual stimulation or supported learning, or included a rich social environment in the form of a stimulating spouse, friends, and institutional affiliations (Deemer, 1989). Like age, education involves more than mere time spent in classrooms. Multiple possibilities help explain why education improves moral development. For example, college aims to develop critical thinking skills and professors are always asking students to explain why, give evidence for opinions, and think for themselves. The social experience of college exposes students to diversity of facts, ideas, people, and cultures. Alternatively, it could be that the people who choose to go to college are more interested in their own development, and college stimulates that (Rest, Narvaez, Bebeau, & Thoma, 1999). Kohlberg (1976) thought it was the process of learning to see things from other people's points of view that provided the key to growth in moral judgment.

Although age and education are the strongest predictors of the DIT's moral development measure known as the P score, "the most striking finding from the literature … is the consistent relationship between DIT P scores and religious beliefs" (Rest, Thoma, Moon, & Getz, 1986, p. 131). Consistently, and perhaps counterintuitively, more fundamental or conservative religious beliefs are correlated with lower levels of moral development in numerous studies (Lawrence, 1978; Parker, 1990; Rest, 1979, 1983, 1986). We wish to point out up front that it is religious *fundamentalism* that is implicated here—the literal interpretation of religious texts such as the Bible or Koran and rigid adherence to those principles, often with intolerance of other views— *not* one's religious affiliation or the strength of one's religious devotion. Some scholars theorize that a higher ethical orientation requires critical and evaluative reasoning that may be opposed to fundamental religious beliefs (Parker, 1990). If orthodox religions teach that it is improper and sinful to question, critique, or scrutinize the church or a divine authority, then people find it harder to move out of the conventional stage of reasoning. Fundamentalist ideologies that prescribe laws or norms and make them binding upon people without question are understood in terms of maintaining norms schemas; divine authority is outside the bounds of human scrutiny or understanding. In one study (Lawrence, 1978), radically fundamental seminarians who could understand postconventional concepts did not use them in making moral decisions. They explained that they were setting aside their own intuitions about what was fair because as mortals, their judgment was fallible. Instead, they turned to religious teachings to tell them what to do. Similarly, other scholars (Glock & Stark, 1996) found that orthodox Christian beliefs were highly correlated with social intolerance, and yet another (Ellis, 1986) concluded that extreme religiosity leads to a greater disregard for the rights of others.

The DIT creators reject the idea that they or Kohlberg, his theory, or the DIT, are antireligious. Indeed, religious directives from transcendent authorities that are incorporated into life experience and therefore not beyond human understanding are postconventional: "Many people of faith have a postconventional understanding of their religion and its moral meaning for their lives" (Rest, Narvaez, Bebeau, & Thoma, 1999, p. 123). Even Kohlberg wrote that religious beliefs influence moral thinking in powerful ways (Kohlberg & Power, 1981), and offered statements about religious beliefs that represented postconventional thinking (e.g., God is the force behind a just society and autonomous personhood; religious faith affirms a person's desire to lead a moral life). This stance is entirely consistent with many contemporary ethical theorists and some ancient ones as well. The final powerful predictor of moral development is political ideology. Typically, conservative attitudes are more supportive of authority and established practices, which describes the conventional level of moral development. Political positions that encourage freedom of thought are more attuned to Postconventional thinking. In DIT studies, self-reported conservatives tend to prefer Conventional statements, and self-reported liberals tend to like Postconventional items.

The DIT creators say that it is natural for political ideology to mirror moral development because political attitudes represent ideas about how people should relate to each other in society; moral judgment also concerns itself with how people should get along in macro situations. In politics, people make decisions about how to relate to others in a larger sense, through laws, institutions, and general practices. Political choices involve choosing how a law or policy affects everyone in society and how society should work generally. Political attitudes mirror the DIT's macro-morality by focusing on what principles should govern us all. The conservative/ liberal scale in political ideology is independent of a particular party—one can be a conservative Democrat or a liberal Democrat, just as one can be a conservative or liberal Republican. Also like the religiosity measure, discriminant validity studies have shown that the DIT is not simply a measure of liberal political attitudes. Both conservative and liberal positions can be staged at Postconventional levels.

Finally, we want to briefly address a common misunderstanding of moral development theory—namely that the work of one scholar "disproves" the work of another. One of the most frequent comments we hear about the field is that Gilligan's work disproved Kohlberg's insights. Her book, *In a Different Voice* (Gilligan, 1982), argued that Kohlberg's theory was biased against women, who preferred to use an ethic of caring for others rather than a justice orientation. She interviewed women who were facing a personal ethical dilemma—whether to have an abortion. Even though Kohlberg had devised his theory to explain ethical reasoning in social situations rather than individual ones such as the abortion question Gilligan studied, he made changes in his theory and instrument to incorporate the ethic of care, or what he called benevolence, in the highest stage of development. When Rest and colleagues developed the DIT, they did include women in their samples and that instrument has not shown any significant gender bias. Reviews of DIT studies show 90% of them find no gender differences (Rest, 1979; Thoma, 1986). When differences are found, it is usually women who score higher, not men. Nevertheless, this belief that Kohlberg is obsolete thanks to Gilligan is an enduring one that persists despite much evidence to the contrary.

## JOURNALISTS AND OTHERS IN MASS COMMUNICATION

The original DIT scholars focused their research on professions with a large moral component including nurses, doctors, dentists, and accountants. They suggest the DIT is especially good at measuring decision-making in uncertain situations. Even though journalism is not technically a profession in the sense that its members are licensed and regulated by independent review boards, the DIT creators include journalism in this category, calling it an "emerging profession" (Rest & Narvaez, 1994, p. xi). We agree; as former professional journalists we are well acquainted with having to make decisions without full information about situations that have no one right answer, or even very good ones. To our knowledge, the first study of journalists using the DIT was a dissertation in 1995 (Westbrook, 1995), which was excerpted for a chapter in Rest and colleagues' book on moral development in the professions (Rest & Narvaez, 1994). Nor are we aware of any further research on these professionals with the DIT until our own pilot study of 72 journalists seven years later (Coleman & Wilkins, 2002). Since then, we and others have completed more research on this important group of professionals.

Our pilot study of 72 journalists showed that they scored fourth highest among all professionals tested with the DIT. The journalists ranked behind seminarians/philosophers, medical students, and physicians, but above dental students, nurses, graduate students, undergraduate college students, veterinary students, and adults in general. The mean P score for the journalists in the first study was 48.17; this is in comparison with the average adult's P score of 40 (for comparison with other professions, see Table 4.2). In order to have confidence in results, social scientists look to replication. So, it was encouraging that the P score of our journalists was virtually the same as the P scores of the 66 journalists in Westbrook's study—48.1. And, furthermore, that our later study of 249 journalists whose news organizations were randomly sampled from around the country was again nearly the same, with a mean P score of 48.68. Larger samples typically produce higher scores, so this slightly (but not statistically significant) higher number is to be expected. In all these studies, journalists scored higher than three groups whose members had higher education levels than the average journalist—dental, veterinary, and graduate students. Recall that education is consistently the best predictor of moral development; as education goes up, so does the mean P score. Yet, these journalists had, on average, a four-year college education, while dental, veterinary, and graduate students have one to two years more education.

We have finished a study of 118 public relations professionals around the country, and they fared similarly to the journalists (Wilkins & Coleman, 2006). The mean P score was 46.2, which puts the PR professionals in sixth place, just below journalists and dental students. Again, except for the journalists, the other groups of professionals all had higher levels of education than the PR professionals. Although this study randomly sampled PR firms around the country, it is by no means the definitive word on the moral development of public relations professionals; cumulative results obtained through replication would give us more confidence.

We issue similar caveats when interpreting the results of a non-random, web-based study of 65 advertising professionals (Cunningham, 2005). The advertisers who responded in this study showed considerably lower levels of ethical reasoning than the journalists or public relations pro fessionals—their mean P score was 31.64, also well below the average P score of 40 for adults in general. They were more similar to the scores of people working in various businesses than other professions. Part of an explanation for this poor showing is the scores on the two advertising-focused dilemmas; the mean P score of 22.7 on these two dilemmas actually pulled down their score on the other dilemmas—more on that later.

In all these studies, we also looked for significant predictors of higher levels of moral judgment. What we found was somewhat consistent with the larger literature, but not on all counts. Religiosity was consistently a predictor of the P score. In both our pilot study and a larger, random sample of journalists, religion was significantly and negatively correlated with these journalists' P scores. In both studies, journalists who said they were more liberal in their beliefs were significantly more likely to score higher than were the religious fundamentalists. Religious fundamentalism had the same negative effect on the public relations professionals' P scores. In that study, we also teased out the difference between fundamentalism and depth of one's religious conviction by including the question: "How religious are you, extremely to not at all?" While those who said they held fundamentalist views showed significantly lower levels of ethical reasoning, those who said they were deeply religious did not show any differences in P scores from the less religious. The advertising study did not ask questions about religion.

Political ideology behaved as it has in other studies only in the study of public relations professionals; in this group, those who rated their political views as more liberal were significantly likely to have higher P scores. This effect did not hold for either study of journalists; advertisers were not asked about their political views.

Surprisingly, age and education were not the major predictors of ethical development in our four studies that they are traditionally. Education approached significance ($p = .06$) in the large sample study of journalists, but not the smaller study of journalists, or the ones of PR professionals and advertisers. We surmise this may have something to do with a lack of variance in education. We have no explanation for the lack of an effect of age considering these respondents ranged from 18 to 75.

Not surprisingly, gender was again not significant in any of the four studies. We also found there were no differences in ethical reasoning abilities between broadcasters and print journalists in either journalism study, although those who had done investigative reporting had significantly higher P scores than those who had not. Various other factors that we studied were significant predictors of better moral judgment, and we invite those interested to read the entire studies (Coleman & Wilkins, 2002, 2004; Cunningham, 2005; Wilkins & Coleman, 2005, 2006).

One common feature of the four studies cited above is the use of domain-specific dilemmas. The DIT creators were adamant for years that the dilemmas should remain the same in order to complete a comparable cycle of research. However, after they devised new dilemmas of their own for a second version of the DIT, called the DIT-2, they began to encourage experimentation with new dilemmas in new formats (Rest, Narvaez, Thoma, & Bebeau, 1999), adding that domain-specific stories can be more predictive of behavior (Rest & Narvaez, 1984). The four studies reviewed here took advantage of that by including two dilemmas specific to journalism, public relations, and advertising. This allowed comparison between the domain-specific dilemmas and the more general dilemmas on the original DIT. In the two journalism studies and the PR study, we found exactly what the DIT creators predicted—that expertise in an area leads to high quality ethical reasoning about those topics (Rest, Narvaez, Bebeau, & Thoma, 1999). In both studies of journalists, the respondents had significantly higher mean P scores for the journalism dilemmas than for the non-journalism dilemmas. The same was true of the PR professionals. The advertising practitioners, however, showed exactly the *opposite* results; their scores on the two advertising dilemmas were actually significantly *lower* than their scores on the non-advertising dilemmas. Using other data they supplied, Cunningham (Cunningham, 2005) theorized that these advertising practitioners were able to reason at a higher level, but suspended that ability when the issues were about advertising and focused instead on financial concerns for themselves, their clients, and agencies. Disturbingly, having worked in the advertising industry longer was significantly predictive of lower levels of ethical reasoning; thus, industry socialization seems to privilege self-serving financial concerns over more universal, social ones.

## OTHER INFLUENCE ON MORAL THINKING

Another approach to the study of moral development has been to devise controlled experiments to see what sorts of interventions or manipulations can help improve people's ethical reasoning. We also have conducted a few experiments on journalists in that vein. Most typically, researchers look to educational interventions such as ethics courses; we examined two different influences that can be found in professional environments, not just college settings—race and the presence of photographs.

In two studies of the effects of race on ethical reasoning, we found that white journalism majors were significantly more likely to use lower quality ethical reasoning when the story subjects were black than when they were white (Coleman, 2003), but that black journalism majors were not (Coleman, 2005). The black future journalists showed the same level of reasoning regardless of the race of the story subjects. This line of research continues with professional journalists of different ethnicities, and expands to include Asian and Hispanic journalists.

In the study of photographs, we found that the presence of a picture of the people in the dilemma significantly improved participants' ethical reasoning. The two experiments identified thinking about the people affected by an ethical situation as important in the process (Coleman, 2007). Visualizing stakeholders is an important component of classical ethical theory, particularly in distributive justice and in many conceptualizations of duty. Providing ethical decision makers with visual information may well evoke these more universal principles, something that has implications for media professionals and members of other professions as well.

## DIRECTIONS FOR FUTURE RESEARCH:
## THE COMPONENTS OF MORAL THINKING

As our research has demonstrated, visual imagery changes moral reasoning. However, life does not happen as a series of still photographs; for most people, most of the time, images move. However, research in psychology has demonstrated that comprehending moving images requires more cognitive capacity (Lang, 2000). In some instances, far from promoting deeper thinking,

TABLE 4.2
**Mean P Scores of Various Professions**

| | |
|---|---|
| Seminarians/philosophers | 65.1 |
| Medical students | 50.2 |
| Practicing physicians | 49.2 |
| Journalists | 48.1 to 48.68 |
| Dental students | 47.6 |
| Public relations professionals | 46.2 |
| Nurses | 46.3 |
| Lawyers | 46 |
| Graduate students | 44.9 |
| Undergraduate students | 43.2 |
| Pharmacy students | 42.8 |
| Veterinary students | 42.2 |
| Navy enlisted men | 41.6 |
| Orthopedic surgeons | 41 |
| Adults in general | 40 |
| Business professionals | 38.13 |
| Accounting undergraduates | 34.8 |
| Accounting auditors | 32.5 |
| Business students | 31.35 to 37.4 |
| Advertising professionals | 31.64 |
| Public relations students | 31.18 |
| High school students | 31 |
| Prison inmates | 23.7 |
| Junior high students | 20 |

*Source:* Compiled by the authors from individual published studies and data
supplied by the Center for the Study of Ethical Development.

moving images—because they demand so much effort to understand—actually retard memory
and retention. Thus, one logical next question is to test whether moving images have the same
impact on moral reasoning as still images do. This question has implications for journalists, who
more and more in these days of convergence, work with moving images. The implications do
not end there. As any student of the field is aware, during the early part of the 21st century, journalism had significant credibility problems, and some of those problems were linked to public
perception about the profession's ethical shortcomings. Because most Americans now get their
news from television, how the average person interprets the ethical content of moving images has
ramifications for understanding audiences' ethical reasoning.

News also increasingly crosses borders and media content is more and more produced for international audiences and by journalists who realize their work speaks to a world-wide audience.
Thus, the study of professional moral development needs to be conducted on non-U.S. journalists, as well. This effort will allow scholars to begin to understand the impact of culture—not just
newsroom culture but also history and country—on journalistic decision making. Philosophically, if some ethical understandings do appear to be universal, and if some patterns of thought
cross the boundaries of nation-state, then this evidence becomes central to the nascent search
for universal norms and understandings (Gert, 1988; Christians, 2002). Culture certainly should
make some difference, and there is preliminary work in the field to suggest it is a difference of
emphasis rather than quality and kind (Rao & Lee 2005). But more systematic work, and work
that can be comparative without being colonial or invasive, would add considerable depth to the
contemporary understandings in the field.

## THE IMPACT OF WORK ITSELF ON MORAL DEVELOPMENT

The existing literature of moral development has relied extensively on the psychological litera-ture of intellectual development. In addition, much of the literature on moral growth focuses on children (e.g., Piaget) or adolescents and undergraduate college students (Perry, 1970). Relatively few studies have examined moral development throughout the first four decades of the human life span (Levinson, 1986) or moral development in people past the age of 35 to 40 (Belenky, 1986; Gilligan, 1982). Only Levinson's work devotes much attention to the impact of work on develop-ment, and in that study, work was emphasized as marking some sorts of moral growth rather than as an influence on that growth. The same is true of *Women's Ways of Knowing* (Belenky, 1986).

Only Erikson (1963) has provided any sort of theoretical map of the links between moral growth and individual development from birth to extreme old age. That theory is linked with life experience in general, and only at certain times focuses on specific actions; for example, the ability to establish and maintain adult, intimate relationships. However, Erikson's theory also establishes a profoundly influential place for the environment, in his words the society into which human beings are born and function. Erikson provides some tantalizing suggestions about what sort of external influences may spur moral adult development and growth. He notes,

> ...We must expand our scope to include the study of the way in which societies lighten the in-escapable conflicts of childhood with a promise of some security, identity, and integrity. In thus reinforcing the values by which the ego exists...societies create the only condition under which human growth is possible.... Yet, political, economic and technical elites, wherever they have accepted the obligation to perfect a new style of living at a logical point in history, have provided men with a high sense of identity and have inspired them to reach new levels of civilization. (Erikson, 1950/1963, pp. 277–278)

Because Erikson is first and foremost a psychoanalyst, his theory places the individual first and links individual development with specific "crises" that all human beings must surmount. But, another group of psychologists—without the lens of Freudian psychoanalysis—have come to remarkably similar conclusions. When Gardner, Csikszentmihalyi, and Damon (2001) note that journalism is a profession profoundly out of joint with itself, they also summon notions of identity, roles, and professionals goals as they are influenced by the world of work in which con-temporary people spend so much of their adult lives. By interviewing professionals "at the top of their game," Gardner and colleagues assured themselves of a sample with both professional vision and the professional career informed by life experience to reflect upon it. As their book demonstrates, these journalists worked and yearned for a profession that was reconnected to its nurturance and sustenance of political society, specifically contemporary democracy. They saw themselves as reflecting that connection but stymied by the powerful economic factors currently influencing media organizations. Authentic alignment, in their terms, meant creating new institu-tions, expanding the functions of, reconfiguring membership in, and reaffirming the values of existing institutions, and taking personal stands (pp. 212–218.) These suggestions are not so far removed from the final four stages of Erikson's adult moral development. Future research should investigate the specific impact of work on moral growth—specifically professional moral devel-opment. In addition, understanding moral growth may encourage philosophical work. For exam-ple, the ethics of care in the psychological literature has generally been separated from classical ethical theory. However, by an in-depth evaluation of the moral growth of professionals, as well as analyzing their individual moral choices, how professionals connect philosophical concepts such as care and duty have remained separated in the academic literature (Wilkins, in press).

One future challenge of moral development research is to tease out the areas of the world of work that can promote or retard moral growth in a professional context. Empirical work, of course, would follow.

## NOTES

1. The DIT is scored as follows: Participants rank 12 issues statements according to how important each one is in making a decision. The statements represent the different stages of schemas that make up the categories developed by Kohlberg as modified by Rest. Participants have five options—from not important to very important—on each statement, the presumption being that if a person has developed a particular schema, say the conventional schema, the participant will rank statements from that stage higher than statements at other stages. The final task is for participants to consider all 12 statements and rank only the top 4 of them in order of importance in decision making. This ranking forms the basis of the P score—a number which reflects the relative importance the person gave only to postconventional statements.
2. The developers of the DIT spent 20 years trying to develop an alternative scoring system that would eliminate "throwing away data," that is, the lower stage items. The P score survived because it consistently gave better trends for the theoretically expected findings, and was relatively easy to compute and interpret (see Rest, Thoma, Narvaez, & Bebeau, 1997).

## REFERENCES

Belenky, M. F. (1986). *Women's ways of knowing: The development of self, voice, and mind.* New York: Basic Books.
Christians, C. (2002). The social ethics of Agnes Heller. In S. L. Bracci & C. G. Christians (Eds), *Moral engagement in public life: Theorists for contemporary ethics* (pp. 53–72). New York: Peter Lang.
Coleman, R. (2003). Race and ethical reasoning: The importance of race to journalistic decision making. *Journalism & Mass Communication Quarterly, 80*(2), 295–310.
Coleman, R. (2005, Aug. 10–13). Color blind: Race and the ethical reasoning of African Americans on journalism dilemmas. Paper presented at the AEJMC Conference, San Antonio, TX.
Coleman, R. (2007). The effect of visuals on ethical reasoning: What's a photograph worth to journalists making moral decisions? *Journalism & Mass Communication Quarterly, 83* (4), 835–850.
Coleman, R., & Wilkins, L. (2002). Searching for the ethical journalist: An exploratory study of the ethical development of news workers. *Journal of Mass Media Ethics, 17*(3), 209–255.
Coleman, R., & Wilkins, L. (2004). The moral development of journalists: A comparison with other professions and a model for predicting high quality ethical reasoning. *Journalism & Mass Communication Quarterly, 81*(3), 511–527.
Cunningham, A. (2005). Advertising practitioners respond: The news is not good. In L. Wilkins & R. Coleman (Eds.), *The moral media: How journalists reason about ethics* (pp. 114–124). Mahwah, NJ: Erlbaum.
Deemer, D. (1989). Moral judgment and life experience. *Moral Education Forum, 14*(2), 11–21.
Ellis, A. (1986). Fanaticism that may lead to a nuclear holocaust: The contributions of scientific counseling and psychotherapy. *Journal of Counseling and Development, 65*(3), 146–151.
Erikson, E. (1950/1963). *Childhood and society.* New York: W. W. Norton.
Fiske, S. T., & Taylor, S. E. (1984). *Social cognition.* Reading, MA: Addison-Wesley.
Gardner, H., Csikszentmihalyi, M., & Damon, W. (2001). *Good work: When excellence and ethics meet.* New York: Basic Books.
Gert, B. (1988). *Morality: A new justification for the moral rules.* New York: Oxford University Press.
Gilligan, C. (1982). *In a different voice: Psychological theory and women's development.* Cambridge, MA: Harvard University Press.

Glock, C., & Stark, R. (1996). *Christian beliefs and anti-Semitism.* New York: Harper & Row.

Kohlberg, L. (1976). Moral stages and moralization: The cognitive developmental approach. In T. Lickona (Ed.), *Moral development and behavior* (pp. 31–53). New York: Holt, Rinehart & Winston.

Kohlberg, L. (1981). *The philosophy of moral development: Moral stages and the idea of justice.* Cambridge, MA: Harper & Row.

Kohlberg, L. (1984). *The psychology of moral development: The nature and validity of moral stages.* San Francisco: Harper & Row.

Kohlberg, L., & Power, C. (1981). Moral development, religious thinking, and the question of a seventh stage. In L. Kohlberg (Ed.), *Essays on moral development: Vol. 1. The philosophy of moral development* (pp. 311–372). New York: Harper & Row.

Lang, A. (2000). The limited capacity model of mediated message processing. *Journal of Communication, 60*(1), 46–70.

Lawrence, J. A. (1978). *The component procedures of moral judgment-making.* Doctoral dissertation, University of Minnesota.

Levinson, D. J. (1986). *The seasons of a man's life.* New York: Ballantine.

Parker, R. J. (1990). The relationship between dogmatism, orthodox Christian beliefs, and ethical judgment. *Counseling and Values, 34*(3), 213–216.

Perry, W. G. (1970). *Forms of intellectual and ethical development in the college years: A scheme.* New York: Holt, Rinehart and Winston.

Piaget, J. (1965). *The moral judgment of the child.* New York: The Free Press.

Rao, S., & Lee, S. T. (2005). Globalizing media ethics: An assessment of university ethics among international political journalists. *Journal of Mass Media Ethics, 20,* (2&3), 99–120.

Rawls, J. (1971). *A theory of justice.* Cambridge, MA: Belknap Press of Harvard University Press.

Rest, J. R. (1979). *Development in judging moral issues.* Minneapolis, MN: University of Minnesota Press.

Rest, J. R. (1983). Morality. In P. H. Mussen (Ed.), *Handbook of child psychology: Vol. 3. Cognitive development* (pp. 556–629). New York: John Wiley.

Rest, J. R. (1986). *Moral development: Advances in research and theory.* New York: Praeger.

Rest, J. R. (1993). Research on moral judgment in college students. In A. Garrod (Ed.), *Approaches to moral development: New research and emerging themes.* New York: Teacher's College Press.

Rest, J. R., & Narvaez, D. (1984). *Supplement to Guide for DIT-1.* Minneapolis, MN: Center for the Study of Ethical Development, University of Minnesota.

Rest, J. R., & Narvaez, D. (Eds.). (1994). *Moral development in the professions: Psychology and applied ethics.* Hillsdale, NJ: Erlbaum.

Rest, J. R., & Narvaez, D. (1998). *Supplement to Guide for DIT-1.* Minneapolis, MN: Center for the Study of Ethical Development, University of Minnesota.

Rest, J. R., Narvaez, D., Bebeau, M. J., & Thoma, S. J. (1999). *Postconventional moral thinking: A neo-Kohlbergian approach.* Mahwah, NJ: Erlbaum.

Rest, J. R., Narvaez, D., Thoma, S., & Bebeau, M. J. (1999). DIT2: Devising and testing a revised instrument of moral judgment. *Journal of Educational Psychology, 91*(4), 644–459.

Rest, J. R., Thoma, S., Moon, Y. L., & Getz, I. (1986). Different cultures, sexes, and religions. In J. R. Rest (Ed.), *Moral development: Advances in research and theory* (pp. 89–132). New York: Praeger.

Rest, J. R., Thoma, S., Narvaez, D., & Bebeau, M. J. (1997). Alchemy and beyond: Indexing the Defining Issues Test. *Journal of Educational Psychology, 89*(3), 498–507.

Thoma, S. (1986). Estimating gender differences in the comprehension and preference of moral issues. *Developmental Review, 6*(2), 165–180.

Westbrook, T. L. (1995). *The cognitive moral development of journalists: Distribution and implications for news production.* University of Texas-Austin.

White, C., Bushnell, N., & Regnemer. (1978). Moral development in Bahamian school children: A three-year examination of Kohlberg's stages of moral development. *Developmental Psychology, 14*(1), 58–65.

Wilkins, L., & Coleman, R. (2005). *The moral media: How journalists reason about ethics.* Mahwah: NJ: Erlbaum.

Wilkins, L., & Coleman, R. (2006, August 2–5). *The moral development of public relations practitioners: A comparison with other professions.* Paper presented at the AEJMC Conference, San Francisco, CA.

Wilkins, L. (in press). Connecting care and duty: How neuroscience and feminist ethics can contribute to understanding professional moral development.

# 5

# The Search for Universals

## Clifford G. Christians and Thomas W. Cooper

The earth's stratosphere is loaded with satellites for citizen information and military deployment. These two global technologies stand in counterpoint. As information increases, we presume to facilitate global understanding. Open communication unfettered and destructive technology restrained—together they yields a working formula for sustaining the globe at this complicated time in human history.

Indeed, communication has facilitated world affairs. The Berlin Wall fell and Gorbachev's Glasnost took hold before a watching world. A new world information order of free flow and communication balance among nations was touted when the cold war's strategy of mutually assured destruction began to fade. Television, radio, and the Internet rallied the United States on 9/11 and nurtured empathy across the globe. In electronic narrative, working-class rescue teams became heroes of national strength and resiliency, even while the media constructed an identity for terrorism. News coverage of Iraq and Afghanistan helps keep the military accountable, and ensures that the abuses at Abu Ghraib prison are inescapable. The Qatar-based Arab network, Al-Jazeera, has refused to promote any government's agenda. Because of the global media, we recognize that conquering in war and winning minds are two different things, and the latter indispensable.

But in reality only rarely do the media serve as democracy's agent and militarism's contradiction. The Persian Gulf War and the Iraq invasion were integrations of electronic communication and military technology. And certainly the war on terrorism is communications-driven as well. Al-Qaeda exists as a cyber network and its strategies are interwoven with television and computers. Meanwhile, electronic profiling of personal data and surveillance of citizen activities continues to multiply, typically motivated by national security or under its guise.

All of these conditions not only raise the question "Don't we need a global media ethic?" but also imply an answer. It is obvious that the media do not exist in a vacuum. Their welfare is determined by their context. In fact, the urgency of a global media ethics that matches the muscle of today's communication technologies has become obvious. Given the power of international media corporations and the high speed electronic technologies which now characterize the media worldwide, it is imperative that ethics be broad and strong enough to equal their universal scope. Otherwise the result is a quiescent ethics, echoing the status quo rather than challenging or contradicting it.

In fact, several worldwide models have been developed or are underway. The Eurocentric ethical canon that is monocultural, parochial, and patriarchal is being replaced by cross-cultural, international frameworks.

## THEORIES OF UNIVERSALS: PROFESSIONAL APPROACHES

Transcendental metaphysical universals that presume foundationalism have been discredited as imperialistic (see Alleyene chapter for additional discussion of this view). Therefore, scholars today doing credible work on universals understand norms to be historically embedded rather than abstract and absolutist. Diversity in culture does not in itself prove philosophical relativism. Relativism is subject to the naturalistic fallacy; that is, "ought" statements cannot be derived from "is" statements since they represent different realms. What exists in a natural setting cannot itself yield normative guidelines. And relativism faces the long-standing contradiction articulated by Karl Mannheim: Those insisting that all cultures are relative must arise above them and in so doing relativism is nullified. The ethical frameworks described below all emphasize cultural diversity while seeking universals that are transcendent. The primary issue is identifying a different kind of universal, one that honors the splendid variety of human life.

Kaarle Nordenstreng opened a pathway by accounting for common values, but diversity also, through professional codes of ethics. Nordenstreng's *The Mass Declaration of UNESCO* (1984) was a pathbreaker in understanding professional ethics internationally through codes of ethics as constellations of media values. A later inventory of 31 codes in Europe identified journalists' accountability to the public, and to their sources and referents, as the primary emphases (Laitila, 1995). Christians and Nordenstreng (2004) put codes of ethics in the larger context of social responsibility theory. Social responsibility thinking has been appearing in different parts of the world, from the Hutchins Commission in the United States to the MacBride Commission to the European Union to public journalism. Codes of ethics contribute also in bringing society to the forefront, if these codes are reoriented from media-centered professionalism to social responsibility as a citizen-based paradigm.

Cooper's *Communication Ethics and Global Change* (1989) was the first comprehensive survey of media ethics across cultures by an international network of media professionals and educators from 13 countries. His study of professional morality identified three protonorms as candidates for universal status. He concluded that one worldwide concern within the apparatus of professional standards and codes is the quest for truth, though often limited to objectivity and accuracy. A second concern, based on the available research data, Cooper defines as a desire among public communicators to work responsibly within the social mores and cultural features in which they operate. He also concludes that freedom of expression is a third imperative across professional media practice. Although stated in different language and to different degrees, free speech is an important component in maintaining accurate human expression.

Claude-Jean Bertrand (2000) advocates media accountability systems (M.A.S.) for enforcing ethical practices in the democratic media worldwide. M.A.S. examines every option in the private sector that fosters the media's responsibility through pressuring media organization and journalists to better serve the public, and thereby depriving the government of a pretext to interfere. All available strategies for media regulation are included—codes of ethics, ombudspersons, news councils (local, regional, national), in-house critics, journalism reviews, accuracy and fairness citizen groups, readers' and viewers' panels, and research institutes. Media accountability systems are more necessary now than ever given the unprecedented privatization and deregulation of electronic media throughout the world. Media accountability systems emphasizing freedom and equality already exist in various forms across the globe, particularly in such countries as Japan, the United Kingdom, Germany, France, Sweden, Israel, Estonia, Portugal, and the United States (Bertrand, 2003, pp. 293–384).

## THEORIES OF UNIVERSALS: PHILOSOPHICAL APPROACHES

There are also several universal frameworks that step outside professional ethics and media institutions to work from the general morality. While having an explicit communication orientation, they are theoretical models rooted in philosophical reflection.

Seyla Benhabib (1992) has developed a principled interactive universalism not subject to the criticism of postmodernists that grand narratives are no longer possible. She defends universalist ideals in moral and political life by addressing the contemporary assault on universals. In the process, she takes seriously the contributions of feminism and communitarianism. In her reformulation of discourse ethics, humans are dialogic selves whose moral agency follows the norms implicit in Habermas' ideal speech situation—universal moral respect and egalitarian reciprocity (Bracci, 2002, pp. 128–130). Her idea of interactive dialogic rationality keeps ethics close to people's everyday experience, so that diversity in cultures is recognized rather than burying differences under an abstract metaphysics.

Kwasi Wiredu (1996) writes out of an African philosophical perspective. The human species lives by language. Every language is similar in its phonemic complexity and all languages serve not merely functional roles but in cultural formation. All languages are translatable into another and understood in doing so. Every normal human being can learn another language and some people are purely bilingual. Through the intrinsic self-reflexivity of natural language, we arbitrate our values and establish our differences and similarities. Languages everywhere are communal giving their speakers particularity, while the shared lingual character of our existence makes intercultural communication possible. Through the commonness of our biologic-cultural identity as *homines sapientes*, we can believe that there are universals while living at the same time in our local communities.

In a study of ethical principles in 13 countries, the sacredness of human life is consistently affirmed as a universal value (Christians and Traber, 1997). The rationale for human action is reverence for life on earth, respect for the organic realm in which human civilization is situated. The veneration of human life represents a universalism from the ground up. Various societies articulate this protonorm in different terms and illustrate it locally, but every culture can bring to the table this fundamental norm for ordering political relationships and such social institutions as the media. There is at least one generality of universal scope underlying systematic ethics. The primal sacredness of life is a protonorm that binds humans into a common oneness. And in our systematic reflection on this foundation of the social order, we recognize that it entails such basic ethical principles as truth, human dignity, and nonviolence.

Cooper's (1998) strategy for understanding our universal humanity is expanding our study from industrial societies to include learning from indigenous groups. He lived with the Shuswap in Canada, Polynesians in Hawaii, and the Rock Point Navajo People to experience first hand their moral perspectives and modes of communication. He documents the *umwelt*, spirituality, respect, and wisdom of Native Peoples for whom communication is a release of stored power—potential energy becoming kinetic energy. He observes that "what outsiders call 'ethics' are derivative from a singular ethic, inseparable from the Great Spirit's law" (Cooper, 1998, p. 163). The Native Nations' emphasis on communion and community, the multilayered character of truth in indigenous cultures, and their integration of heart and mind demonstrate the fundamental human commitment to authentic communication.

Hamelink (2000) appeals to international human rights as the foundation of moral standards for the media. Human rights provide the only universally available principles for the dignity and integrity of all human beings. The world political community has recognized the existence of human rights since the adoption of the UN Charter in 1945, and has accepted international legal machinery for their enforcement. Member states of the United Nations have pledged themselves to promote universal respect for and observance of human rights, the dignity and worth of the human person, social progress, and the right of recognition before the law without discrimination. Therefore, in order to ensure democratic participation, all people have the right of access to communication channels independent of governmental or commercial control.

Nussbaum (1999, 2000, 2006)) uses extensive research into the lives of women in the non-industrial world to argue for overlapping capabilities that are true of humans universally as they work out their existence in everyday life. The common values that emerge from people's daily struggles are bodily health, affiliations of compassion, recreation, emotional development, political participation, rights to goods, and employment. All human beings are capable of fulfilling these functions, and the countless ways of doing them overlap and establish standards for the quality of life across cultures.

Ward (2005) develops a philosophical foundation for global journalism ethics in contractualism. The idea of ethics as social contract stems historically from Hobbes, Locke, Rousseau, and Kant, with Ward preferring the contract theory of John Rawls as the most productive framework. In Ward's contractualism, ethical principles are intersubjective agreements produced by rational discussion in light of common purposes, values, and facts. These restraints on social behavior guide decisions through reasonable dialogue among all interested parties. Ethics is the ongoing project of inventing, applying, and critiquing the basic principles that direct human interaction, define social roles, and justify institutional structures. Ethics for the news media is a set of legitimate but fallible agreements established by fair deliberation between the overarching profession of journalism and the public it serves.

Postcolonial theory is developed by Rao and Wasserman (2007; Wasserman, 2006) into a global perspective on ethics. Normative ideals for the media can only be conceived within the historical and political context that underlies current global power relations. Theoretical ethics ought to be global in their reach but local in conception. Such central propositions in ethics as human dignity must be understood across their symbolic and material axes. Dignity only comes to mean something when radical social change is brought about, otherwise it deepens human dignity for an elite while ignoring the misery of the rest. Ethical principles are not *a priori* but must include the material and discursive conditions to make them possible. The validity of our moral values for the global media is determined by the extent to which they resonate with the voiceless and vulnerable. Postcolonial theory provides both the critical vocabulary and tools for intervention that situate normative values in history while globalizing them simultaneously.

Wilkins (2008) develops a universal theory through neuroscience. In her model, the literature of moral development and feminist ethical theory are interconnected and established globally through neuroscientific research on the human brain. Moral development and the ethics of care in its own way assume that all human beings have the capacity for moral thinking. Ethical reasoning, while linked to experience, is considered an organic part of what it means to think as a human being. Neuropsychology documents that through evolutionary naturalism, the human species has a universal sense of right and wrong. Whether the human moral instinct is a faculty, or hard wired, or best described in other ways still being researched worldwide, this biological inheritance is the ground for universalizing ethics throughout the species.

Universalist positions have discredited themselves over history by breeding totalitarianism. Those who claim knowledge of universal truth typically use it to control or convert dissenters. Universalism is said to threaten diversity, whereas relativism liberates us to reject all oppressive claims to truth. In light of this objection, it must be reiterated that the universalist appeals from Benhabib to Wilkins are not foundational *a prioris*. Interactive universalism, our common lingual identity, the sacredness of life, authentic communication in indigenous culture, international human rights, overlapping capabilities, contractualism, postcolonial theory, and neuroscience in the theoretical models above are not objectivist absolutes. They are presuppositions to which we are committed inescapably; one cannot proceed intellectually without taking something as given. Cartesian rationalism and Kant's formalism presumed noncontingent starting points. These primordial generalities do not. Without protonorms of universal scope, ethical theory and politics are trapped in the distributive fallacy, one ideological bloc presuming to speak for the whole.

A commitment to universals does not eliminate cross-cultural differences in thinking and belief. The only question is whether our values affirm the human spirit or not. The issue is whether these theoretical models enable the media to build a civic philosophy and thereby demonstrate a transformative intent. This is worldview pluralism which allows us to hold our beliefs in good faith and debate them openly rather than be constrained by a superficial consensus. The universal principles described so far do not obstruct cultures and inhibit their development. On the contrary, they liberate us for strategic action and provide a direction for social change.

## SACREDNESS OF LIFE

To understand how these universal theories work regarding the media and media professions, the sacredness-of-life model can be expanded for illustrative purposes (Christians and Traber, 1997). This study starts from a different premise than comparing codes of media ethics around the world. Codes are distillations of the best thinking practitioners can do together on their standards and ideals, and seeking common themes among them is one way to discover cross-cultural agreement.

The sacredness of life emerged from a dissimilar strategy. Philosophers, religious thinkers, cultural leaders, and social theorists were consulted instead of media professionals. The question for them was their starting point: What is the first principle that is non-negotiable among your people, in your religion or culture? What is bedrock for you, the presupposition from which you begin? Aristotle taught us that there must be an unmoved mover. There cannot be infinite regression or knowledge is indeterminate. One cannot act or think without taking something as given. All knowledge begins with presuppositions because we must start somewhere, not because they have been demonstrated to be unequivocally true. First principles are not pure truth in isolation but beliefs about what's best for the world.

Around the question of basic presuppositions, workshops, conferences, and consultations were organized worldwide. Fifty major papers were given in six languages on first principles—ranging from general theories, to communication ethics in Latin America, Africa, Japan, Taiwan, Poland, Brazil, and South Africa, to Arab-Islamic and Judeo-Christian ethics, Hinduism, and Native American mythology. This research on four continents is a limited sample, and ideally the question about basic presuppositions should be asked of all 6,500 living languages in the world and 20,000 people groups. But this study is explicitly international and cross-cultural, and points us in the right direction.

The basic commitment in all the groups they studied is the sacredness of life. Within the natural world is a moral claim on us for its own sake and in its own right. The sacredness of life is a pretheoretical given that makes the moral order possible. The history of how humans have valued their natural world is long and torturous, but the scientific view cannot account for the purposiveness of life. Living nature reproduces itself in terms of its very character. Therefore, within the natural order is a moral claim on us for its own sake and in its own right. As Hans Jonas concludes, "Nature evinces at least one determinate goal, life itself.... With the gaining of this premise, the decisive battle for ethical theory has already been won" (1984, p. 78).

Our duty to preserve life is similar in kind to parental obligation to their offspring. When new life appears, the progenitors do not debate their relationship to it as though their responsibility is a matter of calculating the options with neutral protoplasm. The forbears' duty to their children is an imperative that is timeless and nonnegotiable (cf. Jonas, 1984, ch. 4). Nurturing life has a taken-for-granted character outside subjective preference. From the sacredness of life perspective, the biological world provides a rich arena for seeing the permanent value of human life in its brilliant diversity.

The veneration of life is a protonorm similar in kind to the proto-Indo-European language, a lingual predecessor underlying the Indo-European languages as we know them in history. Reverence for life on earth establishes a level playing floor for cross-cultural collaboration on the ethical foundations of a responsible press. It represents a universalism from the ground up. Various societies articulate this protonorm in different terms and illustrate it locally, but every culture can bring to the table this fundamental norm for ordering political relationships and such social institutions as the press. In this sense, universal solidarity is the basic principle of ethics and the normative core of all human communication.

Human responsibility regarding natural existence contributes the possibility of intrinsic imperatives to moral philosophy. It demonstrates the legitimacy of concluding that collective duty can be cosmic and irrespective of our roles or contracts. This is a protonorm that precedes its elaboration into ethical principles. And its universal scope enables us to avoid the divisiveness of individual interests, cultural practices, and national prerogatives. The primal sacredness of life is a protonorm that binds humans into a common oneness. Out of this primordial generality basic principles emerge such as truth, human dignity, and nonviolence.

Truth is one ethical principle on which various cultures rest. The most fundamental norm of Arab-Islamic communication is truthfulness. Truth is one of the three highest values in the context of the Latin American experience of communication. In Hinduism, truth is the highest dharma and the source of all other virtues. Among the Sushwap of Canada, truth as genuineness and authenticity is central to its indigenous culture. Living with others is inconceivable if we cannot tacitly assume that people are speaking truthfully. Lying, in fact, is so unnatural that machines can measure bodily reactions against it. When we deceive, Dietmar Meith argues, the truth imperative is recognized in advance: "Otherwise there would be no need to justify exceptions as special cases.... Those who relativize truthfulness, who refuse to accept it as an ethical principle, indirectly recognize it as generally valid" (Meith, 1997 p. 89).

In Aristotle's legacy, truth and falsehood are permanently imbalanced: "Falsehood is itself mean and culpable, and truth noble and full of praise" (Aristotle, 1947, bk. 4, ch. 7). We ought not to grant truth and lying equal status and then merely calculate the best results. Lying must be justified while telling the truth need not be. In Bok's elaboration, only in monumental crises or as a last resort, can lying even be considered for moral justification. "Deceit and violence—these are the two forms of deliberative assault on human beings" (Bok, 1999, p. 18). Those who are lied to are resentful, hostile, and suspicious. "Veracity functions as the foundations of relations among human beings; when this trust shatters or wears away, institutions collapse" (Bok, 1999, p. 31).

While Aristotle's predilection toward truth is Greek in its cadence, he speaks to the world and across history. For Hinduism truth is the highest *dharma* and the source of all other virtues. The Truth and Reconciliation Commission in South Africa demonstrated that suffering from apartheid can be healed through truthful testimony. In the Talmud, the liars' punishment is that no one believes them. For the former secretary general of the United Nations, Dag Hammerskjold, "the most dangerous of all dilemmas is when we are obliged to conceal the truth to be victorious" (Jensen, 2000, p. 7). In Gandhi's *satyagrapha* the power of truth through the human spirit eventually wins over force. The fundamental norm of Islamic communication is truthfulness. For the Shuswap tribe in Canada, the truth as genuineness and authenticity is central to culture.

Respecting human dignity is another underlying principle about which there is transnational agreement. Different cultural traditions affirm human dignity in a variety of ways, but together they insist that all human beings have sacred status without exception. Native American discourse is steeped in reverence for life, an interconnectedness among all living forms so that we live in solidarity with others as equal constituents in the web of life. In communalistic African societies, *likute* is loyalty to the community's reputation, to tribal honor. In Latin American societies, insistence on cultural identity is an affirmation of the unique worth of human beings. In Islam, every person has the right to honor and a good reputation. In Judaism and Christianity, dignity is God's irrevocable claim on human beings, not earned, nor bestowed by people or institutions (Moltmann, 1984; Schultziner, 2006). For Confucianism, correct communication practices derive from the larger social etiquette of *li*, that is, respecting the dignity of others. *Homo sapiens* as a species requires within itself respect for its members as a whole.

Nonviolence is a third ethical principle entailed by the sacredness of life, or in negative terms, no harm to the innocent. Mahatma Gandhi and Martin Luther King developed this principle beyond a political strategy into a philosophy of life. For the preeminent theorist of dialogic communication, Emmanuel Levinas, the self-Other relation makes peace normative. When the Other's face appears, the infinite is revealed and I am commanded not to kill (Levinas, 1981, p. 89). Along with *dharma, ahimsa* (nonviolence) forms the basis of the Hindu worldview. In communalistic and indigenous cultures, care for the weak and vulnerable (children, sick, and elderly), and sharing material resources are a matter of course. Death and violence at the World Trade Center, suicide bombings in the Middle East, and the killing of the innocent in Afghanistan and Iraq cut to our deepest being. Along with the public's revulsion against physical abuse at home and our consternation over brutal crimes and savage wars is a glimmer of hope reflecting the validity of this principle.

Out of nonviolence, we articulate ethical theories about not harming the innocent as an obligation that is cosmic and irrespective of our roles or ethnic origin. When peace is an ethical imperative, it is not reduced to the politics of war, but one of three fundamental ways to understand the sacredness of life intrinsic to our humanness. When considering universals, nonviolence is of epoch-making importance: "No survival without a world ethic. No world peace without peace between the religions. No peace between the religions without dialogue" (Kung, 1991, p. xv). The principle of nonviolence promotes a discourse of peaceful coexistence in community life, rather than a focus on peace making between intergovernmental bodies. In Clemencia Rodriguez's "social fabric" approach to peace, open communication is essential, "based on mutual respect, solidarity, and collective enjoyment of public spaces" (2004, p. 3). In terms of this principle understood through the protonorm, "only by invoking the sacredness and inviolability of life, by advocating non-violence and creative resolution, can communicators act morally" (Lee, 2007, p. 52). And the Declaration toward a Global Ethic of the Parliament of the World's Religions in 1993 connects principle and protonorm in the same way. The first of its four "irrevocable directives" is a commitment to a culture of nonviolence and respect for life.

A commitment to universals does not eliminate all differences in what we think and believe. The only question is whether the first presupposition with which we begin affirms the human good or not. The issue is whether our values help to build a civic philosophy and thereby demonstrate a transformative intent. This is worldview pluralism, which allows us to hold our beliefs in good faith and debate them openly rather than be constrained by a superficial consensus. The standard of judgment is not economic or political success, but whether our worldviews and community formations contribute in the long run to truth telling, human dignity, and nonviolence.

When we build our ethical models in universal terms, we have a framework by which to judge the media professions and practices locally. Of the three ethical principles that have arisen from various sections of the world, in communications we have worked the hardest with the first and second—human dignity and truth. Truth is central to communication practice and appears everywhere in our codes of ethics, mission statements, classes, and textbooks on media ethics. We disagree on the details, not always sure what truth means and how it applies. There is still in news a heavy emphasis on facts and unbiased information that no longer is defensible epistemologically. But the general concept of truth is an unwavering imperative. In entertainment media, we insist on realism, on artistic imagery and aesthetic authenticity, as synonyms for truth. In the persuasive arts, advertising and public relations, we consider its antonym, that is, deception, to be absolutely forbidden.

But if we broaden our understanding of truth from the Western Enlightenment tradition to a definition rooted in the universal sacredness of life, the view of truth as accurate information is too narrow. With a framework oriented to the universal, the concept of truth is more sophisticated as disclosure. Truthful statements entail a comprehensive account of the context which gives them meaning. Dietrich Bonhoeffer contends correctly that a truthful account takes hold of the culture, motives, and presuppositions involved (1995, ch. 5). Truth means, in other words, to strike gold, to get at "the core, the essence, the nub, the heart of the matter" (Pippert, 1989, p. 11). No hard line exists between fact and interpretation; therefore, truthful accounts entail adequate and credible interpretations rather than first impressions. The best journalists weave a tapestry of truth from inside the attitudes, culture, and language of the people and events they are actually reporting. Their disclosures ring true on both levels; that is, they are theoretically credible and realistic to those being covered. The reporters' frame of reference is not derived from a free-floating mathematics, but from an inside picture that gets at the heart of the matter. Rather than reducing social issues to the financial and administrative problems defined by politicians, the media disclose the subtlety and nuance that enable readers and viewers to identify the fundamental issues themselves.

And increasingly, human dignity has taken a central position in media ethics. For two decades now, we have worked on ethnic diversity, racist language in news, sexism in advertising. We see gender equality in hiring, and eliminating racism in organizational culture, not as political correctness but as moral imperatives. Human dignity that arrives on our agenda from the universal, takes seriously lives that are loaded with cultural complexity. Our selves are articulated within these decisive contexts of gender, race, class, and religion. A community's polychromatic voices are the arena through which participatory democracy takes place.

The imperative of human dignity grounded in the sacredness of life moves us beyond an individualistic morality of rights to a social ethics of the common good. It enables us to recognize that an urgent issue on the civic agenda at present is to enable the voices of self-discovery and self-affirmation to flourish among a society's cultural groups. A community's moral obligation is not merely treating ethnic differences with fairness, but an explicit commitment to what Charles Taylor calls "the politics of recognition." As he puts it, "Nonrecognition or misrecognition can inflict harm, can be a form of oppression, imprisoning someone in a false, distorted, and reduced mode of being. Due recognition is not just a courtesy we owe people. It is a vital human need" (Taylor, 1994, p. 26). Promoting human dignity does not mean informing a majority audience of racial injustice, for example, but insures those forms of representation from the ground up that generate a critical consciousness for oneself and others. In honoring the human dignity principle, the press reorients multiculturalism from individual rights and political correctness to the larger moral universe of nonhierarchical social relations.

But the third ethical principle, nonviolence, is still underdeveloped. Flickers of peace are emerging on our media ethics agenda, but only glimmers compared to truth, and of late, human dignity. Johan Galtung has developed and applied the principle most systematically with his peace journalism, concerned not simply with the standards of war reporting, but positive peace—

creative, nonviolent resolution of all cultural, social, and political conflicts (e.g., 2004). Peace journalism recognizes that military coverage as a media event feeds the very violence it reports, and therefore is developing the theory and practice of peace initiatives and conflict resolution (Lynch and McGoldrick, 2005). But the broad task remains of bringing this third principle to maturity. Our international magazines and newspapers should articulate, promote, craft, and illustrate the ethics of nonviolence. We need a rich venue at present for doing so—addresses, group discussions, news features, educational multimedia presentations, documentaries, theater, and music—together bringing the idea into its own across cultures and from the bottom up.

## MEDIA TECHNOLOGY

A complicating factor in putting universals to work in communication ethics, is that, unlike many other disciplines, its focus has been changed by technology. While legal, medical, and business ethics, for example, have also been impacted by technical innovation, communication ethics is the only such field in which both the heart and name of the field has shifted from people to machines. As early as 1988, a comprehensive bibliographic study suggested that over 80% of modern writing about communication ethics focused upon media ethics (Cooper, Sullivan, Medaglia, and Weir, 1988). There is neither reason nor research to suggest that the four to one ratio has since decreased.

Historically, many ethicists have argued that external technologies only amplify the presence of eternal ethical issues, so media ethics is merely communication ethics in disguise. However, a significant number of important scholars such as Mumford (1934), White (1962), and Giedion (1969) have suggested that each technology transforms society and may have unintended consequences that need to be addressed ethically.

For example, research on television effects triggers a debate about whether repetitive televised violence may contribute to actual human violence. Computers and satellites provide the possibility for invading national and global privacy in ways that the naked eye and ear cannot. Arguments can be made that almost every medium transforms previous ethical issues and introduces new ones.

Indeed, Marshall McLuhan (1977), Eric McLuhan (1983), and Barrington Nevitt (1985) claim that there are specific laws of the media which, like the laws of nature, are all but indifferent to human intention and action. Although Cooper (1997) found that there were 40 ethical issues associated with cybermedia by the end of the last millennium, three years later he claimed there were 52 such issues (2000) and now has identified 64. Does speed-up in the rate of implementing new technology mean there is also a speed-up in the quantity and impact of ethical issues? Or are such issues old wine in new bottles because there is "nothing new under the sun?"

With the advent of communication speed-up there are many invisible technologies at work which the public cannot detect. Indeed the research presented to the Foundation of Intelligent Physical Agents at their annual conference in Dublin (1998) indicates that the creators of new communication technology have the greatest ethical responsibility. Their hidden engineering systems may be tested in advance but little attention is given to examining their possible effects until after the new technology has been irreversibly introduced into society. Most of the public does not even know what intelligent agents are, let alone their impact upon individuals and groups.

Moreover, it is the interplay of technologies, software upgrades, plug-ins, formats, and innumerable invisible devices that is most difficult to track. In his ground-breaking *Food for Naught* (1974), the seminal Canadian biochemist Ross Hume Hall shows the hidden effects of the interaction of food additives. Although tested in isolation, the additives were untested in combination by nutritionists and government scientists. Similarly, the new media ecology, with a multiplication of new interacting species, also enlarges the world of both hidden and observable ethical problems.

However, to observe these phenomena is not to suggest that machines, rather than people, cause or are accountable for ethical lapses and virtues. People invent and maintain the machines, and are thus responsible for them. Nevertheless a globe of interactive talking machines which outlive the people who invented them is very different from the world of Aristotle and Confucius.

As noted at the outset regarding the urgency of a global ethics, we live in an age when information instruments and weapons technologies are closely linked. In such an age we have learned that, if we are not willing to use communication technologies for humane, prosocial purposes, there are those who will use such technologies for their own darker designs. Hitler's S.S. cameramen, for instance, used film not simply to record Holocaust atrocities but to proudly document their systematic efficiency when introducing accelerated methods of genocide.

Given the concerns that are routinely expressed worldwide about the digital divide, censorship, deceptive advertising, information flow, propaganda, privacy, piracy, pornography, cultural erosion, racial and national stereotyping, violence, and many related problems, there is indeed a need for a global communication ethic. Research cited within and beyond this essay, and written recommendations since Hammurabi, demonstrate that the quest for responsible, truthful, communication practice transcends period and place.

## A FUTURE FOR RESEARCH

So the question of greater concern is not if, but rather how, a global communication ethic may be created and implemented. Harold Innis (1951) recommended that there must be a balance between communication technologies of space and time. A larger requirement for a communication ethic is that there ought to be a balance between eternal communication ethics (that is, approaches transcending time), and external communication ethics (that is, approaches extending across space). The notion of space must now take into account technologies and codes which leap over continents to weave a multicultural mosaic. Such technologies at present extend into outer space (e.g., satellites), inner space (e.g., our media-filled subconscious minds), and global space (e.g., the wired world of seven continents and 24 time zones). A balance between an ethics of space and of time is now required.

And other types of balance cannot be excluded when building a communication ethic suitable to a new millennium sensitivity:

1. A balance between the indigenous and developed world's wisdom and vision.
2. A balance between idealized codes which inspire and policies which accurately depict harsh global realities.
3. Input from both the North and South, and the East and West (as in honoring not only Jewish but also Buddhist ethics and noting where they may be parallel).
4. A balance between universal principles and the particular issues and practices of regions.
5. A balance between the professional and the academic; between technical media and the core origins of communication ethics (speech, written, and performance ethics); between the political and the spiritual; between the codified and the intuitive/oral traditions.

In short, a harmonious inclusiveness which honors cultural and other diversity in fact, not as lip service, is required.

Within the technical world, homeostasis is also essential. New communication technologies are primarily tested by (1) engineers for effectiveness; (2) research and development departments for competitive value; and (3) sales and marketing forces for target audiences. The teams which pretest not only technologies, but also programming and information formats, must also be complemented by ethicists, scientists, policy experts, parents, and community leaders who consider the potential impact of any new medium or product before it is introduced into the community.

A truly global inclusiveness must inform any communication ethics. Peoples such as the Rapa Nui, Zulu, Old Order Brethren, Amish, Dani, and a wide variety of other cultural groups are not usually consulted about world communication policy. Yet they often provide a valuable perspective because of their media blackouts, single source media, (no) advertising stance, and other atypical approaches which force cultures to rethink the conventional wisdom.

Ethical issues often appear after a technology, new program, communication genre, or software platform is introduced into society. Such problems might have been prevented or better understood if presearch (preventive research) had been utilized. Before advertisers export feminine hygiene commercials into the cultures of Pacific Islanders, they need to realize that many island women watching TV will leave the room to avoid public embarrassment. Cross-cultural presearch is necessary. Before Hollywood producers make a film with seemingly harmless initiation rites that will be imitated by hundreds of teenagers (several of whom will be killed), it is wise to involve teens and parents in the test screenings. Before introducing fiber optics communication into the mainstream and unleashing related hazardous waste by-products, multidisciplinary presearch is necessary to study the toxic side effects.

Consequently, a global communication ethics must also be balanced between safe-guarding the future with presearch and learning from our mistakes in the past via case studies. A multidisciplinary approach must seek and employ the wisdom of many thinkers, professions, schools, and peoples. It must take into account not only the original issues of rhetoric such as defamation and deception, but should now include the growing index of techno-issues from cyberspam and flaming to the Hall effect within an elaborate media ecology.

The global communication ethics that is required must not only be balanced, inclusive, and preventive, but also based on a solid foundation of cross-cultural values. A synthesis of research to date suggests that the theories and studies described above provide a notable starting point for identifying those underlying values necessary to build such a unifying ethics. When combined, an overarching analysis of both the Western and indigenous communication ethics research of these scholars yields a list of 16 primary values. Without these 16 interhuman essences and the related values which they imply, any global ethics document would be strictly ornamental. Although several of these values drawn from the authors above overlap, and although other important values must be inferred from the list, the "group of 16" stands as symbolic of what large global populations expect from both individual and professional communication: accountability, social responsibility, truthfulness, free expression, implementation systems (ombudspersons, codes, news councils, etc.), gender and racial equity, community, respect, reciprocity, spirituality, authenticity, human rights, integrity, nonviolence, dignity, and honoring the sacredness of all life.

This list may be easily expanded or contracted into a more detailed or quintessential foundation. Indeed in one sense the most recent commentary by Christians and Nordenstreng (2004), like the previous work of Christians and Traber (1997), suggests the ultimate contraction from 16 into a single protonorm. One implication of their thinking is that the 16th or final value is a bedrock omni-foundation beneath the cornucopia of 15 other values.

This underarching prima-protonorm, which is listed as the final one, might be summarized as "reverence for life" which is also strongly akin to the indigenous emphasis upon "respect for all life." Christians and Traber (1997) argue that nurturing life is a pretheoretical given that makes the moral order possible. For there to be truth, freedom, rights, and all the other 15 basic values, there must first be the existence of life and an ethics committed to preserving it. The other values cannot survive without it.

Hence in a world populated with instruments of destruction and of communication, the latter must be committed to dissolving the former; that is to the honoring and preservation of life. A communication ethic for the 21st century must be rich in its ability to encompass complexity. Yet it must also remain morally simple in its unequivocal purpose, which is to nurture and protect the sacredness of life.

Behind this ethic are the spirits of many peoples. From Martin Buber (1965) there is the commitment that when dialog is genuine the speaker will respectfully "behold his partner as the very one he is" (p. 143). Mahatma Gandhi (1947) teaches that "you must be the change you want to see in the world." From Chief Thomas Littleben (1993) is the advice to "listen with all of yourself and only speak what you know." In Mother Teresa's wisdom, "there is no one who does not deserve our caring communication" (personal communication to Cooper, 1983).

A global communication ethics must be more than a hollow skeleton of worldwide codes and rhetorical declarations. It must be more than notions which are balanced over space and time, inclusive, preventive, and built upon a 16-fold values foundation. To be truly effective such a communication ethics must also be constantly lived and protected by people of every background. These are people who are concerned that, depending upon the choices we human beings make, our current modes of communication may either guide destructive nuclear bombs or heal destroyed nuclear families. These are people who are unafraid to accept Horace Mann's (1859) ultimate challenge: "Be ashamed to die until you have won some victory for humanity."

## REFERENCES

Aristotle (1947). *Nicomachean Ethics.* In R. McKeon (Ed.), *Introduction to Aristotle* (pp. 308–543). New York: The Modern Library.

Benhabib, Seyla (1992). *Situating the Self: Gender, Community and Postmodernism in Contemporary Ethics.* Cambridge, UK: Polity Press.

Bertrand, Claude-Jean (2000). *Media Ethics and Accountability Systems.* Piscataway, NJ and London: Transaction.

Bertrand, Claude-Jean (2003). *An Arsenal for Democracy: Media Accountability Systems.* Cresskill, NJ: Hampton Press.

Bok, Sissela (1999). *Lying: Moral Choice in Public and Private Life.* New York: Vintage Random House.

Bonhoeffer, Dietrich (1955). *Ethics,* H. N. Smith (Trans.). New York: Macmillan.

Bracci, Sharon (2002). "Seyla Benhabib's Interactive Universalism." In Sharon Bracci and Clifford Christians (Eds.), *Moral Engagement in Public Life: Theorists for Contemporary Ethics* (pp. 123–149). New York: Peter Lang.

Buber, Martin (1965). *The Knowledge of Man.* New York: Harper & Row.

Christians, Clifford and Kaarle Nordenstreng (2004). "Social Responsibility Worldwide." *Journal of Mass Media Ethics, 19*(1), 3–28.

Christians, Clifford and Michael Traber (Eds.). (1997). *Communication Ethics and Universal Values.* Thousand Oaks, CA: Sage.

Cooper, Thomas W. (1997). "Alphabetizing and Analyzing the Leading Forty Issues in New Technology Ethics." *Pacific Telecommunications Review, 19*(2), 5–14.

Cooper, Thomas W. (1989). *Communication Ethics and Global Change.* New York: Longman.

Cooper, Thomas W.(1998). *A Time Before Deception: Truth in Communication, Culture, and Ethics.* Santa Fe, NM: Clear Light.

Cooper, Thomas W. with Robert Sullivan, Peter Medaglia, and Christopher Weir (1988). *Television and Ethics: An Annotated Bibliography.* Boston, MA: G. K. Hall.

Galtung, Johan (2004). *Transcend and Transform: An Introduction to Conflict Work* (*Peace by Peaceful Means*). London: Pluto Press.

Gandhi, Mahatma (1947), as quoted in *Globaltribe* (2008), PBS television and KCET-TV, retrieved March 22, 2008, from http://www.pbs.org/kcet/globaltribe.change

Giedion, Siegfried (1969). *Mechanization Takes Command.* New York: W.W. Norton.

Hall, Ross Hume (1974). *Food for Naught: The Decline in Nutrition.* Philadelphia: Lippincott.

Hamelink, Cees (2002). *The Ethics of Cyberspace.* Thousand Oaks, CA: Sage.

Innis, Harold (1951). *The Bias of Communication.* Toronto, ON: University of Toronto Press.

Innis, Harold (1952). *Empire and Communication.* Toronto, ON: University of Toronto Press.

Jensen, Vernon (2000). "Bridging the Millennia: Truth and Trust in Human Communication," Sixth National Communication Ethics Conference, Gull Lake, Michigan, May, pp. 6–7.

Jonas, Hans (1984). *The Imperative of Responsibility.* Chicago: University of Chicago Press.

Jones, Clement (1980). *Mass Media Codes of Ethics and Councils.* Paris: UNESCO.

Kung, Hans (1991). *Global Responsibility: In Search of a New World Ethic.* J. Bowden (Trans.). London: SCM Press.

Laitila, T. (1995). "Journalistic Codes of Ethics in Europe." *European Journal of Communication, 10,* 527–544.

Lee, Philip (2007). "Communication Is Peace: WACC's Mission Today." *Media Development, 54*(1), 49–52.

Littleben, Chief Thomas (1990). Interview with Cooper, Rockpoint Dine (Navajo) Reservation, Rockpoint, AZ.

Lynch, Jake and Annabel McGoldrick (2005). *Peace Journalism.* Stroud, Glos., UK: Hawthorn Press.

Mann, Horace (1859), Commencement address. Yellow Springs, OH: Antioch College Archives.

McLuhan, Eric (1983). Interview, telephone. Philadelphia to Toronto.

McLuhan, Marshall (1974). "At the Moment of Sputnik, The Planet Became a Global Theatre." *Journal of Communication, 24*(1), 48–58.

McLuhan, Marshall (1977). Interview with Cooper, University of Toronto, Toronto, Canada.

Mieth, Dietmar (1997). "The Basic Norm of Truthfulness: Its Ethical Justification and Universality," in Clifford Christians and Michael Traber (Eds.), *Communication Ethics and Universal Values* (pp. 87–104). Thousand Oaks, CA: Sage..

Moltmann, Jurgen (1984). *On Human Dignity: Political Theology and Ethics.* M. Douglas Meeks (Trans.). Philadelphia, PA: Fortress Press.

Mother Teresa (1983). Letter to Cooper, Sri Lanka to Boston.

Mumford, Lewis (1934). *Technics and Civilization.* New York, NY: Harcourt, Brace, and Company.

Nevitt, Barrington (1985). Interview, Toronto, Canada.

Nordenstreng, Kaarle (1984). *The Mass Media Declaration of UNESCO.* Norwood, NJ: Ablex.

Nussbaum, Martha (1999). *Sex and Social Justice.* New York: Oxford University Press.

Nussbaum, Martha (2000). *Women and Human Development: The Capabilities Approach.* Cambridge, UK: Cambridge University Press.

Nussbaum, Martha (2006). *Frontiers of Justice.* Cambridge, MA: Harvard University Press, chs. 4–5.

Pippert, Wesley (1989). *An Ethics of News: A Reporter's Search for Truth.* Washington, D.C.: Georgetown University Press.

Rao, Shakuntala and Herman Wasserman (2007). "Global Journalism Ethics Revisited: A Postcolonial Critique." *Global Media and Communication, 3*(1), 29–50.

Rodriguez, Clemencia (2004). "Communication Is for Peace: Contrasting Approaches." *The Drum Beat,* E-MAGAZINE, *278,* December 6, 2–5

Schultziner, Doron (2006). "A Jewish Conception of Human Dignity." *Journal of Religious Ethics, 34*(4), 663–683.

Taylor, Charles (1994). "The Politics of Recognition." In Amy Gutmann (Ed.), *Multiculturalism: Examining the Politics of Recognition* (pp. 25–73). Princeton, NJ: Princeton University Press.

Ward, Stephen J. A. (2005). "Philosophical Foundations for Global Journalism Ethics." *Journal of Mass Media Ethics, 20*(1), 3–21.

Wasserman, Herman (2006). "Globalized Values and Postcolonial Responses: South African Perspectives on Normative Media Ethics." *The International Communication Gazette, 68*(1), 71–91.

White, Lynn (1962). *Medieval Technology and Social Change.* Oxford, UK: Oxford University Press.

Wilkins, Lee (2007). "Connecting Care and Duty: How Neuroscience and Feminist Ethics Contribute to Understanding Professional Moral Development." In Stephan J. A. Ward and Herman Wasserman (Eds.), *Media Ethics Beyond Borders.* Capetown, SA: Heinemann Publishers.

Wiredu, Kwasi (1996). *Cultural Universals and Particulars: An African Perspective.* Bloomington: Indiana University Press.

# II
# PROFESSIONAL PRACTICE

# 6

# Truth and Objectivity

## Stephen J. A. Ward

Modern journalism ethics was built upon the twin pillars of truth and objectivity. By the early 1900s, journalism textbooks, associations and codes of ethics cited truth and objectivity as fundamental principles of the emerging profession. Truth and objectivity have long roots in journalism, going back to the advent of the periodic news press. The claim to provide accurate and impartial reports or "relations" was made by the editors of the newsbooks of the seventeenth century. Two centuries later, mass commercial newspapers displayed a "veneration of the fact" (Stephens, 1997, p. 244).

Today, the pillars of truth and objectivity show serious wear and tear. To some, the concepts are antiquated, due to at least three factors: First, a corrosive post-modern scepticism about objective truth. Second, a cynicism about the ethics of profit-seeking news organizations. Third, a belief that non-objective journalism is best for an "interactive" media world populated by citizen journalists and bloggers. The result is an *intense* debate about the principles of journalism.

Prima facie, it may appear nonsensical to question truth and objectivity. How could journalism ethics *not* include the duty to seek truth? Shouldn't journalists provide citizens with the most accurate information possible? Truthfulness in communication is imperative for any responsible communicator, let alone powerful news organizations. How can journalists claim to inform citizens if they don't follow objective standards?

These questions raise important considerations but they are an inadequate response. They are naïve historically, politically and epistemologically. Historically, surprise at such doubts forgets that objectivity, as an explicit doctrine, is relatively recent. For most of the 400 years of modern journalism, journalists were expected to be partisan, not impartial. Politically, incredulity forgets that a full-blooded affirmation of truth-seeking and objectivity in journalism is hardly universal. Support for truth-seeking journalism is weak in authoritarian societies. In democracies, at times of insecurity, citizens may support a patriotic journalism that restrains truth-telling and takes the "side" of government. Epistemologically, the assertion that truth and objectivity are obvious principles fails to engage criticism in academia and in journalism. Perhaps other values, such as care or civic engagement, are more important than truth and objectivity (Steiner & Okrusch, 2006).

Therefore, any discussion must begin with the *problem* of truth and objectivity in journalism. The disagreements are too philosophical to admit of simple solution. One can, however, shed light on the problem by examining the evolution of the main theories and showing the way forward. This historical and diagnostic approach guides what follows. I outline how truth and objectivity came to be principles of journalism ethics, and how they came under attack. Then I propose an alternative theory of objectivity.

## TRUTH AND OBJECTIVITY IN JOURNALISM

There are many theories of truth and objectivity. Philosophers have offered theories of truth in terms of "realism" (or correspondence with fact), the coherence of ideas, well-justified belief or successful prediction (Horwich, 1990). But not all theories have played a dominant role in the history of journalism ethics. The practice of journalism has tended to rely on a simple version of the realist notion of truth that stresses the accurate observation of external events. Realism holds that a belief or statement is true if it accurately describes some object, fact or state of affairs in the real world. True beliefs "fit" with or correspond to the world as it really is. False beliefs do not. The realist idea of beliefs "fitting" the world is a natural attitude to take toward questions of truth and falsity. In our everyday lives, when our common sense is not entangled in philosophical doubt, we are all "naïve" realists.

"Realism" also refers to a sophisticated theory of truth developed from antiquity onward. For Plato, truth was not shifting belief about quasi-real objects but certain knowledge of transcendent and truly "real" objects (Cornford, 1968, pp. 217–218). Aristotle in his *Metaphysics* defined truth as "to say of what is that it is, or of what is not that it is not" (1011b22-30, p. 749). Propositions are true or false depending on whether they accurately predicate a property of an object—whether propositions correspond with reality or the facts. Moreover, Aristotle thought that the disciplined, scientific mind is capable of knowing the true causes or external principles of reality.[1] Realist theories explain the "fit" of belief and object in different ways.[2] A simple or "minimalist" realism ignores complicated questions about how ideas correspond to objects by defining truth as such: "A statement (proposition, belief) is true if and only if what the statement says to be the case actually is the case" (Alston, 1996, p. 5). It is true that grass is green if it is the case that grass is green.

Realist theories separate the question of what is truth in general (the concept or property) from *how* we determine what is true. For the realist, truth is not justification. There may be many truths about the world that humans may never know. A justified belief, considered true at time $t_1$ may be shown to be false at time $t_2$ in the future. Why, then, do realists seek justification through standards of evidence? Because they make it more likely that our beliefs are true. Despite the varieties of realism, the essence of realism is that our beliefs are made true by some reality external to my mind. External objects provide an objective check on my beliefs. Historically, journalism's realism has relied on common sense. If a journalist accurately reports on what was said or done, then the report is true. A news photograph is true if it captures an external event without distortion. If not, it is false. Since journalism is a practical craft covering ordinary events, journalists tend to presume that a simple realism and a rough-and-ready empiricism are sufficient to guide their activities.

To situate journalism's idea of objectivity, we need to note that, in Western culture, there have been three senses of objectivity: ontological, epistemological and procedural (Ward, 2005, pp. 14–18; Megill, 1994, pp. 1–20). A belief is ontologically objective if it denotes an independently existing object, property, fact, lawful regularity or state of affairs. Something is ontologically subjective if it is non-existent or exists only in the mind, such as perceptual illusions or hallucinations. Ontological objectivity is closely associated with a realistic theory of truth as correspondence with external objects. Epistemological objectivity refers not to external objects but to the methods and standards by which we come to hold beliefs about objects. Beliefs are epistemically objective if they satisfy our best practices and standards; otherwise they are subjective. Epistemological objectivity requires our beliefs to satisfy a range of standards derived from logic, perception and the canons of inquiry. We seek methods of discovery and standards of evaluation because truth is not directly accessible. Procedural objectivity is the use of objective criteria not to describe an object but to make a fair judgment, such as when we hire employees or award contracts.

Journalistic discussions of objectivity combine all three senses of objectivity. Ontologically, journalists claim they describe things the way things are. Epistemologically, they support their claims by appeal to their sources, their evidence, their methods. They also evoke a procedural sense of objectivity by claiming that they judiciously balanced views and treated sources fairly. Historically, even the editors of the seventeenth-century newsbooks assured readers their reports were true because they used certain methods, such as relying on eye-witnesses and reliable correspondents, and by comparing different reports of the same event (Ward, 2005, pp. 108–115). By the nineteenth century, epistemological objectivity would be the dominant sense of objectivity in journalism. Reporters disciplined their pursuit of news with a complex set of standards and procedures. The standards and rules would form the doctrine of news objectivity or "traditional objectivity" by the 1920s.

## TRADITIONAL JOURNALISM OBJECTIVITY

By "traditional objectivity" I mean the original notion of news objectivity first espoused by North American print journalists in the early 1900s, first advocated by American journalists and then adopted by their Canadian colleagues. Objectivity was never widely popular in European journalism. At the heart of traditional objectivity is the idea that reporters should provide straight, unbiased information without bias or opinion. The idea is summed up by imperatives to "stick to the facts" and to avoid "taking sides."

After the First World War, "objectivity" arrived as an explicit, common term, espoused by leading editors and widely practiced in newsrooms. The term occurred in numerous press codes, articles and textbooks. One of the earliest known uses of journalism "objectivity" is found in Charles G. Ross's *The Writing of News*, published in 1911: "News writing is objective to the last degree in the sense that the writer is not allowed to 'editorialize'" (Ross, 1911, p. 20). Recognition of objectivity as a formal ethical principle can be traced to two major codes of ethics: the 1923 code of the American Society of News Editors (ASNE) and the 1926 code of Sigma Delta Chi, forerunner of the Society of Professional Journalists. The ASNE code, the first national American code, said that anything less than an objective report was "subversive of a fundamental principle of the profession." Impartiality meant a "clear distinction between news reports and expressions of opinion" (Pratte, 1995, pp. 205–207). The principle of objectivity was second only to the principle of truthfulness in the code of Sigma Delta Chi. "Truth is our ultimate goal," said the code. "Objectivity in reporting the news is another goal, which serves as a mark of an experienced professional. It is a standard of performance toward which we strive." Objectivity reached its zenith in the 1940s and 1950s. Brucker saluted objective reporting as one of the "outstanding achievements" of American newspapers (Brucker, 1949, p. 21).

Traditional objectivity can be defined as a type of report:

• A report is objective if and only if it is a factual and accurate recording of an event. It reports only the facts, and eliminates comment, interpretation, and speculation by the reporter. The report is neutral between rival views on an issue.

Traditional objectivity was literally a "doctrine"—a rich web of ideas. The doctrine elaborated on journalism's commonsense realism and empiricism, disciplining it with rules, standards and attitudes. Journalism objectivity was, and is, an ideal implemented in newsrooms by standards and practices. It was, and is, an ideal that helps to distinguish types of story and to organize the content of news products. The ideal can be analyzed into six standards: (1) standard of factuality: reports are based on verified facts; (2) standard of balance and fairness: reports balance and fairly represent the main viewpoints on an issue; (3) standard of non-bias: the reporter's prejudices and interests do not distort reports; (4) standard of independence: journalists are free to report without fear or favour; (5) standard of non-interpretation: reporters do not put their interpretations into reports; (6) standard of neutrality: reporters do not take sides in disputes.

These standards were, and are, operationalized in newsrooms by rules on newsgathering and story construction. All opinion must be clearly attributed to the source, accompanied by direct quotation and careful paraphrasing. Objective practice asks reporters to verify facts by reference to documents, scientific studies, government reports and numerical analysis. To enhance objectivity, reports are written from the detached tone of the third-person. Phrases that indicate a bias or are an unjustified inference from the facts are eliminated or translated into neutral language. The objective style of news writing tends to be the so-called inverted pyramid, which conveys the most important facts, tersely and quickly. By the early 1900s, many mainstream newsrooms were divided into news sections, operating according to these rules of objectivity, and editorial sections where objectivity did not apply. Newspapers were divided into news and opinion.

## WHY TRADITIONAL OBJECTIVITY?

Why would journalists restrain their freedom to publish with an elaborate system of rules? Why did journalists believe that this demanding doctrine was appropriate for the hurly-burly world of journalism? The historical reasons are many. Some major factors were: (1) the objective style fit the emphasis on news that was driving the development of a mass commercial press; (2) increased demand among the public for accurate, updated information, rather than partisan opinion; (3) the need to reduce sensational "yellow" journalism, which raised public criticism; (4) the need to provide professional and ethical standards for a growing craft, and to protect journalists' independence; (5) increased independence of newspapers from political parties and a motivation to publishing news "for everyone"; (6) a scepticism about the ability of undisciplined empiricism to discern the facts and avoid manipulation.

With the rise of the mass commercial press in the second half of the eighteenth century, the primary business of newspapers changed from providing opinion to providing news. Electricity, more powerful printing presses, trains, a national economy and better educated populations in growing urban centres—all combined to create large papers, with staggering increases in circulations and advertising revenue (Baldasty, 1992). The telegraph made rapid transmission of news possible and encouraged a crisp factual style. News agencies, founded on the telegraph, showed journalists how to write objectively. In 1866, Lawrence Gobright of *The Associated Press* in Washington wrote: "My business is merely to communicate facts. My instructions do not allow me to make any comments upon the facts which I communicate" (quoted in Mindich, 1998, p. 109). In society, the public increasingly needed accurate information and was less tolerant of the old partisan opinion press. The newspaper increasingly depended on circulation and advertising revenues, not political parties. It was increasingly written for a wide diasporas of readers at a cheap price, not for a small group of political sympathizers who could afford subscription fees. Yet the growth in reporting was not enough to bring about a devotion to objectivity. Before objectivity could become dominant, the desire for news had to be tempered by a willingness to discipline that desire.

A willingness to restrain journalism, and to articulate norms, grew out of a concern about the excesses of "yellow journalism," the headlong pursuit for the sensational story, as evidenced in the fiercely competing papers of Randolph Hearst and Joseph Pulitzer. In time, the charge of "yellow journalism" would include the first tabloid papers in the 1920s (Campbell, 2001). Another factor was the growing awareness that reporters' chronicles of events were being distorted by their subjectivity, their desire to "sell" the news, interfering press barons and advertisers, and the manipulation of government and corporate propagandists. The rise of the press agent and the success of propaganda during the First World War called for a journalism that tested alleged facts (Schudson, 1978, p. 142). Naïve realism now seemed inadequate. An impulse to chronicle the world was not enough for truthful journalism. The idea grew among leading journalists and journalism associations that journalists, like other professionals, needed an ethics that stressed the reporter's impartiality and the separation of facts and opinion.

By the turn of the century, writers and textbooks were laying down the basics of objectivity. "It is the mission of the reporter to reproduce facts and the opinions of others, not to express his own," wrote Edwin Shuman in 1894. Shuman, the *Chicago Tribune's* literary editor, published the first comprehensive American journalism textbook, *Steps into Journalism*. His book contained the basics of traditional objective journalism: the inverted pyramid style, non-partisanship, detachment, a reliance on observable facts and balance. Shuman quoted approvingly an AP directive to its employees, which stated:

> All expressions of opinion on any matter, all comment, all political, religious or social bias, and especially all personal feeling on any subject, must be avoided. This editorializing is the besetting sin of the country correspondent and a weariness of the flesh to the copy-reader who has to expunge the copy's colourings and invidious remarks about individuals. (Shuman, 1894, pp. 65–66)

The difference between objectivity and the preceding empirical realism was the strictness of its norms and its detailed set of rules. Objective reporters were to be *completely* detached; they were to eliminate *all* of their opinion; they were to report *just* the facts. The traditional language of journalistic objectivity was a language of self-denial, restraint and exclusion.

Objectivity was justified as a method for producing more accurate, truthful reports and more independent professional journalists at a time of growing skepticism about the press. Objective reporting, it was argued, was crucial to egalitarian democracies. Commentary was not enough, and biased (or manipulated) reporting tainted the information supply. Citizens needed objective news about their government to make political judgments for themselves. Journalism, Lippmann claimed, only served democracy if it provided objective information about the world, not "stereotypes" (Lippmann, 1922).

## CHALLENGE AND DECLINE

The heyday of traditional objectivity was from the 1920s to the 1950s in the mainstream broadsheet newspapers of North America. The doctrine was so pervasive that, in 1956, press theorist Theodore Peterson said objectivity was "a fetish" (Peterson, 1956, p. 88). The second half of the century is a story of challenge and decline due to new forms of journalism, new technology and new social conditions. There have been three types of complaint: First, objectivity is too demanding an ideal for journalism and hence objectivity is a "myth." Second, objectivity, even if possible, is undesirable because it forces writers to use restricted formats. It encourages a superficial reporting of official facts. It fails to provide readers with analysis and interpretation. Objectivity ignores other functions of the press such as commenting, campaigning and acting as public watchdog. Finally, objectivity restricts a free press. A democracy is better served by a diverse, opinionated press where all views compete in a marketplace of ideas.

Objectivity was challenged from its inception. Henry Luce, who founded *Time* magazine in the 1920s, dismissed objectivity: "Show me a man who thinks he's objective and I'll show you a liar," Luce declared.[3] He argued that events in a complex world needed to be explained and interpreted. The new magazine "muckrakers" of the early 1900s rejected neutrality in reporting. The emergence of television and radio created more personal forms of media where a strict objective style struggled. In the 1960s, an "adversarial culture" that criticized institutions and fought for civil rights was sceptical of objective experts and detached journalism. Other journalists practiced a subjective "personal" journalism that looked to literature for its inspiration.

In the final decades of the century, online journalism gave further support to interpretive or opinion journalism. New media technology allowed almost anyone with a computer to publish their thoughts, commentary or photos online. The rise of the unprofessional or untrained "citizen journalist" and "blogger" is hailed as the democratization of news media, and adding to the diversity of voices in the public sphere. "Social media"—websites that allow citizens to express opinions on events and to share stories about their lives—attract millions of readers and participants. The primary values of this new media, however, were (and are) different from the primary values of traditional professional journalism ethics. The new media value immediacy, interactivity, sharing and networking, limited editorial checks and gatekeeping, and the expression of bias or opinion in an often "edgy" manner. The primary values of traditional journalism ethics is accuracy and verification, pre-publication checks, objectivity and a restraint on personal opinion. In sum, the trend in media values on the Internet has been to move away from, and to be sceptical of, the ideas of professionalism and objectivity.

In academia, doubts about objectivity arose in the middle of the century. Philosophers, social scientists, activists and others challenged the authority of objective science. Thomas Kuhn's influential writings were interpreted as showing that scientific change was a non-rational "conversion" to a new set of beliefs (Kuhn, 1962). A sociology of knowledge explained knowledge by reference to social causes (Barnes & Bloor, 1982). All knowledge was "socially constructed" (Hacking, 1999). Philosopher Richard Rorty attacked a "Platonism" that believed objective knowledge was a "mirror" of nature (Rorty, 1979). Post-modernists such as Lyotard and Baudrillard questioned the ideas of detached truth and philosophical "meta-narratives"—large historical narratives that make sense of human experience (Connor, 1989). Butler describes the illusive sense of post-modernism as a "realism lost" where people live in a "society of the image" or "simulacra" (Butler, 2002, pp. 110–111). Feminists portrayed objectivity as the value of a patriarchal society that "objectifies" women (Hawkesworth, 1994). Media scholars treated objectivity as the tainted dogma of a dominant corporate media (Hackett & Zhao, 1998). Objective routines protected journalists from criticism (Tuchman, 1978).

Today, the questioning continues. Journalist Martin Bell rejected objectivity for a journalism of "attachment" (Bell, 1998). Jon Katz, an online columnist, said journalists should "abandon the false god of objectivity" for new forms of communication (Katz, 1996). A lead article in the *Columbia Journalism Review*, entitled "Rethinking Objectivity," repeated the complaints cited above (Cunningham, 2003). A public policy center in the United States published a "manifesto for change" in journalism, which noted how objectivity is "less secure in the role of ethical touchstone" while norms such as accountability are increasing in importance (Overholser, 2006, pp. 10–11).

## PRAGMATIC OBJECTIVITY

A century after the doctrine of news objectivity was adopted we arrive at a dead end. Traditional objectivity is a spent ethical force, doubted by journalist and academic alike.

In practice, fewer journalists embrace the ideal, while newsrooms adopt a reporting style that includes perspective and interpretation. Journalism ethics needs to go beyond traditional objectivity. Three options loom: Abandon objectivity and replace it with other principles; "return" to traditional objectivity in newsrooms; redefine objectivity.

Simply abandoning objectivity is not a viable option. Journalists need clear principles to guide their activity. Unfortunately, much criticism of objectivity "deconstructs" the ideal without constructing an alternative. The decline of objectivity has left a vacuum in ethics just as journalism undergoes rapid, disorienting change. A competitive media market prefers attention-grabbing news and opinion, "hot talk" radio shows, and tabloid newsmagazine TV shows. The popular idea that journalists should write with an "edge" is an invitation to bias.

The best option, on my view, is to reform the concepts of truth and objectivity in journalism through philosophical examination. Without a thoughtful reform of objectivity we risk loosing an important restrain on journalism. A new conception of objectivity starts with a diagnosis of where traditional objectivity comes up short. My diagnosis is that, in the late 1800s, when journalists sought a doctrine to discipline the rush for news, they adopted a popular but deeply flawed version of objectivity—a stringent positivism that reduced objectivity to "just the facts." Traditional objectivity was built on an indefensible epistemology, which falsely characterized reporting as passively empirical (Ward, 2005, pp. 77–86). Traditional objectivity was rooted in a misleading metaphor of the journalist as a recording instrument who passively observes and transmits facts. When positivism and its passive model collapsed, so did traditional objectivity. Any new version of objectivity, then, must explain how a non-positivistic objectivity is possible for journalism as *active* inquiry resulting in *interpretations* that involve choice and selection. The central question is: If a news report involves (at least some) interpretation, how can it be objective? How can humans be objective in a world where fact, value, theory and interests are intertwined (see Putnam, 2002)?

My answer is a theory of objectivity, called "pragmatic objectivity." I call the conception "pragmatic" because objectivity is valued, pragmatically, as a means to the goals of truth, fair judgment and ethical action. The claim of objectivity is not absolute but rather a fallible judgment about a belief or report, based on several standards. Works of journalism satisfy the standards to varying degrees. Objectivity comes in different kinds, defined by the goals and practices of the domain in question. Objectivity in law differs from objectivity in journalism, although all forms of objectivity have a common core of general standards. Nor should we apply the standards of objectivity with the same vigour in all circumstances to all forms of stories. The appropriate level of strictness depends on the form of communication. Pragmatic objectivity is a flexible theory, more appropriate for the practical limitations of journalism. Pragmatic objectivity is acutely aware of, and allows for, human failings; it wears a human face.[4]

Pragmatic objectivity defines objectivity epistemologically, as the evaluation of interpretations according to the best available standards (1) of inquiry in general and (2) of the discipline in question. We determine "what is objective from the point of view of our best and most reflective practice" (Putnam, 1994). Pragmatic objectivity is not the reduction of reports to bare facts. It is not the elimination of all interpretation and theorizing. Objectivity is the testing of interpretations, from the mundane to the theoretical. Factual evidence is one standard among many.

The application of pragmatic objectivity to journalism consists of five steps:

## Step 1: Journalism as Active, Truth-Seeking Inquiry

The first step is to re-conceive journalists as active inquirers who should seek to interpret their world as accurately, comprehensively and truthfully as possible. Journalists are not primarily stenographers of fact. Inquiry is the natural activity of a highly evolved organism motivated to understand phenomena as it navigates a perilous environment. The inquirer is a purpose-driven agent in a social setting, constructing interpretations, testing hypotheses and solving problems. Similarly, journalists engage in active, purpose-driven inquiry. They search and interpret, verify and test, balance and judge.

Truth and objectivity remain indispensable norms for pragmatic inquiry. Together, truth and objectivity counter-balance the pressure to twist the truth, to bias the evidence, to force an unwarranted interpretation. Truth, as "achieved understanding," is the "theoretical goal of the practical activity of enquiry" (MacIntyre, 2006, p. 156). Objectivity provides the standards by which to estimate how close we are to the truth.

Truth is important to inquiry because it acts as a presupposition and an ideal of serious inquiry and deliberation. Truth is a presupposition for embarking on study. One inquires about phenomena $x$ to find out some truths about $x$. "Every man is fully satisfied that there is such a thing as truth, or he would not ask any question," wrote C. S. Peirce (quoted in Haack, 1998, p. 22). The idea of truth is required to believe anything, for to believe that $p$ exists is to accept that $p$ is true (Haack, 1997, p. 192). Truth also regulates how we inquire—it demands that we inquire honestly, accurately, diligently, and with disinterest. Truth is not a comforting ideal. It is a hard taskmaster. We cannot acquiesce in wishful thinking or platitudes. Nietzsche said: "Truth has had to be fought for every step of the way, almost everything else dear to our hearts...has had to be sacrificed to it" (Nietzsche, 1968, p. 50).

We need to adopt the goal of truth to make sense of inquiry's adherence to epistemological objectivity. Why struggle to follow objective methods and standards unless we believe that these methods and standards were "truth-directed" or "truth-conducive" (Alston, 1996, p. 242; Moser, 1989, pp. 42–43)? If justification doesn't "count toward truth," why prefer rigorous scientific methods to other dubious methods of acquiring beliefs, such as brainwashing or consulting oracles (Audi 1993, pp. 300–301; Williams, 2002, pp. 127–129)? Furthermore, the distinction between truth and falsity, and the idea of truth-conducive methods, are needed to make other crucial distinctions such as the difference between accuracy and inaccuracy, biased and unbiased, rational persuasion and propaganda. If one really believed that all standards and methods were based only on social conventions, then why inquire?

Truth-seeking is especially important to journalism, socially and politically. It is important that journalists determine whether a country has weapons of mass destruction. It is important that journalists speak truth to power, and that they take responsibility for their own power by refusing to spread unverified rumours. It is important that journalists impartially verify the claims of government and self-interested groups on behalf of the common good. Truth motivates courageous journalism. A gathering of Canadian journalists to recognize journalists who had fought for press freedoms internationally was entitled, "Now Try Writing the Truth."[5] Ethical journalism's endorsement of truth-seeking is well-founded even if there is disagreement on conceptions of truth, and even if our only route to the truth is via interpretation. Pragmatic inquiry in journalism is a truth-oriented process that is fallible, situated and yet non-arbitrary. The process of truth-seeking gradually strips away error, inaccuracy or exaggeration from the initial descriptions of events. Journalism truth is a "protean thing which, like learning, grows as a stalagmite in cave, drop by drop over time" (Kovach & Rosenstiel, 2001, p. 44).

## Step 2: Journalism as an Interpretive Exercise

Journalistic inquiry proceeds through the construction of interpretations that are expressed as news reports, analysis and commentary. In its simplest form, an interpretation places an object under a descriptive or explanatory category. We perceive x *as* a lion in the dark, we interpret x *as* a mocking gesture, we conceive of light *as* quanta of energy. The inquirer can improve his schemes of understanding but he can never completely transcend them. Inquirers interpret phenomena holistically, against a background of conceptual schemes that help us to interpret experience. Interpretation is ubiquitous because humans lack direct, cognitive contact with reality. Even our seemingly direct perceptions of objects are the result of much processing of stimuli by our perceptual system. Therefore, all statements, even factual statements, contain some element of conceptualization, theorizing and evaluation. Statements of fact differ from statements of theory (and other statements) by being more responsive to empirical stimuli and by containing a minimum of speculation.

Pragmatic objectivity denies the possibility of purely factual reports in journalism. News reports hover close to the level of observation but they do not eliminate all interpretation or inferences. A report saying the police chief was "stung" by accusations of wrongdoing and "struggled" to reply is an interpretation. If I report that, "The defence minister is a zealous, misguided, opponent of any budget cuts that might hurt retired soldiers," I mix facts and evaluation. Journalists divide the world into news and non-news, according to their interpretations of significance and novelty.

## Step 3: Objectivity as Holistic Testing of Interpretation

If journalism is the interpretation of events by active inquirers, then the concept of objectivity must be reconceived. Objectivity becomes the process of disciplining our interpretive activity by standards. The idea of objectivity as testing interpretations exists in many domains. Philosophy of science regards scientists as active investigators of nature, whose theories and hypotheses are interpretations that face the objective test of facts, logic and coherence with other knowledge (Thagard, 1992). Philosophical hermeneutics seeks an interpretation of texts against the background of a larger "fusion of horizons" (Gadamer, 2004, p. 305). Objective standards have been studied as normative elements of "epistemic communities" (Cetina, 1999, pp. 1–10). Lynch has argued that there is such a thing as "truth in context"—or truth within conceptual schemes (Lynch, 1998, pp. 101–139). The idea of objective interpretation or "interpretive sufficiency" grounds a basic method of qualitative research in the social sciences. The idea gives rigor to the common idea that there are better and worse interpretations (see Christians, 2005; Denzin & Lincoln, 2000). Longino developed a concept of scientific objectivity "by degree" that depends on whether the social practices of disciplines are open to "transformative criticism" and dialogue (Longino, 1990, p. 76). In law, there are sophisticated theories of objective interpretation (Marmor, 1995). Pragmatic objectivity is part of this movement toward a more nuanced approach to truth and objectivity.

## Step 4: Testing as Based on Generic and Domain-Specific Standards

The objective testing of interpretations uses two levels of standards: generic and domain-specific. Generic objectivity employs (1) an objective attitude and (2) a set of standards suitable for all rational thinking or decision making. Domain-specific objectivity employs standards and rules for the evaluation of inquiry in disciplines. Standards apply generic standards to particular forms of inquiry.

Objective inquirers adopt a generic objective attitude or stance, which consists of a set of virtuous dispositions, such as "open rationality"—to be disposed to give reasons that others could accept—and a love of disinterested truth—a disposition to follow where the facts lead. One applies this attitude by using standards. Three types of generic standards judge the objectivity of any claim or report. There are *empirical standards* that test a belief's agreement with the world; *standards of coherence* that evaluate how consistent a belief is with the rest of what we believe; and *standards of rational debate* that test how fair we have been in representing the claims of others, and in subjecting our claims to the scrutiny to others. The standards of domain-specific objectivity are too numerous and varied to summarize. However, an example helps. A study of the objective efficacy of a new drug requires health researchers to subject the drug to a multi-phased clinical trial. These researchers, of course, adhere to the generic standards of objectivity. But, in addition, they follow standards and methods developed for their domain. The researchers must disprove the null hypothesis, construct a control group, apply triple-blind procedures and evaluate results according to standards of statistical significance.

Journalists and their reports are objective to the degree that they satisfy the two levels of objectivity. Reports must satisfy, to some tolerable degree, the requirements of objectivity in general. That is, reports must be constructed by an objective stance according to the three types of generic standards—empirical standards, coherence standards and standards of rational debate. The empirical standards correspond to the emphasis on factuality in reporting. The standards of coherence correspond with the long tradition in journalism of comparing a claim with existing knowledge and experts. The standards of rational debate correspond with the idea of journalistic fairness, openness, and impartiality. On the second level, reports must satisfy, to some tolerable degree, the standards and rules specific to journalism. Many of these rules and standards exist already as informal practice in newsrooms, or occur in codes of ethics. The rules of accuracy and verification, for instance, provide empirical standards in journalism. Accuracy calls for accurate quotations and paraphrases of statements and the correct use of numbers. Accuracy forbids the manipulation of news images and the use of misleading "reconstructions" of events. Verification calls on reporters to cross-check claims of potential whistleblowers with original documents. Verification standards include rules on the number (and quality) of anonymous sources.

Objective journalism also tests for coherence. Any journalist who has tried to report on an alleged scientific breakthrough knows how important it is to evaluate the claim by appeal to other experts and existing scientific knowledge. Journalists ask: How does this viewpoint fit prevailing knowledge in the field in question? Is it credible? Does it fit with previous similar studies? Standards of rational debate include the demand to include a diversity of views in reports and to fairly represent the views of all groups.

## Step 5: Objectivity Not Opposed to Passion

Pragmatic objectivity rejects a stark opposition between a detached objective journalism and a caring, attached journalism. Pragmatic objectivity is *full* of values and commitments. Disinterestedness means caring so much for the honest truth that one does not allow personal interests to subvert inquiry, or to prejudge the issue. The best journalism is a judicious blend of the romantic and objective impulses. The romantic impulse is a passion for interesting, substantial interpretations. The objective impulse is a passion for justified interpretations. Romantic and objective impulses should work together to produce engaging *and* objectively tested journalism. Journalism based only on passion is reckless; a journalism based only on objectivity is accurate but lacks depth.

## CONCLUSION: THE WAY FORWARD

Whether or not pragmatic objectivity is an adequate theory, the challenge to researchers is clear and formidable. They need to develop a more adequate epistemology of journalism in the midst of a media revolution. The challenges are:

## Theory Building

A new epistemology would include conceptions of truth and objectivity in theory and practice, beyond the sketch of pragmatic objectivity above. Scholars should look for concepts of truth and objectivity in science but also in practices and professions. Only a detailed, thoughtful theory will respond adequately to post-modern scepticism about truth and objectivity.[6] The construction of a "believable concept of truth" is essential for today's communication ethics (Christians, 2005, pp. ix–xi).

## Practical Studies

Researchers need to show how a reformed theory of objectivity would change the practice of journalism in terms of how stories are constructed and evaluated. How would the rules of the newsroom change? What would a new theory of objectivity say about advocacy journalism, citizen journalism and civic journalism?

## New Media, Global Media

Researchers should examine the future of the concepts of journalism objectivity and truth in an age of instant news and multi-media, where bloggers, citizen journalists and others place more emphasis on social communication and the unedited exchange of information than on professional standards of truth and objectivity. Researchers also need to answer the question, "What does 'objectivity' and 'truth' mean in an era of global media with global impact?" In a global era, does objectivity require a cosmopolitan ethics that downplays journalists' patriotic attachment to their own country? What is a "balanced" international story?

The tandem of objectivity and truth, as norms of inquiry and communication, will persist for the foreseeable future despite the challenges. Objectivity has deep roots in human nature. Standards of objectivity will persist so long as humans strive for rigorous, rational understanding and fair social arrangements. Objectivity may be maligned in theory, but journalists continue to use standards to evaluate stories, whether or not they use the term "objectivity." Objectivity looms large where we are dealing with knowledge-seeking and fair decision-making. In society, the public expects its legislatures, government agencies and institutions to make decisions defensible from an objective point of view. We expect the same of judges, labour arbitrators, teachers, referees, peacekeepers and public communicators.

Few people would care to live in a society that has no respect for the concept of objectivity, that sees no virtue in adopting the objective stance and which refuses to guide inquiry by objective standards. Few critics of objectivity would want journalism to abandon objectivity *tout court*. It is one thing to cavil about the myth of objectivity in academia, it is quite another to live in a society that lacks the ideal.

## NOTES

1. Aristotle discusses a proposition's "correspondence with reality" or "facts" in *On Interpretation* (pp. 47, 48, 18a30-40, 19a30-34). In *Metaphysics,* Book Alpha the Lesser, Aristotle identifies the search for truth with the search for causes (993b1-30, p.712–13). In *Nicomachean Ethics*, Aristotle says that both theoretical and practical intellect aim at truth but the practical intellect seeks "truth in agreement with right desire" (1139a30-31, p. 1024).

2. Theories of truth are so varied and sophisticated that this section only attempts to place journalism truth within this tradition, as belonging to the realist camp. For a taxonomy of theories of truth, including the varieties of realism, see Hack (1997), *Evidence and Inquiry* (pp. 188–190).

3. Baughman (1987), *Henry R. Luce and the Rise of the American News Media*, p. 29

4. My theory of pragmatic objectivity owes much to the work of the Harvard philosophers W.V. Quine and Hilary Putnam, and to their pragmatist predecessors, William James and John Dewey. My phrase, objectivity "wears a human face," echoes the title of Putnam's book, *Realism with a Human Face* (1990).

5. "International Press Freedom Awards" presented by Canadian Journalists for Free Expression, Nov. 1, 2006, in Toronto.

6. Theorists of objectivity should not respond to post-modernists by painting them as dangerous relativists undermining all of Western rationality. Rather they should follow Simon Blackburn in *Truth: A Guide* (2005), where he attempts to do justice to both absolutist and relativist traditions.

## REFERENCES

Alston, W. (1996). *A realist conception of truth.* London: Cornell University Press.

Aristotle (2001). *The basic works of Aristotle* (R. McKeon, Ed.). New York: Random House.

Audi, R. (1993). *The structure of justification.* Cambridge, UK: Cambridge University Press.

Baldasty, G. (1992). *The commercialization of the news in the nineteenth century.* Madison, WI: University of Wisconsin.

Barnes, B. & Bloor, D. (1982). Relativism, rationalism and the sociology of knowledge. In M. Hollis & S. Luke (Eds.), *Rationality and relativism* (pp. 21–47). Oxford: Blackwell.

Baughman, J. (1987). *Henry R. Luce and the rise of the American news media.* Boston: Twayne.

Bell, M. (1998). The truth is our currency. *Harvard International Journal of Press/Politics, 3*(1), 102–109.

Blackburn, S. (2005). *Truth: A guide.* Oxford: Oxford University Press.

Brucker, H. (1949). *Freedom of information.* New York: Macmillan.

Butler, C. (2002). *Postmodernism: A very short introduction.* Oxford, UK: Oxford University Press.

Campbell, W. J. (2001). *Yellow journalism: Puncturing the myths, defining the legacies.* Westport, CT: Praeger.

Cetina, K. (1999). *Epistemic cultures: How the sciences make knowledge.* Cambridge, MA.: Harvard University Press.

Christians, C. (2005). Preface. In R. Keeble (Ed.), *Communication ethics today.* Leicester, U.K.: Troubador.

Connor, S. (1989). *Postmodernist culture.* Oxford: Blackwell.

Cornford, F. (1968). *The republic of Plato.* New York: Oxford University Press.

Cunningham, B. (2003). Rethinking objectivity. *Columbia Journalism Review,* (4), 24–32.

Denzin, N. & Lincoln, Y. (Eds.) (2000). *Handbook of qualitative research,* 2nd ed. Thousand Oaks, CA.: Sage.

Gadamer, H. (2004). *Truth and method.* 2nd rev. ed. London: Continuum.

Haack, S. (1997). *Evidence and inquiry: Towards reconstruction in epistemology.* Oxford: Blackwell.

Haack, S. (1998). *Manifesto of a passionate moderate: Unfashionable essays.* Chicago: University of Chicago Press.

Hackett, R. & Zhao, Y. (1998). *Sustaining democracy? Journalism and the politics of objectivity.* Toronto: Garamond Press.

Hacking, I. (1999). *The social construction of what?* Cambridge, MA.: Harvard University Press.

Hawkesworth, M. (1994). From objectivity to objectification. In A. Megill (Ed.), *Rethinking objectivity* (pp. 151–77). London: Duke University Press.

Horwich, P. (1990). *Truth.* Oxford: Basil Blackwell.

Katz, J. (Oct. 9, 1996). No news is good news. *Hotwired.* http://www.hotwired.com.

Kovach, B. & Rosenstiel, T. (2001). *The elements of journalism.* New York: Crown.

Kuhn, T. (1962). *The structure of scientific revolutions*. Chicago: University of Chicago Press.

Lippmann, W. (1922). *Public opinion*. New York: Macmillan.

Longino, H. (1990). *Science as social knowledge*. Princeton, NJ: Princeton University Press.

Lynch, M. (1998). *Truth in context: An essay on pluralism and objectivity*. Cambridge, MA: MIT Press.

MacIntyre, A. (2006). *The tasks of philosophy*. Cambridge, UK: Cambridge University Press.

Marmor, A. (Ed.) (1995). *Law and interpretation: Essays in legal philosophy*. Oxford: Clarendon Press.

Megill, A. (1994). *Rethinking objectivity*. London: Duke University Press.

Mindich, D. (1998). *Just the facts: How "objectivity" came to define American journalism*. New York: New York University Press.

Moser, P. (1989). *Knowledge and evidence*. Cambridge, UK: Cambridge University Press.

Nietzsche, F. (1968). *The twilight of the idols and the AntiChrist* (R. J. Hollingdale, Trans.). Harmondsworth, UK: Penguin.

Overholser, G. (2006). *On behalf of journalism: A manifesto for change*. Annenberg Public Policy Center. Philadelphia: University of Pennsylvania.

Peterson, T. (1956). The social responsibility theory of the press. In F. Siebert, T. Peterson, & W. Schramm, *Four theories of the press* Urbana: University of Illinois Press.

Pratte, Paul. (1995). *Gods within the machine: A history of the American Society of Newspaper Editors, 1923–1993*. Westport: CT: Praeger.

Putnam, H. (1990) *Realism with a human face* (J. Conant, Ed.). Cambridge, MA: Harvard University Press.

Putnam, H. (1994). *Words and life*. Cambridge, MA: Harvard University Press.

Putnam, H. (2002). *The collapse of the fact/value dichotomy and other essays*. Cambridge, MA: Harvard University Press.

Rorty, R. (1979). *Philosophy and the mirror of nature*. Princeton, NJ: Princeton University.

Ross, C. (1911). *The writing of news: A handbook*. New York: Henry Holt.

Schudson, M. (1978).*Discovering of news: A social history of American newspapers*. New York: Basic Books.

Shuman, E. (1894). *Steps into journalism: Helps and hints for young writers*. Evanston, IL: Correspondence School of Journalism.

Steiner, L. & Okrusch, C. (2006). Care as a virtue for journalists. *Journal of Mass Media Ethics, 21*(2 & 3), 102–122.

Stephens, M. (1997). *A history of news: From the drum to the satellite*. Fort Worth, TX: Harcourt Brace.

Thagard, P. (1992). *Conceptual revolutions*. Princeton, NJ: Princeton University Press.

Tuchman, G. (1978). *Making the news: A study in the construction of reality*. New York: Free Press.

Ward, S. J. A. (2005). *The invention of journalism ethics: The path to objectivity and beyond*. Montreal: McGill-Queen's University Press.

Williams, B. (2002). *Truth and truthfulness: An essay in genealogy*. Princeton, NJ: Princeton University Press.

# 7

# Photojournalism Ethics: A 21st-Century Primal Dance of Behavior, Technology, and Ideology

## Julianne H. Newton

Everything that happens is fluid, changeable. After they've passed, events are only as your memory makes them, and they shift shapes over time.—Charles Frazier. (2006, p. 21)

We need our intellectual eyes wide open.—Clifford G. Christians. (2005, p. 3)

The photographer Walter Curtin (1986), who lived through much of the 20th century, once said he was waiting for the day when he could simply blink an eye to take a picture. He would see something, blink, send the electrical impulses down his arm, and transfer the energy of what he saw through the touch of his fingertip to sensitized material. I often wonder how our perceptions of such ethical issues as photographic intrusion, the gaze, or even digital manipulation might shift if we removed the camera from the process of seeing and image making. Would the instant of recording light reflected from people and things become more credible or less so? Would photography, or "light writing," be viewed as more of an extension of human perceptual processes than a process of constructing false realities? Would seeing and creating images be considered processes of thinking and being, parallel with writing words, rather than problematic exercises of power or deception?

Ethical discussions about the practice of photojournalism and the meanings and significances of its resulting artifacts and influences often are sidetracked by general confusion about the nature of seeing and practices related to seeing. Seeing begins and ends in the living organism of the human body. Yet the process of seeing—a biological process—and, by extension, the practices of seeing, have been alternately ennobled/vilified, overrated/underrated, blamed/ignored. This chapter explores photojournalism's role in this normative dialectic by addressing three aspects of seeing: behaviors, technologies and ideologies.

## VISUAL BEHAVIOR

The human visual system is driven by both conscious and nonconscious processes of the brain. We are drawn to movement, brightness, sharpness, and difference as part of our physical surveil-

FIGURE 7.1 Dancing galaxies (NGC 2207 and IC 2163) twirling around each other. Captured by NASA's Spitzer Space Telescope. NASA, ESA/JPL-Caltech/STScI/D. Elmegreen.

lance and self-protection processes. We are particularly drawn to look at violent or sexual activity, the color of blood, a sudden movement or noise. Yet, if we choose to do so, we can ignore the fluttering movement of a golden leaf framed by a ray of sunlight as it spirals downward from a tree limb—or turn away from seeing the suffering of millions of other humans. Both conscious and nonconscious cognitive processes drive human *visual behavior*, which encompasses all the ways we use seeing and imaging in everyday life (Newton, 2004a).

The visual system is part of the larger system of human perception, the physiological and psychological means through which we respond to and make meaning of stimuli. Brain researchers believe at least 75% of information we take in is visual. One matter of debate in cognitive neuroscience is whether we know something when we perceive something (as Aristotle maintained)— or whether knowledge comes afterward (as Descartes maintained), when the brain has processed the stimuli and made meaning by organizing stimuli according to innate and learned patterns. Although contemporary research supports the former as the nonconscious foundation for most decision making (Damasio, 1999; LeDoux, 1996), research also supports the latter in that we can, by drawing on our continuum of experiences, make decisions based on accepting responsibility for our actions (Gazzaniga, 2005). Cognitive neuroscientist Michael Gazzaniga (2005) puts it succinctly: "Brains are automatic, but people are free. Our freedom is found in the interaction of the social world" (p. 99). He explains:

> Most moral judgments are intuitive.... We have a reaction to a situation, or an opinion, and we form a theory as to why we feel the way we do. In short, we have an automatic reaction to a situation—a brain-derived response. Upon feeling that response, we come to believe we are reacting to absolute truths. What I am suggesting is that these moral ideas are generated by our interpreter, by our brains, yet we form a theory about their absolute "rightness." Characterizing the formation of a moral code in this way *puts the challenge directly on us* [emphasis added]. (p. 192)

This *ecology of seeing* through which a human organism gathers and makes use of visual stimuli not only creates and stores images internally but also can create and produce visual stimuli for other humans to see (Newton, 2005). Bodily generated visual stimuli can be as subtle as a tightened muscle in the face or as intricate as a pirouette, as external as our skin or as internal as our dreams. Following Marshall McLuhan (1964), we extend our internal processes of perception and communication via external forms, such as clothing, pen and ink, paper or canvas, light-sensitive film, electronic media and architecture. Each process entails its own set of behaviors. For example, we alter our behaviors when we think we are being observed—either by other humans, or by extension, by seeing devices such as cameras. This tendency is not unique to humans. Heisenberg's principle describes the effect of observation on the *action* of subatomic particles. Yet the changes in human behavior resulting from being observed surprise us. The social psychologist Stanley Milgram (1977a, 1977b) described such unique "photographic behavior" patterns as the tendencies to cheat less on exams and to give more money to charity when we think someone is watching or a camera is recording our actions.

We can further extend behavioral effects to media consumption and production. We have little choice but to consume some forms of media; a highway billboard, for example, casting a nearly nude figure alongside a bottle of beer is likely to grab our attention because of its disproportionate size and distinctive, out-of-context content. Other media we can clearly choose to see or to ignore; a photograph of a war scene from Iraq, for example (see Figure 7.4), may look like dozens of other war scenes from Iraq we've viewed in recent years and hence goes relatively unnoticed within the larger system of media imagery.

## VISUAL TECHNOLOGIES

Moss (2001) offers a useful definition of *technology* as "the means by which human societies interact directly with and adapt to the environment. Technology can also refer to the steps taken, or manufacturing process used, to produce an artifact." The most significant technology, then, for the present discussion, is the brain.

Our bodies evolved to believe what the eyes see, to translate light rays into electrical signals and send them along the optic nerve to the thalamus. From there a rough schema of what we see is quickly—and first—sent to the amygdala, the part of the brain that can signal the body to fight or flee. In the meantime, a more detailed schema of what we see is sent (more slowly in brain time) to the visual cortex for conscious processing (LeDoux, 1996).

We found ways to translate our perception of the multidimensional world into two-dimensional form—first with rough drawings on cave walls, then through drawing and painting on paper and canvas. We created visual symbol systems—writing—to convey the words we had learned to articulate. We devised techniques such as two-dimensional perspective to create the illusion of a third dimension—depth—within a frame limited by height and width. We used Aristotle's observations of the behavior of light rays passing through a hole in a leaf to help us construct a camera obscura for observing the world and to help us draw more realistically. Then we determined processes through which to convert the energy of light to record the reflectances of objects "out there" into forms we could peruse and collect at will. In this way, photography, or light writing, came to be. Added to the reproducible texts we already had created through movable type and printing processes, we quickly determined the usefulness of combining verbal and visual reports of daily occurrences as a means of disseminating information about our world.

Even more profound for the extension of the human perceptual system was learning how to use other wavelengths from the electromagnetic spectrum—radiowaves, for example—to carry sound and other forms of energy across great distances and quickly. But only now, in the 21st century, are we learning how to use the "speed of mind," as McLuhan termed it, to move prosthetic devices and communicate. Through our behaviors, we have learned how to extend the technology of the brain and central nervous system into machines and processes—print publications, motion pictures, television, the Internet, cell phones, virtual games, and images of information, advertising, entertainment, and art.

The point of this gloss of the history of communication technologies is to highlight the extensional properties of contemporary media. They originated with humans. They are still operated and used by humans. Yet we more often blame media technologies than ourselves for abuses of those technologies. The notion of technology itself as morally neutral is contentious (e.g., Bugeja, 2007). This problem can apply to the brain as a technology, as well as what we traditionally consider to be a technology—machines constructed of inanimate materials to accomplish specific tasks. What we too seldom stop to consider is that blaming *mass media* technologies too easily removes responsibility for our *use* of them from the primary mediating entity we can indeed influence through conscious reflection—our own brains.

## VISUAL IDEOLOGIES

For this discussion, I want to define *ethics* as the dynamic process through which we determine how to behave in daily life. *Media ethics*, then, become the dynamic process through which we determine how to create, disseminate, and use human communications to affect behavior. *Communication*s are the messages we create, perceive, and convey via various transmission and reception systems in order to interact with other humans. Our understanding of the meaning of every stimulus is *mediated*, regardless of the source of the stimulus. We know, for example, that anything we think we see directly with our own eyes is a mediated form organized by the brain (Gazzaniga, 2005). That organization process takes time—milliseconds, yes, but time nonetheless—and is influenced by the physiological abilities of our individual brains and by our individual experiences. The great Spanish perspectivist Ortega y Gasset (1941) said it well: "Yo soy yo y mis circunstancias" ("I am myself and my circumstances"). Gazzaniga (2005) believes the seat of the soul (which he calls the interpreter) is a part of the brain that gathers information (stimuli) to create a story of the self. This scientific basis for 21st-century understanding of the self supports the social construction of the self espoused by 19th-century psychologist William James (1890/1962).

Following this line of thought, *visual media* are any form of imagery we organize for internal or external communication. *Visual ethics* are the dynamic process through which we determine how best to create, disseminate, and use image-based stimuli. Inherent in that definition are the behaviors—both conscious and nonconscious—humans enact as perceivers and communicators.

## PHOTOJOURNALISM

A *journal* is a record of daily activities—those behaviors, including thoughts, that may be either internally or externally perceived and recorded. *Photojournalism* is writing with light to report daily activities. That is the basic definition. However, the *practice of photojournalism* connotes far more than that simple definition indicates.

Photojournalism is a professional practice through which visual reporters seek, document, and present moments of time to multiple viewers. As human beings, visual reporters possess varying degrees of skill and talent, preparation and luck, resources and integrity. Their behavior has consequences beyond those of many other professionals' behavior because their products are (1) disseminated as if they are visual facts, and (2) we tend to believe what we see when it looks real. Although a viewer pausing to contemplate an image of photojournalism might be fully capable of distinguishing whether the image is authentic or false, few viewers stop to do so. Images of photojournalism, therefore, carry weight beyond words: the human perceptual system has evolved to first believe what it sees and question only later, if at all.

This inherent authority of images of the real feeds a range of ideological points of view. On one end of the ethical continuum, an idealized photojournalist visually captures history, documenting moments and people for the world's diary. On the other end of the ethical continuum, a photojournalist is little more than a scavenger, a voyeur turning tragedy and victory into commodities for sale through media industries—yet still, and profoundly, human in both origin and use. Similarly, the concept of *photojournalism* evokes a range of ideological attributes: objectivity/subjectivity, power/powerlessness, truth/fiction, document/commodity, self/other, persecutor/victim.

The core of the best photojournalism is an intuitive connection photojournalists feel with all of humanity. This is evidenced in self-sacrificing acceptance of the "call" of photojournalism, which some compare to a spiritual calling, a call that lures those destined to be international seers into solitary personal lives and the willingness to put themselves at ultimate risk for the sake of a picture. The important point to note, however, is that what they do is not really about the picture. What good photojournalists do is seek to understand humankind by understanding human life and showing it to other humans. Good photojournalists seek to know themselves by knowing others, gathering visual information for that part of the brain that weaves the tale of the self, and trying to satiate existential curiosity about the nature of life and death. Good photojournalists operate from a base of hope that in seeking, in seeing, in documenting, the many selves of the world, that world can become known and can move beyond the darkness of fear and loathing engendered by ignorance into the brightness of acceptance and caring engendered by awareness.

All this, from a practice some believe has more in common with pornography (as an exercise of domination, violence, and exploitation) than with enlightenment? Yes.

The simultaneous, conflicting passions of the human drive to know/survive and the fear of knowing/dying fueled the ideology of the biblical location of sin within the feminine, with Eve's hunger for the apple of knowledge and Adam's presumption that without that knowledge, he would dwell forever in the grace of a higher power's Eden.

This classic parable applies to photojournalism. People want to know, and seeing is the primary way we know. More than 75% of the information our brains process is from visual sources. Photographers document and create images based on their abilities to see and know. Other people then see and learn through the photographers' eyes. People are both drawn to look at and repelled by the frightful and the serene. The frightful is too harsh a light, too reflective of our worst attributes as living organisms. The serene can be too soft a light, too reflective of our best attributes as living organisms. The frightful assures us we are alive. The serene is too ordered to be interesting.

Photojournalism embodies a masculine/feminine metaphor for understanding the gaze. The lens looks outward, penetrating space and moment, then receives the light, holding a moment that has the potential to become a frame of collective memory. Through the extension of human vision via photojournalism, seeing and its instruments (such as cameras) are both active agents, extending into space and time to capture and create moments and likenesses, and passive conduits, receiving light to record form and action for later contemplation and communication. It is the technology of the human organism consciously and nonconsciously interacting with the technology of the camera that facilitates the interaction of both active and passive elements of vision.

## ROOTS OF THEORY AND RESEARCH IN PHOTOJOURNALISM ETHICS

We can divide the study of photojournalism ethics into two categories: process and meaning (Newton, 1984). Ethics of *process* in photojournalism refers to how images are gathered, created, and used. Ethics of *meaning* in photojournalism refers to ways in which we interpret images and incorporate them into our meaning systems. *Intentionality* becomes an issue in both categories, which are not mutually exclusive but rather overlap in complex ways in everyday practice. Does a photographer intend to show the truth or to deceive? Does an editor intend to convey the truth of an event or to use an image to startle or draw a reader/viewer? Does a viewer engage an image with the conscious intent to determine authenticity and respect the human framed within? Or does the viewer read the image through the filters of uninformed, nonconscious prejudice, seeing only what she or he chooses to see?

Finding an effective starting point for a review of literature is difficult. We can reasonably argue that the roots of observing the world lie in the survival tools with which the human species evolved: the ability to observe our surroundings, perceive danger and respond, choose and construct environments to protect our young, and create symbols external to the body for communicating with other humans. As noted earlier in this chapter, photography's own technological ontology blossomed from our desire to reproduce realistically what we see in the world around us. If only we could find a *Pencil of Nature*, as William Henry Fox Talbot (1961), the inventor of the paper negative, termed it, we could capture truth. Yet even the image credited as the "world's first photograph" incorporated the hard-to-discern phenomenon of collapsing more than eight hours of shifting highlights and shadows into one still, ambiguous frame (Williams & Newton, 2007).

In middle and late 19th-century Europe and America, the technologies of talbotypes, daguerreotypes, tin types, and cartes de visite became the media for the masses to record self and other. Previously, only the rich had been able to indulge this passion through the use of the masterful hand art of oil painting. Within decades, the painstaking recording of life became a relatively rapid pursuit, collapsing the days, weeks, months required for painting into eight photographic hours, then 30 minutes, then fractions of a second, and now an instant equivalent to the speed of mind. The complexities of the recording technology continued to diminish, evolving from a carefully coated pewter plate, to paper negatives, to the roll film loaded by technicians into George Eastman's Brownie box camera, to 35 mm film loaded by consumers and pros alike, to the instant pictures of Edward Land's Polaroid process, to the digital-image processes proliferating in our 21st-century world.

Important to note here are distinctions among forms of technological advances: (1) *tool* (brain and eye; hand; stylus, brush and pen; camera; computer); (2) *medium* (energy, light, memory, earth, stone, clay, pigment, ink, paint, cloth, chemical, electricity, byte); (3) *container* (living cell; DNA; body, including brain; rock, wall, landscape; token; sculpture; structure; paper; canvas; book; photograph; radio; movie; telephone; television; computer; building). Along the way observer and observed, self and other, mind and body, subject and object shift from what once were considered discrete elements of the processes of knowing into the integrated dialectics of the ecology of knowing in a world made increasingly complex through our own doing.

Photojournalism offers a form of virtual reality through which we experience worlds beyond our own. The people portrayed in images of photojournalism are, in some ways, our avatars, offering journeys to spaces and moments about which we might wonder but never actually visit. Virtual reality informs our understanding of why we are drawn to the real. Through the frame we enter a timeless world of the other by taking on the other's image self—how else can we understand what we see unless we have some memory, some frame of reference for empathy, myth, understanding?

## THE LITERATURE

The literature of photojournalism ethics derives from several strains of thought: (1) the physical sciences, which include principles of physics and biology; (2) the social sciences, which include principles of observation, interaction and annotation; (3) the hermeneutical traditions of philosophy, exploration of discourse practices, artistic expression, and introspection.

Through the physical sciences, we came to understand the properties of energy, particularly the behavior of light as it passes through space, and refracts through and reflects off objects. Our study of the unique behaviors linking observation and being observed originate in the physical responses of atoms and their parts, and emanate outward to include reflexive humans whose behaviors shift when observed by other human eyes as well as by the mechanical eye of the camera (Milgram, 1977a, 1977b).

Through the social sciences, we came to understand the properties of human interaction, particularly the desires for preservation and connection that drive our voyeurism, observational imperative, exoticization of the other, stereotyping, preoccupation with self, and empathic expression of love and hate, joy and sorrow.

Through hermeneutics, we employ dialogue, letters, journals, art, dance, theater, mass and personal media, in the discovery of self through interaction with others, presentation of self through performance, and the self's interaction with self.

For the origins of photojournalism as a specific field, we might look to the 1930s documentary movement promulgated by the U.S. Farm Security Administration, to the picture magazines originating in Europe and then proliferating in the United States, then to the 1960s when photojournalism became part of journalism curricula and blossomed in newspapers as editors learned the readership value of pictures. For ideological exploration of photojournalism, we can look to the decade of the 1970s, which generated Stuart Hall's (1973) exploration of the news photograph, Susan Sontag's (1973) articulation of photography as aggressor, Tuchman's (1978) characterization of news as constructed event, Foucault's (1977) application of panopticism, and such movements in anthropology and sociology as Harper's (1979, 1981) assertion that social science photographers must earn the ethical right to photograph.

Early work in photojournalism ethics focused on both process and meaning. One of the earliest studies, Emily Nottingham's (1978) ethnographic investigation of subject feelings during a photographic event, laid groundwork for Newton's qualitative (1983) and quantitative (1991) examinations of the influence of photographers' behavior on how people felt about being photographed. On the other side of the process continuum is research exploring what editors and photographers think about various practices in photojournalism. Craig Hartley (1981) conducted what may be the first study of such practices as setting up a scene or photographing the victim of a wreck. Sheila Reaves (1995a, 1995b) moved the research discussion into the digital arena with her seminal explorations of the differences between newspaper and magazine editors' views on the ethics of altering images.

Paul Lester produced the first comprehensive publications on photojournalism ethics, editing a report issued by the National Press Photographers Association (1990) and writing his philosophically based book *Photojournalism: The Ethical Approach* (1991). Tagg's (1988) *The Burden of Representation* explores issues of power and commodification of subjects' images through photographic practices, including photojournalism. Gross, Katz, and Ruby (1991) addressed the moral rights of subjects in visual media in their book *Image Ethics*. Through her book *The Burden of Visual Truth: The Role of Photojournalism in Mediating Reality* (2001), Newton extended the discussion to examine the interplay of responsibilities of subjects, photographers, editors, and viewers in the creation and use of photojournalism images.

The last 10 years have seen an explosion of scholarship about the visual, an indication of increased recognition of the prominence of visual forms of communication in contemporary life. Among the most important works are Barbie Zelizer's (1998) explorations of the influence of photojournalism archives on what and how we remember such events as the Holocaust and David Perlmutter's (1998) work on the use of photojournalism images in international politics. Lester (1996) and then Lester and Ross (2003) contributed significantly to our understanding of the potential harms of stereotyping people in media images. Tom Wheeler (2002) explicated the concepts of phototruth and photofiction in the digital age, and outlined his theory of viewer expectations of reality. Gross, Katz, and Ruby edited a second book *Image Ethics in the Digital Age* in 2003. Newton's (2001, 2004b) typology of visual behavior outlined a method for analyzing intersections of ethical issues arising through the creation, dissemination and viewing of photographs of people.

## THE INTERSECTIONS OF BEHAVIORS, TECHNOLOGIES, AND IDEOLOGIES

In photography, *truth* is an ideology, an encoding of information deemed authentic within a frame according to conventions of professional practice (sharp, well exposed, not set up, not digitally manipulated). Yet truth in photojournalism is more about the mindfulness of the seer than the neutrality of a mechanistic technology. Truth in pictures is about truth in self, the search for moments of empathy as gateways to moments of revelation about the story of the self. Here seer and self may be photographer, subject, viewer; each is interchangeable. Yet each is different—never the same.

Applying Foucault (1988), we might say that photojournalism is a "technology of the self," a tool for excavating society and culture for the bones of truth about the "history of the present."

It is here that technology, behavior, and ideology come together. Life itself is energy; self is energy; light is energy. Whether recorded by gelatin silver granules or by a sensor that converts light into digital bits, energy is at play. Laura Marks (1999) argues that this is enough to maintain the organic correspondence so long valued in photography and used as the justification for photography's ability to record "truth."

Yet it is more complicated than that, as we know. Let's take an example, a set of front-page images published by *The Oregonian*, which won the Pulitzer Prize for Public Service in 2002.

On April 2, 2003, *The Oregonian* published a front page (see Figure 7.2) featuring a photograph of a grieving Iraqi father kneeling beside the wooden coffins of his children. By itself, the photograph evokes empathy, engendering a feeling of connection between viewer and subject: one of the greatest—if not *the* greatest—losses a human can face is the death of one's child. For two weeks before the publication of the photograph, Oregonian editors had selected photographs showing U.S. soldiers in battle in the relatively new war in Iraq (Randy Cox, 2003).

That night, after the front page had already been designed, another story from Iraq broke. Missing POW Jessica Lynch had been rescued. With the early deadline for statewide delivery upon them, *Oregonian* editors quickly rebuilt a section of the front page to run the Lynch rescue story as an off-lead on the top left side of the page (see Figure 7.2).

Many Oregonians who received the paper that morning were not pleased with the page design that gave more prominence to a photograph of an Iraqi than to the photograph and accompanying story about Lynch. Readers communicated their negative responses by canceling subscriptions and calling editors to accuse them of being unpatriotic and caring more about Iraqis than U.S. soldiers. By the time the noon April 2 edition of *The Oregonian* hit the Portland streets,

FIGURE 7.2 *The Oregonian*, Sunrise Edition, April 2, 2003. Used with permission.

editors had had time to redesign the front page to feature a large photo of the rescued Jessica Lynch (see Figure 7.3).

What had transpired? Both photographs were true and it is likely that each was selected for front-page, above-the-fold display because of their news value and visual appeal. To some readers, however, the photographs and page designs connoted more than visual reports of news events. Consider a set of possible interpretations of how the images were used. The photograph

Figure 7.3 *The Oregonian*, noon edition, April 2. Used with permission.

of the grieving Iraqi father made clear that the war was harming the innocent; it also focused attention on the "enemy" rather than on U.S. troops. The photograph of Corporal Lynch affirmed U.S. military prowess by portraying a female soldier as a heroine rescued from the enemy by U.S heroes. The first photograph proclaimed the injustice of war on citizens who happen to get in its way, visually reporting a negative aspect of the U.S. invasion of Iraq. The large photograph of a rescued Corporal Lynch affirmed U.S. ability "to make things turn out all right" in the face of an enemy who had captured and perhaps tortured (we learned later how Iraqi medical personnel had helped save Corporal Lynch) a young U.S. woman who had entered the military to get an education.

The photographs were of real people and real events. Yet each came out of and entered into discourses of individual differences, national identity, and international disagreement. One could be read as about loss of innocence, the other as about recovered pride and vindication. Each photograph was contextualized by the front-page design of headlines and text within a newspaper frame—and by the perceptions and biases of reader/viewers.

The next day, April 3, *Oregonian* page 1 editors returned to visual content that was similar to the content they had published for two weeks preceding the breaking of the Lynch story. In Figure 7.4, we see the story of the War in Iraq as it was most acceptable to many U.S. readers/viewers in 2003: U.S. troops marching on Baghdad as fighters for freedom and national security.


## CONCLUSION

We somehow were brought up with the notion that documentary pictures were the equivalent of a testimony that was credible because it was a photograph.

> In other words, the very nature of being photographic was a good enough reason for all of us to consider the photograph as a reliable witness of events in our daily life.... However, upon closer inspection and scrutiny, we start to find all sorts of loopholes that bring up a high degree of doubt to this otherwise empirical comparison between the photograph and reality.—Pedro Meyer (2002)

Mexican photographer Pedro Meyer (1995) is known for images he constructs, through digital processes, to be "true fictions." He believes that the digital process facilitates his ability to communicate truths that are truer than the original images alone. In this way, he calls attention to and makes use of the all-too-real human perceptual principle known as the Gestalt. Formulated by early 20th-century psychologists, the principle asserts the now-classic idea that the whole is greater than the sum of its parts. One way to consider this principle is to consider how different a room looks when we remove one item—a piece of furniture, a painting, a window. The great *Life* magazine picture editor Wilson Hicks articulated the principle in regard to journalism when he noted that putting a picture and words together communicated meaning beyond what either the picture or words alone communicated. To envision this "third effect," try covering up the main headline in one of the sample pages from *The Oregonian*. What if, instead of "U.S. Forces Sweep Past Republican Guard Units," the headline had read, "U.S. Forces Find Lynch in Care of Iraqi Physician"? Or change "Troops Close on Baghdad" to "Troops May Kill Thousands." The content of the images has not changed, but the way our minds perceive and use them to make meaning from the combination of words and images changes dramatically.

When the Gestalt principle is applied through digital manipulation (for example, envision changing Lynch's smile to a sob), the content of the image itself is changed. In art, such as with Meyer's work, the act is considered ethical because the artist seeks to express truths for which there may be no real-world referent. In photojournalism, however, the act is decidedly unethical. Why? Because we expect an image produced and disseminated through journalistic processes to be exactly like the real world. If the image looks real, it should be real. Yet we know that photographers, subjects, editors, and viewers can mislead, deceive, and even lie with images just as they can with words. Intention is not always conscious. Subjects can pose in a certain manner (such as President Bush did when declaring victory in Iraq), photographers can frame a nonrepresenta-

FIGURE 7.4 *The Oregonian*, April 3, Sunrise Edition. Used with permission.

tive part of a scene or use photographic techniques to blur or freeze action, editors can select a nonrepresentative but highly appealing image to report a story, designers can place an image next to words that anchor its meaning erroneously, and viewers can misread (or ignore) the content of an image to support preconceived or even nonconscious ideas about reality.

Photojournalism organizations, such as the National Press Photographers Association (2007), have enacted fairly specific codes of ethics to guide the professional practice of photojournalism.

However, the burden of visual truth must be carried by all those who make and consume images of photojournalism—not just the photographers (Newton, 2001). This assertion is idealistic but possible to a great extent through education about the ways images communicate.

I want to conclude this synopsis of photojournalism's relationship to reality, to technology, to truth, and to contemporary culture through ideological discourse by positing the idea of "reasonable truth," the best truth a human can acquire, given the variables of perception, behavior, culture and institutional practices that affect all understanding between humans (Newton, 2001).

The call to continue the search for a reasonable truth through whatever means available to us is idealistic. It is grounded in Christians' (2005) universal ethics based in the core principle that all life is sacred: "Human beings resonate cross-culturally through their moral imagination with one another. Our mutual humanness is actually an ethical commitment rooted in the moral domains all humans share" (p. 9). Christians writes:

> In the process of invigorating our moral imagination, the ethical media worldwide enable readers and viewers to resonate with other human beings who also struggle in their consciences with human values of a similar sort. Media professionals have enormous opportunities for putting universal protonorms to work—such as the sacredness of life—and enlarging our understanding of what it means to be human. (p. 12)

Christians' universal ethics is supported by a growing group of scientists, exemplified by Michael Gazzaniga (2005), who writes:

> I am convinced that we must commit ourselves to the view that a universal ethics is possible, and that we ought to seek to understand it and define it. It is a staggering idea, and one that on casual thought seems preposterous. Yet there is no way out. We now understand how tendentious our beliefs about the world and the nature of human experience truly are, and how dependent we have become on tales from the past. At some level we all know this. At the same time, our species wants to believe in something, some natural order, and it is the job of modern science to help figure out how that order should be characterized. (p. 178)

I believe photojournalism—or visual journalism as it is sometimes now called—also plays an important role, along with philosophy, art, and science, in helping humankind determine how best to live together in coming centuries. As the great photojournalist Gordon Parks once wrote, "My eyes only act as conduits for my heart" (inscription on photograph).

This chapter has explored photojournalism ethics by journeying through human visual history toward building a broader theory of visual ethics. I have sought to extend understanding of photojournalism beyond political or economic interpretations of media—big or small—toward core human behaviors of seeing, knowing, communicating, and caring.

We need more research about these behaviors to ground our professional practices and consumption of photojournalism images. Pshcyologist Paul Slovic (2007), for example, has determined that viewers respond with more empathy to images of one suffering person than to images of many suffering people. This is in keeping with Christians' (2005) articulation of the need to resolve one/many issues by considering "the many as being reconstituted into the one" (p. 11). Journalism has a long tradition of "humanizing" stories by focusing on individuals. In photojournalism, the "Day in the Life Of" story comes to mind.

We also need research about the current trend toward participatory visual journalism. As Maria Puente (2007) wrote for *USA Today*: "Oh, for the good old days when all we worried about was Big Brother government watching us. Too late: Now we have Little Brother to contend with, too—and he has a camera phone." Interestingly, the teaser for the article read, "Cell phone cameras continue to haunt both celebs and Ordinary Joes. Can morals keep pace with technology?" *USA Today* posed these "quick questions" to its online readers: "Will citizen outrage eventually quell the use of cell phone cameras in public?" Possible answers: "Yes, boredom and social conventions will set in." or "No, this is only the tip of the iceberg."

One example of cell-phone visual reporting is the allegedly unauthorized video of Saddam Hussein dangling from the executioner's rope. Many people decried the posting of the video on the Internet. But we can look at the issue as a photojournalist would: without the crude video, most of us would still have little recourse but to accept the official description of Hussein's execution as dignified and orderly. In other words, we would have believed the official lie. Regardless of whether we think it ethical to *show* the video to the public, we needed the visual evidence in order to *know* what happened.

And to those who say we can no longer use photography or video as evidence, we now have technology that can determine whether digital images are authentic or digitally manipulated. Science journals, such as *The Journal of Cell Biology*, have developed guidelines for using Photoshop to determine whether scientists have altered pixels in the images they submit as evidence to accompany their research publication (Wade, 2006). Professor Hany Farid (2007), a computer scientist who leads Dartmouth's Image Science Group, has developed image authentication software to detect image manipulation. Farid also affirms human visual abilities. In one interesting study, Farid and M. J. Bravo (2007) determined that 10 human observers inspecting 360 images, spending an average of 2.4 seconds on each image, "correctly classified 83% of the photographic images and 82% of the CG [computer-generated] images" (para. 3). Farid and Bravo (2007) wrote, "Even with great advances in computer graphics technology, the human visual system is still very good at distinguishing between computer generated and photographic images" (para. 5).

Viewers of news images can develop their critical observation abilities to interpret what they see with increased clarity. They also might want to embrace serious photojournalism's creative vision, its selective construction of news stories, its carefully crafted construction of features. Visual journalists edit and compile their "findings" just as word journalists record, select, and edit quotes, facts, and descriptions. A core problem is that visual journalists—and viewers of visual news—reject the constructionist nature of visual reporting for fear of delegitimizing its authority. We so distrust the visual (yet we cannot help but trust our eyes) that we cannot fathom trusting a seer other than ourselves. Yet we must, if we are to be fully aware citizens of this diverse globe of ours. Consider, for example, that no amount of carefully selected words can make visible the invisible in the manner evoked by pictures. Photojournalism confronts us with the ambiguities of seeing—indeed with the ambiguity of truth and the processes of knowing.

When we look—really look—into the image in Figure 7.2 of the Iraqi father mourning the deaths of his children, we are confronted by the *self* we see in the *other*, and we cringe at the pain we sense and at the need to acknowledge our own complicity in the father's suffering. In her provocative book *Vision's Invisibles* (2003), philosopher Véronique Fóti (2003) explores the complexities of seeing external forms versus knowing internal realities:

> There really is no antithesis between philosophy's fascination with dimensions of invisibility, on the one hand, and, on the other hand, a cherishing of visuality and sensuous presencing. Their traditional but artificial opposition only abets the impoverishment of sight. If both are to be optimally realized, their opposition needs to be crossed out to allow one to understand them more meaningfully and to bring them into an intimate reciprocity. (p. 8)

Fóti draws on Aristotle and Heidegger to reassert that perceiving is knowing: "envisagement *is* [author's italics] already understanding…" (p. 104). She cautions, however, that vision "is historically and culturally formed and also has its critical powers, which give it the possibility of education, refinement, and transformation" (p. 104). Fóti further invokes an active, "compassionate vision" that is "unconcerned with self." This compassionate vision is "indissociable from what in Buddhist thought is called 'all-accomplishing wisdom' (a wisdom fully realized only enlightened awareness)" or, in Judeo-Christian thought, "a compassion so intolerant of the sight of suffering as to find the power even to restore a dead man to life" (p. 104).

We know, from our history on this planet, that many humans do need guidelines (and laws) for behavior. Humans make those guidelines, too—and they violate them. The answers to the ethical challenges brought to bear via technologies are found in the hearts and minds of human beings.

We have come a long way, as the saying goes, in understanding the complex natures of truth and reality. We may not have satisfactory definitions for either concept, but we can appreciate both their complexity and their centrality to living the ethics-grounded life. Given this desire to understand truth and reality, addressing ethical concerns about the role of photojournalism and its multiple technological forms in contemporary culture is easily mired in confusion about the origins and uses of images of photojournalism.

To get at the ethical core of photojournalism, I have focused on three themes: photojournalism as human behavior, photojournalism as technologically based practice, and photojournalism as ideology. Some would argue that one cannot simultaneously ground a theory of ethics in theories of self-construction and universal values. My goal with this chapter was to demonstrate the value of both/and thinking in regard to self and other, the particular and the universal, and practices—such as photojournalism—that both articulate and evoke on their way to helping us determine reasonable truths for living.

## REFERENCES

Christians, C. G. (2005). Ethical theory in communications research. *Journalism Studies, 6*(1), 3–14.

Cox, R. (2003). Presentation to J204 Visual Communication for Mass Media, School of Journalism and Communication, Allen Hall, University of Oregon.

Curtin, W. (1986). Presentation to Texas Photographic Society, Austin, Texas.

Damasio, A. (1999). *The feeling of what happens.* New York: Harcourt Brace.

Farid, H. (2007). Digital tampering & forensics. Accessed May 10, 2007, from http://www.cs.dartmouth.edu/~farid/research/

Farid, H., & Bravo, M. J. (2007). Photorealistic rendering: How realistic is it? Accessed May 10, 2007, from http://www.cs.dartmouth.edu/farid/publications/vss07.html

Foucault, M. (1977). *Discipline and punish.* A. Sheridan (Trans.). New York: Pantheon Books.

Foucault, M. (1988). Technologies of the self: A seminar with Michel Foucault. Martin, L. H., and Gutman, H. (Eds). Amherst: University of Massachusetts Press.

Fóti, V. M. (2003). *Vision's invisibles: Philosophical explorations.* Albany: State University of New York Press.

Gazzaniga, M. (2005). *The ethical brain.* New York: The Dana Foundation.

Gross, L., Katz, J. S., & Ruby, J. (Eds.). (1991). *Image ethics: The moral rights of subjects in photographs, film, and television.* London: Oxford University Press.

Gross, L., Katz, J. S., & Ruby, J. (Eds.). (2003). *Image ethics in the digital age.* Minneapolis: University of Minnesota Press.

Hall, S. (1973). The determination of news photographs. In S. Cohen & J. Young (Eds.), *The manufacture of news: A reader* (pp. 176–190). London: Constable.

Harper, D. (1979). Life on the road. In J. Wagner (Ed.), *Images of information: Still photography in the social sciences* (pp. 25–42). Beverly Hills, CA: Sage.

Harper, D. (1981). *Good company.* Chicago: University of Chicago Press.

Hartley, C. (1981). *The reactions of photojournalists and the public to hypothetical ethical dilemmas confronting press photographers.* Unpublished master's thesis, University of Texas, Austin.

James, W. (1890/1962). *The principles of psychology.* New York: Smith.

Kobre, K. (2005). *Photojournalism: The professionals' approach,* 5th ed. Boston: Focal Press.

LeDoux, J. (1996). *The emotional brain.* New York: Simon & Schuster.

Lester, P. M. (Ed.). (1990). *NPPA special report: The ethics of photojournalism.* Durham, NC: National Press Photographers Association.

Lester, P. M. (1991). *Photojournalism: The ethical approach.* Mahwah, NJ: Erlbaum.

Lester, P. M. (1996). *Images that injure: Pictorial stereotypes in the media.* Westport, CT: Praeger.

Lester, P. M., & Ross, S. D. (2003). *Images that injure: Pictorial stereotypes in the media* (2nd ed.). Westport, CT: Praeger.

Marks, L. U. (1999). How electrons remember, *Millennium Film Journal, 34*(Fall). Accessed May 7, 2007, from http://mfj-online.org/journalPages/MFJ34/LMarks.html

McLuhan, M. (1964). *Understanding media: The extensions of man.* New York: McGraw-Hill.

Meyer, P. (2002). If you liked documentary work, you are going to love digital images. *ZoneZero.* Accessed February 11, 2007 from http://zonezero.com/default.html

Meyer, P. (1995). *Truths & fictions: A journey from documentary to digital photography.* New York: Aperture Foundation.

Milgram, S. (1977a). The image-freezing machine. *Psychology Today, 10,* 50–54, 108.

Milgram, S. (1977b). *The individual in a social world, essays and experiments.* Reading, MA: Addison-Wesley.

Moss, M. L. (2001). Anthropology 150—Glossary. Accessed February 11, 2007, from http://darkwing.uoregon.edu/~mmoss/GLOSSARY.HTM

National Press Photographers Association (2007). NPPA Code of Ethics. Accessed June 17, 2007, from http://www.nppa.org/professional_development/business_practices/ethics.html

Newton, J. H. (1984). The role of photography in a social science research project in Northern Mexico: A matter of ethics. Unpublished master's thesis, University of Texas, Austin.

Newton, J. H. (1991). In front of the camera: Ethical issues of subject response in photography. Unpublished doctoral dissertation, University of Texas, Austin.

Newton, J. H. (2001). *The burden of visual truth: The role of photojournalism in mediating reality.* Mahwah, NJ: Erlbaum.

Newton, J. H. (2004a). Visual ethics. In K. Smith, G. Barbatsis, S. Moriarty, & K. Kenney, (Eds.), *Handbook of visual communication* (pp. 429–443). Mahwah, NJ: Erlbaum.

Newton, J. H. (2004b). A visual method for visual research: Exploring ethical issues in pictures by applying a typology of visual behavior. In K. Smith, B. Barbatsis, S. Moriarty, & K. Kenney (Eds.), *Handbook of visual communication* (pp. 459–477). Mahwah, NJ: Erlbaum.

Nottingham, E. (1978). From both sides of the lens: Street photojournalism and personal space. Unpublished doctoral dissertation, Indiana University, Bloomington.

Ortega y Gasset, J. (1941). *History as a system and other essays toward a philosophy of history* (Helen Wey, Trans.). New York: W.W. Norton.

Parks, G. (date unknown). Inscription on photograph of Russel Lee by Alan Pogue.

Perlmutter, D. D. (1998). *Photojournalism and foreign policy: Icons of outrage in international crises.* Westport, CT: Praeger.

Puente, M. (February 28, 2007). "Hello to less privacy." USA Today. Accessed on February 28, 2007, from http://www.usatoday.com/tech/news/2007-02-27-cameraphones-privacy_x.htm

Reaves, S. (1995a). Magazines vs. newspapers: Editors have different ethical standards on the digital manipulation of photographs. *Visual Communication Quarterly,* Winter, 4–7.

Reaves, S. (1995b). The vulnerable image: Categories of photos as predictor of digital manipulation. *Journalism & Mass Communication Quarterly,* 706–715.

Slovic, P. (2007). If I look at the mass I will never act: Psychic numbing and genocide. Paper presented at the annual meeting of the AAAS, San Francisco, February 16.

Sontag, S. (1973). *On photography.* New York: Dell.

Talbot, W. H. F. (1961). *The pencil of nature.* Facsimile ed. New York: Da Capo Press. (Original issued serially from 1844 to 1846)

Tagg, J. (1988). *The burden of representation: Essays on photographies and histories.* Basingstoke, UK: Macmillan Education.

Tuchman, G. (1978). *Making news, a study in the construction of reality.* New York: The Free Press.

Wade, N. (2006, January 24). It may look authentic; here's how to tell it isn't. *The New York Times.* Retrieved January 25, 2006, from http://www.nytimes.com/2006/01/24/science/24frau.html?pagewanted=2&th&emc=th

Williams, R., & Newton, J. H. (2007). *Visual communication: Integrating media, art and science.* Mahwah, NJ: Erlbaum.

Zelizer, B. (1998). *Remembering to forget: Holocaust memory through the camera eye.* Chicago: University of Chicago Press.

# 8

# Why Diversity Is an Ethical Issue

## Ginny Whitehouse

The news industry should see diversity as part of its ethical canon, Brislin and Williams wrote for the *Journal of Mass Media Ethics* in 1996. That same year, 69 percent of newspaper editors and broadcast news directors surveyed called diversity an ethical issue (Medsger, 1996, p. 7). Since the mid- to late 1990s, diversity has come to be viewed as a crucial part of accuracy and professionalism. If ethics broadly is concerned with how we live our lives and what we value (Jaksa & Pritchard, 1994, p. 3), then nothing could be more relevant to a discussion of ethics than the way people relate to, perceive, and share stories with those who are different from them. The impact of these stories stretches from shaping international relations to helping create empathy for a next door neighbor (Craig, 2006, p. 9). Alasdair MacIntyre believes that people come to know who they are through stories with interlocking narratives (1984, pp. 214–216). Each person's very identity is created through these stories. "The pervasiveness of news and 'mediated experience' as the source of stories thus makes journalists in a sense, co-authors of moral meaning in contemporary society" (Lambeth, 1992, p. 87).

If one segment of society is ignored, vilified, or even inappropriately sanctified through mass media narratives, then under MacIntyrian logic, those marginalized and the community as a whole is harmed. As an example, Muslim immigrants in Western nations have found themselves particularly vulnerable. After the Sept. 11, 2001, attacks, London's Turkish-speaking immigrants developed what Aksoy (2006) calls a transnational identity to cope with the "us" versus "them" language used by both politicians and journalists. Dominant culture television stations vilified the Turkish- and Arab-language media. The immigrants consumed more English-language media than their white counterparts, in addition to Turkish-and Arab-language media, just trying to understand the complexities of the crisis. Aksoy found that they became more distrustful of all news media, including Turkish- and Arab-language media (2006, p. 927). The result was a media-created ethical dilemma for a vulnerable population struggling to create an identity outside popular narratives. The dominant culture media's tendency toward simplistic, over-generalized interpretations of Islam, the role of women, and jihad have created a "clash of civilizations" narrative and thus contributed to international public policy on war (Ahmad, 2006, p. 980). The opposing frames journalists tend to use in describing conflicts contribute significantly toward increased polarization, therefore reaffirming public perceptions of powerlessness (Jameson & Entman, 2004, p. 38).

Simultaneously, when considering ethics and diversity, there is a need to separate cultural relativism and cultural pluralism. Cultural relativism holds no universal or common norms and in essence espouses: I am good if I do not tell you that you are bad. By its very nature, cultural relativism eliminates the need for ethical debate because it assumes that all judgments are equal (Shaw, 2003, p. 94). By contrast, cultural pluralism allows an array of moral options within parameters of mutuality, or acting with respect for the interdependency of all people (Christians et al., 1993, p. 57) and basic values are shared across societies (Bok, 2002, pp. 13–16). Those values are lived out in different ways in different cultures and subcultures, but identifying commonality provides a starting point for dialogue and connection. Calls for understanding and identifying universal norms should not lead to totalitarian results, but rather a support for cultural diversity (Christians, 2005, p. 6). The 'live and let live' rhetoric common in cultural relativism becomes in reality 'you go live over there' because it denies opportunity for interaction. Relativism simply is impractical because it fails to recognize that injustice or oppression exists, as well as making true relationship among people of differences impossible (Bok, 2002, p. 45). Interaction, relationship, and diverse connections can only occur and be effective within a culturally plural environment as opposed to a culturally relative environment.

## DIVERSITY WITHIN NEWS ORGANIZATIONS

In the last three decades, nearly all the major U.S. professional and educational journalism organizations have included diversity as a primary ethic, value, goal, or mission: American Society of Newspaper Editors (ASNE), Associated Press Managing Editors (APME), Association for Education in Journalism and Mass Communication (AEJMC), Newspaper Association of America (NAA), Radio and Television News Directors Association (RTNDA), Society of Professional Journalists (SPJ), and others. RTNDA also offers a Spanish language option on its website and SPJ offers its Code of Ethics in eight languages. At the same time, national associations for ethnic and minority groups formed and gained an increasing voice, and four associations have come together to create UNITY: Journalists of Color, Inc. When UNITY convened in Washington, DC, in 2004, the dearth of ethnic minority journalists in the nation's capital press corps was emphasized: Within the Washington, DC, newspaper press corps' bureau chiefs, editors, and writers, only one in ten were journalists of color, and only a handful of print journalists of color participate in presidential political campaign coverage and reporting on national public policy (Martin & Pineda, 2004, pp. 1, 16).

Efforts to increase minority recruitment and improve retention have long been part of professional journalism organizations' agendas. In 1978, ASNE set a goal to have minority representation in newsrooms to be at parity with the nation's demographics by 2000. Gain was made, but only at about one percent a year, and the target date was reconfigured to 2025. ASNE and APME partnered together with other groups to create the annual Time-Out for Diversity initiative, encouraging news organizations to consider the changing community demographics particularly amongst children.

ASNE had hoped to reach 18.55 percent for minority representation in newsrooms by 2005, but organizational research that year showed the actual rate was 13.87 percent. That was an increase from the previous year, up by .45 percent. Meanwhile, the nation's ethnic minority population was at 33 percent. ASNE had hoped by 2005 to have 348 newsrooms at demographic parity—177 had reached that goal. ASNE leaders were pleased that some successes had been made, but voiced concern at the level of success. ASNE Diversity Chair Sharon Rosenhause said in a media release: "The country is changing faster and more dramatically than our newspapers and newsrooms.... It takes very determined editors, newspaper and media companies to make a difference and, right now, not enough are" (ASNE, 2006).

Television journalism has fared better than newspapers overall at increasing its ethnic minority presence, with 21.8 percent of the television news workforce being ethnic minorities in 2004. However, only 12.5 percent of the television news directors and 7.4 percent of the general managers were persons of color (Papper, 2004, pp. 24, 28). That means the actual management of news organization and the news content itself is nowhere near as diverse as the ethnicity of on-air news personalities. Having some ethnic minorities in visible positions, such as a television news anchor, indicates to the viewing public that entire news organizations are diverse. This false front becomes particularly problematic because it fuels dominant culture assumptions that racism is neither systemic nor pervasive, and may even relegate racism to past history (Heider, 2002, p. 20).

The blame for lack of parity has been spread throughout media institutions, to a variety of standard newsroom practices, and to education. Students must have internships in order to successfully enter the industry, but many internships are unpaid, thus creating a significant economic disadvantage for those already facing economic challenges. Lower starting salaries in broadcast journalism are an often-cited problem for ethnic minorities leaving university saddled with student loans (Iqbal, 2004, p. 10). Meredes de Uriarte (2003) believes parity has not occurred primarily because numerical integration has been confused with substantive intellectual diversity. Newsroom demographics are not diverse because newsroom culture and news values have not been diversified effectively: "Newsrooms moved forward assuming that they could just find and add minorities without experiencing discomforting cultural change" (p. 36). Once persons of color arrive in management positions, many find that their opportunity to influence news policy is limited by prevailing conventions. Nearly 60 percent of news executives of color reported that they believe they must censor themselves when expressing opinions (Woods, 2002 p. 24). At the same time, ethnic minority journalists report that editors regularly reject their story ideas because they are perceived as biased. The principal of journalistic balance becomes defined as using traditionally accepted sources with predictable conclusions, and accuracy becomes defined as consistency (de Uriarte, 2003, pp. 72–76).

While the mainstream media struggle to recruit and retain people of color, ethnic media organizations, including Spanish-language media, are highly effective at reaching ethnic minorities. Research examining a cross-section of ethnic groups in the United States has shown:

> Forty-five percent of all African American, Hispanic, Asian American, Native American and Arab American adults prefer ethnic television, radio or newspapers to their mainstream counterparts. These "primary consumers" also indicated that they access ethnic media frequently. This means that a staggering 29 million adults (45 percent of the 64 million ethnic adults studied) or a full 13 percent of the entire adult population of the United States, prefer ethnic media to mainstream television, radio, or newspapers. (Bendixenan & Associates, 2005, p. 8)

Yet when national mainstream professional organizations have held conferences and structured dialogs on diversity, the ethnic press is rarely invited to participate and then in very small numbers (de Uriarte, 2003, p. 5).

Research in the area of newsroom diversity must consider more than just horserace figures on the losses and gains of journalists of color. Research must examine specific models of recruitment/retention success and clarify how newsroom culture itself must change in order to meet organizational goals. Research must illustrate how journalists of color throughout the management chain can be given appropriate voice to define news outside dominant culture frames. However, the actual success of diversity efforts will remain limited unless the culture of media organizations changes internally to reflect the diversity of communities covered.

## HOW DIVERSITY IS PORTRAYED

Perhaps one of the best ways to redefine newsroom culture is through research applying intercultural communication scholarship to the ways that the media—from the local weekly sports reporting to national advertising campaigns—gather and disseminate information across diverse groups. Improving professional practice will foster more ethical responses to cultural conflicts and provide the whole community with better understanding of all its parts.

A danger in reviewing the intercultural communication literature is in failing to understand how analysis and categories are made within this academic field. Accuracy is a vital ethical requirement in any research, from journalism to social science. To examine communication trends, intercultural scholars are careful to frame constructs about ethnic groups accurately in the context of tendencies and sociotypes. Sociotypes involve cultural predispositions towards certain activities and behaviors that generally are neutral and defined internally by an ethnic group or are backed by empirical data. For example, asserting that African Americans in the Northeastern United States tend to be Democrats would be an accurate sociotype supported by the research and voting trends (Triandis, 1994, p. 107). Stereotypes by contrast most frequently come from outside the culture, are framed in absolute terms without acknowledging individual difference, are often overly simplistic, and are most frequently negative. If the stereotype is framed as intending to be a positive statement, such as 'all Asians are smart,' the assertion frequently is dismissive of other attributes and makes unsubstantiated generalities (Ting-Toomey, 1999, p.161). Stereotypes then are inaccurate and inappropriate generalizations; sociotypes gain validity because they are defined internally, recognize individual difference, and are supported by verifiable evidence.

The power stereotyping has should first be addressed in the form of privilege because understanding the power of privilege is fundamental to understanding the ethics of diversity. Peggy McIntosh identifies white privilege as an "invisible knapsack of unearned assets...of special provisions, maps, passports, codebooks, visas, clothes, tools, and blank checks." She argues those with privilege "are not taught to recognize their own privileges" and, if acknowledged, they "deny the resulting advantages" (McIntosh, 2000, pp. 115–116). Simply put, the world's media culture is led largely by those with privilege, who ultimately define the narratives of those without privilege. Stereotypes that emerge from those narratives, regardless of intent, perpetuate distrust, misperception, and oppression. A common dominant culture response to avoid stereotyping is to claim colorblindness: The observer asserts that he or she does not see color or ethnicity, only the individual person. However, the assertion is flawed because color and ethnicity are part of identity and denying that identity is a problematic part of white privilege.

Essed argues that white privilege leads those in the dominant culture to assume that nearly everyone makes decisions, including ethical decisions, in the same way, and given the same set of circumstances would come to the same conclusions (1991, p. 189). By extension, that means many dominant culture news managers may assume that all people would select the same news stories. Heider, who studied local television news, determined that news directors tended to believe they were adequately covering their communities, including ethnic minorities, if they had high ratings. "Even if trying to appeal to a large audience has a pluralistic sound to it, it still comes down to a news philosophy that is based on the principal where the majority rules" (2002, p. 29). The result then is coverage of minorities based on what the dominant culture may find interesting, such as festivals and holidays. This practice helps create the illusion that non-European groups are primitive and their cultures belong to the realm of past history.

If particular cultural groups are portrayed only in limited settings, then their entire existence in popular thought becomes limited to those narrow portrayals. Heider calls this incognizant racism: Systematic exclusion and stereotypical inclusion may not be deliberate but nonetheless results in racist news coverage and false narratives (2000, p. 51). In football game coverage, overt racial slurs would not get past Federal Communication Commission legal restrictions, much less any ethical consideration. Nonetheless, sports media research has consistently shown that stereotypes of African Americans are persistent. Billings (2004) examined 162 hours of college and professional football coverage with over 3,800 characterizations of White and Black quarterbacks. While stereotypes connecting race and intelligence appear to be abating, African Americans still are most frequently described as successful because of athletic prowess and White players as failing because of their "lack of innate ability" (p. 207–208). Incognizant racism occurs subtly but still perpetuates false narratives.

One of the most glaring concerns comes in the ways Africans Americans tend to be significantly overrepresented in news images showing the "face of poverty." Gilens' 1996 research found that only 27 percent of the poor in the United States were African American at that time, but African Americans made up 63 percent of the news images of poor people (pp. 516–517). When the images involved working-age younger people, more than half were African American. When the images involved the elderly, only one in five was African American. That meant that the unsympathetic poor—those who might be perceived as able to work—received a considerably disproportionate share of the images. He argues that these images link "being poor" and "being Black" together tightly in the American psyche, creating an inaccurate public perception of what it means to be either Black or impoverished (1999, p. 68). This conclusion was further validated in a 2002 study comparing television viewing with attitudes on race and poverty. The more news that research subjects chose to view on television, the more likely they were to attribute poverty amongst African Americans to lack of motivation instead of lack of economic opportunity (Busselle & Crandall, 2002, p. 269). Additional research is needed to quantify how media portrayals of race and poverty directly impact public policy.

So while African Americans are overrepresented in news stories about poverty, African Americans are underrepresented as victims of crime and as police officers in television network news programs (Dixon, Azocar, & Casas, 2003). Latinos, Asian Americans, and Native Americans are rarely the subjects of stories, thus making their experiences invisible in their communities (Poindexter, Smith, & Heider, 2003). Vargas argues that newspaper coverage perpetuates images of Latinos as an underclass despite increasing economic strengths (2000, p. 268). One in three television news stories on Latinos in 2004 focused entirely on immigration, and no Latino was quoted in half of the stories about Latinos (Subervi, 2005, p. 4). These immigration stories also tend not to consider how U.S. foreign policy shapes instability within Latin American countries and tends to favor depictions of Latinos wanting something in the United States that they could not get at home (De Uriarte, 2003, p. 84). The National Association of Hispanic Journalists expressed particular concern about television news in its 2005 Brownout Report: "What viewers have learned is that too often Latinos are portrayed as problem people living on the fringes of U.S. society" (p. 5).

In prime time entertainment programming, Latino men are portrayed as less articulate than their White or African American counterparts while Latina women are portrayed as having a significantly lower work effort. Latinos make up only 3.9 percent of popular U.S. TV characters, a figure that has been fairly stagnant for more than a decade, even though Latinos make up more than 12.5 percent of the total U.S. population and are emerging as the largest ethnic minority group in the nation (Mastro & Behm-Marowitz, 2005, p. 124). In addition, Latinos make up about 1 percent of the speaking characters in U.S. TV advertisements, and then most frequently appear as oversexed and less intelligent. By contrast, Asians appeared as characters in 2.3 percent of the U.S. TV advertisements, primarily as passively working in technology fields. Native

Americans appeared less than .04 percent, most frequently in advertisements for big retail stores such as Wal-Mart (Mastro & Stern, 2003, pp. 642–643).

Stereotypical portrayals become all the more demeaning when other positive media representation is absent and the ethnic minority experience becomes even more invisible. Journalist Darla Wiese, an Okanagan tribal member, remembers as a child seeking out every popular image of Native Americans she could find, even ones belittling her heritage: "Though no one in my family watched sports, I sought and learned the 'Tomahawk Chop' all for mainstream cultural validation" (2006). Wiese said incognizant racism through the absence of valid Native images may not be deliberate, but nonetheless those negative images fill voids when no alternatives are available. Oklahoma student Sara Mac Martin, who is Choctaw and Lakota, says her high school mascot makes her feel "like my race is being used as a prop" (Beck, 2005).

While some sports teams are reconsidering Native-themed mascots, many high school, university, and professional teams have maintained stereotypical mascots. So many in fact, that the NCAA created new rules that prohibit schools with "hostile or abusive" Indian mascots from hosting its championships and bowls, just as schools in states that fly Confederate flags are prohibited. If schools determined to have offensive Native mascots participate in playoffs, they are barred from displaying Indian nicknames or logos (Wieberg, 2006, p. C3). This may relieve some burden on media organizations who must decide whether using official team names in sports coverage is an overt act of racism. Native American groups estimate that more than 2,000 sports teams across the United States have eliminated Indian mascots since 1970; however, over 1,000 teams choose to continue the practice (*Indian Country Today*, 2005), meaning virtually all U.S. mainstream news organizations are still left with the choice of how to cover these sports teams. Notably, 81 percent of Native leaders have found Native mascots offensive and demeaning (*Indian Country Today*, 2001). In 2003, the Native American Journalists Association formally called for all news organizations to stop publishing or broadcasting all Indian mascot names and images. To date, only five newspapers have accepted this policy in full, though others have chosen to eliminate the use of particularly offensive mascots such as The Cleveland Indians' Chief Wahoo. NAJA argues news organizations do not increase accuracy by identifying teams by Indian mascot; the school or city name achieves the same purpose:

> Our complaint about mascots is that they are racial slurs and stereotypes that are comparable in meaning to the 'n-word' and which should be offensive to all thinking people. We count team names such as Indians to be stereotypes and team names such as redskins, squaws, and red men to be slurs. However, to say one is more acceptable than the other is simply to bargain with racism. (NAJA, 2003, p. 6)

Systematic research is needed to quantify how coverage of teams with Native sports mascots impacts Native American's own identity and the public perception of that identity in light of the virtual absence of Native Americans in other media contexts.

## BLACK/WHITE BINARY

The mascot struggle reflects the experiences that many cultural groups have in the United States, particularly with a dominant culture tendency to frame all ethnic minority experiences by comparing it within a Black-and-White frame. A body of literature, particularly within legal and historical research, has developed surrounding Critical Race Theory and the Black/White Binary (Hutchinson, 2004; Karst, 2003; Perea, 1997).

> Like other paradigms, the Black-White one allows people to simplify and make sense of a complex reality.... The risk is that non-black minority groups, not fitting into the dominant society's idea of race in America, become marginalized, invisible, foreign, un-American. (Delgado & Stefancic, 2001, p. 70)

This binary means, for example, that at the turn of the last century, Chinese immigrants wanting a voice in state courts and Native Americans attempting to gain rights within and outside reservations had to place their experiences and desires for justice within a frame comparing them to the struggles of African slaves seeking U.S. citizenship and voting rights (Davis, 1997, pp. 234–235). Creating a binary frame impacts relations amongst all ethnic minority groups, while at the same time placing White dominant culture as the primary cultural frame contrasted against all others on a pigment continuum. Research is needed to explore the binary systematically, but media critics have long recognized the trend. *The New York Times* 2000 series, "How Race is Lived in America" was particularly criticized by Richard Rodriquez (2000) because it focused almost exclusively (though not entirely as Rodriquez states) on black/white relations:

> The Times has been running a series...concerned exclusively with how "Whites" "Blacks" perceive one another.... Nothing was said in the *Times* about Korean/Mexican relations in L.A. or Haitian-American/African-American relations in Tampa.... The Times found a majority of Black and White Americans regard race relations to be "generally good."

The Black/White binary frame creates three significant communication concerns for the mass media: (1) ignoring or downplaying sections of the American demographic, those whose ancestry originates outside Europe and Africa; (2) emphasizing a continuum with Whites at one end and everyone else at another, thus encouraging an us/them perspective with the "us" being the dominant culture; and finally; (3) ignoring relationships amongst various ethnic groups.

The result is news coverage of the changing American demographic portraying Latinos as 'The New Cool Kids,' with news articles educating the dominant culture about Ricky Martin and Jennifer Lopez (Del Rio, 2005, p. 2, 12–13). The Latinidad identity nonetheless draws from three continents, and involves a myriad of economic profiles, and internal distinctions. The Cuban exile, the Spanish immigrant, and Salvadorian economic refugee are all lumped into a single category along with Asians Americans and other Native Americans. Each ethnic group's experience and marginalization must be considered distinctively. Just as African Americans are not likely to be asked to produce a green card or have strangers accuse them of destroying the nation's automobile industry, few Asian Americans are likely to be berated by strangers for having too many children or being on welfare (Delgado & Stefancic, 2001, pp. 69–70).

Notably, the 15-part *New York Times* series was not exclusively about Blacks and Whites, as Rodriquez states, and included compelling stories about a range of people across economic and political lines. Nonetheless, binary concerns did persist. Four stories out of the 15 considered people other than just Blacks and Whites. Reporter Mireya Navarro considered Houston's construction industry in light of the city's three roughly equal primary ethnic groups in a story headlined: "Bricks, Mortar and Coalition Building; Houston is Nearly Equal Parts Black, Hispanic and Anglo; For 3 Contractors, That Means Working Together." Efforts to resolve tensions between African Americans and Latinos were examined considering Affirmative Action-based contracts. The language though describing African Americans was at best troubling: "Mr. Lewis agrees that Anglos and Latinos get along better. Latinos are less confrontational than blacks, less 'hardheaded,' he said." While it could be argued that this is merely a quote, a stereotype is quoted here without challenge or question. Notably, stereotypes of Anglos were not included in the comparison. The other story concerning Anglo, Latino, and African-American relations involved a reporter going undercover in a Tar Heel, NC, slaughterhouse, where he described how race determines position in bloody, messy work. He came to one clear conclusion: Being poor is painfully hard, regardless of ethnicity (LeDuff, 2000). The series' story on Cuban Americans took another approach: It recast Brown back into a Black and White issue. The headline read: "Best of Friends, Worlds Apart: Joel Ruiz is Black. Achmed Valdés is White. In America They Discovered It Matters" (Ojito, 2000). The fourth story compared the political successes and struggles of Washington Governor Gary Locke, who is Chinese American, and Seattle's King County Executive Ron Sims, who is African American. The headline read: "When to Campaign with Color: An Asian-American Told His Story to Whites and Won. For Black Politicians, It's a Riskier Strategy" (Egan, 2000). While the story itself shared the complexities of race in the lives of two politicians, the headline put the focus back squarely on how the dominant culture views people of color. The headline becomes of greater concern because the Locke/Sims story was the only one in the series where no person described as White was a primary player. All 14 other stories prominently profiled at least one White person, which led Rodriquez (2000) to his conclusion:

> Whites were portrayed as being at the very center of contemporary American life…. Persons of liberal disposition and politics. Rather like the readers of the *Times*. So with every article, White readers were reassured that they remain at the center of our national life—which is exactly where they expect to be.

## IMPROVEMENT POSSIBLE BUT AT A COST

The primary reason why U.S. news coverage of the nation's ethnic minorities has not improved is simple: to make substantive changes costs money and time, and in the news business, time is money. Ethnic minority coverage is better, considering both the perception within minority communities and the facts judged by content analysis, in places where resources are devoted to those communities. Providing resources means at least in part sending journalists to spend time within ethnic cultural groups: That means time to build relationships with sources while not working a particular story. While *The New York Times* series was fraught with concerns about who was left out and how the dominant culture was framed, the model it presented for time, space, and energy in reporting deserves recognition. Other news organizations are striving to make similar efforts. Reporter Lourdes Leslie Medrano spent a month in the Minneapolis-St. Paul area just listening to people as she prepared a series on the "Faces of Islam" before and after the September 11, 2001, attacks. She went to mosques and sat with women as they prayed. She visited Muslim schools and eventually developed relationships with the family of two of the students (Whitehouse, 2002, p. 17). The time spent both to build relationships and then develop the story allowed Medrano Leslie to create images that both validated the Muslim community and explained its richness to those outside it. She wrote:

> "Aminah, it's time to pray," Adam called out to her the other day as he and his mother, Fatma Ahmed, knelt on prayer rugs…. "It's like eating," he said. "If I don't eat, I'm hungry. If I don't pray, I feel empty." As an observant Muslim, Adam said he was saddened by the Sept. 11 hijacking attacks and is angry at those who carried it out, supposedly in the name of Islam. "Islam does not stand for this kind of atrocities," he said. "This is a religion about making peace; our greeting is 'Peace be upon you, As-Salaam aleikum.'" (2001, p. 1A)

The story showed a family's daily life in a way accessible to many cultural groups, but developing the relationships to get to the story meant that Leslie Medrano was not producing high volumes of copy while working on this one.

Recognizing that not all people within any group perceive time in the same way, Western culture, and by extension Western media culture, tends to emphasize a product-oriented, time-driven approach to doing business and gathering information. On the other hand, many ethnic minorities come from what has come to be called collectivist societies. Within these societies, resources including information may be shared with those within a group or where a relationship already exists, but not with strangers (Triandis, 1994, p. 166). That means for an individualistic Western journalist, relationships become a byproduct of good reporting because the relationship develops as information is shared. By contrast, ethnic minority sources may be quite reticent to share in-group knowledge with a stranger whose motives are unknown, particularly when past experiences have been negative. Requests for information also involve white privilege. White journalists, like most White Americans, tend to presume that "every interaction is a blank slate," said Intercultural Communication Scholar Judith Martin (quoted in Whitehouse, 2002, p. 21).

Those from marginalized groups may approach such encounters quite differently—with all the cultural memory of previous oppression.

Focusing on meeting deadlines and quick story turnaround tells those in ethnic minority communities that their experiences are unimportant. One reason ethnic minority journalists may continue to leave the field is because they are forced to capitalize on relationships like commodities, and to do so at a rapid speed. The very nature of accepted news practice may run up against cultural ethical norms.

Research is needed to both quantify and qualify the impact Western-style deadline emphasis has on how collectivist ethnic minority communities are covered. The ethics of source exploitation need careful exploration, particularly within the context of individualist and collectivist societies' interpretation of relationship, as well as study of how these factors impact minority journalist retention.

## POSSIBILITIES AND PERILS OF FEATURES

One resolution to this deadline conflict is to develop deliberately more teams of journalists who produce and write feature stories outside the festival and crisis frame, and place ethnic minorities with the scope of the broader communities where they live. De Uriarte believes feature stories may humanize the very statistics that frequently stereotype. De Uriarte points to nationwide prison enrollment statistics which may reveal the actual number of African-American men in prison, but don't consider "the various limitations on those men's experience, including class and gender. You might hear about budget constraints. But you don't talk about literacy. You don't have the context of the problem, just a lot of statistics and an easy formula.... You don't know if you have other options than just hiring more lawyers" (Whitehouse, 2002, p. 21).

The problem though with encouraging feature stories on ethnicity is that, unless deliberately structured as part of a long-term plan, the stories most often are framed in a way that appeals to the dominant culture. Features can become a means to ignore the complexities of the issue addressed because they are placed in a section of the newspaper or broadcast designed to make audience feel good. For example, both national and local news organizations periodically discover that Americans other than celebrities are adopting children internationally. NBC Nightly News aired such a story as on October 28, 2006, as a closing package concerning single mothers traveling to Asia to adopt children. Two Caucasian single professional women were profiled: one packing her suitcase to go to Vietnam then being interviewed in front of her living room hearth; the other carving pumpkins with her two Chinese-American daughters, aged two and six. (Notably the only demographic difference between this author and the second woman was that my oldest daughter would not turn six until the following week.) Both in the preview and the story body, the women were described as "older and wiser with much to give." While certainly some feminist critique could be given to consider the gendered language, the story itself was gentle and one dimensional: good women with money finding fulfillment in creating a family with orphans. Numerous additional story frames could have been included:

1. Anything about the daughters themselves.
2. Anything about the children's home country culture as practiced in the United States.
3. Anything about attitudes within the Chinese or Vietnamese communities concerning attitudes toward adoption.
4. Anything about the adoption process and an explanation of the numbers of international adoptions worldwide.
5. Anything about adoptive parents who are not White.
6. Anything about the challenges and joys of single parenting, a list that is varied and long, and extends far beyond having enough money.

Coverage of these issues however would not have contributed to the primary function of that particular NBC feature: to have a happy, feel-good story to close the newscast. Most important, happy and feel good are defined by the dominant culture. For feature stories then to provide the necessary depth, news organizations must reconsider the role of feature story itself. The need for change though cannot be adequately addressed by story form unless models are deliberately created and followed; the real change must come in changing the way information is gathered and disseminated.

## RESEARCH NEEDS

Triandis argues that anyone seeking information across cultures cannot escape bias, including ethnocentric tendencies toward using our own culture as the standard of comparison. Simply saying "I will strive to be unbiased" is not enough. Triandis' ethical recommendations for cross-cultural researchers' techniques to avoid bias (1994, p. 85) can be adapted to the practice journalism:

- Explanation of the differences amongst cultures should be embedded within the descriptions of similarities. Cultural differences can and should be considered, but recognizing that ethnic groups are part of the larger community. A predominantly African-American church is still a church, like others in most communities. Its religious practices do not need to be portrayed as foreign or quaintly odd.
- Multiple methods of gathering information are used. That means listening to multiple voices within a community over time and recognizing diverse leadership within diverse communities. No one person can speak for all people of color, or for an individual ethnic group within a community.
- Qualitative information through interviews is used to clarify and explain quantitative reports. De Uriarte offered an example of this in her description earlier of African-American men in prisons.
- Conclusions reached about a culture are sociotypes consistent with how those within that group would define themselves, and stereotypes are removed.
- The information is gathered in an ethical way, meaning that the sources are treated as people with value rather than merely a means to getting a story.

Unfortunately developing these techniques, just as developing complex stories, takes time and is therefore expensive to facilitate and apply in practice.

The very language used to describe experience becomes even more problematic. Post-modern cultural critic Jean-François Lyotard (1988) suggested that marginalized peoples face differend, where key terms have different meanings from one group to another. The concept of Auschwitz means one thing for a Jewish Holocaust survivor and another for a Holocaust denier (p. 9). If the survivor chooses to respond with strong empirical proof, the human angst gets lost in the data. If the survivor offers a hard-told drama of experience, then the universal evidence is called into question. Similarly, Native Americans struggle to explain the differend over mascots, tomahawks, and eagle feathers, and Hawaiians struggle with the differend of island sovereignty (Heider, 2000, p. 50). Delgado and Stefancic emphasize that European Americans balk at the suggestion that the descendents of slaves might seek financial reparation, when no slave or slave-holder is living and the practice was made illegal well over a century ago. The result then is that the very concept of justice is differend (2001, p. 44). Yet the nature of privilege denies that differend even exists. A white television news director told de Uriarte in her research for ASNE: "A story is story. I would hope diversity issues would not come into play" (p. 89). The result of differend is that journalists and their ethnic minority sources may use different words, languages, or codes, and that difference results in misconceptions and even the negation of the minority experience. If a primary function of media is to give voice to the voiceless, then journalistic models should be created to give voice with a new language offsetting differend and offer evidence through research of the models' effectiveness.

Polarization in language becomes an increasing concern when groups with different viewpoints must rely on news media to get information on each other. When that happens, the news coverage itself can escalate conflict. For example, whaling rights have at times become a particularly volatile issue in the Pacific Northwest. The Makah Tribe members periodically hunt whale in Neah Bay, Washington, but has only captured two since 1994 when the gray whale was taken off the endangered species list. Tribal elders believe that most venomous comments were selected for sound bites—not only from the Makah but also the predominately white anti-whalers. Shelley Means, from the Oglala Lakota and Ojibwe tribes and an environmental justice associate with the Washington Association of Churches, said she came to believe:

> anti-whalers were irrational, that they would say anything and do anything to protect a whale, even if that meant endangering the life of people that I care about in Neah Bay.... I got those images from the media in the protests—the focus was on the most vulgar of the demonstrators. I imagined that that translated across the movement, that that was whom I would encounter when I drove to Port Angeles and stopped at the local grocery store. I was afraid for the people in my community. (Whitehouse, 2002, p. 19)

Those supporting and opposing whaling were surprised to discover that each believed the media generally favored the other, and that both sides believed their own positions had been significantly misrepresented. One whaling opponent described media depictions of the controversy as "Cowboys and Indians on the water."

Therefore, despite the journalistic conventions of objectivity and removal of bias, the media presence contributed to conflict. Similar accusations come in nearly every racial conflict. Additional research is needed to document how basic journalistic forms, such as quote or sound byte selection, contribute to conflict because the very foundational practices of journalism are created and defined by privilege. Journalism academics have long maintained that media conventions do not change because they are comfortable for those who control them (Schudson, 1978; Gans, 1980). Schudson explained in 1995: "Standard practices are not, of course, neutral inventions.

They have biases of their own" (p. 83). Those standard practices, the biases that formed them, and the biases that they produce need careful examination to offer additional evidence of impact and opportunity for revision.

Notably, this chapter has focused on ethnic diversity with limited reference to class, gender, and religious diversity, and no reference to a host of other factors, including sexuality, disability, or geography. Each of these and other diversity concerns requires intense and careful consideration. Just as the experience of one ethnic group cannot be equated to the experience of another, the issues facing ethnic diversity cannot to be superimposed upon all marginalized peoples. Therefore additional research needs to identify and explore carefully each group's concerns beyond which has been outlined in this chapter.

Finally, research is needed to explain the financial prospects of doing better diversity coverage. News organizations frequently cite better coverage of ethnic minorities as part of its ethic and stated commitment to covering all of the community served. However, real change may not occur until there is extensive and widely publicized evidence that such coverage is profitable, so profitable that the effort needed to create culture change is worthwhile. Otherwise, the news about ethnic minorities in the United States will continue to look as it has looked: with festivals and crises, with stereotypes and marginalization, with statistics without context, and most damningly, with ethnic minorities expected to frame their experiences in a way that makes sense to the dominant culture, or to face no coverage at all.

# REFERENCES

Ahmad, F. (2006) British Muslim perceptions on news coverage of September 11. *Journal of Ethnic and Migration Studies, 32,* 961–982.

Aksoy, A. (2006). Transnational virtues and cool loyalties: Responses of Turkish-Speaking migrants in London to September 11. *Journal of Ethnic and Migration Studies, 32,* 928–946.

ASNE. (2006, April 25). Media Release: ASNE census shows newsroom diversity grows slightly. Retrieved November 29, 2006 from http://www.asne.org/index.cfm?id=6264.

Beck, H. (2005, Jan. 31) Take me out of the ball game. *Wiretap Magazine.* Retrieved October 20, 2006 from http://www.wiretapmag.org/stories/21115/.

Bendixen & Associates. (2005). The ethnic media in America: The giant hidden in plain   sight.   Research conducted for New California Media, in partnership with the  Center for American Progress and the Leadership Conference on Civil Rights  Education Fund.

Billings, A. (2004). Depicting the quarterback in Black and White: A content analysis of college and professional football broadcast commentary. *Howard Journal of Communications, 15,* 201–210.

Bok, S. (2002) *Common values.* Columbia, MO: University of Missouri Press.

Brislin, T., & N. Williams (1996). Beyond diversity: Expanding the canon in  journalism ethics. *Journal of Mass Media Ethics, 11,* 16–27.

Busselle, R. & H. Crandall. (2002). Television viewing and perceptions about race  Differences in socioeconomic success. *Journal of Broadcasting and Electronic Media, 46,* 265–283.

Christians, C. (2005). Ethical theory in communication research. *Journalism Studies, 6,* 3–14.

Christians, C., Ferré, J., & Fackler F. (1993). *Good news: Social ethics and the press.* New York: Oxford University Press.

Craig, D. (2006). *The ethics of the story.* Lanham, MD: Rowman & Littlefield.

Davis, A. D. (1997). Identity notes, part one: Playing in the light. In R. Delgado & J. Stefancic (Eds.), *Critical White studies: Looking behind the mirror* (pp. 231–238). Philadelphia: Temple University Press.

Delgado, R. & S. Stefancic. (2001). *Critical race theory.* New York: New York University Press.

Del Rio, E. (2005). *Latinos, U.S. news magazines, and multiculturalism as a form of professional bias.* Presented at the annual meetings of the International Communication Association, New York.

De Uriarte, M. L. (2003). *Diversity disconnects: From class room to news room*. Report to the American Society of Newspaper Editors. Funded by the Ford Foundation.

Dixon, T. L., Azocar C. L., & Casas, M. (2003). The portrayal of race and crime on television network news. *Journal of Broadcasting & Electronic Media, 47*, 498–523.

Egan, T. (2000, June 20) When to campaign with color. *The New York Times*, A1.

Essed, P. (1991). *Understanding everyday racism: An interdisciplinary theory*. Newbury Park, CA: Sage.

Gans, H. (1980) *Deciding what's news*. New York: Vintage Books.

Gilens, M. (1996) Race and poverty in America: Public misperceptions and the American news media. *Public Opinion Quarterly, 60*, 515–541.

Gilens. M. (1999). *Why Americans hate welfare*. Chicago: University of Chicago Press.

Heider, D. (2002). *White news: Why local news programs don't cover people of color*. Mahwah, NJ: Erlbaum.

Hutchinson, D.L. (2004). Critical race theory: History, evolution and new frontiers. *American University Law Review, 53*, 1187–1215.

*Indian Country Today*. (2001, Aug. 7). American Indian opinion leaders: American Indian mascots. Retrieved October 20, 2006, from http://www.indiancountry.com/content.cfm?id=43.

*Indian Country Today*. (2005, Aug. 11). Abusive mascots still a serious issue. Retrieved October 20, 2006 from http://www.indiancountry.com/content.cfm?id=1096411388.

Iqbal, A. (2004, Aug. 4). Dearth of men of color in TV reporting persists. *TheUnity News,* 10.

Jaksa, J. & Pritchard, M. (1994). *Communication ethics: Methods of analysis*. Belmont, CA: Wadsworth.

Jameson, J. K. & R. M. Entman. (2004). The role of journalism in democratic conflict management. *Harvard International Journal of Press & Politics, 9*, 38–59.

Karst, K. L. (2003). Law, cultural conflict, and the socialization of children. *California Law Review, 93*, 967–1028.

Lambeth, E. B. (1992). *Committed journalism: An ethic for the profession*. Bloomington: Indiana University Press.

LeDuff, C. (2000, June 16). At a slaughterhouse, some things never die: Who kills, who cuts, who bosses can depend on race. *The New York Times*.

Lyotard, J. F. (1988). *The differend: Phrases in dispute* (G. Van Den Abbeele, Trans.). Minneapolis: University of Minnesota Press.

MacIntyre, A. (1984). *After virtue*. Notre Dame, IN: Notre Dame Press.

Martin, T. & S. Pineda. (2004, August 4). Washington press corps virtually all white. *The Unity News,* 1.

Mastro, D. E. & E. Behm-Marowitz. (2005). Latino representation in prime time. *Journalism and Mass Communication Quarterly, 82*, 110–130.

Mastro, D. E. & S. R. Stern. (2003). Representations of race in television commercials: A content analysis of prime-time advertising, *47*, 638–647.

McIntosh, P. (2000). White privilege: Unpacking the invisible knapsack. In J. Noel (Ed.), *Notable selections in multicultural education* (pp. 115–120). Guilford, CT: Dushkin/McGraw-Hill.

Medrano L. L. (2001, November 23). Faces of Islam: A family centered on faith. *The Minneapolis Star Tribune*, p. 1A.

Medsger, B. (1996). *Winds of change: Challenges confronting journalism education*. Arlington, VA: Freedom Forum.

Native American Journalists Association. (2003). *Reading Red report*. Retrieved October 20, 2006 from http://www.naja.com/resources/publications/2003_reading-red.pdf.

Navarro, M. (2008, July 13). Bricks, Mortar and Coalition Building. *New York Times*, p. A1.

Ojito, M. (2000, June 5). Best of friends, worlds apart: Joel Ruiz is Black. Achmed Valdés is White. In America they discovered it matters. *New York Times*.

Papper, B. (2004, July/August). Recovering lost ground. *RTNDA Communicator*, pp. 24–28.

Perea, J. E. (1997). The Black/White binary paradigm of race: The "normal science" of American racial thought. *California Law Review, 85*, 1213–1258.

Poindexter, P. M., Smith, L., & Heider, D. (2003). Race and ethnicity in local television news: Framing, story assignments, and source selections. *Journal of Broadcasting & Electronic Media, 47*, 524–536.

Rodriquez, R. (2000, July 13). How race really is lived in American. *Salon.com*. Retrieved October 31, 2006, from http://archive.salon.com/news/feature/2000/07/13/race/index.html.

Schudson, M. (1978). *Discovering the news: A social history of American newspapers*. New York: Basic Books.

Schudson, M. (1995). *The power of news*. Cambridge, MA: Harvard University Press.

Shaw, W. (2003). Relativism in ethics. In J. Boss (Ed.), *Perspectives on ethics* (pp. 90–95). New York: McGraw-Hill.

Subervi, F. (2005) Network brownout report 2005: The portrayal of Latinos and Latino  issues on network television news 2004, With a Retrospect to 1995. Produced for the National Association of Hispanic Journalists.

Ting-Toomey, S. (1999). *Communicating across cultures*. New York: Guilford.

Triandis, H. C. (1994). *Culture and social behavior*. New York: McGraw-Hill.

Vargas, L. (2000). Genderizing Latino news: An analysis of a local newspaper's coverage of Latino current affairs. *Critical Studies in Mass Communication, 17*, 261–293.

Whitehouse, V. (2002, December). Taking time. *The Quill, 90*, 16–22.

Wieberg, S. (2006, February 26). Bolder NCAA faces up to new challenges. *USA Today*, p. C3.

Wiese, D. (2006, Sept. 15). Chief is reflection of American Indian education. *The Dispatch* (Moline, IL. Quad-Cities Online Edition) Retrieved September 16, 2006 from http://qconline.com/qcnews/archives/qco/sections.cgi?press=display&id=306221&query=&print=1.

Woods, K. (2002). *McCormick fellowship initiative report to the industry: Do we check it at the door?* Chicago: McCormick Tribune Foundation.

# 9

# The Ethics of Advocacy: Moral Reasoning in the Practice of Public Relations

## Sherry Baker

Each realm of work has a central mission, which reflects a basic societal need and which the practitioner should feel committed to realizing.... All practitioners should be able to state the core traditional mission of their own fields.... A good way of clarifying this sense of mission is to ask: "Why should society reward the kind of work that I do with status and certain privileges?" (Gardner Csikszentmihalyi, & Damon, 2001, p. 10)

As advocates in the marketplace of ideas, public relations professionals should strive to further the ideals of democratic institutions. Whether in business or government or non-profit practice, the common good is served only when the "voices" of special interests present their views in ways that advance informed decision making and contribute to the well-being of the greater society. (Fitzpatrick and Bronstein, 2006, p. xi)

Increased visibility or profitability should only be a means to some more important social and individual end.... The moral end in public relations..."must center around respect for that indi vidual to whom the particular persuasive effort is directed":...it must enable or empower those to whom it is directed to make good decisions and voluntary choices for themselves. (Baker, 2006, p. 17)

## INTRODUCTION: THE FIELD OF ADVOCACY ETHICS

Advocacy ethics as an area of inquiry arises from a concern about practices of persuasion that operate only on the basis of what is *effective* in the quest to achieve advocacy objectives, without sufficient regard for the basic moral principles that might be violated, or the people and interests that might be harmed in the process. In broad terms, the field of advocacy ethics pushes back against the (Adam) Smithian notion that "out of self-interest...harmonious societies grow" (Kagan, 1998, p. 189). It challenges from a variety of perspectives the assumption that *caveat emptor* (let the buyer beware), and related attitudes, is a legitimate moral position for advocates to embrace (Patterson & Wilkins, 2005, p. 61; Baker, 1999a).

While several professions (such as public relations, marketing, advertising, sales, law, and politics) engage in advocacy and persuasion, and share core ethical issues and considerations, the discussion here focuses primarily on the ethics of public relations (pr) practices.

A robust body of literature has emerged in recent years that addresses multiple facets of advocacy ethics from a wide variety of perspectives. This body of work, taken together, comprises an attempt by scholars and practitioners to find useful ways to conceptualize, contextualize, and apply ethical principles to the issues of advocacy and persuasion. The following is list of areas explored and developed within the literature of the field, in no particular order. This typology or categorization, while not necessarily complete, should be helpful for contextualizing particular articles or studies one might be reading, writing, or conducting. (The decision-making models discussed in this chapter, for example, fall primarily under category 8.)

1. Classical ethical theory
2. Applied ethics
3. Philosophical foundations of the ethics of advocacy
4. Historical accounts of advocacy theory, philosophy, and practices
5. Application of basic ethical principles to advocacy (truth, loyalty, etc.)
6. Identification of ethical problems and issues in the practice of advocacy
7. Development of ethical norms and theory specific to advocacy
8. Decision-making models specific to advocacy ethics
9. Discussions of the ethics of particular practices in advocacy (political pr, word-of-mouth marketing, etc.)
10. Characteristics/virtues of ethical advocates
11. Motivations and justifications of practitioners, clients and corporations
12. Practitioners' attitudes and practices relating to advocacy issues and ethics
13. Audience (customer/receiver) attitudes and responses relating to advocacy practices, issues, and ethics
14. Codes of ethics
15. Procedural models for incorporating ethics into routine public relations practices
16. Assessing for ethics in practitioners, employees, organizations, and professions
17. Case studies in advocacy.

The discussions of these topics unfolds in a variety of ways, from descriptive to normative, from specific to general, and from concrete to abstract, all contributing in their own way to the overall discussion and richness of the field of advocacy ethics. Despite its breadth and depth, however, advocacy ethics as a field is inquiry is relatively new as compared to similar scholarship relating to other professional areas such as medicine, law, and journalism. There is still much to be done. In a speech entitled "Ethics in the 21st Century," Dr. Clifford Christians (2006) presented a guiding focus that he said should direct the efforts of applied *media* ethicists in the future. They are applicable as well to advocacy ethics.

1. Ethicists must develop normative theory—taking a stand as to what is right and wrong. They must establish norms and guidelines, and not be neutral. "The best of philosophy throughout the ages is normative" (Christians, 2006).
2. Ethicists must structure their normative theories within *general moral principles* as opposed to professional practices (which may be too narrow and like-minded). The preoc-

cupation of ethicists should be with the moral dimensions of everyday life which apply to diverse humanity (Christians, 2006).

3. Ethicists must *expand and invigorate the Western ethical canon* by including ethical perspectives from other cultural traditions, and developing an ethics that is cosmopolitan and culturally inclusive. Ethicists must expand their vision and recognize an obligation to others beyond their own communities (Christians, 2006).

4. Ethicists must develop an *ethics of being* rather than of rationalism. The ethics of virtue is a perennial problem in all traditions, and it must be developed (Christians, 2006).

5. Ethicists must articulate a case for *realism against relativism*. There are physical realities in the universe that we all share as human beings, and some values are universal—such as reverence for life on earth. These universal realities, rather than cultural relativism, should be the basis of our ethics (Christians, 2006).

## FOCUS OF THE CHAPTER

This chapter focuses primarily on moral reasoning in advocacy ethics. The chapter begins by exploring the theoretical ground for advocacy ethics, or the social and societal sources from which arise the moral requirement for professional advocates to behave ethically. Then, moving more closely to moral behavior and decision making, it examines moral temptations, ethical dilemma paradigms, and ethical issues faced by practitioners in public relations practice. Three models for moral reasoning are reviewed—each taking a different approach to ethical decision making in the practices of advocacy. The question of the relationship between moral reasoning (knowing the right thing to do) and moral behavior (actually doing the right thing) is then explored, as is the relationship between ethical behavior in the workplace, and the practitioner's sense of personal well-being. The chapter concludes with a discussion about moral perspective-taking.

Taken together, the chapter provides an overview of the central concerns, considerations, and conversations that are represented in the literature of public relations ethics. The ultimate objectives of the chapter are to increase understanding of the basic ethical issues in advocacy, to provide various tools by which practitioners might think through ethical issues relating to the practices of advocacy, and to emphasize the ways in which ethical behavior in professional practice leads one not only to do good, but to experience personal growth, fulfillment, and a sense of living a life that is worthwhile.

## THE THEORETICAL GROUND FOR ADVOCACY ETHICS

### A Conventional Model

Ground: "a source of standards or norms which are binding on a certain class or group of agents." (Koehn, 1994, p. 8)

This section explores the theoretical ground or source from which arises the moral requirement for professional advocates to behave ethically, and suggests that this ground is best conceptualized within a covenantal model of advocacy.

Daryl Koehn (1994) has written that a profession "is a set of norm-governed practices grounded in a relationship of trust between professionals and clients...and potential clients" (Koehn, 1994, p. 8). The centrality of the relationship between the professional advocate and the client, however, does not assume that the advocate is a service provider whose only responsibility is to service client desires (Baker, 2002, p. 194). Professional advocates have additional moral duties to self and others connected to the functions they perform. "The professional must have a highly internalized sense of responsibility; must be bound to monitor his/her own behavior" (Baker, 2002, p. 196, citing Koehn, 1994, pp. 55–56, 65).

While the professional's key responsibility is to the client, the professional/client relationship exists within the larger context of professional responsibility to society.

> Professionals, then, are not exclusively client-oriented; they are not unconditional loyal servants of the individual client at hand.... Rather, the client is an individual member of a community before whom the professional has made a "profession." (Baker, 2002, p. 198, citing Koehn, 1994, pp. 173–174)

The covenantal model is based in professionals' and clients' responsibilities to each other and to the public good. The following list summarizes key points in the covenantal model as the theoretical ground of advocacy ethics.

- The ground of advocacy ethics consists in a covenantal relationship of trust between advocate and client, and between advocate and society.
- The loyalty of the advocate to the client does not sanction promoting the client's interest to the direct sacrifice of the well-being of other members of the public.
- The professional encourages ethical behavior on the part of the client.
- The professional serves the client's good, but the client also is obligated to act in ways that engender that good.
- The professional advocate does not serve client whim, but client good, and is not obligated further if the client does not behave in ways that foster that good. (For example, clients are responsible to conduct their affairs reputably rather than expecting the advocate to spin away disreputable behaviors.)
- The professional refuses to engage personally in unethical practices even if, or merely because, the client requests or demands it.
- The professional refuses to promote evil or to represent clients and causes that directly result in harm to others (see Baker, 2002, pp. 200–201).

## MORAL TEMPTATION AND ETHICAL DILEMMAS IN PUBLIC RELATIONS PRACTICE

When faced with a situation that has ethical implications, is one actually dealing with a genuine ethical dilemma, or is one simply tempted to do something that clearly is wrong? The distinction drawn by Kidder (1995) is that ethical dilemmas are right-versus-right situations and moral temptations are right-versus-wrong situations.

> Ethical dilemmas have good and right arguments to commend them on all sides of the situation. They require careful moral reasoning to arrive at the most appropriate action. Right-versus-wrong issues, on the other hand, are *moral temptations*. They do not require deep philosophical/ethical analysis because they are simply wrong from the outset. (Baker, 1997, p. 200, italics added; Kidder, 1995, p. 184)

This distinction allows practitioners and decision makers to clarify the nature of the decision they are dealing with. If the ethical course of action is not clear, they are grappling with a true ethical dilemma, and must engage in moral reasoning to arrive at a morally justifiable course of action. If, on the other hand, they can acknowledge that they know what their moral responsibilities are in the situation, but are inclined to do otherwise—they can recognize that they are being enticed by a moral temptation. In this case, their only choice is whether to do the right thing.

Assuming that a genuine ethical dilemma (not a moral temptation) has presented itself, Kidder writes that there are four value sets that are so fundamental to the right-versus-right choices all of us face that they can be called *dilemma paradigms*. These four paradigms are (1) truth versus loyalty; (2) individual versus community; (3) short-term versus long-term; and (4) justice versus mercy. Kidder says these are the classic tensions in most ethical dilemmas (Baker, 1997, p. 200, citing Kidder, 1995, p. 18).

The paradigm of truth versus loyalty sets honesty in opposition with allegiance, fidelity, and promise-keeping. Individual versus community pits self or us against them or others. Short-term is concerned with immediate needs and desires (the now) as opposed to long-term which is concerned with future goals or prospects (the then). Finally, justice is concerned with fairness and equity which sometimes comes into opposition with compassion and empathy (Baker, 1997, p. 201).

These conflicting value paradigms (especially the first three) are useful for broadly conceptualizing the moral dilemmas inherent in the practice of public relations. Truthfulness versus loyalty, for example, is a core ethical dilemma in advocacy. What are the limits of loyalty to corporation or client as balanced against the moral requirements of truthfulness in communications? Individual versus community (us versus them) also is a central ethical dilemma in advocacy. Should people behave solely in a self-interested (us) manner, or should their concerns also be with receivers of their persuasive messages (them)? Short-term versus long-term considerations are critical, and are related to each of the other paradigms. Should practitioners make their decisions in a particular circumstance based upon the best short term consequences—or should they act with a primary consideration for long-term interests?

As these questions make evident, the dilemma paradigms overlap and interrelate. In the practice of public relations, for example, the truth versus loyalty dilemma spills over into the us versus them dilemma. Should practitioners and decision makers engage in partial truths in their own self-interest (an emphasis on "us"), or should their concerns be with receivers of their persuasive messages (an emphasis on "them") in providing others with the truthful information they need to make rational decisions about an issue? Similarly with regard to short-term versus long-term considerations, is long term interest served best by truth or by loyalty; by an emphasis on us or on them?

Kidder acknowledges that neither side of the dilemma paradigms invariably is right. Nevertheless, he argues that all things being equal (when both sides of the argument have equal weight or good arguments to support them), he would choose truth over loyalty, community over individual, long-term over short-term, and mercy over justice (Baker, 1997, pp. 201–202; Kidder, 1995, pp. 219–221). It is up to the individual or corporation to decide which should take precedence in any given situation, and to be able to justify their decision.

Table 9.1 lists some examples of ethical issues that arise in the practice of public relations. It includes several categories of pr activities (such as advocacy through front groups, and communicating across cultures) that raise particular ethical challenges. The items and activities listed are diverse, and they illustrate that while in some circumstances and contexts, a practitioner clearly might be dealing with a moral temptation, it is more likely that the complexity of the issues and activities involved present difficult and challenging ethical dilemmas.

## TABLE 9.1
### Ethical Issues and Ethically Challenging Activities in the Practice of Public Relations

* Deception, partial truth, misrepresentation
* Spinning news events
* Objectivity versus advocacy in news releases
* Partial (vs. full) disclosure
* Plagiarism
* Bartering for favorable coverage
* Kickbacks
* Keeping confidences
* Lying for a good cause
* Initiating disclosure vs. responding to demands for information
* Lack of transparency
* Being transparent against client wishes
* Collecting and interpreting research data
* Taking credit for another's work
* Disagreements with management
* Concealing illegal acts
* Legal/ethical confusion
* Recalls
* Conflicts of interest
* Unfairness
* Greed and self-interest
* Careerism (at the expense of others)
* Sensationalism
* Exaggerated threats of harm
* Creating unnecessary fear
* Lobbying and political advocacy
* Failure to be responsible and accountable for one's actions
* Strategic risk communication
* Public diplomacy

* Advocacy for activist groups
* Communicating across cultures
* Poor taste
* Invasions of privacy
* Pandering to the lower instincts
* Inappropriate resource allocation
* Stereotyping; typecasting
* Lack of concern for social responsibility and the common good
* Lack of respect for persons in providing information to inform their decision making
* Plagiarism
* Copyright infringement
* Crisis management
* Corporate philanthropy
* Whistle blowing
* Virtual organizations
* Front groups waging "grassroots" campaigns
* Gifts and Junkets
* Marketing practices
* Marketing to children
* Word-of-mouth marketing
* Questionable product lines
* Employee safety
* Employee diversity
* Environment-related activities
* Multinational corporate issues: status of women and children, hiring practices, treatment of animals, & working with governments with different values, etc.

*Partial list of ethical issues as identified in Baker (1997); in six public relations textbooks: Bagin and Fulginiti (2005); Guth and Marsh (2006); Lattimore et al. (2004); Newsom, Turk, and Kruckeberg (2007); Seitel (2004); Treadwell and Treadwell (2004); and in Bivins (2006); Palenchar and Heath (2006); Seib (2006); Hon (2006); Wright (2006).

## TOOLS FOR MORAL REASONING IN ADVOCACY

In their foreword to a seminal special double issue on ethics and professional persuasion in the *Journal of Mass Media Ethics*, editors Ralph Barney and Jay Black wrote that "a major frustration of professionals in media fields is the academics who don't provide definitive answers to the important questions" (Barney & Black, 2001, p. 73).

> When a professional queries an expert, and expects a "this is what to do" answer, she or he often finds the response lays out a myriad of alternatives, perhaps without even a hierarchy. If, for the professional, closure and solution are discussion goals, scholars exalt discussion with closure low in priority. And so it is, perhaps in spades, with media ethics, particularly on a topic as prickly as professional persuasion. (Barney & Black, 2001, p. 73)

Applied ethicists often are hesitant to make definitive statements as to what general behaviors and practices are ethical or unethical. This is because nuances in facts, circumstances, potential outcomes, and the actors involved (including their motivations) often can be determinative of an appropriate course of action. Applied ethicists do, however, strive to provide ways by which practitioners can think about and clarify moral issues and thus find for themselves, through their own reasoning processes, ethically justifiable, if not definitive, answers to important questions.

Professional codes of ethics are examples of tools designed for moral reasoning in the practice of public relations. These include codes of ethics for the Public Relations Society of America (PRSA), the International Association of Business Communicators (IABC), the Global Alliance for Public Relations and Communication Management (all available online), and the codes of ethics of individual corporations and workplaces.

Additional aids in systematic moral reasoning are classical ethical theories that help focus one's attention on various aspects of a moral dilemma. The utilitarian perspective, for example, draws attention to finding in any situation the action that will result in the greatest good for the greatest number, and Kant's categorical imperative requires that as a matter of moral duty one must identify and act upon correct principles—those maxims that one would want everyone to honor in similar situations.

The three models reviewed below take classical ethical theory into account in developing rubrics for systematic moral reflection in the applied area of advocacy and public relations practices. Taken together, they constitute a set of tools by which to facilitate clear thinking and moral reasoning about various aspects of advocacy. They are designed to make the ethics of advocacy "accessible, teachable, applicable, behavior-influencing and empowering for practitioners, students, and instructors" of professional persuasive communications (Baker, 2006, p. 25).

## Five Baselines Model for Assessing Motivations and Justifications in Advocacy

The motivations that drive one's actions are an important issue in ethics, as is the moral requirement that one should be able to explain or justify one's actions. The "Five Baselines" framework below (adapted from Baker, 1999b) "allows conceptual clarity both about differing motivations that underlie action in professional persuasive communication and differing grounds or baselines from which action is justified" (Baker, 1999b, p. 79). The five baselines (to be explained below) are: Raw Self-Interest; Entitlement; Enlightened Self-Interest; Social Responsibility; and Kingdom of Ends. As the structure of the framework implies (beginning with Raw Self-interest and ending with the Kingdom of Ends), each successive baseline represents higher moral ground than the one before it (Baker, 1999b, p. 69).

1. The *Raw Self-Interest* baseline assumes legitimacy in pure self-interested egoism or looking out for oneself, even to the detriment of others. It assumes that advocates may use society for their own benefit, "even if it is damaging to the social order" (Baker, 1999b, pp. 70–71). While many may act according to this standard, it clearly is not a morally justifiable position.

2. *The Entitlement Model* represents the position that all clients, legal products, and causes are entitled to professional assistance and representation (despite their moral indefensibility); that professional persuaders have a right to advocate for legal products and causes, even if they are harmful; that *caveat emptor* [let the buyer beware] is a morally acceptable position; that clients and advocates have no responsibility for the negative effects on others that result from their legal persuasive communications; that professional communicators have a responsibility to serve their clients well despite potential harm to society or personal moral aversion; and that if a product or cause is legal, its promotion is ethically justifiable (Baker, 1999a, p. 1).

The Entitlement baseline asserts communicator rights and entitlements "without the balancing acceptance of ethical responsibility for one's behavior and for the welfare of others.

Essentially, the model fails the basic ethical requirement that people take responsibility for the effects of their actions on others" (Baker, 1999a, p. 20.)

3. The *Enlightened Self-Interest* baseline assumes that "businesses do well (financially) by doing good (ethically), and it is, therefore, in their bottom-line interest to engage in good deeds and ethical behavior" (Baker, 1999b, p. 73). This baseline has much to recommend it, in that it encourages ethical behavior (albeit by providing economic incentives). However, this approach assumes that all actions should result eventually in a reward to self or corporation (Baker, 1999b, p. 75). By this rationale, if an action or policy did not result in bettering a bottom-line interest, it would not be justified, even if it were the morally correct thing to do.

Martinson (1994) has cautioned that enlightened self-interest "ignores the social dimension of ethics, the concern for the common good. It fails as an ethical baseline because ethics 'is about doing what is right where others, both individually and collectively, are concerned'" (Baker, 1999b, p. 75, quoting Martinson, 1994, p. 106).

4. The *Social Responsibility* baseline takes Martinson's concerns into account. This baseline assumes that persons in society are interdependent, and that "the focus of one's actions and moral reasoning should be on *responsibilities* to others and to community.

5. The name of the *Kingdom of Ends* baseline derives from Kant's well-known categorical imperative. The defining characteristic of the Kingdom of Ends as a guiding model for behavior in advocacy is that...

> People should always act by those maxims (laws of conduct) to which they would want everyone to adhere if we all lived in an ideal community, a community in which everyone always is moral, one in which all people were treated as ends in themselves rather than as means to someone else's ends. (Baker, 1999b, p. 78)

The Kingdom of Ends baseline assumes that professional communicators can contribute to creating the kind of world in which they would wish to live, and in which the rights, needs, and interests of others are respected.

## The TARES Test: Five Principles for Ethical Persuasion

The TARES Test (Baker & Martinson, 2001) is comprised of five principles that articulate the basic moral duties of advocates: Truthfulness (of the message); Authenticity (of the persuader); Respect (for the persuadee); Equity (of the appeal); and Social Responsibility (for the common good). "All ethical persuasive practices, according to this model, will take place within the boundaries of these five prima facie duties or principles of action" (Baker, 2006, p. 17).

The TARES Test is designed to be comprehensive, in that it addresses ethical principles relating to all elements of an advocacy message or campaign—the message, the advocate, the receiver(s) of the message, the conduct and elements of the advocacy campaign, and society as a whole. The test asserts an ethical requirement that the *message* must be *true*; the *advocate* must be an *authentic* representative of the cause or message; *receivers* of the advocacy message must be *shown respect* by empowering them to make good decisions and voluntary choices for themselves; the persuasive *campaign* must be *fair* in every respect; and the *product or service* advocated, as well as the *campaign* itself, must be *socially responsible* for the common good of society.

The following are questions that practitioners might ask themselves from the perspective of the TARES Test.

*Truthfulness (of the Message)*: Is the message factually accurate and also truthful? Does it deceive overtly or covertly? Does it lead people to believe what I myself do not believe (Bok, 1999, p. 13)? Does it satisfy the listener's information requirements?

*Authenticity (of the Advocate)*: Am I acting with integrity? Do I endorse this message? Would I take personal responsibility for it? Would I persuade those I care about to do this? Do I believe that people will benefit from this?

*Respect for the Persuadee (or receiver of the message):* Have I respected the interests of others? Have I given them substantially complete information so they can make good decisions? Have I made them aware of the source of this message?

*Equity of the Appeal (or the Advocacy or PR campaign)*: Is this campaign fair? Does it take unfair advantage of receivers of the message? Is it fair to targeted or vulnerable audiences? Have I made the communication understandable to those to whom it is directed? Have I fairly communicated the benefits, risks, costs, and harms?

*Social Responsibility (for the Common Good)*: Will the cause I am promoting result in benefits or harm to individuals or to society? Is this cause responsible to the best interests of the public?

A sincere and well-intentioned consideration of all elements and principles of the TARES Test should lead practitioners of advocacy and persuasion to morally justifiable decisions.

## The Principled Advocate versus the Pathological Partisan: A Model of Opposing Archetypes of Public Relations Practitioners

Usually, discussions of applied ethics center on what one should *do*—what actions one should take. Virtue (or character) ethics takes a different perspective. The central question is not "What should I *do*?" but rather "What sort of person should I *become*?" (Pojman, 2006, p. 156, italics added; Baker, 2006, p. 4, in press).Character or virtue ethics is "the arena of the virtues and the vices" (MacIntyre, 1984, p. 168). A moral virtue is a "disposition to follow the moral rules" (Gert, 1998, p. 284), while a moral vice is a disposition to violate a moral rule when there is a conflict between the rule and one's own interests or inclinations (Gert, 1998, p. 283; Baker, 2006, p. 5, in press).

Moral virtues have corresponding moral vices...just as moral vices have corresponding moral virtues. (For example, the virtue of truthfulness has a corresponding vice of deceitfulness.) Virtue and vice are developed by and exhibited in habitual actions and consistency of behavior.

MacIntyre writes that *practices* provide "the arena in which the virtues are exhibited" (MacIntyre, 1984, p. 187; Baker, 2006, p. 13, in press). Public relations and advocacy are examples of such practices.

> A good human being is one who benefits her or himself and others...both qua human being and also characteristically qua the exemplary discharge of particular roles or functions *within the context of particular* kinds of practice. (MacIntyre, 2002, p. 65, italics added)

Persons who represent the embodiment of the virtues are ideal persons (or ideal types), moral exemplars, or moral heroes. "These are role models, who teach us all what it is to be moral by example, not by precept. Their lives inspire us to live better lives, to be better people" (Pojman, 2005, p. 166). This moral exemplar aspect of the virtue perspective can facilitate decision making, and can be action guiding, in that one might either look to the example of *particular* role models (whom one knows or knows about) to influence behavior, or one might ask oneself more theoretically what a virtuous person would do in similar circumstances (Hursthouse, 1999, p. 36; Baker, 2006, p. 12, in press). The virtue perspective also is action guiding in that each virtue generates a prescription (such as "do what is honest") and each vice generates a prohibition (such as "do not do what is dishonest"). Hursthouse calls these rules of virtue ethics "v-rules." V-rules are virtue-based prescriptions, or vice-based prohibitions (Hursthouse, 1999, pp. 36–37; Baker, 2006, p. 12, in press).

As mentioned above, virtue ethics also is related to the issue of "becoming." According to MacIntyre, we are the authors of the narratives of our own lives, and the virtues (or vices) are "components of the narrative unity of life" (MacIntyre, 1984, pp. 215, 222–223; Baker, 2006, p. 13, in press). Lebacqz proposes that this notion of the coherence of one's life story is one tool by which virtue ethics provides guidance for action. One would ask oneself if a particular contemplated action fits his or her life story—if it lends integrity to him or her, or rather if it threatens his or her integrity. One might ask, "Which act has the most integrity in terms of the kind of person I want to *become*? (Lebacqz, 1985, pp. 85-86, italics added; Baker, 2006, p. 14, in press).

The model (Table 9.2) of The Principled Advocate versus The Pathological Partisan (Baker, 2006, p. 27, in press) is based in the virtue ethics perspective. As discussed above, virtue ethics focuses on the actors (or advocates) themselves, rather than on the acts they perform. It asserts that good people (people who possess the virtues) will do the right thing; and that people who do the right thing will *become* virtuous. One *becomes* a virtuous or Principled Advocate by habitually engaging in ethical practices of advocacy. Conversely, one becomes a Pathological Partisan by habitually engaging in unethical practices of advocacy (Baker, 2006, p. 15, in press).

The term "Pathological Partisan" has been adopted from the philosopher Sissela Bok. According to Bok, the virtue of loyalty, taken to an extreme, can become the vice of pathological partisanship. A Pathological Partisan "uses loyalty as a justification to condone abuses in the name of a cause.... [Pathological Partisans] blind themselves to the kind of harm they are doing to those on the outside" of their cause (Bok, 1988; Baker, 2006, p. 16, in press).

**TABLE 9.2**

**The Principled Advocate versus the Pathological Partisan: A Model of Opposing Archetypes of Public Relations and Advertising Practitioners**

| The principled advocate | The pathological partisan |
|---|---|
| Advocates for noble (morally justifiable) causes with moral virtue, principled motives and means. | Abandons moral virtues, principles, and values in support of a cause. |
| As one habitually enacts the virtues in practice, one becomes a Principled Advocate. | As one habitually enacts the vices in practice, one becomes a Pathological Partisan. |
| **VIRTUES** $\longleftarrow$ | $\longrightarrow$ **VICES** |
| Humility (acknowledges one's moral responsibility) | Arrogance (exempts oneself from moral responsibility) |
| Truth | Deceit |
| Transparency | Secrecy (Opacity) |
| Respect (for others' right to self-determination | Manipulation (of others for one's own ends) |
| Concern (for others) | Disregard (for others) |
| Authenticity | Artifice |
| Equity | Injustice |
| Social Responsibility (for the common good) | Raw Self-Interest (to the detriment of others) |

The virtues and vices generate "v-rules." Each virtue generates a prescription ("be truthful"); each vice generates a prohibition ("do not deceive") (Hursthouse, 1999, p. 36). The model is a continuum. "The virtues and the vices are such that as a person moves away from one end of the scale, she necessarily moves toward the other" (Gert, 1998, p. 284).
*Source*: Baker, 2006, p. 27.

The Principled Advocate advocates for noble (or morally justifiable) causes with moral virtue, and with principled motives and means. He or she embodies and enacts the virtues of humility, truth, transparency, respect and concern for others, authenticity, equity, and social responsibility.

The Pathological Partisan, by contrast, abandons moral virtues, principles, and values in support of a cause. He or she embodies and enacts the vices of arrogance, deceit, secrecy, manipulation, disregard for others, artifice, injustice, and raw self-interest.

The virtues of truthfulness, authenticity, respect, equity, and social responsibility are familiar from the TARES Test. Their corresponding vices (deceit, artifice, manipulation of others for one's own ends, injustice, and raw self-interest) appear in The Principled Advocate vs. The Pathological Partisan model. The additional virtues of humility, concern for others, and transparency (together with their corresponding vices of arrogance, disregard for others, and secrecy/opacity) have been added as a contribution from the virtue ethics perspective. Humility involves, in part, the recognition that one is fallible and vulnerable, and that morality applies to oneself as it does to everyone else (Gert, 1998, p. 306; Baker, 2006, pp. 7, 18, in press). Humility's opposing vice is arrogance, which includes "the view that one is exempt from some or all of the moral requirements to which all other moral agents are subject" (Gert, 1998, p. 306; Baker, 2006, p. 7, in press).

The virtue of concern (humane concern or concern for the common good) relates to the notion of mutual dependence (MacIntyre, 2002). Concern for others "goes beyond the more rational notion of respecting the rights of others.... [Concern] would include treating people with respect, but would be motivated by care for them and their welfare as fellow vulnerable human beings" (Baker, 2006, p. 18, in press). Disregard for others is the corresponding vice.

Finally, the virtue of transparency is a key element in the profile of the Principled Advocate. Transparency relates to the characteristics of openness and penetrability.

> In public relations and advertising practices this virtue would be enacted by freely volunteering information that others have a legitimate need to know; being accountable for one's actions, words, and decisions; [and] being candid and open. (Rawls, 2006; cited in Baker, 2006, p. 18)

The vice corresponding to transparency is secrecy (or opacity) which would involve, in part, failing to be forthcoming, and hiding or obscuring information that others have a legitimate need to know.

The critical and significant essence of this model is the graphic opposition of the antithetical virtues and vices. However, it should be noted that the model also is constructed such that the Principled Advocate and the Pathological Partisan are conceptual constructs at opposite ends of a *scale*. In practice, the virtues and vices in the model should be viewed as if on a continuum. "As a person moves away from one end of the scale, she necessarily moves toward the other" (Gert, 1998, p. 284; Baker, 2006, p. 5, in press).

The virtue ethics perspective can be applied in moral reasoning by seeking advice from or following the example of a role model, a moral exemplar, or an admired colleague; by contemplating if a particular course of action would enact particular virtues or vices identified in the model, or if a particular decision would lead one to become more like a Principled Advocate or a Pathological Partisan; or by asking oneself if a particular action would augment or diminish one's integrity and good reputation.

Gardner et al. (2001), invoke virtue ethics themes in their book *Good Work: When Excellence and Ethics Meet.* Among the concerns that sparked their interest in studying good work was "*the loss of powerful 'heroic' role models* that inspire the younger members of a profession..."

(p. xi, italics added). They define good work as "work of expert quality that benefits the broader society" or is "socially responsible" (Gardner et al., 2001, p. xi). They write that a central element of identity is moral, and that people must determine for themselves "what lines they will not cross and why they will not cross them" (Gardner et al., 2001, p. 11). They propose that we experience work as "good" when it is "something that allows the full expression of *what is best in us*..." (p. 5, italics added). Doing good work "*feels* good" for those individuals who are "wholly engaged in activities that exhibit the highest sense of responsibility" (Gardner et al., 2001, p. 5).

Doing good work creates "*a holistic sense of identity*: a person's deeply felt convictions about who she is, and what matters most to her existence as a worker, a citizen, and a human being" (Gardner et al., p. 11).

## THE MORAL PERSPECTIVE

The models presented above are designed to assist practitioners of advocacy to arrive at decisions about morally appropriate and justifiable courses of action. Sometimes, however, knowing what one *should* do does not always determine what one actually *does*.

James Rest (1994) has proposed a theory of the determinants of moral behavior. He writes that there are four psychological components that must be in place for people to behave ethically:

> (1) Moral Sensitivity (awareness of possible lines of action, and of how our actions might affect other people); (2) Moral Judgment (the ability to use moral reasoning to determine what behaviors are morally justifiable); (3) Moral Motivation (the desire to prioritize moral values over competing values); and (4) Moral Character (having the courage and ego strength to do the right thing, despite the costs and difficulties in doing so). (Baker, 2007, citing Rest, 1994, pp. 22–25)

All four psychological components are necessary for moral behavior to occur, and "moral failure can occur because of deficiency in any [one] component" (Rest, 1994, p. 24). One must have enough moral sensitivity to recognize an ethical issue when it presents itself (such as a situation or communication that could cause harm to others). One must have also the moral judgment or moral reasoning skills to be able decide the right thing to do. Further, one must have the motivation to prioritize and act on moral values, even when those values come into conflict with other cherished values and priorities (such as economic gain or career success). Even when moral sensitivity, moral judgment and the desire to prioritize moral values are in place, one must also have enough "ego strength, perseverance, backbone, toughness, strength of conviction, and courage" under pressure to do the right thing (Rest, 1994, p. 24).

Kidder (1995) has written that "*standing up for values* is the defining feature of moral courage" (Kidder, 1995, p. 3, italics added). It is moral courage that "lifts values from the theoretical to the practical and carries us beyond ethical reasoning into principled action" (p. 3).

The models for systematic moral reasoning discussed in this chapter relate primarily to Rest's Moral Judgment element (no. 2) in that they provide tools by which to determine what behaviors are morally justifiable in the practices of public relations. Nevertheless, a deep understanding of the underlying philosophical assumptions of the models also should contribute to the other three elements by augmenting sensitivity to moral issues in advocacy, increasing the desire to prioritize moral values over other conflicting values, and strengthening the practitioner's courage to do the right thing.

Rest's "moral sensitivity" component is related to the concept of "the moral point of view" (Pojman, 2005, p. 34) or moral perspective. Moral perspective involves, in part, the recognition that one's actions have consequences for others as well as for oneself. It involves the process of considering and caring about the ramifications of one's actions for others. Bok (1999) refers repeatedly to this perspective when she asks her readers to broaden their view about deception. She writes that liars often deceive to achieve some advantage for self, with insufficient consideration for the harms that result from those deceptions to those lied to (the dupes). Often, liars deceive to gain power over others; to help themselves achieve their objectives by diminishing the knowledge and power of the dupes in the situation.

*Power* is an important concept for advocates and public relations practitioners to consider. Communicators are powerful. The information they disseminate (or withhold) has the power to inform (or misinform) individuals and the public, to shape their assumptions about truth and reality, and to influence their decision-making, spending, attitudes, votes, choices, behaviors, and lifestyles. Like deception, the vices of arrogance, unwarranted secrecy, manipulation, disregard for others, artifice, injustice and raw self-interest all operate in one way or another to assist the Pathological Partisan to withhold power from others, and to garner it for themselves or their clients.

John Rawls's (1971) Veil of Ignorance exercise provides a useful conceptual tool by which to help facilitate the moral perspective. In this exercise, when a decision is to be made, one imagines everyone who will be affected by the decision to be standing behind a veil of ignorance, in an "original position" where everyone is equal in value, humanity, and power. Behind the veil, "no one knows his situation in society, nor his natural assets, and therefore no one is in a position to tailor principles to his advantage" (Rawls, 1971, p. 139). The objective is to make a decision that will be fair to all stakeholders when they step out from behind the veil and assume their identities in society. The process of decision-making from a position behind the veil thus "represents a genuine reconciliation of interests" (Rawls, 1971, p. 142). One result of the perspective-taking or "reflective equilibrium" provided by the deliberative veil of ignorance process is that "weaker parties will be protected" (Patterson & Wilkins, 2005, p. 143). The ethical perspective gained from behind the veil would discourage practices of advocacy that are designed to take unfair advantage of parties who are in weaker positions than advocates for a variety of reasons, including a lack of necessary and truthful information.

Nothing in this chapter is meant to imply that advocates and pr practitioners should not be competitive, or that they should have no interest in achieving their worthy professional objectives. The injunction against raw self-interest (unfettered egoism) that is achieved with disregard for the interests of others is not an injunction against legitimate self-interest. The theories, principles and models suggested in this paper do, however, suggest means by which practitioners can achieve and act upon the moral perspective in which personal interests and those of others can be properly balanced.

Louis Pojman (2005) has written about this issue that "Martin Luther, the great Protestant reformer, once said that humanity is like a man who, when mounting a horse, always falls off on the opposite side, especially when he tries to overcompensate for his previous exaggerations" (p. 42). Pojman suggests that we should accept neither the "Sucker altruism of the morality of self-effacement" nor the "Cheater's preoccupation with self-exaltation that robs the self of the deepest joys in life" (p. 42).

This recognition of the rights and needs of others is the essence of the moral perspective, and it should propel the practitioner toward what Roy Peter Clark of the Poynter Institute has called the "green light" (versus the "red light") view of ethics. Red light ethics *proscribe*. They focus on restraint, suggesting what one ought *not* to do. Green light ethics, by contrast, *prescribe*. They mobilize creative energies and resources; they focus on mission and results, power and duty—on what one *ought* to do. Red light ethics constrain; green light ethics empower (Black & Steele, 1991, p. 9).

This chapter's discussion of public relations and advocacy ethics, and the decision-making models presented, are intended to augment this empowering green light effect—to contribute to the development of the moral perspective in this field; to encourage practitioners to use their talent and power as communicators for worthy purposes, with moral means, while also achieving noble professional objectives and becoming persons of integrity.

## REFERENCES

Bagin, D., & Fulginiti, A. (2005). *Practical Public Relations: Theories and Techniques That Make a Difference*. Dubuque, Iowa: Kendall/Hunt.

Baker, Sherry (1997). "Applying Kidder's ethical decision-making checklist to media ethics." *Journal of Mass Media Ethics*, Vol. 12, No. 4, pp. 197–210.

Baker, Sherry (1999a). "The Entitlement Model: A morally bankrupt baseline for justification of marketing practices. *Research in Marketing*, Vol. 15, pp. 1–23.

Baker, Sherry (1999b). "Five Baselines for Justification in Persuasion." *Journal of Mass Media Ethics*, Vol. 14, No. 2, pp. 69–81.

Baker, Sherry (2002). "The Theoretical Ground for Public Relations Practice and Ethics: A Koehnian Analysis." *Journal of Business Ethics*, Vol. 35, pp. 191–205.

Baker, Sherry (2006). "The Virtuous Advocate versus The Pathological Partisan: A Model of Opposing Archetypes of Public Relations and Advertising Practitioners (A Virtue Ethics Approach to Applied Ethics for Public Relations and Advertising Practitioners)." Paper presented to: Association for Education in Journalism and Mass Communication, San Francisco, CA, August.

Baker, Sherry (in press). "The Model of the Principled Advocate and the Pathological Partisan: A Virtue Ethics Construct of Opposing Archetypes of Public Relations and Advertising Practitioners." *Journal of Mass Media Ethics*.

Baker, Sherry, & Martinson, David L. (2001). "The TARES Test: Five principles for ethical persuasion." *Journal of Mass Media Ethics*, Vol. 16, Nos. 2&3, pp. 148–175.

Barney, Ralph & Black, Jay (2001). "Foreword." *Journal of Mass Media Ethics*, Vol. 16, Nos. 2 & 3, pp. 73–77.

Bivins, Thomas H. (2006). "Responsibility and Accountability," in *Ethics in Public Relations: Responsible Advocacy*, Kathy Fitzpatrick & Carolyn Bronstein, eds. Thousand Oaks, CA: Sage, pp. 19–38.

Black, Jay, & Steele, Bob (1991). "Red Light Ethics vs. Green Light Ethics." Protocol: NPPA Photojournalism Ethics. Presented at the Annual Convention of the National Press Photographers Association, Washington, D.C., July.

Bok, Sissela (1988). "Sissela Bok: Ethicist" (1988). PBS interview with Bill Moyers. Distributed by Films for the Humanities and Sciences.

Bok, Sissela (1999). *Lying: Moral Choice in Public and Private Life*. New York: Vintage Books.

Christians, Clifford (August, 2006). "Ethics in the 21st Century." Paper presented at the Association for Education in Journalism and Mass Communication. San Francisco, CA.

Fitzpatrick, Kathy, & Bronstein, Carolyn, eds. (2006). *Ethics in Public Relations: Responsible Advocacy*. Thousand Oaks, CA: Sage.

Gardner, Howard, Csikszentmihalyi, Mihaly, & Damon, William (2001). *Good Work: When Excellence and Ethics Meet*. New York: Basic Books.

Gert, Bernard (1998). *Morality: Its Nature and Justification*. New York: Oxford University Press.

Guth, D. W., & Marsh, C. (2006). *Public Relations: a Values-Driven Approach* (3rd ed.). Upper Saddle River, NJ: Pearson Education.

Hon, Linda (2006. "Negotiating Relationships With Activist Publics," in *Ethics in Public Relations: Responsible Advocacy*, in Kathy Fitzpatrick & Carolyn Bronstein, eds. Thousand Oaks, CA: Sage, pp. 53–70.

Hursthouse, Rosalind (2001). *On Virtue Ethics*. Oxford: Oxford University Press.

Kagan, Jerome (1998). *Three Seductive Ideas*. Cambridge, MA: Harvard University Press.

Kidder, Rushworth (1995). *How Good People Make Tough Choices*. New York: Morrow.

Kidder, Rushworth (2005). *Moral Courage*. New York: Morrow.

Koehn, Daryl (1994). *The Ground of Professional Ethics*. New York: Routledge.

Lebacqz, Karen(1985). *Professional Ethics*. Nashville, TN: Abingdon Press.

Lattimore, D., Baskin, O., Heiman, S. T., Toth, E. L., & Van Leuven, J. K. (2004). *Public Relations: The Profession and the Practice* (5th ed.). New York: McGraw- Hill.

MacIntyre, Alasdair (1984). *After Virtue: A Study in Moral Theory* (2nd ed.). Notre Dame, IN: University of Notre Dame Press.

MacIntyre, Alasdair (2002). *Dependent Rational Animals: Why Human Beings Need the Virtues*. Chicago: Open Court. The Paul Carus Lecture Series 20, 1999.

Martinson, David (1994). "Enlightened Self-Interest Fails as an Ethical Baseline in Public Relations." *Journal of Mass Media Ethics*, Vol. 9, pp. 100–108.

Newsom, D., Turk, J. D., & Kruckeberg, D. (2007). *This is PR: the Realities of Public Relations* (9th ed.). Belmont, CA: Thomson Wadsworth.

Palenchar, Michael J., & Heath, Robert L. (2006). "Responsible Advocacy Through Strategic Risk Communication," in *Ethics in Public Relations: Responsible Advocacy*, Kathy Fitzpatrick & Carolyn Bronstein, eds. Thousand Oaks, CA: Sage, pp. 131–154.

Patterson, Philip, & Wilkins, Lee (2005). *Media Ethics: Issues and Cases* (5th ed.). Boston: McGraw-Hill.

Pojman, Louis P. (2005). *How Should We Live? An Introduction to Ethics*. Belmont, CA: Thomson Wadsworth.

Pojman, Louis P. (2006). *Ethics: Discovering Right and Wrong*. Belmont, CA: Thomson Wadsworth.

Rawls, John (1971). *A Theory of Justice*. Cambridge, MA: Harvard University Press.

Rest, James (1994). "Background: Theory and Research,", in *Moral Development in the Professions*, James R. Rest & Darcia Narvaez, eds. Hillsdale, NJ: Erlbaum.

Seib, Philip (2006). "The Ethics of Public Diplomacy," in *Ethics in Public Relations: Responsible Advocacy*, Kathy Fitzpatrick & Carolyn Bronstein, eds. Thousand Oaks, CA: Sage, pp. 155–170.

Seitel, F. P. (2004). *The Practice of Public Relations*, 9th ed. Upper Saddle River, NJ: Pearson Prentice Hall.

Treadwell, P. F., & Treadwell, J. B. (2004). *Public Relations Writing: Principles in Practice*, rev. ed. Thousand Oaks, CA: Sage.

Wright, Donald K. (2006). "Advocacy Across Borders," in *Ethics in Public Relations: Responsible Advocacy*, Kathy Fitzpatrick & Carolyn Bronstein, eds. Thousand Oaks, CA: Sage, pp. 171–190.

# 10

# The Ethics of Propaganda and the Propaganda of Ethics

## Jay Black

## INTRODUCTION

This chapter opens with examples of the "new propaganda" permeating today's public communications. It then explores shifting definitions of propaganda, noting contributions from diverse disciplines: political science, philosophy, social psychology, education, semantics, and communication theory. These definitions remind us that how we define propaganda most assuredly determines whether we perceive the enterprise to be ethical or unethical. This section of the chapter is followed by a consideration of the social psychology and semantics of propaganda, given the significance of belief systems and language behaviors in producing, consuming, and critically comprehending the phenomenon. Finally, the entire enterprise is redefined in a way that should inform further studies of this pervasive and oft-lamented component of modern society.

Several premises underlie the discussion:

Propaganda is inevitable in today's media mix. It is not a question of "if" our society and its institutions engage in propaganda; it is rather a question of "how." It is not just what the "bad guys" do; modern media systems are perfectly honed to be agents of propaganda, with modern media audiences its willing recipients.

Propaganda has become problematic in part because the lines have blurred among the information, persuasion, and entertainment functions of media. Implications for ethics are striking, for those who would be successful propagandists, those who would avoid being propagandists, and those who would care to be more sophisticated targets for and students of propaganda.

## THE NEW PROPAGANDA: TRUTHINESS, FAKE NEWS, AND INFO-GANDA

A quick rundown of recent media activities highlights the nature of "new propaganda"—the blurring of truth and fiction ("truthiness" is the descriptor coined by TV comedian Steven Colbert, "fake news" has been popularized by Jon Stewart, and "info-ganda" is a term suggested by one of Stewart's "fake correspondents," Rob Corddry—all of Comedy Central). Some of the media activities are nurtured by the government; others are strictly in-house productions. The following examples demonstrate how modern government and modern media have developed a troubling symbiotic relationship, despite the Government Accountability Office's repeated holdings that government-made news segments may constitute improper "covert propaganda" (Barstow & Stein, 2005).

The George W. Bush administration has spent billions of dollars on domestic and international propaganda—more than $1.6 billion between 2003 and early 2005, according to a Government Accounting Office report (Rich, 2006, p. 172). The money went to a wide range of advertising and public relations campaigns and to 131 media organizations and eight individual members of the media:

- The Department of Health and Human Services (HHS) paid syndicated newspaper columnists to promote the administration's marriage incentives, and along with the State Department, Transportation Security Administration, Agriculture Department, and other federal agencies produced numerous video news releases (VNRs) to tout the administration's various programs. Many of the VNRs, hosted by pseudo-journalists Karen Ryan and Alberto Garcia, aired on dozens of financially strapped, news-hungry local television stations which never identified the reports' sources. The *New York Times* reported that at least 20 federal agencies had produced and distributed hundreds of fake news programs between 2002 and 2005 (Barstow & Stein, 2005).
- The Department of Education budgeted $240,000 in taxpayer's money to pay newspaper columnist and broadcast talk-show host Armstrong Williams to promote the administration's No Child Left Behind program during the 2004 election year (Rich, 2006, p. 168).
- The Defense Department (with more than $1.1 billion in promotional contracts between 2003 and 2005) and the Pentagon's Psychological Operations unit paid a fledgling Washington, DC public relations firm, The Lincoln Group, more than $130 million to engage in various propaganda activities. In one campaign, Iraqi journalists were paid to publish pro-American news stories—written by American military personnel—in Iraqi newspapers. Secretary of Defense Donald Rumsfeld described the fake news stories as a "non-traditional means" of getting "accurate information" to the Iraqi people (Rich, 2006,p. 174), and said that America would be remiss if it didn't pay off foreign media (Wasserman, 2006). An internal Pentagon review concluded that these activities violated neither law nor governmental policy (Shanker, 2006).
- The Defense Department and its Office of Cuba Broadcasting paid hundreds of thousands of dollars over the past several years to ten Miami, Florida veteran news journalists to produce programs for Radio Martí and TV Martí. Martí programming, intended to undermine the communist government of Fidel Castro, cannot be broadcast within the United States because of anti-propaganda laws. Several of the journalists were subsequently fired from their Florida news jobs, and ethicists said the Martí appearances violated the principles of an independent press (Corral, 2006).
- Meanwhile, there is no shortage of examples of the media doing this sort of thing on their own, *sans* governmental instigation, including a $6 billion (and growing) surreptitious global business known as "product placement" or "embedded advertising" (Elliott, 2005; Petrecca, 2006):
  - Over a 10-month period in 2005 and 2006, the Center for Media and Democracy (CMD) documented 77 cases of local television stations' blatant use of video news releases. When the VNRs are sent to the stations their sponsors are identified, but there is almost never anything within the VNRs themselves that tell audiences who is paying the piper (Farsetta, 2006).
  - Product placement has long been a staple of Hollywood films, but the planting of branded products or services—embedded advertising—has found its way into commercial

television entertainment and news programs, video games, magazines, newspapers, and, most recently, children's books. And, for decades, it has been hard to separate advertising from editorial content in mass circulation magazines (Lamb, 2005).

- Recently, however, the practice of undisclosed paid promotions has spread across media, showing up in places once considered off limits to such tactics:
  - Television news programs' lifestyle segments devoted to a particular brand or product are shamelessly promoted by the brand's spokesperson while being interviewed by the segment's host; the deals are brokered by the marketing department, with disclosures, if any, appearing for only a split second during the closing credits (Product placement, 2007);
  - "Branded entertainment" product placements are becoming staples on soap operas, reality programs, or other shows because viewers electronically zip and zap commercials (Barnes, 2005; Elliott, 2005; Turow, 2006);
  - Mainstream newspapers are not immune; $65 million traded hands for product placements in newspapers in 2005, with "advertorials" either paid for directly or bartered (Lamb, 2005);
  - Authors and publishers of children's and juvenile books have made deals with marketers to mention a few brand names in their novels (Petrecca, 2006; techdirt, 2007);
  - The Internet has become the brave new world of not just product placement, but of concept placement. For several months in 2006, the vastly popular YouTube.com carried the "cryptic video musings of a fresh-faced teenager" in what most thought to be a legitimate and intimate diary. Turns out "Lonelygirl15" was an actress, the musings were scripted, and the whole thing a promotion for an upcoming movie (Heffernan & Zeller, 2006);
  - The fact/fiction ("faction") friction seemed to peak in early 2006 when Jamey Frey, author of a memoir *A Million Little Piece*, which had been widely touted by Oprah Winfrey, admitted that substantial portions of his "true life story" had been fictionalized to make the story more compelling (Associated Press, 2006; Deggans, 2006).

These examples cut across the information/persuasion/entertainment media. However, it can be argued that the major challenge of propaganda in modern media is to those who gather, report, and consume news. This is because those in this particular media arena have a greater obligation to "get things right" for democratic self-government than do the entertainers or all the special persuaders and their audiences.

This is not to say the propaganda of entertainment and persuasion is insignificant. But most recognize infomercials and advertorials when we see them—although the game is getting more sophisticated. When journalists misuse their tools, melding information, persuasion, and entertainment; when they blur the lines between facts, inferences, and values judgments, we ought to be concerned. Meanwhile, those of us who consume their propaganda—especially the propaganda that fits comfortably into our belief systems and doesn't challenge us to be better citizens—can rightfully be called unethical propagandees in large part because we have placed our self-interest above the interests of others and the community on a daily, and sometimes hourly, basis.

## SHIFTING PERSPECTIVES ON PROPAGANDA

### Early Approaches to Propaganda

One implication of the term "propaganda," when it was first used in the sociological sense by the Roman Catholic Church, was to the spreading of ideas that would not occur naturally, but only via a cultivated or artificial generation. In 1622 the Vatican established the *Congregatio de Propaganda Fide*, or "Congregation for the Propaganda of Faith," to harmonize the content and teaching of faith in its missions and consolidate its power. This early form of propaganda was considered by the Church to be a moral endeavor (Combs & Nimmo 1993, p. 201).

Over time the term took on more negative connotations; in a semantic sense, propaganda became value-laden; in an ethical sense, it was seen as immoral. In 1842 W. T. Brande, writing in the *Dictionary of Science, Literature and Art*, called propaganda something "applied to modern political language as a term of reproach to secret associations for the spread of opinions and principles which are viewed by most governments with horror and aversion" (Qualter, 1962, p. 4).

After World War I, R. J. R. G. Wreford (1923) maintained that propaganda had retained its pejorative connotations as "a hideous word" typical of an age noted for its "etymological bastardy" (Qualter, 1962, p. 7). At that time, the forces of propaganda, public relations, and psychological warfare had become inextricably intertwined in the public's mind. Social scientists and propaganda analysts, strongly influenced by models of behaviorism, tended to depict a gullible public readily manipulated by forces over which it had little control (Institute for Propaganda Analysis, 1937; Lee & Lee, 1988). This depiction offended humanists and progressives. (For a good treatment of this, see Michael Sproule, 1989, 1997.)

Distinguishing between education and propaganda has been difficult. Martin wrote:

> Education aims at independence of judgment. Propaganda offers ready-made opinions for the unthinking herd. Education and propaganda are directly opposed both in aim and method. The educator aims at a slow process of development; the propagandist, at quick results. The educator tries to tell people *how* to think; the propagandist, *what* to think. The educator strives to develop individual responsibility; the propagandist, mass effects. The educator fails unless he achieves an open mind; the propagandist unless he achieves a closed mind. (Martin, 1929, p. 145)

Doob (1935) added:

> If individuals are controlled through the use of suggestion…then the process may be called propaganda, regardless of whether or not the propagandist intends to exercise the control. (p. 80)

Harold Lasswell (1927) offered the first attempt to systematically define propaganda to assure some degree of validity and reliability in studies of the phenomenon. Propaganda, Lasswell wrote, is "the control of opinion by significant symbols, or, so to speak, more concretely and less accurately, by stories, rumors, reports, pictures, and other forms of social communications" (p. 627). Nearly a decade later, George Catlin (1936) defined propaganda as the mental instillation by any appropriate means, emotional or intellectual, of certain views.

The 1930s and 1940s saw propaganda's definitions reflecting social science's struggles between behaviorism (the "stimulus response" model) and a more value neutral stance. At the same time, propaganda was applied to increasingly broad categories of social and political phenomena.

Edgar Henderson (1943) proposed that no definition of propaganda can succeed unless it meets several requirements: (1) it must be objective; (2) it must be psychological, or at least socio-psychological, rather than sociological or axiological; (3) it must include all the cases without being so broad as to become fuzzy; (4) it must differentiate the phenomenon from both similar and related phenomena; (5) it must throw new light on the phenomenon itself, making possible a new understanding and systematization of known facts concerning the phenomenon, and suggesting new problems for investigation (p. 71). Given these criteria, Henderson claimed previous definitions fell short, and proposed that "Propaganda is a process which deliberately attempts through persuasion-techniques to secure from the propagandee, before he can deliberate freely, the responses desired by the propagandist" (p. 83). Stanley Cunningham (2002) has implied that the psychological bias reflected in Henderson's definition dominated the field for several decades, removing "profoundly philosophical determinants"—including considerations of ethics—from discourse about propaganda (p. 5).

## THE PAST HALF-CENTURY

After World War II, propaganda was often defined in accordance with constantly shifting perspectives on political theory and the processes/effects and structures/functions of mass communication. Increasingly, however, as media and organized persuasion enterprises *in and of themselves* were seen to have diminished mind-molding influences, definitions of propaganda shifted.

French social philosopher Jacques Ellul (1964, 1965), whose ideas have significantly informed the propaganda research agenda in recent decades, held a sophisticated view construing propaganda as a popular euphemism for the totality of persuasive components of culture. Ellul (1965) saw a world in which numerous elements of society were oriented toward the manipulation of individuals and groups, and thereby defined propaganda as "a set of methods employed by an organized group that wants to bring about the active or passive participation in its actions of a mass of individuals, psychologically unified through psychological manipulations and incorporated in an organization" (p. 61). Propaganda performs an indispensable function in society, according to Ellul (1965):

> Propaganda is the inevitable result of the various components of the technological society, and plays so central a role in the life of that society that no economic or political development can take place without the influence of its great power. Human Relations in social relationships, advertising or Human Engineering in the economy, propaganda in the strictest sense in the field of politics—the need for psychological influence to spur allegiance and action is everywhere the decisive factor, which progress demands and which the individual seeks in order to be delivered from his own self. (p. 160)

Ellul (1965) focused more on the culturally pervasive nature of what he called "sociological" and "integration" propaganda. What Ellul (1965) defined as "the penetration of an ideology by means of its sociological context" (p. 63) is particularly germane to a study of mass media propaganda. Advertising, public relations, and the culturally persuasive components of entertainment media are definitely involved in the "spreading of a certain style of life" (p. 63) and all converge toward the same point. Meanwhile, news reporting that emerges from and reflects a dominant—some call it "hegemonic"—worldview would certainly qualify as integration propaganda, as would any news reporting that perpetuates closed-mindedness and undue reliance upon authority.

In a sense sociological propaganda is reversed from political propaganda, because in political propaganda the ideology is spread through the mass media to get the public to accept some political or economic structure or to participate in some action, while in sociological propaganda, the existing economic, political, and sociological factors progressively allow an ideology to penetrate individuals or masses. Ellul (1965) called the latter a sort of "persuasion from within a progressive adaptation to a certain order of things, a certain concept of human relations, which unconsciously molds individuals and makes them conform to society" (pp. 63–64). In contemporary society this is a "long-term propaganda, a self-reproducing propaganda that seeks to obtain stable behavior, to adapt the individual to his everyday life, to reshape his thoughts and behavior in terms of the permanent social setting" (p. 74).

It is significant that those who produce sociological or integration propaganda often do so unconsciously, given how thoroughly (and perhaps blindly) they themselves are invested in the values and belief systems being promulgated. Besides, if one is an unintentional "integration" propagandist merely seeking to maintain the status quo, one's efforts would seem to be *prima facie* praiseworthy and educational. However, when considering propaganda as a whole, Ellul (1981) concluded that the enterprise was pernicious and immoral—a view shared by many but not all other students of the subject. Ellul argued that pervasive and potent propaganda that creates a world of fantasy, myth, and delusion is anathema to ethics because (1) the existence of power in the hands of propagandists does not mean it is right for them to use it (that is—ought problem); (2) propaganda destroys a sense of history and continuity so necessary for a moral life; and (3) by supplanting the search for truth with imposed truth, propaganda destroys the basis for mutual thoughtful interpersonal communication and thus the essential ingredients of an ethical existence (Ellul, 1981, pp. 159–77; Johannesen, 1983/1990, p. 116; Combs & Nimmo, 1993, p. 202; and Cunningham, 1992). Ellul's broad concepts of propaganda in contemporary society have influenced many scholars; for example, Gordon (1971) and Merrill and Lowenstein (1971).

An honest appraisal of propaganda scholarship shows a void of what Cunningham (2001, 2002) called front-line academic research between the 1950s and early 1980s. Cunningham has gone so far as to call propaganda a theoretically undeveloped notion during that period, and to laud the recent Ellulian-motivated resurgence of propaganda scholarship. Some of that recent research and commentary (see esp. Combs & Nimmo, 1993; Cunningham, 2002; Edelstein, 1997; Frankfurt, 2005; Jowett & O'Donnell, 1999; Penny, 2005; Pratkanis & Aronson, 1991; Smith, 1989; Solomon, 2005; Sproule, 1989, 1997; Taylor, 2003) has painted propaganda with a wider brush that covers the canvas of media, popular culture, and politics. While much of that scholarship posits that propaganda is systematic and purposive, others recognize the likelihood of unconscious or accidental propaganda, produced by unwitting agents of the persuasion industry.

## HOW TO DETECT PROPAGANDA

In his 2000 book *Lies We Live By*, Carl Hausman offered "ten warning signs that the message you are reading, seeing, or hearing is propagandistic in nature." The "signs" were drawn largely from the Institute for Propaganda Analysis of the late 1930s, but incorporate some contemporary concern about mass media propaganda:

1. The person presenting the message figuratively turns over card after card after card and everything squares with the message. All the cards are in the dealer's favor, and turn over exactly at the right time. If you get the gut feeling the deck is stacked, it probably is.
2. The message contains vague, but appealing, terms, such as "red-blooded Americans" or "progressive freethinkers."
3. The message contains vague, but somehow repellant, terms, like "card-carrying member of the ACLU."
4. There are many references to vague authority. "Professors at leading universities say…" Who are they? What universities? Or there are many testimonials when the connection between the person (usually famous) and the message are tenuous.
5. The message tries to convince you to do something because everybody else is doing it. You don't want to be left off the bandwagon.
6. The message or the messenger appeals to "plain folks." Be on guard when someone, particularly someone with a lot of power and money, tries to convince you that he or she is just one of the "ordinary people."

7. Name-calling is used as a device to reinforce the message. Note, for example, whether the messenger uses words like "terrorist" or "freedom fighter."
8. The whole message seems deliberately confusing.
9. The message centers on transferring the attributes of one thing, like the Bible or the flag, to another person or thing.
10. The attribution is biased. Be on guard when sources are not quoted as "Smith said," but rather "Smith gloated" or "Smith tried to defend his actions by saying...."(Carl Hausman, 2000. *Lies we live by: Defeating double-talk and deception in advertising, politics, and the media.* New York: Routledge, pp. 136–137)

Media scholar Alex Edelstein, in his 1997 book *Total Propaganda: From Mass Culture to Popular* Culture, said "old propaganda" is traditionally employed by the government or the socially and economically influential members in "a hierarchical mass culture, in which only a few speak to many," and it is intended for "the control and manipulation of mass cultures." He contrasts this with the "new propaganda" inherent in a broadly participant popular culture "with its bedrock of First Amendment rights, knowledge, egalitarianism, and access to communication" (p. 5).

Canadian philosopher Stanley Cunningham (1992, 2001, 2002), has argued strenuously against both the value-free definitions posed by social scientists and the value-laden definitions replete with unsupported assertions offered by pundits. In their stead he has insisted that the cultural or mass-mediated environmental phenomenon can only be fully understood in terms of articulated theory and method, and that defining the term per se is "neither possible nor necessary" (2002, p. 176). To that end, he proposed an eleven-paragraph description of propaganda in a chapter titled "The Metaphysics of Propaganda" (2002, pp. 176–178). Among other considerations, Cunningham insisted that propaganda is not morally neutral, that it is counterfeit or pseudocommunication:

> Because it inverts principal epistemic values such as truth and truthfulness, reasoning and knowledge, and because of its wholesale negative impact upon voluntariness and human agency, and because it also exploits and reinforces a society's moral weaknesses, propaganda is not ethically neutral. Rather, it is an inherently unethical social phenomenon. (2002, p. 176)

Although reluctant to offer a simple definition of propaganda, Cunningham (2001) did not hesitate to characterize the phenomenon in terms of the serious ethical challenges it poses:

> Propaganda comprises a whole family of epistemic disservices abetted mostly (but not entirely) by the media: It poses as genuine information and knowledge when, in fact, it generates little more than ungrounded belief and tenacious convictions; it prefers credibility, actual belief states, and mere impressions to knowledge; it supplies ersatz assurances and certainties; it skews perceptions; it systematically disregards superior epistemic values such as truth, understanding, and knowledge; and it discourages reasoning and a healthy respect for rigor, evidence, and procedural safeguards. In sum, what really defines propaganda is its utter indifference to superior epistemic values and their safeguards in both the propagandist and the propagandee. (p. 139)

## THE SOCIAL PSYCHOLOGY OF PROPAGANDA

Scholarly analyses of propaganda tend to focus on either the political or philosophic or semantic/rhetorical nature of the beast. An equally intriguing set of insights can be offered by social psychologists, concerned as they are with the nature of belief and value systems and the various psychological needs that a phenomenon such as propaganda tends to fulfill. A truncated look at some of this literature in instructive for a holistic understanding of the ethics of propaganda, propagandists, and propagandees in contemporary society.

Harold Lasswell said as far back as 1936 that technological western democracies are characterized by circumstances that give rise to two general categories of need fulfillment: catharsis and readjustment. By catharsis he referred to the discharge of tension with a minimum of change in overt social relationships; by readjustment, the removal of the symbolic or material source of insecurity (1947, p. 403). Citizens overwhelmed by powerlessness and anomie turned instead to their own affairs; they became privatized. The past half-century's concerns over media propaganda have been based on the often stated assumption that one responsibility of a democratic media system is to encourage an open-minded citizenry—that is, a people who are curious, questioning, unwilling to accept simple pat answers to complex situations, etc. (Kovach & Rosensteil, 2001). Mental freedom, the argument goes, comes when people have the capacity, and exercise the capacity, to weigh numerous sides of controversies (political, personal, economic, etc.) and come to their own rational decisions, relatively free of outside constraints.

## The Open and Closed Mind

A growing body of research on perception and belief systems seems to be concluding that individuals constantly strive for cognitive balance and that individuals will select and rely upon information consistent with their basic perceptions. Donohew and Palmgreen (1971), for instance, showed that open-minded journalists underwent a great deal of stress when having to report information they weren't inclined to believe or agree with, because the open-minded journalists' self-concepts demanded that they fairly evaluate all issues. Closed-minded journalists, on the other hand, underwent much less stress because it was easy for them to make snap decisions consistent with their basic worldviews (pp. 627–639, 666).

Social psychologist Milton Rokeach, in his seminal work *The Open and Closed Mind* (1960), concluded empirically that the degree to which a person's belief system is open or closed is the extent to which the person can receive, evaluate, and act on relevant information received from the outside on its own intrinsic merits, unencumbered by irrelevant factors in the situation arising from within the person or from the outside (p. 57). To Rokeach, open-minded individuals seek out sources (media and otherwise) that challenge them to think for themselves, rather than sources that offer overly simplified answers to complex problems. Closed-minded or dogmatic media consumers, on the other hand, seek out and relish the opposite kinds of messages (Rokeach, 1954, 1960, 1964).

Several of Rokeach's validated insights (Vacchiano et al., 1969) into open- and closed-mindedness are helpful when studying propaganda: the belief-disbelief dimensions; the central, intermediate, and peripheral dimensions; and the time-perspective dimensions. Let us consider each of them in turn.

1. *The belief-disbelief dimensions.* A person's belief system represents all the beliefs, sets, expectancies, or hypotheses, conscious and unconscious, which that person at a given time accepts as true of the world he or she lives in; the disbelief system, or series of subsystems, reflects the same dimensions that the person rejects as false (Rokeach, 1960, p. 33). This total framework, or composite of systems, includes not only what is usually referred to as "ideology" (i.e., the type of thoughts and attitudes based largely on communication *per se*), but also highly personalized pre-ideological beliefs, beliefs that are undoubtedly formed by a composite of influences. Rokeach evaluated the basic belief-disbelief systems in terms of their isolation and differentiation. By

isolation he meant the perceived lack of relationship between beliefs that may be intrinsically related to each other; by differentiation, the degree of articulation or richness of detail within the basic system and its various parts.

While we cannot safely say that propaganda has created the basic nature or degree of isolation and differentiation between belief and disbelief systems, it is fascinating to note the parallels between the commonly expressed goals of propaganda and the shortcomings Rokeach pointed out in the isolation and differentiation characteristics of the dogmatic individual. The most fundamental conditions of the closed-minded individual are the high magnitude of rejection of all disbelief systems, and little differentiation within the disbelief system (Rokeach, 1960, p. 61). A dogmatic propagandist or propagandee would thus have the following behaviors, as described by Ellul (1965): offering relatively rigid responses to complex issues; being relatively unimaginative, with a tendency to stereotype; being sterile with regard to socio-political process; being unable to adjust to situations other than those created by propaganda; seeing the world in terms of strict opposites; being involved in unreal conflicts created and blown up by propaganda; giving everything his or her own narrow interpretation, depriving facts of their real meaning or order to integrate them into his or her own system and given them an emotional coloration (p. 167).

2. *The central-intermediate-peripheral dimensions.* Rokeach (1960, 1964) conceived of beliefs as existing in either three or five non-rigidly outlined layers: a *central region* (or central regions, positive and negative), representing a person's primitive and relatively impervious-to-change beliefs about the nature of the physical world, the nature of the "self," and the "generalized other"; an *intermediate region*, representing the beliefs a person has in and about the nature of authority and the people who line up with authority, on whom a person depends to help form a picture of the world to be lived in; and a *peripheral region* (or peripheral regions), representing the beliefs derived consciously or unconsciously from authority, beliefs that fill up the details of a person's frame of reference.

In studying these dimensions, Rokeach focused on the degree to which people receive and act upon communication that helps them round out their pictures of the world and the degree of reliance placed upon authority figures (rational, tentative reliance for the non-dogmatists, arbitrary, absolute reliance for the dogmatists). Change of primitive beliefs is difficult to effect. A smart propagandist knows it would be a waste of time to directly attack such central beliefs. However, a successful propagandist will take advantage of those beliefs, will nuance them, will employ authority figures creatively, and will play rhetorical and semantic games with them, doing much of the propagandizing at the peripheral or inconsequential level of beliefs, where slogans, brand names, and other insignificant rhetoric are employed and where media provide conversational items, social status, and a bit of self-worth. Meanwhile, propaganda would seem to work best on the open-minded in cases when the propaganda gives the appearance of employing multiple and contrasting authorities, when individuals are led to believe they can pick and choose for themselves—from authorities and prejudices pre-selected by the propagandist!

Selective attention, perception, and retention are artifices of the central-intermediate-peripheral belief system—how and what we choose to attend to, be cognizant of, and recall depends largely upon how those three dimensions of our belief system line up. It follows, then, that the dogmatist is seemingly unaware of the interconnectedness of the three regions, while the open-minded is more cognizant and hence, less vulnerable to propaganda.

3. *The time-perspective continuum.* The place of a time-perspective dimension in a consideration of belief systems is based on Rokeach's conclusion that the way a person feels about the past, present, and future as they relate to each other is an important part of that person's entire view on the world. To the relatively open-minded person, the past, present, and future are all represented within the belief-disbelief dimension in such a way that the person sees them as being

related to each other. The relatively closed-minded person, on the other hand, has a narrow time perspective. The closed-minded person would have a simplistic concept of causes and effects; the open-minded would think in terms of multiple causality, and in terms of concomitants rather than simple causality.

Propaganda, it follows from the above, is far more likely to be created by and aimed at the closed-minded who have a time-perspective disconnect.

## Belief Systems and Media Propaganda

One of the dominant themes in media criticism for much of past half-century or so has been the tendency of media to mitigate against open-mindedness. The body of literature is vast, and only a snapshot of it appears here.

Gilbert Seldes (1957) expressed fear that the mass media had begun to inculcate in the audience a weakened sense of discrimination, a heightening of stereotypical thinking patterns, a tendency toward conformity and dependence (pp. 26, 50–62).

A decade earlier, Harold Lasky (1948) had observed that

> The real power of the press comes from the effect of its continuous repetition of an attitude reflected in facts which its readers have no chance to check, or by its ability to surround these facts by an environment of suggestion which, often half-consciously, seeps its way into the mind of the reader and forms his premises for him without his even being aware that they are really prejudices to which he has scarcely given a moment of thought. (p. 670).

Likewise Charles Wright (1959) expressed similar concerns. The mid-century views of Seldes, Lasky, and Wright do not depart radically from the 1922 lamentations of Walter Lippmann concerning the stereotypical pictures in the heads of people. The logic of Jacques Ellul (1965) is compelling in this regard, as he argued that people in a technological society *need* to be propagandized, to be "integrated into society" via media. Modern citizens, Ellul concluded, therefore condemn themselves to lives of successive moments, discontinuous and fragmented— and the news media are largely responsible.

The hapless victims of information overload seek out propaganda as a means of ordering the chaos, according to Ellul. Propaganda gives them explanations for all the news, so that it is classified into easily identifiable categories of good and bad, right and wrong, worth-worrying-about and not-worth-worrying-about, etc. The propagandees allow themselves to be propagandized, to have their cognitive horizons narrowed. Ellul argued people are doubly reassured by propaganda because it tells them the reasons behind developments and because it promises a solution for all the problems that would otherwise seem insoluble. "Just as information is necessary for awareness, propaganda is necessary to prevent this awareness from being desperate," Ellul concluded (1965, pp. 146–147).

If our nature is to eschew dissonance and move toward a homeostatic mental set, the crazy quilt patterns of information we receive from our mass media would certainly drive us to some superior authority of information or belief that would help us make more sense of our world. Propaganda thus becomes inevitable.

Most of the foregoing emphasizes the propagandee's belief system, showing parallels between dogmatic personality types and the "typical" propagandee. Not much of a case has been made to maintain that propagandists themselves possess the basic characteristics of the dogmatist, but there is much evidence suggesting that communicators who are intentionally and consciously operating as propagandists recognize that one of their basic tasks is to keep the minds of their propagandees closed. Unconscious propagandists are another matter. They may have unconsciously absorbed the belief and value system that they propagate in their daily integration or socialization propaganda. Their unexamined propagandistic lives reflect a cognitive system that has slammed as tightly shut as those of the authorities for whom they blindly "spin" and as the most gullible of their propaganda's recipients.

As Donohew and Palmgreen (1971) implied, it appears to be difficult and stressful for both media practitioners and media consumers to retain pluralistic orientations. But if media personnel and audiences never find themselves concerned over contradictory information, facts that don't add up, opinions that don't cause them to stop and think, then they are being closed-minded purveyors and passive receivers of propaganda.

## THE SEMANTICS OF PROPAGANDA

Many academic findings are highly consistent with the body of knowledge referred to as "general semantics." This is not surprising, given how much the scholars have in common: All are interested in how people perceive the world and how they subsequently communicate their perceptions or misperceptions. General semantics, a field of study framed by Alfred Korzybski (1933/1948) in *Science and Sanity*, assesses human's unique symbolic behavior. At the heart of the field is the argument that unscientific or "Aristotelian" assumptions about language and reality result in semantically inadequate or inappropriate behavior.

Numerous empirical studies of general semantics reinforce these original suppositions. Studies of children and adults trained in general semantics principles have demonstrated that semantic awareness results in such diverse achievements as improved perceptual, speaking, reading, and writing skills (Berger, 1965; Glorfield, 1966; Haney, 1962–1963; Livingston, 1966; Ralph, 1972; True, 1966; Weaver, 1949; Weiss, 1959; Westover, 1959), generalized intelligence (Haney, 1962–1963; Steele, 1972), decreased prejudice (J. A. Black, 1972), decreased dogmatism (J. J. Black, 1974; Goldberg, 1965), and decreased rigidity (J. J. Black, 1974).

General semanticists' descriptions of sophisticated ("sane") language behavior include— but are not limited to—awareness that (1) our language is not our reality, but is an inevitably imperfect abstraction of that reality; (2) unless we're careful, our language usually reveals more about our own biases than it does about the persons or objects we're describing; (3) people and situations have unlimited characteristics; the world is in a constant process of change; our perceptions and language abilities are limited; (4) a fact is not an inference and an inference is not a value judgment; (5) different people will perceive the world differently, and we should accept authority figures', sources', and witnesses' viewpoints as being the result of imperfect human perceptual processes, and not as absolute truth; and (6) persons and situations are rarely if ever two-valued; propositions do not have to be either "true" or "false," specified ways of behaving do not have to be either "right" or "wrong," "black" or "white"; continuum-thinking or an infinite-valued orientation is a more valid way to perceive the world than an Aristotelian two-valued orientation (Bois, 1966; Chase, 1938, 1954; Hayakawa, 1939, 1941, 1949, 1954, 1962; Johnson, 1946; Korzybski, 1948; Lee, 1941, 1949; see also *Etcetera: A Review of General Semantics*, a quarterly published by the International Society for General Semantics).

Emerging from this literature are conclusions about a series of semantic patterns that typify the semantically sophisticated or unsophisticated individual. The patterns are highly reflective of Rokeach's typologies of the open-minded or closed-minded individual and of propaganda analysts' descriptions of the non-propagandistic or propagandistic individual.

Specific semantic problems for the journalist can be identified, and semantic solutions to those problems can be proposed. Although presented in polarized form, they are best understood in terms of a continuum:

1. *Problem: the blurring of abstraction levels*: Problems arise when journalists carelessly jump within and among different levels of abstraction, when they leave the impression that "that's the way it is," when they draw inferences and value judgments without sharing with their readers and viewers the hard data (if any) used to move to those higher levels of abstraction.

   *Alternative to blurring levels of abstraction*: Journalists should know, and show, the differences between objects, statements of fact, inferences, and value judgments. They should remember that abstraction is the inevitable process of narrowing and reducing data from the real world and from human's limited ability to observe it.

   Journalists would do well to tell what someone or something "does" rather than what it "is." The order of abstraction should go from fact, to description, to inference, to value judgment; journalists should show their evidence so audiences can follow the same logical pattern. As David Ignatius (Just the facts? 1999) explained in the *Washington Monthly*, journalists would do well to follow the 1950s advice of J. Russell Wiggins, who said that "The reader deserves one clean shot at the facts" (Just the facts? p. 26).

   > The ethics of journalism…must be based on the simple truth that every journalist knows the difference between the distortion that comes from subtracting observed data and the distortion that comes from adding invented data.—John Hersey, "The Legend on the License," The Yale Review, 72, No. 2, February 1986, p. 290.

2. *Problem: the tendencies toward "allness"*: Problems arise when journalists act as though they have seen all they need to (or could possibly) see, have described all they need to (or could possibly) describe, and have concluded all they need to (or could possibly) conclude. They are genuinely surprised when they find exceptions to their dogmatic view of reality, and then they write stories about what they (but few others) find sensational or bizarre. They make unqualified predictions based on what they pass off as complete evidence. They forget that their sources and news subjects are very likely not to be objective, but find no reason to go beyond the truncated versions of "absolute truth" the sources offer up to interviewers

   *Alternative to "Allness"*: Journalists should be conscious of "etcetera," aware that while their descriptions may be adequate, they are not complete: People can never see, or say, everything that needs to be seen or said about an individual or situation, so they shouldn't pretend they're doing otherwise. Semantically sophisticated writing is characterized by "etc" terms. Journalism that seeks alternatives to "allness" is filled with answers to "how much" and "to what extent" questions; the journalistic dialogue encourages statements of theory and hypotheses, rather than absolute law. To achieve this, reporters are driven by boundless curiosity and dissatisfaction with simplistic explanations of complex issues.

   Humility and ethics require that journalists don't leave the impression that they have exhausted the territory.

3. *Problem: the "two-valued orientation"*: Semantic and ethical problems arise when the world—and all its sub-sets of data—are arbitrarily divided into mutually exclusive, polarized opposites.

   Objectivity means giving all sides a fair hearing, but not treating all sides equally…. So objectivity must go hand in hand with morality. (Christiane Amanpour, "Just the facts?" *The Washington Monthly*, Jan./Feb., 1999, p. 23)

*Alternative to the "two-valued orientation"*: To demonstrate a multi-valued orientation, the use of "etcetera" is helpful. It reminds reporters and audiences that persons and situations are rarely if ever two-valued; that propositions do not have to be either "true" or "false," specified ways of behaving do not have to be either "right" or "wrong," "black" or "white," that continuum-thinking or an infinite-valued orientation is a more intellectually honest way to perceive and communicate about the world than an Aristotelian two-valued orientation.

Indeed, a multi-valued journalist relishes subtlety in sources, subjects, and stories, and processes dissonance with a certain amount of comfort.

4. *Problem: the "is of identity"*: When journalists ask "What is?" or "Who is?" the answers tend to be stereotypes. The questions, and answers, may make reporters and audiences appear unconscious of myriad individual differences among individuals, situations, and problems. "Truth claims" can emerge from observation and scientific evidence, or from unverifiable bases such as faith, aesthetics, authority, intuition, or philosophy. Problems arise when journalists fail to recognize which is which.

When "to be" verbs are used as an equal sign they suggest that language is equated to reality. To do so is to set up false-to-fact relationships, resulting in stereotypes, labels, name-calling, and instant classification of individuals, groups, situations, and so forth. Such behaviors ignore the fact that language is only an imperfect abstraction of reality.

*Alternative to the "is of identity"*: Semantically sophisticated journalists seek nuances. They use verbs of "non-identity." They separate nouns with qualifying verbs (if only in their heads). They do whatever it takes to differentiate among people, situations, and problems.

5. *Problem: the "is of predication"*: When people use "to be" verbs between nouns and adjectives ("he is stupid," "she is beautiful," etc.), or when they carelessly employ adjectives to affirm qualities, they may be assuming falsely that everyone else sees the qualities in the same way, through the same viewfinder.

*Alternative to the "is of predication"*: Reporters are advised to be conscious of their selectivity and projections by qualifying problematic noun/adjective relationships.

Competent journalists not only use these constructs in their own conclusions, but ask questions in such a way that interviewees are encouraged to use them also.

6. *Problem: being time-bound*: The time-bound ahistorical journalist apparently fails to understand or appreciate the interconnectedness of time and development, the interrelationship of past, present, and future. Such a journalist dwells on the past, fixates narrowly on the present, or dreams idly of the future.

*Alternative to being time-bound*: Change is the constant companion for the semantically sophisticated journalist. Life is gestalt—anything is the cause and result of everything. Conscientious journalists need not be obsessed by past/present/future interrelationships, but do well to appreciate them. They should be curious about their heritage, learn from their mistakes, and remain guardedly optimistic.

## "Attitude Reporting" and "Articlesclerosis"

One reason to conflate general semantics, belief systems, and propaganda theory is to address a general category of the new propaganda in the media. Some have called it "Attitude Reporting," but a better term might be "Articlesclerosis—the hardening of the articles." Blurring of inverted pyramid and narrative styles of writing, of fact and opinion, of detailed description and value judgment, of straight information and distracting entertainment, of objectivity and subjectivity, are the characteristics of journalism-cum-propaganda. "We are increasingly inserting ourselves between our readers and the information they need, and that surely counts as an ethical problem" (Brown 2001, p. 38). Brown faulted his profession for two practices that violate traditional norms and are ethically disquieting: first, a patronizing and condescending story-telling approach to everyday stories ("in an effort to attract people who don't much care about the news"), the second, "oh-so-cunning, supercilious" and "smarty-pants" reporting of politics, in an effort "to impress people who spend altogether too much time trying to outmaneuver us" (Brown 2001, p. 38)

David Ignatius (1999), veteran reporter and editor, said that:

> The biggest danger I encountered in my years as an editor was a reflective cynicism among some reporters that led them to assume they knew what a story was about, before they had actually done the reporting. They would begin with an assumption of who the good guys and bad guys were, and then organize the facts around that hypothesis. Sometimes, reporters were so confident about their *a priori* hypothesis that they would make only the most perfunctory, last-minute efforts to contact the "bad guys." (Just the facts? p. 27)

## PROPAGANDA REFRAMED

We can now amalgamate these insights into a conceptualization about the propagandistic nature of contemporary society. The picture that emerges of propagandists/propaganda/propagandees and their opposites, as uncovered by the preceding discussions, reveals several definite patterns of semantic/belief systems/ethical/etc. behavior. Note that on the one hand the dogmatist (typical of propagandist and propagandee, and revealed in the manifest content of propaganda) seeks psychological closure whether rational or not; appears to be driven by irrational inner forces; has an extreme reliance upon authority figures; reflects a narrow time perspective; and displays little sense of discrimination among fact/inference/value judgment. On the other hand, the non-dogmatist faces a constant struggle to remain open-minded by evaluating information on its own merits; is governed by self-actualizing forces rather than irrational inner forces; discriminates between/among messages and sources and has tentative reliance upon authority figures; recognizes and deals with contradictions, incomplete pictures of reality, and the interrelationship of past, present, and future; and moves comfortably and rationally among levels of abstraction (fact, inference, value judgment).

The above typologies help lead us to an original definition of propaganda, one that partially meets the criteria laid down sixty years ago by Henderson (1943): It is socio-psychological, broad without being fuzzy, differentiates propaganda from similar and related phenomena, and sheds new light on the phenomena. In addition, it describes the characteristics of the propagandists, the propaganda they produce, and the propagandees—something sorely lacking in many other definitions. Finally—and significantly—it injects the philosophic notion of ethics into the enterprise.

The definition is as follows:

While it may or may not emanate from individuals or institutions with demonstrably closed minds, the manifest content of propaganda contains characteristics one associates with dogmatism or closed-mindedness; while it may or may not be intended as propaganda, this type of communication seems non-creative and appears to have as its purpose the evaluative narrowing of its receivers. While creative communication accepts pluralism and displays expectations that its receivers should conduct further investigations of its observations, allegations, and conclusions, propaganda does not appear to do so. Rather, propaganda is characterized by at least the following half-dozen specific characteristics:

1. A heavy or undue reliance on authority figures and spokespersons, rather than empirical validation, to establish its truths, conclusions, or impressions.
2. The utilization of unverified and perhaps unverifiable abstract nouns, adjectives, adverbs, and physical representations, rather than empirical validation, to establish its truths, conclusions, or impressions.
3. A finalistic or fixed view of people, institutions, and situations, divided into broad, all-inclusive categories of in groups (friends) and out-groups (enemies), beliefs and disbeliefs, situations to be accepted or rejected *in toto*.
4. A reduction of situations into readily identifiable cause and effect relationships, ignoring multiple causality of events.
5. A time perspective characterized by an overemphasis or underemphasis on the past, present, or future as disconnected periods, rather than a demonstrated consciousness of time flow.
6. A greater emphasis on conflict than on cooperation among people, institutions, and situations.

This definition encourages a broad-based investigation of public communications behavior along a propaganda–non-propaganda continuum. Practitioners and observers of media and persuasion could use this definition to assess their own and their media's performance.

The definition applies to the news/information as well as to entertainment and persuasion functions in the media. Many criticisms of the supposedly objective aspects of media are entirely compatible with the above standards. Meanwhile, since most people expect the advertisements, public relations programs, editorials, and opinion columns to be non-objective and persuasive, if not outright biased, they may tend to avoid analyzing such messages for propagandistic content. However, because those persuasive messages can and should be able to meet their basic objectives *without* being unduly propagandistic, they should be held to the higher standards of non-propaganda. (For what it's worth, persuasive media that are propagandistic, as defined herein, would seem to be less likely to attract and convince open-minded media consumers than to reinforce the biases of the closed-minded true believers, which raises an intriguing question about persuaders' ethical motives.)

## CONCLUSIONS

This chapter does not suggest that the necessity for mediating reality and merchandising ideas, goods, and services inevitably results in propaganda: Far from it. But we do suggest that when there is a pattern of behavior on the part of participants in the communications exchange that repeatedly finds them dogmatically jumping to conclusions, making undue use of authority, basing assumptions on faulty premises, and otherwise engaging in inappropriate semantic behavior, then we can say they are engaging in propaganda. They may be doing it unconsciously. They may not be attempting to propagandize or even be aware that their efforts can be seen as propagandistic or know that they are falling victim to propaganda. It may just be that their view of the world, their belief systems, their personal and institutional loyalties, and their semantic behaviors are propagandistic.

But this doesn't excuse them.

It is sometimes said, among ethicists, that we should never attribute to malice what can be explained by ignorance. That aphorism certainly applies to propaganda, a phenomenon too many observers have defined as an inherently immoral enterprise that corrupts all who go near it. If we consider propaganda in less value-laden terms, we may recognize ways all participants in the communications exchange can proceed intelligently through the swamp, and we can make informed judgments about the ethics of particular aspects of our communications rather than indicting the entire enterprise.

It is possible to conduct public relations, advertising, and persuasion campaigns, plus the vast gamut of informational journalism efforts, without being *unduly* propagandistic.

In a politically competitive democracy and a commercially competitive free enterprise system, mass communication functions by allowing a competitive arena in which the advocates of all can do battle. What many call propaganda therefore becomes part of that open marketplace of ideas; it is not only inevitable, but may be desirable that there are *openly recognizable and competing propagandas* in a democratic society, propagandas that challenge all of us—producers and consumers—to wisely sift and sort through them.

A fully functioning democratic society needs pluralism in its persuasion and information, and not the narrow-minded, self-serving propaganda some communicators inject—wittingly or unwittingly—into their communications and which, it seems, far too many media audience members unconsciously and uncritically consume. Open-mindedness and mass communications efforts need not be mutually exclusive.

## REFERENCES

Associated Press. (2006, January 27). "You betrayed millions." *St. Petersburg Times*, p. 2b.

Barnes, B. (2005, January 22). For advertising dollars, daytime TV plugs away. *St. Petersburg Times*, pp. 1e, 4e.

Barstow, D., & Stein, R. (2005, March 13). The message machine: How the government makes news; Under Bush, a new age of prepackaged news. *The New York Times*. Accessed 25 March 2005 at http://query. nytimes.com/search/restricted/article?res=F50914FC3E580C708DDDAA0894DD404482

Berger, I. (1965). Eleven common sense principles about language: Student writing examined for logic and clarity. In M. Judine (Ed.), *A guide for evaluating student compositions: A collection of readings*. Champaign, IL: National Council of Teachers of English.

Bernays, E. L. (1928). *Propaganda*. New York: Liveright.

Black, J. A. (1972, March). A language approach to prejudice. *Etcetera, 29*, 9–11.

Black, J. (1974). General semantics, belief systems, and propaganda: Interrelationships in journalism. Unpublished PhD dissertation, University of Missouri.

Black, J. J. (1977–1978). Another perspective on mass media propaganda. *General Semantics Bulletin, 44/45*, 92–104.

Black, J. (2001). Semantics and ethics of propaganda. *Journal of Mass Media Ethics, 16*, 121–137.

Bois, J. S. (1966). *The art of awareness*. Dubuque, Iowa: Wm. C. Brown.

Brown, F. (2001, January-February). Keep it straightforward. *Quill Magazine*, p. 38.

Burnett, N. (1989). Ideology and propaganda: Toward an integrative approach, in T. J. Smith III (Ed.), *Propaganda: A pluralistic perspective* (pp. 127–137). New York: Praeger.

Catlin, G. E. G. (1936). Propaganda as a function of democratic government, in H. W. Childs, (Ed.) *Propaganda and dictatorship: A collection of papers*. Princeton, NJ: Princeton University Press.

Chase, S. (1938). *The tyranny of words*. New York: Harcourt, Brace.

Chase, S. (1954). *The power of words*. New York: Harcourt, Brace.

Cole, R. (Ed.). (1998). *The encyclopedia of propaganda*. Armonk, NY: Sharpe.

Combs, J. E., & Nimmo, D. (1993). *The new propaganda: The dictatorship of palaver in contemporary politics*. White Plains, NY: Longman.

Corral, O. (2006, Sept. 8). 10 Miami journalists take U.S. pay. *MiamiHerald*.com. http://www.miami.com.

Cunningham, S. (1992). Sorting out the ethics of propaganda. *Communication Studies, 43*, 233–245.

Cunningham, S. (2001). Responding to propaganda: An ethical enterprise. *Journal of Mass Media Ethics 16*, 138–147.

Cunningham, S. (2002). *The idea of propaganda: A reconstruction.* Westport, CT: Praeger.

Deggans, E. (2006, January 22). Truth, lies and bestsellers. *St. Petersburg Times*, p. 5.

Donohew, L., & Palmgreen, P. (1971, Winter). An investigation of "mechanisms" of information selection. *Journalism Quarterly, 48*, 627–639, 666.

Doob, L. W. (1935). *Propaganda, its psychology and technique.* New York: Henry Holt.

Edelstein, A. (1997). *Total propaganda: From mass culture to popular culture.* Mahwah, NJ: Erlbaum.

Elliott, S. (2005 B, March 29). More products get roles in shows, and marketers wonder if they're getting their money's worth. *The New York Times.* http://www.nytimes.com/2005/03/29/business/media

Ellul, J. (1964). *The technological society,* New York: Vintage Books.

Ellul, J. (1965). *Propaganda: The formation of men's attitudes.* New York: Alfred A. Knopf.

Ellul, J. (1981). The ethics of propaganda: Propaganda, innocence, and amorality. *Communication, 6*(2), 159–177.

Farsetta, D. (2006, March 16). Fake TV news: Widespread and undisclosed. http://www.prwatch.org/fak-enews/execsummary

Frankfurt, H. G. (2005). *On bullshit.* Princeton, NJ: Princeton University Press.

Glorfield, L. E. (1966). Effects of a limited semantics methodology on the writing improvement of college freshmen. Unpublished PhD dissertation, University of Denver.

Goldberg, A. (1965, March). The effects of a laboratory course in general semantics. *Etcetera, 22*, 19–24.

Gordon, G. N. (1971). *Persuasion: The theory and practice of manipulative communication.* New York: Hastings House.

Haney, W. V. (1962–1963). The uncritical inference test: Applications. *General Semantics Bulletin, 28–29*, 34–37.

Hausman, C. (2000). *Lies we live by.* New York: Routledge.

Hayakawa, S. I. (1939, April). General semantics and propaganda. *Public Opinion Quarterly, 3*, 197–205.

Hayakawa, S. I. (1941). *Language in action.* New York: Harcourt, Brace.

Hayakawa, S. I. (1949). *Language in thought and action.* New York: Harcourt, Brace.

Hayakawa, S. I. (1954). *Language, meaning and maturity.* New York: Harper &Brothers

Hayakawa, S. I. (Ed.) (1962). *The use and misuse of language.* Greenwich, CT: Fawcett.

Heffernan, V., & Zeller, T. (2006, Sept. 13). Well, it turns out that Lonelygirl really wasn't. *The New York Times*, C1, C9.

Henderson, E. H. (1943). Toward a definition of propaganda. *Journal of Social Psychology, 18*, 71–87.

Henning, A. F. (1932). *Ethics and practices in journalism.* New York: Long & Smith.

Ignatius, D. (1999, January/February). Just the facts? *Washington Monthly*, p. 27.

Institute for Propaganda Analysis. (1937, November). How to detect propaganda, *Propaganda Analysis, 1*, 1–4.

Jensen, J. V. (1997). *Ethical issues in the communication process.* Mahwah, NJ: Erlbaum.

Johannesen, R. L. (1983). *Ethics in human communication,* 2nd ed. Prospect, IL.: Waveland Press.

Johannesen, R. L. (1990). *Ethics in human communication,* 3rd. ed. Prospect, IL.: Waveland Press.

Johnson, W. (1946). *People in quandaries: The semantics of personal adjustment.* New York: Harper & Brothers.

Jowett, G. S., & O' Donnell, V. (1999). *Propaganda and persuasion.* Thousand Oaks, CA: Sage.

Just the facts? (1999, January/February). *The Washington Monthly*, pp., 22–35.

Kieran, M. (Ed.) (1998). *Media ethics: A philosophical approach.* New York: Routledge.

Korzybski, A. H. (1948). *Science and sanity: An introduction to non-Aristotelian systems and general semantics,* 4th ed. Lakeville CT: Non-Aristotelian Library. (Original work published 1933)

Kovach, B., & Rosensteil, T. (2001). *The elements of journalism: What newspeople should know and the public should expect.* New York: Crown.

Lamb, G. M. (2005, Sept. 29). Product placement pushes into print. *The Christian Science Monitor.* Accessed 24 February 2007 at http://www.csmonitor.com/2005/0929/p12s-wmgn.html

Lasky, H. (1948). *American democracy*. New York: Viking Press.

Lasswell, H. D. (1927). *Propaganda technique in the world war*. New York: Knopf.

Lasswell, H. D. (1947). The scope of research on propaganda and dictatorship. In H. L. Childs (Ed.), *Propaganda and dictatorship: A collection of papers*. New York: International Universities Press.

Lee, A. M. (1952). *How to understand propaganda*. New York: Rinehardt.

Lee, I. J. (1941). *Language habits in human affairs: An introduction to general semantics*. New York: Harper Brothers.

Lee, I. J. (1949). *The language of wisdom and folly: Background readings in semantics*. New York: Harper Brothers.

Lee, A. M. & Lee, E. B. (1988). An influential ghost: The institute for propaganda analysis. *Propaganda Review, 3*, 10 14.

Lippmann, W. (1922). *Public opinion*. New York: Macmillan.

Livingston, H. (1966, June). Can the effects of general semantics be measured? *Etcetera, 23*, 254–258.

MacDonald, J. F. (1989). Propaganda and order in modern society, in T. J. Smith III (Ed.), *Propaganda: A pluralistic perspective*. New York: Praeger, pp. 23–35.

Martin, E. D. (1929). Our invisible masters. *Forum, 81*, 142–145.

Martin, L. J. (1958). *International propaganda: Its legal and diplomatic control*. Minneapolis: University of Minnesota Press.

Merrill, J. C. (1997). *Journalism ethics: Philosophical foundations for news media*. New York: St. Martin's Press.

Merrill, J. C., & Lowenstein, R. L. (1971). *Media, messages, and men: new perspectives in communication*. New York: David McKay.

Penny, L. (2005). *Your call is important to us: The truth about BULLSHIT*. New York: Crown.

Petrecca, L. (2006, Sept. 11). Authors strike deals to squeeze in a few brand names. *USA Today*, 8B.

Pratkanis, A. & Aronson, E. (1992). *Age of propaganda: The everyday use and abuse of persuasion*. New York: W. H. Freeman.

Qualter, T. H. (1962). *Propaganda and psychological warfare*. New York: Random House.

Ralph, R. S. (1972, March). Measuring effects of general semantics on personality adjustment in elementary school. *Etcetera, 29*, 13–19.

Rich, M. (2006, June 12). Product placement deals make leap from film to books. *The New York Times*. Accessed 25 February, 2007 from nytimes.com.

Ritch, F. (2006). *The greatest story ever sold: The decline and fall of truth from 9/11 to Katrina*. New York: Penguin Press.

Rokeach, M. (1954). The nature and meaning of dogmatism. *Psychological Review, 61*, 194–206.

Rokeach, M. (1960). *The open and closed mind: Investigations into the nature of belief systems and personality systems*. New York: Basic Books.

Rokeach, M. (1964, September). Images of the consumer's mind on and off Madison Avenue. *Etcetera, 31*, 264–273.

Seldes, G. (1957). *The new mass media: Challenge to a free society*. Washington, D.C.: American Association of University Women.

Shanker, T. (2006, March 22). No breach seen in work in Iraq on propaganda. *New York Times*.

Smith, T. J. III (Ed.) (1989). *Propaganda: A pluralistic perspective*. New York: Praeger.

Solomon, N. (2005). *War made easy: How presidents and pundits keep spinning us to death*. Hoboken, NJ: John Wiley.

Snow, N. (2003). *Information war*. New York: Seven Stories Press.

Sproule, J. M. (1989). Social responses to twentieth-century propaganda, in T. D. Smith (Ed.), *Propaganda: A pluralistic perspective*. New York: Praeger, pp. 5–22.

Sproule, J. M. (1997). *Propaganda and democracy: The American experience of media and mass persuasion*. Cambridge, UK: Cambridge University Press.

Steele, H. C. (1972, March). Assessing intelligence: Some semantic implications. *Etcetera, 29*, 21–26.

SourceWatch (2006, August 28). Product placement. Accessed 24 February 2007 at http://www.sourcewatch.org/index.php?title=Product_placement

Taylor, P. M. (2003). *Munitions of the mind: A history of propaganda from the ancient world to the present day,* 3rd ed. Manchester: Manchester University Press.

Techdirt (2007, February 21). Product placement or a novel? Does it make a difference? Accessed 26 February 2007 from http://techdirt.com/articles/20070220/163903.shtml

True, S. (1966, Spring). A study of the relation of general semantics and creativity. *The Journal of Experimental Education, 24*, 34–40.

Turow, J. (2006, August 27). Hidden messages: Is new technology empowering consumers—or marketers? *The Boston Globe*, http://www.boston.com

Vacchiano, R. B., Strauss, P. S., & Hochman, L. (1969, December). The open and closed mind: A review of dogmatism. *Psychological Bulletin 71*, 261–273.

Wasserman, E. (2006, April 3). All the propaganda that's fit to print. *The Miami Herald Herald.com*: http://www.miami.com

Weaver, E. H. (1949). An approach to language behavior from the point of view of general semantics. Unpublished PhD dissertation, Northwestern University.

Westover, L. M. (1959). A study of the semantic orientation of inexperienced and experienced public speakers. Unpublished PhD dissertation, University of Denver.

Weiss, T. N. (1959). The construction and validation of an "Is of Identity" test. *General Semantics Bulletin, 24–25.,* 69–80.

Wreford, R. J. R. G. (1923). Propaganda, evil and good. *The Nineteenth Century and After, 92,* 514–524.

Wright, C. R. (1959). *Mass communications: A sociological perspective.* New York: Random House.

# 11

# Perspectives on Pornography Demand Ethical Critique

## Wendy Wyatt and Kris E. Bunton

It takes no more than a cursory review of the literature on pornography to discover the very deep divides that permeate attitudes about the practice. Scholarship on pornography from the political, psychological, sociological, legal, economic, religious, and, of course, ethical traditions reveal that pornography has been hotly contested for years, and the debate shows little sign of ending. Like other disputed issues, most perspectives on pornography have come to represent one of two polarized positions: the strident anti-porn view and the equally strident anti-censorship view.

Part I of this chapter examines the state of scholarship on pornography framed around the two polarized perspectives. First, we include a discussion of the competing views, and we lay out various definitions of pornography for consideration. (None of those definitions includes child pornography, which we believe is beyond the justification of any moral system and which has long been deemed illegal and thus excluded from any constitutional protections for expression.) We also summarize the actions and reactions that each side has pursued to further its agenda. We then turn to a critique of the current framing and raise issues that we believe need to be considered in any discussion of pornography's ethical implications.

## THE POLARIZATION OF PORNOGRAPHY

### Anti-Pornography Activists and the Call for Legal Remedies

The anti-pornography position, also called the absolutist position, began developing in the 1970s when anti-pornography feminists formed an unlikely partnership with moral conservatives to work toward a common cause: increasing prosecutions under existing obscenity laws and introducing new laws against pornography. For moral conservatives, pornography threatens "the family and the moral fabric of society" (Berger, Searles, & Cottle, 1991, p. 1). Anti-pornography feminists, on the other hand, claim that pornography reifies the traditional gender order and causes harm to women.

In the 1980s, as the gender order in the real world was being challenged but representations of that order via pornography remained stagnant, the feminist emphasis on pornography became axiomatic (Hardy, 2000). From the anti-pornography perspective, this emphasis can be illustrated through three events. The first represents the views of anti-pornography feminists; the second gives a nod to the feminist position but more than anything highlights the views of moral conservatives; and the third demonstrates that the two positions—while fundamentally different—have, in many instances, merged.

## Anti-Pornography Feminism

Central to the anti-pornography feminist perspective is the belief that pornography is a male discourse that helps naturalize hegemony, which is characteristic of women's oppression. According to anti-pornography feminists, the primary social sphere of male power resides in the area of sexuality (MacKinnon, 1982), and so "the ways and means of pornography are the ways and means of male power" (Dworkin, 1981, p. 24). Women, on the other hand, are victims, the "objects" of a cycle of abuse that has pornography at its center.

For anti-pornography feminists, pornography is not only a form of misogyny and coercive sexuality, it is a system of sexual exploitation and female sexual slavery and a method of socialization that causes and perpetuates acts of violence against women. Pornography does nothing less than define who women are based on the way men see them (Berger, Searles, & Cottle, 1991). These forms, systems, and methods that help us define "woman" exist not only as fantasy or a mere idea, but rather as sexual reality; anti-pornography feminists claim that pornography is "a concrete, discriminatory social practice that institutionalizes the inferiority and subordination" of women to men (p. 37). The representational practices of pornography, therefore, become indistinguishable from actual sexual practices, and gender power imbalances are further naturalized.

In the 1970s, anti-pornography feminists formed groups such as the San Francisco-based Women Against Violence in Pornography (1976) and the New York-based Women Against Pornography (1978), both of which organized local demonstrations and protests. But their cause gained national exposure in 1983 when Andrea Dworkin and Catharine MacKinnon introduced an anti-pornography civil rights ordinance in Minneapolis. Until that time, pornography was legislated only if it met the definition of obscenity as set forth by U.S. Supreme Court Chief Justice Warren Burger in the 1973 *Miller v. California* ruling. This obscenity test had three conditions:

> (1) whether the average person, applying contemporary community standards would find that the work, taken as a whole, appeals to the prurient interest, (b) whether the work depicts or describes, in a patently offensive way, sexual conduct specifically defined by the applicable state law, and (c) whether the work, taken as whole, lacks serious literary, artistic, political, or scientific value. (Gunther, 1991, p. 1109)

For Dworkin and MacKinnon, obscenity laws did not suffice. Pornographic words and images were not only *about* subordination, they themselves *subordinated*. Whether or not they met the legal requirements of obscenity, pornographic words and images could have no value because they could not be used in non-derogatory ways (Tirell, 1999, p. 228). The proposed ordinance, therefore, defined pornography as a practice that discriminates against women, and it gave women the option of civil suit against those whose involvement with pornography caused them harm.

Under the ordinance, pornography was defined as "the graphic sexually explicit subordination of women, whether in pictures or in words, that also includes one or more of the following" (Gunther, 1991, p. 1127):

> (1) Women are presented as sexual objects who enjoy pain or humiliation; or (2) Women are presented as sexual objects who experience sexual pleasure in being raped; or (3) Women are presented as sexual objects tied up or cut up or mutilated or bruised or physically hurt, or as dis-

membered or truncated or fragmented or severed into body parts; or (4) Women are presented in scenarios of degradation, injury, abasement, torture, shown as filthy or inferior, bleeding, bruised, or hurt in a context that makes these conditions sexual; or (6) Women are presented as sexual objects for domination, conquest, violation, exploitation, possession, or use, or through postures or positions of servility or submission or display. (p. 1127)

The Minneapolis City Council twice passed the ordinance, and the mayor twice vetoed it. In 1984, a similar ordinance was introduced in Indianapolis. This time, the ordinance did pass at the city level but soon after was declared unconstitutional in Federal District Court and reaffirmed as unconstitutional on appeal in the Seventh Circuit Court of Appeals and then in the U.S. Supreme Court (Berger, Searles, & Cottle, 1991).

The justification Indianapolis offered for passing the ordinance—and a premise the appellate court accepted even while striking down the ordinance—was the claim that pornography *affects* peoples' thoughts and actions. People often act in accordance with words and images to which they are exposed. Men who see women depicted as subordinate are more likely to believe these women are subordinate and treat them as such (Gunther, 1991, p. 1129).

## ANTI-PORNOGRAPHY MORAL CONSERVATIVES

The "harmful effects" argument used by anti-pornography feminists is also one familiar to moral conservatives. In fact, this group put pornography's harmful effects front and center during hearings for the 1986 Attorney General's Commission on Pornography, more commonly known as the Meese Commission. But for moral conservatives, the harm of pornography is not the subordination of women but pornography's potential for causing sexual lust and sexual acts that lead to the disintegration of society's established institutions, particularly those of marriage and family.

President Ronald Reagan established the commission, and Attorney General Edwin Meese appointed its 11 members, seven of whom had taken previous public stands against pornography. The commission's official charter was to "determine the nature, extent, and impact on society of pornography in the United States, and to make specific recommendations to the Attorney General concerning more effective ways in which the spread of pornography could be contained, consistent with constitutional guarantees" (Attorney General's Commission on Pornography, Final Report, 1986, p. ix).

This was not the first commission to investigate such issues. In 1970, the Commission on Obscenity and Pornography concluded that no anti-social effects resulted from pornography. However, following the release of the 1970 report, the U.S. Senate passed a resolution condemning it, and President Richard Nixon warned about permissive attitudes toward pornography, claiming they would threaten our social order and moral principles (Kendrick, 1987, p. 219).

During 14 months in 1985 and 1986, the Meese Commission brought forth scores of witnesses to testify in more than 300 hours of public hearings and business meetings. Most heavily represented among the witnesses were law enforcement officers and spokespeople from conservative anti-pornography groups, but social scientists, representatives of the anti-pornography feminist position, and a handful of civil libertarians and anti-censorship feminists were also given an opportunity to speak. Although the traditional religious-conservative view of pornography dominated the beliefs of most of the 11 commissioners, members also attempted to draw on feminist discourse and social science research in order to "modernize" their own moralistically based anti-pornography position (Vance, 1986).

The Meese Commission's goal in looking to social science research was to refute the research cited by the 1970 commission, and in some ways it did. At the end of the section on "Social and

Behavioral Science Research Analysis" in the Meese Commission's final report comes a brief subsection titled "An Integration of the Research Findings." The subsection states:

> It is clear that the conclusion of "no negative effects" advanced by the 1970 Commission is no longer tenable. It is also clear that catharsis, as an explanatory model for the impact of pornography, is simply unwarranted by evidence in this area, nor has catharsis fared well in the general area of mass media effects and anti-social behavior.
> This is not to say, however, that the evidence as a whole is comprehensive enough or definitive enough. While we have learned much more since 1970, even more areas remain to be explored. (Attorney General's Commission, Final Report on Pornography, p. 289)

The Meese commissioners were unable to agree on a definition of pornography, but they did identify four classes of sexually explicit images: (1) images that are violent; (2) images that are not violent but degrading; (3) images that are not violent and not degrading; and (4) images that portray nudity but are not sexually explicit. According to the commissioners, existing social science evidence showed clear negative effects with the first two classes of images (Berger, Searles, & Cottle, 1991).

The second modernizing perspective—feminist discourse—became the one from which the commission eventually drew most heavily. However, this discourse came not from well-known anti-pornography feminists such as Dworkin, but rather from anecdotal evidence provided by "victims of pornography." One of the commission's most famous victims was Linda Marchiano (formerly Linda Lovelace of the movie *Deep Throat*), who testified about the "sexual coercion and moral decadence" pervasive in the pornography industry (Berger, Searles, & Cottle, 1991, p. 26). These stories ended up trumping the arguments of Dworkin and other anti-pornography feminists who had always argued against obscenity laws, claiming they reflected "a moralistic and anti-sexual tradition which could only harm women" (Vance, 1993, p. 37). Given the commission's conservative constituency and agenda, it would never attack obscenity laws. Therefore, while the commission "happily assimilated the rhetoric of anti-pornography feminists, it decisively rejected their remedies" (p. 37).

The commission's nearly 2,000-page final report claimed that the pre-eminent harms caused by porn were not sin and immorality, but rather violence—violence to women, to men, to children, to homosexuals, to marriage, and to families. The commission gave 92 recommendations for increased enforcement of obscenity laws as well as the passage of new laws (Vance, 1993). The commission also called for local citizen action groups to "canvass local bookstores and newsstands for offensive items, report [them] to the police, monitor prosecutions and sentencing, and organize demonstrations and boycotts" (Vance, 1986, p. 81).

## The Melding of Anti-Pornography Positions

At the end of the 1980s, the anti-pornography position had orchestrated two major efforts. The proposed civil rights ordinances represented the values of one group—anti-pornography feminists—while the Meese Commission largely symbolized the values of another—moral conservatives. Although the two groups began by proposing different tactics and opposing remedies, and even though their fundamental beliefs were poles apart, this unlikely duo continued to cross paths when the 1980s ended. In some cases, the tactics, remedies, and fundamental beliefs of the two groups became less distinct.

In 1992, for example, anti-pornography feminists were successful in temporarily shutting down an art exhibit about prostitution at the University of Michigan. The exhibit, which included several documentary films created by women, was commissioned as part of a conference titled

"Prostitution—From Academia to Activism" (Vance, 1993). While the conference was supposed to feature competing views, some participants from the anti-pornography perspective refused to participate if the exhibit stood.

What critics of the threatened boycott pointed out, however, is that much of the material in the films had esthetic, intellectual, and political merit; the films were decontextualized when they were called porn (Vance, 1993). The result was that the campaign of the anti-pornography feminists aligned with moral conservatives in their use of the term "pornography" to describe any material with sexual content or a theme the viewer could find objectionable (Vance, 1993). According to at least one anti-censorship feminist, the Michigan case "shatters the illusion that restricting sexual imagery for feminist purposes is distinguishable from fundamentalist censorship—either in method or consequence" (¶ 21).

## ANTI-CENSORSHIP ACTIVISTS AND THE ARGUMENT FOR RESIGNIFICATION

If the anti-pornography position emerged as a response to pornography and its harms, anti-censorship groups such as the Anti-Sexism Campaign and Feminists Against Censorship formed largely as a response to anti-pornography activism. Although the anti-censorship perspective has not garnered as much public attention and media coverage as the anti-pornography position, according to some scholars, it tends to hold higher academic ground (Hardy, 2000). This anti-censorship position includes both anti-censorship feminists and civil libertarians, and it puts forth two primary arguments: pornography has potential benefits, and censorship has real harms.

Civil libertarians flatly reject regulation of pornography as illegal and unethical infringement by government or pressure groups. The American Civil Liberties Union states, "Censorship, the suppression of words, images, or ideas that are 'offensive,' happens whenever some people succeed in imposing their personal political or moral values on others" (ACLU, ¶ 1). The ACLU bases its rejection of censorship on two fundamental principles in First Amendment law. First is content neutrality, which holds that government cannot censor expression merely because it offends. "In the context of art and entertainment, this means tolerating some works that we might find offensive, insulting, outrageous—or just plain bad" (ACLU, ¶ 5). The second principle is that of imminent harm. As the ACLU states, "Expression may be restricted only if it will clearly cause direct and imminent harm to an important societal interest" (¶ 6). According to the ACLU's position, censorship of pornography must be rejected under this principle because "no causal link between exposure to sexually explicit material and anti-social or violent behavior has ever been scientifically established, in spite of many efforts to do so" (¶ 9).

The ACLU's president, Nadine Strossen, has gone so far as to suggest that feminists have a special obligation to reject censorship of pornography. Strossen suggests censorship of pornography is essentially paternalistic and harmful to women who earn their living as sex workers or who wish to explore their sexual identities. Further, she suggests censorship of pornography harms relatively powerless groups such as feminists and lesbians. "As is true for all relatively disempowered groups, women have a special stake in preserving our system of free expression. For those women who find certain 'pornographic' imagery troubling, their most effective weapon is to raise their voices and say so" (Strossen, 1994, p. 243).

The first response that anti-censorship feminists make to those who seek to restrict pornography is that women's victimization has been overemphasized. Most women, they say, would call most of their sexual experiences consensual (Berger, Searles, & Cottle, 1991). The problem is that sexually expressive women have come to be seen as victims of male propaganda and male violence. If women enjoy sex—and they don't hide it—they are viewed as expressing men's sexuality. Anti-censorship feminists are, therefore, fighting for women's freedom of sexual investigation and expression (Assiter & Carol, 1993).

What's more, anti-censorship feminists argue, simply removing words and images does nothing to change the larger culture. Questions ought to be asked about the roots of a culture that is so hostile to women. How, for example, did men achieve their symbolic power over women, and how can this be changed? For anti-censorship feminists, pornography is not violence and does not cause violence; instead, that violence is a symptom rather than a source of women's oppression (Hardy, 2000). Alison Assiter and Avedon Carol are two leading figures in the feminist anti-censorship movement who claimed that before anti-pornography activism began, "it would have seemed ludicrous to treat pornography or sadomasochism as anything other than, at worst, mere symptoms of sexist culture, and sheer time-wasting to attack those supposed symptoms while leaving the causal foundations of sexism unremarked" (Assiter & Carol, 1993, p. 8). Yet, they maintain, this is exactly what the anti-pornography movement has done.

What's needed, then, is "free and unfettered erotic expression" because that expression is the "best means for the diverse transformation of the hegemonic form" (Hardy, 2000, p. 79). Pornography, anti-censorship feminists maintain, can serve as a tool of discourse.

> It is only because censorship was reduced and the language of sexuality became a common part of our ordinary lives that we were able to spread the word on sexual issues, publish the insights of our own consciousness-raising groups, read women's own descriptions of the parts of our bodies that polite society kept hidden and secret, and begin to understand the extent to which the sex dualism had robbed us. (Assiter & Carol, 1993, p. 4)

The attitude that derogatory words and images may have some redeeming value has led anti-censorship feminists to be described as reclaimers. Pornography, they say, can be reclaimed, resignified, and, in turn, given liberating—rather than subordinating—power (Tirrell, 1999).

This liberating power has already been demonstrated by some of the new forms of pornographic expression produced by women. The Black Lace series of "domesticated porn" is one example of a product line written by women and marketed to women, although critics point out that the owners are still men (Ciclitira, 2004). Other companies, however, are owned and run by women. Former pornography star Candida Royalle formed Femme Productions, and her plot-oriented films featuring portrayals of older women, mothers, and married couples provide "an emotional context and motivation for sex" (Berger, Searles, & Cottle, 1991, p. 45). Pornography from a woman's perspective can also be found on Internet sites run by women for women and in the growing selection of lesbian pornography, which features women writers, producers, and directors. The idea behind all these endeavors is that "porn does not always perpetuate male power over female bodies" (Ong, 2005, ¶ 8). And these new forms of pornography, along with the more "traditional" materials, are not turning women away. In the United States, for example, women buy an estimated 40 percent of adult videos (Gibson, 2004, p. 60).

Another benefit of pornography relates to our need for fantasy. Many anti-censorship feminists tend to subscribe to a psychoanalytic theory of pornography as fantasy, a fantasy that is otherwise denied cultural expression (Hardy, 2000). Lynne Segal, for instance, claims that relations of domination and submission connect to oedipal and pre-oedipal desires, and "psychoanalytic readings suggest a way of understanding the bizarrely 'pornographic nature of our fantasy life'" (Segal cited in Hardy, 2000, p. 85). This focus on pornography as fantasy that emerges from psychic forces has been "expedient" for anti-censorship feminists because it makes the "erotic preoccupation with power seem less threatening and politically problematic" (Hardy, 2000, p. 85). Critics of this view, not surprisingly, argue that taking refuge in a purely psychoanalytic account ignores compelling cultural issues.

Finally, a key critique by anti-censorship feminists of those who advocate restrictions is that the harms of censorship are far worse than the harms of pornography. While anti-pornography feminists (but not necessarily moral conservatives) want to make a distinction between objectionable pornography and acceptable erotica, it is impossible, anti-censorship feminists argue, to define where to draw the line. That line, therefore, becomes arbitrary, and moralistic prudery often prevails. What the distinction usually amounts to is something like Ellen Wills' sarcastic description: "What I like is erotica, and what you like is pornographic" (Wills cited in Assiter and Carol, 1993, p. 28). With definitions as flexible as this, anti-censorship feminists warn that even sex education materials could be deemed pornographic and therefore restricted. What's more, anti-censorship feminists such as Judith Butler argue that censorship further marginalizes those who are already marginalized (Hardy, 2000). The anti-pornography position shows an indifference to class privilege and a lack of concern for sex workers.

In the end, anti-censorship feminists and civil libertarians claim that their anti-pornography counterparts reject the interpretive schemes that demonstrate the complexity and ambiguity of sexually explicit images as well as viewer responses (Vance 1993). In response, anti-pornography feminists and moral conservatives question how people who claim a feminist position and concern for the plight of women can be so reluctant to criticize a practice that clearly produces harm.

## AN ETHICAL CRITIQUE OF PORNOGRAPHY

### The Problem with Polarization

For more than 30 years, two diametrically opposed positions on pornography have almost entirely controlled the discourse about it. Anti-pornography feminists and moral conservatives act to regulate pornography, and anti-censorship feminists and civil libertarians then react. The debate has assumed an almost circular identity as the same arguments surface and resurface time and time again.

The opposing positions of the moral conservatives and civil libertarians are relatively clear, and the roots of both positions can be traced to unambiguous foundational ideas. However, the arguments presented by feminists are messier; each side of the pornography debate has appropriated the idea of "feminism" to help make its case. This made the debate within feminism highly politicized—so politicized, in fact, that Carol Clover called pornography "the feminist issue" of the 1990s (Gibson & Gibson, 1993, p. 1). In more aggressive terms, Assiter and Carol called the debate within feminism a "sexual battlefield" (1993, p. vii).

Arguments presented by anti-pornography feminists and anti-censorship feminists are clearly important, and when analyzing the landscape of the pornography debate, both positions deserve commendation as well as criticism. Anti-pornography feminists—along with their moral conservative partners—recognize and speak against a practice that has distinct potential for harm and one that has helped perpetuate the hegemonic order. But their proposed remedies fail to address the culture of hostility toward women and often end up actually attacking women. On the other hand, anti-censorship feminists—together with civil libertarians—recognize that our culture, rather than pornography, is the source of women's oppression, and they are cognizant of the real harms of censorship. But in making their arguments, anti-censorship advocates appear unwilling to offer any critique of hegemonic heterosexual eroticism; in making their claims for resignification, they fail to speak to the *signification* and the harms produced by pornographic images and texts.

Anyone with an interest in the ethics of pornography will come across much from the two polarized positions before ever discovering the voices that argue for something beyond—or perhaps between—the strident positions of the anti-pornography and anti-censorship activists. When these voices do emerge, however, they make an important point: The polarized camps' attempts to advance their own arguments ignore complexity in the issues surrounding pornography.

The first complication involves people—particularly women—who are conflicted about pornography. The same women can both defend pornography based on personal pleasure and criticize it based on political ideas. Likewise, some women may use pornography as a tool to explore their sexuality but resist being complicit in it. In a series of semi-structured interviews conducted by British psychologist Karen Ciclitira in 2004, women reported that the negative politicization of pornography exacerbated "guilt, shame and confusion about their own sexuality" (Ciclitara, 2004, p. 297). One of Ciclitira's subjects described the conflict like this:

> I have this real porn dilemma, which is probably why I've never been into it in a big way anyway, because half of me wants to look and um explore and desire and, and go as far as I can go, an and another half of me is *very* aware that the people who *make* those kinds of images films, or whatever, are maybe *not* doing it out of a *free* choice, an I and I know, I'd like to think that I am aware of that, and so because I don't want to support an industry that is you know er abusing people, then I don't want pornography, but because I want to explore my own sexuality, I want to reassure myself about my own sexuality. I want to explore my own potential then, I do want it. So I have this kind of half of me does and half of me doesn't thing, the whole time I'm, I'm watching it.... (p. 292–293, emphasis in original)

Just as many women have come to believe that enjoying pornography and being a feminist are incompatible, the same can be said about men who enjoy pornography but are committed to an egalitarian relationship with a female partner. The men are apt to either reject pornography because of its symbolic subordination of women or retain it as a guilty secret. This conflict over pornography has led both women and men to believe they must choose between their erotic pleasures and their ethical commitments (Hardy, 2000).

A second complication involves social scientific effects research. Both anti-pornography and anti-censorship feminists make claims to it, but, in fact, the findings cannot be completely allied with either camp. The bulk of social science research into pornography has been conducted in experimental settings and has focused on men's attitudes and behaviors. It has also tended to favor a distinction between strictly sexually explicit materials and materials that combine sexual themes with violence or degradation toward women (Scott, 2004, p. 295). A leading scholar in the study of pornography's effects, Daniel Linz, said if we know anything about antisocial behaviors that stem from exposure to pornography, it is that "1) for the average person, the message of violence as pleasurable to the woman must be present for negative effects to occur; and 2) for other forms of pornography, the effects are an interaction between personality characteristics and exposure" (Linz, 2004, ¶ 13).

A seminal study by Linz, Edward Donnerstein, and Steven Penrod (1984) involved showing male college students films that were either sexually explicit, sexually explicit and violent, or not sexually explicit but violent. The study concluded that the men who viewed films that were only sexually explicit showed no negative effects. Conversely, men who saw films depicting violence toward women in a sexual context—whether the films were sexually explicit or not—viewed women as significantly less worthy as people. Britain Scott (in press) noted that other experiments involving men have yielded similar findings.

> Exposure to sexually violent material increases men's sexual callousness toward women and lowers their support of sexual equality (e.g. Zillmann and Bryant, 1982), desensitizes men to violence

against women and increases men's acceptance of rape myths such as "all women secretly want to be raped" (e.g., Malamuth & Check, 1981), and increases aggression toward women in the laboratory. (e.g., Donnerstein & Berkowitz, 1981)

Similar negative effects have been found for men's exposure to degrading material—that which contains male dominance, female availability, penis worship, female insatiability, or objectification of women (Scott, 2004). Again, however, material that is sexually explicit but nondegrading has not led to the same negative attitudes and behaviors. Once research moves out of the laboratory, the effects of sexually explicit materials are "almost certainly a joint function of the personality characteristics of the individual who seeks out such materials and of exposure to such materials per se" (Linz, 2004, ¶ 15). Beyond pornography use, factors such as family violence, delinquency, attitudes supporting violence, sexual promiscuity, and hostile masculinity can all correlate with sexual aggression against women (Malamuth, Addison, & Koss, 2000).

Most psychological research on pornography focuses on men's responses to material designed for men. In recognizing the limits of this approach and responding to the growth of sexually explicit material geared toward women, some researchers such as Ciclitara have begun to investigate women's responses to pornography. Scholars have included women participants in experimental studies and have collected women's accounts of their experiences with pornography. Experimental research on women and pornography shows that women tend to respond more positively to sexually explicit material made for them than materials designed for men. When that material includes violent or degrading words or images, women respond less positively. The experimental research, however, "does not have much to say about how pornography might directly harm women" (Scott, in press).

Moving beyond the laboratory, accounts of battered women's experiences with pornography show that "pornography is associated with many cases of sexual violence and that from the perspective of these women, pornography suggested ways to harm the women as was, itself, part of the harm inflicted upon them" (Scott, 2004, p. 300). Women in non-abusive relationships have also talked about their experiences with pornography, explaining that their partners' use of pornography has affected their views of their partner, of their relationship, and of their self-esteem and sexual desirability (Scott, in press).

What does the effects research mean for the anti-pornography versus anti-censorship argument? Anti-pornography feminists habitually point to a causal relationship between pornography and violent behavior, but they run the risk of overstating the argument. Although pornography can be associated with violence, the causal link has not been established. What's more, a good deal of sexually explicit material is neither violent nor degrading and cannot be connected to violent behavior. Conversely, anti-censorship feminists readily point to the dubiousness of studies conducted in artificial settings and the lack of definitive effects. Likewise, they note that recent studies have exonerated non-violent pornography and that research should explore material in the media that is violent but not sexual, which anti-censorship feminists claim is a much greater problem with more substantiating evidence.

## AN ALTERNATIVE APPROACH

With problems evident in the two polarized positions on pornography, perhaps it is time to put more effort into seeking voices that call for a different response and introduce alternative views. One voice already circulating is that of British sociologist Simon Hardy (2000), who has called for an ethical critique of pornography that works within rather than against eroticism. Hardy recognizes the need for critique that is so evident in the anti-pornography position but also the commitment to and desire for expression that comes out strongly in the anti-censorship view. In developing his critique, Hardy looks to the work of Anthony Giddens and his claim that in our times, the realm of intimacy has been transformed into a site of moral and political negotiation where sexuality plays a special role in the ongoing reformation of gender relations and self-identities. The social structural domain of gender where principles of equality are generally upheld operates in stark contrast to the symbolic domain of the erotic where representations have been associated with a particular form of hegemonic heterosexuality in which the power of men over women is "tirelessly presented as the natural condition of heterosexual pleasure" (Hardy, 2004, p. 88). Hardy argues that, in theory, eroticism could be used "to bind fast *any* configuration of gender: conventional or unconventional, symmetrical or asymmetrical," but until new ways of representing heterosexuality emerge, many are "forced in a real sense to choose between erotic pleasures and ethical commitments" (pp. 88–89).

For Hardy, the "revolution which is elsewhere transforming gender relations" needs to move into the erotic realm and fill the gaps between the real hegemonic practice of current erotica and the ideal version of egalitarian erotic discourse (p. 89). This would be an eroticism that exults love of equals; it would naturalize and help institute a counter-hegemonic heterosexuality founded on the modern principle of equality. This is resignification with a critical eye; it shares the commitment to expression that the anti-censorship position champions but brings with it the skeptical perspective of the anti-pornography position. Here skepticism of eroticism is retained "even as we engage with it and in it" (p. 92).

## CONSIDERATIONS FOR AN ETHICAL CRITIQUE

Hardy's approach to pornography—one that allows for erotic expression but also employs strategies of critique—is, in our minds, a more ethically defensible approach than either the unyielding anti-pornography or anti-censorship positions. Legal remedies are not the answer. In addition to serving as only Band-Aids that cover up symptoms but fail to treat the disease, legal remedies could never draw a clear line between acceptable erotica and unacceptable pornography. What's more, texts and images that are not sexually explicit per se but contain themes of sexual degradation or sexualized violence have begun flooding the media. The "everyday pornography" on network television—think *Law & Order: Special Victims Unit*—contains texts and images that are allowed on the public airwaves but that fit many criteria shown by social scientists to be associated with troubling attitudes and behaviors by those who consume them.

If pornography is to remain within legal bounds, however, it must not go uncriticized. Incorporated into an ethical critique should be several considerations. First, the critique must refuse to politicize the literature on effects; the social scientific research must be seen for what it is. As research on Internet pornography use begins to emerge, this imperative becomes even more important. While it is certainly clear that the Web has introduced a brand new medium for pornography—one with a global reach and one that certainly raises new questions about the potential harms of pornography—the temptation to exaggerate or take out of context effects of viewing Internet pornography must be resisted. Consider, for instance, this testimony given in November 2004 by Dr. Judith Reisman, president of the Institute for Media Education, before a U.S. Senate subcommittee on the science behind pornography addiction.

> Thanks to the latest advances in neuroscience, we now know that pornographic visual images imprint and alter the brain, triggering an instant, involuntary, but lasting, biochemical memory trail, arguably, subverting the First Amendment by overriding the cognitive speech process. This is true

of so-called "soft-core" and "hard-core" pornography. And once new neurochemical pathways are established they are difficult or impossible to delete. (Reisman, 2004, ¶ 2)

In response to Reisman's claim that "media erotic fantasies become deeply imbedded, commonly coarsening, confusing, motivating and addicting many of those exposed" (¶ 3), Daniel Linz argued that, in fact, many powerful images leave strong memory traces, and Reisman's claim that pornography is somehow unique is without credible evidence. Linz added that the notions of pornography addiction generally and online sex addiction in particular are "highly questionable to most scientists" (Linz, 2004, ¶ 5).

In addition to representing the social scientific research fairly, an ethical critique of pornography should also encourage more research on the variety of reactions that both heterosexual and lesbian women of all classes, races, and ages may have to pornography produced by both men and women. As research continues to move out of the artificial conditions of the laboratory and becomes more inclusive of women's perspectives, a more sophisticated understanding of the nuances behind the use of pornography should emerge that will better inform the critique.

Beyond taking into account how social scientific research informs our thinking about pornography, an ethical critique must consider new questions and challenges introduced by technological innovations. Emerging technologies have led not only to the global phenomenon of Internet pornography, but to the ability to digitally manipulate or even digitally create it. Does it matter, for instance, if someone or something portrayed in a pornographic image isn't real?

The business of pornography is another important topic for consideration. While pornographic content has received much attention, an ethical critique must be all-encompassing; it must address the entire process from writing and production to marketing and distribution. Germaine Greer has argued that pornography has nothing to do with freedom to express images; it is, rather, a business that "uses and abuses those who provide the imagery but also the fantasy-ridden sub-potent public, mostly male, that pays for its product" (Greer cited in Ciclitara, 2004, p. 298). While the analysis may not work in all instances, the condemnation is worthy of reflection.

The proliferation of everyday pornography was mentioned earlier as a challenge to instituting legal limits, but it is worth mentioning again under the umbrella of an ethical critique. We are now seeing an increasingly brazen pushing of the boundaries in media that are not considered traditional homes for pornography. The most obvious example is network television, where dramas routinely feature plots that focus on sexual deviance and violence toward women. *Playboy* magazine may be stocked behind the counter at the local convenience store, but *CSI: Crime Scene Investigation* is available on broadcast network TV for all to see. Advertisements in women's and men's magazines also include sexist, degrading, and even violent images of women. Although they may not be sexually explicit, the messages of these shows and advertisements can raise as many questions as more traditional pornographic materials do. Any ethical critique must include in its domain the everyday pornography we so often encounter.

It's clear that most of the concern about pornography centers around the treatment of women by men. Anti-pornography feminists speak of the subordination of women through pictures and words, and anti-censorship feminists respond that these derogatory images and words can and should be reclaimed. Neither group would refute that many pornographic texts are misogynous. But what about words and images that degrade men? Sadomasochistic books and videos—one of pornography's most popular genres—feature plots in which females are dominant, in which "men perform as objects, or as virtual sex slaves to women" (Assiter & Carol, 1993). Here the tables are turned, and the message becomes not one of misogyny but misandry. An ethical critique of pornography must take into account the instances where hate is inflicted by women onto men.

Finally, an ethical critique must raise the question of whether the meaning of pornography changes if its texts are co-defined by men and women together. Feminists on both sides of the pornography debate would agree that the primary social sphere of male power now resides in the area of sexuality. Does *pornography* become simply *erotica* when the hegemonic nature of the texts' production and content becomes a more egalitarian, relational enterprise?

In the end, it may be impossible to convince either moral conservatives or civil libertarians of the merits of an approach to pornography that allows for expression but also mandates critique. But for the feminists, perhaps there is hope. Within the rhetoric of both anti-pornography and anti-censorship feminists are important concerns that deserve to be heeded, and only a willingness from both sides to hear the claims of the other can bring with it an opportunity to both respect women and leave room for erotic pleasure.

## REFERENCES

ACLU (American Civil Liberties Union). What is censorship? <www.aclu.org/freespeech/censorship/26611res20060830.html> Retrieved October 26, 2006.

Assiter, A., and Carol, A. (1993). *Bad Girls and Dirty Pictures: The Challenge to Reclaim Feminism.* London: Pluto Press.

*Attorney General's Commission on Pornography, Final Report of the.* (1986). Nashville, TN: Rutledge Hill Press.

Berger, R. J., Searles, P., & Cottle, C. E. (Eds.). (1991). *Feminism and Pornography.* New York: Praeger.

Ciclitira, K. (2004). Pornography, women and feminism: Beyond pleasure and politics. *Sexualities, 7(3),* 281–301.

Donnerstein, E., & Berkowitz, L. (1981). Victim reactions in aggressive-erotic films as a factor in violence against women. *Journal of Personality and Social Psychology, 41,* 710–724.

Dworkin, A. (1981). *Pornography: Men Possessing Women.* New York: Perigee.

Gibson, P. C. (Ed.). (2004). *More Dirty Looks: Gender, Pornography and Power.* London: British Film Institute.

Gibson, P. C., & Gibson, R. (Eds.). (1993). *Dirty Looks: Women, Pornography and Power.* London: British Film Institute.

Gunther, G. (1991). *Constitutional Law* (12th ed.). Westbury, NY: The Foundation Press.

Hardy, S. (2000). Feminist iconoclasm and the problem of eroticism. *Sexualities 3(1),* 77–96.

Kendrick, W. (1987). *The Secret Museum: Pornography in Modern Culture.* New York: Viking Press.

Linz, D. (2004). Response to Testimony before the United States Senate, Subcommittee on Science, Technology, and Space of the Committee on Commerce, Science and Transportation on The Science Behind Pornography Addiction. <www.freespeechcoalition.com/dan_linz.htm> Retrieved October 19, 2006.

Linz, D., Donnerstein, E., & Penrod, S. (1984). The effects of long-term exposure to filmed violence against women. *Journal of Communication, 34,* 130–147.

MacKinnon, C. (1982). Feminism, Marxism, method, and the state: An agenda for theory. *Signs, 7,* 515–544.

Malamuth, N. M., Addison, T., & Koss, M. (2000). Pornography and sexual aggression: Are there reliable effects? *Annual Review of Sex Research, 11,* 26–91.

Malamuth, N. M., & Check, J. V. P. (1981). The effects of mass media exposure on acceptance of violence against women: A field experiment. *Journal of Research in Personality, 15,* 436–446.

*Marvin Miller v. California,* 413 U.S. 15, 93 S.Ct. 2607, 37 L.Ed.2d 419, 1 Med.L.Rptr. 1441 (1973).

Ong, J. S. (2005). Parsing the perverse. Book review of *More Dirty Looks: Gender, Pornography and Power.* Available at <www.latrobe.edu.au/screeningthepast/reviews/rev_18/JObr18a.html> Retrieved August17, 2006.

Reisman, J. (November 18, 2004). Testimony before the Subcommittee on Science, Technology and Space of the Committee on Commerce, Science and Transportation on The Science Behind Pornography

Addiction. <http://commerce.senate.gov/hearings/testimony.cfm?id=1343&wit_id=3910> Retrieved October 19, 2006.

Scott, B. A. (2004) Women and pornography: What we don't know can hurt us. In J. C. Chrisler, C. Golden, & P. D. Rozee, (Eds.), *Lectures on the Psychology of Women* (3rd ed., pp. 292–309). Boston: McGraw-Hill.

Scott, B. A. (in press) Women and pornography: What we don't know can hurt us. In J. C. Chrisler, C. Golden, & P. D. Rozee, (Eds.), *Lectures on the Psychology of Women* (4th ed.). Boston: McGraw-Hill.

Strossen, N. (1994). A feminist critique of 'the' feminist critique of pornography. In D. E. Lively, D. E Roberts, & R. L. Weaver, (Eds.), *First Amendment Anthology* (pp. 235–243). Cincinnati, Ohio: Anderson Publishing. (Original work published 1993)

Tirrell, L. (1999). Pornographic subordination. In C. Card, (Ed.), *On Feminist Ethics and Politics* (pp. 226–243). Lawrence, KS: University Press of Kansas.

Vance, C. (1993). Feminist fundamentalism: Women against images. *Art in America 1(9)*, 35(4). Retrieved from InfoTrac OneFile, June 29, 2006.

Vance, C. (1986). The Meese Commission on the road. *The Nation, 243(3)*, 76–82.

Zillmann, D., & Bryant, J. (1982). Pornography, sexual callousness, and the trivialization of rape. *Journal of Communication, 32(4)*, 10–21.

# 12

# Violence

## Patrick Lee Plaisance

Shortly after Miramax released *Reservoir Dogs*, the modern-day gangster film debut by Quentin Tarantino, film critic Stanley Kauffmann published a self-reflective review describing the movie as being "crammed with murders." More interesting, however, was the acclaimed film critic's rumination on the use and prevalence of violence in movies today. The movie clearly made Kauffmann stop a moment and think about the effects of violent content on audiences. But his moment was fleeting, and his review remained stuck on relatively derivative questions of aesthetics—at one point, Kauffmann wondered whether Tarantino, Hollywood's latest star director, didn't simply make the film just because he could—whether *Reservoir Dogs* was produced "just for the sake of its making, the application of style to sheer slaughter."

"Adjustment to changing values is the prime law of the twentieth century," Kauffmann wrote, "but once in a while a film comes along that makes me imagine that everyone has a mental compass on the subject of violence and that I must tap mine to make sure it's not stuck" (1992, p. 31). It is both unsurprising and unfortunate that Kauffmann typed "mental compass" instead of "moral compass." Far be it from a prominent film critic to question or challenge the effects of such gratuitous bloodletting on moral grounds. Even his "tapping" seems to be understood as an exercise in righteous futility: Kauffmann never hints at what the compass actually tells him. The implication is that, in our violence-soaked media culture, only the gesture of conscience matters. Our considered response as moral agents, as long as we continue to watch, does not.

Many behavioral researchers and media ethicists, however, beg to differ. More than three decades of rigorous research has compellingly documented the negative effects of violent media content on certain populations and how exposure to such content appears to contribute to aggressive and antisocial behavior. And while free-speech and commercially driven interests tend to override others considerations in the public discourse, the field of ethics provides numerous ways not only to tap our moral compasses when it comes to violent media content, but to understand the resulting compass readings so that we can talk more compellingly about our obligations as moral beings in the media world. Clear ethical thinking about the nature of respect, duty, harm and accountability, as applied to both media consumers and producers, can help turn moral claims that strike many as unrealistic and ineffective into a more useful framework with which to critique violent media content. This chapter will provide a brief survey of the research documenting the effects of violent media content on audiences, discuss the nature of the potential "harm" posed by such content, and suggest ways to more effectively incorporate ethical theory into our responses to violence in the media.

## PATTERNS OF VIOLENT CONTENT

Policymakers, researchers, and politicians began expressing concern over the effects of violent television content in the 1950s. In the early 1970s, researchers estimated that by age of 14, the average child witnessed more than 11,000 murders on television (Bartholow, Dill, Anderson & Lindsay, 2003, p. 4). But a 1995 study showed that the average American child now witnesses more than 10,000 violent crimes *each year* on television (Signorielli, Gerbner & Morgan, 1995). This trend of ever-prevalent violent content continues despite pledges by industry groups to actively monitor and limit violent content. The Network Television Association vowed to do so in 1992. In 1993, the National Cable Television Association condemned the "gratuitous use of violence depicted as an easy and convenient solution to human problems" and vowed to "strive to reduce the frequency of such exploitative uses of violence" (Bartholow et al., 2003, p. 4). Regardless, levels of violent content have remained high. For prime-time programming, television audiences witness on average five violent acts per hour, and 20 times per hour on so-called children's programming (Strasburger & Wilson, 2002).

## VIOLENCE IN TELEVISION AND MOVIE ENTERTAINMENT

Violence is a staple of television and movie fare. But several studies of television violence have shown frequencies and levels of violent TV content to be quite stable over the last few decades— and in some cases even decreasing (Gerbner et al., 1994, as cited in Comstock & Scharrer, 1999, p. 66). But those frequencies—and several compelling contextual factors—are sobering. Overall, 57 percent of television programming features violent content. Of that, 73 percent contain scenes in which the violence is unpunished, 58 percent feature violence without showing any signs of pain, and 39 percent contain violent scenes that include humor (National Television Violence Study, 1996). Regarding what's on the local movie theater screen, violence dominates in a similar way. The percentage of PG-rated films that have come out of Hollywood has steadily declined. There is more violence in G-rated films than ever before (Yokota & Thompson, 2000).

## VIOLENCE IN VIDEO GAMES

The overwhelming majority of children play video games daily or weekly. About 15 percent of young men entering college play at least one hour of video games per day in an average week (Cooperative Institutional Research Program, 1999). In the early 1990s, one study found that 85 percent of the most popular video games were dominated by violent themes or content. Researchers also have found that such overwhelmingly violent games were the favorites of young children; in 1996, researchers reported that by far, large majorities of fourth-grade girls and boys said their favorite games were violent ones (Buchman & Funk, 1996).

## VIOLENCE IN NEWS

Crime is a staple of television news. According to Graber (1996), nearly half of all the news items covered in tabloid news magazine shows such as "Inside Edition" dealt with crime-related stories. On "Dateline NBC," "60 Minutes," and other similar network news shows, one of every four items is crime-related. Studies on television crime news over the last two decades have all shown the same pattern: Focus is consistently on crimes such as burglary and homicide instead of white-collar offenses, on crimes against people and less on those involving property; and most coverage is focused on initial stages of accusation and investigation and not on the later stages of prosecution and sentencing (Comstock & Scharrer, 1999, p. 126).

## EFFECTS OF VIOLENT CONTENT

Decades of experimental and survey research has painted a compelling picture of the negative effects of violent media content. In 1969, the National Commission on the Causes and Prevention of Violence concluded that "violence in television programs can and does have adverse effects upon audiences (cited in Bartholow et al., p. 4). In 1972, the report by the Surgeon General's Scientific Advisory Committee on Television and Social Behavior concluded that "there is a causative relationship between televised violence and subsequent antisocial behavior." Several credible organizations have gone on record over the last two decades in stating that media violence is one of the causes of aggression in society. These include the American Medical Association, the American Academy of Pediatrics, The American Psychological Association, the National Institute of Mental Health, the National Institutes of Health, and the American Academy of Child and Adolescent Psychiatry. In their survey of the research on effects of media violence, Sparks and Sparks (2002) concluded that "numerous reviews by researchers, professional associations and organizations all agree that exposure to media violence is causally related to aggressive behavior" (p. 273). Since 1977, at least eight "meta-analyses"—sophisticated statistical assessments that cluster different studies on the same topic to estimate the overall magnitude of relationships among variables—have been conducted with research projects that have examined questions of effects of violent media content. All of them

> make it irrefutably clear that children and teenagers who view greater amounts of violent television and movie portrayals are more likely to behave in an aggressive and antisocial manner.... This is an outcome that holds for all ages, both genders...and occurs across both experimental designs, where causation can be inferred, and nonexperimental survey designs, which produce data describing everyday occurrences. (Comstock & Scharrer, 2003, p. 207, 222)

In one notable study, researchers following the viewing patterns of children in the United States and four other countries established a strong relationship between children's level of viewing and their aggressive behavior (Huesmann & Eron, 1986). About 60 percent of the children were tracked down 15 years later. The result? According to Huesmann (2005):

> [The] children's exposure to media violence between ages 6 and 9 correlates significantly with a composite of 11 different kinds of measures of their aggression taken 15 years later when they were 21 to 25 years old.... [T]hese results certainly add credence to the conclusion that childhood exposure to violence in the media has lasting effects on behavior through a high-level process of imitation in which cognitions that control aggressive behavior are acquired. (pp. 262, 264)

Critics of media-effects research and apologists for the television industry often cite the apparently low "effect size" produced by these studies—the correlational statistic that reports what percentage of an overall effect (i.e., aggressive behavior) can be attributed with confidence to a certain stimulus (i.e., exposure to media violence). The effect size of the best studies and meta-analyses, however, are *higher* than that of other public-health research programs that have resulted in proactive policy decisions to protect certain populations from identified threats. These include exposure to lead and IQ scores among children, nicotine patch adoption and smoking cessation, calcium intake and bone mass, homework and academic achievement, and women's self-examination and extent of breast cancer (Comstock & Scharrer, 2003, p. 217; Bushman & Anderson, 2001, p. 481). A 2001 meta-analysis of research exploring the effects of violent video games also concluded that there is a correlation between video-game play and examples of aggressive behavior, but that the effect size is smaller than that found with television violence (Sherry, 2001).

Defenders of the television and movie industries also have long argued that violent content, instead of stimulating imitative acts and aggressive tendencies, actually provides a cathartic outlet. In one characteristic comment, legendary film director Alfred Hitchcock said, "One of television's greatest contributions is that it brought murder back into the home where it belongs. Seeing a murder on television can be good therapy. It can help work off one's antagonism" (Myers, 1999, p. 412). Extensive research, however, suggests that catharsis simply doesn't occur; there are dissenting views (Signorielli, 1990; Gunter, 1994), but the evidence "overwhelmingly shows that media violence has quite the opposite effect than that which is predicted by catharsis" (Strasburger & Wilson, 2003, p. 78).

Researchers have found that very different cognitive and behavior modeling processes help explain both short-term and long-term effects of violent content in increasing the likelihood of aggressive behavior.

## SHORT-TERM EFFECTS

*Priming* occurs when an observed stimulus serves to activate other neural activity that is associated with aggressive thoughts or behaviors. The excited "nodes" then may become more likely to influence behavior (Berkowitz, 1993). *Excitation transfer* refers to when, after a violent stimulus, a subsequent provocation may be perceived as more pronounced than it is because of the emotional response to the previous observed violence (Zillmann, 1983). *Imitation* refers to the natural tendency of children and young primates to imitate whomever they observe. The observation of specific aggressive behaviors around them increases the likelihood of children behaving in the same way (Bandura, 1977). Research by Berkowitz (1993) also suggests that children who have viewed a violent movie "are slower...to intervene" when they witness a fight erupting among other children (pp. 223–224).

## LONG-TERM EFFECTS

Children and young adults engage regularly in *observational learning* that can establish schemas about a hostile world, "scripts" for problem-solving that rely on aggression and general beliefs about the acceptability of aggression (Bushman & Huesmann, 2001). *Desensitization* occurs over repeated exposure to violence so that innate negative responses to observing violence are tempered through habituation, and proactive aggression can become more likely. The theory of *cultivation* argues that people who are heavy television viewers will "cultivate" a view of the world that is much more crime-ridden and violent than it actually is (Gerbner & Gross, 1976). Gerbner and his colleagues have referred to the resulting effect as the "mean world syndrome."

## APPLICATION OF ETHICS THEORY TO VIOLENT CONTENT

Violence is a serious ethical issue, Clifford Christians said, because "it violates the persons-as-ends principle" that constitutes the cornerstone of our moral obligations, according to Kant and other theorists (2004, p. 28). When we are clear about the legitimate reasons *why* types of violent content are so ubiquitous—whether as attention-getting techniques for largely commercial purposes or as valuable artistic depictions or honest efforts to reflect its occurrence in society—then we can minimize muddied thinking and self-validating ideological exchanges, and instead more effectively exercise our moral compass and bring to bear the full power of ethics.

## VIOLENCE: ARTISTIC CLAIMS

Violent content is defended and justified on artistic grounds when such depictions serve to help carry out an aesthetic vision of our world. Art helps us make meaning of our variegated existence. Violence is part of the natural and human realm. To reflexively denounce violent depictions as never justifiable stunts the aesthetic needs of all of us, threatens to sanitize reality, and reduces art to either an exercise in cheap sentimentalism or to a propagandistic tool: The fullness of the Aristotelian enterprise of the virtuous life is denied. From this perspective, one could say that the function of the artistic impulse, and the maintenance of its integrity, requires access to the brutal as much as it does to the divine. Our diverse moral sensibilities and prioritization of values, of course, mean that the boundary between artistic integrity and gratuitous gore is continually contested—hence the moralistic claims and the "mental compass" moments of Kauffmann and the rest of us over *Reservoir Dogs* and other provocations. If we keep in mind the deliberative essence of ethics, we see that it is in this debate that our Aristotelian selves live and breathe.

While a life of virtue implies an openness to life's rich pageant as we search for our zones of moderation and manifest our moral agency in social action, artistic integrity requires a Kantian imperative of freedom. Even in the context of the effects research surveyed above, a censor's impulse to limit or "cleanse" film and video depictions of violence can threaten to undermine the capacity for reason and the exercise of free will that all humans require. Our moral obligation to respect and cultivate both is central to Kant's system of moral agency.

## VIOLENCE: JOURNALISTIC CLAIMS

"If it bleeds, it leads." The cynical adage signals a key element of news, particularly for broadcast media. Stories featuring crime, suffering, tragic loss and shattered lives exploit our primal human impulses of surveillance and dramatic narrative. Stories involving violence rarely get old for journalists because they promise compelling verbal and visual images that never fail to draw and hold audiences, which translate into high ratings. Moreover, they are obligatory if journalism is to carry out one of its core functions of public service by representing the march of human events in all its dimensions. To sanitize reality by minimizing or marginalizing the presence and intensity of violence would be both hypocritical and paternalistic. Ignatieff (1997) and other theorists argue that modern forms of ethnic conflict, such as in Bosnia and Rwanda, demand that journalists become moral witnesses who must insist that such atrocities be given special attention. Yet most journalists are keenly aware of the fine distinction between unflinching reportage and rubbernecking voyeurism. How much violence and how much graphic gore is too much are questions that constantly dominate reporter and editor listservs and journalistic Websites. Characteristic was the debate among journalists around the world struggling to decide just how much to show of the brutal attacks on American security contractors in Fallujah, Iraq, in March 2004. Many news organizations relied on narrative descriptions of the charred bodies being dragged through the streets and strung up on bridges; video clips showing them never made it on the air at most broadcast outlets, and were relegated to websites that featured advisory warnings.

Readers and viewers also are served daily buffets of crime-related stories and stories focusing on violent aftermath because they so easily fit the twin journalistic imperatives of newsworthiness and expediency. In an environment of constant deadlines, journalists are often simply in a *reactive* mode, focusing and reporting on the latest *consequences* of decisions, acts and policies on various individuals or groups. Violent events are often the result of something—of a regional or ethnic conflict, of psychological and social disorders, of failed diplomatic efforts. Investigating the *causes* of violent outcomes is more difficult and often requires much more time and resources. Additionally, media sociologists also have shown that the news decisions of television news producers are often driven by "good visuals" (Abbott & Brassfield, 1989). Stories that come with compelling visuals and footage will get airtime; more difficult stories, which often do not lend themselves to visual storytelling (i.e., the Enron scandal) will either receive late or marginal attention or none at all. Crime news also is extremely cheap to produce; all that is required is a police scanner, a TV truck, and a camera. This insistence that all news be visual, as well as the fixation on consequences rather than on causes, constitutes two of the four distorting forces of television as a news medium, Ignatieff argues. The other two are television's "artificial constraints" of the 30-minute format—"The time disciplines of the news genre militate against the minimum moral requirement of engagement with another person's suffering" (1997, p. 29)—and television's tendency to commodify human tragedy:

> A dishonor is done when the flow of television news reduces all the world's horror to identical commodities. In a culture overwhelmed by the volume of promiscuous representation, there must be some practice by which the real—the instant when a real body is struck, abused or violated—is given a place of special attention, a demarcation that insists that it be seen. (p. 30)

## VIOLENCE: ECONOMIC CLAIMS

As we have seen, values of artistic integrity and journalistic autonomy are given significant weight in our deliberation over the ethics of violent media content. But the game changes when the justifications for violent content leave either of these arenas and the *motive* for using violence can be described another way. When the rationale becomes based on economic or marketing claims, the thinness of any ethical justification for its use is thrown into stark relief. The commonly used justifications for the use of violence may present compelling economic, financial or marketing arguments, but these cannot be mistaken for *ethical* arguments when they fail to take into account how the use of media violence does or does not serve our moral obligations. Indeed, one might argue that, from an epistemological perspective, ethics theory and its focus on negotiating among competing, *legitimate* moral claims would suggest that there is little to discuss in this realm: While we may claim that gratuitous and commercially-motivated use of violent content represents a moral failure, it doesn't actually provide much of an ethical dilemma at all. "Gratuitous cheapening of life to expand ratings, in terms of Aristotle's teleological model, is a reprehensible misuse of human beings as means to base ends," Christians suggested (2004, p. 28). In his 1994 book, *Selling Out America's Children*, Walsh discusses how television programming and advertising, two key influences in American culture today, work together to shape our values. The top priority for media executives is to draw audiences that they can reliably deliver to advertisers promoting their products. We see pervasive messages that include sex, violence and humor because those topics, or frames, reliably capture audience attention. So it is no surprise that researchers and policymakers have concluded that media executives are consequently creating programming that depends largely on images and contexts that trade on violence, sex and the enshrinement of consumerism. "In this respect, media executives are profiting from a product that is unhealthy for those who consume it, particularly children" (Walsh, 1994, p. 10).

Violence is a consistently reliable and effective marketing tool because it attracts the attention of male adolescents, which is a demographic segment that is intensely sought after by advertisers. Violent content presents a more universal language compared with "complex, dialogue-based stories" and is easier to produce (Groebel, 2001, p. 255). Gerbner, Morgan and Signorelli (1994) argued that violent content is prominent in global or exported media because it requires very little verbal translation, whereas humor, despite its value as an attention-getting tool, often is culture-bound and difficult to translate.

Some studies suggest, however, that violent entertainment content, while effective in drawing eyeballs, actually may undermine the friendly, receptive "environment" that companies want media outlets to provide for their advertising. From a media economics perspective, in other words, addiction to violent fare as an attention-getting tool may become self-defeating. Gerbner concluded that "the most highly rated programs are seldom violent" (cited in Hamilton, 1998, p. 32). Hamilton (1998) reported that when theatrically produced movies are shown on television along with warnings about content (for violence, nudity or language), "broadcasters run more network promotions and fewer general ads, consistent with the theory that warnings cause advertiser pullouts that lower prices" (p. 165). Other more compelling recent research has suggested that strong viewer emotional response to violent content—specifically, anger—actually interferes with viewer ability to recall advertising embedded in the content (Bushman & Phillips, 2001).

The very prevalence of media violence can serve to discourage and trivialize any exploration of the issue's ethical dimension. If research was able to document a "positive" cathartic effect, how might that allow us to argue that violent depictions intended to provide a relatively innocuous method of "venting" one's stress or aggression is justified in terms of ethical use of media? We might say such a utilitarian description of violent content spares society actual (read: greater) harm that may otherwise occur without such a social release valve. We might say that the harm inherent in the actual media content is outweighed by the existence of a positive public effect. But even if a cathartic effect of media violence were demonstrated to exist, we would not so easily be able to justify such content on the grounds of expediency if in fact it offered a cinematic repudiation of our duty of non-injury. We are well-aware that the means we use to accomplish our goals say as much about us as the ends themselves. The use of the theory of utility itself here raises other problems, which will be discussed later, regarding how we articulate public good and how the theory invites a reliance on gross generalizations rather than a serious consideration of how we might weigh competing values.

## MEDIA VIOLENCE AND OUR MORAL AGENCY

It is useful to consider how ethics theory helps us clarify the stakes involved in violent content and its effects that we have outlined here. Ethics helps us "delineate responsibility" among various stakeholders, as Christians said; it enables us to press the question of "whether producers of violent entertainment can dismiss their responsibility by claiming to give the public what it wants" (2004, p. 28). Developing a credible *normative* ethics theory remains difficult due to the demands of media practitioners' daily problems and routines and the predominance of rather simplistic utilitarian conventions and guidelines. But the preceding survey of the research documenting the effects of violent media content provides evidence that a deontological, duty-based approach is more effective in our efforts to develop an ethical framework with which to judge violent content, rather than a consequentialist approach.

## DIMENSIONS OF HARM POSED BY VIOLENT CONTENT

Even as using a duty-based moral framework provides a more effective way to judge the ethics of using violence in media content, it is still valuable to have a firm grasp of the nature of the potential harm that can result. As we have seen, the question of whether violent media content has an effect is no longer a serious one. And the existence of such effects does not necessarily raise a question of ethics. To be considered a compelling ethics question we must determine the relative *harmfulness* of those effects. Some dimensions, or forms, of this harm may be readily apparent: the priming potential of some violent cues to foster endorsement of antisocial behavior in children, for example, could clearly be said to pose a legitimate harm. Research also has suggested that men who watch pornographic material are likely to express "desensitized" attitudes toward women (Harris, 1994; Traudt, 2005). Theorists also have long argued that advertising that sexualizes, marginalizes and generally devalues women as objects is harmful because it undermines girls' self-esteem by promoting impossible and restrictive norms of beauty and femininity (Silverstein, Perdue, Peterson & Kelly, 1986; Myers & Biocca, 1992). In these and other cases, the claims of harm are much more concrete and significant than mere claims of being offended by violent or sexual content. It can be argued that, in these areas, research strongly suggests that actual "harm" has indeed occurred. Others may be less concrete or verifiable: How much violence against women can be directly attributed to the objectification and hypersexualization of young women in advertising?

Several theorists have been concerned about building a universal framework for moral responsibility for the assessment of harm and justifying standards about the "blameworthiness" of anyone who chooses not to prevent harm. Harris (1973), for example, claimed that to discover that a person is morally responsible for external harm is to discover that she is both causally responsible for it and morally to blame. Consequently, we must use a definition of harm that is more specific than the way many armchair media critics may understand it. The National Television Violence Study, among the most comprehensive studies to track the content of televised programming, offered the following definition of violence:

> Any overt depiction of a credible threat of physical force or the actual beings. Violence also includes certain depictions of physically harmful use of such force intended to physically harm an animate being or group of consequences against an animate being or group that occurs as a result of unseen violent means. Thus there are three primary types of violent depictions: credible threats, behavioral acts, and harmful consequences. (1998, p. 41)

Potter (1999) explored what he called the "profound" difference between what the public considers violent and how researchers conceptualize violence. The public often express outrage and concern when audience members are "shocked" or "offended" by what they see—what registers most viscerally with many viewers is the *graphicness* of the media violence. This is why many parents do not seem to be concerned with violence in children's cartoons, even though research has documented that such cartoons feature some of the highest rates of violence found in the media. While the public is concerned with being shocked by what they watch, scientists are concerned whether certain audiences will be harmed by what they watch, regardless of whether it can be called shocking or not (Bartholow et al., 2003, p. 4). Indeed, using terms such as "shocking" or "graphic" as measures of violent content denies the long-term cultivation and desensitization processes that researchers have recorded.

## HARM AND THE INADEQUACY OF UTILITARIAN THEORY

Though the conventions of media practice may have a "natural affinity" with utilitarian approaches, as Christians said, the theory elaborated on by John Stuart Mill and which has become the basis for much of our majoritarian democratic policy making is actually ill-suited for guiding ethical deliberations of media practitioners. Critics have argued that the limitations of Mill's approach point up a general failure of utilitarianism to account for fundamental injustices or address how unequal distribution of goods and wealth raise questions about moral agency. Utilitarianism goes wrong, Arneson argues, "in regarding only aggregate totals or averages of welfare while ignoring altogether the value of equal distribution of welfare among persons.... [I]t is polemically slanted insofar as it highlights harmonious, rosy possibilities and ignores equally likely but more troublesome cases which pose acute conflicts of distribution" (Arneson, 1997, pp. 87, 92). This objection also reflects a more general problem with Mill's overall argument for his theory of utility in guiding decision making. Having as our object the achievement of the greatest benefit for the largest number of people is clearly a noble thing. And Mill, in his efforts to build a usable framework to help ensure a harmonious social life, never lets us understate or dismiss the centrality of individual freedom as a driving value. But the devil, for most utilitarian theorists, has always been in the details—in the practical application of Mill's abstract claims. Who determines the nature of the potential harm involved? How are we defining "benefit," and is our focus on the short term or on the long term? Noting the work of Charles Taylor, Christians said utilitarianism certainly is very appealing in part because of its promise to provide a single principle to help us adjudicate conflicts. But the abstractness of the theory of utility leaves practitioners grappling—often unproductively—with fundamental questions about the nature of a supposed benefit, the exact membership of groups that may benefit or suffer from a decision, and whether immediate or long-term impacts are considered. In the end, the theory of utility offers an exactness that is not exact at all, representing only a "semblance of validity" as policymakers and potential stakeholders dismiss or marginalize whatever factors that cannot be quantified. Christians (2004) outlines several other deficiencies of utility:

> [Utilitarianism] depends on making accurate measurements of the consequences, when in everyday affairs, the results of our choices are often blurred, at least in the long term. In addition, utilitarians view society as a collection of individuals, each with his or her own desires and goals. Thus, institutions and structures are not analyzed in a sophisticated manner, and an atomistic, procedural view of democracy is presumed. Moreover, the principle of the greatest public benefit applies only to societies in which certain nonutilitarian standards of decency prevail. (p. 21)

The theory spelled out in Mill's famous *On Liberty* and other essays is understandably a landmark in social and political theory and undergirds much of our majoritarian democratic ideals: And rightly so. But Mill is much less useful in the realm of ethics because he invites blanket assumptions and gross generalizations on the kinds of key questions just mentioned. By maintaining such a high level of abstraction, Mill also discourages serious explorations into the various types and dimensions of harm. Indeed, his abstraction results in some significant contradictions, particularly when we try to apply his utilitarian framework to media behavior.

## REFINING OUR CONCEPTION OF HARM

In his landmark work, *Harm to Others*, social philosopher Joel Feinberg builds a largely legalistic framework for properly understanding the notion of harm and how it should be handled by the law and the courts. He discusses various dimensions of "injuring" or "wronging" others and how different kinds of harm should be punished. According to Feinberg, a harm is an act or state that "sets back" the interest of someone else, such as her reasonable interest in her career, health, reputation, or privacy. This "setting back" of someone's interest has to be concrete—it has to be something that explicitly makes the person's state of affairs, or his or her ability to attain reasonable goals, worse off than if the act had not been done. And it must be something that "sets back" important desires, like raising a family or accomplishing a long-term project, and not more trivial interests such as seeing a movie or walking a dog. "Not everything that we dislike or resent, and wish to avoid, is harmful to us," Feinberg writes (1984, p. 45). "[It is critical that we distinguish] between the harmful conditions and *all* the various unhappy and unwanted physical and mental states that are not states of harm in themselves" (p. 47).

Behavioral research also suggests that largely negative effects of violent media content may pose an altogether different sort of harm because of the often unconscious way aggressive modeling can be imitated. As noted earlier, imitation is among the cognitive processes that researchers have pointed to as a likely cause of short-term effects of violent content on aggressive behavior. Heyes (2001, 2004), Meltzoff and Decety (2003; Meltzoff, 2004) and other researchers have established how imitative learning processes, far from being the mindless, childlike repetition of actions scientists once thought, are elaborate methods of goal emulation with diverse "ends/ means" structures. They are more complex than scientists once believed, yet they also are largely automatic. We don't think about them. Susan Hurley (2004) suggested the ethical implications of our exposure to violent media content is enormous. "Ironically, imitative tendencies that bypass autonomous deliberative processes may well be symptomatic of the way our distinctively human and rational minds are built," she suggested (p. 177). If this "deliberative bypass" occurs with regularity over a range of behaviors, there is no reason that imitative learning regarding the violence we see in the media should be exempt from it—whether we acknowledge this process or not. And that, Hurley argued, raises troubling questions about our autonomous agency as audience members.

If it is true, as recent cognitive-processing research has suggested, that we *have little or no control* over the negative effects of violent media content due to unconscious imitative-learning processes, does that provide compelling ethical grounds for limiting or restricting such violent content to ensure our autonomy? A Kantian approach might argue that the answer is yes: Actions that violate the persons-as-ends principle include those that undermine or subvert the exercise of our autonomous agency, or free will. Exposure to violent media content that triggers unconscious imitative behaviors could represent a failure of our primary duty to respect every individual's free will and capacity for reason. Hurley, however, also adopts a utilitarian approach that draws on Mill's harm principle to promote similar moral claims. The results of research on imitative learning and its implication of audiences being involuntarily affected by violent content pose significant challenges to our assumptions about liberal political theory and human autonomy:

Prevention of such harm to third parties provides a strong reason (or "compelling interest") for liberal government to interfere with violent entertainment, and is not effectively blocked by the rationales for giving special protection to freedom of speech, since these are very weakly engaged by violent entertainment.... The power of the media industry over the public should be compared to the power of government as a potential threat to autonomy. Moreover, as we've seen, there is good reason to believe that many effects of violent entertainment on audiences are unconscious and automatic and bypass autonomous deliberative process. Audience autonomy would arguably be increased, not decreased, if such influences were reduced. (2004, p. 189, 194–195)

## DUTY VERSUS CONSEQUENCE

There is a paradox in the linkage between the moral duties the best theorists have embedded in the communicative act—duties of transparency, of non-injury, of respect for the dignity of the individual and of the engagement of a public—and the consequentialist purposes that we understand such messages to have. Media messages are intended to advance ideas, to inform, to persuade, to provoke, to soothe, to stimulate, to narcotize: We want our messages to have an *effect*. When it comes to violent media content, nearly three decades of extensive research has made it clear: Certain viewers, with certain predispositions, will likely exhibit more aggressive behavior under certain conditions after repeated and long-term exposure to certain types of portrayals of violence. But as the string of preceding qualifiers suggests, this effect is highly nuanced, contingent and multidimensional. And neurologists and cognitive psychologists have just begun to understand the behavioral effects of much of our messages. They also are making clear how our reception and processing of messages is profoundly contextual and intersubjective. In this sense, our cultural tendency to look to a consequentialist ethical system for guidance, with its assumptions of clear, quantifiable and unambiguous results to point to, can seem to be quite absurd. Again, Christians provides a valuable perspective:

> In the full range of human relationships, we ordinarily recognize that fulfilling promises, preventing injury, providing equal distribution, and relieving distress are moral imperatives. But utilitarianism as a single-considerations theory renders irrelevant other moral demands that conflict with it. In some of the most crucial issues we face at present, utility is not an adequate guide—for understanding distributive justice, diversity in popular culture, violence in television and cinema, truth-telling, digital manipulation, conflict of interest, and so forth. (p. 22)

A straightforward consequentialist approach is more likely to exempt us from moral accountability than it is to clarify our moral responsibilities. The only acceptable approach is that which begins by acknowledging our moral duties to others as outlined by the works of Kant, Ross and others. Our ethical deliberations, then, will rightly focus on whether or not our communicative acts represent appropriate attempts to balance conflicting duties.

While we all acknowledge that we have a fundamental duty not to harm others if we're serious about our obligations as moral agents, "the fact that an act will cause harm is invariably a moral reason not to do it, though not necessarily an overriding one," theorists point out (McNaughton & Rawling, p. 432). This is one reason why moral philosopher W. D. Ross and his discussion of our often-conflicting prima facie duties can be helpful. While Mill never lets us underestimate the respect and weight owed to our idea of liberty, and Kant requires us to fully consider what it means to be morally obligated to treat others in certain ways, Ross illuminates how we may weigh competing obligations. "He allows us to think of moral conflict not as conflicts of duties but as a conflict of moral reasons," moral philosopher Philip Stratton-Lake says

(2002, p. xxxviii). Ross is clear about the duties that we have, including avoidance of harm, but his system is largely dependent on context. Any broad generalizations about duty that do not sufficiently consider the facts of a specific case carry little weight in Ross's system. He cautions that it is a mistake to presume in any ethical deliberation that "every act that is our duty is so for one and the same reason." "[N]o act is ever, in virtue of falling under some general description, necessarily actually right; its rightness depends on its whole nature and not on any element of it" (Ross, 1930/2002, pp. 24, 33).

## DIRECTIONS FOR FUTURE RESEARCH

Efforts to develop media ethics theory that draws from cognition research have only recently begun. As the field of media ethics continues to mature, theorists who are well-grounded in both duty-based and consequentialist approaches in moral philosophy will be invaluable in helping shape public debate and policy decisions regarding violent media content. If patterns of observed media effects hold true and as mediated images continue to pervade culture, questions of ethics, standards and responsibility will only increase in urgency and immediacy. Yet such social-science research and ethical theorizing seem to exist on tracks that rarely intersect. One philosopher recently noted the "irony" in the fact that research on aggression and violence has developed specific meanings around these words "independently of much reference to or involvement by philosophers" (Bäck, 2004, p. 219). This chapter has preliminarily raised questions involving our conceptions of autonomous agency, the multiple dimensions of harm and assignment of responsibility; each of these and other questions require further explication to broaden and deepen our understanding in the context of violent media content.

Clearly, media ethics theory must largely be built on the empirical evidence emerging from research on cognitive and behavioral effects if we are to avoid reductive exchanges and ineffective moralizing. Our ethical deliberation on questions of autonomous agency, dimensions of harm and responsibility must be rooted in the facts as we know them. As Hurley (2004) suggested, the largely unconscious way we appear to imitate behaviors raises fundamental questions about the *control* we can claim to have as media consumers. What value priorities, then, can we say should drive decisions of media producers about content and exposure? How might our "altered states" as autonomous agents affect how social and political theory, including the premium placed on utility, is brought to bear on our judgments regarding media exposure?

The research on negative effects of violent content also poses an important opportunity for media ethics theorists to clarify our understanding of the "harm" involved and how the different dimensions of harm affect the moral claims we can make. When can we say harm actually "sets back" a legitimate social interest or threatens to do so, and how might Feinberg's criteria for regulating such harm (1984) help us in our ethics theorizing? Ethicists also can draw on the disparate realms of cognition research and media sociology to explore how a distributive justice theory might shape our judgments on harmful media effects. Using the contractualist framework of Rawls (1971), ethics theorists could consider the validity of regulatory arguments based on protecting society's least advantaged or most vulnerable audiences and on the nature of the harm involved.

Christians (2004) focused on the responsibility issue; media ethics theory has much to contribute in "delineating responsibility" (p. 28), he claimed. There is no question of the need for ethicists to continue work to clarify the public debate over how to establish levels of responsibility among corporate media executives, producers, policy makers and audience members. But unidirectional claims of responsibility, particularly for media content, presuppose a rather simplistic understanding of the term. Compelling models of *accountability* are needed that harness the concept's "dynamic of interaction" between the claims of autonomous agents and their values (Plaisance, 2000).

Potter (2003) outlined several areas where more focused media-effects research is urgently needed: to try to further document types of effects other than "disinhibition" processes and fear responses; to produce more definitive assessment of long-term effects through longitudinal and panel studies; to explore positive, "prosocial" effects, which may in fact be stronger than the negative effects that have preoccupied researchers for three decades; to delineate types and degrees of effects from violence in print, video and audio-based media. All of these areas include significant ethical dimensions that cannot be ignored if we are to take seriously ideas such as moral obligation, autonomous agency, non-injury and accountability.

# REFERENCES

Abbott, E. A., & Brassfield, L. T. (1989). "Comparing decisions on releases by TV and newspaper gatekeepers." *Journalism Quarterly, 66* (4), 853–856.

Arneson, R. J. (1997). "Paternalism, Utility and Fairness." In *Mill's 'On Liberty': Critical Essays*, G. Dworkin (Ed.). Lanham, MD: Rowman & Littlefield.

Bäck, A. (2004). "Thinking clearly about violence." *Philosophical Studies, 117* (1–2), 219–230.

Bandura, A. (1977). *Social learning theory*. Englewood Cliffs, NJ: Prentice Hall.

Bartholow, B. D., Dill, K. E., Anderson, K. B. & Lindsay, J. J. (2003). "The proliferation of media violence and its economic underpinnings." In *Media violence and children*, D. A. Gentile (Ed.). Westport, CT: Praeger.

Berkowitz, L. (1993). *Aggression: Its causes, consequences and control*. New York: McGraw-Hill.

Buchman, D. D., & Funk, J. B. (1996). "Video and computer games in the '90s: Children's time commitment and game preference." *Children Today, 24*, 12–16.

Bushman, B. J., & Anderson, C. A. (2001, June/July). "Media violence and the American public: Scientific facts versus media misinformation." *American Psychologist, 56* (6/7), 477–489.

Bushman, B., & Huesmann, L. (2001). "Effects of television violence on aggression." In *Handbook of children and the media*, D. Singer & J. Singer (Eds.). Thousand Oaks, CA: Sage.

Bushman, B. J., & Phillips, C. M. (2001). "If the television program bleeds, memory for the advertisement recedes." *Current Directions in Psychological Science, 10*, 44–47.

Christians, C. G. (2004). "Ethical and normative perspectives." In *The Sage handbook of media studies*, J. D. H. Downing (Ed.). Thousand Oaks, CA: Sage.

Comstock, G., & Scharrer, E. (1999). *Television: What's on, who's watching and what it means*. San Diego, CA: Academic Press.

Comstock, G., & Scharrer, E. (2003). "Meta-analyzing the controversy over television violence and aggression." In *Media violence and children*, D. A. Gentile (Ed.). Westport, CT: Praeger.

Cooperative Institutional Research Program. (1999). *Cooperative Institutional Research Program survey results*. Ames, IA: Office of Institutional Research.

Feinberg, J. (1984). *Harm to others: The moral limits of the criminal law*. New York: Oxford University Press.

Gerbner, G., & Gross, L. (1976). "Living with television: The violence profile." *Journal of Communication, 26*, 173–199.

Gerbner, G., Morgan, M. & Signorielli, N. (1994). *Television violence profile No. 16*. Philadelphia, PA: Annenburg School of Communication, University of Pennsylvania.

Graber, D. A. (1996). "Say it with pictures." *Annals of the American Academy of Political and Social Science, 546*, 85–96.

Groebel, J. (2001). "Media violence in cross-cultural perspective: A global study on children's media behavior and some educational implications." In *Handbook of children and the media*, D. Singer & J. Singer (Eds.). Thousand Oaks, CA: Sage.

Gunter, B. (1994). "The question of media violence." In *Media effects: Advances in theory and research*, J. Bryant & D. Zillmann (Eds.). Hillsdale, NJ: Erlbaum.

Hamilton, J. T. (1998). *Channeling violence: The economic market for violent television programming.* Princeton, NJ: Princeton University Press.

Harris, J. (1973). "The Marxist conception of violence." *Philosophy and Public Affairs, 3*, 192–220.

Harris, R. J. (1994). *A cognitive psychology of mass communication* (2nd ed.). Hillsdale, NJ: Erlbaum.

Heyes, C. (2001). "Causes and consequences of imitation." *Trends in Cognitive Sciences, 5* (6), 227–280.

Heyes, C. (2004). "Imitation by association." In *Perspectives on Imitation: From neuroscience to social science. Vol. 1: Mechanisms of imitation and imitation in animals*, S. Hurley & N. Chater (Eds.). Cambridge, MA: MIT Press.

Huesmann, L. R. (2005). "Imitation and the effects of observing media violence on behavior." In *Perspectives on imitation: From neuroscience to social science. Vol. 2: Imitation, human development and culture*, S. Hurley & N. Chater (Eds.). Cambridge, MA: MIT Press.

Huesmann, L., & Eron, L. (1986). *Television and the aggressive child: A cross-national comparison*. Hillsdale, NJ: Erlbaum.

Hurley, S. (2004). "Imitation, media violence and freedom of speech." *Philosophical Studies, 117* (1-2), 165–217.

Ignatieff, M. (1997). *The warrior's honor: Ethnic war and the modern conscience*. New York: Henry Holt.

Kauffmann, S. (1992, November 23). "Blood lines." *The New Republic, 207* (22), 30–31.

McNaughton, D., & Rawling, P. (2006). "Deontology." In *The Oxford handbook of ethical theory*, D. Copp (Ed.). New York: Oxford University Press.

Meltzoff, A. (2004). "Imitation and other minds: The 'Like Me' hypothesis." In *Perspectives on Imitation: From neuroscience to social science. Vol. 2: Imitation, human development and culture*, S. Hurley & N. Chater (Eds.). Cambridge, MA: MIT Press.

Meltzoff, A., & Decety, J. (2003). "What imitation tells us about social cognition: A rapprochement between developmental psychology and cognitive neuroscience." *Philosophical Transactions of the Royal Society of London B, 358*, 491–500.

Myers, D. G. (1999). *Social psychology* (6th ed.). Boston: McGraw-Hill.

Myers, P. N., & Biocca, F. A. (1992). "The elastic body image: The effect of television advertising and programming on body image distortions in young women." *Journal of Communication, 42*, 108–133.

National Television Violence Study. (1996). *National television violence study: Scientific papers, 1994–1995.* Studio City, CA: Mediascope.

National Television Violence Study. (1998). *National television violence study: Vol. 3*. Santa Barbara: University of California, Santa Barbara, Center for Communication and Social Policy.

Plaisance, P. L. (2000). "The concept of media accountability reconsidered." *Journal of Mass Media Ethics, 15* (4), 257–268.

Potter, J. W. (1999). *On media violence*. Thousand Oaks, CA: Sage.

Potter, J. W. (2003). "The frontiers of media research." In *Media violence and children*, D. A. Gentile (Ed.). Westport, CT: Praeger.

Rawls, J. (1971). *A theory of justice*. Cambridge, MA: Belknap Press.

Ross, W. D. (1930/2002). *The right and the good*, P. Stratton-Lake (Ed.) Oxford: Clarendon Press.

Sherry, J. L. (2001). "The effects of violent video games on aggression: A meta-analysis." *Human Communication Research, 27* (3), 409–431.

Signorielli, N. (1990). "Television's mean and dangerous world: A continuation of the cultural indicators perspective. In *Cultivation analysis: New directions in media effects research*, N. Signorielli & M. Morgan (Eds.). Newbury Park, CA: Sage.

Signorielli, N., Gerbner, G. & Morgan, M. (1995). "Violence on television: The cultural indicators project." *Journal of Broadcasting and Electronic Media, 39*, 278–283.

Silverstein, B., Perdue, L. Peterson, B. & Kelly, E. (1986). "The role of mass media in promoting a thin standard of bodily attractiveness for women." *Sex Roles, 14*, 519–532.

Sparks, G. G., & Sparks, C. W. (2002). "Effects of media violence." In *Media effects: Advances in theory and research* (2nd ed.), J. Bryant & D. Zillmann (Eds.). Mahwah, NJ: Erlbaum.

Strasburger, V. C., & Wilson, B. J. (2002). *Children, adolescents and the media.* Thousand Oaks, CA: Sage.

Strasburger, V. C., & Wilson, B. J. (2003). "Television violence." In *Media violence and children,* D. A. Gentile (Ed.). Westport, CT: Praeger.

Stratton-Lake, P. (Ed.). (2002). Introduction. In *The right and the good,* W. D. Ross (Ed.). Oxford: Clarendon Press.

Traudt, P. J. (2005). *Media, audiences, effects: An introduction to the study of media content and audience analysis.* Boston: Allyn & Bacon.

Walsh, D. A. (1994). *Selling out America's children: How America puts profits before values—and what parents can do.* Minneapolis, MN: Fairview Press.

Yakota, F., & Thompson, K. M. (2000). "Violence in G-rated animated films." *Journal of the American Medical Association, 283,* 2716–2720.

Zillmann, D. (1983). "Transfer of excitation in emotional behavior." In *Social psychophysiology: A sourcebook,* J. Cacioppo & R. Petty (Eds.). New York: Guilford.

# 13

# The Eroding Boundaries between News and Entertainment and What They Mean for Democratic Politics

## Bruce A. Williams and Michael X. Delli Carpini

### INTRODUCTION: THE CHALLENGE OF THE NEW MEDIA ENVIRONMENT

In March of 2002 ABC entered into negotiations with late night talk show host David Letterman in an attempt to lure him from CBS to replace *Nightline*, hosted by Ted Koppel. When the story became public, it was prominently covered in the press, making the front page of *The New York Times* two days in a row and the nightly news broadcasts of all the networks except, not coincidentally, ABC. Outrage erupted over the network's efforts to replace an award winning, twenty-year-old news program with a comedy and celebrity driven entertainment show. Typical were comments by Alex Jones of the widely respected Joan Shorenstein Center on the Press, Politics and Public Policy at Harvard, who said in *USA Today* that the proposed replacement would "be a body blow to news in this country as we know it.... This is a genuine breach of the covenant between a company that has stewardship of a great news organization and the American public" (cited in Johnson & Levin 2002).

While most press commentary agreed about the body blow to democratic politics, there were a few dissenters. *New York Times* columnist Frank Rich quoted Roger Ailes, the chairman of Fox News, who said: "There are a lot of people who don't think there's a hell of a lot of difference these days between news and comedy." Rich went on: "That's not entirely facetious. Young viewers who ditch their parents' news sources often do get their news from Jon Stewart's *Daily Show* and other comic venues that not infrequently have more insight and command of the facts than, say, the Ken and Barbie dolls lately recruited as news 'personalities' to stem the hemorrhaging at *CNN*" (Rich 2002)

In the end the immediate controversy was resolved, in a fashion, when Letterman announced that he would remain at CBS and ABC offered a "lukewarm" commitment to *Nightline*. But, the larger issues underlying this particular case are far from resolved and are the subject of frequent debate among media practitioners, critics, and scholars. While this debate takes various forms, at its heart is the now commonplace observation that the quality information citizens need is less and less available in an American media system dominated by "infotainment": a blurring of the lines between "news" and "entertainment." Typically, this blurring is viewed with alarm, seen as a sometimes economic, sometimes cultural challenge to journalism's preeminent status as the nation's gatekeeper of the public interest. But what *is* the difference between news and entertainment, between *Nightline* and *The Letterman Show*?

In this chapter, we argue that anxiety over the rise of infotainment is less about the blurring of lines between news and entertainment (lines virtually impossible to draw in any intellectually satisfying way) and more about uncertainty resulting from the dramatic changes occurring in the media environment over the last two decades. These changes have enormous consequences for the ways in which political information is and will be produced, consumed, and circulated in the 21st century. A sophisticated understanding of the potentials and pitfalls for democracy of this new media environment depends upon an historical and ethical perspective that is not dependent upon *a priori* assumptions, rooted in dubious conclusions from the recent past, about the appropriate forms or sources of political information. We suggest a more pragmatic approach, drawing upon the historical development of what we call media regimes in the United States and their role in structuring the patterns and practices of ordinary citizens as they search for political information.

## MEDIA REGIMES AND CITIZENSHIP

For our purposes, we define a media regime as an historically specific more or less stable institutional arrangement of the state, culture, and economy that structures how mediated information is provided to the public. Once in place, a media regime organizes the gates through which information about culture, politics, and economics passes, thus shaping the *discursive environment* in which such topics are discussed, understood, and acted on. At most points in time, the structure of this gate-keeping process is invisible, with elites, citizens, and scholars tacitly accepting as natural and unproblematic the rules by which information is disseminated. Controversy, when it occurs, centers on perceived violations of the rules rather than on the appropriateness of the rules themselves. A good example is when a journalist is seen as violating the norms of objectivity or the confidentiality of an anonymous source.

Periodically, however, economic, cultural, political, or technological changes lead to disjunctures between existing media regimes and actual practices (for example, when new technologies, such as cable or the Internet, challenge the dominant role of a particular set of media elites, such as the news divisions of the television networks). When the contradictions between existing rules and actual practice become too great to ignore, normally unexamined assumptions underlying a particular media regime become more visible and more likely to be challenged, opening up the possibility of "regime change." Robert McChesney defines such moments as "critical junctures," while Paul Starr defines such periods as "constitutive moments" (McChesney 2007; Starr 2004). As McChesney argues, we are at just such a critical juncture. It is revealing to recall briefly past critical junctures and the resulting debates and policies over media and democracy which shaped previous American media regimes.

For example, economic, political, and cultural changes occurring during the early part of the 20th century, coupled with the emergence of radio and later television, challenged the existing media regime (dominated by newspapers and their owners). This disjuncture set off a series of very public struggles over fundamental issues such as the relative merits of newspapers versus radio or television as a source of public information, the appropriate balance between public and private ownership, commercialization, which elites should communicate with the polity and how should they do so, and even the appropriate role of citizens in a democracy (McChesney 1993).

By the middle of the 20th century, a more or less stable new media regime had emerged. It consisted of the increasing dominance of electronic over print media, concentrated ownership of a shrinking number of media outlets, a public service obligation imposed on radio and television networks in exchange for the use of the public airwaves, and, finally, heightened status for professional journalists who would mediate between political leaders and the citizenry. It was through the emergence of this new regime (called "The Golden Age of Broadcast News" by Jon Katz 1997), with its particular combination of media institutions, norms, processes and actors, that familiar distinctions such as news versus entertainment and the central role of professional journalists as gatekeepers came to take on their unquestioned, authoritative meaning.

In this regime, the "news media" became gatekeepers of the public agenda, the source of information about pressing issues of the day, and the public space in which (mainly elites) debated these issues. Significantly, this regime depended upon a limited number of gates through which political information would pass to citizens: the three network news broadcasts and a single newspaper for most Americans. The vigorous defenders of Ted Koppel and *Nightline* whom we discussed at the beginning of this chapter accepted the assumptions of this media regime.

Much academic research buttressed the underlying assumptions of this regime. Based upon decades of survey research, it was assumed that the public was largely uninterested in politics and could only be periodically roused around elections, or in times of crisis. This generally apathetic and poorly informed citizenry would receive all they needed to know about the political world if they turned to the evening news for 30 minutes a day, and perhaps, for the more engaged, read a newspaper or news magazine. Once tuned in, professional journalists would provide citizens with the information they needed to make wise decisions—primarily by voting.

When it came to examining the political influence of the media, scholars focused almost exclusively on media explicitly labeled as political by producers: news broadcasts, news and editorial sections of print media, political advertisements, and so forth. It's also significant that from the early days of empirical communications research by Paul Lazarsfeld and his colleagues in the 1940s (Lazarsfeld, Berelson, & Gaudet 1944) through the methodologically sophisticated work of scholars like Donald Kinder, Shanto Iyengar (1987, 1991; Iyengar & Reeves 1997), Diana Mutz et al. (1996), or Robert Entman (1989, 2004), the centrality of media gatekeeping has been assumed. Almost without exception, researchers assumed (sometimes explicitly, more often implicitly) that between the booming, buzzing, blooming confusion of the political world and the limited time and capacity of ordinary citizens stood professional journalists who, in negotiation with political elites, would determine what information passed through these gates to the general public. It was primarily at a limited number of such gates that the public would gather to learn abut politics.

From the perspective of the early 21st century, it is clear that this whole line of analysis and the media regime within which it is situated emerged from a very particular media environment. The basic features of this environment and how much has changed over the last two decades is illustrated by the fact that in 1982, the year in which Iyengar and Kinder (1987) were doing their influential research on the political influence of the broadcast news, the average American home received 10 television channels, 20% of American homes had a VCR, fewer than two million personal computers were sold, and the Internet, DVDs, cell phones, satellite television, and so forth were not available to a mass market.[1]

Since that time, however, changes in the media environment have severely undermined the regime of the "Golden Age of Broadcast Journalism." The average American household now has access to more than a hundred television channels and three out of four households have more than one set. By 2003, 90% of homes had VCRs or DVD players. Consequently, television sets are often tuned to different channels in different rooms and any given channel has a far smaller and often much more homogenous audience than in the past. Industry types call this phenomenon audience fragmentation and it means that the days of a family gathering together on the couch watching the same show are dying out for good. Further, by 2004 annual PC sales had grown to 178 million and nearly three in four U.S. households had an Internet connection (45% of which were high speed connections).

These and numerous other technological changes (from the remote control to TiVo) have made it easier to time shift, skip through commercials, or avoid broadcast media entirely. This exponentially increases the number and type of gates through which mediated information flows, and in the process profoundly changes the way citizens choose their media diet. The result of these developments has been greater variation than at any point in history in the quantity, form, content, and sources of the mediated information consumed by individual Americans. At the same time, these changes have blurred the distinction between "political" and "non-political" media and genres, eroded the gate-keeping and agenda-setting roles of the news media, muddied the line between producers and consumers of media, and challenged the professional bases of modern journalism.

Nowhere are these changes more evident than when it comes to the increasingly fragmented and segmented audiences for political information. So, by 2006 the audience for network news had shrunk by half from over 40 million viewers per night in the 1980s (Ahonen 2006). Even more telling, while the average American is 35 years old, the average age of those watching network news is about 60 (those who get their news from the online sites of the network news divisions are between 10 and 15 years younger). Those who grew up in the "Golden Age of Broadcast News" tend to be those who still seek their political information from the gatekeepers established during that media regime.

Younger people seek out information differently. By the 2004 elections, a poll conducted by the Pew Research Center for the People and the Press reported that 21% of 18- to 29-year-olds named *The Daily Show* and *Saturday Night Live* as their regular source of campaign news (up from 9% in 2000). Twenty-three percent in this group named one of the three nightly network news broadcasts as their source of campaign news (down from 39% in 2000). The figures for those who regularly seek out political information on the Internet are similarly skewed by generation (Pew Research Center for the People and the Press 2004b).

These changes have been regularly noted by many scholars and journalists. However, they have been viewed from the perspective of the very media regime that is being challenged. As a result, the breakdown of distinctions such as that between news and entertainment, the emergence of a hybrid form labeled infotainment, the declining influence of professional journalists, and so forth, are seen as a crisis of democracy itself. Viewed from a broader historical vantage, however, it is the the "Golden Age of Broadcast News" that is exceptional in its attempts to limit politically-relevant media to a single genre ("news") and a single authority ("professional journalists"). Indeed, despite the seeming naturalness of the distinction between news and entertainment, it is remarkably difficult to identify the characteristics upon which this distinction is based. In fact, it is difficult—we would argue impossible—to articulate a theoretically useful definition of this distinction (Williams & Delli Carpini 2000).

We want to avoid such irresolvable and ultimately pointless definitional disputes about appropriate and inappropriate sources of political information. Instead we begin with the assumption that a central criterion for judging any media regime in a democratic society is how well it fosters a more informed citizenry. By this standard, the lamented "Golden Age of Broadcast Journalism" did a remarkably poor job. As many scholars have noted, despite dramatic increases in the average level of education and an increase in access to sources of information, Americans in the 1980s showed no improvement in levels of political knowledge as compared to the earliest days of survey research in the 1940s (Entman 1989; Delli Carpini & Keeter 1996). As well, the era of the Golden Age witnessed precipitous declines in virtually all forms of political participation. We are not arguing that the Golden Age, and the rise of its dominant medium television, caused these trends, only that this media regime clearly did nothing to improve matters.

Keeping the limitations of the Golden Age in mind, what does it mean that young people regularly get their political information from non-traditional sources labeled as "entertainment" and not news? Consider the Pew Research Center poll we discussed above, which asked four questions about current affairs (Pew Research Center for the People and the Press 2004b).[2] The survey then calculated the percentage of respondents who got all four questions correct according to their self-reported primary source of news and found the following ranking: *Daily Show* = 47%; *O'Reilly Factor* = 47%; Talk radio = 45%; PBS' *The NewsHour* = 46%; Sunday Political Talk Shows = 44%: National Public Radio = 36%; Daily Newspaper = 34%; Nightly Network News = 33%.[3] We draw the conclusion that those who rely on non-traditional sources of information are certainly no less informed than those who rely on traditional news sources and there is evidence that they may, in fact, be better informed.

A careful analysis of the Pew data by Dannagal Young and Russell Tisinger, (2006) reveal that our understanding of how young people gather political information is obscured by employing untenable distinctions between news and entertainment. They find, for example, that young people are not replacing one source of information (traditional news outlets) with another (late night comedians), rather:

> …individuals use diverse forms of content to create political understanding, regardless whether that content is on the NBC *Nightly News* or a late-night comedy program. And while some news producers may be uncomfortable with the notion that shows like *The Daily Show* might play an important role, perhaps their growing relevance speaks to a larger trend in the information environment. (Young & Tisinger 2006: 130)

It turns out that those who report that they rely on late night comedians are *more* likely, not less likely, than those who do not rely on such shows, to also learn from other, more traditional sources of political information.

Moreover, the simplistic distinction between news and entertainment obscures the significant differences between shows lumped within one or another of these categories. So, for example, much of what appears on network news broadcasts, or in a newspaper is concerned with celebrity lifestyles (or styles of death in the case of Anna Nichole Smith), fashion, television and movie reviews, and other topics usually denigrated as entertainment or infotainment. Conversely, as Young and Tisinger point out, the humor on *The Daily Show* depends upon irony and satire, assuming a basic knowledge of the events being satirized. In contrast, Letterman and Leno's jokes tend to be structured around incongruity and do not depend upon detailed knowledge of the specific issues upon which the joke is based.

To us, these findings suggest that the panic over young people turning to new or non-traditional sources of political information is at least as much about the challenges to institutionalized elite control over political information as it is about the quality and democratic implications of the way some citizens learn, or fail to learn, about politics. What is needed are ways of understanding the changes in the information environment which are not dependent upon outmoded or ill defined distinctions between sources of information, but rather which allow us to fully grasp the democratic potentials and pitfalls of a changing media environment.

This is not to say that many elements of the collapsed golden age are not worthy of salvaging. It is not saying that past regimes, when the lines between genres were less clear, did not suffer from their own shortcomings. And it is not saying that the new media environment is simply a return to the past.

It is to say, however, that like it or not, the answers about media and democracy provided by the Golden Age are suspect and that the new media environment opens up both new democratic possibilities as well as new threats. At the very least, changes in the media environment challenges what we think we know about political communications to the extent that our knowledge assumes the existence of a media regime that no longer exists. Moreover, if we want to foreground media's role in fostering an informed citizenry, it is vital to focus on how ordinary citizens understand the emerging media regime. As with scholars, ordinary citizens operate on a set of assumptions conditioned by past experience with media and have given much less careful thought to the features of the new media environment and the new regime it will both shape and be shaped by.

In research bearing on this question, Press, Williams, Moore and Johnson (2005) had thirty-five individuals from all walks of life keep media diaries during the three months around the 2004 election. Supplemented by face-to-face interviews and focus group discussions, the project results provide insight into how subjects thought about or discussed public issues, and the use of media (old and new) in these deliberations. Mirroring the arguments of Young and Tisinger (2006), Press et al. found that their subjects moved seamlessly between different sources of political information, making few distinctions between old and new media or between traditional and non-traditional sources. Even more importantly, most subjects had absorbed the assumptions about political information in the Golden Age—they were quick to criticize what they saw as biased political coverage by journalists and expressed a desire for neutral sources of information.[4] Overall, subjects were quite critical about the potential short-comings of political information received from the gatekeepers defined by the Golden Age. However, when it came to the myriad sources of information available through new media and through non-traditional outlets, subjects were much less critical and tended to adopt an uncritical enthusiasm for its possibilities.

In short, these findings, and others like them, indicate a need for understanding the new media environment on its own terms and focusing on its implications for fostering an informed and engaged citizenry. Such understanding is vital if the media regime that will emerge over the next decades is to take full advantage of the potentials in the new media environment for enhancing democratic life. In the balance of this chapter, we try to suggest some ways to more productively understand the new media environment in ways that will allow its democratic potentials to be maximized as a new media regime develops. First, what is needed are definitions of politically-relevant mediated information that are not rooted in a now moribund Golden Age, but rather more suited to the new media environment. It is also important to develop normative criteria that can be used in public debate about the changes that are taking place.

Politically-relevant mediated information is a concept that is always essentially contestable, in need of continuous definition and explicit discussion and debate.[5] The new media environment both limits the ability of professional journalists to limit and control the number of gates through which political information flows and so places more responsibility with ordinary citizens who now must sort through an often seemingly bewildering number of sources and types of political information. The interactivity of the Internet and the ease with which almost anyone with a handheld video camera or audio recorder can make information available to large numbers of people blurs the very line between producers and consumers of mediated political information. As policies and practices of a new media regime emerge, careful scholarly analysis and public deliberation emphasizing democratic values is necessary, if we are to avoid a regime aimed solely at maximizing the new media environment's potential for furthering corporate interests, rather than democratic potentials. As in the past, journalists, political elites, and scholars have a role to play in this public debate, but so too do movie producers, television writers, musicians—and most importantly, ordinary citizens themselves. In short, we think that the new media environment creates new responsibilities for all who hold and view the tremendously expanded media soap box.

## DEFINING AND EVALUATING POLITICALLY-RELEVANT MEDIA

To begin it is important to shift from categorizing politically-relevant media by genre (for example news versus drama), content (for example, fact versus fiction) or source (for example, journalist versus actor) to categorizing by utility. That is, the extent to which any communication is politically relevant is dependent on what it does—*its potential use*—rather than what it says, who says it, and how it is said.

We argue that, in a democratic polity, politically-relevant communications are those that shape opportunities for understanding, deliberating about, and acting on the relationships among: (1) the conditions of one's day-to-day life; (2) the day-to-day life of fellow members of the community; and (3) the norms and structures of power that shape these relationships. It is the connection among these three elements that constitutes for us the inevitably contested, but nonetheless central definition of political relevance.

What purchase does such a definition bring us? First, it moves us away from a priori categorizations based solely on genre, focusing instead on the full range of mediated messages with which citizens interact. A Jay Leno monologue that satirically points out the political ignorance of the general public, a scene from the HBO series *The Wire* exploring racial injustice in our legal system, or an Internet chatroom discussion of Al Gore's *An Inconvenient Truth* are all as politically-relevant as a newspaper or the nightly news.

Second, and more importantly, our definition shifts the fundamental question from *if* a particular mediated message is politically relevant to *how* it is relevant. For example, the insider coverage of campaign strategy and horse race frames that make up much of news coverage of elections may be politically relevant, but this relevance often comes from a tendency to limit rather than enhance opportunities for understanding, deliberating about, and acting on the relationship among the conditions of day-to-life and the norms and structures of power that shape these relationships (Patterson 1993). If we suggest that much of the content of news broadcasts and political talk shows is politically debilitating, it is more difficult to blame the public for not paying attention to the issues raised on such shows. It certainly casts doubt on using awareness of such coverage as a hallmark of good citizenship and civic engagement.

The new media environment does more than simply make it difficult for citizens and scholars to determine what is or is not political communication. It also has challenged the criteria by which one assesses the media's impact on democratic politics. Historically, much of the debate and changing consensus over the appropriate role of the media in American democracy has been based on assumptions about who should (or is able to) participate in politics and so who is in need of the information to do so effectively.

The concept of "community" in our definition of political relevance is meant to signal the importance of this question. One of the greatest powers of the mass media is to help define the community to which individuals think of themselves as belonging. This is a central act in democratic politics which underlies notions of moral responsibility. As citizens are left more and more to themselves to sift through the myriad gates through which politically relevant information flows to them, the possibilities for redefining the political community expand.

Defining the communities to which we see ourselves belonging is central to the normative implications of politically-relevant media. As John Dewey observed,

> To learn to be human is to develop through the give and take of communication an effective sense of being an individually distinctive member of a community; one who understands and appreciates its beliefs, desires and methods, and who contributes to a further conversion of organic powers into human resources and values (1927: 154, emphasis added).

Philosopher Onora O'Neill (1996) argues that in defining moral responsibilities, we need to carefully and consistently define the individuals who are members of our own moral community. So, for example, if we consume inexpensive food and clothing whose price is dependent upon low paid foreign labor, it is morally inconsistent to then say that we have no responsibility to such laborers simply because they live in far-away lands about which we know little and care less. Whether we like it or not they have become members of our moral community because our own day-to-day life is dependent upon the conditions of their day-to-day life (and vice versa). The modern media are central to constructing, revealing, and at times disguising the communities to which we belong.

It's easy to dismiss emerging virtual communities, moral communities, or communities of interest as less real or meaningful than more traditional, place-based ones. It is also easy to argue that such connections can and have been made prior to the emergence of new media. Certainly both these points have merit, but it is important not to overstate them.

Consider, for example, the sense of moral outrage and collective self-reflection that accompanied the failure of local residents to come to Kitty Genovese's aid as she was attacked on a Queens, New York street in 1964. Ms. Genovese's neighbors were blamed because *they saw (or heard) her plight and failed to act* in a situation where action was possible (at least by calling the police). In addition, national broadcast news and newspaper coverage of the incident sparked citizens around the country to reflect on the loss of community. This broader reflection did not, however, carry with it any deep-seated sense of obligation to act for viewers or readers—Ms. Genovese was not *their* neighbor. In the current environment it is increasingly the case that media audiences are more like Ms. Genovese's neighbors than like the viewers and readers of her story.

We increasingly find ourselves in mediated situations where we come know other people (at least as well as Ms. Genovese's neighbors knew her), where we see these people in need of help, where we have a real economic, cultural, or political connection to them, and where it is possible for us to do something. This creates new and heretofore unimaginable communities of moral obligation—obligations which cannot be defined mechanistically, but rather are essentially contestable and in need of constant public discussion and clarification. This is even more true when we consider the specific interactive capabilities of the Internet. During the American-led invasion of Iraq in 2003, for example, bloggers, like the "Baghdad Blogger," were able to communicate their experiences of being under bombardment to millions of Internet users around the world (Pax 2003). This brought "enemy" civilians into our own community of moral obligation in ways almost impossible in past conflicts. This is not an unproblematic development, of course, it raises questions about the ability of the public to critically analyze such information, the implications for those who have access to new media versus those who do not (victims of genocide in Darfur, for instance), who has greater access to our resulting community of moral inclusion and so forth. Our point is that such potentials are new to the media system we now live in and need to be openly debated and discussed as we cast policies that will institutionalize a new media regime.

We are not arguing that the new media environment will inevitably lead to either improved or degraded notions of community—this will ultimately depend on how new media is used. Rather it is to suggest that in this new environment we must be aware of the political relevance of a much more varied set of communication genres and technologies. This new environment changes—for better or worse—current notions of community and the moral and political obligations associated with them.

With this in mind, we suggest four qualities of politically-relevant media that are likely to influence the practice of democratic politics. We believe that these qualities—what we label transparency, pluralism, verisimilitude, and practice—salvage the spirit and intent of past efforts to create a democratic media environment, while taking into consideration both the limitations of these earlier efforts and the new promise and pitfalls of the new media environment. We offer these criteria not because they are the only ones possible, but rather to open up discursive space for an explicit consideration of the relationship between a new media environment and democratic politics in the 21st century

## TRANSPARENCY

By this term we mean that the audience of any mediated message must know who is speaking to them. It is related to the traditional journalistic norms of revealing one's sources, including a by-line, and acknowledging when a story involves the economic interests of the media organization. But transparency is more encompassing. It is as important to know the sources, biases, intentions, and so forth of Jon Stewart as Brian Williams; to know the economic interests of a movie studio as a newspaper chain; and to know the "sources" of a screenwriter as a reporter.

## PLURALISM

Pluralism is the openness of the media environment to diverse points of view and the ease of access to these views. It is related to the traditional notions of balance and equal time, but again we see pluralism as a much broader concept.

New technology and the blurring of out-dated distinctions in genres increases the possibility for either a much richer conversation that includes a more diverse set of viewpoints or a more homogeneous one that implicitly limits debate. The increasing ability to target audiences coupled with the ability of audiences to pick and choose the information they attend to makes it quite possible that public discourse will become more fragmented even as it becomes more controlled by a small number of media corporations.

## VERISIMILITUDE

We use the word "verisimilitude" not in its meaning as "the appearance or illusion of truth" (though this definition should always be kept in mind), but rather "the likelihood or probability of truth." It acknowledges the uncertainty of things, while also recognizing the importance of seeking common understanding through efforts to approach the truth.

When we talk about verisimilitude in the media, we mean the assumption that sources of political communications take responsibility for the truth claims they explicitly and implicitly make, even if these claims are not strictly verifiable in any formal sense. This is as applicable to a newspaper or network news broadcast as it is to documentaries like *Fahrenheit 9/11* and *An Inconvenient Truth*, more traditional Hollywood movies like *Good Night, and Good Luck* and *Breach*, or to television series like *Law and Order* and *CSI: Miami*.

## PRACTICE

Finally, we suggest the concept of *practice*. We mean this in two senses: first, as in modeling, rehearsing, preparing, and learning for civic engagement; and second as actual engagement and participation, be it in further deliberation or more direct forms of political activity.

The Internet provides the most obvious example of how one might assess the democratic utility of the media by considering its potential for encouraging and facilitating democratic practice. As it is it provides numerous opportunities for citizens to both learn and act: from deliberating about issues of the day, to contacting public officials, to contributing money to political causes, to finding opportunities to volunteer in one's local community, to participating in national and even global movements. But there is no guarantee that this evolving medium will continue to develop its political potential—compared to the creativity and resources that have gone into making the Internet a good and safe place to shop, efforts to make it a good and safe place to both prepare for and actually engage in political action seem malnourished.

## CONCLUSIONS

The challenge in this new media environment is not to determine how to recreate the authoritative political information hierarchy of the past—for better or worse that battle has already been lost. Instead, the challenge is to create a media regime that provides the opportunities for a wide variety of voices, interests, and perspectives to vie for the public's attention and action. We believe that such an environment is preferable—more democratic—to assuming a priori that any particular group or interest should have the power to set the agenda. But whether one agrees with this assessment or not, there is no returning to the past system in which a limited set of elites served as sole gatekeepers and agenda setters.

Ultimately the new information environment requires not just a new definition of political relevance and democratic utility, but also an expanded definition of democratic citizenship. The distinctions between political, cultural, and economic elites, between information producers and consumers, even between elites and "the masses" are becoming more fluid. Consequently, notions of press responsibility that underlie traditional models of media and politics must be expanded to other individuals and institutions that influence politically relevant media texts. Similarly, notions of civic responsibility that are applied to the general public must be expanded to also apply to traditional political, cultural, and economic elites—to any individual or organization that is given access to the media soapbox in our expanded public square.

In the end, the issues raised by the changing media environment are not unlike those underlying the debate between John Dewey and Walter Lippmann of nearly a century ago. At its core remains the issue of the limitations of the public—the public and its problems as Dewey called it. As the position of journalists as authoritative gatekeepers declines, citizens are left more on their own to sort through competing perspectives and multiple sources of political information available to them. So, the critical capacities and interests of the public—media literacy—again becomes a central problem for democratic life. Like Dewey we see this problem as one that is the responsibility of all of us, the media included, to overcome.

## NOTES

1. All figures on the changes in the structure of the media environment are *from Statistical Abstract of the United States*, 2005 and *TV Dimensions 2004* (Media Dynamics, Inc). Internet statistics from http://www.websiteoptimization.com/bw/0403/.
2. The questions and the percentage of respondents answering correctly were: 79% were able to recall that Martha Stewart had been found guilty in her then recent trial; in an open-ended question, 71% volunteered that al Qaeda or Osama bin Laden were behind the September 11 attacks; 56% knew that the Republicans currently maintained a majority in the House of Representatives; and 55% were able to correctly estimate the current number of U.S. military deaths in Iraq.
3. These findings are generally supported by a range of other polls, including one testing levels of knowledge about candidates in the 2004 presidential election (Pew Research Center for the People and the Press 2004a).
4. These findings were supported by a Pew Foundation survey which found that a large majority of subjects expressed a desire for news with "no point of view," rather than news from their own political perspective (2004a).
5. The meaning of any concept or issue varies over time and among different people. Certain concepts, however, are likely to generate a greater variety of meaning by their very nature:

   When disagreement does not simply reflect different readings of evidence within a fully shared system of concepts, we can say that a conceptual dispute has arisen. When the concept involved is appraisive in that the state of affairs it describes is a valued achievement, when the practice described is internally complex in that its characterization involves references to several dimensions, and when the agreed and contested rules of application are relatively open, enabling parties to interpret even those shared rules differently as new and unforeseen situations arise, then the concept in question is an "essentially contested concept. (Connolly 1983: 10)

## REFERENCES

Ahonen, T. T. (2006, August 16). TV broadcast news lost half of its audience from peak—CBS now simulcasts online. *Financial Times*, p. 1A.

Connolly, W. E. (1983). *The terms of political discourse* (2nd ed.). Princeton, NJ: Princeton University Press.

Delli Carpini, M. X., & Keeter, S. (1996). *What Americans know about politics and why it matters*. New Haven, CT: Yale University Press.

Dewey, J. (1927). *The public and its problems*. New York: Henry Holt.

Entman, R. M. (1989). *Democracy without citizens: Media and the decay of American politics*. New York: Oxford University Press.

Entman, R. M. (2004). *Projections of power: Framing news, public opinion, and U.S. foreign policy*. Chicago: University of Chicago Press.

Iyengar, S. (1991). *Is anyone responsible? How television frames political issues*. Chicago: University of Chicago Press.

Iyengar, S., & Kinder, D. R. (1987). *News that matters: Television and American opinion*. Chicago: University of Chicago Press.

Iyengar, S., & Reeves, R. (1997). *Do the media govern? Politicians, voters, and reporters in America*. Thousand Oaks, CA: Sage.

Johnson, P., & Levin, G. (2002, March 4, 2002). It's not just Koppel vs. Letterman. *USA Today*, p. 1D.

Katz, J. (1997). *Media rants: Postpolitics in the digital nation*. San Francisco, CA: Hardwired.

Kinder, D., & Pax, S. (2003, June 4). Baghdad blogger. *Guardian Unlimited*,

Lazarsfeld, P. F., Berelson, B., & Gaudet, H. (1944). *The people's choice: How the voter makes up his mind in a presidential campaign*. New York: Duell, Sloan & Pearce.

McChesney, R. (2007). *The real communication revolution: Critical junctures and the future of media*. New York: New Press.

McChesney, R. W. (1993). *Telecommunications, mass media, and democracy: The battle for the control of U.S. broadcasting, 1928–1935*. New York: Oxford University Press.

Mutz, D. C., Sniderman, P. M., & Brody, R. A. (1996). *Political persuasion and attitude change*. Ann Arbor: University of Michigan Press.

O'Neill, O. (1996). *Towards justice and virtue: A constructive account of practical reasoning*. New York: Cambridge University Press.

Patterson, T. E. (1993). *Out of order*. New York: A. Knopf.

Pew Research Center for the People and the Press. (2004). *Cable and internet loom large in fragmented political news universe perceptions of partisan bias seen as growing, especially by democrats*. Washington D.C.: Pew Research Center for the People and the Press.

Pew Research Center for the People and the Press. (2004). *News audiences increasingly politicized online news audience larger, more diverse*. Washington D.C.: Pew Research Center for the People and the Press. Retrieved from http://people-press.org/reports/display.php3?ReportID=215

Press, A. L., Williams, B. A., Moore, E., & Johnson, C. (2005). Connecting the private to the public: Media and the future of public life. Paper presented at the Annual Meeting of the American Political Science Association.

Rich, F. (2002). Live by showbiz, die by showbiz. *The New York Times*, A15.

Starr, P. (2004). *The creation of the media: Political origins of modern communications*. New York: Basic Books.

Williams, B. A., & Delli Carpini, M. X. (2000). Unchained reaction: The collapse of media gatekeeping and the Clinton-Lewinsky scandal. *Journalism: Theory, Practice, Critique, 1*(1), 61–85.

Young, D. G., & Tisinger, R. M. (2006). Dispelling late-night myths: News consumption among late-night comedy viewers and the predictors of exposure to various late-night shows. *Harvard International Journal of Press/Politics, 11*(3), 113–134.

# 14

# What Can We Get Away With?
# The Ethics of Art and Entertainment
# in the Neoliberal World

## Angharad N. Valdivia

**Vignette 1**

The Art Institute of Chicago in spring of 2007 (February 17–May 12, 2007) showcased an exhibition entitled, *Cézanne to Picasso: Ambroise Vollard, Patron of the Avant Garde*. Organized by the Art Institute in conjunction and collaboration with the Metropolitan Museum of Art in New York City as well as the Musée D'Orsay and Réunion des Musées Nationaux, both of Paris, France, the exhibition brought together works by Paul Cézanne, Paul Gauguin, Vincent Van Gogh, Pierre Bonnard, Aristide Maillol, Henri Matisse, Pablo Picasso, and Edouard Vuillard. The group of artists ranges from the Spanish to the Dutch though most are French. The subjects of the paintings come from all walks of life, especially given the Impressionist, post-Impressionist, and the Fauve's tendency to represent the everyday and, until then, those considered too lowly to be the subjects of paintings. The collection of paintings, given the vicissitudes of art and war, as well as of circulation of art in global markets, came from a range of private and museum collections in the United States, Canada, Europe, including a significant number of the Gauguins loaned by the Hermitage in St. Petersburg, Russia. In sum, this is a transnational enterprise that exhibits a collection of art originally produced by a transnational group of artists whose works now circulate in transnational circuits.

What is missing, of course, are any female artists. However, not missing are the not so subtle ethical issues that relate to the production, collection, and exhibition of art. 1890s Paris was, as we suspect the art world continues to be, a very conservative, tight community of elite understanding about what is art and who is an artist. New schools of art as well as new artists had then, as they still have, a difficult time breaking into the circles of circulation and exhibition. It took a visionary such as Ambroise Vollard to bring to light, as it were, the works of many artists who are now enshrined at the core of our cultural heritage as cosmopolitan citizens of the Western World. The thought of Picasso literally throwing himself at Vollard so he would exhibit his work rattles one's senses. The ethical issues about whose work Vollard chose and, as important then as it is now, especially for a starving artist, the level of financial commitment and remuneration remain at the forefront of whose art survives and endures.

As it turns out, Vollard became a very rich man by showcasing the work of previously unknown artists. Some artists did not mind. Cézanne, for example, was independently wealthy so he appreciated any chance for his artwork to circulate. Gauguin, on the other hand, was living hand to mouth and greatly resented the fact that while Vollard grew richer through the sale of his works, Gauguin was barely able to continue producing his artwork. Gauguin's effort to shield himself from Vollard's uncanny ability to buy low and sell high proved to be mostly futile as no matter whom he left his paintings with, they mostly eventually ended up with Vollard who made tidy profits from all of them. We can also speculate that at least Gauguin had a troubled relationship with Vollard which was better than none at all. How many other artists did not manage even that and we have, as a result, not heard about them? Certainly, few had the opportunity that Matisse had to secure another exhibition patron and be able to later refuse Vollard's offers.

I begin with this example of Vollard and the Parisian art scene at the turn of last century (1890s–1920s) to underscore the continuities about issues of circulation and exhibition of art and other entertainment media despite much ahistorical assertion that all of these are new issues. Artists and other cultural producers then and now face complex ethical and economic issues that are transnational and complex. The thin line between agency and structure faced Van Gogh as much as it faces Eminem, Britney Spears, Marianne Pearl, Don Imus, and Mira Nair, to name but a few contemporary entertainment figures that cross media, nations, and genres. Issues of representation as they overlap with ethical issues remain now as they existed then. Granted, there wasn't a huge public outcry when Gauguin used Tahitian natives as the backdrop and foreground of his most famous works of art, such as the canonical "Where Do We Come From? What Are We? Where Are We Going?" (1897), but the use and representation of "others" remains at the core of ethical discussions today. Otherwise shock jock Don Imus's remarks about the Rutgers' girl's basketball team would not have caused the outbreak it did, resulting in Imus's firing and the bleeding of usage of the "n" word into critiques of hip hop, rap, talk radio in general, and who gets to use which words to refer to each other.

## Vignette 2

On April 4, 2007 in his *Imus in the Morning* radio show on the CBS radio network, speaking about the then ongoing women's basketball season, Don Imus referred to the Cinderella Rutgers team as "nappy-headed hos." The ensuing debate and ramifications of that statement included Imus's firing on April 12. Tellingly of how far we have veered from ethical sensibilities, Imus's lawyers sued CBS not because his freedom of speech had been violated but rather for the fact that CBS had not used the delay button, which implicitly meant that they knew that his comment was going on the air. The controversy extended to a wide ranging discussion of issues of race, gender and class——after all his comment succinctly highlighted all three of these vectors of difference. This discussion wrapped in the ongoing debate about misogyny in rap and hip hop music, who gets to use the n-word, or indeed any racial in-group specific slang as popular culture makes ethnic cross-dressing a desirable and marketable strategy of youth identity, and where is the line of good taste when so much of entertainment seems to revel in the flaunting of previous codes of sensitivity and politeness? A *Time* magazine article entitled "Who Can Say What?" (Poniewozik, 2007) included the following in its exploration of recent challenging contributors to the ethics of contemporary entertainment: Sacha Baron Cohen of *Borat: Cultural Learnings of America for Make Benefit Glorious Nation of Kazakhstan*, Quentin

Tarrantino, the star of the Sara Silverman Program, *South Park*, Ann Coulter, Michael Richards (the comedian who racially assaulted his heckler), Chris Rock, Rosie O'Donnell, Mel Gibson, Ludacris, Ted Danson, Jimmy the Greek, and many others. The list above includes comedians, political pundits, sports commentators, talk show hostesses, television shows, movie actors and directors—in sum, a range of those appearing in entertainment media today. All of them crossed that illusory line of ethics, art, and entertainment with a wide range of ramifications from none at all to delivering apologies and experiencing temporary loss of employment. In sum the repercussions were few and temporary.

The ongoing discussion continues to skirt issues of ethics, while Imus's lawyers focused on network culpability (the network was at fault for not pushing the red button), network executives and pundits turn to the issue of intent—did Imus "intend" to hurt people? Thus Sean Ross of radio research firm Edison Media Research asks:

> Are you saying you can't entertain without saying racial slurs or talking about assaulting prominent women? I would hope that these people see themselves as having more to say.... But the bigger issue is, I don't know what anyone who makes any of these comments means. I don't think it's because it's a deeply held opinion and they say they're doing it as comics to be provocative, which is maybe even worse. (quoted in Kaufman, 2007)

So here the issue becomes one of intent and provocation. Indeed much of the coverage centers around issues of "shock jocks" whose provocative style garners high ratings and therefore high profits for both radio and television networks. Many have "solved" the Imus controversy by suggesting that he, like fellow shock jock Howard Stern, just move over to satellite networks like Sirius and avoid Federal Communication Commission rules and any ethical issues altogether.

## Vignette 3

Having touched on issues of art and broadcast news/entertainment, another historically enduring concern in media studies has been that of children and youth. Millions of dollars and of journal article pages have been devoted to the area of children and the media. We treat this as an ethical concern because we implicitly assume that we must simultaneously protect our children and invest in them all that is good because they will become the adults of tomorrow. If we cannot ethically bring up our young, how can we expect to have an ethical society? Children and youth, as I read the other day in an airport sign, are part of our present but 100% of our future. Drawing on decades of studies wherein both advertisers and the media industry have sought to downplay the strong effects model, a research team composed of the foremost scholars in the field of children and the media (Anderson et al., 2003) found that "research on violent television and films, video games, and music reveals unequivocal evidence that media violence increases the likelihood of aggressive and violent behavior in both immediate and long-term contexts" (p. 81). This project updates previous research on two fronts. First it provides stronger evidence of short and long term effects. Second, it includes a wider range of media than just television—especially music and video games.

Violence, however, is not the only ethical issue arising out of entertainment media and our children. Other issues include overexposure to commercialization, poor eating habits, and, recently foregrounded in Hollywood films, the glamorization of smoking. In sum, this speaks to the ethics of product placement in mainstream media (Galician, 2004; Wenner, 2004).

In an article on health, Kluger (2007), drawing on research published in the Lancet and Pediatrics medical journals, connects the recent popularity of onscreen smoking in Hollywood movies to the recruitment of a new generation of smokers. Not only do recent studies suggest that exposure to these movies increases the likelihood of smoking but also that those from nonsmoking homes are more affected. The glamorous representation of smoking, in such films as *The Black Dahlia* (2006), starring Scarlett Johansson, apparently sanitizes what those from smoking households experience negatively at the level of smell and vision (stuff like stinky clothes, dirty ashtrays). Both health experts and children advocates worry about the ethical implications of glamorizing smoking for children who have no exposure to its bad and ugly side effects. However, they have to battle against an industry that both down plays effects and that is far more responsive to the profit motive than to ethical issues. Seldom do we get the hand wringing guilt brought on by the diagnosis of cancer. Such was the case when screenwriter Joe Eszterhaus wrote an op-ed piece in the *New York Times*, following throat cancer, about how he had contributed to the promotion of cigarette smoking to young audiences and how he wished he could take it back (Watson, 2004). More often health and children advocates are relegated to talks with Hollywood executives, the same people who strike lucrative tie-in deals with tobacco companies—*Thank You for Smoking* (2005), for instance, was a satirical treatment of this Hollywood–tobacco industry collaboration. This third vignette takes us full circle to the Parisian vignette in that the study of the ethics of art and entertainment must be considered in a global context where the profit motive is so strong as to nearly trump all other concerns.

## ETHICS OF ENTERTAINMENT AND ART WITHIN MEDIA STUDIES

The ethics of art and entertainment in the contemporary world generate many issues that need to be considered. Carroll (2000) documents the ongoing philosophical interest in the connections between ethics and aesthetics dating back to Plato and continuing into the eighteenth century. However, due to a variety of reasons beyond the scope of this chapter, having to do with tensions between utilitarian and Kantian philosophy, until recently there has been a two-century neglect of the connections. Contemporary ethicists treat art and entertainment media as the same category. For example in his exhaustive overview of recent research in art and ethical criticism, Carroll (2000) includes examples of Hollywood (*In and Out*) and European film, including the infamous Nazi-era *Triumph of the Will* by Leni Riefensthal, opera, literature (Shakespeare, Jane Austin, Herman Melville), paintings, etc. At a point in the essay he asks:

> There are so many kinds of art which mandate so many different kinds of audience responses. What if any significance do the Sex Pistols, the Egyptian pyramids, and Rembrandt's *Girl Sleeping* have in common? Why imagine there is a global criterion applicable to all arts? (p. 358)

This quote suggests that from an ethicist's perspective, approaches to art and entertainment are at least similar if not inseparable. I use that quote for a number of reasons. First it points to the important issue of reception. Second it covers a wide range of artistic forms, across time, space, and media. Third it points to the difficulty of developing one standard. Fourth, it acknowledges the "global," even if in a generic sense.

Within communication and media studies, Christians (2000, 2004, 2005) and Christians and Nordenstreng (2004) underscore the historical, theoretical, and philosophical of ethics and media studies (see Christians, 2005). Issues of truth, voice, authenticity, appropriation, and representation are principles to strive for even if routinely violated in a world that is mostly ruled by a capitalist transnational system that claims amorality but borders on and crosses right into immorality. Christians (2004) suggests that the study of media ethics is a rather new undertaking, with its news component predating more recent entertainment and art focus. Yet the study of ethics overlaps with older traditions within the field of media studies. We care about ethics because we hope that "media can contribute to high quality social dialogue" (Christians, 2000, p. 182). Can truth telling, for instance, be a moral standard that we should expect from media professionals? Christians foregrounds this value:

> Truth telling is the ethical framework that fundamentally reorders the media's professional culture and enables them to enrich social dialogue rather than undermine it. (p. 182)

Truth telling is inextricably linked to professional codes of objectivity for those producing, for example, television entertainment, who still have to abide by professional guidelines (Katan & Straniero-Sergio, 2001). We need to remember, however, that these guidelines may vary on a country by country basis, and even on a region by region basis, especially if the country is large or fragmented. For instance, the First Amendment is not a global law. It is part of the U.S. Constitution. To assert its primacy across the globe smacks of imperialist ethics—somewhat of a contradiction in terms.

While there are still educators and politicians who strive to draw the thin line between art and entertainment, blurring of these lines is evident both in aesthetic theory (see Carroll, 2000) and in media and cultural studies. The traditional separation between information/education and entertainment/leisure has been thoroughly challenged, both by scholars and by new media genres. In particular hybrid genres of "infotainment" shows such as some forms of talk shows, entertainment news, and the inclusion of celebrity culture in most U.S. news venues ranging from CNN to the recent redesign of *Time* magazine, which makes it look more like *People* than a news magazine, should prompt us to reconsider the tenets of liberal philosophy that undergird so much of media production and ethics.

The fact that Comedy Central, a U.S. cable network, has a Pulitzer Prize winning news show, the Daily Show, should tip us off that people are consuming news differently from before. Granting a show in a comedy network more attention and legitimacy than traditional venues such as the prestige press and news networks—for the Pulitzer Prize is about hallowed standards of journalism—suggests a production, audience, and critic shift in valuation. Whereas information was deemed to be the core of liberal philosophy's privileging of the educational and democratic components of the media, the latter, entertainment/leisure, were, until quite recently the discarded and derided material that we now know as popular culture. However as many cultural studies scholars haven noted (see Giles & Middleton, 1999; Japp et al., 2005; Storey, 2003), the genres of art and entertainment not only educate us all but are nearly impossible to separate from the genres of news and information. They are all material produced within culture, and as such they circulate cultural understandings which in turn we are shaped by and we shape. This cultural turn has spurred media ethics scholars (e.g., Good & Dillon, 2002; Katan & Straniero-Sergio, 2001; Smoot Egan, 2004; Watson, 2004) to pursue arts and entertainment as a primary focus. In fact, dating back to the 1980s scholars sought to connect the literature and research on the visual to that of ethics (Gross et al., 1989).

The global dimension of art and entertainment, though treated by some as a new thing, really has concerned philosophers for centuries and, more recently, media theorists since the eighties. Thus Communication Ethics and Global Change (Cooper, 1989) explored, on a country-by-country basis, ethical issues of the media. That national focus, though still important, is lately being complemented by a transnational approach that takes hybridity, at the level of genre and of population, as central. For example, in an essay about Italian television and hybrid genres Katan and Straniero-Sergio (2001) remind us that there is cultural variability to measures of sincerity. González (in press) builds much of his work on border youth on different approaches and valuations of humor between the United States and Mexico.

Unsurprisingly measures of good taste and of sexual explicitness also vary cross-culturally. For example, German over-the-air television broadcasts frontal nudity after 10 p.m. while U.S. television is far more restrained in matters of sexuality and nudity. On the other hand, the level of violence in U.S. television seems to be unchecked whereas in other countries there are stricter guidelines for this type of content. Similarly there is a wide range of tolerance for representations of gender in general and women in particular throughout the globe. Nonetheless, as media circulates globally and populations experience forced or voluntary mobility, some form of professional ethics that apply transnationally seem to be in order. The fact is that art and entertainment circulate globally, that not all global players are equally empowered, and thus ethical components must be thought about in those terms.

While it is logical and intuitive that professional ethics would relate to entertainment, the study of the ethics of art and entertainment also implicitly overlaps with the dominant social scientific paradigm of the "effects" tradition within U. S. communication and media studies.[1] Ethics is to the humanist as effects is to the scientific approach. In fact, one might say that it is the implicit ethical concern that drives the effects tradition. Why would we care about children and youth and the media were it not for a normative concern? Why would community standards be of importance if negative effects, in the sense of anti-social and disruptive implications, were not part of the picture? The inclusion of children and youth, moreover, reinforces the move from a focus on news and information to entertainment and art. Even education is moving from a straightforward delivery of information to a more entertaining delivery that might attract a longer attention span and bigger, or at least, more desirable target audiences. Tate Modern in London, England employs intricate interactive audiovisual pads for children to navigate the extensive collection and unusual building.[2] Nearly all major museums, such as the Chicago Art Institute and the Metropolitan Museum of Art in New York or the Prado in Madrid and the already mentioned Tate Modern make efforts to connect the art to children's modern and hi-tech sensibilities.

Why is it, then, that media and art are combined to provide a suitable and entertaining option for children? Part of the answer must be that children travel with parents and this strategy brings in a bigger total of visitors. However, another part is the normative belief that art makes us all better citizens, an Arnoldian vestige that is still strong. Maybe an art literate child will be a more tolerant, creative, cosmopolitan adult? Here we have an instance where ethical issues function against the backdrop of implicit effects. More often, as in the case with violence, consumerism, and smoking, effects function against the implicit backdrop of ethics. Both times they are intertwined for effects and ethics really inform each other. In a cultural climate wherein scientific evidence is the most authoritative, both government and industry demand that if not proof at least strong correlations and contributing factors be demonstrated before any corrective steps are taken.

Another major area of media studies that predates and greatly overlaps with the study of the ethics of art and entertainment is the political economy of communications, a normative theory that examines power in media (McQuail, 2005). As Christians (2004) begins in his essay "Ethical and Normative Perspectives," media ethics are about "recognizing the power of mass communications in today's global world" (p. 19). Issues of power in a transnational context are of major concern to scholars of political economy. We cannot discuss anything in the contemporary world, and certainly not media and entertainment, without attention paid to the global political economy of media industries (Herman & McChesney, 1997; Mosco, 2004; Schiller, 2007). Again, as with effects, the concern with concentrated ownership and control of the media across the globe implicitly references the potential that the profit motive will trump any moral or ethical sensibilities. Although Marx called capitalism an "amoral" system, many currently would argue that it is downright immoral. What some call globalization but what is widely acknowledged as a form of not only speedy and widespread global interconnectivity but also one that is accompanied by concentrations of ownership and control, has immense ethical implications for both the global North and South. New technologies may use new modalities of delivery but are being subsumed under very traditional corporate structures such as the most powerful contemporary Diaspora, transnational capital. In fact, just as with radio and television, the same networks/conglomerates appear prominently with new media, though with some newcomers to be sure. Whereas in the 1970s the United States appeared as a nearly undisputed hegemony on global communications, both in hardware and software, by 2007 Jeremy Tunstall revised the title of his original book *The Media Are American* (1977) to *The Media Were American* (2008).

Thirty years have seen the rise of other global participants but we must not lose sight of the fact that the United States is still a major player in global communications (Morley, 2004). In many markets the United States remains a prominent if not dominant presence in terms of media, software, and genres. Synergy and convergence in terms of ownership and media delivery mean that art and other forms of entertainment are likely to be circulated, distributed, and exhibited by the same conglomerate. Hollywood product placements are influenced by these synergies though the most successful participant, and probably the original synergy conglomerate, is Disney. Representing itself as a family friendly conglomerate, Disney has created new ventures so as to be able to reach less than family friendly audiences, such as Buena Vista pictures, purveyors of PG fare.

The reason to discuss issues of synergy, conglomerates, and transnational media concentration is that the type of footloose capital that characterizes the contemporary neoliberal era has no patience with ethics. When ethics interferes with productivity and profit, mobility can always be the answer. Whereas Don Imus has to respond within a national space, albeit temporarily, transnational corporations have the luxury of exploring other countries in case of ethical violations ranging from content to poor treatment of workers.

As a result, art and entertainment ethics have to be globally considered although ethical issues are usually approached on a case-by-case basis. For instance, if we consider the First Amendment to the U. S. Constitution as one of the backbones of ethical approaches in media content, then we have to realize this is a national issue. However, the fact that media, entertainment, and art are now usually transnationally produced and, certainly, transnationally distributed, makes many U.S.-based media issues global ones. That we are exporting capitalism goes without saying. That exportation has to include some degree of glocalization—that is, the acknowledgment that products have to be somewhat tailored to a local situation, even in the case of McDonald's—is also a crucial component of a successful transnational strategy. Yet as Herbert Schiller (1989) encouraged us to ask long ago, what else are we exporting? Is it a way of life beyond just media genres and particular products? Are we exporting anorexia, for example? Or bad eating habits? Smoking and violence? Contributing to the growing existence of violent adults? Lest we assume a media-centric approach, the issue of contributing to a climate rather than causing an effect remains at the core of ethical research in the media.

Given the contemporary global climate wherein neoliberalism, with its drive for privatization and commoditization go nearly unchecked, art and entertainment as profitable components of a globally produced and circulating media circuit of culture have to be analyzed in terms of ethics and be subject to some form of ethical standards. The problem, of course, lies in the tension for some form of global ethical standard, or protonorm, and the need to pay attention to cultural differences and sensibilities. We certainly would not advocate deploying, yet again, another imperialistically conceived standard yet we must be able to voice, as global citizens, some ethical concerns that will value the sanctity of life and the environment. Christians and Nordenstreng (2004) suggest:

> Instead, universal ethical principles are the most appropriate framework, and the cross-cultural axis around which these principles revolve is the sacredness of human life. Embedded in the protonorm of human sacredness are such ethical principles as human dignity, truthtelling, and nonmaleficence. These principles are citizen ethics rather than professional ethics.... (p. 3)

In an effort to develop a protonorm with global sensitivity and agreement, the participants in the above project sought to bring the issue of ethics and media to something all could agree with: human sacredness. As an ethical standard, if human sacredness is violated, no matter what the cultural context, a line has been crossed and all of us as members of a global community ought to censure it and work toward its correction and disappearance. As well, the move from professional to citizen ethic broadens the scope to not just media producers but to all of us who are enveloped in a media world as citizens striving for democracy. It is a different language but a similar sentiment to Cornell West, the philosopher, who advocates love and hope as forms of ethical engagements in contemporary life (McPhail, 2002). This extends issues of ethics of art and entertainment to reception to be sure. In fact many of the essays in Japp et al. (2005) are:

> [G]rounded in the assumption that humans construct meaning in and through symbol systems and that these constructions are imbued with ethical implications and rhetorical potential. (p.8)

Extending art and entertainment ethics to the audience, and more inclusively, to the citizenry brings up questions of enfranchisement, especially along the lines of difference. One difference already mentioned, that of age, resonates with media scholars as we, all of us implicitly adult, are guardians of their welfare. Other components of difference such as transnational experience are also included in approaches that seek to develop ethics for global change or establish a protonorm. Still the two most often mentioned categories of difference, gender and race, remain to be discussed.

As Ella Shohat (1991) notes, race is always present in media, whether explicitly, at an "epidermal" level, or implicitly. Contemporary scholars of race and gender historicize this remark as well as document it persistence. All three vignettes at the beginning of this chapter illustrate this point. First, the art collector's world was mostly a white one representing whiteness. The ethical implications of Gauguin's representations of natives in relation to nature and to the implicit superiority of the European subject were explored after his death (see Dorra, 2007). Indeed the popularity of his Tahitian work was fully posthumous. Nonetheless his paintings speak to issues of race, voice, and representation that are so central to an ethical engagement with issues of the ethics of art and entertainment (hooks, 1995; Valdivia, 2002). Who represents whom and for what purposes, is a question that guides contemporary ethics of art and entertainment. How are narratives of racial difference, deployed to curtail social justice, included in art and entertainment?

In vignette 2, the Don Imus controversy, issues of race and representation are explicitly and immediately apparent. That it took nearly a week for the CBS radio network to take a stance on the comment is what is surprising. Imus's remarks represented a largely underclass group of mostly African-American basketball players in relation to narratives of race that code African-American women as sexually deviant and permanently members of the underclass "hos" and as unable to conform to Eurocentric ideals of beauty—"nappy headed." The reaction from many different constituencies was immediate in its ethical critique. What does a comment like this tell girls/women in general and African-American girls/women in particular? Was the fact that the team was composed of high achieving college students not relevant to the residual coding of all women of color as underclass? What was the racial implication being made in relation to other women's basketball teams composed mostly of white players? Was this any different than former Penn State women's basketball coach Renee Portland's public remarks that her team harbored no lesbians? Who was the implicit listener of the show in particular and that type of shock radio in general? What does it tell us that such shows are highly rated and that their hosts make millions of dollars a year to spew exactly such comments? Did the FCC and community standards have a responsibility to ban such remarks? Some advertisers did not wait—American Express, Staples, and Procter & Gamble pulled out. Imus responded:

> This phrase that I use, it originated in the black community. That didn't give me a right to use it, but that's where it originated. Who calls who that and why? We need to know that. I need to know that. (Poniewozik, 2007, p. 35)

In a multicultural world in which many previously marginalized, oppressed, or unacknowledged populations are beginning to gain a voice and representation in relation to the ethics of art and entertainment, these questions have no easy answers. In fact these very same gaffes have happened to many other public figures, with differential effects. The immediate link to the frequent use of this word as well as many others in rap, hip hop, and the comedy of Chris Rock, for example, was inevitable. Feminists, white and black, weighed in on the misogyny of music and comedy. If anything can be said of the Imus case, it opened up a discussion that many did not want to enter. It simultaneously highlighted the huge profits to be made from racist and sexist programming. The question that seems to guide these shock jocks is not what is ethical but what can we get away with?

Vignette 3, children and youth and smoking, implicitly took up issues of race and gender. Much of the children and the media literature had implicitly recruited us to approve of the normalization of white middle-class childhood with class and race difference usually coding in for deviance. Unstated in the concern for the stronger effects upon children who do not live in smoking families is that these are white middle-class children we are talking about. We are implicitly assuming that smoking is more prevalent in racialized and working-class families. In fact Hollywood never stopped representing smoking, but until recently it was used as a code for precisely working- or underclass, deviant, or people of color. The recent change in representation is that the epitome of beauty, heterosexuality, and white femininity, Scarlett Johansson, is now the one smoking. This is troubling because this can potentially recruit "our" children, the children of the implicit reader of *Time* magazine, in its entire *People*-like splendor.

In fact smoking does violate the protonorm, the sanctity of human life, because it has been scientifically proven to cause cancer. It also affects us all through second hand smoke. The effects are material as well as biological. Not only does the body deteriorate, but the health costs to U.S. taxpayers and the economy, in terms of lost hours of work, are huge. There are ethical issues with the glamorized representation of smoking for it encourages behavior that threatens the sanctity of life. Yet, as with the other vignettes, there is the tension between ethical considerations and the profit motive. While shameless marketing of cigarettes to children is largely frowned upon, the prevalent use of product placement in Hollywood film (Galician, 2004; Wenner, 2004) is a way around the ethics of entertainment. The complicit avoidance of mainstream media to picture celebrities smoking, dating back to Jackie-O who died of cancer, to present-day starlets such as

Paris Hilton and Lindsay Lohan, speaks much more of an effort to shield special people from the stigma of smoking than our population from its glamorization.

## CONCLUSION

I have charted a path of consideration of art and entertainment as forms of popular culture that have been a concern to philosophers and more recently media scholars as well as to the general public. After a brief two-century break, the ethics of art and entertainment have returned to the attention of philosophers. Yet as Christians and Carroll note, contemporary discussions might deal with newer technologies but they echo issues dating back to Plato. Using three vignettes as a device to discuss ethical issues in art and entertainment, we can see that issues of appropriation, transnational flows, and race and gender are both long-standing and enduring. That race and gender are discussed more contemporarily does not mean that the issues were not present in Plato's or Vollard's time. What has accelerated is the global concentration of ownership and control of the media. While this does not imply some simplistic model of dominance, it does have major ramifications for ethics. At a national level, the drive for profit trumps ethical principles in all but the most extreme cases. With Don Imus it remains to be seen whether his remarks will permanently hurt his career. If previous shock jock controversies are any indication, he will return stronger and better paid than before.

At a transnational level, our ability to export mass quantities of entertainment and the synergistic capabilities to circulate art in tandem with other forms of entertainment potentially means that we are exporting our ethics. The effort to come up with a universal agreement about a set of ethics of entertainment has resulted in human sacredness as a protonorm. That remains a guiding form at the level of principle. Yet at the level of practice what seems to be most operative is the range of things that a person or corporation can get away with. Ethical guidelines are just that—guidelines. It remains up to all of us as global citizens to strive for a more just and ethical media. Thus Christians and Nordenstreng's (2004) change from professionals to ethics both universalizes and democratizes the practice and enforcement of ethics.

## NOTES

1. I single out the United States because the dominant paradigm speaks to the endurance of positivism within the U.S. academy. Communication and media studies globally do not necessarily deploy the same paradigms, or at least the same dominant paradigms.
2. From an anecdotal perspective, the Tate Modern electronic pad was a total hit with my seven and twenty-two-year-olds. My mother and I could not figure out how to use it!

## REFERENCES

Anderson, C. A., L. Berkowitz, E. Donnerstein, L. R. Huesmann, J. D. Johnson, D. Linz, N. M. Malamuth, & E. Wartella (2003). The influence of media violence on youth. *Psychological Science in the Public Interest, 4*:3, 81.

Carroll, N. (2000). Art and Ethical Criticism: An Overview of Recent Directions in Research. *Ethics. 110*: 2, 350–387.

Christians, C. (2000). Social Dialogue and Media Ethics. *Ethical Perspectives. 7*:2–3, 182–193.

Christians, C. (2004). Ethical and Normative Perspectives. In J. H. Downing (Ed.), *The Sage Handbook of Media Studies* (pp. 19–40). Thousand Oaks, CA: Sage.

Christians, C. (2005). Foreword. In P. Patterson & L. Wilkins (Eds.), *Media Ethics: Issues and Cases*. Boston: McGraw-Hill.

Christians, C., & K. Nordenstreng (2004). Social Responsibility Worldwide. *Journal of Mass Media Ethics, 19*:1, 3–28.

Cooper, T. W. (Ed.). (1989). *Communication Ethics and Global Change*. White Plains, NY: Longman.

Dorra, H. (2007). *The Symbolism of Paul Gauguin: Erotica, Exotica, and the Great Dilemmas of Humanity*. Berkeley: University of California Press.

Galician, M. (Ed.). (2004). *Handbook of Product Placement in the Mass Media: New Strategies in Marketing Theory, Practice, Trends, and Ethics*. New York: Best Business Books.

Giles, J., & T. Middleton. (1999). *Studying Culture: A Practical Introduction*. Oxford, UK: Blackwell.

González, D. (in press). Watching Over the Border: A Case Study of the Mexico-United States Television and Youth Audience. In A. N. Valdivia (Ed.), *Latina/o Communication Studies Today*. New York: Peter Lang.

Good, H., & M. J. Dillon (2002). *Media Ethics Goes to the Movies*. Westport, CT: Praeger.

Gross, L., J. S. Katz, & J. Ruby (Eds.). (1989). *Image Ethics: The Moral Rights of Subjects in Photographs, Film, and Television*. New York: Oxford University Press.

Herman, E. S., & R. McChesney. (1997). *Global Media: The New Missionaries of Corporate Capitalism*. London: Cassell.

hooks, b. (1994). *Teaching to Transgress: Education as the Practice of Freedom*. New York: Routledge.

hooks, b. (1995). *Art on My Mind: Visual Politics*. New York: New Press.

Japp, P. M., M. Meister, & D. K. Japp (Eds.). (2005). *Communication Ethics, Media, & Popular Culture*. New York: Peter Lang.

Katan, D., & F. Straniero-Sergio (2001). *Look Who's Talking: The Ethics of Entertainment and Talkshow Interpreting*. The Translator.

Kaufman, G. (2007). Is Shock Radio Dead? More Potty-Mouthed DJs Join Don Imus in Doghouse: Bad Boys of Radio Living on Borrowed Time as Sexist, Slur-Filled Gags Garner Suspensions, Firings. Retrieved May 15 2007 6:12 pm EDT from http://www.Mtvnews.com.

Kluger, J. (2007, April 23). Hollywood's Smoke Alarm. *Time*, 59–61.

McPhail, M. L. (2002). Race, Coherence, and Moral Knowledge: Cornel West's Rhetoric and Politics of Convergence. In S. L. Bracci & C. G. Christians (Eds.), *Moral Engagement in Public Life: Theorists for Contemporary Ethics*. New York: Peter Lang.

McQuail, D. (2005). *McQuail's Mass Communication Theory* (5th ed.). London: Sage.

Morley, D. (2006). Globalisation and Cultural Imperialism Reconsidered: Old Questions in New Guises. In J. Curran a& D, Morley (Eds.), *Media and Cultural Theory* (pp. 30–43). New York: Routledge.

Mosco, V. (2004). *The Digital Sublime: Myth, Power, and Cyberspace*. Cambridge, MA: MIT Press.

Poniewozik, J. (2007, April 23). Who Can Say What? *Time*, 32–38.

Schiller, D. (2007). *How to Think about Information*. Urbana: University of Illinois Press.

Schiller, H. (1989). *Culture Inc. The Corporate Takeover of Public Expression*. New York: Oxford University Press.

Shohat, E. (1991). Ethnicities in Relation: Toward a Multicultural Reading of American Cinema. In L. Friedman (Ed.), *Unspeakable Images: Ethnicity and the American Cinema* (pp. 215–250). Urbana: University of Illinois Press,

Smoot Egan, K. (2004). The Ethics of Entertainment Television: Applying Paul Ricoeur's Spiral of Mimesis for Authenticity as a Moral Standard. *Journal of Popular film and Television. 34*:1, 158–166.

Storey, J. (2003). *Inventing Popular Culture: From Folklore to Globalization*. Oxford, UK: Blackwell.

Tunstall, J. (1977). *The Media Are American*. New York: Columbia University Press.

Tunstall, J. (2008). *The Media Were American: US Mass Media in Decline*. New York: Oxford University Press.

Valdivia, A. N. (2002). bell hooks: Ethics from the Margins. *Qualitative Inquiry, 8*:3.

Watson, M. A. (2004). Ethics in Entertainment Television: Introduction. *Journal of Popular Film and Television. 34*:1, 146–148.

Wenner, L. A. (2004). On the Ethics of Product Placement in Media Entertainment. In M. Galician (Ed.), *Handbook of Product Placement in the Mass Media: New Strategies in Marketing Theory, Practice, Trends, and Ethics* (pp. 101–132). Binghamton, NY: Best Business Books.

# III
# CONCRETE ISSUES

# 15

# Justice as a Journalistic Value and Goal

## David A. Craig

When reporters uncover corruption in a city police department, they are upholding justice as a value of journalism. When editors plan a series aimed at inequities in availability of housing by race, they are making justice one of their goals. Whenever journalists do stories that point out unfairness in how people are treated, justice lies in the background even if it is not explicitly on the minds of reporters and editors.

A commitment to justice has a long tradition in journalism. Investigative reporting from the work of the muckrakers in the early 20th century to contemporary investigations of individual and social problems (Protess et al., 1991; J. S. Serrin & W. Serrin, 2002; Tichi, 2004) has often addressed topics with justice implications. But justice is served by reporting across a variety of beats—for example, through political stories that explain candidate positions on important social issues and medical stories that help people navigate the complexities of the healthcare system.

While journalists have been pursuing stories that involve dimensions of justice, media scholars have been reflecting in recent decades on what justice means, many of them drawing on historical or current lines of thinking from philosophy, political theory, and psychology. This thinking is important to journalism students and practitioners because it offers ways to more carefully and systematically apply concepts of justice to journalism, as well as to critically evaluate how journalists think about justice and have actually applied it. Despite the attention to justice by thoughtful and caring journalists, it would be easy for this concern to be squeezed out of stories under the pressure of competition and profit.

This chapter will provide an overview of what media scholars have said about justice. It will then focus on an important aspect of the topic that has received relatively little attention: how justice as an ethical value can be used to critique and improve coverage of topics in which justice is an important dimension of the story itself. The chapter will close with suggestions for additional research on justice as a value and goal of journalism.

## LITERATURE AND CONCEPTS

When media scholars examine justice, they are stepping into an area that has been a long-time concern of philosophers and political theorists, as well as a matter addressed by psychologists who think about how people develop in their moral reasoning. Before discussing the variety of thinking about justice in media scholarship, it is appropriate to offer a definition that crosses several scholarly traditions about what justice means. Beauchamp and Childress (2001), writing in the context of medical ethics, state that a variety of philosophical perspectives "interpret justice as fair, equitable, and appropriate treatment in light of what is due or owed to persons" (p. 226). Although it comes from outside the field of journalism, this definition effectively summarizes important concerns implicit in journalists' consideration of justice as a value to guide coverage and a goal of coverage. Beyond this broad definition, though, a variety of differences in emphasis and substance are evident in the notions of justice that scholars have applied to journalism. This section will examine several strands of thinking in media scholarship that relate to justice: work based on utilitarianism, the egalitarianism of John Rawls (1971), communitarianism, and moral development theory (including discussion of feminist, care based critiques of justice), and finally other work rooted in a variety of perspectives.

## UTILITARIAN-BASED PERSPECTIVES

Utilitarianism, particularly the version developed by John Stuart Mill in the 19th century, has been a prominent perspective in media ethics textbooks. This perspective's focus on the weighing of goods and harms to maximize benefit has brought attention to the importance of considering consequences in journalistic decisions. Several books (Bivins, 2004; Christians, Rotzoll, Fackler, McKee, & Woods, 2005; Day, 2006; Patterson & Wilkins, 2005; Smith, 2003) include summaries of utilitarianism of varying lengths with application to journalism. Most of these discussions do not explicitly relate utilitarianism to justice—though the connection is implied in Patterson and Wilkins's discussion of utilitarianism as a justification for investigative reporting that may harm the subject in the interest of the general welfare (p. 11).

Mill, however, did explicitly connect justice and utility. In his view, people's rights ought to be defended because of the benefit of protecting their security—an "extraordinarily important and impressive kind of utility" (2003, p. 226). For Mill, justice based on utility is "the chief part, and incomparably the most sacred and binding part, of all morality" (p. 231). Bivins's (2004) discussion of utilitarianism does acknowledge the linkage that Mill made between justice and utility, noting (p. 97) that Mill pointed to the importance of several dimensions of justice including giving to those who are deserving and not showing partiality.

## PERSPECTIVES RELATED TO RAWLS

Just as Mill's theory was one of the most influential to grow out of the 19th century, John Rawls's theory of justice—developed in the book by that name (1971)—was one of the most prominent perspectives on justice from the 20th. Rawls regards justice fundamentally as a notion of fairness to members of society that grows out of a hypothetical "original position" in which "no one knows his place in society, his class position or social status, nor does any one know his fortune in the distribution of natural assets and abilities, his intelligence, strength, and the like.... The principles of justice are chosen behind a veil of ignorance" (p. 12). Working from this vantage point, it is expected that people will be sensitive to those who are least advantaged, allowing inequalities only if they benefit those people (pp. 14–15). Beauchamp and Childress (2001) called Rawls's theory "the major contemporary example of qualified egalitarianism" (p. 234).

As with utilitarianism, several books on media ethics (Christians et al., 2005; Day, 2006; Patterson & Wilkins, 2005; Smith, 2003) discuss and apply Rawls's perspective at least briefly.

For example, Patterson and Wilkins (2005, pp. 142–143) suggest that the veil of ignorance can be helpful when considering whether journalists should photograph or talk with survivors of an airline crash at the scene. Behind the veil of ignorance, the stakeholders—such as a reporter, a survivor, a family member, and a reader—would not know which position they would occupy when they emerged and would therefore be sensitive to considerations of need to know and right to privacy from a variety of perspectives.

Lambeth (1992) also drew on Rawls's perspective in presenting justice as part of a framework of five principles for ethical decision making in journalism—a framework that is of central importance in media ethics scholarship because of its systematic incorporation of both justice and other important considerations such as truth-telling and freedom. Lambeth argued that Rawls provided a strong theoretical grounding for the watchdog role of the news media. A journalist acting in the interest of justice should ask critical questions in covering the major institutions of society—questions such as: "Are agreed-upon rules and procedures followed consistently and uniformly? Are some groups or classes of persons enjoying more than their fair share of goods or bearing more than their fair share of the burdens?" (p. 29). Lambeth's framework in turn formed the theoretical basis for a study by Hadley (1989) of how television news directors viewed ethical questions.

## COMMUNITARIAN PERSPECTIVES

A third perspective on justice, communitarianism, developed in the late 20th century. Some thinkers who have been called communitarians, such as Robert Bellah and his colleagues (Bellah, Madsen, Sullivan, Swidler, & Tipton, 1985, 1991), have reacted to what they see as a negative impact of overemphasis on individualism, particularly in American society. Others, such as Michael Sandel (1982), have argued that the very view of the person that underlies liberal political theory's emphasis on the individual is wrong (Mulhall & Swift, 1992; Craig, 1996). Sandel argues that Rawls viewed the self incorrectly as independent of particular aims or attachments to others and to a community. This conception of self would make people unable to make more than arbitrary choices about the principles of justice (Kukathas & Pettit, 1990). Communitarianism undergirds a strong notion of justice by making people's connection to one another central to their lives.

Christians, Ferré, and Fackler (1993) carried communitarian thought into the realm of theory about the proper role of the news media in society. They argued that justice must be a central goal of journalism:

> A press nurtured by communitarian ethics requires more of itself than fair treatment of events deemed worthy of coverage. Under the notion that justice itself—and not merely haphazard public enlightenment—is a *telos* of the press, the news-media system stands under obligation to tell the stories that justice requires. (p. 93)

In this application, just journalism means speaking up for people who are "abused or ignored by established power" (p. 92). More specifically, Christians and his colleagues ask: "Is the press a voice for the unemployed, food-stamp recipients, Appalachian miners, the urban poor, Hispanics in rural shacks, the elderly, women discriminated against in hiring and promotion, ethnic minorities with no future in North America's downsizing economy?" (p. 92). This perspective provides a robust justification for why journalists should make the needs of marginalized people a priority.

## WORKS DISCUSSING MORAL DEVELOPMENT THEORY

Several media scholars have examined work in moral development theory, which addresses how people develop in their thinking about ethical matters. In particular, scholars have drawn on Kohlberg's (1981) work, which places priority on justice as a universal ethical principle. Some of them have contrasted it with the work of feminist scholar Carol Gilligan (1982), who emphasizes care and the interaction of people in relationships.

- Barger (2003) used Kohlberg's moral development theory to evaluate moral language in newspaper columns and letters to the editor. She found that most arguments did not rise to Kohlberg's postconventional level, in which fairness and justice become central considerations.
- Wilkins and Coleman (2005) used the Defining Issues Test, which was influenced by Kohlberg's framework, to evaluate how journalists think through ethical decisions. A disturbing finding was that students showed lower levels of ethical reasoning when evaluating photos that showed black rather than white people. Spurred by this finding, the authors called for a renewed emphasis on social justice in the teaching of journalism ethics.
- Lind (1996) evaluated the presence of justice and care orientations in viewers' evaluation of ethically controversial television news stories. She found that considerations of justice, emphasizing issues such as objectivity, were considerably more prevalent than considerations of care, emphasizing matters such as benefits and harms—but that both were commonly used. The orientation varied depending on story topic.
- Steiner and Okrusch (2006) criticized a justice-based model for journalism built on rights—what they see as the prevailing ethical foundation for journalism in the United States—as too "thin" (p. 103) and explored the contribution of care to the strengthening of journalism ethics, urging journalists to "care toward justice" (p. 116). They suggested that public journalism has already melded the two and argued that "incorporation of some revised ethic of care would help revitalize a stronger and more philosophically and politically defensible concept of justice and (human) rights" (p. 119).

## OTHER PERSPECTIVES ON JUSTICE

The ethical issue of justice has also been stated or implied in other work on journalism. Brislin (1992) applied just war theory developed historically in Christian theology to create a model of just journalism in which issues including intention, degree of harm, and alternatives are considered in evaluating the ethics of actions that, like war, would be extreme—in a journalistic context, actions such as deception or invasion of privacy. Pippert (1989), in a book focused on truth as an ethical value, argued that reporters who seek truth will also uncover issues of justice. He said this aspect of stories will emerge in coverage of a variety of topics from civil rights to sports and business if reporters look for it. "The mass media must take note of wrong and oppressive conditions in our society and write stories for the express purpose of bringing about justice and peace" (p. 43). Ettema and Glasser (1998), while not explicitly focusing on justice as an ethical value, argued strongly that investigative reporters are making moral judgments throughout their work as they cover stories of wrongdoing in society.

## JUSTICE AS A VALUE FOR CRITIQUING NEWS COVERAGE

As the previous discussion of concepts and literature makes clear, scholars have thought about justice and applied this principle to journalism from a variety of perspectives. Some of this work has raised questions to guide coverage or suggested topics for attention. This section will explore another framework (Craig, 1997, 1999) that uses justice and related considerations as a tool to critique and improve news coverage—particularly coverage in which justice is an important dimension of the story itself. This framework and the questions it implies will be presented, followed by discussion of the relevance of these questions to coverage of medicine and science, business, and other topics.

### A Framework for Evaluating Coverage

Ethical concerns including justice are important angles in coverage of topics ranging from genetic testing to the conduct of corporate executives. Across professions, from medicine to business to law, justice is a relevant consideration for journalists in evaluating the work of practitioners in these fields and the broader institutional context in which they function. The work of Lambeth (1992) paved the way for systematic evaluation of coverage of professions by urging that journalists ask justice-based questions and report in depth on what advances or hinders excellence in specific professions. Building on this work, Craig (1997, 1999) proposed a framework for evaluating and improving coverage of issues in professions and society. The framework regards some—but not comprehensive—coverage of the ethical dimension as an ethical obligation of journalists covering issues with important ethical implications. Because of the limitations imposed by time and space constraints and other factors, journalists cannot be expected to write thoroughly about justice and other ethical issues in all or even most stories. However, they should pay some attention to these issues in the overall coverage of a topic that raises important ethical issues or in individual stories that are intended to examine it in depth. This argument is consistent with social responsibility (Commission on Freedom of the Press, 1947; Siebert, Peterson, & Schramm, 1956) and communitarian (Christians et al., 1993) theories about what the role of the press should be, since the assumption is that journalists should make it a priority to serve society rather than simply to present information.

Evaluation of the place of justice and other ethical issues can be done more specifically under this framework by examining four criteria for evaluating the adequacy of coverage. Although the framework goes beyond considerations of justice, each component of it can help in evaluation of how well relevant issues of justice are being portrayed in stories.

- Levels of analysis: ethical issues in areas such as medicine, business, and government play out in settings that involve not only the decisions of individuals but also the organizational/institutional, professional, and social contexts in which they function. Good coverage should pay attention to more than one level of analysis. In relation to justice specifically, consideration of multiple levels is important because organizations provide important constraints on the ability of individuals to act justly or receive justice. At their best, they may help to foster justice on behalf of individuals. Professional expectations and norms similarly may, on the positive side, encourage just decision making and treatment of people, or they may leave room for unjust practices. The broader social environment may encourage or discourage just behavior, depending, for example, on whether fair treatment of minorities is becoming more or less of an expectation in the broader society.

- Relevant parties: numerous parties such as doctors and executives, institutions such as hospitals and corporations, and professional bodies may play a part in decisions that have implications for justice. In a story involving both professions and the public, it is important to include nonprofessionals such as patients as well as professionals such as doctors as sources. Good coverage should pay attention to several relevant parties and not just professionals if others are important parts of the story. Consideration of relevant parties is important in examining justice not only because a wide array of people and groups may foster or hinder justice, but also because parties that may have more power—such as physicians or insurance companies—can easily act unjustly at the expense of more vulnerable parties such as patients.
- Legal and regulatory issues: these are often important considerations in stories because they put constraints on the decisions of the relevant parties, and because they may themselves foster or limit exercise of justice. Stories should devote some attention to relevant legal and regulatory concerns. Legal and regulatory limitations may be relevant in a wide range of topics such as conduct of corporate executives and corporations, the work of scientists and doctors, and the development and exercise of policies by government agencies.
- Ethical issues, questions, and themes: coverage of topics with important ethical implications should, most centrally, provide some attention to the ethical dimension itself. This means that the story should address issues that are important in ethical theories—such as duties (including justice and, from theological ethics, sensitivity to human needs) and consequences (both benefits and harms). Where relevant, issues from other perspectives such as the feminist ethic of care (Gilligan, 1982) could be addressed. Reporters should also deal with ethical questions and themes—for example, when human life begins—that may emerge in reporting but not fit neatly into one theoretical perspective.

In relation to justice, consideration of the emphases that come from different theories can point to questions that will help journalists shed light on the ways that different aspects of justice are relevant in a story. For example, Mill (2003) linked the value of rights to utility and specifically to the protection of people's security. Therefore, utilitarianism would suggest that journalists ask whether and how the security of individuals or groups is being protected or compromised, by, for example, a decision about the use of pension funds by a corporation. Mill also pointed to the importance of avoiding partiality, which suggests that journalists should ask whether parties in a story are acting in a way to treat some people better at the expense of others. Rawls (1971) related justice to a veil of ignorance behind which people would consider the least advantaged and not allow inequalities that harm them. In this light, journalists could ask whether policies under debate at the federal or state levels of government would avoid inequalities that hurt these parties, a consideration relevant, for example, in choosing how to distribute funding for public schools across a state. Communitarian perspectives on justice also place special priority on the needs of the marginalized (Christians et al., 1993). Informed by communitarianism, journalists might place even more priority on considering how government policies or corporate decisions provide or fail to provide for the needs of people who have little voice or power.

## Application to Medical and Science Coverage

Consideration of justice and related issues out of this framework can help sharpen the questions used to plan or critique coverage of topics in medicine and science. Many subjects in these areas touch on issues of life and death, or the quality of life, so the justice issues they raise have profound implications for individuals and society. Therefore, these are particularly important issues for journalists to "get right" for readers and viewers.

The application of this framework will become clearer by reference to coverage of two topics with profound implications for justice: genetic testing and physician-assisted suicide.

Advances in genetic research in recent years have included the discovery of genes connected with diseases such as breast cancer and Alzheimer's. Some of these discoveries have led to the development of tests for whether people have the genes. The ethical challenges created by development of these tests are significant (Craig, 1997, 2000b). It is usually uncertain whether people who test positive will actually develop the disease, and they may find that no treatment is available and may face difficulty getting insurance or encounter discrimination in employment. As the framework makes clear, however, consideration of the ethical challenges connected with genetic testing needs to go beyond the individual level to examine the obligations of healthcare institutions, companies developing the tests, insurance companies, and employers. Professional norms and expectations are also important to examine, as are the social expectations and stigmas attached to diseases. Sources should include a variety of parties such as doctors and patients, insurance executives, test developers, and family members of patients. It is important to explain what laws and regulations govern the development and use of genetic testing.

The other part of the framework, consideration of the ethical dimension itself, calls for careful thought about how perspectives on justice may bring to light important journalistic questions that may be going unanswered, or may bear further development in in-depth stories. For example, Mill's (2003) linkage of rights to utility and the protection of security suggests that journalists should ask whether and how policy makers are helping to guard against genetic discrimination. Rawls's (1971) veil of ignorance would suggest that all parties, including test developers and insurance companies, should consider how to protect the most vulnerable parties, patients or future patients, from harm that might come from indiscriminate disclosure of test results. Communitarianism (Christians et al., 1993) would call for similar questions in the defense of vulnerable parties and would underline the need for inclusion of the voices of those parties as sources in stories on discrimination concerns.

A story in *Time* (discussed in Craig, 1997, 2000b) provides an example of inclusion of this kind of voice:

> Consider the case of Vickie Reis, a 42-year-old farmer who lives in Northern California. Six years ago, Reis told an emergency-room doctor treating her for bronchitis that her sister had died of cystic fibrosis, an incurable lung ailment. The physician then tested the woman and found that she bore a single copy of the CF gene. But as any first-year genetics student knows, it takes two copies of the damaged gene for a person to develop this disease. Even so, Reis' medical record subsequently contained the information about her cf gene, and she was repeatedly denied health insurance. "I had never had any symptoms of the disease," she notes. "But the fact that I carried the gene was enough to leave a big shadow on my medical history." (Gorman, Nash, Park, Thompson, & Weingarten, 1995, p. 61)

By including this anecdote, Christine Gorman et al. highlighted a justice-related problem by pointing out a situation in which insurance was denied, apparently without strong medical evidence.

As with genetic testing, the framework points to important justice-related concerns about physician-assisted suicide. Physician-assisted suicide and euthanasia have come to public attention in American society in recent years through events such as the U.S. Supreme Court's ruling rejecting the existence of a fundamental constitutional right to assisted suicide (*Vacco v. Quill*, 1997; *Washington v. Glucksberg*, 1997), the state of Oregon's approval of a law permitting assisted suicide, and Dr. Jack Kevorkian's assisted suicides and finally a trial stemming from his killing of a man on television. The framework would suggest that thorough coverage of assisted suicide consider the needs and views of individuals such as terminally ill patients, their families, and doctors, but also the priorities and practices of institutions such as hospitals and hospices. At the professional level, consideration of traditional and current ethical standards for medical practice is important. For this issue, society's views of death, dying, and pain are also important. Few stories will deal with all of these issues in depth, but the best coverage, in stories on this topic as a whole, should address all of these levels.

The framework further points to the need for a range of parties as sources that would include physicians, professional leaders in medical ethics, policy makers, and especially older or more medically vulnerable people—those who might be most directly affected by laws allowing assisted suicide and be most susceptible to abuse. In this topic, the need to understand and explain their legal and regulatory constraints is particularly evident. Finally, consideration of the ethical dimension itself again sheds light on relevant issues of justice. Mill's (2003) recognition of impartiality as a dimension of justice suggests that journalists should, in covering policy debates related to assisted suicide, ask how policies provide for fair distribution of end-of-life care so that people with or without insurance can receive good palliative care to manage severe pain. Rawls's (1971) theory of justice would suggest that any inequalities in care for the terminally ill should benefit the least advantaged—again pointing to important policy questions that lie in the background of consideration of the ethics of assisted suicide. A communitarian (Christians et al., 1993) view of justice would ask how a community bound together by mutual concern would want to care for individuals gravely ill at the end of life. This perspective, for example, would support stories of people who volunteer to spend time with patients in cancer wards or hospices.

Journalistic language that draws attention to justice is evident in an analytical piece by Mary Rourke that ran in the *Los Angeles Times* "Southern California Living" section (discussed in Craig, 2000a, 2002) after Kevorkian went beyond assisted suicide and gave a man a lethal injection on a videotape shown on CBS News' "60 Minutes." In one paragraph, Rourke wrote:

> By his very public acts, Kevorkian has forced urgent health-care problems to the center of attention. Most of them have to do with how we treat the dying. Lack of adequate pain medication and lack of support for good nursing homes, spiritual care and hospices—in which the dying are allowed to end life naturally, with pain control—are key concerns. (Rourke, 1998, p. E1)

The concerns the writer raises about insufficient end-of-life care and pain control imply that an injustice is being done when this kind of care is lacking.

In coverage of both genetic testing and physician-assisted suicide, justice issues can emerge when journalists ask critical questions about ethical implications beyond merely the level of the individual, get to a broad range of sources, set the topic in legal and regulatory context, and consider issues that theories of justice would raise. This kind of analysis can inform scholarly evaluation of coverage as well as the planning of coverage in these topics and others in science and medicine.

## APPLICATION TO BUSINESS COVERAGE

Business coverage, which sometimes overlaps with medical and science coverage, is another area in which considering multiple levels of analysis, breadth of sourcing, legal backdrop, and issues from ethical theory can shed light on strengths and weaknesses of stories and point to ways that justice issues can be portrayed more effectively. Individual business owners, executives, and employees make decisions themselves, but they do so as part of organizations that must provide goods or services and care for the needs of their own people. Professional expectations for ethical practice in business in turn influence the organizational culture, and the priorities of society related to money and its appropriate uses put a larger frame around the ethical choices that business people make. Stories that profile businesses or explain their decisions need to take into account these multiple levels and use a variety of sources within them—both people within the organization and customers as well as critical observers outside. In addition, laws and regulations provide at least a minimum standard for ethical conduct. Perspectives on justice from ethical theory may again, as in the case of medical coverage, raise important questions about the treatment of more vulnerable parties—such as employees and families facing layoffs or loss of pension plans, and community members living near environmentally hazardous plants or mines.

Coverage of scandals involving corporations and executives in the opening years of the 21st century provides an example of a topic related to business in which the framework sheds light on justice-related implications. Several companies including Enron, WorldCom, and Tyco made headlines over the conduct of their executives and the fallout it had for employees and their families.

In-depth coverage of these scandals should include a range of sources including not only executives, employees, and families but also observers such as business ethicists who are able to make informed, critical evaluations of executives' conduct and of the corporate and professional cultures. Clearly in this case, since legal action was brought against numerous executives, the legal system's effort to bring justice—at least ideally—in these cases is important to consider as well. As for considerations from theories of justice, the issues are similar to those raised in the discussion of medicine and science coverage—particularly consideration of the security and well-being of the parties most vulnerable in these situations, especially employees and families who have considerably less ability to recover financially than the highly paid executives at the top.

Particularly important for business stories, the coverage should include these individuals as sources and subjects but should also carefully scrutinize the corporate culture they lived in or were affected by—and the professional and social climates as broader context. Decisions that were made harming employees' pensions and financial futures represent unjust treatment that cannot be fully understood without this broader background.

Magazine pieces about the string of scandals in 2001 and 2002 (discussed in Craig & Turner, 2003) included cover stories and other investigative articles that were built on substantial reporting but also included strong commentary that drives home the ethical implications of corporate conduct. These pieces went beyond the individual to explore the organizational, professional, and even social levels. For example, a piece in *BusinessWeek* (Byrne, France, & Zellner, 2002) said many academics who had presented Enron as a model in the late 1990s

> are now scurrying to distill the cultural and leadership lessons from the debacle. Their conclusion so far: Enron didn't fail just because of improper accounting or alleged corruption at the top. It also failed because of its entrepreneurial culture—the very reason Enron attracted so much attention and acclaim. The unrelenting emphasis on earnings growth and individual initiative, coupled with a shocking absence of the usual corporate checks and balances, tipped the culture from one that rewarded aggressive strategy to one that increasingly relied on unethical corner-cutting. (Byrne et al., 2002, p. 118)

Enron's problems are thus presented as being issues of organizational culture—a point developed throughout the story. Although justice is not discussed directly, the focus on the culture as one dependent on unethical practices shows how the foundation was laid for unjust conduct.

A cover story in *Fortune* (Gimein, Dash, Munoz, & Sung, 2002) addresses ethics at the broader level of the profession. After pointing to the "ever-lengthening parade of corporate villains," the article criticizes the ethics of the business world:

> These people and a handful of others are the poster children for the "infectious greed" that Fed chairman Alan Greenspan described recently to Congress. But by now, with the feverish flush of the new economy recognizable as a symptom not of a passion but of an illness, it has also become clear that the mores and practices that characterize this greed suffused the business world far beyond Enron and Tyco, Adelphia and WorldCom. (Gimein et al., 2002, p. 64)

The story establishes evidence for this statement using an analysis of stock sales by executives and directors for more than 1,035 companies that were losing money. The study found that "a total haul of $23 billion went to 466 insiders at the 25 corporations where the executives cashed out the most" (Gimein et al., 2002). By setting the corporate scandals in broad professional context, through in-depth reporting, the story sets a broader backdrop for consideration of the justice of practices by many at the top of the corporate world—though again justice is not directly mentioned.

## OTHER TOPICS FOR APPLICATION

Beyond coverage of medicine, science, and business, coverage of a variety of other topics could benefit from systematic evaluation with an eye to how justice is addressed. Here are three areas in which these considerations are relevant:

- Conduct of public officials (Craig, 1999). In the context of election coverage or ongoing evaluation of officials' work, journalists can consider questions such as: Is there evidence of favoritism toward better-funded or more powerful interests in the decisions and priorities of a member of Congress? In dealing with the development or implementation of social services policies, is an agency head pushing for careful consideration of the interests of those who might be hurt because they are economically vulnerable? These questions echo one raised by Lambeth (1992) in his discussion of justice building on Rawls (1971): "Are some groups or classes of persons enjoying more than their fair share of goods or bearing more than their fair share of the burdens?" (Lambeth, 1992, p. 29). This kind of reporting calls for use of a broad array of sources—including people with a variety of views inside government and others outside.
- Debates over government policy. Stories on policy topics may work either during election season when candidates are debating policy positions or at other times when Congress or state governments are considering legislation. It is particularly important to evaluate the potential impact of policy choices on individuals, affected organizations, and the residents of the state or nation as a whole. Clearly the legal and regulatory background is important to report. In order to carefully evaluate the possible harm to more vulnerable stakeholders, it is important to listen to the evaluations of lawmakers with a variety of views, as well as policy analysts and academics with expertise, and individuals who may be affected. But because of the potentially complex and far-reaching impact of policy decisions, it is important for journalists not to rely too heavily on anecdotal accounts of hurting individuals, even though a communitarian perspective on justice (Christians et al., 1993) would call for some of these voices to be included. Consideration of justice at the social level demands

that sources include people with knowledge to evaluate potential long-term and less obvious consequences, thereby helping to ensure that the interests of the least advantaged that are so important in both communitarian and Rawlsian ethics are served.

- The practices of journalists themselves. Writers who evaluate the work of journalists can help shed light on whether reporters are actually doing a good job covering topics with justice-related implications. These critical analysts may be media writers for large news organizations, public editors or ombudsmen who write independent evaluations of an organization's work, other commentators for print and broadcast media, or bloggers who evaluate the work of journalists online. These writers can provide a form of accountability for journalists through critical evaluation of the depth and breadth of coverage of a topic, particularly the ways in which justice issues were discussed.

For all these topics, systematic evaluation of sources, levels, legal backdrop, and facets of justice can lead to both better coverage and more thorough scholarly assessment.

## AREAS FOR FURTHER RESEARCH

In order to advance both scholarly understanding and professional practice, it is important for researchers to do additional critical evaluation of how justice and related issues are addressed in news coverage, to strengthen the conceptual foundation for application of justice to journalistic practice, to explore journalists' own views of justice as a value and goal, and to extend the analysis beyond journalism to persuasion and entertainment.

As the discussion above shows, some explicit scholarly attention has been given to how justice as a value has been stated or implied in coverage, as well as to the context of sourcing, levels at which justice issues played out, and legal considerations that may promote justice or limit it. However, much of this attention has been focused on coverage of medicine and science (e.g., Craig, 2000b, 2002) or business (Craig & Turner, 2003). As already suggested, important justice-related questions can be raised about the work of government officials, the development of public policy, and the work of journalists themselves. Beyond these, a variety of other topics have justice implications—for example, the decisions and practices of religious institutions and the priorities of professional and college sports. The door is wide open for in-depth qualitative evaluations of coverage or broad-scale quantitative analyses. In particular, given Wilkins and Coleman's (2005) findings about a lowering of moral reasoning level based on race, it is important to evaluate how racial issues are being covered across a variety of beats.

In addition to extending the analyses to a wide array of topics, researchers should consider how justice issues are or should be addressed across a range of journalistic genres. An obvious area of focus would be investigative reporting because of the powerful moral implications of journalistic examinations of wrongdoing (Ettema & Glasser, 1998). Researchers could examine how investigative reporters have thought through and written about dimensions of justice in coverage of, for example, police corruption. Narrative journalism is another journalistic form in which compelling writing can draw attention to social needs or simply to the plight of individuals (Craig, 2006). Journalists who do in-depth narrative features sometimes use the storytelling devices of the novelist to drive home to readers or viewers the ways that injustices affect people in their daily lives. Through content analyses (qualitative or quantitative) and interviews with writers, researchers could shed light on how and why justice issues were portrayed.

In addition, the development of online journalism raises distinctive questions in which justice could be an important consideration. Multimedia projects making the most of powerful video, audio, and still photography have the potential to highlight stories of injustice in compelling ways. Content analyses could explore whether projects addressing social concerns such as homelessness are making the most of the narrative power of multiple media forms. Blogs, another important component of online journalism, also have interesting justice implications. By inviting comments from the audience, bloggers can foster debate over the practices of government, medical, and business institutions and the conduct of individuals. Those bloggers who include their own opinions in their postings may also help to spur discussion. Content analyses of blogs could evaluate the quality and nature of the analysis and discussion that they bring to the public. More generally, the interactivity and feedback capability of the Internet open the potential for interaction of a wide array of voices, whether through blogs, discussion forums, or audio or video segments. But the extent to which this potential is being realized should be closely evaluated through research on the content of this communication.

Another important area for further research is additional systematic thinking about the conceptual foundations for justice in ethical theory and what different perspectives distinctively contribute to evaluation of justice in coverage—as well as the nature of justice as a goal of journalism. As the review of concepts and literature in this chapter shows, media scholars have brought a variety of perspectives on justice to the table for application or critique, including perspectives based on utilitarianism, Rawls's egalitarianism, communitarianism, and moral development theory. However, greater conceptual clarity and more precise application are still needed. For example:

- If both Rawls's (1971) and Christians et al.'s (1993) notions of justice place priority on the needs of the disadvantaged, what differences in priority for journalistic practice do their conceptual distinctives suggest? The particular focus in communitarian media ethics on giving voice to individuals might call for a priority on stories highlighting these narratives, but if Rawls also gives priority to the least advantaged, would his perspective call for anything different?
- What are the distinctives and similarities between the notions of care growing out of feminist ethics and the conception of justice in communitarian ethics? Unlike rights-based notions of justice growing out of the liberal tradition or built on Kohlberg's moral development theory, communitarian justice focuses on people in relationship with others—as do feminist ethics of care. Even though these other conceptions of justice have been set against notions of care (e.g., Steiner & Okrusch, 2006), justice in communitarianism has much common ground with care-based ethics. How would these two perspectives inform the work of journalism differently?

Finally, it is important to evaluate journalists' own perspectives on justice as a value and goal of their work. Journalists across a variety of beats and genres could be interviewed to shed further light on the importance they place on justice as a value, how they define it, and how they view it in relation to other journalistic values. Wilkins and Coleman's (2005) work uncovered weaknesses in moral reasoning related to justice, underlining further the importance of exploring journalists' views of this value and whether and how they regard it as an appropriate goal of journalism. Bringing their views to light may help to expose ways their understanding and application can be sharpened.

Beyond exploring implications for journalism, researchers could extend their evaluation of justice-related concerns to other media areas that have gotten less attention from ethics scholars. Persuasive communication by public relations and advertising practitioners is filled with justice implications. For example, advocacy for a particular public policy or business decision may advance or hinder the fair treatment of vulnerable parties in a community. Advertising for an expensive product may raise questions of social justice if it explicitly targets people with little ability to pay. Some previous scholarly work such as Baker and Martinson's development of the TARES Test (2001) has already explored justice-related concerns as they apply to persuasion. However, consideration of justice in public relations and advertising with additional attention to analysis at the levels of individual, organization, profession, and society might further sharpen discussion of what constitutes ethical practice. In the entertainment world, justice-based analysis could shed light on a variety of issues such as the fairness of portrayal of older people and minorities; the casting and treatment of reality show participants for the sake of humor; and broader considerations of the responsibility of movie, television, and music producers to society. While critics have made much of the need for responsible practice in entertainment media, the scholarly field of entertainment ethics, which could help foster careful and dispassionate analysis, is in its infancy. Careful consideration of justice in the development of entertainment ethics research would help ensure that entertainment products and processes are evaluated at a variety of levels and from multiple theoretical perspectives, not treated in an overly simplified manner.

## REFERENCES

Baker, S., & Martinson, D. (2001). The TARES test: Five principles for ethical persuasion. *Journal of Mass Media Ethics, 16,* 148–175.

Barger, W. (2003). Moral language in newspaper commentary: A Kohlbergian analysis. *Journal of Mass Media Ethics, 18,* 29–43.

Beauchamp, T. L., & Childress, J. F. (2001). *Principles of biomedical ethics* (5th ed.). New York: Oxford University Press.

Bellah, R., Madsen, R., Sullivan, W., Swidler, A., & Tipton, S. (1985). *Habits of the heart: Individualism and commitment in American life.* New York: Harper & Row.

Bellah, R., Madsen, R., Sullivan, W., Swidler, A., & Tipton, S. (1991). *The good society.* New York: Knopf.

Bivins, T. (2004). *Mixed media: Moral distinctions in advertising, public relations, and journalism.* Mahwah, NJ: Erlbaum.

Brislin, T. (1992). "Just journalism": A moral debate framework. *Journal of Mass Media Ethics, 7,* 209–219.

Byrne, J. A., France, M., & Zellner, W. (2002, February 25). "The environment was ripe for abuse." *Business Week,* pp. 118–120.

Christians, C. G., Rotzoll, K. B., Fackler, M., McKee, K. B., & Woods, R. H. (2005). *Media ethics: Cases and moral reasoning* (7th ed.). Boston: Pearson.

Christians, C. G., Ferré, J. P., & Fackler, P. M. (1993). *Good news: Social ethics and the press.* New York: Oxford University Press.

Commission on Freedom of the Press. (1947). *A free and responsible press.* Chicago: University of Chicago Press.

Craig, D. (2006). *The ethics of the story: Using narrative techniques responsibly in journalism.* Lanham, MD: Rowman & Littlefield.

Craig, D. A. (1996). Communitarian journalism(s): Clearing conceptual landscapes. *Journal of Mass Media Ethics, 11,* 107–118.

Craig, D. A. (1997). Covering the ethics angle: Toward a method to evaluate and improve how journalists portray the ethical dimension of professions and society (Doctoral dissertation, University of Missouri-Columbia, 1997). *Dissertation Abstracts International, 59* (02), 1999.

Craig, D. A. (1999). A framework for evaluating coverage of ethics in professions and society. *Journal of Mass Media Ethics, 14,* 16–27.

Craig, D. A. (2000a, August). *Covering the ethics of death: An exploration of three model approaches.* Paper presented at the meeting of the Association for Education in Journalism and Mass Communication, Phoenix, AZ.

Craig, D. A. (2000b). Ethical language and themes in news coverage of genetic testing. *Journalism & Mass Communication Quarterly, 77,* 160–174.

Craig, D. A. (2002). Covering ethics through analysis and commentary: A case study. *Journal of Mass Media Ethics, 17,* 53–68.

Craig, D. A., & Turner, K. T. (2003, July). *Bad apples or rotten culture? Media discourse on the corporate scandals of 2001 and 2002.* Paper presented at the meeting of the Association for Education in Journalism and Mass Communication, Kansas City, MO.

Day, L. A. (2006). *Ethics in media communications: Cases and controversies* (5th ed.). Belmont, CA: Thomson Wadsworth.

Ettema, J. S., & Glasser, T. G. (1998). *Custodians of conscience: Investigative journalism and public virtue.* New York: Columbia University Press.

Gilligan, C. (1982). *In a different voice: Psychological theory and women's development.* Cambridge, MA: Harvard University Press.

Gimein, M., Dash, E., Munoz, L., & Sung, J. (2002, September 2). You bought. They sold. *Fortune,* 64–74.

Gorman, C., Nash, J. M., Park, A., Thompson, D., & Weingarten, T. (1995, April 10). The doctor's crystal ball. *Time,* 60–62.

Hadley, R. (1989). Television news ethics: A survey of television news directors. *Journal of Mass Media Ethics, 4,* 249–264.

Kohlberg, L. (1981). *Essays on moral development.* San Francisco: Harper & Row.

Kukathas, C., & Pettit, P. (1990). *Rawls: A theory of justice and its critics.* Stanford, CA: Stanford University Press.

Lambeth, E. B. (1992). *Committed journalism: An ethic for the profession* (2nd ed.). Bloomington, IN: Indiana University Press.

Lind, R. A. (1996). Care and justice in audience evaluations of ethics in TV news. *Journal of Mass Media Ethics, 11,* 82–94.

Mill, J. S. (2003). On the connexion between justice and utility. In Mary Warnock (Ed.), Utilitarianism *and* On liberty: *Including Mill's* "Essay on Bentham" *and selections from the writings of Jeremy Bentham and John Austin* (2nd ed., pp. 216–235). Malden, MA: Blackwell.

Mulhall, S., & Swift, A. (1992). *Liberals and communitarians.* Oxford, UK: Blackwell.

Patterson, P., & Wilkins, L. (2005). *Media ethics: Issues & cases* (5th ed.). Boston: McGraw-Hill.

Pippert, W. G. (1989). *An ethics of news: A reporter's search for truth.* Washington, D.C.: Georgetown University Press.

Protess, D. L., Cook, F. L, Doppelt, J. C., Ettema, J. S., Gordon, M. T., Leff, D. R. et al. (1991). *The journalism of outrage: Investigative reporting and agenda building in America.* New York: Guilford Press.

Rawls, J. (1971). *A theory of justice.* Cambridge, MA: Belknap Press of Harvard University Press.

Rourke, M. (1998, November 25). Kevorkian's latest act raises new concerns. *Los Angeles Times,* p. E1.

Sandel, M. (1982). *Liberalism and the limits of justice.* Cambridge, UK: Cambridge University Press.

Serrin, J. S., & Serrin, W. (Eds.). (2002). *Muckraking! The journalism that changed America.* New York: New Press.

Siebert, F. S., Peterson, T., & Schramm, W. (1956). *Four theories of the press.* Urbana: University of Illinois Press.

Smith, R. F. (2003). *Groping for ethics in journalism* (5th ed.). Ames, IA: Iowa State University Press.

Steiner, L., & Okrusch, C. M. (2006). Care as a virtue for journalists. *Journal of Mass Media Ethics, 21,* 102–122.

Tichi, C. (2004). *Exposés and excess: Muckraking in America, 1900–2000.* Philadelphia: University of Pennsylvania Press.

*Vacco v. Quill,* 521 U.S. 793 (1997).

*Washington v. Glucksberg,* 521 U.S. 702 (1997).

Wilkins, L., & Coleman, R. (2005). *The moral media: How journalists reason about ethics.* Mahwah, NJ: Erlbaum.

# 16

# Transparency in Journalism: Meanings, Merits, and Risks

## Stephanie Craft and Kyle Heim

As public opinion polls continue to chart increasingly negative attitudes toward the news media, transparency has been embraced as a method by which journalists can reestablish trust with the public. Some newspapers have turned to ombudsman's columns to pull back the curtain and explain the newsgathering process. Others have invited readers to witness the process firsthand by opening their news meetings to the public. Mistakes that once would have been acknowledged with a terse correction might today merit a "note to readers" detailing how or why the error occurred.

The growth and increasing accessibility of the Internet have made it possible for nearly anyone with an opinion and some computer skills to become a media critic and for journalists to shed the limitations of space and time to disseminate information. As bloggers take the conventional news media to task and, in their own developing style of discourse, privilege openness over other principles of traditional journalism, pressure on traditional journalists to explain and justify their actions has increased.

For all its popularity and its potential importance to addressing journalistic and public concerns, however, discussion of transparency has suffered from a lack of clarity in its definition. This lack of explication hinders both academic inquiry into the role transparency could or should play in journalistic practices and journalism's ability to create new or better ways to respond to its critics, reconnect with its audience and fulfill its ethical obligations.

The arguments for transparency's importance seem to rest on basic norms of journalism practice that ultimately are grounded in a definition of journalism as having a distinct public or democratic purpose. Generally speaking, such arguments note the public's need for a certain kind and quality of information to aid in self-governance and community sustenance and journalism's unique qualifications for providing that information. That the public relies on this information creates an obligation for journalism to perform in ways that bolster public trust in the information; and transparency, it follows, is one tool for bolstering that trust. But does that conclusion necessarily follow? Answering that question will require much more clarity regarding what transparency is and requires. What is unclear in the many ways "transparency" is invoked in discussion and takes form in practice is precisely *what* needs to be transparent—Motives? Processes? Information?—in order for journalism to fulfill its more general obligation and *how* it should do so. Also unclear is whether transparency of any of those things, in whatever "amount," is actually a means to producing the desired effect. There may be reasons, in fact, to think that transparency can be counterproductive.

This chapter will attempt to sort through some of the confusion surrounding transparency in the hopes of pointing toward a conceptualization of it that is more amenable to theorizing as well as to practice. First, we will identify how transparency has been defined and employed in journalism and other domains, paying particular attention to the implications of two primary ways in which it has been conceptualized. Second, we will examine what transparency's value consists in as well as its relationship to media accountability and credibility. Third, we will consider the possible dangers of transparency, including implications of too much transparency, and suggest avenues for future research to clarify transparency and justify it as means to achieving the kind of accountability and improved media credibility people seem to want.

## WHAT IS TRANSPARENCY?

A pivotal moment in charting the course of journalistic transparency came on September 26, 2000, when *The New York Times* published an editor's note reflecting on its coverage of Wen Ho Lee, a scientist at the Los Alamos National Laboratory in New Mexico who had been arrested on suspicion of giving secrets about U.S. nuclear weapons to China. Critics had charged that the *Times'* initial reporting of the case amounted to a witch hunt, contributing to the Justice Department's overzealous prosecution of Lee, who ended up pleading guilty to one count of mishandling secret information. Acknowledging that the newspaper's coverage had ignited a firestorm of controversy, the *Times* editors told their readers:

> As a rule, we prefer to let our reporting speak for itself. In this extraordinary case, the outcome of the prosecution and the accusations leveled at this newspaper may have left many readers with questions about our coverage. That confusion—and the stakes involved, a man's liberty and reputation—convince us that a public accounting is warranted. (*New York Times*, 2000, p. A2)

The *Times* admitted that its coverage had fallen short and vowed that its journalists would go back and do more reporting. This frank self-assessment did not fit the profile of a typical editor's note. The note was neither a correction nor an outright apology, but instead offered a rare glimpse into the newsgathering process, signaling the start of "the modern era in transparency at *The New York Times*" (Rosen, 2004).

Some news organizations have embraced this modern era of transparency in earnest. In July 2004, 24 top media executives, journalists, and consultants gathered at an Aspen Institute conference, where they called for a presumption of openness in American journalism and concluded that journalists ought to be "as transparent as practical" (Ziomek, 2005). Recommendations included virtual newsroom tours on news organizations' websites, weekly editors' columns reviewing the week's news events, corrections policies that go beyond the standard corrections box on page 2, and explanations whenever anonymous sources are used (Ziomek, 2005).

While transparency may have only recently become part of journalists' vernacular, it has deeper roots in other disciplines. The push for greater transparency in the news media can be seen as part of a global trend toward transparency in such diverse areas as corporate financial reporting, monetary policy, international politics, and food and tobacco labeling. Several forces have contributed to this clamor for transparency. Globalization and the spread of democracy have created a more integrated and interdependent world where it can be critical to understand the actions and motives of people thousands of miles away. At the same time, advances in information technology have made it harder than ever to keep secrets. In the past, governments or corporations (or news organizations) could easily control the flow of information, but today the Internet has empowered individuals and grassroots organizations to learn, share their knowledge, and mobilize. It is important to note, as Wasserman (2006) does, that while transparency emerged in other domains as a response to corruption, claims of bias and not corruption have prompted calls for transparency in the news media.

Transparency's rise in rhetoric and practice has not been accompanied by much consensus on how best to define or measure it. Indeed, definitions of any kind are rare. Until we better understand what transparency is, what it involves, it will be difficult if not impossible to know whether it is worth promoting and whether it is likely to actually produce greater accountability or trust. Addressing this basic question also can help us understand which efforts to promote transparency would be most effective.

We should start by distinguishing two questions: First, when people call for greater transparency, *what* do they want to be transparent? To take the case of journalism, is it the methods used to gather and verify information, how newsroom resources affect editorial choices, why certain stories are pursued and others aren't, or perhaps all of those things and many others that need to be transparent? Second, what is it for a relevant thing to be *transparent*? When, for example, does explaining how a decision to pursue a particular story was made count as being transparent and how is the explanation of the decision made transparent?

If we start with the second question, we can note that transparency appears in two distinct but related guises in the scholarly literatures of political science, international affairs, and business as well as journalism—as availability of information and as disclosure of it.[1] As "availability," transparency is passive. It refers to a state in which documents, statistics, procedures, motives, and intentions are open to public view. In the business literature, Bushman, Piotroski, and Smith (2004) exemplify this perspective, calling corporate transparency "the availability of firm-specific information to those outside publicly traded firms." Likewise Tapscott and Ticoll (2003) consider transparency to be "the accessibility of information to stakeholders of institutions, regarding matters that affect their interests" (p. 22).

Definitions, as they exist, in the political science literature also focus on availability, though the structures by which information is made available, and not the information alone, are accorded importance. Finel and Lord (1999), for example, refer to transparency as "legal, political and institutional structures that make information about the internal characteristics of a government and society available to actors both inside and outside of the domestic political system" (p. 316).

The notion of transparency as availability shares common ground with the theory of information ethics advanced by Luciano Floridi, in which the "infosphere"—"the collected sum of information itself"—is central (see Hongladarom, 2004, for a brief overview).

> Floridi's information ethics is predicated on the idea that ethical norms are based on the size of the infosphere—on whether the norms do improve or impoverish the infosphere. This works well if everything in the infosphere is *transparent*; that is, if any and all the information contained in the infosphere is readily available to be discerned and made use of by anybody who enters it. (Hongladarom, 2004, p. 92, emphasis in original)

As "disclosure," transparency is active, connoting a process for bringing information into view. The 2005 report of the Aspen Institute conference offers a definition reflective of the disclosure perspective: "In journalism, transparent organizations open the processes by which facts, situations, events, and opinions are sorted, sifted, made sense of, and presented" (p. 4).

Transparency has become common practice on the Internet, where bloggers often disclose their methods and motives as they post information about current events. Writing about the ethics of blogging, Mitchell and Steele (2005) equated transparency with disclosure in three key areas: the principles you hold, the processes you follow, and the person you are. In the diplomacy arena, Florini traces the evolution of transparency as a political norm to the Cold War when the United States, challenging the traditional presumption of secrecy about military affairs, argued that the Soviet Union was *obliged to provide* certain types of information about itself to other states (Florini, 1996, emphasis added).

In the scant scholarly research in journalism, transparency has been defined in terms of disclosure and providing explanation. Singer (2006) argues that transparency covers "truthful disclosure before and during an act as well as after it has been taken" (p. 13). Rupar (2006) analyzed 674 New Zealand newspaper articles about genetic engineering to determine whether a lack of transparency in the newsgathering process had an impact on the meaning of news. Transparency was operationalized as the presence or absence of explanation: Articles in the "explained" category clearly described the input of sources behind the stories, while "unexplained" articles did not include such sourcing. Almost two-thirds of the articles fell into the unexplained category.

The availability and disclosure perspectives often seem to overlap in the literature, as when Mitchell (1998) equates promoting transparency with "fostering the acquisition, analysis and dissemination of regular, prompt and accurate regime-relevant information" (p. 109), or O'Neill (2002) promotes transparency as "checkability," encompassing information as well as the capacity for others to verify that information. Kovach and Rosenstiel (2001) offer the "Rule of Transparency" for journalism, which calls for "embedding in the news reports a sense of how the story came to be and why it was presented as it was" (Kovach & Rosenstiel, 2001, p. 83). The rule essentially applies scientific standards of verification to journalistic practice. Just as a scientist reports the research methods used to test a hypothesis and any limitations of the research, the journalist provides any information that readers need to assess the reliability of the news account. Similarly, Hongladarom contends that the "infosphere" must include structures for making sense of available information: "For a piece of information to be transparent is just for it to enter the representation system that gives it value" (p. 94).

On a practical level, the distinction between availability and disclosure suggests different ways of making something transparent. Let's consider the implications by returning to the journalistic example regarding how a decision to pursue a story was made. How could the explanation of the decision-making method be made transparently available? One option would be for a news organization to offer an explanation of the decision when asked. Another might be to post a list of commonly used criteria of newsworthiness to the news organization's website. Readers and viewers could consult the rubric to figure out how any story matches up. Approaching the example from the disclosure perspective, we see more active options. Making that decision transparent could take the form of including an editor's note with each story explaining its newsworthiness, or an editor's blog in which he or she offers reasons for each story presented during the newscast or in the paper.

We need not consider availability and disclosure to be competing or mutually exclusive perspectives. Still, their interchangeable use in the scholarly literature and trade press confuses efforts to understand what transparency is and requires. Making the distinction has theoretical implications for considering when availability is appropriate or "enough" to accomplish the aims of transparency and when more active disclosure seems warranted. Either case, however, assumes we can know *how* to make a thing transparent. Even then, we still must address whether all things of that kind must always be transparent or how determinations of the necessity of transparency on some occasions and not others are to be made. Let's leave aside the issue of the general applicability of openness and consider something— motives—which seem to be especially difficult to render transparent.

Returning to our earlier example, let's imagine that the issue isn't the method by which the decision to pursue a story was made but the motives of the decision makers employing that method. If one were to take the availability perspective, it might suffice for the decision makers merely to respond to questions about their motives. Under the disclosure perspective, a more active offering of explanation, perhaps in the form of an editor's note accompanying the story, might be required. Providing such an account, whether passively or actively, depends on knowing one's motives and being able to communicate them. This is no easy hurdle to clear. Human beings are capable both of self-deception and a lack of self-awareness, so we cannot assume that the motives a person ascribes to himself are his actual motives. Moreover, we cannot assume that the reader or viewer will understand those motives, even if they are the "real" ones, in the way the journalist understands them.

This scenario and its attendant difficulties call to mind the ideal speech situation in Jürgen Habermas's discourse ethics. Habermas's work, on discourse ethics as well as the idea of the public sphere, has influenced a number of scholars interested in ways that journalism might invigorate public dialogue and its own relationship with the public. Transparency is an important component of the ideal speech situation, enabling each participant in a discourse to perfectly know and understand the motives and intentions of the other participant. As Sinekopova (2005) points out, this ideal of transparency is possible only if one considers language to be a transparent medium, capable of transmitting pure meaning. In his discussion of scholarly interpretations of Rousseau's views regarding transparency in political life, Marks (2001) offers a definition that also suggests a difficulty in achieving genuine transparency of motives. He writes: "What exactly is transparency? Simply put, it is a state in which we experience things, ourselves and other people as they really are, in which appearance corresponds to reality" (p. 623). While such transparency is already difficult in the face-to-face encounter of the ideal speech situation, it is unclear whether it is even possible to achieve in the mediated encounters between journalists and their audiences.

It goes beyond our purposes here to settle the question of whether or how well the pictures in our heads correspond with the world outside, as Lippmann (1922) might have put it. For now it is enough to say that, even if perfect transparency is unattainable, it is reasonable to consider circumstances or practices as affording more or less transparency relative to others. We point out the special challenges of motive transparency not because the extreme case helps us to highlight problems with transparency more generally, but because concern about motives, more than other aspects of journalistic performance, may be what is propelling recent calls for transparency. Given that journalists already open many aspects of their work to public view—identifying sources, correcting errors, declaring potential conflicts of interest—much of the additional information that proponents of greater transparency seem to want relates more to intentions than facts, to providing an account more than to making information available. While all of this suggests a preference for the disclosure type of transparency, the type that leans toward accountability, it is important to point out that transparency is not the same thing as accountability. Transparency refers to revealing what might otherwise be hidden, such as the motives or decisions we've previously discussed. Accountability refers to making a case for why those revealed decisions or motives were reasonable. For example, *New York Times* editor Bill Keller, in revealing the decisions behind his newspaper's story about secret government wire-tapping, went beyond merely revealing how the story was pursued to justifying the pursuit. Transparency's connection to accountability will be briefly addressed in the next section.

## THE VALUE OF TRANSPARENCY

That transparency has been defined variously, vaguely, or not at all should not suggest doubt about its value. Indeed, it seems to be taken for granted that transparency is good and worth promoting. Transparency is seen as an indispensable element of public accountability and a necessary condition for promoting public trust in institutions (e.g., the news media, the government, the securities market). Underlying these values is transparency's contribution to truth seeking and truth telling. Overall, transparency's value is seen as primarily instrumental. It is a means through which greater accountability may be achieved, credibility may be enhanced, and truth may be told.[2]

Historically, transparency has been touted as a safeguard against corruption. Calls for greater openness have given risen to such organizations as Transparency International (http://transparency.org/), a global network that fights corruption by promoting transparency in elections, public administration, procurement, and business. Transparency in international affairs has been advocated as a way to foster cooperation and defuse tension. When nations make their political motives clear, they can ease mutual suspicion and fear, enabling them to work together to prevent conflict escalation (Finel & Lord, 2002). Transparency also has been invoked as a way to increase trust among investors, consumers, and regulators. After financial fraud led to the demise of U.S. corporate giants Enron and WorldCom, Congress responded by passing the Sarbanes-Oxley Act, requiring greater information disclosure from publicly traded companies and their auditors (Tapscott & Ticoll, 2003).

In journalism, too, transparency is valued for its role in creating and sustaining trust. Numerous studies have tracked declining trust in the mainstream news media, showing that many readers do not believe what they read and think that journalists are biased or out of touch with their audience (American Society of Newspaper Editors, 1999). To rebuild public trust, the ASNE study recommended that journalists make a greater effort to explain the editorial decision-making process to readers (Urban, 2002). In a 1999 speech announcing the study's findings, Edward Seaton, editor of the *Manhattan* (Kan.) *Mercury*, told journalists that "explaining reasons for our practices will soften a lot of the negative perceptions. We need clear statements, in writing, about what constitutes acceptable journalistic practice.... And they should be published so readers can understand and evaluate our decisions" (Seaton, 1999).

This implied linkage among readers' ability to witness, to evaluate, and, therefore, to trust, indicates the valued role transparency plays in facilitating journalistic accountability. Indeed, providing an account is seen as an affirmative moral duty of professionals (Newton, Hodges, & Keith, 2004). But to whom are journalists accountable, and for what? There are no simple answers. "Accountability" is often used interchangeably with "responsibility," though McQuail (2003) and Hodges (Newton, Hodges, & Keith 2004) are among the scholars who argue that it is essential to distinguish the two. Hodges offers the following definitions:

> The issue of responsibility is: To what social needs should we expect journalists to respond ably?
> The issue of accountability is: How might society call on journalists to explain and justify the ways they perform the responsibilities given them? (Newton et al., 2004, p. 173)

The news media are generally averse to allowing external parties to define their responsibilities or to following formal procedures for answering criticisms of how they discharge them, as McQuail (2003) notes. Transparency, engaged in voluntarily, seems directed at overcoming this general aversion and at least signaling a willingness to give the public more information to aid in its evaluation of performance and to answer to criticism of that performance.[3]

Plaisance (2006) grounds transparency's value in meeting journalists' ethical obligation of respect for persons. "Transparency is tightly bound up with the Kantian duty of acting in ways that respect the humanity—or, more precisely, the rational capacity and the free will to exercise that capacity—of others. We fail in this regard when we are not upfront about our intent or purpose" (Plaisance, 2006, p. 23). This link to the principle of humanity also is manifest in the trust and credibility transparency encourages, Plaisance argues. "[I]f we have a proper understanding of the concept of transparency, in fact it ought to "limit" deception and misinformation.... Even if transparency is not always sufficient condition for more ethical behavior, its absence is a prerequisite for deception, which, as we know, presents serious challenges for anyone who values ethical behavior" (pp. 9–10).

Transparency's value also is bound up with journalists' pursuit of truth. Singer (2006) determined that bloggers enact traditional journalistic norms regarding transparency, autonomy, and allegiance to truth, but differ in their enthusiasm and methods for meeting them. She notes that codes of ethics for blogging place a premium on transparency, elevating it to the level truth occupies for traditional journalists. She concludes: "What truth is to journalists, transparency is to bloggers" (p. 18). McQuail (2003) also notes that in assessing media quality, particularly as it relates to truth telling, key criteria include "demonstrability" and "openness" or "transparency of purpose" (pp. 76–77).

Advocates also argue that transparency fosters dialogue between journalists and their audiences. Such dialogue is valued for its own sake as well as for its contribution to promoting trust. Steven A. Smith (2005), editor of *The Spokesman-Review* newspaper in Spokane, Washington, said the ASNE's call for more explanation laid the foundation for the "transparent newsroom," in which citizens are "partners in the news conversation," not passive consumers (p. 44). Smith characterized the transparent newsroom as the opposite of fortress journalism, in which a newspaper walls itself off from the communities it covers.

## THE DANGERS OF TRANSPARENCY

Advocates of transparency contend that it can help impede corruption, limit deception, increase trust, and encourage dialogue and mutual understanding.[4] These are powerful reasons to promote it. What, if anything, might temper our enthusiasm for doing so? The prospect of pursuing transparency and achieving none of these positive outcomes would certainly be disappointing, as the failed pursuit would represent a waste of time, energy and other precious resources. That the hoped-for good outcomes might not occur, however, is a trivial reason not to promote transparency. Rather, we need to consider the potential for increased transparency to create new problems at least as troublesome as those it is intended to solve or, worse, exacerbate the very problems transparency is meant to cure.

First, let's consider the potential for transparency to serve interests that may be antithetical to independent journalism. Taking a cue from political philosophy, we note that transparency is not necessarily neutral. Garvey (2000), contrasting Bakhtin's views on transparency with those of Habermas, notes that while both men "recognize the theoretical connection between communicative transparency and the ethical value of sincerity," Bakhtin "associates transparency with the power that social interests can bring to bear on a discourse" (pp. 376–377). In short, Bakhtin sees transparency as a potential threat to autonomy in that it cannot be politically neutral. While forcing government policies into the light probably does not pose a threat, the issue "gets cloudier" as one moves closer to transparency of self, Garvey argues. (We offer the mundane example that few people would agree that completely transparent interactions with one's family over Thanksgiving dinner would be desirable.) Others have noted that transparency must be weighed against the need to keep some information out of public reach. For example, international negotiations often require diplomatic secrecy, and many of the superpower arms control agreements signed during the Cold War might not have been achieved had the United States insisted on greater levels of transparency (Mitchell, 1998).

Speaking about journalism specifically, Wasserman (2006) makes the similar argument that transparency might hinder rather than help independent journalism. He points in particular to transparency of journalistic processes, suggesting that what we have been calling the disclosure perspective here does not give journalists the room they need to do good work.

> The problem goes to the nature of journalism, which is practiced in a state of continual tension between private and public spheres. As public as the reporter's orientation is, journalism relies on an untidy, creative and collaborative process of debate, argumentation and muted conflict. I think that is how journalists strive to understand the realities they are then supposed to represent to the public via news. That process needs a space and needs a degree of privacy.
>
> I would strongly agree that the news media need to be held accountable publicly for the results of that process, especially when those results are badly flawed. But that is not the same as saying that the process itself should be routinely conducted in public view…. (Wasserman, May 10, 2006)

Wasserman questions whether calls for transparency are, in fact, politically motivated, making their interference with journalism practice more troublesome. Proponents, he contends, are more concerned with an alleged "ideological pollution" in journalism than with accuracy or fairness. "The point is not to hold media accountable, but make certain media discountable, by asserting that the journalism those media organizations provide is programmatic and ideological—is little better than propaganda—and cannot be trusted" (Wasserman, 2006).

Another way in which the risk of promoting transparency might exceed the reward is what O'Neill (2002) characterizes as almost an inverse relationship between transparency and trust. While certain relationships—with one's family or doctor, for example—involve high degrees of trust without correspondingly high levels of transparency, it appears that "public distrust has grown in the very years in which openness and transparency have been so avidly pursued" (p. 69). O'Neill's explanation for this counterintuitive observation: While transparency may be able to eliminate secrecy, it cannot eliminate the kind of deception or deliberate misinformation that produces distrust. The flood of available information—ever more so due to greater and more widespread technological capacity—compounds the problem.

Indeed, scholars have issued the caution that, taken to the extreme, transparency can be counterproductive, bombarding people with so much information that it becomes nearly impossible to separate the "signal" from the "noise." Balkin (1999) likened this to the discovery process in a court case. Faced with a request to release sensitive information, a legal team may adopt the seemingly counterintuitive strategy of over-compliance, producing so many documents that the other side lacks the time or ability to find the relevant information (Balkin, 1999, p. 395). As Florini (1999) explained: "In a cynical view, if you really want to hide information, the best thing to do is to bury it in a flood of data" (p. 9). The point has been made in journalism as well. An *American Journalism Review* article titled "Too Transparent?" began by observing: "You can almost hear the hot air seeping from our bloated egos, replaced by groveling apologies and overwrought explanations to our fleeing readers" (Smolkin, 2006, p. 16). The article questioned whether the pressure for journalists to explain themselves is spiraling out of control and quoted one former newspaper editor who noted the virtue in transparency but said, "We may well have gone overboard" (p. 16).

O'Neill agrees, connecting trust not to the amount of available information but to what one is able to do with the information. "We place and refuse trust not because we have torrents of information (more is not always better), but because we can trace *specific* bits of information and *specific* undertakings to *particular* sources on whose veracity and reliability we can run some checks" (p. 76, emphasis in original). Given that journalism is conducted in such a way that those specifics and particulars are already—transparently—available, we are left to wonder about the value of increased transparency of less checkable information such as motives or even methods and processes. In fact, that less easily verified information might be a breeding ground for the kind of deception that O'Neill and others worry about. Motives, we have noted, are particularly difficult to make transparent. To be sure, knowing a communicator's motives is to have some basis for critiquing what is communicated and whether those motives conflict with some general expectation about good performance. Transparency in this sense is anticipatory. It anticipates what people need to know to make sense of what is being communicated. However, if my motives are suspect, the requirement to be transparent might create an incentive for me to hide my actions and motives even more carefully.

Finally, there is the danger that transparency may be aimed at the wrong things and distract attention from what is really important. As Strathern (2000) puts it, "What does visibility conceal?" (p. 310). This question suggests a two-stage process. First, it seems reasonable to say that those things that can most easily be rendered transparent are what, in fact, will be made transparent, whether or not those things are especially relevant to the overall goals of greater transparency. Second, the "easy" things that have been made transparent are reified as the important things or even as transparency itself. Strathern, examining such reification in higher education evaluation techniques, writes:

> Here indeed is a world which has institutionalized second-order description. In the case of higher education auditing, it has done so through an assumption that a university is first and foremost an organisation whose performance as an organisation can be observed. A second assumption is that publicity and visibility make for transparency of operation. This rests in the proposition that if procedures and methods are open to scrutiny, then the organization is open to critique and ultimately to improvement. Transparency is in turn embedded in certain practices (artefacts, technologies) of accountability, epitomized by the notion of "audit.".... Such practices cannot be made fully transparent simply because there is no substitute for the kind of experiential and implicit knowledge crucial to expertise, and which involves trust of the practitioners. (Strathern, 2000, p. 313)

It is far from a settled question, then, whether transparency can make the important or merely the easy more visible. This would seem to apply not just to higher education, but to any knowledge organization, like journalism, featuring "experiential and implicit knowledge crucial to expertise." Let's make this conclusion a bit more concrete by considering examples from journalism. If it were easiest to ask reporters to make the sources of information in their stories transparent—fully identify them, indicate why their views are considered worthy of inclusion in the story—then doing would constitute being transparent. That practice has the added benefit of being empirically observable and measurable, so the public could assess for themselves how well the reporters were doing in meeting the expectation of transparency. Notice how much more difficult it would be to make transparent an editor's or publisher's decisions about how newsroom resources (human and financial) are deployed, and how the fact that news organizations do not typically reveal such information is not considered a blow to transparency. Which of these kinds of information, sources or resources, is more important? It is not difficult to make an argument for the importance of both, but notice how unlikely it is that we would get both.

## GOING FORWARD

Certainly we do not mean to present a false choice—between transparency of certain things and not others, or even between transparency and opacity more generally—only to highlight some of the practical and theoretical difficulties the push for transparency presents. As this overview of the potential advantages and disadvantages in pursuing transparency makes clear, more research is needed on at least two fronts. First, it is imperative to provide a justification for transparency, given the risks of pursuing it, that goes beyond merely acknowledging that accountability depends on a certain level of transparency. Plaisance (2006) has begun to explore such a theoretical foundation in Kant's principle of humanity; other perspectives are needed as well.

Second, empirical work addressing public reactions to transparency efforts or, more specifically, to the kind of journalism featuring relatively greater transparency, would go a long way toward determining whether transparency actually achieves the goods its proponents trumpet. For example, one could test the link between transparency and credibility experimentally. Does the presence or absence of an explanatory editor's note alter reader perceptions of a news story's credibility? Are stories featuring more information about a reporter's background considered more credible than stories that do not include that information? Additionally, we would encourage research to explore goods other than credibility that greater transparency might produce. In some sense, to focus on credibility is to focus on the needs of the news organization, not the readers or viewers. Examining transparency from the perspective of interactivity, for example, might include addressing what methods of transparency—blogs, editor's notes, forums—work best for the readers and viewers. What level of interactivity is necessary for something to be considered transparent enough?

In general, empirical work ought to examine the best ways of being transparent, of making information available and disclosing intentions. To this last point we might add that, in our view, for transparency to mean little more than availability is a meager conceptualization indeed. If transparency does not connote a more active type of disclosure, then it does not appear to add much to how journalism is currently practiced.

## NOTES

1. A similar distinction appears in the international relations literature. Bishop (2004) notes the contrast between transparency that aids monitoring or "internal" transparency (common in trade agreements) and transparency that includes public participation in decision-making processes, or "external" transparency. Bishop also notes the frequent conflation of these two concepts, in part because "often one is seen as a means to the other" (p. 13).

2. A case for transparency's intrinsic value also could be made. That is, transparency as a variety of truthfulness, and not merely a state that allows one to ascertain or verify the truth, would be valuable in itself. We will not pursue that more fine-grained argument here, as it goes beyond the purposes of this discussion.

3. What we have in mind here is what McQuail and others call the "answerability" model of accountability. As distinguished from the "liability" model, answerability focuses "on the quality of performance rather than on specific harm caused" (McQuail, 2003, p. 204).

4. However, the empirical evidence supporting some of these effects is limited. Rupar (2006) found that the absence of transparency—defined as explanation—"leads to the disappearance of context in the story and loss of the journalist's place within that context" (p. 134), which hinders establishing dialogue. A content analysis by Nemeth and Sanders (2001) concluded that many practices that have been linked to transparency—letters to the editor, correction boxes, and ombudsman columns—in

fact constitute a "truncated dialogue" that contributes little to a meaningful discussion of newspaper performance (p. 58). Correction boxes and ombudsman columns were more likely to focus on objective errors than on deeper questions about newsroom practices. Letters to the editor often presented the letter writers' views about public issues rather than observations about the newspaper's performance (Nemeth & Sanders, 2001). There also is little empirical evidence documenting the relationship between greater transparency and public trust. Furthermore, the mere release of information is no guarantee of policy success. Weil et al. (2006) noted that "whether and how new information is used to further public objectives depends upon its incorporation into complex chains of comprehension, action, and response" (p. 157).

## REFERENCES

American Society of Newspaper Editors. (1999, August 10). Examining our credibility: Perspectives of the public and the press: The findings in brief. Retrieved December 14, 2006, from http://www.asne.org/kiosk/reports/99reports/ 1999examiningourcredibility/p5-6_findings.html.

Balkin, J. M. (1999). How mass media simulate political transparency. *Cultural Values, 3*(4), 393–413.

Bishop, C. (August 2004). The internationalization of secrecy: A look at transparency within the World Trade Organization. Unpublished master's thesis, University of Missouri, Columbia.

Bushman, R. M., Piotroski, J. D., & Smith, A. J. (2004). What determines corporate transparency? *Journal of Accounting Research, 42*(2), 207–252.

Finel, B. I., & Lord, K. M. (1999). The surprising logic of transparency. *International Studies Quarterly, 43*(2), 315–339.

Finel, B. I., & Lord, K. M. (Eds.) (2002). *Power and conflict in the age of transparency.* New York: Palgrave Macmillan.

Florini, A. M. (1996). The evolution of international norms. *International Studies Quarterly, 40*(3), 363–389.

Florini, A. M. (1999, April). *Does the invisible hand need a transparent glove? The politics of transparency.* Paper prepared for the Annual World Bank Conference on Development Economics, Washington, D.C.

Garvey, T. G. (2000). The value of opacity: A Bakhtinian analysis of Habermas' discourse ethics. *Philosophy and Rhetoric, 33*(4), 370–390.

Hongladarom, S. (2004). Making information transparent as a means to close the global digital divide. *Minds and Machines, 14*, 85–99.

Kovach, B., & Rosenstiel, T. (2001). *The elements of journalism: What newspeople should know and the public should expect.* New York: Three Rivers Press.

Lippmann, W. (1922). *Public opinion.* New York: The Free Press.

Marks, J. (2001). Jean-Jacques Rousseau, Michael Sandel and the politics of transparency. *Polity, 33*(4), 619–642.

McQuail, D. (2003). *Media accountability and freedom of publication.* Oxford: Oxford University Press.

Mitchell, B., & Steele, B. (2005, January). *Earn your own trust, roll your own ethics: Transparency and beyond.* Paper presented at the conference Blogging, Journalism, and Credibility: Battleground and Common Ground at Harvard University, Cambridge, MA. Retrieved October 31, 2006, from http://www.poynter.org/content/resource_popup_view.asp?id=34211.

Mitchell, R. B. (1998). Sources of transparency: Information systems in international regimes. *International Studies Quarterly, 42*(1), 109–130.

Nemeth, N., & Sanders, C. (2001). Meaningful discussion of performance missing. *Newspaper Research Journal, 22*(2), 52–64.

Newton, L., Hodges, L., & Keith, S. (2004). Accountability in the professions: Accountability in journalism. *Journal of Mass Media Ethics, 19*(3&4), 166–190.

*New York Times*, editors. (2000, September 26). The *Times* and Wen Ho Lee. *The New York Times*, p. A2.

O'Neill, O. (2002). *A question of trust.* Cambridge: Cambridge University Press.

Plaisance, P. L. (2006). *Transparency: An assessment of the Kantian roots of a key element in media ethics practice.* Paper presented at the annual meeting of the Association for Education in Journalism and Mass Communication, August.

Rosen, J. (2004, May 29). From Wen Ho Lee to Judy Miller: The transparency era at the *New York Times, PressThink,* Retrieved October 31, 2006, from http://journalism.nyu.edu/pubzone/weblogs/press-think/2004/05/29/lee_note.html.

Rupar, V. (2006). How did you find that out? Transparency of the newsgathering process and the meaning of news: A case study of New Zealand journalism. *Journalism Studies, 7*(1), 127–143.

Seaton, E. (1999, November 29). Committee of Concerned Journalists: Explaining yourself. Retrieved December 14, 2006, from http://www.concernedjournalists.org/node/307.

Sinekopova, G. V. (2006). Building the public sphere: Bases and biases. *Journal of Communication, 56,* 505–522.

Singer, J. (2006). *Truth and transparency: Bloggers' challenge to professional autonomy in defining and enacting two journalistic norms.* Paper presented at the annual meeting of the Association for Education in Journalism and Mass Communication, August.

Smith, S. A. (2005). A newsroom's fortress walls collapse. *Nieman Reports, 59*(3), 44–45.

Smolkin, R. (2006, April/May). Too transparent? *American Journalism Review, 28*(2), 16–23.

Strathern, M. (2000). The tyranny of transparency. *British Educational Research Journal, 26*(3), 309–321.

Tapscott, D., & Ticoll, D. (2003). *The naked corporation: How the age of transparency will revolutionize business.* New York: Free Press.

Urban, C. (2002, August 12) American Society of Newspaper Editors: Overview: Building reader trust. Retrieved October 31, 2006, from http://www.asne.org/credibilityhandbook/brt/overview.htm.

Wasserman, E. (2006, May 10). *Transparency and quality journalism.* Speech to the Forum Folha de Jornalismo, Sao Paulo, Brazil.

Weil, D., Fung, A., Graham, M., & Fagotto, E. (2006). The effectiveness of regulatory disclosure policies. *Journal of Policy Analysis and Management, 25*(1), 155–181.

Ziomek, J. (2005). *Journalism, transparency and the public trust.* A report of the eighth annual Aspen Institute Conference on Journalism and Society. Retrieved October 31, 2006, from http://www.aspeninstitute.org/atf/cf/%7BDEB6F227-659B-4EC8-8F84-8DF23CA704F5%7D/JOURTRANSPTEXT.PDF.

# 17

# Conflict of Interest Enters a New Age

## Edward Wasserman

Conflict of interest is so familiar in its basics that it is virtually a cultural archetype of journalistic corruption. It is the financial writer who owns stock in the company she is profiling, the politics reporter who accepts a weekend junket from a rich officeholder, the publisher who kills a story about an advertiser caught up in an anti-prostitution sweep, the TV network whose news operation soft-pedals a legislative proposal that will save its parent company billions.

Broadly, conflict of interest comprises a variety of instances where undeclared obligations or loyalties exist that might plausibly intervene between journalists or journalism organizations and the public they principally serve. The conflict takes the form of an interposed set of rival objectives, usually invisible to the audience, that the journalist would reasonably be expected to be mindful of and which could influence his or her judgment governing the reporting or its presentation. Although the traditional notion of "interests" suggests a material stake rather than a personal bond, the conception is not so narrow; any valued relationship may suffice to produce a conflict (Borden & Pritchard 2001).

A common thread among the various conceptions of conflicts is the danger they pose to trust. In that respect their importance is not reducible to the possible distortions a specific conflict might engender in a given story. The notion has power as an archetype of cultural villainy because it implicates the fundamental trustworthiness of communications. Trust, as Annette Baier (2004) reminds us, is quite different from reliance. It is an expression of a belief not just in the technical competence but in the good will of the other, especially when the power, knowledge, and capacity of the two parties are widely unequal and when the trusted party necessarily operates within a wide grant of autonomy and self-direction. Nothing strikes quite so hard at the basics of communicative trust than the suspicion that messages are motivated and shaped by selfish interests the other party is deliberately concealing.

But it is not correct to view conflicts solely, or even primarily, as the extraordinary intrusion of contaminants external to the practice of journalism that sully some otherwise pristine purity of regard. The logic of conflict of interest equally implicates routine features of the organizational sociology of contemporary journalism that normally go unchallenged. The beat system itself, whose rationale requires nurturing a stable network of useful informants, contains strong incentives to use or withhold information to sustain those relations (Wasserman 2007). The White House correspondent who learns the aging president catnaps during Cabinet meetings understands reporting that may cost him his access, and consequently, his coveted beat. What about the columnist who vets potential topics with an eye to those that will get him on TV talk shows and thence onto the lucrative speaker circuit (Fallows 1992)? Or the city editor who hungers for a big national prize, and devotes an outsized proportion of her staff to a glamorous and sensational project at the expense of important, but less prize-worthy, matters?

If we drill down further, to the level of political economy, what makes conflict of interest yet more perplexing is that its logic incriminates the economic essentials of news in a commercial setting. A news operation that is dependent on advertising is under unrelenting pressure to assess coverage options by their appeal to desirable demographics, not by their broad value to an informed citizenry (Davis & Craft, 2000). Redeploying staff from foreign bureaus to lucrative travel or fitness sections, or upping the advertising minutes in a half-hour newscast, may have economic justification, but is still a response to conflicts of interest.

Those vexing elements related to organizational sociology and political economy are captured in the formulation offered by Black, Steele, and Barney (1999): "Conflicts of interest occur when individuals face competing loyalties to a source or to their own self-interest, or to their organization's economic needs as opposed to the information needs of the public" (p. 115). The value of that formulation lies in its breadth.

In a larger sense, then, the problem of conflicts derives from the reality that journalists are necessarily embedded in the organizations that employ them and the communities they serve. They practice journalism within interpenetrating layers of obligation and duty—personal, professional, institutional—and balance the demands of multiple constituencies: sources, colleagues, bosses, competitors, family, posterity, and above all one hopes, the public. All have more or less legitimate claims on the journalist's loyalty. Their needs sometimes coincide and sometimes clash, and those areas of agreement and discord are etched into the journalism that results. Journalists suffer or benefit from what they do in ways that may not be evident, and their understanding of those private consequences cannot help but color their professional performance.

Does that mean journalism is necessarily corrupt? No, but as a truth-telling practice it is inevitably a negotiated approximation, and the notion that it can be practiced within a hermetic zone of undiluted dedication to the public good is impossible to sustain. Instead, conflicts of interest are best seen as an inescapable feature of the terrain that journalists navigate, which cannot be purged, but must be managed, more or less well, more or less ethically.

## CONFLICTS INVOLVING NON-JOURNALISTS

Conflict of interest is a concern for non-journalist communicators as well, where it takes different forms, particularly for public relations practitioners and producers of fictional entertainment. Among PR practitioners, who unlike journalists operate under an explicit agent–client model, the classic conflict occurs when the practitioner has an undisclosed, rivalrous commitment to a party other than the client (Public Relations Society of America [PRSA] 2000). The standard terms of client relations forbid such entanglements, and in that regard they are not ethically vexing; they are correctly prohibited.

Lately, conflict of interest has emerged as a high-profile problem for PR practitioners in another way: when they engineer concealment so that their influence remains invisible. The typical case is when practitioners contrive to make the views they are paid to propagate appear, falsely, as if they arose freely from supposedly independent commentators (Elliott 2005; Boehlert 2005). There is no conflict with the client's interests; indeed, the whole point of the ruse is to advance those interests. The wrong resides in paying someone to pose as an arm's-length participant in public discourse when he is not.

Although this is forbidden, it is fair to ask whether the practitioner who suborns the deception has a conflict of interest at all. Certainly not in the usual sense: His loyalty to the client is undiluted. But an ethically significant conflict still exists. It derives from the practitioner's duty to respect conditions of honest public discourse, which makes possible the principled advocacy to which the profession is committed. In its essentials, the problem is no different from a journalistic conflict: An undisclosed loyalty intercedes between the commentator and the public, which is deceived into presuming the commentator's independence.

A second area of conflict affecting non-journalists affects those who create fictional content. This is product placement (Levin 2006; Byrne 2006; Elliott 2006), in which marketers pay producers to integrate branded goods and services into scripts for TV, film or theater. Although the chief argument for product placement is economic—to overcome the decline in traditional advertising—it has advocates on the creative side as well, who argue that realism demands that the make-believe environments fictional characters inhabit be rich in brands. The practice is typically criticized as sneaky; its wrongness consists of failing to alert the audience to the promotional subterfuge. But the placements are problematic because they arise from a conflict of interests that is furtively resolved to favor influences that ought to take a backseat to creative integrity. The conflict is with an audience expectation that content is shaped primarily by the demands of artistic coherence. This critique posits that audiences have a right to expect that a fictional character's choice of consumer goods is revealing of her personality and lifestyle, and that plots are driven by dramatic imperatives unrelated to showing off such products in an alluring way.

Whether in fiction, public relations or journalism, what makes the conflict of interest insidious is that it is not readily detectable from the substance of the communication itself. Unlike other wrongs communicators commit—inaccuracies, unfairness, plagiarism—conflict of interest derives from an off-stage influence that cannot be easily inferred.

## HISTORICAL RUN-UP

Identifying conflict of interest as a distinct problem first required articulating broader principles of communicative ethics, such as independence and objectivity. Until those emerged as values, the notion of a conflict could have no normative bite: A hidden loyalty cannot constitute a conflict without some principal obligation it can conflict with. Moreover, on the level of political culture, only after the idea was advanced that the journalist has some public duty did it make sense to deplore private influences that might subvert it.

Although the term itself dates only to the mid-20th century (Davis 2001, p. 17), it is possible to detect in early expressions of journalistic objectivity the first signs of sensitivity to what we now call conflict of interest. In his history of journalism ethics, Stephen Ward (2004) identifies, starting in 17th century England, two sources of objectivity as a professional norm. The first was the rise of periodic publishing, an economic model based on building return business. The publisher's wish not just to reach today's readers but to ensure they came back for the next issue spawned standards of reliability and trustworthiness that, though not explicitly couched in conflict of interest language, were the rhetorical equivalent of a claim to be addressing the public with clean hands.

In the century that followed, Ward argues (chapter 4), that marketplace incentive was joined by a robust conception of the informed public as a political force, allied to a press whose leanings were subject to open speculation and critique. Although the press was anything but free of competing loyalties, the notion that it had a principal duty to the public was born in this period, and a fuller conception of conflict of interests became possible.

In the United States the idea that journalists have a primary loyalty to the public good took modern form in the late 19th and early 20th centuries, apace with the emergence of news media as large-scale profit-driven industrial enterprises, the rise of the mass-circulation ad-support model, and the movement of journalism toward self-identification as both a professional practice and a tool of popular sovereignty (Schudson 2003; Iggers 1999). It is argued that "institutional conflicts of interest"—the idea that powerfully corrupting pressures on journalists originate within their own businesses—emerged only later, with the late 20th century rise of media conglomerates whose wide-ranging operations sought "synergies" with their news divisions (Davis & Craft 2000). While the potential for improper influence is surely greater in a diversified enterprise, early concerns about the corrupting influence of undisclosed private entanglements also focused on internal pressures.

Those concerns were evident in the first U.S. industry-wide ethics code, that of the American Society of Newspaper Editors in 1926, which warned: "Freedom from all obligations except that of fidelity to the public interest is vital," and, "Promotion of any private interest contrary to the general welfare, for whatever reason, is not compatible with honest journalism...." A decade later, the American Newspaper Guild code identified several areas related to conflicts of interest, such as taking money for PR work and withholding coverage on matters that clashed with the wishes of newspaper owners (Wilkins & Brennen 2003). By 1984, the inaugural issue of the *Journal of Mass Media Ethics* found most codes assigned central importance to conflicts of interest, and addressed such matters as extracurricular political involvements and outside income.

## CONTEMPORARY APPROACHES

The main thrust of contemporary codes is twofold; forbidding activities that might either bind journalists to individuals or entities affected by news coverage, or be construed by others as creating such bonds. Hence the frequent reference to avoiding "the appearance" of conflict, the elevation of "perceived" conflicts to coequal status with the real thing, and the emphasis on "credibility," which inevitably relates to ways that news organizations are viewed by the public.

Naturally, codes routinely restrict or prohibit gifts and trips from news sources, outside employment with entities that figure in the news, use of company letterheads "for personal gain," free meals and the like. But they also widen the sweep of conflicts rules well beyond material corruption to embrace activities whose effects on journalism are hard to discern—and which may not constitute ethical breaches at all. Among them are actions that might expose employers to public reproach, dilute their brands, deny them credit or payment for outside work employees do, and otherwise put them at a commercial disadvantage—without, however, necessarily affecting the information and commentary delivered to the public, which constitutes the journalist's main duty. A valid question is whether the language of professional ethics is being conscripted to serve narrow institutional interests.

"The principle of independence calls on journalists to remain free of associations or activities that may compromise their integrity or damage their credibility," the authors of *Doing Ethics* write (Black et al. 1999, p. 119). They offer the example of a local TV news anchor who donates to a political candidate. But why is that wrong? Admittedly the anchor's action, once known, may harm his public acceptability, just as some customers might not patronize a hardware store whose owner supports a particular office-seeker. But is that a conflict of interest—an undisclosed loyalty that quietly skews the services the public receives—or a business problem?

Suppose an anchor emcees a political rally. *Doing Ethics* suggests she has relinquished her independence as a journalist. But has she? True, she has declared a political preference. But is that a waiver of independence—or an expression of it? She is not dependent on the candidate. She is free to change her allegiance at any time. Her autonomy, in that respect, is unaffected.

To be sure, this is a challenge to the station's acceptability among a broad political spectrum of audience members, and the station may have good reason to prohibit her activities. But if this analysis of conflicts is to have any clarity or precision we must ask whether that prohibition would be rooted in ethics or in straightforward brand-management. Imagine a different station in the same community that cultivates a strongly partisan appeal. It might well not only tolerate but encourage its evening anchor to appear publicly at political rallies of a certain stripe, reasoning that *its* "credibility" would actually be enhanced. Would that station be ethically obtuse? Or are we not in the realm of ethics at all?

On the other hand, consider the Denver TV news director whose husband is running for governor (Black, Steele, & Barney 1999). Plainly, she has an interest in the career of a public official. With such a senior position the range of policies—social, economic, cultural—that are implicated is vast. It is inconceivable that she would be able to handle her journalistic duties blind to her perception of her husband's political needs. Nor should she be placed in a position where she must choose between being a conscientious newswoman and a caring spouse. This is an irreconcilable conflict, and is ethically untenable.

But many prohibitions have no comparable justification. The *New York Times* code (2004) is largely a meditation on conflicts of interest, and places extraordinary emphasis on the obligation of employees to protect the newspaper from any hint that it is not utterly impervious to outside influence. The code also prohibits employees, on conflict-of-interest grounds, from selling book deals without first giving the Times publishing arm a chance to bid. The *Miami Herald* bars employees from campaign fund-raising concerts (Poynter 2004), even if they pay full freight and their passion is the music, not the politics.

Again, these may be perfectly sensible restrictions to enforce discipline for the good of the employer and maintain brand uniformity for purposes of marketplace positioning. But they are clothed in the discourse of professional ethics and that, it would seem, is misleading. Moreover, these instances belong to the questionable tradition of fixing conflicts of interest as primarily, if not exclusively, matters of personal temptation and dereliction, rather than a broad-gauge challenge on all levels—the institutional and industrial as well as the individual.

Let us conclude this contemporary survey with a word on business journalism: Almost universally, business reporting staffs are forbidden to report on matters in which they or their families have financial interest (Society of Business Editors and Writers n.d.). Many organizations view that prohibition as too narrow. Dow Jones (2004) focuses on short-term holdings, the idea being that news can indeed move markets but only momentarily. Hence *Wall Street Journal* employees may not hold financial instruments for less than six months.

What about financial commentators whose franchises are based on their being "in the market" and who talk openly about what they own and why (Glaser 2003)? Typically, disclosure is said to neutralize the harm of any influence their holdings might bring to bear, since the audience is able to put their analyses in the right context. But the matter is more complicated than something simple candor can fix. A sophisticated market player will be mindful of the possible impact of anything she says on the value of her holdings. Disclosing purchase plans might drive up an asset's price. Disclosure doesn't resolve all conflicts and doesn't even fully identify the many ways in which investment might bias analysis. It only eliminates deception. The larger issue is whether the investing public should be denied the benefit of street-smart advice from self-described market players because of involvements it evidently accepts as sufficiently transparent.

Conflicts are emerging as an emblematic problem in the evolving media world, thanks to the conglomeration of media-owning companies, which brings pressure to reflect a wide range of institutional interests in deciding how or whether to cover specific matters (Davis & Craft 2000). Was it likely that the company that owns CBS, having already offered her a TV movie and a book deal, would unleash its news division on determining whether Jessica Lynch was indeed the war hero the Pentagon claimed (Wasserman 2003)? Is the owner of CBS right in keeping a foreign head of state from commenting on a sensational allegation he let drop until its "60 Minutes" news program could air it in full—in a report timed to coincide with publication of his memoir by its publishing house affiliate (Wasserman 2006, Oct. 2)?

The emerging media world also comprises non-traditional communicators—Internet-based bloggers, for instance—who work outside customary employment relationships. Conflict rules focused on such matters as moonlighting (Limor & Himelboim 2006) are nearly unintelligible to people whose careers consist of serial moonlighting: They are writing a magazine article for one paymaster, copywriting for another, editing for a third, consulting, teaching, working on a novel. How can loyalties to one employer be kept from tainting performance for the next?

## A TYPOLOGY

The way in which the conflict of interest has metastasized into a vague, catchall criticism of a great number of activities suggests a need for more systematic analysis.

In the field of news and topical commentary, conflicts—actual, potential or apparent—vary along two key dimensions: the degree to which they are endemic to the practice of journalism, and the degree to which they are consequential, meaning it is highly plausible that they will have discernible effects on what the journalist produces.

### Dimension 1: From the Endemic to the Extraneous

Conflicts are endemic to the degree they derive from the nexus of institutional, professional and personal relationships in which the journalist works. They are extraneous to the degree they are external to those relationships.

Examples of endemic conflicts: Reporters rely on the cooperation of sources to whom they are also supposed to be adversarial. That reliance may oblige the reporter to ignore newsworthy stories that, if published, would damage ongoing relationships that enhance the reporter's effectiveness and career success (Wasserman 2007). That is a conflict inherent to the practice. Similarly, the TV station manager who kills a story that would imperil a fat advertising contract is responding to a structural reality of ad dependency: Advertisers may withhold support from news that does not support them. That does not mean the manager's decision is ethically sound, which it almost certainly is not. But it is a response to a conflict endemic to commercial news.

By contrast, consider a reporter's decision to campaign on her own time for a political candidate. That is not a response to challenges or opportunities inherent in her journalism. If she stayed home as a citizen, her work as a journalist would be unaffected. Likewise, if a reporter buys property whose value could be affected by things he writes, the purchase is not one of those tough decisions he must weigh as part of his job. The conflict created by the purchase arises from concerns external to his journalism, and in that respect is non-endemic: Nothing in the practice of journalism itself gives rise to it.

Is that distinction nothing more than the difference between avoidable conflicts and unavoidable ones? The realms do overlap. But avoidability is a judgment I would prefer not to import to the discussion. True, endemic conflicts are harder to avoid without harming operational performance. But non-endemic conflicts too are avoidable only at a price. Take the reporter's outside electoral advocacy: If her enthusiasms were solely journalistic, such activity would be easy to avoid. But the reporter is also a citizen, and prohibiting her political engagement curtails a fundamental right we normally cherish. Similarly, the reporter who buys into a neighborhood on the brink of revival is only applying his hard-won realty expertise to the kind of private investing decision that people of similar means regard as a basic entitlement. To be sure, the conflict is avoidable—but only when the cost of curtailment is regarded as acceptable. Hence, avoidability rests on an implied ethical priority assigned to the duties associated with being a journalist. It is not necessary to make that judgment to determine that the conflicts are extraneous to the journalist's role obligations.

## Dimension 2: From Conflicts with Clear Impact to Those Without

Some conflicts seem more laden with consequence than others. While it is easy to adduce loyalties or obligations that seem certain to affect reporting, the opposite is harder to imagine. What is an inconsequential conflict? Yet, as we saw, news organizations routinely promulgate rules barring them. A sports writer might be disciplined under a conflict-of-interest prohibition for attending a political fundraising concert even though he will never write about any campaign event. A politics reporter could face limits on her investments not because they might tilt her stories one way or another, but because her employer covets a reputation for integrity. Are those restrictions justified?

It is important to be skeptical about the appropriation of ethics language into the vocabulary of workplace supervision and institutional brand management. But there may still be a principled reason to forbid some activities or entanglements that have no direct, immediate or substantive effect on the journalist's output: They may still clash with the reporter's duties in real ways. Suppose the outside activities are so controversial that some potential informants are deterred from talking to the reporter and some potential readers distrust what he writes. The education writer who is a high-profile abortion rights activist might find her ability to report and to reach her readers impaired (Elliott n.d.). Journalists are communicators, and they must have people willing to talk to them and listen to them.

Similarly, outside commitments may induce a reporter to privilege certain obligations that ought to be subordinated to a primary duty to the public. Consider celebrity journalism, in which journalists are rewarded with lavish fees on the speaker circuit once they establish themselves by appearing on high-profile talk shows. They have a huge incentive to anticipate, in their day jobs, the kind of topics and treatments that will make them talking heads on TV. That unacknowledged agenda might plausibly guide their journalism toward covering some things and ignoring others. Hence, even though it lacks the specificity of consequence we normally associate with conflicts of interest, we still have the classic rudiments of a conflict, where the journalist allows a set of interceding loyalties to stand between content and audience, burdening the message with undisclosed purpose and entitling her to rewards unrelated to her obligation to serve her public ably and independently.

None of these conflicts has a clearly discernible impact on a particular area of coverage. Yet each defines alignments that, it is reasonable to presume, affect the journalist's inclination to scrutinize entities she ought to cover, her ability to approach and be received by individuals she ought to be talking with, and her capacity to be regarded as credible by the public to whom she is speaking. So the argument that these may indeed be conflicts of interest seems sound.

Hence, we have two legitimate dimensions of conflicts to consider: The degree to which they arise from the ways in which journalism is practiced and institutionalized, and the degree to which they have readily discernible consequence on facts and commentary delivered to the public.

## HANDLING CONFLICTS

Does that typology offer clues as to how to handle conflicts of interest and mitigate the harm they cause?

Before looking at how to handle conflicts, we need first to finish addressing the question implied above: How to tell whether one actually exists. The question is keenly important because of the prevalence of bans on so-called perceived conflicts—itself a troubling concept. Perceptions, after all, are not usually considered valid reasons for moral action unless they are accurate. A venerable tradition in moral philosophy insists on the fallibility of perception and the need to subject it to rigorous verification. The alternative is to say, in effect, "There's nothing wrong with the action except that others might view it as objectionable." Such a statement privileges the ill-founded opinion of outsiders as ethically authoritative, rather than as a view that needs to be disputed, corrected or disregarded. Sometimes "the public" is wrong; sometimes "the public" may not even be audible above the din of special pleadings whose real purpose is to discredit and disarm a news organization.

In our formulation, if it is determined that the activities or relationships that seem problematic do not or are not likely to have a plausible impact on the quality of journalism delivered to the public, we do not have a conflict of interest, real or potential. The problem is a misperception, and the solution is to show that it is a misperception so that a reasonable outsider will agree. M. Davis (2001) argues this in his discussion of "apparent" conflicts of interest, which he defines as situations where no conflict exists but an outsider might be justified in suspecting one. The way to address that, he suggests, is "by making available enough information to show that there is no actual or potential conflict" (p. 18). Still and all, if the suspect activities keep the journalist from doing her job effectively and she refuses to curtail them, she might have to be shifted or fired. But that is a workforce management issue, not a response to ethical wrongdoing. If management bows to bigotry or ignorance under the guise of eliminating a conflict of interest it may well not only be committing an injustice but aggravating it with misrepresentation.

What about conflicts that are found to be not just apparent but real. In general, remedies come in three varieties: eliminate the conflict, disclose it or manage it. How effective—and how available—those remedies are will depend on the specifics of the conflict and whether it is endemic or not, and consequential or not.

### Elimination

Clearly, this is the most effective response to a genuine conflict of interest. It could take the form of severing the outside relationships or commitments that are problematic, or restructuring the specific duties or assignments that are causing the conflict.

By their nature, non-endemic conflicts are ideal candidates for being eliminated without harm to important processes or relationships. That is not to suggest such conflicts can be eliminated without cost, which may well involve abridging employee freedoms. Even if getting rid of non-endemic conflicts may not threaten business as usual, it still comes at a cost that is not trivial.

The logic of this analysis is that anti-conflict rules need to be firmly based in a well-founded fear of impaired journalism; vague concern that outsiders might criticize a reporter's off-duty activities is unlikely to meet that test.

Endemic conflicts are more intractable. How can anyone eliminate the indebtedness a reporter feels toward a useful source or the corporate manager's insistence on scaling back state-house bureaus to raise the news division's contribution to the consolidated bottom line? Endemic conflicts usually cannot be eliminated.

## Disclosure

What Louis Day (1997) calls the "moral minimum," disclosure amounts to alerting the public to otherwise hidden loyalties or obligations that might influence what they see or hear. It is rarely an entirely satisfactory response. First, disclosure by and large cannot be specific as to how the outside entanglement might skew the journalism. If readers are supposed to be forewarned to bias by knowing the writer used to work for the subject of the story, they may still not have a clue as to what direction that bias may lean toward. Second, even if the disclosure suggests a broad direction of improper influence, it does nothing to rid the report of it or to indicate its extent. Third, conflict may manifest itself not just in bias, but in impaired professional judgment. Disclosure does not enable the reader to compensate fully for that impairment (Davis 2001, p. 12). Fourth, some powerfully consequential conflicts may be impossible ethically to disclose. Take the negotiation with a news source that obligates the reporter to withhold a good story now in hopes of a better story later. The reporter has a duty to conceal that negotiation, yet it impinges on his duty to the public.

How does disclosure relate to the typology of conflicts? Disclosure is a response that works best with conflicts that are non-endemic—that is, do not implicate basic journalistic processes—and most illuminating with conflicts that are explicitly consequential, where the link between conflict and content is clearest. It does little to mitigate endemic conflicts, in part because those are the conflicts that are least susceptible to being disclosed, and if used as a response to conflicts that are not clearly consequential—meaning they affect predisposition and context, not the substance of produced work—are liable to be unintelligible.

## Managing Conflicts

At the outset, I suggested that conflicts of interest are an inescapable feature of the terrain on which journalism is practiced, and derive, in part, from the reality that journalists work within a nexus of overlapping obligations, most of them perfectly legitimate. The conventional responses to conflicts are elimination or disclosure. But they help most with conflicts that are the least vexing: conflicts that are non-endemic—meaning they do not arise from either the nature of the work, the character of its commercial setting or the boundaries of its institutional structure—and which are plainly consequential, in that they clearly affect the content the journalist produces.

Endemic conflicts work a subtler, longer-term and, I suggest, ultimately more corrupting influence on the independence of journalism, and typically have consequences toward the less discernible side of the scale. Accordingly, other techniques of management may be appropriate, including:

*Fostering In-House Discourse.* Internal disclosure of conflicts may produce benefits that public disclosure does not. (It may be valuable if the public overhears this discourse, and more valuable still if members of the public participate. But the key purpose is encouraging self-awareness and self-criticism among journalists themselves.) The problem of conflicts is one that people in the communications professions experience directly and personally.

*Providing Internal Oversight.*   Endemic conflicts of interest require vigilance and a commitment to keep them from corrupting coverage to the detriment of the public entitlement to significant information. Who watches for sacred cows? Are they not emblematic of endemic dangers to journalistic independence? If the organization has a news ombudsman or public editor, is that person a customer-service supervisor—or is she fully empowered to look for ways that institutional or commercial inducements shape coverage?

*Segregating Functions.*   A typical professional conflict arises when the same individual is expected to fulfill more than one role in regard to the same client (Stark 2001). News organizations, in the name of calibrating editorial operations to business goals, have in recent years given senior editors financial incentives linked not to journalistic success but to cost containment or revenue enhancement (Downie & Kaiser 2003). Managing endemic conflicts honestly requires encouraging them to be made manifest and then addressing them forthrightly. That argues for returning to the traditional church–state distinction and re-segregating news from commerce (Stark 2001).

*Superintending Duties.*   Creating fixed areas of editorial responsibility (e.g., beats) encourages staff to develop durable loyalties to outside constituencies, and sometimes even to view their own prospects as dependent on the success of those constituencies. A reporter covering a presidential campaign might well view her future and her candidate's future as intertwined; that might incline her toward favorable coverage of the candidate, in the hope that victory would land both of them in the White House. Staff should be rotated regularly; fixed beats should be understood as a boon to expertise but also a threat to reportorial independence and an incubator for endemic conflicts.

## CONCLUDING THOUGHTS ON NEW MEDIA

While combating conflicts is a cornerstone of the ethic that is normally thought constitutive of journalistic professionalism, that view is not universally shared by the growing corps of New Media practitioners who believe what they do—reporting and commenting on matters of public significance—is essentially journalism. Some see conflict rules as a fig leaf that conceals a chronic refusal of traditional journalists to own up to biases they are prone to and help propagate. But while the blogosphere has been acutely sensitive to evidence of undeclared political affections, it has thus far been less mindful of commercial influences. Its emerging economic model lacks the transparency of conventional news operations, and private payment in exchange for influence appears to be en route to becoming not just incidental, but integral to some successful blogs.

The continuing problem is to safeguard a professional space for independently gathering and sharing publicly significant information and comment. The conflict of interest is a concept that reflects some of the most potent threats to that space. Finding ways to avert, brand and neutralize the harm of such conflicts remains one of the most difficult challenges facing contemporary journalism.

## EPILOGUE: FUTURE DIRECTIONS

This analysis suggests several promising directions of inquiry, among them:

1. *Effects on content*: It is posited that conflicts may have real impact on what journalists produce. But is there evidence they do? And if so, how can those effects be identified and catalogued, and related to the different types of conflicts analyzed here?
2. *Attitudes toward conflicts*: How journalists view various kinds of conflicts and with what degree of tolerance may vary with rank, gender, medium, years of service, race, ethnicity and, indeed, coverage area.
3. *Public perceptions of conflicts*: Journalists often base their views of conflicts on the public's presumed opinions, yet without solid information about what the public actually thinks about the nature, incidence and acceptability of conflicts. What says the public— and which public?
4. *Conflicts and enforcement:* How do organizations decide which conflicts require disciplinary response, and what determines the harshness or mildness of that response?
5. *Endemic conflicts:* What steps do news organizations take to insulate their news from internal influences arising from material commitments or obligations of their ownership? Which steps appear most successful?

## REFERENCES

Alterman, Eric. (2003). *What Liberal Media? The Truth about Bias and the News.* New York: Basic Books.

American Society of Newspaper Editors, Code of Ethics or Canons of Journalism. (1923). Retrieved May 4, 2007, from http://ethics.iit.edu/codes/coe/amer.soc.newspaper.editors.1923.html

Baier, Annette. (1994). *Moral Prejudices: Essays on Ethics.* Cambridge, MA: Harvard University Press.

Black, Jay, Steele, Bob, & Barney, Ralph. (1999). *Doing Ethics in Journalism: A Handbook with Case Studies* (3rd ed.). Boston: Allyn & Bacon.

Boehlert, Eric (2005, January 12). No Pundit Left Behind. *Salon.com.* Retrieved May 4, 2007, from http://dir.salon.com/story/news/feature/2005/01/12/armstrong/index.html

Borden, Sandra L., & Pritchard, Michael S. (2001). Conflict of Interest in Journalism. In M. Davis & A. Stark (Eds.), *Conflict of Interest in the Professions* (pp. 73–92). New York: Oxford University Press.

Byrne, Bridget. (2006, July 16) "And Now, a (Scripted) Word from our Sponsors." *Washington Post*, p. N07.

Davis, Charles, & Craft, Stephanie. (2000). New Media Synergy: Emergence of Institutional Conflicts of Interest. *Journal of Mass Media Ethics, 15(4),* 219–231.

Davis, Michael. (2001). Introduction. In M. Davis, & A. Stark (Eds.), *Conflict of Interest in the Professions* (pp. 3–19). New York: Oxford University Press.

Davis, Michael, & Elliston, Frederick A. (1986). Introduction to Part IV, Conflict of Interest. In M. Davis & F. A. Elliston (Eds.), *Ethics and the Legal Profession* (pp. 279–282). New York: Prometheus Books.

Day, Louis A. (1997) *Ethics in Media Communications* (2nd ed.). New York: Wadsworth.

Dow Jones & Co. Code of Conduct. (2004). Retrieved May 4, 2007, from http://209.85.165.104/search?q=cache:ndlBHjdwDMsJ:www.shareholder.om/dowjones/downloads/CG_Conduct.pdf

Downie, Leonard, & Kaiser, Robert. (2003). *The News About the News: American Journalism in Peril.* New York: Vintage.

Drinkard, Jim. (2005, January 14). President Criticizes Education Dept.'s Payout to Williams. *USA Today,* p. 9A.

Elliott, Deni. (n.d.). Freedom of Political Expression: Do Journalists Forfeit Their Right? Retrieved Jan. 12, 2007, from Indiana School of Journalism Ethics Case Pages archived at http://www.journalism.indiana.edu/Ethics/freepol.html

Elliott, Stuart. (2005, January 19). Strong Stands Taken as the Public Relations Industry Debates Payments Made to a Commentator. *New York Times*. Retrieved May 4, 2007 from http://select.nytimes.com/search/restricted/article?res=F30E10FF385C0C7A8DDDA80894DD404482

Elliott, Stuart. (2006, 16 August). A Column on (Your Product Here) Placement. *New York Times*. Retrieved May 4, 2007 from http://select.nytimes.com/search/restricted/article?res=F3091FF73C5A0C758DDDA10894DE404482

Fallows, James. (1992). *Breaking the News: How the Media Undermine American Democracy*. New York: Vintage Books.

Fitzpatrick, Kathy. (2006). Baselines for Ethical Advocacy in the "Marketplace of Ideas." In Kathy Fitzpatrick & Carolyn Bronstein (Eds.), *Ethics in Public Relations: Responsible Advocacy* (pp. 1–19). Thousand Oaks, CA: Sage.

Glaser, Mark. (2003, August 26). For Business Journalists, Credibility is Never More than a Trade Away. *Online Journalism Review* .Retrieved from http://209.85.165.104/search?q=cache:QutRM3WnWHcJ:www.ojr.org/ojrglaser/1061942243.php

Iggers, Jeremy. (1999). *Good News, Bad News: Journalism Ethics and the Public Interest*. Boulder, CO: Westview Press.

Levin, Gary. (2006, September 20). The Newest Characters on TV Shows: Product Plugs. *USA Today*, p. A1.

Limor, Yehiel, & Himelboim, Itai. (2006). Journalism and Moonlighting: An International Comparison of 242 Codes of Ethics. *Journal of Mass Media Ethics, 21(4)*, 265–285.

*The New York Times, Ethical Journalism: A Handbook of Values and Practices for the News and Editorial Departments*. (2004). Retrieved February 8, 2007, from http://www.nytco.com/pdf/NYT_Ethical_Journalism_0904.pdf

Poynter Institute. (2004). Memo from *Miami Herald* executive editor Tom Fiedler. Retrieved August 31, 2004, from the Poynter Institute website, http://poynter.org/forum/view_post.asp?id=7901

Public Relations Society of America, Code of Ethics. (2000). Retrieved February 8, 2007, from http://www.prssa.org/downloads/codeofethics.pdf. http://a.abclocal.go.com/three/kgo/prsacodeofethics.pdf

Schudson, Michael. (1978). *Discovering the News*. New York: Basic Books.

Shudson, Michael. (2003). *The Sociology of News*. New York: W.W. Norton.

Shudson, Michael. (2000). The Sociology of News Production Revisited (Again). In James Curran & Michael Gurevitch (Eds.), *Mass Media and Society* (3rd ed., pp. 175–201). New York: Oxford University Press.

Society of Business Editors and Writers, Code of Ethics. (n.d.). Retrieved February 4, 2007, from http://www2.sabew.org/sabewweb.nsf/e0087b5460c4a721862569c2005f85a/7ef63c713fcb012a86256ace0058a191!OpenDocument

Stark, Andrew. (2001). Comparing Conflict of Interest across the Professions. In M. Davis & A. Stark (Eds.), *Conflict of Interest in the Professions* (pp. 335–353). New York: Oxford University Press.

Ward, Stephen J. A. (2004). *The Invention of Journalism Ethics: The Path to Objectivity and Beyond*. Montreal: McGill-Queen's University Press.

Wasserman, Edward. (2003, June 30). *The Lessons of Jessica Lynch for Media Monopoly*. Retrieved May 4, 2007, from Washington and Lee University Knight Professor of Journalism Ethics Web site http://journalism.wlu.edu/knight/2003/06-30-03.html

Wasserman, Edward. (2005a, January 25). *Ideas for Sale in the Commentary Arena*. Retrieved May 4, 2007, from Washington and Lee University Knight Professor of Journalism Ethics Web site http://journalism.wlu.edu/knight/2005/01-2405.html

Wasserman, Edward. (2005b, August 8). *Needed: Ethics from the Bottom Up*. Retrieved May 4, 2007, from Washington and Lee University Knight Professor of Journalism Ethics Web site http://journalism.wlu.edu/knight/2005/08-08-05.html

Wasserman, Edward. (2005c, October 17). *Selling the Blogosphere*. Retrieved May 4, 2007, from Washington and Lee University Knight Professor of Journalism Ethics Web site http://journalism.wlu.edu/knight/2005/10-1705.html

Wasserman Edward. (2006a, January 9). *The Lobbyist and the Media*. RetrievedMay 4, 2007, from Washington and Lee University Knight Professor of Journalism Ethics Web site http://journalism.wlu.edu/knight/2006/01 092006.htm

Wasserman, Edward. (2006b, August 3). *The Ethics of Product Placement*. Panel Presentation presented August 2006, Magazine, Media Ethics and Advertising divisions, Annual Conference, Association of Educators in Journalism and Mass Communication. Retrieved May 4, 2007, from Washington and Lee University, Knight Professor of Journalism Ethics Web site: http://journalism.wlu.edu/knight/Lectures/08-03-2006.htm

Wasserman, Edward. (2006c, October 2). *Holding News Until the Time is Right*. Retrieved May 4, 2007, from Washington and Lee University Knigh Professor of Journalism Ethics Web site http://journalism.wlu.edu/knight/2006/10-02-2006.html

Wasserman, Edward. (2006d, November 27). *Holding the Line On News Pollution*. Retrieved May 4, 2007, from Washington and Lee University Knight Professor of Journalism Ethics Web site http://journalism.wlu.edu/knight/2006/11-27-2006.htm

Wasserman, Edward. (2006, December 25). *Can the Internet Be Saved?* Retrieved May 4, 2007, from Washington and Lee University, Knight Professor of Journalism Ethics Web site http://journalism.wlu.edu/knight/2006/1225-2006.htm

Wasserman, Edward. (2007, January 8). The Insidious Corruption of Beats. Retrieved May 4, 2007, from Washington and Lee University Knight Professor of Journalism Ethics Web site http://journalism.wlu.edu/knight/2007/01-08-2007.htm_

Wilkins, Lee, & Brennen, Bonnie. Conflicted Interests, Contested Terrain: Journalism Ethics Codes Then and Now. (2003). Media Ethics Division, AEJMC 2003 Annual Conference. Retrieved May 4, 2007, from http://eric.ed.gov/ERICDocs/data/ericdocs2/content_storage_01/0000000/80/23/b0/4a.pdf

# 18

# Digital Ethics in Autonomous Systems

## Michael Bugeja

Autonomy is the very condition of technological development—Jacques Ellul (2003)

In the future, communities formed by ideas will be as strong as those formed by the forces of physical proximity—Nicholas Negroponte (1998)

What happens to the public trust when U.S. democracy's most indispensable element, an independent, community-based press, merges with an amoral autonomous system whose features may obliterate or obfuscate space, culture, and time? In that question lies the whole of digital ethics in the practice of journalism as Fourth Estate, or watchdog over government and other privileged or powerful social entities.

Answers are far-reaching because consumers in the early 21st century have made new media and communication technology their No. 1 life activity. The average American spends more time consuming media and using technology via video, audio, and portable communication devices, than any other human activity, including eating and sleeping, according to findings of a Middletown Media Studies report (Ball State University, 2005). Moreover, a recent medical study concludes that 1 in 8 Americans are addicted to Internet (Stanford University, 2006). To put that into perspective, 1 in 13 Americans are addicted to alcohol (National Institute on Alcohol Abuse and Alcoholism, 2006). Given the unprecedented levels of consumer use, news organizations continue to migrate online in a converged diversified "world" whose hallmarks include 57 million weblogs that double in number every 236 days with many of the most influential sponsored by traditional media (Sifry, 2006). Media technology also assists revenue generation. Predictably, online advertising revenue in 2005 rose by 25 percent from the previous year as news organizations continued to "find" subscribers in virtual rather than in local habitats (State of the News Media, 2006).

Since its inception, the news media have been grounded in the physical. Historically they have existed apart from the niche outlets of magazines and entertainment programming targeting subscribers, listeners, viewers, or clientele via the demographics and psychographics of consumer profiling. The sharper is the profiling, the stronger is the brand; the stronger the brand, the greater the revenue. David Miller, writing in the March 2006 issue of *Ideas: The Magazine of Newspaper Marketing*, states the objective of newspaper branding is "to create a differentiating and durable strategic position of relevant value. Whether it is real or perceived, the idea is that it would be difficult for your competitors to replicate it" (p. 10). Replicating news that happens in real space, culture, and time is the objective of objective journalism. Traditionally, the only real variants in spot news and beat reporting—terms associated with physical proximity, by the way—are the scope, breadth, and depth of fact compilation and presentation. When airliners crash into buildings, the public requires event replication in print and on air from as many sources as possible to comprehend the dimensions of the tragedy. Newspaper branding often overlooks this fundamental criterion of a free press as social steward. According to Miller, consumer branding is essential if newspapers are to meet the demands of the Internet age. He argues that newspapers have not enjoyed much success in making the transformation because of several factors, including the capitol investment in presses and trucks—symbols of physical proximity.

In a telling remark indirectly associated with media ethics, Miller states:

> Stewardship of the public trust remains central to the identity of most newsrooms. But perhaps newspapers are now structured on promises of value, such as independence and objectivity, which fail to substantially exist in the minds of consumers.
> Even if it were a perception that could be re-kindled, how much additional purchase intent would it generate? (p. 12)

News grounded in space, culture, and time continues to ensure the public trust. Jefferson's famous axiom—that he would prefer newspapers without government providing people could read and those newspapers could be delivered—is at the heart of public education and liberty in the United States. Moreover, an informed, educated populace fulfills both deontological and utilitarian visions, defining civic duty as well as providing the greatest good for the greatest number. This chapter investigates whether those outcomes are altered online as media corporations focus increasingly on revenue rather than stewardship.

Our brightest journalism minds continue to debate the facts, values, principles, and loyalties of stewardship. However, when addressing them in technological environs, they often confront "the paralyzing complexity of the Internet" that raises "a new ensemble of ethical and legal challenges for which journalism does not yet have a nuanced understanding or even a full vocabulary" (Challenger & Friend, 2001, pp. 258, 267). This abridged apprehension and vocabulary are likely associated with universal principles eroding in spheres lacking linear, cultural, and physical dimensions. The French philosopher Jacques Ellul (1912–1994) noted that the nature of technology neither endures "any moral judgment" nor tolerates "any insertion of morality" in the technician's work (2003, p. 394). Might he then contend that ethical principles metamorphose in amoral autonomous spheres? If so, the medium is not the message, but the moral.

Conversely, technology advocates such as Nicholas Negroponte (1995), co-founder and director of the Massachusetts Institute of Technology Media lab, believe that the "medium is not the message in a digital world" but "an embodiment of it" (p. 71) through which text messaging (variant of the telegraph); telephone; still and moving images; animation; sound recordings; books; radio and television; film; animation; and print—each of which altered culture historically according to McLuhanesque theory—converge. If Internet obliterates time and physical place, does convergence also obfuscate culture? This exploratory analysis addresses that and other nuanced effects of digital ethics in autonomous systems.

## UNIVERSAL REVIEWS: AN ELLULIAN OR NEGROPONTEAN FUTURE?

One of the most prescient works about the morality of autonomous systems was Neil Postman's *Amusing Ourselves to Death* (1985), which opens with a comparison of the Orwellian vs. Huxleyan technological world orders. Although Postman was discussing broadcast technology, he upholds the Ellulian perspective in embracing Huxley's vision in which no technologically omnipotent Big Brother deprives people of their morality and cultural history because "people will come to love their oppression, to adore the technologies that undo their capacities to think" (p. viii). Postman predicts an autonomous system that would not ban democratizing information but provide so much trivializing data that "truth would be drowned in a sea of irrelevance" (p. viii).

Nicholas Negroponte overlooks that outcome. "Yes, we are now in a digital age," he wrote in 1998, "to whatever degree our culture, infrastructure, and economy (in that order) allow us." In his final column in *Wired*, Negroponte forecast an optimistic future that would transform space, culture, and time. Digitized ideas would be as powerful as those formed by physical proximity. Local governance would abound in a virtual global environment rendering territory meaningless. We would lead asynchronous lives during which prime time would be "my time" in pajamas.

Negroponte's most famous work, *being digital* (1995), is worth evaluating today in as much as it foreshadowed the virtual world in which most of us, especially in journalism and journalism education, dwell for most of our digital day. Before exploring this world theoretically, and investigating technology's impact on universal principles, it behooves us to state how space, culture, and time may be obliterated or obfuscated by computing technologies, quoting Negroponte in both subheads and text:

- *Place without Space*: "[T]he post-information age will remove the limitations of geography. Digital living will include less and less dependence upon being in a specific place at a specific time, and the transmission of place itself will start to become possible" (p. 165).
- *Being Asynchronous*: "A face-to-face or telephone conversation is real time and synchronous while email is not.... The advantage is less about voice and more about off-line processing and time shifting" (p. 167).
- *Mediumlessness*: "Thinking about multimedia needs to include ideas about the fluid movement from one medium to the next.... [M]ultimedia involves translating one dimension (time) into another dimension (space)" (pp. 72, 73).

Place without space and being asynchronous are self-explanatory; but mediumlessness requires theoretical grounding because it relates to culture. McLuhan, of course, is the standard here in his most important work, *Understanding Media: The Extensions of Man*," in which the word "culture" is the third word of his opening paragraph:

In a culture like ours, long accustomed to splitting and dividing all things as a means of control, it is sometimes a bit of a shock to be reminded that, in operational and practical fact, the medium is the message. That is merely to say that the personal and social consequences of any medium—that is, of any extension of ourselves—result from the new scale that is introduced into our affairs by each extension of ourselves, or by any new technology. (p. 7)

In other words, culture adapts to the autonomous system of technology, which is why we see passersby ignoring others and seemingly speaking to themselves using cell phones in the digital street. This effect went unforeseen by some of our most astute social activists, chief among them, Parker J. Palmer who wrote about the universality of place in 1981 in *The Company of Strangers*, calling the street our most public place, for there we meet strangers with whom we interact, even when nobody speaks. People send a message through the channel of their bodies in real place, acknowledging that "we occupy the same territory, belong to the same human community" (p. 39). Within a few years of their introduction to society, cell phones altered our ancient human bond: No longer did we belong together in community; instead, we belonged to a rate plan offering rollover minutes and ring tones. How did this happen under the radar of our conscience, coloring how we view the world and each other?

As Postman (1993) explains, "embedded in every tool is an ideological bias, a predisposition to construct the world as one thing rather than another, to value one thing over another, to amplify one sense or skill or attitude more loudly than another," hence altering culture (p. 13). Cell phone users altered the interpersonal culture of community, elevating the value of people and places somewhere else over those in physical proximity (Bugeja, 2004). Media history records how each device—from the telegraph and telephone in the 19th century to the radio and television of the 20th century—not only changed culture but also how journalists covered it. Hence, the "mediumlessness" of multimedia's streaming text, images, sound, video, animation and interaction may homogenize culture in addition to splitting rather than extending human senses (as well as consciousness).[1] Ironically, Negroponte states this in his futuristic proclamation: "In the next millennium, we will find that we are talking as much or more with machines than we are with humans" (1995, p. 145).

Ellul would be horrified by that pronouncement. He predicted different outcomes on the theory that autonomous technological systems often neglect primary human needs, especially conscientious ones involving unifying principles by which to gauge and govern our thoughts, words, and deeds. He saw technology as an inhuman, self-determining organism ("an end in itself") whose autonomy transformed centuries' old systems "while being scarcely modified in its own features" (p. 386). Ellul did not live long enough to witness completely the digital era's impact on the news industry, although his theories presaged technology's impact on culture, especially on the economy:

> Like political authority, an economic system that challenges the technological imperative is doomed.
>
> It is not economic law that imposes itself on the technological phenomenon; it is the law of technology which orders and ordains, orients and modifies the economy. Economics is a necessary agent. It is neither the determining factor nor the principle of orientation. Technology obeys its own determination, it realizes itself. (p. 392)

In other words, apply technology to the economy, and the economy henceforth is about technology (think NASDAQ). Apply it to politics, and politics henceforth is about technology (think Kennedy-Nixon debates). Apply it to education, and education henceforth is about technology (think *Sesame Street*). Apply it to journalism, and journalism henceforth is about technology (think convergence). Moreover, because technology is autonomous and independent of everything, *it cannot be blamed for anything*.

Ellul, perhaps more than any other philosopher, associated technology's applied outcomes with moral principles. He theorized technology does not advance the moral ideal nor endure moral judgment (p. 394). As such, he argued, technology cannot be halted for a moral reason. Situational ethics, long associated with the practice of journalism, is just one more technological effect, "quite convenient for putting up with anything" (p. 395). If morality is constantly redefined to augment the latest technological feature, then it has effectively negated the existence of universals.

This is evident in the ethics of social networks, which have effectively refined friendship for the emerging generation. MySpace ranked for a time the most visited Internet site, claiming 4.46 percent of all Internet visits (Hitwise, July 11, 2006). Increasingly popular are mobile social networks, or MoSoSos, which use global positioning system technologies to alert users via cell phone, laptop, or other portable device when someone from their "affinity groups" are in physical space. MoSoSo users market themselves by creating Web profiles that inform others about their interests and pursuits, including their romantic availability. According to *Wired News*, "Not surprisingly, MoSoSos are ideal for hooking up young, active professionals tied to their mobile phones or laptops, and they're starting to take off" (Terdiman, 2005).

Again we see yet another erosion of the universality of place. It is one thing to speak to a friend on a cell phone and ignore strangers in the public street; it is quite another to navigate those streets with a "life remote control," tuning in to those who share our marketing profiles rather than our space. Rather than relying on principles such as justice or fairness, which have defined friendships in community since Aristotle, social network users market themselves like products in virtual or physical space. The McLuhan aphorism, *All advertising advertises advertising*, now applies to how we see ourselves and others through the social norm of "egocasting." No other current ethicist has defined the current age more precisely than Christine Rosen who conceived the term "egocasting" in her continuing studies of technology's effect on human relationships. In her watershed essay, "The Age of Egocasting," Rosen notes how the most powerful of new technologies "encourage not the cultivation of taste, but the numbing repetition of fetish. And they contribute to what might be called 'egocasting,' the thoroughly personalized and extremely narrow pursuit of one's personal taste" (2004–2005).

Rosen, a resident fellow at the Ethics and Public Policy Center, notes that it is no surprise that users of social networks "have a tendency to describe themselves like products and to develop their own vocabulary to describe the pseudo-relationships such networks foster" (personal correspondence, November 11, 2005). She states that users often speak about "*friending* rather than building *friendships*." Digital-based friendships appeal to the ego rather than the conscience, she says,

> with the number of successful targets listed on their pages as evidence of any given person's appeal. This is a more acquisitive practice—collecting friends like consumer goods--rather than the older understanding of building friendships gradually, over time, and with the assumption of lasting mutual obligations. On the Internet, everything can be had on demand; why not friends? Such an attitude has long-term consequences for the younger generation's understanding of relationships. It is ironic that the technologies we embrace and praise for the degree of control they give us individually also give marketers and advertisers the most direct window into our psyche and buying habits they've ever had.

Contemplating friendship, Rosen like Aristotle focuses on the justice of "lasting mutual obligations." Friendship is a social *contract*, not a social contact among fellow online voyagers that can be added or deleted on demand with a mere click of the keys. In *The Nicomachean Ethics* as translated by David Ross (1998), friends possess "common property" evaluated by the level of truthfulness in real space and time, "for friendship depends on community" (p. 207). Aristotle evaluates friendship in space, culture, and time, using the term "fellow voyagers" literally and linearly in association with the social contract. "We may see even in our travels," he writes, "how near and dear every man is to every other. Friendship seems too to hold states together..." (p. 192). Gestures of friends in the public street are universal, Aristotle observes, even when we are unfamiliar with the country and its customs. According to him, such friendship is especially prized by lawgivers because it expels faction, unifies society, and becomes "the truest form of justice" (p. 193). In fact, the greater the friendship the more intense the demands of justice, especially truth, which also endures across space, culture, and time. While it is true that friendship, in and of itself, may have little to do with the practice of journalism, the principles that define friendship—justice, responsibility, truth, and trust—relate directly to digital ethics, the public trust, and the question at hand: whether universals metamorphose in autonomous systems that may obliterate or obfuscate physical dimensions.

In discussing universal principles, Deni Elliott uses a crystalline metaphor:

> Viewed from a wide angle, the world's communities and subcommunities appear to be an array of values, a colorful moral kaleidoscope. But these dissimilarities among values, as striking as they are, mask the similarity behind the "colors"—the species-specific "crystals" that create discernible and consistent patterns amid the array of value-colors. The argument for universal values, like moral development theories, builds on the notion of similarities among human behavior that stretch across space, culture, and time. (1997, p. 68)

In a word, Elliott grounds universals in physical realities rather than in asynchronous, acultural, virtual dimensions. Moreover, her conclusion about the social nature of the human being— "namely the need for being-in-community" (p. 80)—adds another moral yardstick by which we can gauge whether principles metamorphose or remain intact in autonomous technological systems: "Moral reasoning and consciousness are not, primarily, about our individual selves but about judgments on actions, or intended actions, regarding others. The socialization of the moral being takes place in the individual's relationships with others" (p. 80). Thus, a measurement of the applicability of universals is to ask whether online content is about others (associated with community) or ourselves (associated with marketing).

In this, technology gives up the ethical ghost. The means by which technology obliterates space and time and obfuscates culture are encyclopedic and grist for theories. But its nature, as that of the scorpion, is stingingly obvious. "What has the essence of technology to do with revealing?" questions Heidegger: "The answer: everything" (2003, p. 255). What current communication technology reveals, along with the practice of journalism in the digital age, often appears to be a singular objective: revenue generation.

Alas, the generation of news has never been particularly cost-effective. For centuries, new technology has been introduced into newsrooms and studios to cut down costs. With each new invention, reporters distanced themselves from the sources and locales. Telegraphs bridged the divide between Europe and the North America in the 19th century, and telephones eliminated the need to travel to interview newsmakers. During the third televised presidential debate, Richard Nixon argued from a studio in Los Angeles and John F. Kennedy, from a studio in New York, joined together "by a network of electronic facilities which permits each candidate to see and hear the other" (The Third Kennedy-Nixon Debate). Despite newsroom and studio innovation, technology remained a one-way delivery system. With the advent of digital technology, however, interactivity created two-way systems with fees often applied in each direction, multiplied by the number of media converging in any one device. Revenue rose along with consolidation. In the early 1980s, 50 major communication companies controlled most of the media. By 2003, Ben H. Bagdikian writes in *The New Media Monopoly*, that number reduced to five: Time Warner, Disney, Murdoch's News Corporation (Australia), Viacom, and Bertelsmann (Germany). "Today, none of the dominant media companies bother with dominance merely in a single medium. Their strategy has been to have major holdings in all the media, from newspapers to movie studios. This gives each of the five corporations and their leaders more communications power than was exercised by any despot or dictatorship in history" (2004, p. 3).

In Bagdikian's view media owners emphasize fiduciary responsibility rather than social responsibility. This can be documented, in part. In 2004, the "State of the News Media" report documented these disturbing trends:

- Between the recession of 1991–2000, newspaper advertising revenues climbed 60 percent with profits rising 207 percent. Increases in newsroom personnel were about 3 percent, "most of which then got wiped away during the 2001 downturn."
- Newspapers have about 2,200 fewer newsroom employees today than in 1990 with "work once done by printers and composing room workers" migrating to the newsroom, adding more jobs "related to production rather than news gathering."
- Data collected by Joe Foote, dean of the Gaylord College at the University of Oklahoma, indicate the number of network correspondents "since the 1980s has been cut by a third," with workload increasing by 30 percent during the same period.
- In local television, "average workload increased 20 percent between 1998 and 2002," and "59 percent of news directors reported either budget cuts or staff cuts in 2002."

The 2005 "State of the News Media" report notes the consequences of these practices—a larger trend in American journalism to repackage and present information, rather than gather it. And there were additional cuts as well:

> "The New York Times would cut nearly 60 people from its newsroom, the Los Angeles Times 85; Knight Ridder's San Jose Mercury News cut 16%, the Philadelphia Inquirer 15%—and that after cutting another 15% only five years earlier. By November, investors frustrated by poor financial performance forced one of the most cost-conscious newspaper chains of all, Knight Ridder, to be put up for sale."

The 2006 "State of the News Media" reports a continuation of cost-cutting measures to increase revenue growth, noting that "full-time professional employment at daily newspapers fell by 600 during 2005."

In his aptly named book, *Knightfall: Knight Ridder and How the Erosion of Newspaper Journalism is Putting Democracy at Risk*, Davis Merritt discusses how the focus on profit has compromised the news industry's social mission, including its commitment to the universal principle of social responsibility, thereby jeopardizing U.S. democracy. According to Merritt, "The question is whether newspaper journalism can be successfully migrated to new technologies—the Internet or whatever might succeed it—before it becomes extinct, suffocated like the dinosaurs by the impact of the twenty-first century giant meteor labeled greed" (p. 1).

In reviewing the Ellulian vs. Negropontean worlds, one might conclude that, at the least, the autonomy of technological systems is an unfriendly host to universal principles, primarily because marketing addresses the ego rather than the conscience. Technological systems reflect the intentions of their interfaces, reducing human nature to the demographics and psychographics of marketing through which we increasingly focus on ourselves, rather than on others. As Ben H. Bagdikian observes in *The New Media Monopoly*, the collective ego is fed daily by commercials targeting users through their own interactive technologies describing "with some precision [their] income, education, occupation, and spending habits" (p. 230). The focus, then, is not on duty, happiness, or the common good but on the ego's appetites, to which marketing appeals. Moreover, the ego is its own autonomous system which, like technology, neither endures nor tolerates moral judgment. The marriage of ego and technology in a milieu that blurs space, culture, and time seemingly underwrites profit rather than principles. What, precisely, are those principles and how might they be applied in the digital era? What role, if any, do journalists have in ensuring that they do? How can media ethicists assist in all of those endeavors?

## UNIVERSAL METHODS: THE DIMENSIONS OF PRINCIPLES

In a 2006 keynote address at the International Communication Association, sociologist and author Manuel Castells waxed philosophic about the millions of blogs worldwide accounting for an explosion of "I" mass media across cultures. In the question and answer session, Castells was asked: "For centuries in Occidental culture there has been a philosophical debate, entirely conjectural, that universal principles exist or do not exist. We now have some empirical evidence to answer this question. Given the expanse of the blogosphere across cultures, are there any philosophical patterns that qualify now as universal, from Jeremy Bentham's happiness principle to Immanuel Kant's duty principle to John Locke's natural law?"[2] After some reflection, Castells answered affirmatively: "The longing for freedom."

That longing in and of itself is not a universal principle but the desire for one. Nevertheless, freedom is associated with human nature and need, secular and religious. It also rises to the sacred through the notion of free will. Indeed, in her treatise on universal values and moral development, cited earlier, Deni Elliott references a survey of representative samples of adult populations from 13 countries and concomitant cultures out of which a list of uniformities were compiled by sociologist Handley Cantril in 1965:

1. Satisfaction of survival needs;
2. Physical and psychological security;
3. Sufficient order and certainty to allow for predictability;
4. Pleasure: both physical and psychological excitement and enjoyment;
5. Freedom to act on ideas and plans for improvement of self and context;
6. Freedom to make choices;
7. Freedom to act on choices;
8. Personal identity and integrity; a sense of dignity;
9. Feeling of worthwhileness;
10. A system of beliefs to which they can commit themselves;
11. Trust in the system on which they depend (cited in Elliott, 1997, p. 71).

The term "freedom" appears in three of the 11 across cultural needs (Nos. 4–7). Assigning universal precepts to the others is a rhetorical rather than ethical exercise. However, with that disclaimer, one can discern these universal principles from the above list: the sanctity of life (Nos. 1, 2), justice/fairness (No. 3), pleasure/happiness (Nos. 4, 9), responsibility/duty (No. 10), integrity/dignity (No. 8), trust (No. 11).

Philosopher Christina Hoff Sommers (September 12, 1993) substitutes the term "moral absolutes" for Cantril's "uniformities," noting that these behaviors are clearly right or wrong and not subject to serious debate in any culture:

1. It is wrong to mistreat a child.
2. It is wrong to humiliate someone.
3. It is wrong to torment an animal.
4. It is wrong to think only of yourself.
5. It is wrong to steal, to lie, to break promises.
6. It is right to be considerate and respectful of others.
7. It is right to be charitable and generous (p. 16).

Explicating those tenets, one can assign to "sanctity of life" Nos. 1–3, with these other universals rounding out the remaining list: responsibility/duty (No. 4), truth/trust (No. 5), respect (No. 6), and generosity (No. 7).

Thus, we can compile from these lists a lexicon of universals: dignity, duty, fairness, freedom, generosity, happiness, integrity, justice, pleasure, respect, responsibility, sanctity of life, truth, and trust. We might further elevate these universal tenets of human nature to the status of "protonorm" as much a part of the genetic code as an ethics code. The sacredness of life as a protonorm was articulated by Clifford Christians (1997, pp. 6–8) who identified three categories into which the above universals easily fall:

- *Human dignity*: dignity, duty, fairness, freedom, integrity, justice, responsibility, trust.
- *Truth-telling*: truth.
- *Nonviolence*: generosity, happiness, pleasure, respect, sanctity of life.

According to Christians, "The primal sacredness of life is a protonorm that binds humans into a common oneness. And in our systematic reflection on this primordial generality, we recognize that it entails such basic ethical principles as human dignity, truth, and nonviolence" (pp. 12–13). Christians concludes that a commitment to universals, grounded ontologically, not only is pluralistic but simplistic conceptually, easily related to the practice of journalism: "The only question is whether our values affirm the human good or not. As our philosophies of life and beliefs are lobbied within the public sphere, we have a responsibility to make public the course we favor and to demonstrate in what manner it advances our common citizenship" (p. 18).

Again, however, even in Christians as in Deni Elliott, we confront the central issue on which this chapter is based: Do universals, or even protonorms, metamorphose or remain intact when transported to virtual realms that obliterate or obfuscate space, culture, and time? The whole of Christians' persuasive argument about the common oneness of humans is based on "reverence for life on earth, for the organic whole, for the *physical realm* [emphasis added] in which human civilization is situated" (1997, p. 7).

In as much as human civilization is merely reflected in (with varying degrees of truth) but not situated in the virtual realm where humans "dwell" for most of their digital day, how, if at all, do communication technologies affirm good, condemn evil, and advance our common citizenship—tenets articulated in the Society of Professional Journalists' code of ethics, which uphold these ideals?[3]

Heidegger's concept of technology's nature—that of revealing—offers scant evidence that universal ideals are upheld in the global village of Internet. First of all, the village may be global in that content is generated on every continent; however, when viewed by way of what, precisely, is accessed, the Web is as American as a *USA Today* pie chart. Of the top 30 most accessed Internet sites, Asia claims four and Europe, one, according to the *International Herald Tribune*, which reports:

> Like most of the world's pop culture and brands, the rest of the Internet's most sought-after brands of information and entertainment are dominated by U.S. companies. In this case, replace Disney, Coca-Cola and McDonald's products with Microsoft, Yahoo and Google Web pages. That makes the discussions somewhat moot this week in Athens, where the first Internet Governance Forum is trying to come to grips with the more abstract issue of political control. In Athens, the buzz is about diversity, access, human rights, security and openness, not YouTube, Office Live and iTunes. (Shannon 2006)

Diversity, human rights, security, and openness (freedom) may qualify as universals philosophically but not technologically, whose autonomous systems elevate their own subsystems (Microsoft, Yahoo, Google) over historically powerful corporate brands, including Coca-Cola. Ellul's vision as opposed to Negroponte's seemingly is upheld in that Web content cannot be controlled by ethics or even politics, as Ellul prophesied. Evaluating his theories, Robert C. Scharff and V. Dusek write that human hubris assumes that we can control technology when, in fact, we ourselves are simultaneously blind and beholden to its autonomous systems: Typically, they state, it is characteristic for technology advocates to overestimate their own skills at controlling content that negatively affects society:

> Scientists and engineers display embarrassing naïveté and shallowness in dealing with the social impact of technology. Politicians are driven by ideological assumptions rather than knowledge in their efforts to direct or regulate technical practices. And ordinary citizens and consumers are seriously uninformed about both the technical practices and social realities that dominate everyday life. (2003, p. 383)

Technology, said to be efficient and convenient, has lived up to that billing in many ways in the newsroom and broadcast booth as well as in the consumer's household and workplace. What is efficient or convenient is not necessarily moral, however; and the average user may be blind to that effect. Indeed, Ellul theorizes that technological systems inevitably entrance all involved, often viewed as a creative force that displaces traditional morality, "which is now regarded as merely something lingering 'inside' our minds" (Scharff & Dusek, p. 383). That effect is revealed in the current day with data about usage of the most accessed online content, challenging even Heiddegger's hope of formulating a free relationship to technology—"a way of living with technology that does not allow it to warp, confuse, and lay waste our nature" (Dreyfus & Spinosa, 2003, p. 315). That nature is said to be rooted in moral law expressed in the sanctity of principles that transcend space, culture, and time. Negropontean predictions about "place without space," "mediumlessness," and "being asynchronous" seem inherently at odds with his own ethical ideals perhaps best articulated in his "One Laptop per Child (OLPT)" initiative, a non-profit humanitarian project producing "a flexible, ultra low-cost, power-efficient, responsive, durable machine with which nations of the emerging world can leapfrog decades of development—immediately transforming the content and quality of their children's learning" (OLPT, 2006). Given content most apt to be accessed, along with what search engines are apt to display, this project—despite its noble intentions—typically fails to factor how technology warps, confuses, and lays waste to the very principles on which Negroponte, as OLPT chairman, has bookmarked his aspirations.

Technological predictions, however humane, "have become the 'airport reading' of the world—a substitute for beach reading in a harried age, just as predictable but a lot less engaging, celebrating not the steamy pleasures of physical reality but the disembodied pleasures of virtual reality" (p. 63), argues Rosalind Williams (2006), director of MIT's Program in Science, Technology, and Society. She elaborates on the digital evangelism of futuristic predictions—technology "will read our thoughts" and "lift us out of the mud of localism to digital globalism"—noting that historians, in particular, are wary of such exaggerated claims (p. 63).

Historian Theodore Roszak, author of *The Making of a Counter Culture* and *The Cult of Information*, has disputed Negropontean claims for decades. "How does the mind think?" he asks. "Not by assembling information, but by applying the intellectual patterns we call 'ideas' to experience. This is something we would not expect machines to do" (personal correspondence, October 11, 2006). Roszak's advice is to commit fiercely to refuting the technologist's claim that the mind is just another machine and to affirm "that thinking with your own naked wits is a pure animal joy that cannot be programmed, and that great culture begins with an imagination on fire. We should remind our children at every turn that more great literature and more great science were accomplished with the quill pen than by the fastest microchip that will ever be invented" (personal correspondence, October 11, 2006). Great journalism, like great literature and science, is an outgrowth of critical thinking without which we are left to contemplate Roszak's greatest fear: *that technology will reduce the mind to the level of a machine*. A focus on the dimensions of universal principles—and our duty as journalists to safeguard them—may ward off such a future. The problem is, increasingly, the practice of journalism in the digital age is virtual, mediumless, and asynchronous.

## UNIVERSAL CHALLENGE: RESURRECTING THE DIMENSIONS

This chapter thus far has noted that universal principles historically and philosophically have been grounded in the physical dimensions of space, culture, and time, which the nature of technology at best obfuscates and at worst, obliterates. Hence, Ellul's vision seems verified at least in part in as much as Negropontean predictions of a humane, ideal-driven digital world appear yet unrealized when typical use of Internet technologies is explored. The challenge then is to keep focused not only on universal principles but on how they can be applied using technology as tool to cover space, culture, and time or to facilitate such interactions in real rather than virtual community. It also can be argued that the virtual, mediumless, and asynchronous qualities of the Negropontean world have not given society a global village as promised but a global mall (Bugeja, 2005b, p. 8) with an emphasis on entertainment, consumer-profiling, and profit. Digital technologies are said to appeal to the ego rather than to the conscience, intensifying "our collective voyeuristic urges" in a technological society saturated by amusement (Gross, Katz, & Ruby, 2003, p. xi, 95). It also has been noted earlier that such saturation is good for business. As David Scott (2006) writes in *I.T. Wars: Managing the Business-Technology Weave in the New Millennium*,

> Business is routinely conducted twenty-four hours a day, seven days a week. Organizations are increasing their global outreach. Travel no longer means that people are out-of-the-loop. Because people can stay connected to their work they often find, or at least feel, that they must stay connected. The requirement for effective business and information systems, their proper utilization, and the pressure for the most return possible has never been greater. (p. 1)

Such an assessment also applies to the business of journalism. In 1971 in *The Information Machines*, journalist and educator Ben Bagdikian wrote:

> It has taken two hundred years of the Industrial Revolution for men to realize that they are not very good at predicting the consequences of their inventions: to the surprise of almost everyone, automobiles changed sex habits. Information devices are no exception: machines for mass communications produce unexpected changes in the relationship of the individual to his society. (p. 1)

The consequences of convergence in journalism also have been surprising, as earlier citations attest, with the focus increasingly on fiduciary rather than social responsibility. Some believe the goal of digital ethics, then, is to resurrect and apply principles associated with stewardship of the public trust. However, that may not happen unless new media practitioners re-emphasize physical dimensions rather than virtual ones. Many prominent journalists and journalism educators are attempting to do just that, including Geneva Overholser, who views the existence of new media platforms as uplifting. Overholser, former editor of *The Des Moines Register* and chair of the

Pulitzer Prize Board, has served on the editorial board of *The New York Times* and as ombudsman of *The Washington Post*. She also is Curtis B. Hurley Chair in Public Affairs Reporting Missouri School of Journalism, Washington bureau. "Though many have seen the proliferation of new media," she states, "the fast pace of change, as unsettling, I would say its existence on the contrary holds the promise of returning to the media some of the ethical energy that our recent difficulties have leached out" (personal correspondence, July 17, 2006).

Overholser believes that putting the emphasis on moral rather than technological convergence can help fulfill the media's public service role, especially after years of struggle with the high-profit, low-reinvestment model for media, which has demoralized so many in the business. By focusing on the physical dimensions of space (beat and local coverage), culture (diversity and international reporting), and time (context and story follow-up), the values of public-service journalism can be passed on to new generations reared in a technological environment. Overholser further believes that revitalization in media will occur when educators and professionals refocus on the enduring democratic traditions of social responsibility. "This arrival of hope and potential has profound ethical implications, for the new possibilities can energize the most talented people in journalism and bring the best of journalism back to communities across the country. By marrying venerable tradition to new financial arrangements we can restore vigor to a woebegone media world, that it might better fulfill its ethical obligations" (personal correspondence, July 17, 2006).

Practical methods for doing so, however, often run against the grain of productivity emphasized in the converged newsroom. "Good journalism is expensive," states Dick Doak, senior editorial page writer for The Des Moines Register. "You've got to be willing to set a writer free for a couple weeks, not to produce anything but to dig around. You have to send them to seminars and let them travel wherever their sources are. That's very expensive and doesn't produce immediate results. With all the bottom line pressures you have to produce something every day," especially with competition from "Internet and cable TV with instant feedback" (personal correspondence, February 1, 2005). Ethicist Lee Wilkins, professor at the Missouri School of Journalism, notes that she has heard newspaper editors complaining about this phenomenon for the past 15 years. The situation has become more critical now, however, because technology and corporate practice facilitate the indoors behavior. "We don't talk about this very much," she says, but getting out of your chair and into the community "is an element of accurate, credible, contextualized news, which we ethics folks call 'authenticity'" (personal correspondence, May 15, 2006). According to the tenet of authenticity, journalists cannot report entirely truthfully unless they do so physically and face-to-face with their sources. "Reporters who venture outdoors on assignments or beats tend to view their communities with a more professional, critical eye. They don't look at issues "in terms of what is good for me," Wilkins adds, but "what is good for the citizen next-door or the neighbor and the neighbor's child" (personal correspondence, February 1, 2005).

The focus on citizenship, in particular, has been associated with journalism as Fourth Estate, again guided by the theory of social responsibility. In *New Media and American Politics*, Richard Davis and Diana Owen (1998) argue that "the new media are quantitatively different from the mainstream press. They do not simply represent a variation of the established news media" but offer more opportunities for interactive political analysis, enabling "the public's ability to become actors, rather than merely spectators, in the realm of media politics" (p. 7). Conversely, the authors state, new media's promise "is undercut by the commercial and entertainment imperatives that drive them. In reality, the political role of new media is ancillary. The new media are political when politics pays. Thus the new media's role in the political realm is volatile. Their educational function is incomplete and sporadic" (p. 7). As such, these commercial imperatives dilute and at times undermine Overholser's wish for new media to return journalism to public service. Undoubtedly, the potential is there, as Davis and Owen believe, noting that the proliferation of media platforms have multiplied choices so that "citizens can now more sharply tailor their media habits to suit their life-styles, tastes, and needs" (p. 163). Unfortunately, lifestyles, tastes and needs are associated with consumer profiling rather than journalism ethics. When an industry obliterates or obfuscates the dimensions of real community—physical place, local culture, and linear time—all that remains is market niche, which technology can segment, compile, and appeal to in the form of "branding," which began discussion in this chapter. We have come full circle, confronting how journalists can maintain stewardship of the public trust communicating through an autonomous system that routinely clusters the public into consumer groups.

## UNIVERSAL CONCLUSIONS: AN ETHICS OF DUTY

The suggestion that technology is an autonomous system contradicts the popular belief that it is just a tool. (If so, ethicists could simply focus on how the tool was being used, and for what purpose.) In one sense, technology really is a tool in that it gets a job done. The word "tool" is generic, though; a hammer and a hacksaw are tools. Journalism education typically emphasizes how to use the tool so that, metaphorically, we are not pounding nails with a hacksaw and cutting wood with a hammer. Digital ethics, however, demands more of us. First, we need to determine what the interface or application of a device is programmed to do so that we can analyze whether we are using it responsibly. We also have to measure not only the content of our messages but the systems that deliver them. Finally, we have to ascertain whether principles that define ethical journalism are diluted by those systems, adjusting for the consequences of that in our coverage.

The ultimate challenge of digital ethics not only involves persuading the public that an independent, objective news industry is in its best interest; journalists also must overcome (a) the use of autonomous technology to enhance profit of media companies; (b) the shift in priorities from social to fiduciary responsibility; and (c) the obliteration or obfuscation of universal principles filtered through market-driven corporate policies and computer practices that are inherently amoral, acultural, and asynchronous.

Historians such as Theodore Roszak and Rosalind Williams approach technological issues three dimensionally, especially in assessing technology's impact over time—past, present, and future. Williams, in particular, articulates "the cultural paradox" of the digital age, which "engenders both a sense of liberating possibilities and a sense of oppression," noting that as "information technology keeps reinforcing its dominance in terms defined by the market, other forms of sociability get selected out" (2006, p. 66). To prevent that outcome, we require an ethic beyond the consequences of utilitarianism whose focus is on the future, and one that takes into account the historian's linear time zones of past as well as future.

In an ethics of consequences, writes Clifford Christians, "only the future counts with respect to what is morally significant, and not the past," whereas an ethics of duty "covers the entire time frame (2006, pp. 60–61). In making a case for such an ethic guided by universal principles of human dignity, truth, and nonviolence, Christians reminds us about the value of physical, cultural, and linear dimensions. "Social systems precede their occupants and endure after them. Therefore, morally appropriate action intends community" (p. 62). Moreover, he argues, "our selfhood is not fashioned out of thin air" (p. 62).

Thin air is the foundation of Internet technologies whose asynchronous systems tend to homogenize according to the dictates of consumerism rather than the dimensions of culture or the universals of ethics. Nonetheless, as Christians notes, an ethics of duty requires communicators "to know ethical principles that they share with the public at large—truth-telling, justice, human dignity, keeping one's promises, no harm to the innocent, and so forth" (p. 66). In this, ethicists and practitioners may find the key to realize optimistic assessments of new technology, from Negroponte to Overholser. Admittedly, this chapter on digital ethics was meant to spur debate, not only about the nature of human beings but also about the nature of technology, so that educators and practitioners can contemplate how universal principles apply online via an ethic of duty.

Recommendations for future study might include:

- Online journalists should adjust for the virtual dimensions of space without place, mediumlessness, and asynchrony.
- Being mindful of what Internet technologies may obliterate or obfuscate is the first step toward maintaining standards and relevance.
- In addition to significance and interest, online news values should emphasize locality, culture, and time.
  - The objective is to spark interaction not only online but also in community.
- The practice of journalism should happen in real space interpersonally, augmented by the virtual databases of computer-assisted reporting.
  - Journalists must witness the public interpersonally to safeguard the public trust.
- Coverage should be assessed by universals that ensure the public trust, namely dignity, duty, fairness, freedom, integrity, justice, responsibility, trust, truth, generosity, happiness, pleasure, respect and, above all, sanctity of life.
  - Universal principles not only ensure standards of social responsibility but also a comprehensive, relevant, balanced news report grounded in the physical dimensions of space, culture, and time.

Finally, in analyzing the works of Clifford Christians, Deni Elliot, and others cited here, concerning universal principles, future study also may focus more comprehensively on how moral theories grounded in space, culture, and time make the leap to cyberspace. This preliminary analysis suggests that principles do not naturally apply or even reveal themselves in autonomous technological systems that are ends in themselves. Christians, with his scholarship on Jacques Ellul, understands the social consequences of technology and has written convincingly on the journalistic merits of an ethics of duty. It will require an ethicist of his erudition and acumen to ascertain conclusively whether principles remain in tact or metamorphose in virtual environments and how, if at all, journalists can adjust for space without place, mediumlessness, and asynchrony.

## NOTES

1. In *Interpersonal Divide: The Search for Community in a Technological Age* (Oxford University Press, 2005), Michael Bugeja makes the case that McLuhan's (1964/2002) biological model of technology's extending human senses is largely erroneous. He uses a physics model to explain how communication technology splits the senses by locating users in both real and virtual space, such as occurs when a person uses a cell phone while driving (pp. 122–141).
2. The question put to Manuel Castells was asked on June 19, 2006 following his speech to open the 56th annual International Communication Conference in Dresden, Germany. The author of this chapter asked it.
3. The SPJ preamble (1996) states: "Members of the Society of Professional Journalists believe that public enlightenment is the forerunner of justice and the foundation of democracy. The duty of the journalist is to further those ends by seeking truth and providing a fair and comprehensive account of

events and issues. Conscientious journalists from all media and specialties strive to serve the public with thoroughness and honesty. Professional integrity is the cornerstone of a journalist's credibility. Members of the Society share a dedication to ethical behavior and adopt this code to declare the Society's principles and standards of practice."

# REFERENCES

Aristotle (1998). *The Nicomachean Ethics* (Trans. David Ross). Oxford: Oxford University Press.

Bagdikian, Ben H. (1971). *The Information Machines.* New York: Harper & Row.

Bagdikian, Ben H. (2004). *The New Media Monopoly.* Boston: Beacon.

Ball State University News Center. (2005, September 23). Average person spends more time using media than anything else. Retrieved November 23, 2006 from http://www.bsu.edu/news/article/0,1370,--36658,00.html

Bugeja, Michael (2004, July 30). Unshaken Hands in the Digital Street. *The Chronicle of Higher Education,* p. B5.

Bugeja, Michael (2005b). *Interpersonal Divide: The Search for Community in a Technological Age.* New York: Oxford University Press.

Challenger, Donald, & Friend, Cecilia (2001). Fruit of the Poisonous Tree: Journalistic Ethics and Voice-Mail Surveillance. *Journal of Mass Media Ethics,* Vol. 16, No. 4, 255–272

Christians, Clifford (1997). The Ethics of Being in a Communications Context. In *Communication Ethics and Universal Values,* Clifford Christians & Michael Traber (Eds.). Thousand Oaks, CA: Sage.

Christians, Clifford (2006). The Case for Communitarian Ethics. In *Contemporary Media Ethics: A Practical Guide for Students, Scholars and Professionals,* Mitchell Land & Bill W. Hornaday (Eds.). Spokane, WA: Marquette Books.

Davis, Richard, & Owen, Diana (1998). *New Media and American Politics.* New York: Oxford University Press.

Dreyfus, Hubert L., & Spinosa, Charles (2003). Heidegger and Borgman on How to Affirm Technology. In *Philosophy of Technology: The Technological Condition,* Robert C. Scharff & V. Dusek (Eds.) . Malden, MA: Blackwell.

Eliott, Deni (1997). Universal Values and Moral Development Theories. In *Communication Ethics and Universal Values,* Clifford Christians & Michael Traber (Eds.). Thousand Oaks, CA: Sage.

Ellul, Jacques (2003). The "Autonomy" of the Technological Phenomenon. In *Philosophy of Technology: The Technological Condition,* Robert C. Scharff & V. Dusek (Eds.). Malden, MA: Blackwell.

Gross, Larry, Katz, John Stuart, & Ruby, Jay (Eds.). (2003). *Image Ethics in the Digital Age.* Minneapolis: University of Minnesota Press.

Heidegger, Martin (2003). The Question Concerning Technology. In *Philosophy of Technology: The Technological Condition,* Robert C. Scharff & V. Dusek (Eds.). Malden, MA: Blackwell.

Hitwise. (2006, July 11). MySpace is the Number One Website in the United States. Retrieved Dec. 8, 2006 from http://www.hitwise.com.au/press-center/hitwiseHS2004/social-networking-june-2006.php

McLuhan, Marshall (2002). *Understanding Media: The Extensions of Man.* Cambridge, MA: MIT Press. (Original work published in 1964).

Merritt, Davis (2005). *Knightfall: Knight Ridder and How the Erosion of Newspaper Journalism is Putting Democracy at Risk.* New York: AMACOM/American Management Association.

Miller, David (2006, March). Finding the Reason to Be: Creating a Durable Brand Identity. *Ideas: The Magazine of Newspaper Marketing,* pp. 9–13.

National Institute on Alcohol Abuse and Alcoholism. (2006). Are specific groups of people more likely to have problems? Retrieved November 26, 2006 from http://www.niaaa.nih.gov/FAQs/General-English/FAQ9.htm

Negroponte, Nicholas (1995). *being digital.* New York: Knopf.

Negroponte, Nicholas (1998, December). Beyond Digital. Retrieved November 23, 2006 from http://web.media.mit.edu/~nicholas/Wired/WIRED6-12.html

One Laptop per Child/ (2006). Home page. Retrieved December 9, 2006 from http://laptop.org/

Palmer, Parker J. (1981). *The Company of Strangers.* New York: Crossroad.

Postman, Neil (1985). *Amusing Ourselves to Death: Public Discourse in the Age of Showbusiness.* New York: Penguin.

Postman, Neil (1993). *Technopoly: The Surrender of Culture to Technology.* New York: Vintage.

Rosen, Christine (Fall 2004/Winter 2005). The Age of Egocasting. *The New Atlantis.* Retrieved December 8, 2006 from http://www.thenewatlantis.com/archive/7/rosen.htm.

"The Third Kennedy-Nixon Debate," October 13, retrieved Feb. 25, 2007 from http://www.jfklibrary.org/Historical+Resources/Archives/Reference+Desk/Speeches/JFK/JFK+Pre-Pres/Third+Presidential+Debate+101360.htm

Scharff, R. C., & Dusek, V. (Eds.).(2003). *Philosophy of Technology: The Technological Condition,* Malden, MA: Blackwell.

Scott, David (2006). *I.T. Wars: Managing the Business-Technology Weave in the New Millennium.* Charleston, SC: Booksurge.

Shannon, Victoria (2006, November 1). Content vs. Control. *The International Herald Tribune.* Retrieved December 9, 2006 from http://www.iht.com/articles/2006/11/01/business/ptend02.php

Sifry, Dave (2006, October). State of the Blogosphere. Retrieved November 26, 2006 from http://www.technorati.com/weblog/2006/11/161.html

Society of Professional Journalists' Code of Ethics (1996). Preamble. Retrieved December 9, 2006 from http://www.spj.org/ethicscode.asp

Sommers, Christina Hoff (1993, September 12). Teaching the Virtues. *Chicago Tribune Magazine* reprint, p. 16.

Stanford University (2006, October 17). Internet addiction: Stanford study seeks to define whether it's a problem. Retrieved November 23, 2006 from http://mednews.stanford.edu/releases/2006/october/internet.html

State of the News Media (2004). Overview. Retrieved December 8, 2006 from http://www.stateofthenewsmedia.org/narrative_overview_newsinvestment.asp?media=1

State of the News Media (2005). Overview. Retrieved December 8, 2006 from http://www.stateofthenewsmedia.org/2006/narrative_overview_intro.asp?media=1

State of the News Media (2006a). Economics. Retrieved November 23, 2006 from http://www.stateofthemedia.com/2006/narrative_overview_economics.asp?cat=5&media=1

State of the News Media (2006b, May 8). Intro. Retrieved December 8, 2006 from http://stateofthemedia.org/2006/narrative_newspapers_newsinvestment.asp

Terdiman, Daniel (2005, March 8,). MoSoSos Not So So-So. *Wired News.* Retrieved December 8, 2006 from http://www.wired.com/news/culture/0,1284,66813,00.html?tw=wn_tophead_4

Williams, Rosalind (2006). History as Technological Change. In *Society, Ethics, and Technology,* Morton E. Winston, & Ralph D. Edelbach (Eds.). Belmont, CA: Thomson/Wadsworth.

# 19

# Peace Journalism

## Seow Ting Lee

## INTRODUCTION

Peace journalism is a child of its time, a reaction to fractured politics and a growing disenchantment with journalistic norms that fan conflict, inadvertently or otherwise. Peace journalism was first proposed in the 1970s by Norwegian peace studies founder Johan Galtung, who envisioned it as a self-conscious, working concept for journalists covering war and conflict (Lynch & McGoldrick, 2006). Galtung (1998a), who made a strong case for rerouting journalism to a "high road" for peace, was critical of the "low road" taken by news media in chasing wars and the elites who run them, fixating on a win-lose outcome, and simplifying the parties to two combatants slugging it out in a sports arena. War reporting is also influenced by a military command perspective: news is about who advances, who capitulates, while losses are recorded in terms of tangible human casualties and material damage. Galtung urged journalists to take the "high road" of peace journalism that focused on conflict transformation: "As people, groups, countries and groups of countries seem to stand in each other's way (that is what conflict is about) there is a clear danger of violence. But in conflict there is also a clear opportunity for human progress, using the conflict to find new ways, transforming the conflict creatively so that the opportunities take the upper hand—without violence."

By taking an advocacy, interpretative approach, the peace journalist concentrates on stories that highlight peace initiatives; tone down ethnic and religious differences; prevent further conflict; focus on the structure of society; and promote conflict resolution, reconstruction, and reconciliation. Galtung (1998b, 2000, 2002) observed that traditional war journalism is modeled after sports journalism, with a focus on winning in a zero-sum game. Similarly, the reporting of peace negotiations is modeled after court journalism. Participants are portrayed as verbal pugilists: what is newsworthy is about who outsmarts the other, and who maintains his original position. In Galtung's vision, peace journalism is modeled after health journalism. A good health reporter describes a patient's battle against cancer and yet informs readers about the disease's causes as well as the full range of cures and preventive measures. According to Lynch and McGoldrick's (2006) definition, "[p]eace journalism is when editors and reporters make choices—of what stories to report and about how to report them—that create opportunities for society at large to consider and value non-violent responses to conflict" (p. 5).

## TWO NEWS VALUES: OBJECTIVITY AND CONFLICT

War reporting is a journalistic litmus test because journalists have to navigate an ethical minefield filled with critical questions about the accuracy and fairness of their coverage, the consequences of reportage, and personal safety. War reporting is shaped by two major journalistic values: objectivity and conflict. At first glance, peace journalism runs counter to the time-honored journalistic value of objectivity that sees the journalist as a detached and unbiased mirror of reality. As a neutral bystander, the journalist strives for detachment from internal biases and external influences while striking a midpoint between competing viewpoints through eyewitness accounts of events, and corroboration of facts with multiple sources to achieve balance. According to Iggers (1998): "Although few journalists still defend objectivity, it remains one of the greatest obstacles to their playing a more responsible and constructive role in public life" (p. 91). If this is true, responsible journalism should be about intervention, as argued by McGoldrick and Lynch (2000): "The choice is about the ethics of that intervention—therefore the question becomes 'what can I do with my intervention to enhance the prospects for peace?'"

Many advocates of peace journalism thus view the approach as a moral imperative, especially in a world wracked with pessimism about the role of reason in solving conflict. As a goal-oriented strategy, peace journalism is premised upon journalists' conscious, active, and formal engagement of specific working principles to promote peace. Two misconceptions about peace journalism must be dispelled. Peace journalism does not rely on actions that are unconscious, informal, or aimed only at avoiding harm; for example, steering clear of inflammatory reporting that may provoke violence. The principle of "doing no harm" rests upon a lower moral foundation when compared to the principle of "doing good" that peace journalism aspires to do. Galtung (1968) distinguishes between "negative peace" and "positive peace"; the former refers to the absence of organized violence between nations or religious, racial, ethnic groups, while the latter is defined as patterns of cooperation and integration. In Galtung's reckoning, the latter supersedes the former—thus opening up a role for peace journalism.

In war reporting, objectivity is used to justify journalists' disinterested moral autonomy from being swayed by the parties involved in a conflict. However, journalistic objectivity may cause more harm than good. As noted by Hackett (1989), "Objective journalism's respect for the prevailing social standards of decency and good taste likely mutes reportage of the brutality of war, and the suffering of victims, helping to turn war into a watchable spectacle rather than an insufferable obscenity" (pp. 10–11). Objective reporting's focus on facts and overt events, "devalues ideas and fragments experience, thus making complex social phenomena more difficult to understand" (Iggers, 1998, pp. 106–107). Hackett's and Iggers's arguments make a moral case for advocacy journalism—the non-objective, self-conscious intervention by journalists premised in public journalism, development journalism, and peace journalism.

Factual reporting of war is a chimera; the ingredients of war—patriotism, national interest, anger, censorship, and propaganda—conspire to prevent objective and truthful accounts of a conflict (see Carruthers, 2000; Dardis, 2006; Iggers, 1998; Knightley, 1975, 2004; Michael, 2006; Van Ginneken, 1998). Pedelty (1995) showed how institutional influences shaped the reporting of the civil war in El Salvador in the 1980s by comparing two reports about the shooting down of a U.S. military helicopter. Written by the same correspondent, one report was for an American paper, and the other for a European paper. The former validated the anger of U.S. officials to legitimize the release of aid to fight the rebels, but the latter sympathized with the rebels. Similar findings, which abound in the literature of war reporting, are consistent with Knightley's (1975) observation, in paraphrasing U.S. Senator Hiram Johnson's famous remark in 1917 that in war truth is the first casualty. Galtung (1998b), however, argued that truth is only the second victim in war; the first is peace. Truth telling, even when it is achievable, is not enough because "[t]ruth journalism alone is not peace journalism." War reporting requires some degree of separation from the military but embedded or similar programs in which journalists travel and report alongside military units—embraced warmly by war reporters desperate to gain access to battlefields—further compromise objectivity (see Haig et al., 2006, Paul & Kim, 2004; Pfau et al., 2004; Rosenblum, 1979). "A reporter who travels with one army, sharing C-ration peanut butter and watching friends fall dead, finds it hard to separate himself from the men around him" (Rosenblum, 1979, p. 173).

War reporting is grounded in the notion of conflict as a significant news value. The drama of discord inherent in antagonistic and opposing actions, fuelled by a related news value—violence, appeals to journalists and their audiences alike. As a result, war reporting is often sensational and a mere device to boost circulations and ratings (Toffler & Toffler, 1994; Hachten, 1999; Allen & Seaton, 1999) although Galtung himself was skeptical of the claim that violence sells; he viewed it as an excuse panned out by incompetent journalists: "To say that violence is the only thing that sells is to insult humanity" (Galtung, 2000, p. 163). Journalistic preoccupation with conflict drives war journalism to be characterized by an identification with one or the home side of the war; military triumphantist language; an action orientation; and a superficial narrative with little context, background, or historical perspective. The news value of conflict further renders consensus-building efforts non-newsworthy. Journalists often ignore peace negotiations unless the proceedings are accompanied by violent or verbally explosive sideshows. Peace journalism subscribes to universal protonorms of nonviolence and respect for human dignity, which many journalists have cast aside in their pursuit of what they consider to be far worthier goals—professional values of objectivity and newsworthiness. In a sense, the peace journalist has grappled with and succeeded in answering the fundamental question: Am I a human being first or a journalist first?

Like public journalism and development journalism, peace journalism is grounded in communitarian philosophy—namely the commitment to the idea of civic participation, the understanding of social justice as a moral imperative, and the view that the value and sacredness of the individual are realized only in and through communities. Christians, Ferré, and Fackler (1993) urged journalists to abandon libertarianism in favor of communitarianism by adopting a new journalistic standard that gives priority to civic transformation. The idea that journalists have an active and conscious role in promoting peace is controversial nonetheless. The term "peace journalism" invokes strong reactions, many of them unfavorable. Unfortunately, peace is an overused, nebulous, and often misunderstood word; its inherent idealism does not seem to fit in with the mood of pessimism governing these trying times. The term "peace journalism" was coined by Galtung more than three decades ago, but as a practice, it has not gained wide acceptance among journalists nor attracted adequate attention from researchers.

In August 1993, Galtung founded TRANSCEND (www.transcend.org), a non-profit organization, to advance his ideas of peace, including peace journalism. In the late 1990s, his ideas were picked up by U.K.-based Conflict and Peace Forums (CPF) that refined his model through a series of dialogues with journalists. The CPF published four booklets: The Peace Journalism Option (Lynch, 1998), What Are Journalists For? (Lynch, 1999), Using Conflict Analysis in Reporting (Lynch, 2000), and Reporting the World (2002)—that are mainly how-to manuals based on anecdotes. Just as journalists are more interested in covering war than peace, much has been written and studied about the role of the media in war, but little about their role in peace. Although there exists an excellent body of literature and research on war journalism (e.g., Allan & Zelizer,

2004; Carruthers, 2000; Dardis, 2006; Dimitrova, 2006; Hallin, 1986, 1987; Hallin & Gitlin, 1994; Iyengar & Simon, 1994; Knightley, 1975, 2004; Lang & Lang, 1994; Seib, 2004, Tumber & Palmer, 2004), most of the work on peace journalism is philosophical or normative, outlining its benefits and detailing how it can be implemented (e.g., Galtung, 1986, 1998b, 2002; Lynch, 1998; McGoldrick & Lynch, 2000; Lynch, 2003a, 2003b, Lynch & McGoldrick, 2006). There is little research on peace journalism, which is all the more relevant today in a world wracked with strife and conflict. Few studies have operationalized peace journalism.

The subsequent sections of this chapter will review four studies about the framing of war and conflict which are based on Galtung's framework of peace/war journalism, and discuss the implications of the findings as well as directions for future research.

## OPERATIONALIZING GALTUNG'S IDEAS

I was introduced to peace journalism by Filipino media scholar Maslog C. Crispin, who has developed and taught modules in peace journalism as part of his courses in international/intercultural communication in Asia, Norway, and the United States. Maslog is also author of *A Manual on Peace Reporting in Mindanao* (1990). Our collaboration resulted in several publications; the first was Lee and Maslog (2005). The *Journal of Communication* study is the first to offer a quantitative contribution to a topic that has received mostly normative and anecdotal discussion. By operationalizing Galtung's classification of war/peace journalism, the study focused on four Asian conflicts: the Kashmir dispute between India and Pakistan; the Tamil Tiger uprising in Sri Lanka; the Aceh and Maluku civil wars in Indonesia; and the Mindanao separatist movement in the Philippines.

The study shows that news coverage of these conflicts is dominated by a war journalism frame. The Indian and Pakistani coverage of the Kashmir issue reveals the strongest war journalism framing while the coverage of the Tamil Tiger movement and the Mindanao conflict by the Sri Lankan and the Philippine newspapers suggests a more promising peace journalism framing. The three most salient indicators of peace journalism are the avoidance of demonizing language, a non-partisan approach, and a multi-party orientation. The war journalism frame is supported by a focus on the here and now, an elite orientation, and a dichotomy of good and bad. Based on a similar peace journalism research framework, my co-researchers and I published two other studies in 2006 that expanded our scope of study to the 2003 War in Iraq. An *Asian Journal of Communication* article examined how five Asian countries framed the war in Iraq (Maslog, Lee, & Kim, 2006) while an *International Communication Gazette* article compared the framing of Asian conflicts with that of the war in Iraq (Lee, Maslog, & Kim, 2006). A forthcoming work (Kim, Lee, & Maslog, 2009) focuses on the framing of Asian conflicts by vernacular newspapers. These four studies will be discussed in greater detail in this chapter.

Theoretically, peace journalism is supported by framing theory. There is no one standard definition of framing (Entman, 1993; McCombs, Lopez-Escobar, & Llamas, 2000; Scheufele, 1999) but broadly, news framing refers to the process of organizing a news story, thematically, stylistically, and factually, to convey a specific story line. According to Entman (1993), "to frame is to select some aspects of a perceived reality and make them more salient in a communicating text, in such a way as to promote a particular problem definition, causal interpretation, moral evaluation, and/or treatment recommendation for the item described" (p. 52). Tankard et al. (1991) described a media frame as "the central organizing idea for news content that supplies a context and suggests what the issue is through the use of selection, emphasis, exclusion and elaboration" (p. 3). Frames package key ideas, stock phrases, and stereotypical images to bolster a particular interpretation. Through repetition, placement, and reinforcement, the texts and images provide a dominant interpretation more readily perceivable, acceptable, and memorable than other interpretations (Entman, 1991).

McCombs, Shaw, and Weaver (1997) argued that the concepts of agenda-setting and framing represent a convergence, in that framing is an extension of agenda-setting. In fact, the concept of framing has been explicated as second-level agenda setting (Jasperson et al., 1998; McCombs, 1994; McCombs & Bell, 1996; McCombs & Evatt, 1995; McCombs, Shaw, & Weaver, 1997). Object salience is transmitted in the first level of the agenda setting process. In the second level, framing, or indicator salience, illustrates how the media tell us *how* to think about something—a reprise of Bernard Cohen's famous statement that the media tell us what to think about. Framing is found to activate specific thoughts and ideas for news audiences, as seen in the vast body of framing effects research (e.g., Iyengar, 1991; McLeod & Detenber, 1999; Price, Tewksbury, & Powers, 1997; Schuck & de Vreese, 2006; Sotirovic, 2000; Thorson, 2006; Wilnat et al., 2006).

A number of studies have focused on the framing of war reporting. Gamson (1992) identified four frames used in the framing of the Arab-Israeli conflict: strategic interests, feuding neighbors, Arab intransigence, and Israeli expansionism. Wolfsfeld (1997) found that the media's pursuit of "drama" frames in the Middle East conflict accorded the extremists from both sides more than their due share of air time, while drowning voices calling for peace. Carruthers (2000) suggested that the media, subjected to state and military censorship, employed the same values and priorities in reporting conflict as in covering other events. As a result, media become willing accomplices in wartime propaganda, and may help instigate conflict. Pfau et al. (2004) found that the embedded journalist coverage of the 2003 war in Iraq was framed more favorably toward the U.S. military than non-embedded reporting. Lawrence (2006), who studied the coverage of the Abu Ghraib prison abuse scandal in American newspapers, found a framing homogeneity that can be explained by institutionalist theory.

## War and Peace: Two Competing Frames

Galtung viewed peace journalism and war journalism as two competing frames. His classification of war journalism and peace journalism is based on four broad practice and linguistic orientations: peace/conflict, truth, people, and solutions. In contrast, war journalism is oriented in war/violence, propaganda, elites, and victory. Galtung's labeling of peace journalism as both peace- and conflict-oriented may appear paradoxical but in reality, peace-oriented journalists must first accept that a conflict exists, and explore conflict formations by identifying the parties, goals, and issues involved. The journalist understands the conflict's historical and cultural roots, and by giving voice to all parties (not only two opposing sides), creates empathy and understanding without resorting to emotionally-charged devices. Through careful, consistent, and conscientious application of peace journalism practices, the peace journalist hopes to create a setting in which the causes of and possible solutions to the conflict become transparent. Other peace journalism approaches include taking a preventive advocacy stance—for example, editorials and columns urging reconciliation and focusing on common ground rather than on vengeance, retaliation, and differences—and emphasizing the invisible effects of violence (e.g., emotional trauma, and damage to the social structure). In contrast, war journalism plays up conflict as an arena where participants are grouped starkly into two opposing sides ("them vs. us") in a zero-sum game, and focuses on the visible effects of war (casualties and damage to property).

Galtung's classification of war/peace journalism was expanded by McGoldrick and Lynch (2000) and Lynch and McGoldrick (2006) into 17 good practices in covering war. Advice to journalists included focusing on solutions, reporting on long-term and invisible effects, orientating the news on ordinary people, reporting about all sides, and using precise language. Maslog (1990) offered a similar peace journalism manual based on the Mindanao conflict that clarifies differences between Muslims and Christians and, more importantly, their common ground. Advice included avoiding mention of culturally offensive issues such as pork consumption and polygamous practices. Another important principle is linguistic accuracy. "Rebels" should be identified as dissidents of a particular political group, and not simply as "Muslim rebels."

## Peace Journalism in Coverage of Asian Conflicts (Lee & Maslog, 2005)

In our research, a news frame is defined as an interpretive structure that sets specific events within a comprehensive context. Based on Galtung's classification of war/peace journalism, our first study posed two research questions: (1) Does the news coverage of the four Asian conflicts reflect war journalism and war journalism frames, and are there differences in framing with different conflicts? (2) What are the salient indicators of war/peace journalism manifest in the news coverage of these conflicts?

The 1,338 stories were harvested from the 10 English-language newspapers from five Asian countries—India: *Times of India* (122 stories); *Hindustan Times* (137); *Statesman* (91); Pakistan: *Dawn* (131); *Pakistan News Service* (261); The Philippines: *Philippine Daily Inquirer* (122); *Philippine Star* (61); Indonesia: *Jakarta Post* (189); and Sri Lanka: *Daily News & Sunday Observer* (145); *Daily Mirror* (79). The unit of analysis was the individual story, a definition that included "hard" news, features, opinion pieces, and letters to the editor.[1]

The coding categories involved 13 indicators of war journalism and 13 indicators of peace journalism (see Appendix). These indicators, used to elicit from the body text of each story which frame—war or peace journalism—dominated the narrative, comprised two themes: approach and language. The approach-based criteria included: (1) reactivity, (2) visibility of effects of war, (3) elite orientation, (4) differences, (5) focus on here and now, (6) good and bad dichotomy, (7) party involvement, (8) partisanship, (9) winning orientation, and (10) continuity of reports. The language-based criteria focused on language that was (1) demonizing, (2) victimizing, and (3) emotive.

## A Dominant War Journalism Framing

Of the 1,338 stories, 749 stories (56%) were framed as war journalism, compared to 478 stories (35.7%) framed as peace journalism, and 111 neutral stories (8.3%). Overall in the sample, the war journalism frame was more dominant than peace journalism or neutral frames, $\chi^2(2, N = 1,338) = 459.771, p<.0001$. Country-wise, there was a significant difference in war/peace/neutral framing of stories, $\chi^2(4, N = 1,338) = 150.834, p<.001$; Cramer's $V = .237, p<.001$. The strongest war journalism framing was found in the Kashmir coverage by Pakistani and Indian newspapers, followed by Indonesian, Philippines, and Sri Lankan papers' coverage of their respective conflicts. Conversely, the strongest peace journalism framing was from Sri Lanka, followed by the Philippines, Indonesia, India, and Pakistan. The following section discusses the patterns of framing for each country's newspapers.

*India-Pakistan (Kashmir).*   There was a significantly higher proportion of war journalism frames observed in Pakistani papers (74.2%) than for Indian papers (63.7%), $\chi^2(2, N = 742) = 10.886, p<.005$; Cramer's $V = .121, p<.005$. The distribution of war/peace/neutral stories also differed among the five newspapers, $\chi^2(8, N = 742) = 23.104, p<.005$; Cramer's

$V = .125$, $p<.005$. The strongest war journalism framing is seen in the *Pakistan News Service*; nearly 80% of its stories were framed as war journalism, followed by the *Statesmen* (67%), *Hindustan Times* (66.4%), *Pakistan Dawn* (65.6%), and *Times of India* (59%). The *Pakistan News Service*, a national news agency, has the highest number of war journalism frames among the 10 news outlets examined in the content analysis.

*Indonesia.* There was a significant difference in the distribution of war/peace/neutral frames in the *Jakarta Post*; 48% of its stories were framed as war journalism, compared to 41.8% framed as peace journalism, and 10.1% neutral stories, $\chi^2(2, N = 189) = 47.238$, $p<.001$. The *Jakarta Post* published 110 articles on the Free Aceh movement, and 79 on the Maluku conflict. Comparing the Aceh and Maluku conflicts, however, 37.31% of articles about Aceh were framed as war journalism compared to 54.5% peace journalism, and 8.2% neutral. In contrast, the Maluku stories showed a more salient war journalism frame—63.3% compared to 24.1% peace journalism, and 12.7% neutral. Clearly, the *Jakarta Post*'s coverage of the two conflicts did not share the same framing pattern, $\chi^2(2, N = 189) = 17.610$, $p<.001$; Cramer's $V = .305$, $p<.001$.

*Sri Lanka.* The LTTE (Liberation Tigers of Tamil Eelam) coverage by Sri Lankan papers showed the strongest peace journalism framing. Of the 224 stories, more peace journalism stories were observed—58.0% compared to 30.8% war journalism stories, and 11.2% neutral stories, $\chi^2(2, N = 224) = 74.473$, $p<.001$. There was a significant difference between the two papers, $\chi^2(2, N = 224) = 7.080$, $p<.05$; Cramer's $V = .178$, $p<.05$, with more peace journalism frames in the *Daily Mirror* than in the *Daily News & Sunday Observer*. There was also a significant difference before and after the December 2001 ceasefire between the Sri Lankan government and the LTTE, $\chi^2(2, N = 224) = 30.199$, $p<.001$; Cramer's $V = .367$, $p<.001$. Prior to the ceasefire, the two papers demonstrated a significant framing difference, $\chi^2(2, N=224)=14.377$, $p<.001$; Cramer's $V=.199$, $p<.05$. Before the ceasefire, *the Daily News & Sunday Observer* produced 51.5% of war journalism stories, compared to 38.4% of peace journalism stories, and 10.1% neutral stories. After the ceasefire, its war journalism stories dropped to 4.3% while peace journalism stories increased to 89.1%. Before the ceasefire, the *Daily Mirror* published 20.4% war journalism stories, 59.3% peace journalism stories, and 20.4% neutral stories. After the ceasefire, its war journalism stories remained at 20.0% while peace journalism stories increased to 76.0%. As a result of an increase in peace journalism stories, there was no significant difference in the post-ceasefire distribution of war/peace journalism stories between the two papers, $\chi^2(2, N = 224) = 4.538$, $p<.103$. With the ceasefire, there was a change from war journalism to peace journalism framing in the *Daily News & Sunday Observer* but the change was less obvious in the *Daily Mirror* because it had a strong peace journalism framing prior to the ceasefire.

*The Philippines.* The framing of war/peace journalism stories was less clear. Although the newspapers produced more peace journalism stories compared to war journalism stories, statistical significance was absent, $\chi^2(1, N = 171) = 2.579$, $p<.108$. There was a significant difference in the distribution of war/peace/neutral frames between the *Philippine Daily Inquirer* and the *Philippine Star*, $\chi^2(2, N=183)=6.840$, $p<.05$; Cramer's $V=.193$, $p<.05$, with more peace journalism stories in the *Daily Inquirer* compared to the *Star*.

Indicators of War Journalism and Peace Journalism

Based on a frequency of 5,220, the three most salient indicators of war journalism were: a focus on the here and now (17.6%), an elite orientation (15.4%), and a dichotomy of the good and the bad (10.3%). Through a here-and-now perspective, the war journalism stories confined a conflict to a closed space and time, with little exploration of the causes and long-term effects of the conflict. Reporting only on the here and now is a common journalistic practice, focusing on only what is happening in the battlefield, the military clashes and the casualties, with very little background. Stories tended to focus on elites—political leaders and military officials—as actors and sources while ignoring the foot soldiers who fight the wars and the civilians who suffer the consequences of wars. Dichotomizing between the bad guys and the good guys involves casting simplistic moral judgments about the parties involved, and assigning blame to the party who started conflict. For example, the *Pakistan News Service* reported: "The Indian government's fake elections held in the valley will not deter them. Despite giving them the right to self-determination, the Indian government had stepped up its brutal activities against innocent people in occupied Kashmir" ("Indian election drama not alternative to Kashmir cause," April 5, 2002).

The three most salient indicators of peace journalism, based on a frequency of 9,104, were avoidance of demonizing language (15.9%), non-partisanship (13.8%), and multi-party orientation (12.8%). In avoiding demonizing language, the journalists provided precise titles or descriptions to players. By being non-partisan, stories were not biased for one side or another. In pursuing a multi-party orientation, stories gave a voice to the many parties involved, treating them with dignity. For example, the Sri Lankan *Daily Mirror* covered the work of a peace group: "The Peace Support Group in a statement signed by prominent activists (names) said it was abundantly clear that the electorate had endorsed a re-vitalization of the peace process and dialogue with the LTTE" ("A mandate for peace, grab it"; December 12, 2001).

The Kashmir coverage, which showed the most salient war journalism framing, was dependent on the following indicators (based on a frequency of 3,558): a focus on the here and now (15.4%), the use of elites as actors and sources (14.1%), a partisan approach (11.0%), and emphasis on differences (9.7%). The Sri Lankan newspapers' coverage of the Tamil Tigers, which exhibited the strongest peace journalism framing, was supported by the following indicators (based on a frequency of 1,148): an avoidance of good-bad label (13.5%), a non-partisan focus (12.9%), a multi-party orientation (10.4%), and a win-win approach (10.1%).

## Other Findings of Interest

There was no relationship between story type (news, feature, or opinion) and distribution of war journalism and peace journalism stories, $\chi^2(6, N = 1,338) = 8.612$, p<.197. Of the 1,338 stories, 76.1% were "hard" news stories, 10.0% were features, 9.0% were opinion pieces including editorials, and 4.9% were "others" that included letters to the editor and speech transcripts. Whether a story was written as hard news, a feature, or an opinion piece had no bearing on the framing of the story. However, there was a positive correlation between story length (in paragraphs) and peace journalism (r = .156, p<.001). The longer the story, the more likely it was framed as peace journalism. Conversely, there was a negative relationship between story length and war journalism (r = -.186, p<.001). Conceivably, longer stories allow journalists time and effort to investigate an issue or event more fully and thoughtfully, and to go beyond reporting of facts into providing analysis.

Foreign wire stories contain more war journalism frames and fewer peace journalism frames than stories produced by local sources including the papers' own correspondents, $\chi^2(2, N = 1,338) = 7.964$, p<.05. About 10% of stories were produced by foreign wire services such as AP, CNN, BBC, Reuters, and AFP. That the majority—89.8%—were produced by local sources was unsurprising given the conflicts' local nature. Of the stories produced locally, 96.2% were written by the newspapers' own reporters, compared to 1.3% sourced from national news agencies, and

2.4% contributed by freelancers, academics, and the public. One explanation is that reporting by foreign wire services is less involved and more detached (as seen in the shorter stories; stories produced by local sources are significantly longer than stories produced by foreign wire services, t(1,336) = 6.133, p<.0005. The mean length of a locally sourced story is 12.98 paragraphs compared to 8.77 for a foreign wire story. Another explanation is that Western foreign news agencies tend to report violence and conflict more saliently than any other news from developing countries (e.g., Hachten, 1999; Hachten & Scotton, 2006; Hess, 1996; Riffe, Aust, Jone, Shoemaker, & Sundar, 1994; Rosenblum, 1979). The actions of foreign governments, when connected to violence and conflict, are more likely to be reported by U.S. media than other types of news. Not surprisingly, war journalism framing prevailed more in foreign wire copy than in local copy.

Following the study on Asian newspaper coverage of regional conflicts, we expanded our research to the coverage of the Iraq War and vernacular newspapers. The next section summarizes the findings of the three follow-up studies.

## The Iraq War

Maslog, Lee, and Kim (2006) examined how the coverage of the war in Iraq by news organizations from India, Pakistan, Sri Lanka, Indonesia, and the Philippines was framed according to Galtung's principles of peace and war journalism. The findings, based on a content analysis of 442 stories from eight newspapers, suggest a slight peace journalism framing. Religion and sourcing are two significant factors shaping the framing of the conflict, and support for the war and for its protagonists (Americans/British vs. Iraqis). Newspapers from the non-Muslim countries, except the Philippines, have a stronger war journalism framing, and are more supportive of the war and of the Americans/British than the newspapers from the Muslim countries, which are more supportive of the Iraqis. Stories from foreign wire services have a stronger war journalism framing—consistent with earlier findings—and show more support for the war and for the Americans/British than stories written by the papers' own correspondents.

## Comparing Asian conflicts and the Iraq War

Lee, Maslog, and Kim (2006) examined the coverage of the War in Iraq and Asian conflicts by eight Asian newspapers to compare the framing of two different levels of conflicts—international and local. A content analysis of 1,558 stories from India, Pakistan, Sri Lanka, the Philippines, and Indonesia on the war in Iraq and their own local conflicts showed that the Asian press used a war journalism frame in covering local conflicts but deployed a peace journalism frame in covering the war in Iraq. Hard news was dominated by war journalism framing, while features and opinion pieces were shaped by peace journalism. Foreign-sourced stories from wire services contained more war journalism frames and fewer peace journalism frames than locally-produced stories written by the papers' own correspondents, again supporting the findings of the previous two peace journalism studies.

## The Vernacular Press

The earlier studies discussed above focused on English-language Asian newspapers but the fourth study (Kim, Lee, & Maslog, 2009) concentrated on the vernacular press. In many Asian countries, the Western-language press has a long history harking back to Western colonial rule. Despite stiff competition from their vernacular counterparts, the English-language papers continue to be viewed as status symbols, with strong circulations and advertising revenues. Although the vernacular press is perceived as being less metropolitan and sophisticated, and is often marginal-ized from the mainstream media, it plays a significant role in shaping mass opinion because it includes the largest-circulation newspapers in the respective countries (Waslekar, 1995). It has been suggested that vernacular newspapers, unlike the national-level media in Asia (that most English-language newspapers belong to), are more likely to be swayed by communal feelings to the extent of inciting violence with irresponsible reporting (Chenoy, 2002; Khan, 2003; Press Council of India, 2003).

Kim, Lee, and Maslog (2009) examined the peace/war journalism framing of three Asian conflicts—Kashmir, the Tamil Tiger movement, and the Aceh/Maluku civil wars—by eight ver-nacular newspapers from India, Pakistan, Sri Lanka, and Indonesia. The findings from the con-tent analysis of 864 stories support the results of the previous studies. First, the coverage of the conflicts was dominated by war journalism framing, the strongest of which is the case of Kashmir that generated the strongest war journalism framing among four regional conflicts analyzed in the study of 10 English-language Asian newspapers. Second, the most salient indicators of peace journalism included avoidance of emotive language, avoidance of demonizing language, people-orientation, and non-partisanship, while the most salient indicators of war journalism included focus on the here and now, dichotomy of the good and the bad, elite-orientation, and focus on differences. Third, there were significant relationships between war/peace journalism framing and story attributes. Stories that are longer and are written as features and opinion pieces instead of shorter or hard news were more likely to be framed as peace journalism.

## IMPLICATIONS AND DIRECTIONS FOR FUTURE RESEARCH

As exploratory research, the four studies of Asian English-language and vernacular presses op-erationalized and measured the principles of peace journalism advanced by Johan Galtung—ideas that have garnered only normative and anecdotal discussion. It is hoped that the findings and subsequent work can help mass media training institutions to customize peace journalism programs, and build a case for offering such courses, as well as generate hypotheses for examin-ing the framing effects of war/peace journalism on public opinion and policy-making.

Clearly, the coverage of the four Asian conflicts is dominated by war journalism. Pakistan and India, embroiled in a decades-old territorial battle over Kashmir, have demonstrated through their five newspapers that media adopt a knee-jerk, unreflecting kind of coverage of conflicts, with little consideration for long-term, peaceful solutions. The strong war journalism framing by Indian and Pakistani papers is not unexpected; the two countries have fought three wars, includ-ing two over the mostly Muslim region of Kashmir, which was divided between them after inde-pendence from Britain in 1947. Among the conflicts examined, Kashmir is the most acrimonious, involving not only the divisive factor of religion but also the minefield of national sovereignty, demonstrating that a country's media are not likely to remain neutral in a conflict involving its government (see Bennett, 2003; Carruthers, 2000; Hiebert, 2003; Keeble, 1998; Knightley, 1975, 2004; Reese & Buckalew, 1994; Van Ginneken, 1998). In the study that compared the framing of local and international, the Asian newspapers relied on war journalism framing to cover local conflicts, but used peace journalism framing to cover the Iraq War. Conceivably, the coverage of a local conflict reflected its government's stand, be it in a war against another country or against rebels within the country's borders. Conversely, the five Asian countries' lack of direct involve-ment in the war in Iraq may have permitted their newspapers to adopt a more detached and conciliatory stance. The overall strong peace journalism framing could also be attributed to the widespread objection in the Asian countries to the U.S.-led military action in Iraq, and a desire among Asian governments to see a more peaceful resolution to the situation in Iraq. Despite assertions of objectivity among journalists, coverage of war is often shaped by national interest, which is perhaps the biggest obstacle to peace journalism.

The case of Sri Lanka may offer some encouragement to peace journalists. That a significant number of stories were framed as peace journalism may be surprising for a country that has faced two decades of violence. A possible explanation is the fact that the August 1, 2001 to February 28, 2002 period of analysis overlapped with government and LTTE efforts to negotiate for a peace treaty under international pressure, although violence persisted. Are peace journalism stories a simple reaction to developments in a conflict (i.e., ongoing negotiations) or genuine, self-conscious intervention by journalists to help promote peace? Journalists may find it difficult to escape the influence of context. The shift from war journalism framing to peace journalism by Sri Lankan papers after the December 2001 ceasefire agreement may reflect a conscious effort by journalists to promote peace through peace journalism. But it is also possible that the change of government and attendant changes in policy toward the LTTE could have motivated journalists' peaceful disposition. Certainly, the measure of a true peace journalist lies in his work *during* a conflict, not *after* the conflict. There is an extensive body of literature documenting governmental influence on the work of journalists in conflicts (e.g., Bennett, 2003; Carruthers, 2000; Combs, 1993; Hiebert, 2003; Keeble, 1998; Lawrence, 2006; Lynch, 2003a, 2003b; Reese & Buckalew, 1994). One small dose of comfort does come from the *Daily Mirror*'s strong peace journalism framing prior to the ceasefire although the true picture for the *Daily News & Sunday Observer*'s strong war framing prior to the ceasefire is less clear.

What is clear is that media outlets within the same cultural and political context do not frame the same event the same way. Another example of context-shaped coverage is the *Jakarta Post*'s dissimilar framing of the Maluku and Aceh conflicts. At the time of the study, the Indonesian government and the GAM (Free Aceh Movement) were on their way to the negotiating table. The Swiss-based Henry Dunant Centre brokered a peace deal between the two parties on December 9, 2002, a major breakthrough in 26 years of hostilities. Hence, a stronger peace journalism framing was evident in the coverage of Aceh. In the case of Maluku, the conflict was still raging, hence the stronger war journalism framing. Similarly the higher number of peace journalism stories in the Asian newspapers' coverage of the Iraq War was encouraging but peace journalism is a self-conscious concept. The peace journalism framing of the Iraq War may be more reflective of caution in reporting a controversial military engagement initiated by a superpower in a distant land than genuine desire to promote peace and seek solutions. More research is needed, especially at the levels of news gate keeping.

Although there are promising signs in the use of peace journalism frames in Sri Lanka and the Philippines, and in the Asian newspapers' coverage of the Iraq War, a closer examination of the patterns of war journalism and peace journalism indicators reveals that peace journalism framing is still highly dependent on criteria of a less interventionist nature, for example, an avoidance of good-bad labels, a non-partisan approach, a multi-party orientation, and an avoidance of demonizing language. These four indicators, although important in the overall scheme of peace journalism laid out by Galtung, are mere extensions of the objectivity credo: reporting the facts as they are. Galtung (1998) believed that truth telling as a guiding journalistic principle in war reporting is simply inadequate: "[T]ruth journalism alone is not peace journalism." These indicators do not truly exemplify a strong contributory, pro-active role by journalists to seek and offer creative solutions and to pave a way for peace and conflict resolution. For example, journalists often simplify storytelling by allowing only a set of villains and a set of victims. The inclusion of a multi-party orientation is a significant step forward in the peace journalism calculus but it does not take the story significantly beyond reporting the facts or telling the truth.

Journalists' dependence on peace journalism practices that are less interventionist in nature can be explained by the dominance of the libertarian notion of the public sphere as a value-free area where individuals freely exploit a wealth of disparate information based on their own personal interpretations and needs. In such a public sphere, the values and identities of individuals, including that of journalists and their work, are obscured by professional aspirations to facilitate purely utilitarian relationships based on satisfying individual/professional goals without adequate consideration for universal protonorms such as nonviolence and respect for human dignity. Unlike the libertarian tradition, the communitarian ethic openly accepts the peace journalist as an interventionist—insofar as that intervention allows the inclusion of a journalist's values and participation in a community's dialogue, consensus building, civic transformation, and a commitment to social justice. In the controversy over peace journalism one sees the clash between two different levels of values—universal and professional, that is best captured by the fundamental question: Am I a human being first or a journalist first? In principle, peace journalism is closer to Carol Gilligan's ethics of care than the more established ethics of justice. In seeking conflict resolution, peace journalism avoids dichotomizing between the victims and the villains, and emphasizing the differences between them. Instead it prefers to focus on their common ground and sustainable relationships; most customary practices of settling disputes (assigning blame, vilifying the wrongdoer, and righting wrongs with punitive actions) are merely short-term solutions that do not lead to genuine reconciliation and lasting peace.

In the four studies, the pattern of salient indicators supporting the peace journalism frame consistently falls short of Galtung's characterization of peace journalism as an advocacy and interpretive approach oriented in peace-conflict, people, truth, and solution. While there is some demonstration of the journalists' deeper understanding of the conflict by mapping it out as consisting of many parties, there is little in terms of a solution-seeking approach, and more disappointingly, not many peace journalism stories are supported by a people-orientation. With little focus on ordinary people and treating them with dignity, and without finding out what whether their position as stated by the elites are reflective of the true feelings on the ground, there is little that journalists can do to empower the ordinary people. The work of journalists follows predictable rituals, and reliance on elites and on official sources that they perceive to be authoritative, credible, knowledgeable, and powerful, is one of them. The peace journalism frame also did not receive adequate support in terms of journalists focusing on a conflict's causes and consequences. Without this understanding, solutions—and social justice—are hard to come by.

The relationships between peace journalism and story attributes such as sourcing, length, and type of story need further investigation. Why does the war journalism frame prevailed more in foreign wire services copy than in locally produced copy? The finding of significant differences in war/peace journalism frames between the locally-produced stories and foreign wire stories is supported by the literature (e.g., Hachten, 1999; Hess, 1996; Riffe, Aust, Jone, Shoemaker, & Sundar, 1994; Rosenblum, 1979). Foreign wire copy or the stories originating from Western news agencies tend to emphasize war/conflict/violence. Foreign news is preoccupied with conflict and violence in which developing nations are described as the scenes of disasters or violence.

One could argue that published foreign wire stories may reflect to some extent a newspaper's framing of the War in Iraq as some gate keeping is involved in selecting which foreign wire stories are published and which are not. In general, however, foreign wire copy, according to newsroom routines, are used to describe and convey daily situation updates of the war, and do not undergo much editing. The positive relationships between hard news and war journalism framing, and between features/opinions and peace journalism framing suggest that the inverted pyramid style of writing and an overemphasis on objectivity and traditional news values such as conflict and violence, other than national interest, may be major obstacles to peace journalism.

If peace journalism were to succeed, journalists must first reassess their notions of hard news, objectivity and traditional news values. The relationship between story length and war/ peace journalism framing suggests that with longer stories, journalists have more opportunities to investigate an issue or event more fully and thoughtfully. Longer stories allow journalists to move beyond reporting of facts into analysis and interpretation, and exploration of the causes and alternatives (as supported by the significant relationships between features/opinion pieces and peace journalism framing). However, newshole allotment to war reporting is a complex affair, subject to not only editorial judgment but also economic considerations, given a shrinking newshole and a shift of focus to entertainment and celebrity news. In the case of the American media, Sept 11 marked a turning point: the shrinking newshole for foreign news became a story of the past as the terrorist threat from abroad and U.S. military involvement in Afghanistan and Iraq renewed interest in foreign news and increased foreign news coverage. But in reality, these stories continued to rely on traditional news values—conflict and American interest—and are little more than American news with a foreign dateline as aptly described by Larson (1984).

Several research papers have attempted to apply peace journalism to breaking news, but this category of news, characterized by their brevity and main function in the news business as information updates, may not be the best unit of analysis. The practice of peace journalism requires a significant amount of journalistic reflection and analysis—elements typically not found in breaking news. Future research should also consider television news, and attempt to apply Galtung's framework to visual images of war. Many of the coding categories used for assessing narrative content were conceived by Galtung as a form of pre-publication criteria, suggesting that another potential locus of research lies in the newsgathering stage.

Many studies have conveyed the concept of framing as an unconscious act (shaped by journalistic routines, social norms and values, time pressures, organizational culture and constraints, etc.; see Shoemaker & Reese, 1996; Tuchman, 1978) but theoretically, framing studies have neglected to explore framing as a conscious act by journalists. As noted by Gamson (1989), the motives behind a journalist's framing of the news can be unconscious, but may also involve intent. Scheufele (1999) rightly observed that this particular link between journalists' individual-level variables and media frames "deserves more attention than it has received" (p.117). The concepts of reciprocity, intent and motive in news framing—with the attendant implications—warrant a closer examination, especially in the news coverage of war, where a potent cocktail—national interest, patriotism, religious differences, censorship, propaganda—can be found.

Framing effects research has found that news consumers respond to journalists' framing of a socially important event rather than to the actual event itself. Peace journalism, as a conscious and deliberate act by journalists, can offer significant insights on a hitherto unexplored aspect of framing theory. Indeed, if framing can be a conscious act involving intent, journalists must then confront the issues of moral accountability, and can no longer seek refuge in the notion that how they cover the news is merely shaped by journalistic routines, social norms, and organizational cultures and constraints that are beyond their control. Tehranian (2002) suggests that the locus of media ethics be expanded from the individual journalist to institutions, nation-states and international communities in order to advance peace journalism. This is a laudable proposal indeed, as more is needed institutionally, be it in the form of infrastructure or sanction, to support ethical journalistic work. But until journalists covering war and conflict are willing to acknowledge and overcome their internal biases and external influences, rethink their over-reliance on objectivity and detachment, and break free of the professional shackles that detract from universal protonorms of nonviolence and respect for human dignity, peace journalism will always remain a child of its time, never to come of age.

## NOTES

1. The stories, content analyzed by six mass communication graduate students, were harvested from the most recent peak periods of the conflicts (some of which date back at least five decades) at the time of the study. When the number of peace journalism indicators exceeded the indicators for war journalism, the story was classified as peace journalism. When war journalism indicators exceeded peace journalism indicators, the story was classified as war journalism. Equal scores denoted neutral stories. The war journalism index ranged from 0 to 13, with a mean of 3.90 and a standard deviation of 2.60 (Cronbach's alpha = .72). The peace journalism index ranged from 0 to 13, with a mean of 2.98 and a standard deviation of 2.73 (Cronbach's alpha = .78). Other variables studied include the story type (news, feature, or opinion), story length, and source (local, foreign/national news agencies, wire service). In terms of intercoder reliability, a coding of 100 stories produced Scott's pi between .76 and .93, with only one indicator (continuity of reports) recording a value of below.

## APPENDIX 19.1
### Coding Categories

| War journalism approach | Peace journalism approach |
|---|---|
| 1. Reactive (waits for war to break out, or about to break out, before reporting) | 1. Proactive (anticipates, starts reporting long before war breaks out) |
| 2. Reports mainly on visible effects of war (casualties, dead and wounded, damage to property) | 2. Reports on the invisible effects of war (emotional trauma, damage to society and culture) |
| 3. Elite-oriented (focuses on leaders and elites as actors and sources of information) | 3. People-oriented (focuses on common people as actors and sources of information) |
| 4. Focuses mainly on differences that led to the conflict | 4. Reports the areas of agreement that might lead to a solution to the conflict |
| 5. Focuses mainly on the here and now | 5. Reports causes and consequences of the conflict |
| 6. Dichotomizes between the good guys and bad guys, the victims and villains | 6. Avoids labeling of good guys and bad guys |
| 7. Two-party orientation (one party wins, one party loses) | 7. Multi-party orientation (gives voice to many parties involved in conflict) |
| 8. Partisan (biased for one side in the conflict) | 8. Non-partisan (neutral, not taking sides) |
| 9. Zero-sum orientation (one goal: to win) | 9. Win-win orientation (many goals and issues; solution-oriented) |
| 10. Stops reporting with the peace treaty signing and ceasefire, and heads for another war elsewhere | 10. Stays on and reports aftermath of war—the reconstruction, rehabilitation, and the implementation of peace treaty |
| *Language* | |
| 11. Uses victimizing language (e.g., destitute, devastated, defenseless, pathetic, tragic, demoralized) which only tells what had been done to people | 11. Avoids victimizing language, reports what has been done and could be done by people, and how they are coping |
| 12. Uses demonizing language (e.g., vicious, cruel, brutal, barbaric, inhuman, tyrant, savage, ruthless, terrorist, extremist, fanatic, fundamentalist) | 12. Avoids demonizing language (and uses more neutral and precise descriptions, titles or names) |
| 13. Uses emotive words (e.g., genocide, assassination, massacre, and systematic) | 13. Objective and moderate (avoids emotive words, reserves the strongest language only for the gravest situation, and does not exaggerate) |

# REFERENCES

Allen, T., & Seaton, J. (1999). *The media of conflict: War reporting and representations of ethnic violence.* London: Zed Books.

Allan, S., & Zelizer, B. (Eds.). (2004). *Reporting war: Journalism in wartime.* London and New York: Routledge.

Bennett, W. L. (2003). Operation perfect storm: The press and the Iraq war [Electronic version]. *Political Communication Report, 13*(3). Retrieved February 10, 2007, from http://www.ou.edu/policom/1303_2003_fall/Bennett.htm

Carruthers, S. L. (2000). *The media at war: Communication and conflict in the twentieth century.* New York: St Martin's Press.

Chenoy, A. M., (2002, June 4). Gujarat carnage: The politics of gender in the politics of hate Anuradha M. Chenoy. *Aman Ekta Manch Digest, 3.* Retrieved on November 7, 2006, from http://www.onlinevolunteers.org/gujarat/news/articles/gender-politics.htm

Christians, C. G., Ferré, J., & Fackler, P. (1993). *Good news.* New York: Oxford University Press.

Combs, J. (1993). From the Great War to the Gulf War: In R. Denton (Ed.), *Popular entertainment and the legitimation of warfare: The media and the Persian Gulf War* (pp. 277–231). Westport, CT: Praeger.

Conflict and Peace Forums. (2002). Reporting the world. Retrieved May 23, 2003, from www.transcend.org/Peace%20Journalism%205.doc

Dardis, F. E. (2006, October/December). Military accord, media discord: A cross-national comparison of UK vs. US press coverage of Iraq War protest. *International Communication Gazette, 68*(5–6), 409–426.

Dimitrova, D. V. (2006, Fall). Episodic frames dominate early coverage of Iraq War in newyorktimes.com. *Newspaper Research Journal, 27*(2), 79–83.

Entman, R. (1991). Framing U.S. coverage of international news: Contrasts in narratives of the KAL and Iran Air incidents. *Journal of Communication, 41*(4), 6–27.

Entman, R. (1993). Framing: Toward clarification of a fractured paradigm. *Journal of Communication, 43*(4), 51–58.

Galtung, J. (1968). Peace. In D. Sills (Ed.), *International Encyclopedia of Social Sciences* (pp. 487–496). New York: Macmillan.

Galtung, J. (1986). On the role of the media in worldwide security and peace. In T. Varis (Ed.), *Peace and Communication* (pp. 249–266). San Jose, Costa Rica: Universidad para La Paz.

Galtung, J. (1998a, December 1,). High road, low road: Charting the course for peace journalism. *Track Two, 7*(4). Retrieved February 10, 2007, from http://ccrweb.ccr.uct.ac.za/archive/two/7_4/p07_highroad_lowroad.html

Galtung, J. (1998b, September 3–6) *Peace journalism: What, why, who, how, when, where.* Presented in the workshop "What are journalists for?" TRANSCEND, Taplow Court.

Galtung, J. (2000). The task of peace journalism. *Ethical Perspectives, 7*(2–3), 162–167.

Galtung, J. (2002). Media: Peace journalism. Retrieved Sept 25, 2003, from https://www.nicr.ca/programs/PeaceJournalism.htm

Gamson. W. A. (1989). News as framing: Comments on Graber. *American Behavioral Scientist, 33,* 157–166.

Gamson, W. A. (1992). *Talking politics.* New York: Cambridge University Press.

Hachten, W. A. (1999). *The world news prism: Changing media of international communication.* Ames, Iowa: University of Iowa Press.

Hachten, W. A., & Scotton, J. (2006). *The world news prism: Global information in a satellite age.* (7th ed.). Boston: Blackwell.

Hackett, R. A. (1989, May). *Spaces for dissent: The press and the politics of peace in Canada.* Paper presented at the Annual Conference of the International Communication Association, San Francisco.

Haig, M. M., Pfau, M., Danesi, J., Tallmon, R., Bunko, T., Nyberg, S., Thompson, B., Babin, C., Cardella, S., Mink, M., & Temple, B. (2006). A comparison of embedded and nonembedded print coverage of the U.S. invasion and occupation of Iraq. *The Harvard International Journal of Press/Politics, 11*(2), 139–153.

Hallin, D. C. (1986). *The uncensored war.* New York: Oxford University Press.

Hallin, D. C. (1987). Hegemony: The American news media from Vietnam to El Salvador, a study of ideological change and its limits. In D. Paletz (Ed.), *Political communication research* (pp. 3–25). Norwood, NJ: Ablex.

Hallin, D. C., & Gitlin, T. (1994). The Gulf war as popular culture and TV drama. In W. L. Bennett & D. L. Paletz (Eds.), *Taken by storm: The media, public opinion, and U.S. foreign policy in the Gulf War* (pp. 149–163). Chicago: University of Chicago Press.

Hess, S. (1996). *International news and foreign correspondents.* Washington, D.C.: Brookings Institute.

Hiebert, R.E. (2003). Public relations and propaganda in framing the Iraq war: A preliminary review [Electronic version]. *Public Relations Review, 29,* 243–255.

Iggers, J. (1998). *Good news, bad news: Journalism ethics and the public interest.* Boulder, CO: Westview.

Iyengar, S. (1991). *Is anyone responsible? How television frames political issues.* Chicago: University of Chicago Press.

Iyengar, S., & Simon, A. (1994). News coverage of the Gulf crisis and public opinion. In W. L. Bennett & D. L. Paletz (Eds.), *Taken by storm: The media, public opinion, and U.S. foreign policy in the Gulf War* (pp. 167–186). Chicago: University of Chicago Press.

Jasperson, A. E., Shah, D.V., Watts, M., Faber, R. J., & Fan, D. P. (1998). Framing and the public agenda: Media effects on the importance of the federal budget deficit. *Political Communication, 15,* 205–224.

Keeble, Richard. (1998). Not the Gulf war: A study of the UK press coverage of the 1991 and 1998 Iraq crises. In P. Lee (Ed.), *The media and the Persian Gulf War* (pp. 5–15). London: World Association for Christian Communication.

Khan, T. (2003). Small town news: Gujarat in the media and memory of Aligarh. Unpublished M.A. thesis, Univeristy of London, September 23, 2003. Retrieved February 7, 2007, from http://bocs.hu/India/taran-khan-disstn.htm

Kim, H. S., Lee, S. T., & Maslog, C. C. (2009) Peacemakers or warmongers? Asian news media coverage of conflicts. *Journal of Global Mass Communication,* January.

Knightley, P. (1975). *The first casualty.* New York: Harcourt Brace Jovanovitch.

Knightley, P. (2004). *The war correspondent as hero and myth-maker from the Crimea to Iraq.* Baltimore, MD: Johns Hopkins University Press.

Lang, G. E., & Lang, K. (1994). The press as prologue: Media coverage of Saddam's Iraq 1979–1990. In W. L. Bennett & D. L. Paletz (Eds.), *Taken by storm: the media, public opinion, and U.S. foreign policy in the Gulf War* (pp. 43–62). Chicago: University of Chicago Press.

Larson, J. F. (1984). *Television's windows on the world: International affairs coverage on the U.S. networks.* Norwood, NJ: Ablex.

Lawrence, R. (2006, April–June). Seeing the whole board: New institutional analysis of news content. *Political Communication, 23*(2), 225–230.

Lee, S., & Maslog, C. C. (2005, June). War or peace journalism? Asian newspaper coverage of regional conflicts. *Journal of Communication, 55*(2), 311–329.

Lee, S., Maslog, C. C., & Kim, H. (2006, November). Asia's local conflicts and the war in Iraq: A comparative framing analysis. *The International Communication Gazette, 68*(5–6), 499–518.

Lynch, J. (1998). The peace journalism option. Conflict and peace forums. Retrieved May 20, 2003, from http://www.conflictandpeace.org/6pub/3pub.html

Lynch, J. (1999). What are journalists for? Conflict and peace forums. Retrieved May 20, 2003, from http://www.conflictandpeace.org/6pub/2pub.html

Lynch, J. (2000). Using conflict analysis in reporting. Conflict and peace forums. Retrieved May 20, 2003, from http://www.transnational.org/features/2000/LynchPart1.html

Lynch, J. (2003a, February 19). *Iraq: Broadening the agenda.* Retrieved October 16, 2003, from http://www.basicint.org/iraqconflict/Pubs/Discussion%20Papers/DS190203.htm

Lynch, J. (2003b, July 15). *Reporting Iraq: What went right?* Retrieved October 16, 2003, from http://www.basicint.org/iraqconflict/Pubs/Discussion%20Papers/DS080903.htm

Lynch, J., & McGoldrick, A. (2006). *Peace journalism.* London: Hawthorn Press.

Maslog, C. C. (1990). *A manual on peace reporting in Mindanao.* Manila: Philippine Press Institute.

Maslog, C. C., Lee, S., & Kim, H. (2006, March). Framing analysis of a conflict: How five Asian countries covered the War in Iraq. *Asian Journal of Communication, 16*(1), 19–39.

McCombs, M. (1994). The future agenda for agenda setting research. *Journal of Mass Communication Studies, 45,* 181–117.

McCombs. M., & Bell, T. (1996). The agenda-setting role of mass communication. In M. Salwen & D. Stacks (Eds.), *An integrated approach to communication theory and research* (pp. 93–110). Mahwah, NJ: Erlbaum.

McCombs. M., & Evatt, D. (1995). Los temas y los aspectos: Explorando una nueva dimension de la agenda setting. [Objects and indicators: Exploring a new dimension of agenda-setting.] *Communication y Sociedad 8*(1), 7–32.

McCombs, M., Lopez-Escobar, E., & Llamas, J. P. (2000). Setting the agenda of indicators in the 1996 Spanish General Election. *Journal of Communication, 50*(2), 77–92.

McCombs, M., Shaw, D. L., & Weaver, D. (1997). *Communication and democracy: Exploring the intellectual frontiers in agenda-setting theory.* Mahwah, NJ: Erlbaum.

McGoldrick, A., & Lynch, J. (2000). Peace journalism—How to do it. Retrieved on June 2, 2003, from http://www.transcend.org/pjmanual.htm

McLeod, D. M., & Detenber, B. H. (1999). Framing effects of television news coverage of social protest. *Journal of Communication, 49,* 3–23.

Michael, R. (2006). Mainstream news media, an objective approach, and the march to war in Iraq. *Journal of Mass Media Ethics, 21*(1), 4–29.

Paul, C., & Kim, J. J. (2004). *Reporters on the battlefield: The embedded press system in historical context.* Pittsburgh, PA: Rand Corporation.

Pedelty, M. (1995). *War stories: the culture of foreign correspondents.* New York: Routledge.

Pfau, M., Haigh, M., Gettle, M., Donelly, M., Scott, G., Warr, D., & Wittenberg, E. (2004). Embedding journalists in military combat units: Impact on newspaper story frames and tone. *Journalism & Mass Communication Quarterly, 81*(1), 74–88.

Press Council of India. (2003). Communal violence in Gujarat: Role of the media. Retrieved on November 6, 2005, from http://www.hvk.org/specialrepo/pci/

Price, V., Tewksbury, D., & Powers, E. (1997). Switching trains of thought: The impact of news frames on readers' cognitive responses. *Communication Research, 24,* 481–506.

Reese, S., & Buckalew, B. (1994, March). The militarism of local television: The routine framing of the Persian Gulf war. *Critical Studies in Mass Communication, 12*(1), 40–59.

Riffe, D., Aust, C., Jone, T., Shoemaker, B., & Sundar, S. (1994). The shrinking foreign news hole of the New York Times. *Newspaper Research Journal, 15*(3), 74–88.

Rosenblum, M. (1979). *Coups and earthquakes: Reporting the Third World for America.* New York: Harper & Row.

Schuck, A., & de Vreese, C. H. (2006). Between risk and opportunity: News framing and its effects on public support for EU enlargement. *Journal of Communication, 21*(1), 5–32.

Scheufele, D. A. (1999). Framing as a theory of media effects. *Journal of Communication, 49*(1), 101–120.

Schuck, A. R. T., & de Vreese, C. H. (2006). Between risk and opportunity: News framing and its effects on public support for EU enlargement. *European Journal of Communication, 21*(1), 5–32.

Seib, P. (2004). *Beyond the front lines: How the news media cover a world shaped by war.* New York: Macmillan.

Shoemaker, P., & Reese, Shoemaker, Pamela, & Reese, Stephen. (1996). *Mediating the message: Theories of influences on mass media content* (2nd ed.). White Plains, NY: Longman.

Sotirovic, M. (2000). Effects of media use in audience framing and support for welfare. *Mass Communication and Society, 3,* 269–296.

Tankard, J., Hendrickson, L., Silberman, J., Bliss, K., & Ghanem, S. (1991, August). *Media frames: Approaches to conceptualization and measurement.* Paper presented at the annual convention of the Association for Education in Journalism and Mass Communication, Boston, MA.

Tehranian, M. (2002). Peace journalism: Negotiating global media ethics. *The Harvard International Journal of Press/Politics, 7*(2), 58–83.

Thorson, E. (2006). Print news and health psychology. *Journal of Health Psychology, 11*(2), 175–182.

Toffler, A., & Toffler, H. (1994). *War and anti-war: Survival at the dawn of the 21st century.* Boston: Little, Brown.

Tuchman, G. (1978). *Making news: A study in the construction of reality.* Beverly Hills, CA: Sage.

Tumber, H., & Palmer, J. (2004). *Media at war: The Iraq crisis.* London: Sage.

Van Ginneken, J. (1998). *Understanding global news: A critical introduction.* Thousand Oaks, CA: Sage.

Waslekar, S. (1995). Track-two diplomacy in South Asia. Bombay, India: International Center for Peace Initiatives. Retrieved on Nov 6, 2005, from http://www.acdis.uiuc.edu/Research/OPs/Waslekar/Waslekar.pdf

Wolfsfeld, G. (1997). Promoting peace through the news media: Some initial lessons from the peace process, *Harvard International Journal of Press/Politics, 2*(2), 52–70.

Willnat, L., Aw, A., Hamdy, N. N., He, Z., Menayang, V., La Porte, M. T., Sanders, K., Tamam, E. (2006). Media use, anti-Americanism and international support for the Iraq war. *International Communication Gazette, 68*(5–6), 533–550.

# 20

# Privacy and the Press

## Lou Hodges

Privacy is an issue of unparalleled importance in the modern world. You must take your shoes off to board an airplane! The ability of government, corporations and journalists to invade the lives of private citizens has dramatically increased through the advent of ever more sensitive listening devices, chemical drug tests, DNA, credit files and widely distributed medical files. All the more strange, cell phones now incorporate cameras. No citizen can escape the probing eye.

As our *ability* to invade privacy has increased, so too has our *willingness* to invade. The evidence: Witness *USA Today*'s probing, in 1992, into Arthur Ashe's illness; mainline media revealing, in 1991, Patricia Bowman's identity as William Kennedy Smith's rape accuser; or even Senate demands, in 1993, for the private diaries of Senator Bob Packwood. These three events seem to have defined journalistic practice at the end of the 20th century.

At the beginning of the 21st century, even more sophisticated invasions of personal privacy appeared. Cell phones now contain cameras. DNA revealed the identity of the father of Anna Nicole Smith's child. Each of these cases involves public intrusion into private matters as well as revelation of private information in the public forum. All of that lends new urgency to the question of how can we decide, and by what criteria, when an invasion of an individual's private life is morally justified? How should (can) we distinguish between the private life and the public life of individual citizens?

Totally apart from questions of ethics, the issue of privacy has become significant for the press in terms of its own self-interest, a matter of prudence. Though many people show interest in private information about others, many others are offended by journalists' conduct, and that has led to increased distrust of the press. When we see reporters poking microphones into the face of a mother who has just witnessed a fire that killed her three children, most of us are morally outraged. (It is interesting that we witness such behavior because other photojournalists show their fellow journalists in action!) Is it surprising that journalists enjoy low public esteem?

The classic case of journalists' invasion of personal privacy in the 20th century is that of Arthur Ashe, this time as an example of the invasion of privacy and the public response (American Press Institute, 1992). Having won at Wimbledon and in the U.S. Open, Ashe in the 1970s was ranked No. 1 in the tennis world. After brain surgery in 1988, he learned that he was infected with HIV, the virus that causes AIDS, as a result of a blood transfusion in 1983. Many of his friends, including a number of reporters, knew of his condition and kept his secret. But in 1993 *USA Today* sent a reporter to ask Ashe about his having the virus. Ashe did not answer the question, and he was told that the newspaper would pursue the story. Although he had wanted to make his own statement later in his own way and at a time of his own choosing, Ashe called a news conference the next day and announced to the world, against his will, that he had AIDS. Gene Policinski (1992), sports editor for *USA Today,* with the support of senior executives, offered the lame and question-begging excuse: "The news was that one of the great athletes of this century had a fatal illness—and that the illness was AIDS. By any journalist's definition, that's news." Public response to what *USA Today* did to Ashe was strongly negative, as was the response of responsible journalists all over the country.

Most people who have had things to say about the newspaper's moral irresponsibility and insensitivity to Ashe's interests would acknowledge the paper's legal right to do what it did. The concern was over the absence of a moral right to do what was perfectly legal. It is that moral focus that concerns us here.

This chapter addresses five fundamental questions about privacy and the ethics of journalistic behavior regarding privacy. They are: (1) What precisely is the definition and meaning of "privacy"? (2) What, if anything, in the human condition is the ground of the need for privacy? (3) In a democratic state, is there a presumed individual *right* to privacy? (4) How might journalists reasonably establish their own standards for reconciling moral tensions between an individual's *need* for privacy in relation to the *need* of citizens to know about that individual? (5) What moral *guidelines,* not absolute rules, should journalists follow when reporting on the private lives of several categories of people?

## THE NATURE OF PRIVACY

To think about the ethics of privacy, one must begin by examining the meaning of the word. We have had basic agreement on definitions for over twenty-five years. Sissela Bok (1982, pp. 10–11) defined privacy as "the condition of being protected from unwanted access by others—either physical access, personal information, or attention." Alan Westin (1967, p. 7) identifies privacy with "the claim of individuals, groups, or institutions to determine for themselves when, how, and to what extent information about them is communicated to others."

Morton Levine (1980, p. 19) shares some of Westin's language but expands the definition slightly when he writes: "[Privacy] is the maintenance of a personal life-space within which the individual has a chance to be an individual, to exercise and experience his own uniqueness."

Similar themes appear in A. C. Breckenridge (1980, p. 1):

> Privacy, in my view, is the rightful claim of the individual to determine the extent to which he wishes to share of himself with others and his control over the time, place, and circumstances to communicate to others. It means his right to withdraw or to participate as he sees fit. It is also the individual's right to control dissemination of information about himself; it is his own personal possession.

Perhaps Judge Thomas Cooley (1988, p. 29) put it most succinctly when he identified privacy as "the right to be let alone."

The language I prefer comes from Alan Westin, as quoted in *Dietemann v. Time, Inc.* (449 F.2d 245 [1971]). "The claim," he says about privacy, "is not so much one of total secrecy as it is of the right to *define* one's circle of intimacy—to choose who shall see beneath the quotidian mask. Loss of control over which 'face' one puts on may result in literal loss of self-identity."

Circles of Intimacy: The visual image of "circles of intimacy" is helpful for an understanding of what we mean by privacy. It invites us to imagine ourselves standing at the center of a series of concentric circles of intimacy in which the degree of intimacy diminishes from the innermost circle outward.

Just examine your own life. In the innermost circle you are alone. Some things about yourself you and you alone know—fantasies, unarticulated hopes, memories—and you would feel (and *be*) violated and invaded if someone learned those things *against your will*. You occupy the second circle with at least one other person, perhaps a spouse, sometimes a professional, such as a member of the clergy, a lawyer, a doctor, or a college counselor. In this second circle you share intimacies that you want only the one other person to know. You reveal yourself, some of your innermost being. With the spouse the revelations are, or should be if the relationship is to endure, reciprocal. If the other is your doctor or your counselor or your minister, the revelation is largely one-directional. The point is that in this second circle you are in the primary private relation with one other human being. The bond is fiduciary. The relationship rests on trust, trust that the one to whom you have revealed yourself will neither betray the trust nor use the revelation to your disadvantage. Our law recognizes the importance of these primary relationships by not requiring spouses to testify against each other and by protecting the lawyer/client relationship.

The third circle from center contains other people to whom you are very close. Under one circumstance it may include your family. In the collegiate environment, it might incorporate close friends, fellow fraternity or sorority members, athletic or debate teammates. Whoever is in this circle with you comes to know things about you that you would not want to be "public" knowledge. You reveal some of your peculiarities—perhaps your flaws, your dreams—because you are confident that the people in this circle will not use that information to your detriment. The key moral ingredient, of course, is that you are in control over who does and does not get access to your private information.

One can extend this image of circles to the outermost imaginable circle, the least intimate, which encompasses all humanity. There are some things about yourself that you would not object to all humanity knowing. Those things constitute your most "public" self.

In terms of this picture, to have privacy is to possess control over your circles of intimacy, to determine who enters each one and who does not. You may choose to be a very "private" person, bent on concealing yourself, or you may be very "public," willing to share intimacies widely with others. Whichever you choose to be, the important issue morally is your right to decide just how public or private you will be.

## THE NEED FOR PRIVACY

Most people acknowledge the *desire* for privacy, the desire to control access to their circles of intimacy. Few seem to understand the individual *need* for privacy. People seem to intuit instinctively the importance of privacy for civilized existence. Many, of course, plead for privacy in order to hide their misdeeds. Question: Should they enjoy the same right to privacy as those who wish to hide their personal longings?

But can our desire for privacy be related to a real human need? Yes. Privacy plays a central role in human affairs. Without some degree of privacy, civilized life would not be possible. The ability to control access to our circles of intimacy meets any number of basic human needs, but the two that seem uppermost are the psychological and the political.

### The Psychological Need

Psychologically, privacy is a precondition for developing a sense of self, an awareness of the boundaries between the self and others. One author, Constance T. Fischer (1980, pp. 37 ff.), uses

Erik Erikson's description of the stages of human development from infancy to maturity. People need private relations, she notes, in order to "try out" new poses, future selves, without fear of ridiculing intrusion by others. Privacy provides the opportunity to imagine possible futures without commitment to any until several have been projected. It provides opportunities to examine fantasies, dreams, hopes, etc., through intimate interaction with trusted others. Privacy shields against the stifling effect of convention. In that way it protects the emerging, still-disordered self while simultaneously allowing for the continuation of custom and convention that are so essential for social order.

In other words, control over our circles of intimacy is necessary if we are to have some control over who we are, over what kind of person we are and wish to become. It gives us a chance to develop our own particular identity, that unique self-consciousness that sets us up as distinct from, but always a part of, the world and the larger mass of humanity. The human need for privacy seems self-evident to anyone who imagines what it would be like never to be alone, never to entertain a private thought or perform a private act. George Orwell's *1984* is a sufficient reminder!

The psychological need for privacy is recognized in the law as well. Edward J. Blaustein, for example, noted that "Our law of privacy attempts to preserve individuality by placing sanctions upon outrageous or unreasonable violation of the conditions for its sustenance." Without it, he added, "an individual merges with the mass" (1964, p. 962).

## The Political Need

Orwell points also to the need for privacy as a shield against the power of the state. The more one knows about individuals the easier it is to influence, manipulate, or even control them. In fact, some scholars argue that liberal democracy is unthinkable without effective guarantees of privacy. One writer, Robert C. Neville (1980, p. 25), puts it this way:

> Precisely because the state is seen as the agency of the citizen's own authority, its independent power is feared, and limitations on the power of the state, such as the Bill of Rights, were established in order to protect private life. Privacy then comes to be viewed as that area of personal life in which the state should make no claim, at least not without due process designed to protect privacy. One of the strong connotations of privacy today is the negative sense that it is where others have no right to intrude.

In this negative sense, freedom from government control, privacy is central to the liberal democratic ideal. Historically, totalitarian societies have used high visibility—the near absence of privacy—as a major ingredient in their drive to produce a homogeneous and servile populace. "Nor is it any mere coincidence," one source (Dionisopoulos and Ducat, 1976) notes, "that accounts for the fact that, in a free democratic society, public affairs are usually marked by openness and private affairs are normally shielded from view, while, in totalitarian states, the reverse is generally true." (The link between privacy and the liberal ideal is explored also in Fuller, 1960; Polanyi, 1951).

Liberal democracy employs privacy as a check on the state. That fact is based on the recognition that to have knowledge about a person is to hold power over that person. One who has no privacy, one who is completely open, is readily coerced. Politically speaking, privacy represents the power to control access to one's self, and thus it conveys some capacity to resist the coercive power of the state.

In this sense, the U.S. Patriot Act (Uniting and Strengthening America by Providing Tools Required to Intercept and Obstruct Terrorism) has special significance. Signed into law hurriedly six weeks after September 11, 2001 and renewed in March 2006, this legislation shifts the Department of Justice's goal from prosecuting terrorists to preventing terrorism. Among its controversial provisions dealing with privacy, it grants to the FBI what its critics call overbroad access to the confidential records of citizens if needed for the clandestine intelligence of suspected terrorism (http://action.aclu.org/reformthepatriotact/). The news media should be vitally involved in providing awareness of these privacy issues as they intersect with the provisions of a democratic state. It seems clear, then, that because privacy is essential to meeting basic psychological and political needs it must not be taken lightly. Indeed, privacy lies at the very heart of the most cherished values of western civilization: freedom, the dignity of humankind, and individual autonomy. Believing as we do in the basic right and duty of individual human beings to work out their destiny in community with others, our civilization developed ways of protecting privacy. As another writer (Bier, 1980, p. x) states:

> With increasing attention to, and recognition of, human dignity in Western society in recent centuries and particularly in recent years, there has come a parallel emphasis on human rights, and central to the cluster of human rights is the right to privacy.

We may now turn our attention from the need for and importance of privacy to the question of a right to privacy.

## THE RIGHT TO PRIVACY

Surprisingly, articulated claims to a right to privacy do not go far back in history. No specific right to privacy is guaranteed by the Bill of Rights, though it is reasonable to claim that privacy is assumed as necessary to the protection from government violation of other rights. In the law, tort claims based specifically on the right to privacy began to be recognized only in the 20th century. The now-famous law review article by Warren and Brandeis (1890) is widely credited with precipitating the 20th-century law of privacy. It was "the law review article that launched a tort."

Though the law of privacy is both important and expanding, it is not our concern here. We are concerned, rather, with the fundamental issue of privacy as an individual's *moral right* to control the entrance of others into one's circles of intimacy. (Moral discourse always has primacy over legal discourse because those who make laws have to know the moral/social goals their laws should be designed to achieve.)

The claim of a moral right to privacy grows ultimately from certain premises about the very nature of the human being. Individually we are unique entities possessing our own personal identities, memories, hopes, and goals. Thus individuals need to identify the boundaries, physical and spiritual, that set them apart as separate entities. We are in part autonomous beings, self-ruling, self-directing. Because privacy—defined as control over access to *one's* circles of intimacy—is essential to self-identity and self-direction, democracy asserts privacy as a right.

### A Countervailing Right

But the right to privacy is not absolute. It stands besides a countervailing right of others to know quite a lot about us as individuals. The moral issues are framed by these two legitimate rights—the individual right to a measure of privacy and the right of others to know some things about the individual.

The claim to a right to privacy grows out of some observations about human nature and human need, and so does the claim to a right to know about others. Because we are individual beings, we have a need (right) for privacy; because we are social beings, we have a need (right) to know many things about others. Individuals have a special need to know quite a lot about those who have power over them. Paradoxically, a person's very image of herself is shaped in large measure by the way others perceive her, so for that reason we need to know just how others perceive us.

Moreover, our sense of individual purpose and destiny is inextricably tied to the fortunes, purposes, and destinies of others. What they do has effects on us and we have effects on them. These observations may be summed up this way: Because humans are individual beings, the total elimination of privacy would eliminate human existence as we know it; and, because we are social beings, the elevation of privacy to absolute status would likewise render human existence impossible.

These claims to competing rights, taken together, frame the moral problem: Just when, in specific cases, should civil societies allow intrusion on private affairs (by government, commercial organizations, the press), and under what conditions should they forbid it? Where should society draw the moral line between society's need (and right) to know and the individual's need (and right) not to reveal? To put the issue in more specific terms, what should the responsible journalist take into account in drawing that line while gathering and disseminating information?

## JOURNALISM AND PRIVACY

The privacy issue arises at two points in the reporting process. The first is at the point of gathering information, where decisions have to be made by the journalist about *intrusion* into the lives of subjects. The second is at the point of deciding what to publish, where decisions are made about what private facts are appropriate for *dissemination*. Journalists at the second point are positioned to determine for the subject what circle of intimacy the public may justifiably enter.

Whether journalists are concerned about gathering or disseminating, the general questions are these: Under what conditions is a journalist justified in gathering and reporting information about a person against that person's will? Where should reporters and editors draw the line between the private and the public self? What in specific cases justifies an invasion of individual privacy by journalists? When is it just to override an individual's right to privacy for the public good?

### A Formal Criterion

I suggest the following as the formal criterion: It is just for a journalist to violate the privacy of an individual only if information about that individual is of overriding public importance and the public need cannot be met by other means. As a formal criterion, of course, this does not tell us what information to publish in specific cases, but it does provide a test for any particular decision on privacy.

Note that this criterion does not permit invasion of privacy to obtain and publish information that the public is interested in but that is not important for the public to know. The mere fact that the public is curious about private information or conduct is not sufficient reason to obtain and publish it against the will of the person reported on.

"Curiosity" is the psychological ground of many of our "interests." Most of us have a kind of healthy curiosity, or inquisitiveness, about the world around us. But we also are capable of such things as "morbid curiosity" and "prurient interest." Clearly, the latter two are not grounds for invading someone's privacy, though they are the criteria that gossip sheets use. But even the healthy form of curiosity, where the public is legitimately interested in a story, should ordinarily not be allowed to override an individual's privacy. That is simply because no genuine need would be served, and the invasion does cause harm.

The mere fact that people want to know is not enough to warrant the harm done to an individual by an invasion of his or her circles of intimacy. Any significant harm to the individual outweighs public curiosity in every imaginable case. To deny a person control over her circles of intimacy is to deny that person a measure of personal dignity. Loss of control of intimacy poses a threat to one's sense of self. It deprives one of a measure of control over oneself. Better that the public be deprived of an interesting story than that journalists harm the individual about whom that story could be written. There are enough interesting stories about interesting people, which we can publish with their permission, without hearing about those who do not want to be in the news. On those grounds the principle of overriding public importance would rule out "interest" as a sufficient test.

But what would that principle allow? How might reporters and editors determine, in particular cases, what is and what is not important enough to justify an invasion of privacy? It is not possible, of course, to establish rules that are narrow enough to determine specific cases in ways that eliminate the need for careful thought. But it is possible to state some general criteria, or tests that can guide the journalist through decisions and help her test them. After all, journalists on a daily basis make judgments about the relative importance of stories.

So far I have proposed the general principle of overriding public importance as a general criterion. It remains to suggest how that principle might function when applied to particular cases and classes of cases. Perhaps the following "guidelines" will provide food for thought and analysis.

## SOME PRIVACY GUIDELINES

### Public Officials

*In reporting on public officials we should publish private information, even against their will, if their private activity might reasonably have a significant effect on their official performance.*

It is of overwhelming importance in a democracy that the people know what their governors are doing. That knowledge is essential for responsible citizenship. The higher ranking the official, the more power that person has to improve or wreck lives. Thus it is in the public interest to know anything about those officials that might affect their wielding of power or their discharge of the public trust. And that can include almost everything—health, leisure activities, marital condition, personal taste, and countless other subjects. But there are limits even for the highest-ranking officials. The story must pass the test of having significance for the official's capacity or willingness to perform official duties.

In a democratic state, citizens have reason to want the lives of officials open to public scrutiny. Openness is essential if the public is to hold them accountable, and public people usually know that most of their privacy is lost once they enter public life. For instance, consider the case of presidential hemorrhoids (this is an actual case!). Ordinarily, it is of no public significance that some poor soul suffers from that ailment. But in the case of the President of the United States even that becomes important news: We don't want him in pain while he is making foreign policy decisions. Also, when the President visits the hospital, it is important that the public know why, that the visit was for hemorrhoids and not a brain tumor. Similarly, the sexual activities of a senator would usually not be of importance to citizens, but when he puts his paramour on the public payroll it becomes important.

Historically, much has been made over extramarital sexual behavior by high officials. Americans seem concerned over marital infidelity and sexual harassment of employees by their employees. Because private sexual activity between consenting adults, even outside marriage, poses little or no threat to performance of public duty, that activity is arguably not a legitimate public concern under our standard. Does it, then, have a place in legitimate news? Sexual harassment, however, is quite another matter. The one being harassed gives no consent and is typically the victim of abuse of power. It is important to readers to know about harassment, but usually not about mere infidelity.

## Public Figures

*In reporting on public figures, we should publish private information, even against their will, if their private activity might significantly affect their performance of duties to their publics.*

The "public figure" category includes top officials in private organizations, including senior executives in industry, business, labor, education, philanthropic organizations, and the like. News about them is important because of the power and authority they wield over others, both within and outside their own organizations. What is good for General Motors may or may not be good for the country, but what General Motors does surely affects the country. For example, questions of health and medical condition, which are private matters for most citizens, are of legitimate public concern insofar as they could have a significant effect on performance.

The public needs to know about those individuals who sit in private seats of power, because power can corrupt whether in the public or the private sector. It is because of their power that public figures are more than merely interesting, and their reduced right to privacy is morally acceptable.

Just as for public officials, the test of importance would not justify publishing everything we can get about public figures. Some privacy should be preserved. It is difficult to imagine, for example, why the public would need to know of an executive's enjoyment of homosexual rather than heterosexual companions. How could that orientation significantly affect job performance? In general, however, in reporting on the privately powerful a bias toward openness rather than privacy and secrecy is warranted, and the greater their power the lower their threshold of privacy.

## Celebrities

*We should publish private information about celebrities if readers are interested in having that information, provided that the information does no serious harm to the celebrity as a person.* (The criterion of "interest" surpasses that of "importance.")

Under the law celebrities are public figures, but morally they are different. John Wayne was important because of his influence as a role model.

By "celebrities" we mean such categories as movie stars, TV personalities, ball players and the like. On the one hand, they surely have some right to privacy. On the other hand, their professional life succeeds or fails depending on their ability to become public. Their admirers are "fans" in part because of the kind of people they are, and fans want to know what the celebrity is like in real life. By their choice of occupation or social function, essentially entertainment, celebrities must waive all but the narrowest measure of privacy.

Carol Burnett (1983) expressed it well:

> A public figure has little in the way of private life. That's a fact of life for those involved in careers that increase public visibility; with increased visibility comes natural curiosity to know more about the person.
>
> That the public feels a kind of intimacy with familiar figures is certainly understandable. Once an individual has achieved public recognition—almost always accomplished through willing participation—it is a journalist's prerogative to report information that he or she feels the public is interested in, or should know.
>
> It's also the journalist's responsibility to make certain what is reported is correct.... Someone said that if you don't want something quoted, don't say it, and if you don't want something reported, don't do it. The injury is done in quoting what wasn't said, or in reporting what wasn't done.

People like Burnett are thus willing, or at least resigned, to sacrifice a significant measure of privacy for other rewards. Even so, while it is interesting to know about the private doings of celebrities, it is not very important in the larger scheme of things. It is important, however, that journalists do celebrities no harm by reporting conditions over which the celebrity has no control. The Arthur Ashe AIDS story is the perfect example. So, beyond the harm principle the moral criteria seem to be "interest" and "accuracy." Entertainers are usually interesting people, and as human beings we need interesting stories about interesting people. And there is nothing wrong with being interested in them. They can add a measure of spice to life's sometimes drab menu.

## Temporarily Newsworthy Heroes

*In reporting on people who have performed heroic acts, we should publish only that private information that relates directly to the newsworthy act.*

Common citizens from time to time do things, unusual acts of heroism, which for a moment put them in the limelight. Perhaps the classic case of the last century is that of Oliver Sipple (Elliott and Linsky, 1982). On September 22, 1975, Sipple deflected the gun that Sarah Jane Moore was about to fire at then-president Gerald Ford. Sipple probably saved Ford's life. Because of his heroic act it is both important and interesting that we know something about Sipple, where he came from, what he does, whether anything in his background helped him know how to deflect the gun or to generate the reflexes to do it. It was relevant, for example, that he was a former Marine. But it was not important to know certain personal matters not related to the action that made him a momentary hero. The fact of his homosexual orientation, which he did not want generally known and which his family did not know about, was clearly not relevant to his action, so there was no overriding public need that would justify publishing that fact of his private life. Nevertheless, a gossip columnist with the *San Francisco Chronicle* reported that Sipple was gay. His family did not know of his homosexuality, and when they learned of it they abandoned him. He died in abject poverty and alone. Positive harm was done by publication of information about his homosexuality, which had nothing whatsoever to do with his heroic deed.

Thus, in the case of the temporarily newsworthy hero, I suggest the guideline of publishing only that private information related directly to the newsworthy act itself. That person should have the moral right to keep everything else private if he or she wishes.

## Criminals

*In reporting on criminal behavior we should report all aspects of the criminal's private life that might help us to understand the criminal and his or her acts.*

Society needs to have the clearest understanding of criminal behavior and of the criminal mind. The more severe the crime, i.e., the more damaging the crime to individuals and society, the more justified journalists are in probing the criminal's private life for clues that contribute to an understanding of the *person,* not merely of her criminal act. One might reasonably argue also that a person who has chosen to commit a criminal act has by that choice given up rights that society normally confers. Should the right to privacy be among them? Yes, insofar as investigating the criminal's private affairs may help society in dealing with criminal conduct. Thus the journalistic bias should be in the direction of openness and revelation rather than secrecy and privacy.

On this point, however, a special word of caution is in order. An accused person is not a criminal until she has been tried and convicted. This guideline should not apply to people merely *suspected* of crime, not even those already arrested and bound for trial. Moreover, pre-trial publicity can be seriously damaging to due process and fair trial, and for that reason editorial judgments must be made with special caution. There is a risk of causing serious damage to innocent people if we probe into the private lives of mere suspects. A just society still presumes innocence until guilt is proven.

## Innocent Victims of Crime and Tragedy

*We should report about crime and tragedy victims only information that they give us permission to publish.*

This is a special category of people with special needs and vulnerability who are frequently treated badly by the press. In a Virginia hamlet, for example, a policeman was murdered in the line of duty and the community and many nearby communities were much bestirred by this event. The media gave the entire affair extensive coverage. On the day of the slain officer's funeral, a local television news crew showed up at the cemetery and with a long-distance lens filmed, and subsequently broadcast, the grieving widow leaving the cemetery. The reporters did not know whether she minded being seen on the news in the state of grief. It seems arguable that if she wanted to work out her tears in the privacy and warmth of family and friends, she should have every right to do so. She should have the right to choose not to appear on TV. The public, though perhaps interested, had nothing important to gain by observing her under those conditions.

Likewise there is little public good to come from the frequent journalistic (mostly television) practice of dispatching a reporter to a burning house to film and interview the owner/victim. The burning house, the cause and extent of the fire, the danger of wood stoves, the leaking gas line are publicly important, but not the private grief of the owner. Is it really news or just drama? In such circumstances, moreover, is it not possible to tell the important story of tragedy without interviewing or filming the victim. If the victim does not want to talk to the news media, the journalist who insists on doing so places an added burden on that victim. Why? If he is filmed against his will, the victim has lost yet more control of his life than the loss occasioned by the fire. That loss is not balanced by a public gain. Why should the victim's privacy be violated? Does he not have a right to be let alone?

Among the most hotly debated examples of reporting on victims are those involving rape and sexual molestation (Lake, 1991). It is unfortunate, but nevertheless true, that a social stigma still attaches to victims of rape. That is largely because many people continue to think of rape as a "sex crime" when it is in fact a particularly heinous form of violent crime. Rape victims who are identified in the media ordinarily suffer the consequences of the stigma, thus adding to the harm already caused by the rape itself. Another moral concern is the effect of public identification upon victims' willingness to report actual rape. Victims who not only have to endure a public trial but who also receive media publicity are discouraged from reporting the fact that they had been raped. For these reasons nearly all news organizations have policies against identifying rape victims without their consent (Overholser, 1989).

A few organizations, however, always identify victims. They usually make two arguments in favor of doing so. First, they believe that reporting victims' names will help overcome the social stigma (Sanders, 1980, p.8). Such thinking is seriously flawed, however, because there are better ways of fighting the stigma, i.e., reporting on the crime of rape and using names of only those victims who give consent. Also, to report victims' names for that reason is merely to use individuals as mere means to others' ends, which violates one of the basic moral rules.

Second, organizations that identify rape victims sometimes argue that out of fairness we should report the accuser/victim if we report the accused/perpetrator. That thinking too is flawed because there are morally valid reasons for identifying the accused that do not apply to the accuser. People need to know about arrests so as to keep watch on police.

For all these reasons, moral analysis requires that rape victims not be identified in news reports without their consent. Sufficient numbers of them will consent, and reporting on those who do will gradually erode the stigma.

## Adult Relatives of the Prominent

*We should report on them only because of the significance of what they do, not because of their family ties.*

Relatives of the prominent (rich, powerful?) are often treated differently from the rest of us. Why? One argument is that all members of a prominent family derive social benefits precisely because of a prominent relative. Therefore, they should also bear the burdens of prominence. That argument rests on some theory of just allocation of benefits and burdens. What it does not consider is the damaging effect of publicity on the prominent person who had no control over the conduct of the relative. The President, for example, should neither be harmed by nor benefit from whatever his "long-lost brother" did or does.

It is not *important* that the public be told about relatives, but they are nevertheless of *interest* to the public. Is that adequate justification for making the families public against their will? Arguably not: If they have not sought prominence, and if they wish to be let alone, they should be. Like other citizens, they should be reported on because of the significance of what they do, not because of what family members do. If they want to remain behind the scenes, why should they not be allowed to do so?

There are circumstances, however, in which relatives of the prominent give up much of their right to privacy. For example, some years ago, Senator Ted Kennedy, a candidate for reelection, had made every effort to use his wife Joan as a major political asset. She was shown in the campaign as a devoted wife, loving mother and constant companion, a person much to be admired. During the campaign, however, she had a traffic accident, apparently while under the influence of alcohol, and smashed a car or two. The wreck, ordinarily not newsworthy, was reported by Roger Mudd on CBS News. Mudd (in an academic seminar at Washington and Lee University) reasoned that because she had been shown as an asset to her husband, she was newsworthy when she became a liability, and that justified broadcasting news about a rather unspectacular traffic accident. Because the senator had tried to persuade people to vote for him because of her, he made her a public figure. Thus when she became a liability, journalists were obligated to show her presumably darker side. Should that change the applicable guidelines?

The reader should refine and extend this list of possible guidelines for policy on privacy and the press. Most journalists have such guidelines, but they are rarely articulated. They should be stated so that journalists may more effectively examine and evaluate their own norms.

## SUMMARY CONCLUSION

One who possesses privacy possesses control over the entrance of others into her circles of intimacy. The possession of privacy is of utmost importance to individuals and societies for psychological reasons (need for individual identity and autonomy) and for political reasons (to curtail the power of the state). But morally speaking, the moral *right* to privacy must be limited by recognition of the *need* of others to know. Thus in reporting on individuals, journalists should temper invasions of privacy in particular cases by applying the test of the public's real need to know.

## REFERENCES

American Press Institute. (1992). *The Public, Privacy and the Press.* Reston, VA: American Press Institute.

Bier, William C. (1980). *Privacy: A Vanishing Value?* New York: Fordham University Press.

Blaustein, Edward J. (1964). "Privacy as an Aspect of Human Dignity: An Answer to Dean Prosser." *New York University Law Review,* 39: 962–1007.

Bok, Sissela. (1982). *Secrets: On the Ethics of Concealment and Revelation.* New York: Pantheon Books.

Breckenridge, Adam Carlyle (1980). *The Right to Privacy.* Lincoln: University of Nebraska Press.

Burnett, Carol (1983). "Once Printed, Words Have Nine Lives." *USA Today,* 16 May, A-10.

Cooley, Thomas M. (1988). *A Treatise on the Law of Torts.* 2nd ed. Chicago: Callaghan.

Dionisopoulos, P. Allan, and Craig R. Ducat (1976).*The Right to Privacy: Essays and Cases.* St. Paul: West.

Elliott, Deni, and Martin Linsky. (September, 1982). "The Oliver Sipple Story: The Questions It Raises for the Press." *The Bulletin of the American Society of Newspaper Editors,* 8–9.

Lon Fuller, *The Morality of Law.* New Haven, CT: Yale University Press, 1969.

Fischer, Constance T. (1980)."Privacy and Human Development." In *Privacy: A Vanishing Value?* ed. William C. Bier, S. J., 35–37. New York: Fordham University Press,

Lake, James Burges. (1991). "Of Crime and Consequence: Should Newspapers Report Rape Complainants' Names?" *Journal of Mass Media Ethics,* 6(2): 106–118.

Levine, Morton H. (1980) "Privacy in the Tradition of the Western World." In *Privacy: A Vanishing Value?* ed. William C. Bier, S.J., 3–21. New York: Fordham University Press.

Neville, Robert C. (1980). "Various Meanings of Privacy: A Philosophical Analysis." In *Privacy: A Vanishing Value?* ed. William C. Bier, S.J., 22–33. New York: Fordham University Press.

Overholser, Geneva(1989, November)."We Should Not Have to Keep Hiding Rape," *The Bulletin of the American Society of Newspaper Editors,* 32.

Polanyi, Michael (1951). *The Logic of Liberty.* Chicago: University of Chicago Press.

Policinski, Gene (1992, July/August). "The Arthur Ashe AIDS Story Is News." *The Bulletin of the American Society of Newspaper Editors,* 17.

Sanders, William B. (1980). *Rape and Woman's Identity.* Beverly Hills, CA: Sage, 1980.

Warren, Samuel D. and Louis D. Brandeis (1890, December 15). "The Right to Privacy," *Harvard Law Review,* 4 193–220.

Westin, Alan F. (1967). *Privacy and Freedom.* New York: Atheneum.

# IV
# INSTITUTIONAL CONSIDERATIONS

# 21

# Buddhist Moral Ethics: Intend No Harm, Intend to Be of Benefit

## S. Holly Stocking

Once there was an Indian prince who led an easy, protected life. Cut off from the miseries of others, he did not know obvious suffering. Of regal bearing and possessed of many talents, he likely saw himself as a relatively independent person, able to function and accomplish many things without the help of others. As yet untouched by death, he likely lived, as most of us do, as if he were going to live forever.

But sometime in his twenties, restless and sensing there was more to life than material pleasure and accomplishment, the prince left home to seek Enlightenment. For years, he wandered among people from all walks of life, awakening to others' pain and suffering and to his own. Then one day, as he sat in deep meditation under a bodhi tree, his ordinary perceptions dissolved like a dream. With diamond-like clarity, the prince realized that no one—not even a prince—is immune to suffering, and that none of us is separate or permanent. To the contrary, we all suffer more than we realize; we are profoundly interdependent, affected by and affecting others more than we know, and nothing lasts—not our wealth, not our friends or families, not even our precious self. With this, the prince's heart burst open to a love and compassion deeper than anything he had ever known, and for 45 years, until his death at 80, Prince Siddhartha—now the Buddha or "awakened one"—taught to others the vast wisdom-knowledge that had roused his slumbering heart and brought him indescribable peace.

The teachings of the Buddha are vast and have taken many forms in the last 2500 years, but basic to all is the notion of our potential for good. Echoing developing findings in science, the Buddha taught that everyone has the capacity for love and compassion. What is more, he taught that each of us without exception has the potential to extend love and compassion not just to friends and family, but to strangers, and even enemies. This remarkable potential is like a seed buried within us. The problem, as the Buddha saw it, is that this seed is frequently hidden from view, covered over by weeds, or negativities, rooted in ignorance. All too often, the fast-growing weeds deny this seed much needed sunlight and other nourishment, so the seed lies dormant. In rare moments, when ordinary awareness is stripped away by life-threatening events, this seed may crack open and our positive potential thrust its way to the surface: We can see this when a hurricane or tsunami drowns a city, and moved by compassion, people rush to help total strangers; we can see it, too, when cancer or some other life-threatening calamity strikes us as individuals, and suddenly deeper priorities grow clear.[1] More commonly, we unintentionally act in ways that stifle our positive potential and hide it, even from ourselves.

While it is true that tragedies can bring out the best in people, it was the Buddha's view that we don't have to wait for obvious life-shattering events to awaken our potential to love others and express compassion. For those with the capacity for discipline, he taught a system of moral ethics that can create the causes and conditions for it to arise and flower in the ordinary course of daily life. This ethical system involves the twin disciplines of weeding out negativities and actively providing the positive nourishment that feeds our positive potential. Or put another way, it is the discipline of abandoning negative or non-virtuous actions that prevent us from living out this potential, and it is the complementary discipline of adopting positive, helpful actions that show us, in very concrete ways, just who we and others can be. By engaging in these inter-related disciplines of the heart, we can gradually uproot the ignorance that leads to suffering and nourish the seed of love and compassion that leads to happiness.

The chapter that follows describes the Buddhist system of ethics, drawing on classic texts and commentaries written by Tibetan Buddhist teachers and supplemented by recent renderings aimed at Westerners.[2] Though I have made an effort to stay as close as possible to the most authoritative of these sources, much has had to be simplified for a non-Buddhist audience; those who seek to learn more should consult the original texts mentioned here, along with others. I also have taken the liberty of reducing the complementary ethical principles in Buddhism to "Intend No Harm," and "Intend to Be of Benefit." I have done this not just for simplicity's sake, but also to draw attention to the importance of intention. In Buddhist ethics, our actions are important, but our intentions are even more important. If we lie with a negative intention, it is very different than if we lie with a purely positive one. This is of great importance.

In addition to describing this ethical system, the chapter discusses the implications and applications of Buddhist moral ethics for mass media practice and for research and scholarship. Though Buddhist ethics bears strong similarities to traditional modes of reasoning taught in media ethics classes, there are also some intriguing differences. In applying this ancient ethical system to contemporary media practice, it is my hope to broaden existing normative approaches to ethical decision making in the media and to spur comparative studies of media ethics.

This discussion of Buddhist ethics is a natural response to the call in recent years to add non-Western voices to conversations about media ethics. Although Buddhist moral ethics remains one of the least familiar areas of Buddhist thought for Westerners, Buddhism itself is no longer a stranger. Increasing numbers of Buddhist students are migrating to the West, showing up in classrooms and giving impetus to efforts to globalize our understandings and teaching of ethics. Many Westerners without religious faith have found in the teachings wisdom to guide their lives. And even people whose ethics are deeply centered in other faiths have found in the teachings of Buddha much that enhances their own abilities to minimize suffering in themselves and others, and to maximize happiness. If nothing else, perhaps this discussion of Buddhist ethics will work to enlarge readers' understanding of their own ethical principles, deepening their awareness of their intentions and actions and the presumed effects of both on all who engage in media practice.

## ESSENTIALS OF BUDDHIST ETHICS

Buddhist ethics has sometimes been boiled down to this injunction: "*Help* others if you can, but if you cannot, at least refrain from *hurting* others." This explains in part why intending no harm is typically mentioned first in discussions of this system of ethics; intending no harm to others is the *least* we can do.

## Intend No Harm

Few of us intend to harm others. And yet we do, all the time. Caught doing something we know we should not be doing, we may tell a little lie. Discovering an umbrella or borrowed book in the back seat of our car, we may decide to keep it, knowing full well it belongs to an acquaintance, but liking it so much we don't give it back. Or cut off in traffic, we may hurl expletives out the car window. These may seem like small things, and they are, relative to other, more harmful acts chronicled every day in the mass media. But if we were honest and kept track, we might count up many such negative acts in our daily lives.

What makes these actions "negative" is the negative mind that generates them and the harm they do or suffering they cause that we often overlook. Road rage, for example, comes from a mind that wants everything to go our own way and is less concerned about others than about ourselves. Such rage may ruin the mood of the errant driver, and that person in turn may lash out at others, generating far-reaching unintended consequences. But even if our anger doesn't irritate the other person, it may disturb any peace of mind we might have had.

And these are not the only harms that negative actions can do. If we believe—as the Buddha believed—that what goes around comes around, our actions will bring us long-term consequences. Among other things, they will increase our familiarity with anger, making it easier to get angry the next time, at another stranger perhaps, or even a partner or a friend, and that person, reacting in turn to our anger, may hurl expletives back at us. Finally, we will make it much harder for the potential for good within us to stir to life and grow.

The Buddha saw very clearly the immediate and long-range harms that people do all the time to themselves as well as to others, and so counseled those he taught to abandon actions that cause harm. The particular actions he recommended that people abandon are ones that he saw most often contribute to personal unhappiness and community disharmony. In Tibetan Buddhism, which provides the basis for this chapter, ten such actions have come down through the ages; though there are many other non-virtuous behaviors in addition to the ten identified here, most are thought to be contained inside these.[3]

Echoing five of the "thou shalt not's" of the Ten Commandments of Christianity, the ten actions include killing, stealing, sexual misconduct, lying, and covetousness. But in addition, they include divisive speech, which is intended to disrupt harmonious relationships between individuals and groups; hurtful speech, which is intended to hurt someone's feelings; idle chatter or gossip, which is any talk that whiles away the time, without meaning or purpose; malice or ill will, which contrary to love, is the wish that others will come to harm; and holding wrong views, which includes (but is not limited to) ignoring or minimizing the fact that our actions have consequences (ignoring, in other words, the law of cause-and-effect, or karma).[4]

In Tibetan Buddhism, these ten actions are placed behind three "doors" representing our connection to the outside world: the door of the body, the door of speech, and the door of the mind, and they are ordered in a way that emphasizes their presumed destructiveness to self and others, as noted in the chart below.

1. Killing
2. Stealing          BODY
3. Sexual Misconduct

---

4. Lying
5. Divisive Speech          SPEECH

6. Hurtful Speech
7. Idle Chatter

---

8. Covetousness
9. Malice                    MIND
10. Holding Wrong Views

Under this ethical system, non-virtuous actions of the BODY (1–3) are generally presumed to be worse than those of SPEECH (4–7), by virtue of the relative amount of suffering they tend to cause. Of these, killing is generally regarded as the most destructive to others and ourselves and idle chatter (or gossip) the least harmful, with all those in between listed in descending order of destructiveness. A moral agent seeking to minimize the amount of harm his actions are likely to inflict on himself and others should thus seek to eliminate those actions of body and speech presumed to cause the most harm.

The last three non-virtuous actions, those of the MIND (8–10), are presumed to be causes of all the other non-virtues (1–7) and for this reason are generally considered the most destructive of all. Malice, for example, can lead us to say hurtful things. And covetousness, which is the desire to possess what others have, can lead some of us to take what hasn't been offered (or steal) or to become sexually involved with someone else's partner (one form of sexual misconduct).[5] Indeed, the placement of actions of the mind at the bottom of the list suggests that such actions are at the "root" of all the other non-virtuous actions that cause suffering (though, importantly, their order of destructiveness is reversed, with the top action, covetousness, considered the least destructive of the three non-virtuous actions of the mind, and the bottom action, holding wrong views, considered the most destructive). While this would appear to suggest a need to abandon these actions above all others, actions of the mind are also considered the hardest to abandon, as they are implicated, in varying ways, in all the other actions.[6] The good news is that because they are implicated in all the other actions, the more we work to abandon the non-virtuous actions of body and speech, the more we create the causes and conditions for abandoning non-virtues of the mind as well.

Not only does the amount of destructiveness associated with each non-virtuous action vary under this ethical system, but also within each action, there can be gradations of harm. Not all lies are equal, in other words. Some lies are worse than others, depending on a variety of factors, including the intention behind our actions, the method we use in taking the action, the object of the action, how often we commit the action, and whether or not we engage in positive actions to offset the negatives.[7]

Of all of these factors that affect the severity of a non-virtuous action, the most important is intention. In Buddhist thought, a non-virtuous action by its nature arises from a negative mind and can never be virtuous. However, some actions can be more severely negative than others as a function of the nature and strength of the intention. For example, if we kill out of jealousy or rage or with malicious delight it is a far more harmful action than if we kill with great reluctance, wishing we did not have to kill at all. Likewise, if we engage in divisive speech, which creates or reinforces a divide between people, and we do it with the explicit intention of stirring things up so people will hurt one another, it's far more harmful than if we do it while engaging in mindless gossip.

Such statements must not be misunderstood. Just because all lies are not equal does not mean that lies are condoned in this system of moral ethics. There may be rare exceptions when lies can be told, not out of ignorance, but with clear awareness of what is at stake and compassion for everyone involved (in which case the lies are not considered non-virtuous at all; see next section, below). However, lies that arise from the kind of mindless, negative thinking that makes us separate from and more important than others (what we might call non-virtuous lies) are never condoned. This is because such lies do harm.

If we look carefully enough, it is possible to see the harm for ourselves. If we lie about something we have done (if we have strayed, say, from a committed relationship out of desirous attachment for someone else), we deny the person we are lying to the freedom to choose a course of action based on the truth. If discovered, our lie just adds to that person's distrust of us. Even if our lie is not found out, we know in our hearts we have lied, and we know from experience that our lying this time may make it necessary to lie again later; it may also make it easier to lie the next time, which if the lying goes on long enough can lead to an habitual tendency to lie. All this lying takes a lot of energy too, energy that might better be invested in more positive activities. Buddhist guidelines for moral conduct may not be absolutist, in the sense of prohibiting all lies, but they are clear that lies (and other non-virtuous actions that arise from a negative mind) generally do harm to ourselves and others, and if we want to minimize harm and create the causes and conditions that make it easier for our better qualities to arise, we should abandon as many of these actions as we can.

Abandoning non-virtuous actions (which is itself considered "virtuous" action in this system) is typically not something that can be done overnight. Especially if we have engaged in negative actions frequently enough to have made them into habits, it can require a great deal of discipline to change our ways. Knowing this, some Buddhists take vows for a day, or a week, or a month, to not indulge in a certain action, checking up on themselves with regularity, and if they slip, expressing regrets, taking other actions to repair any damage, and recommitting themselves to more positive actions. Others simply work to be mindful of every time they are tempted to engage in a particular negative action, and recognizing their actions could cause harm, work to find alternatives. Most people who exercise ethical restraint in these ways come to understand that even with the best of intentions they will make mistakes; all we can do is do the best we can, and over time, make improvements. To do nothing is to allow and create the causes and conditions for continued harm and suffering.

## Intend to Be of Benefit

But it would be a mistake to limit ethics to the moral injunction to *intend no harm.* Just as the *first* obligation of medical doctors has traditionally been thought to be to do no harm (*primum non nocere*), the larger obligation of physicians is to prevent and cure diseases, or, as we're discussing it here, to be of benefit. Likewise, in Buddhism, the least we can do to maximize our positive potential is to do no harm, but the most important thing to do is to be of help. Indeed, given the massive amount of suffering in the world, we should do everything we can to open our hearts to be of benefit, "applying steady, continuous effort" (Gyatso, 1995, p. 383).

The positive actions we can take to be of benefit are countless. Indeed, writers on Buddhist ethics often end their lists of things to do with a simple "etc." or "and so forth." Actions that remove others' ignorance, especially ignorance of our deep connections to one another and our responsibilities for each other, may be especially beneficial. One writer lists, as examples of positive actions, any work that alleviates others' suffering, removes dangers which threaten and arouse fears in others, consoles others, teaches skills that others need and don't possess, and helps others in ways appropriate to their views and customs (Gyatso 1995, p. 454 ff.). By engaging in these and other positive actions, we nourish our own positive qualities, creating the causes and conditions for them to grow quickly and well, and for our own ultimate happiness.

As with abandoning harmful actions, our intention is critical to being of benefit. With a pure intention to be of benefit, it is possible in some circumstances to engage in an action like lying that with other motivations would be non-virtuous. In the Buddhist system of ethics, such an action can be positive, provided it is truly motivated by love and compassion for everyone involved (and not just for the most obvious "victims" in a situation).

Again, the apparent flexibility of this ethical system should not be misunderstood. Because so much of our mind tends to be rooted in ignorance, it can be easy to imagine we have the best of intentions, when in fact we may not, we may simply be striving for an outcome that will get us what we think we want, while hurting someone else along the way. Buddhism stresses that every one of us without exception wants to be relieved of suffering and to attain happiness; this is so even as we habitually chase after things that bring nothing but suffering. In this, despite superficial differences, we are alike. Given our fundamental similarities, everyone is deserving of our compassion. No one, regardless of station, is inherently more important than another.[8] So if we do engage in an action like lying, we should make sure our intention is to benefit *everyone* involved.

Finally, cultivating actions that are intended to benefit others is every bit as much a discipline as abandoning non-virtuous actions. Some Buddhists make it a practice to engage in particular kinds of positive actions over a period of time; actively consoling others, for example, through volunteer activities in a hospice or hospital. In this way, they gradually nourish the seeds of love and compassion. Over time, their hearts grow warmer and more open and more and more used to attending to others' needs as well as to their own.

## IMPLICATIONS OF BUDDHIST ETHICS FOR MEDIA PRACTICE

Little, if anything, appears to have been written about the implications of Buddhist ethics for media practice.[9] However, for media professionals, who have in their hands the power to both reflect and contribute to suffering, Buddhist ethics appears to offer general guidance for how to practice in ways that will diminish suffering and maximize happiness. It appears to offer guidance related to the type of work we choose to do and the way in which we choose to do that work. It is also flexible enough to offer guidance for making decisions when particular values clash, as they do in ethical dilemmas.

### Guidance for the Type of Work One Chooses to Do

If we assume, as Buddhism does, that our own happiness depends on the happiness of others and that everything we do affects others, and if we further assume that we are not independent moral agents but are affected by a variety of social influences (an assumption supported by recent scholarship; see Voakes, 1997), then the kind of work we choose to do, and for whom, matters. If we seek to reduce suffering and generate happiness for ourselves and others, we should refrain, for example, from taking a position in a company that has a reputation for lying or stealing and in other ways cutting ethical corners. Likewise, we should refrain from using our media skills on behalf of a company whose primary products, like alcohol or cigarettes, enable people to abuse their bodies and increase the chances that they will die prematurely. And it will be beneficial to refrain from working for a firm that greedily puts profits or ratings ahead of sound ethics.

It also will be helpful to seek out work that encourages us to actively benefit others, jobs in which the primary purpose is to assist people in need, to give a voice to the voiceless, for instance, and to promote products and services (e.g., medicines and educational materials or hospice care for the dying and programs that feed the hungry) that will improve peoples' quality of life or give people access to basic human rights.

It will be beneficial, in short, to avoid a livelihood that does harm and seek instead what some Buddhist traditions call "right livelihood," work that avoids harmful actions and that encourages helpful actions instead.

This is not to say that we are going to always be free to choose our occupation or place of employment. If we have limited opportunities or a family to support, for example, we may not have the luxury of choosing the work we do or the company we work for. But where we can make choices in the best long-term interests of others, and ourselves, we should try to do so.

## Guidance for Doing the Job

Buddhist ethics not only offers useful guidance for the kind of media jobs to seek; it also offers guidance for conducting ourselves in *whatever* media work we choose to do.

If we seek to follow Buddhist prescriptions for abandoning non-virtuous actions in our work, we would want to think twice, for example, before:

- producing a story or other media message that endangers a life (killing);
- wrongly appropriating intellectual property off the Internet or snatching from ordinary people privacy that is not freely given (stealing);
- using sex as a mere seduction to gain access to information from a source or competitor (sexual misconduct);
- using deception to gain information from a source or competitor, or hiring actors or creating front groups to promote causes without identifying who they represent (lying);
- using labels and information that stereotype groups and magnify a divide between "us" and "them" (divisive speech);
- producing programs or writing blogs that make thoughtless use of abusive language (hurtful speech);
- generating stories about celebrities or others that are little more than titillating gossip and as a result distract us from more meaningful work and lead others to not take us seriously (idle chatter).

To the extent that these and other questionable actions arise from a negative mind, we should exercise restraint. Only with a positive mind, with the pure intention to be of benefit to *everyone* involved, should we consider engaging in them.

Consider an opportunity to report on the wayward behavior of a major celebrity. If we are considering such reporting out of greed—because it would gain ratings or hits from a celebrity-crazed audience or because it would keep up with or beat out the competition—it would be best to refrain from such reporting. On the other hand, if we have the pure intention to provide information that will help both the celebrity and those who feed on celebrity to understand the pressures that fame and material wealth can place on a vulnerable personality, then reporting on this wayward behavior may be justified.

The challenge is to be sure we aren't fooling ourselves. As noted earlier, it is extraordinarily easy in our ignorance to pull the wool over our eyes; people can rationalize all kinds of negative behaviors. Given this, engaging in actions that are generally defined as non-virtuous (actions like lying, for example) is almost never recommended. If there is an alternative action we might take, we should definitely explore it.

Of course Buddhist ethics not only offers guidelines for the kinds of actions we should try to abandon when doing our jobs, it also encourages people to look for ways to be of benefit. This can mean finding ways to use our knowledge and talents to actively reduce ignorance and relieve others of their suffering. This might mean producing stories that give voice to those who have been deprived of basic human rights, so that solutions can be found, and relief granted. It might mean investigating dangers in the environment, so authorities can clean them up. It might mean offering "news you can use"—for example, science-based stories on conflict resolution, so people can learn ways to resolve conflicts with co-workers, playground bullies, and members of their own families. If one is in PR or advertising, it might mean doing *pro bono* media relations work or producing television commercials for organizations that help victims of hunger, violence, or turbulent weather.

But actively working to relieve others of their suffering is not the only beneficial thing we can do. We can also actively work to celebrate the loving and compassionate deeds of ordinary people, deeds that otherwise would go unremarked. His Holiness the Dalai Lama, has expressed this in his popular book *Ethics for the New Millennium*:

> When the media focuses (sic) too closely on the negative aspects of human nature, there is a danger that we become persuaded that violence and aggression are its principal characteristics. This is a mistake, I believe. The fact that violence is newsworthy suggests the very opposite. Good news is not remarked on precisely because there is so much of it. Consider that at any given moment there must be hundreds of millions of acts of kindness taking place around the world. Although there will undoubtedly be many acts of violence in progress at the same time, their number is surely much less. If therefore, the media is (sic) to be ethically responsible, it needs to reflect that simple fact. (Dalai Lama, 1999, 186)

The late Harvard University scientist Stephen Jay Gould made a similar point following the terrorist attacks on Sept 11, 2001, which gave Americans a close-up look at the human capacity to inflict harm. In Gould's words, "Every spectacular incidence of evil will be balanced by 10,000 acts of kindness, too often unnoted and invisible as the 'ordinary' efforts of a vast majority." And "when an unprecedented act of evil so threatens to distort our perceptions of ordinary human behavior," human beings have "a duty, almost a holy responsibility, to record and honor the victorious weight of these innumerable little kindnesses" (Gould, 2001, A23).

Put another way, if the media spew out negative information all the time, people may come to regard the world as a fearful place, full of people who are greedy, corrupt, hateful, and threatening. On the other hand, if the media also run positive stories—if they show ordinary people helping a city rebuild after an horrendous flood or if they show children organizing campaigns to feed hungry children on the other side of the globe—people may come to see the potential for the good that they and others possess. What media professionals focus on, whether it is positive, negative, or trivial, thus matters, to us all.

## Guidelines for Ethical Dilemmas

Buddhist ethics can also have implications for decision making in ethical dilemmas, situations in which values conflict and there is no clear right answer.

Consider a case in which a television reporter has received a tip that institutionalized adults with developmental disabilities are being abused by their caregivers. The tipster is certain the institution won't allow in reporters. Lying in this system of ethics is generally presumed wrong. But is it impermissible in the interests of righting another wrong for a journalist to lie about her identity to secure a staff job and then document the abuse with a hidden camera?

In Buddhist ethics, our first obligation is to do no harm. Since lying is generally presumed harmful, we should make great effort to find a way to do the story without lying. Is it possible, for example, to get the story by talking to the tipster and other staff members inside the institution that this person trusts? If there is another way to get the story, we should.[10]

But let's say we discover there *is* no way to do the story without lying. Wouldn't it be okay, out of compassion for the victims, to lie to the few to benefit the many? If we assume, as Buddhist ethics do, that everyone without exception is deserving of compassion, then deliberately harming one group for the sake of another, even if the second group would benefit, would be questionable. In this particular case, it might be better to ask the tipster to go to the authorities. Let government officials do the investigating. This would avoid the harm that lying presumably would do to ourselves and to those lied to, and at the same time it would benefit the victims by exposing their suffering (and, incidentally, benefit the perpetrators by interrupting their negative deeds, which will only bring them grief). We can always bring the mistreatment to the public's attention, once it is exposed by authorities. Admittedly that will not be the kind of story we can run during sweeps week or submit for journalistic prizes (a very real drawback of this particular approach for the business of media), but if we are truly seeking to do no harm and be of benefit, we wouldn't want to do the story just to gain audience share or garner prizes in any event, as such reasons arise from covetousness or greed, which are themselves non-virtuous actions of the mind.

But let's imagine, for sake of argument, that the authorities are corrupt, taking bribes from the institution to not investigate the allegations of mistreatment. In such a circumstance, going to authorities is not an option. Wouldn't refusing to do the story, when we have the opportunity to bring this mistreatment to light and the attendant corruption as well, make the journalist complicit in the continuing suffering of the victims and the ongoing corruption? Does lying remain impermissible even when it is the only way to do a story that could stop the harm that others are doing and be of benefit?

Any system of ethics that lists ten non-virtuous actions may appear on the surface to be rigidly moralistic. But in this case, it is not. As noted earlier, an action under this system can be more or less right as a function of a host of factors. Of these factors, the most important is our intention or motivation. If we are experiencing such outrage that we can't wait to get inside the institution to film and punish the caretakers, this is not a positive mind; it is, in fact a mind seized by malice; given this negative state of mind, the use of deception would be considered non-virtuous, presumably harming not just others, but ourselves as well.

On the other hand, if our intention is to help everyone involved, including the caretakers, who presumably will suffer even more with respect to their long-term happiness if allowed to continue, the lie could be considered virtuous, and justified. Jail time for the caretakers, from this perspective, would tend to be regarded as preferable to allowing the caretakers to continue what they are doing because at least it would put a stop to actions that harm not just their victims, but themselves.

Our intention, if it is positive, will likely have direct implications for the reporting and framing of the story. Whereas traditional investigative journalism typically reflects outrage over the actions of one set of people (and for this reason is often called the "journalism of outrage"), this other kind of journalism (what might be called the "journalism of compassion") will reflect compassion for everyone involved. More precisely, it will reflect the realization that every one of us has not only the capacity for good, but also a capacity—at varying times and in varying degrees—to get caught up in situations that lead to harmful actions. Reporting may thus include, in addition to investigation of the qualities of individual staff members, investigation of staff-patient ratios, length of workdays, job qualifications and hiring practices, and other causes and conditions that have contributed to this sad state of affairs.[11]

Obviously, a report that shows caretakers beating up helpless adults is going to be shocking and generate outrage, but we can hope that the piece, if motivated by compassion, will also provide information that will enable viewers to move beyond these initial visceral reactions to an understanding of the complexity of factors that have converged to produce wrong actions and suffering. It is possible to imagine such a story garnering professional prizes and high ratings, no less than a story that is done for other reasons. It may not always be possible for our work to be both ethical as this system of ethics defines it *and* good for business, but if we are truly interested in using our work to help reduce suffering and generate happiness, it is a goal worth striving toward.

## IMPLICATIONS FOR RESEARCH AND SCHOLARSHIP

Buddhist ethics presents challenges to both normative and descriptive scholars of media ethics.

### Normative Ethics

In many ways, Buddhist ethics resembles classical ethical reasoning from a Western, Christian-dominated tradition. However, there are also striking differences, both significant and subtle, that deserve exploration by normative scholars.

The similarities:

- Buddhist ethics shares with the utilitarian ethics of John Stuart Mill a concern for maximizing happiness and minimizing harm and a recognition that actions can have harmful (or beneficial) consequences that contribute to both.
- It appears similar to the rule-based system of Immanuel Kant, which counsels actions that conform to rules or duties that respect the dignity of all and that we would want everyone to follow.
- It shares with the ethics of Aristotle a concern for cultivating positive moral habits.

The differences lie in the details:

- Unlike utilitarian ethics (at least the version of utilitarian ethics most widely taught in our field), Buddhist ethics does not determine the moral worth of an action as a function of its calculated potential to maximize the happiness of, and minimize the harm to, the greatest number of actors in the immediate situation. Instead, on the assumption that all beings without exception deserve happiness and relief from suffering, it seeks to maximize happiness and minimize harm with respect to everyone in the immediate situation and also with respect to everyone who might be subsequently affected by the actions. In doing so, it presumes that some actions are more likely than others to maximize happiness and minimize harm now and in the future. It's not that this system ignores the potential consequences of actions for individual actors in the immediate situation. However, it rejects choosing an action merely on that basis. In this system, of far more importance than calculated consequences is our motivation or intention. On the assumption that the mind guides all our physical and verbal actions, the emphasis is on thoughts and feelings, which can be trained and controlled over time, rather than on what arises in the moment on the outside, which in any event is usually beyond one's immediate control.
- Although Buddhist ethics appears to share with Kantian reasoning an emphasis on universal principles that have long-range consequences for individuals and society, it does not

ignore immediate consequences as Kantian reasoning does; immediate consequences do figure in this system, they simply are less important than other factors, especially intention. There are other important differences too. Kantian rules or duties are so absolutist that they make it difficult to know what to do when actions adhering to different rules or duties conflict in a given situation. Buddhist ethics, on the other hand, weighs various actions according to their general ability to inflict harm, allowing us to make choices depending upon the presumed degree of harm we might inflict with a given option. In this sense it comes closer to William David Ross's weighing of *prima facie* rules or duties, which makes decision-making possible when rules or duties conflict. But Buddhist ethics departs in some critical ways from Ross's system too. These include the fact that Buddhist ethics attends to *additional* factors that can mitigate the moral weight of a particular action, including (but not limited to) our intention or motivation.

- Buddhist ethics would appear to most closely resemble Aristotelian ethics with its concern for cultivating positive moral habits and character. However, it can be argued that Buddhist ethics provides more specific guides to moral action than Aristotelian ethics; at least it provides more than the simplified versions of Aristotelian ethics often taught in media ethics classrooms, which do not identify specific acts of virtue other than actions that flow out of cardinal virtues that lie between "extremes."[12] Technically, Buddhist ethics are not concerned either, as Aristotelian ethics are, with cultivating character, for character implies a sense of self that is separate from others and stable, which in Buddhist philosophy is a distortion of a reality that is profoundly interdependent and (despite individual and collective denials to the contrary) impermanent.

- As should by now be clear, of particular importance in Buddhist ethics is restraint of non-virtuous actions of the *mind*. The actions of the mind identified in the context of moral ethics are particular forms of attachment, anger and ignorance, which arise out of our need to protect and advance a separate, permanent sense of self, and are presumed to be a root cause of suffering. In cultivating moral ethics, we assume responsibility for restraining our mental activities (which include thoughts and emotions), as well as our physical and verbal actions.

Scholars interested in comparative ethics would do well to delineate these and other similarities and differences and to compare in given situations the reasoning and outcomes of this system against other ethical systems. Of particular interest might be comparisons to John Rawls's veil of ignorance, communitarianism, and perhaps most importantly, the ethics of care. It could also be beneficial to compare how these differing systems fare under the ever shifting and complex conditions for moral choice.

## Descriptive Ethics

For scholars with descriptive interests, at least two challenges present themselves. Although Buddhist thought is not always conceived of as religious, there are enough similarities to traditional faith systems to make scholarship on the interplay of religious and professional norms of relevance to this project. Sociological research on mass media practice on the part of those who identify themselves as Christians suggests that when professional and religious norms clash in the workplace, professional norms take precedence (Schmalzauer 1999). But this literature, which includes a monograph by Boeyink (1998), also suggests that where there is no conflict, there is considerable room for the application of religious ethics in one's work; the journalists find niches and strategies that allow them to live out their religious values. When Buddhist journalists work in the media, do they likewise bow to professional norms when they conflict with Buddhist principles? And how do the niches and strategies they find for expressing their values compare with those identified by workers who identify themselves as Christians?

In a related vein, when practitioners who practice Buddhist ethics encounter ethical dilemmas in the workplace, do they make different choices from those that Christian practitioners might make? If and when Buddhist-dominated countries adopt Western-style codes of ethics, are the provisions of the codes interpreted in different ways than they would be in the West, as one might expect based on the developing work of Wasserman (in press) and others?

## CONCLUSIONS

Buddhist moral ethics, while unfamiliar to many in the West, offers a measure of guidance for the kind of work media professionals may choose, for the ways they may do their work, and for ethical quandaries. While this system from the East shares similarities with ethical systems of the West, there appear to be important differences, which deserve to be explored by normative and descriptive scholars alike.

Will Buddhist ethics lead to different decisions by media practitioners? And if it does, will these decisions, in turn, affect the extent to which media content reflects and contributes to suffering?

The value of this system for media scholarship and practice in the West will depend on its perceived promise for raising new questions, offering new insights, and affecting the ethics of practitioners in positive ways. If this chapter does nothing but open the discussion of these matters, it will have served a useful purpose.

## ACKNOWLEDGMENTS

I am indebted to many Buddhist teachers who have taught in word and deed these and other lessons in moral ethics. Most especially I am indebted to Kyabje Dagom Rinpoche, formerly of Nepal Ganden Monlam Chenmo in Katmandu, Nepal; Ven. Geshe Kuten Lama and Ven. Jamyang, resident teachers of the Dagom Gaden Tensung Ling Monastery (DGTL) in Bloomington, IN, and Geshe Lobsang Sopa of the Trijang Buddhist Institute in Northfield, VT, for their immeasurable kindness and assistance. In addition, I am grateful to Lisa Farnsworth, Suzy Fulkerson, and Bill Timberlake of DGTL, and Margo Pierce of the Gaden Samdrupling Monastery in Cincinnati, for reading and commenting on earlier drafts of this chapter. While many have helped make this chapter possible, I accept full responsibility for any errors of fact or interpretation.

Send all correspondence to: S. Holly Stocking, Indiana University School of Journalism, Ernie Pyle Hall, Bloomington, IN 47405.

## NOTES

1. The bestselling book *Tuesdays with Morrie* by Mitch Albom provides a good example of the latter.
2. The most scholarly source is a teaching by the late Pabongka Rinpoche based on 15th century teachings for monastics in the Gelupga lineage of Tibetan Buddhism by Tibetan Buddhist teacher Lama Tsongkapa. This source, which is on the stages of the path (or lamrim), comes in two translations: a 1991 translation, *Liberation in the palm of your hand: A concise discourse on the path to enlightenment* and

a three-volume translation, *Liberation in our hands: Part one: Preliminaries (1990), Part two: Fundamentals (1994) and Part three: The ultimate goals (2001).* A more condensed scholarly source on the stages of the path is Geshe Kelsang Gyatso's *Joyful path of good fortune: The complete Buddhist path to enlightenment.* Other, less scholarly and more wide-ranging sources on Buddhist ethics include His Holiness the Dalai Lama's *Ethics for the new millennium* and the book by Jonathan Landaw with Stephan Bodian, *Buddhism for dummies,* a surprisingly accurate rendering of Buddhist ethics (in its many variations), written by a former English translator for His Holiness the Dalai Lama.

3. The thinking behind asking followers to abandon non-virtuous actions is the same across traditions of Buddhism, though the precise actions, in kind and number, vary slightly. See Landaw with Bodian (2003, p 227).

4. The law of cause-and-effect, or karma, states that over the long run, if not immediately, positive causes will have positive effects, and negative causes will have negative effects. Because actions have consequences, how we act matters. Karma is thus not the passive thing that many Westerners mistakenly believe it to be, but something we ourselves influence with every choice we make: If we make the positive choice to abandon actions that are motivated by narrowly selfish interests and if we adopt instead actions that are motivated by genuine love and compassion and the wish to be of benefit, the law of karma says that we can have confidence that at some point (a point we may not be able to see clearly right now), we will experience the positive consequences of those choices; it will grow easier and easier to act in ways that will feed the positive seed within us, allowing it to rise up, grow, and flower. Over time, we will "reap what we sow."

5. An important caveat is in order here: While it is generally true that actions of the mind are more destructive than actions of body and speech by virtue of their involvement in these other actions, it is also true that an action of the mind that is *merely* an action of the mind is going to be less destructive than an action of the mind that is accompanied by an action of body or speech; so, for example, if we covet a person's hat (an action of the mind), but do not actually steal the hat (an action of the body), it is going to be less destructive than if we both covet the hat and actually steal it.

6. Another caveat is in order: Covetousness, malice, and holding wrong views aren't the only actions of the mind that can be causes of the non-virtuous actions of body and speech identified here; they are, though, important ones.

7. To be more specific:
   - The intention behind our actions. For example, if we lie out of revenge, with a strong intention to hurt someone, it is presumed more destructive than if we lie just to get out of something.
   - The method we use in taking the action. If we develop an elaborate lie, embroidered with details intended to deceive, for example, it is generally considered worse than if we lie by indirection or omission. Likewise, if we involve others in the deception, it is worse than if we alone deceive.
   - The object of the action. If we lie to people who have been especially kind to us, for example, it is presumed to be more destructive than if we lie to strangers, not because strangers are inherently less important than those who have been especially kind (they are not; ultimately, all beings are equally valuable), but because the amount of suffering those who have been kind to us are likely to experience is likely to be greater.
   - How often we commit the action. If we lie regularly, for instance, it is much worse than if we lie only occasionally, as a last resort.
   - Whether or not we engage in positive actions to offset the negatives. If we engage in negative actions only, it is far worse than if we engage in negative actions supplemented by actions that benefit others.

8. Though, as indicated earlier, some may be hurt more by our actions than others.

9. One exception is a previous book chapter by the author, "A Teacher's Last Lesson: Love Each Other or Die," in Howard Good's edited volume, *Desperately seeking ethics: A guide to media conduct.* That chapter is not explicitly about Buddhist ethics, but it is based on ethical principles from this system.

10. This is consistent with many professional and organizational codes of ethics, which counsel journalists to use deception to gather a story only as a last resort.

11. From a Buddhist perspective, there would be even deeper causes to explore, but these are not causes that would be easily conveyed in the news.

12. Some scholars might argue—as one reviewer of this chapter did—that this is "too restrictive of Aristotle." In the words of this reviewer, "some versions do limit themselves to acts of virtue constrained by the cardinal virtues, but not all. And to claim that Buddhist ethics provides more specific guides to moral action doesn't give enough credence to Aristotle's phronesis, practical wisdom." Given my own inabilities to address this critique, I will leave this to scholars of ethics to sort out in future comparisons of Aristotle and Buddhist ethics.

## REFERENCES

Albom, M. (1997). *Tuesdays with Morrie: An old man, a young man, and life's greatest lesson.* New York: Doubleday.

Boeyink, D. (1998, June). A search for meaning in the media, in D. H. Smith & R B. Miller (Eds.). *Religion, Morality and the Professions in America, monograph series* (pp. 10–27). Bloomington, IN: Indiana University Poynter Center for the Study of Ethics and American Institutions.

Dalai Lama, His Holiness (1999). *Ethics for the new millennium.* New York: Riverhead Books.

Gould, S. J. (2001). A time of gifts. *New York Times,* Sept. 26, A23.

Gyatso, Geshe Kelsang (1995). *Joyful path of good fortune: The complete Buddhist path to enlightenment.* London: Tharpa Publications.

Landaw, J. with Bodian, S, (2003). *Buddhism for dummies.* New York: Wiley.

Pabongka Rinpoche (1991). *Liberation in the palm of your hand.* Trijang Rinpoche (Ed.) and Michael Richards (Translator). Somerville, MA: Wisdom Publications.

Pabongka Rinpoche (1990, 1994, 2001). *Liberation in our hands. Part one: Preliminaries, Part two: Fundamentals, Part three: The ultimate goals.* Trijang Rinpoche with Sermey Khensur Lobsang Tharchin and Artemus B. Engle (Translators). Howell, NJ: Mahayana Sutra and Tantra Press.

Schmalzauer, J. (1999). Between professional and religious worlds: Catholics and Evangelicals in American religion. *Sociology of Religion, 60,* No. 4, 363–386.

Voakes, P. S. (1997). Social influences on journalists' decision making in ethical situations. *Journal of Mass Media Ethics, 12*(1), 18–35.

Wasserman, H. & De Beer, A. S. (in press). Glimpses through the windowpane: A South African perspective on universal media ethics, in Fortner, R.S. & Fackler. P.M. (eds.) *Ethics and evil in the public sphere: Media, universal values & global development.* Creskill, NY: Hampton Press.

# 22

# Communitarianism

## Mark Fackler

Every relationship is a mutual action—Ferdinand Tönnies

### INTRODUCTION: A DEFINITION AND EXAMPLES

Communitarianism is the social strategy which distinguishes peace-loving virtues from greed-hoarding impulses. Communitarianism argues for the former because, in the main, human experience has shown that people prosper when tribalism and egoism give way to generosity and fair-play as first order responses. Even Genghis Khan, the Asian general whose total-war ferocity shook the 13th century, demonstrated that consistent fairness and truth telling built empire faster and with less bloodshed than any medieval code of honor, encrusted with class and heavy with elitism and privilege (Weatherford, 2004, xix). Community grows under a regime of predictable good will tending toward fearless communication of dissent and negotiated hierarchies of function attentive to the advantage of the least powerful members.

Communitarianism is both ontology and praxis. As a way of being, it is evident primarily in the middle-range bonds of trust and loyalty that come voluntarily to persons who understand that fulfillment, happiness, and eudaemonia evolve through relationships and never in isolation from them. The practice of communitarianism varies from sports fandom to blogging to church or party membership. In every way not forced by the state that people combine for cooperative action and sustain their mutual effort without corruption, communitarianism is evident. Communitarians claim that such praxis is a non-negotiable priority in any successful life. This practice is ideally first experienced in family (Kirkpatrick, 1986, 173). Actions that typify family-care then extend to larger and more diverse groups by those who properly understand their identity and vocation. The number of sociologists and commentators who have exploited this movement from family-care to community is legion. Ferdinand Tönnies captures the heart of it in his classic distinction between Gesellschaft and Gemeinschaft (Tönnies, 33).

The identity of the individual in communitarian theory emerges as an ontological recognition of the primacy of relationships. The communitarian "is a person whose identity and fulfillment are inextricably bound up with relations and communities. Other people are constitutive of rather than instrumental to my identity and well-being as a person" (Fergusson, 1998, 143). This reorientation agitates against the Enlightenment notion of the autonomous individual, who may for purposes of survival or economic improvement freely choose to align with others. Rather, communitarianism insists that mutuality defines and constitutes the person. Without relationships, and therefore communicative sharing, the idea of personhood vanishes. Understanding and defining oneself as a person requires knowing and comparing that "self" with others. Under a communitarian rubric, the person is not incorporated or absorbed in the Other, as in communalism, but establishes a distinctive ontological identity in nexus with others, never isolated or free-floating. John MacMurray explains:

> The self is constituted by its relation to the other; this relationship is necessary personal...the idea of an isolated agent is self-contradictory. Any agent is necessarily in relation to the other. (cited in Kirkpatrick, 1986, 173)

## APPLICATION TO THE MASS MEDIA

Inklings of communitarianism as a basis for an ethic of mass media show in the establishment of public broadcasting agencies, independent of government and mandated to public service. The BBC and particularly its World Service exhibit early ambitions to serve the common good. Consider that long after British colonial control in Africa and Asia ended, the BBC has been a media mainstay across those continents. In the U.S., broadcasting and later the motion picture industry demonstrated that public service regulation—or with the Hays' Office, industry self-regulation—seemed a foothold for communitarian sentiments as "the Invisible Empire of the Air" (inventor Lee De Forest's term) and screen developed their immense influence and fortunes (Lewis, 1958, 1).

The most impressive prelude to communitarianism, in terms of anchoring media responsibility, was the Commission on Freedom of the Press chaired by Robert Maynard Hutchins in the 1940s. The commission's findings were published in *A Free and Responsible Press* in 1947 and given academic currency by the worldwide influence of that little after-thought book by Siebert, Peterson, and Schramm in 1956, Four Theories of the Press. The Illinois scholars called Hutchins's work the social responsibility theory of the press, highlighting the commissioners' call for a media that would serve the public, challenge state power, and give voice to those on the margins.

Among the leaders of academe, business, and public policy whom Hutchins recruited to his panel, none wrote more on the moral life and media than William Ernest Hocking, who celebrated communication as the essential human responsibility. No person can live a truly human life as recluse, ignoring the commonweal, Hocking contended. Consciousness and thought require the filling of the space between, the zone of the relation.

> Whatever one's final philosophy, it can never be held as a purely private result. As a supposed body of truth about the living world, there is inseparable from it the impulse to knead it into the self-consciousness of the world. (Hocking, 1926, 319)

Hocking's colleague on the commission, theologian Reinhold Niebuhr, joined paradox and promise to his vision for social justice through value-rich mediated news and entertainment. Love—other-minded care—was the ultimate social norm, he insisted. To be effective in public affairs, love must find expression in norms of justice (Niebuhr, 1957, xiii).

Of the five goals for mass media reform recommended by the Hutchins commission, the second and fourth were most coherent with later communitarian themes: to be (2) a forum for the exchange of comment and criticism, and provide (4) the presentation and clarification of the goals and values of the society (Leigh, 1947, 23, 27). These commonplace recommendations were assailed by mid-century media chiefs but embraced by subsequent generations around the world.

Hutchins himself is remembered as a champion of the Great Conversation, values-based dialogue that extends from the beginning of human ethical reflection to a present sorely in need of ethical refreshment. No obscurantist, Hutchins wanted "the voices of the Great Conversation to be heard again because we think they may help us to learn to live better now" (Hutchins, 1954, 3). Hutchins's optimism about a renewal of civil discourse was mirrored by each of his commissioners. Archibald MacLeish, the last surviving member, made repeated reference to the relation-between as "imagination," the basis of human dignity.

> The real defense of freedom is imagination, that feeling-life of the mind which naturally knows because it involves itself in its knowing, puts itself in the place where its thought goes. (MacLeish, 20)

Following the thinking of Hocking, Niebuhr, and Hutchins, communitarians challenge modern Western notions of press and public, built as they are on Lockean and capitalist presuppositions. Western moral systems, assuming an individualist base, require that the press tell the truth in order that well-informed decision makers (voters and policy makers) have access to accurate, current, and unbiased data. Communitarianism reorganizes these requirements: truth celebrates values hammered out through dialogue, debate, and compromise. The press is the most influential means of publicizing the dialogue on values. In classical liberal media theory, one might legitimately claim that speech rights are absolute—a natural right. Conscience is the supreme moral guide and unfettered speech the first requirement of an open marketplace of ideas. A communitarian speaking about media responsibility would consult as a first priority the needs, wants, ambitions, and wisdom of his or her community. Public or civic journalism reflects this second-effort at democratic cooperation (Rosen, 1999, 19).

Currently communitarianism wrestles with its identity and direction in the face of a dominant atomistic-contractarian model of community, or anti-community, as Kirkpatrick explains (1986, 137). Kwame Appiah (2006) prefers the term "cosmopolitanism" and cites the Cynics of the fourth century B.C. as the first who were self-consciously "citizens of the cosmos." Local loyalties were insufficiently tribal to account for the moral obligations borne by all humans for all others. Appiah points to the first-order obligation of developing "habits of coexistence: conversations in its older meaning, of living together, association" (Appiah, 2006, xix).

Appiah's roots in the Akan culture of West Africa serve as a bridge between Western scholars dealing with the wreckage of Enlightenment individualism and African scholars exploring the depth of intersubjectivity, which appears as self-evident truth in that region, unencumbered by Enlightenment bias. Another Akan scholar, Kwasi Wiredu, situates communitarianism in the immediate life-world of harmonized interests and mutual well-being. Had the ancient Akan people written a classic ethics, mutual aid would have been the keynote, not rationalist appeals to duty or injunction revealed by special circumstance, as in Christianity, Judaism, and Islam (Wiredu, 1996, 99).

The Congolese scholar Benezet Bujo contends that loyalty based on clan and tribe rightly enlarges to a "world community [of] every single human person." Using the rhetorical style of his own region, Bujo cites an adage from Burundi:

> "If one member of the family has eaten dog-meat, all the members of the clan are disgraced." To eat the flesh of a dog is disgraceful for the Burundi; one who does so should not think that he alone can bear responsibility as an individual for this deed...the wicked conduct of one member infringes the dignity of all. (Bujo, 2001, 115)

Without doubt the history of violence in Africa is as brutal and malicious as the record of any other region, yet Bujo's starting point for the development of personhood remains fixed at a relational nexus. A child's sense of self and other begins with the first encounter and depends entirely on the care of others. A name is rendered based on relational realities. One grows into care-providing roles, without surrendering the need for care oneself. Violations of the social bond are reckoned as morally blameworthy, and celebrations as communal joy. Large-scale violations—wars in the Sudan and northern Uganda for instance—must be forgotten and people reconciled as *sine qua non* to a future. The miniscule and debatable distinction between Hutu and Tutsi which has turned rivers red in Burundi and Rwanda must evaporate as Bujo's communitarianism translates into social policy there. Communitarian ontology cannot abide perpetual exclusion. Nor can it coherently ordain a cultural hierarchy justifying hegemony or economic domination. Neither colonialism nor traditional culture's gender stereotypes survive communitarian critique. In Native American and other non-Western cultures, the embrace of the Other characteristic of communitarianism includes one's forebears and unobservable "spirits and life essences" not excluding animals, birds, even rivers and mountains (Brown, 2004, 172).

In the 1980s a surge of interest in communications studies followed the work of Charles Taylor, Robert Bellah, and the translations of Jacques Ellul's seminal works. In each scholar's core was the notion that Enlightenment liberalism had sacrificed fundamental human connectedness. The result was a new sense of boredom and disconnected. Novelist Walker Percy described it as "lost in the cosmos" (Percy, 73). For Taylor, the intellectual life of the West, wrapped so tightly in bonds of empiricism, rationalism, and individual rights, had narrowed its "horizons," diminishing its notion of humanity (Taylor, 1989, 27). For Ellul, the drive to efficiency (*la technique*) characterized all modern bureaucracy, abrogating any possibility of genuine freedom and cooperation (Ellul, 1964, 6). Bellah's revealing interviews portrayed a culture groping for meaningful relationships, unsatisfied with the status symbols of rationalistic success (Bellah, 1996, 3). Later Robert Putnam described the loss of social capital in the economized West as he mused over the demise of team sports and a new entertainment market in privatized game-playing. He noted that a "generalized game playing" (I'll do this for you without expecting anything specific back from you, in the confident expectation that someone else will do something for me) born of community trust no longer typifies American life (Putnam, 2000, 21).

In communication studies, Clifford Christians and others associated with the journal *Critical Studies in Mass Communication* sought an alternative theory of the self on which to construct and apply the values of progressive democratic media systems. For Christians, mere tinkering with questions of order, freedom, or tradition failed to address root problems. He pressed toward an ontological breakthrough that affirmed the primacy of relationship and refuted the stand-alone person who then chooses his or her social connections based on market potential or other pragmatic calculations.

Christians' ontology required that common problems of communications ethics and liberal speech/press law be completely reformulated to accommodate persons-in-community. He urged that media operators recast their social vocation, but stopped short of offering to the press a nuanced format or stipulating a code of communitarian media ethics. Rather, his work provided broad parameters intending to reset the principles by which press and public would come to understand their democratic responsibilities. Mutuality replaced individual rights as a first principle. Freedom to speak could no longer start from assertions of the untamed conscience, but rather from a prior regard for the Other, in the language of Emmanuel Levinas. The intellectual work of Ellul, Habermas, Levinas, and feminist communitarians sustained Christians's challenge to the Enlightenment standard (Christians, 1993, 185).

## A THEORETICAL CRITIQUE AND HISTORIC COUNTERPOINT

Christians's applied work in media ethics and press theory drew libertarian critics to the barricades. John C. Merrill, a classical liberal who promotes ethics as individual choice and personal reason, has been a prolific opponent of the trend to situate journalistic responsibility in communitarian terms.

> The twentieth century has spawned a new breed of articulate and very vocal [moral guides] who claim to know what the press should be to be responsible to society. They have shifted, and are continuing to shift, the concept of press freedom from an emphasis on individual media freedom to a stress on a kind of social freedom to have a responsible press. (Merrill, 1989, 28)

In startling cold-war era rhetoric, Merrill drove home his worries over a communitarian turn in American media ethics (1989, 214):

> Absolutes and universal norms are fit only for "operatniks" functioning in an authoritarian system and not for self-valuing journalists in "open" societies.

In a recent effort to revive the Enlightenment liberalism of Locke, Voltaire, Mill, and Jefferson, Merrill finds in communitarianism an effort to give a humane face to the profit-based corporate journalism driven by accountants and edited, as it were, by attorneys. "This new trend was attempting to inject the public into editorial decision-making and to shift journalism's stance from one of neutrality and non-involvement to one of advocacy and involvement." Finally, it's "only a new way of trying to succeed… Nothing new here" (Merrill, 1998, 2).

Another strident critic of the communitarian turn, Carl Hausman, ventured that the pomposity and moral judgmentalism in Christians' popular media ethics text was offensive to working journalists, however convincing the book's arguments might be to "college freshman" (Hausman, 1992, 176).

But of course, it was not college freshman alone who were turning their intellectual and practical attention toward communitarian theory. While communitarianism has ancient roots, there was indeed something new here. Paradigms were changing; seasoned verities concerning reason and abstract principle were giving way to new combinations of theory and praxis, often in response to human suffering unexplained by the air-tight abstractions of rationalism. A new millennium's hope of economic prosperity and global friendship seemed like shallow rhetoric. Following the epochal attack on the World Trade Center in New York, shallowness gave way to the heated rhetoric of the War on Terror. Prospects for peace grew increasingly elusive and the systematic coherence of rationalist polity showed itself to be a human wrecking-ball. Trust diminished, well past already low levels across geographic and ideological divides. No strong solutions presented to growing tensions and bloodshed in regions of the Middle East. Federico Mayor, former head of UNESCO, reflecting on a new millennium and the task ahead for human development, said (Mayor, 2001, 5):

> We cannot fail to observe the increase in soul-sickness at the very heart of the most prosperous societies and social categories which seem best protected from misfortune. The heart itself seems prey to a curious void. Indifference and passivity grow. There is an ethical desert. Passions and emotions are blunted. People's eyes are empty and solidarity evaporates. Grey areas expand. Amnesia wins out. The future seems unreadable. We witness the divorce between forecast and plan. Long-term vision is discredited. Now and then we are truly sick at heart. Will the twenty-first

century be the century of artificial paradises, real hell and the overwhelming increase in depression hinted at by present statistics? Will it be characterized by the massacres, anomie, violence, pandemics....

Then this champion of the developing world challenges readers: "The moment of truth has arrived—the fate of the human race itself may be at stake, so weighty will be the combination of dangers jeopardizing our future" (Mayor, 5).

These extended quotations are meant to convey the passion of world observers for whom the development of a communitarian ethos is a choice for survival, if perhaps also human prosperity. The urgency of the debate as Mayor expresses it carries implications far beyond published treatises or academic theories. Peoples and regions wait for participatory democracy, free and open public expression of core values, and the robust vitalizing power of hope. Mayor forbids that we consign communitarianism to academic discourse while political dialogue crumbles and resources for health and nutrition are wasted by corruption and environmental degradation.

## COMMUNITARIANISM UNDERSTOOD IN CONTRAST TO CLASSICAL LIBERALISM

Essential progress, however, cannot sidestep intellectual attention, particularly as communitarianism challenges liberalism's cultural values and reorients Western notions of personhood and primary loyalties.

Agnes Heller, building on Hannah Arendt's reflections on totalitarianism, began in the 1980s to develop a social ethic around a community's commitment to a common good. Heller departed from the model of social ethics built on autonomous moral agents applying rules consistently. Her critical turn, mentored by Georg Lukacs (1885–1971), adopted a complex and integrated view of the moral life of communities emerging from principled wisdom accumulated from the everyday life of good people, people who choose to suffer wrongdoing rather than perpetrate injustice, people participating in communal-collective deliberation (Christians, 2002, 53).

Jean Bethke Elshtain reacts to a communitarianism which insists on social sameness forced upon civil society in the interests, supposedly, of the many faces of the oppressed. A healthy community is well aware of its differences and rightly celebrates those civic practices which promote democratic dialogue and principled compromise over bland appeals to eliminate color, gender, or lifestyle. At the center of communitarianism is not uniformity, but core values that affirm the dignity of the other with this first response: listen and learn. Good education explores human variability while "cultivating civic sentiments"—making relationships valuable (Ehlstain, 264).

Philip Selznick laments that communitarian responsibility and accountability are second-tier values in most thinking about how to do corporate life better. He presents re-energized themes of mutuality and stewardship as antidotes to a civic culture too stressed over the breakup of personal virtues and too sentimentally fixed on personal care to face the systemic malaise that seems to characterize contemporary life. "Obligations are...supported by love, but they arise and persist even when love is absent or hard to sustain" (Selznick, 62).

## CONTEMPORARY CHALLENGES

Progress in academic theory building, essential to cultural and knowledge revolutions, is never a blueprint. As the end of the first decade of the new millennium looms, communitarianism appears vulnerable to an array of counter-community forces. One need only note the defining day of this decade, 9/11/01, as a telling and tragic example of the loathing which communitarianism tries so arduously to counterbalance. The aftermath of that event has fueled suspicion that years of hard work rebuilding international trust may finally prove to be a failed strategy.

Whatever one may say about the stunning imbalance of power in the world, the 9/11 attacks struck at the heart of relations between peoples. No matter the hegemonic influence of global business represented by the Twin Towers, or the righteous fury of a jihadist, murder cannot be a communitarian response to unfairness or long-held grievance. The response of Western powers to the attack, initially supported by much of the world, fell far short of communitarian restraint and has yet to demonstrate that relations between people trumps suspicion and security concerns. The world seems more tense, more divided, more in need of peaceful, negotiated, dialogical resolution that ever. Communitarianism appears to be a theory without global application.

Aside from armed conflict and strategic terror—if shooting wars miraculously ceased—communitarianism would still confront the immensely influential and entrenched global business movement that acts in every way as aggressively and totalizingly as the several armies facing off in the War on Terror. Google buys YouTube. Viacom buys MTV. News Corp buys MySpace. Media convergence offers programming in new bundles, but not more or better anything, just reconfigured and sold in packages advertised as new symbols of success. The integrated capability of information technology may not spell a more integrated social planet. Why should it? Fortunes are in the balance, and fortunes matter at every level of power. Communitarianism, were it hijacked by the fortune builders or made a tool of the image sellers, would cease to be. Yet as a theoretical module opposing globalized fortune building or cultural sameness, globalized persons-as-consumers, communitarianism appears pathetically short on persuasive appeal.

Communitarianism faces an entrenched ideology in radical religion. To the degree that the Bishop Tutus and Ghandis and Dalais Lamas—peace-seeking leaders of religious movements—weigh in on the side of generosity and reconciliation, the world's competing faiths may have a season when relations between their peoples move closely to approximate the ideals which constitute the public core of their respective teachings. But sentiments are fragile. When Pope Benedict XVI quoted a medieval expositor critical of Islamic extremism in a speech in September 2006, he claimed only to be delivering an academic lecture. Around the world the reaction to this segment of his speech shows how easily (or naively) a scratch becomes a laceration, a bump becomes a blister broken and infectious. Fires destroyed remote properties and attacks on persons placated the bruised honor of Islamic movements. In such times, the bonds of sympathy touted as fundamental to communitarian relations appear as flimsy as a British parliamentarian's outspoken preference that Muslim women unveil their faces when they meet him. A world of edgy, intimidated religionists appears to be on the alert for infractions that permit a show of loyalty by drawing all but unbridgeable boundaries between faiths. Salman Rushdie survived his fatwa, but fatwa or its equivalent as tools of social negotiation, will almost surely survive him. Opposed to them are democratic rhetoricians who placate millions with repetition and post-cold-war belligerence.

Other critics have renewed perennial questions concerning communitarianism's subtle deconstruction of the West's most treasured value, freedom. Does communitarianism subvert liberty? Insofar as liberty has been understood since the Enlightenment as the right to self-ownership, communitarianism would appear to challenge and redesign. The assumed natural rights of the liberal tradition and the freedom to express those rights in a manner suiting the self are nearly synonymous with the West's shake-out of feudalism. For communitarian critic Charles Fried (2007), the conceptual question opens a host of political dilemmas: Is state prohibition of prostitution an infringement of the liberty of contract (a sale negotiated to each party's free consent)? Do anti-sex-for-sale laws reflect a community's protection of unfairly victimized weak-side bargainers on the one hand, and the long-term payees of unwanted pregnancies on the other?

Equally difficult are questions of virtual behavior: on what basis other than a community's interest in negotiated ideas of sexual purity may it impose restrictions on liberty to access graphics or other mediated forms of sex? When the restraint on liberty smacks at a biological drive so human that without it survival is jeopardized, has the community clearly overstepped? That overstep is as common as the librarian's software filter, and the FCC's imposing a tax on entertainment which draws its audience specifically in proportion to its sexual arousal. Are not all of these rules and laws examples of communitarianism's reduction of free space to an inch beyond another's nose? The common square is flattened when sensitivities as different as music preferences steal variety and entrepreneurship, replacing color with a sheen of gray. In a communitarian world, Fried implies, the worst crime is offense against a hypersensitive victims' advocate (Fried, 2007, 125).

Indeed, communitarianism may appear counter-intuitive. Martha Nussbaum notes that living bodies go "from here to there, from birth to death, never fused with any other—we are hungry and joyful and loving and needy one by one…and always continue to have separate brains and voices and stomachs" (Nussbaum, 1984, 62). We seem to carry on, each one, much as the liberal vision of individualism describes it. The hunger of the one must be relieved before hunger is relieved. No communal hunger program succeeds without very distinct bodies receiving bread. Communitarians appear to be amassing a crowd and calling the group a new reality. But hunger is felt by persons alone.

In the shadow of militarism, profit monopolies, religionists bent on mutual annihilation, and classical liberals suspicious of group-think, what are the chances communitarianism will provide the tipping point for peaceable societies and sustainable progress?

## COMMUNITARIANISM AND HISTORIC SYNTHESIS

Communitarianism has emerged in recent decades with the earmarks of a historical synthesis that bodes well for its enduring appeal. The crumbling of the Berlin Wall in 1989 signaled the end of communalism, the idea that personal identities must be submerged into the greater identity of the state. Historical work on the regimes of the late Joseph Stalin and Mao Tse-tung darken prospects that communalism will soon appear by popular choice (Chang and Halliday, 2005, 3). Likewise, atomistic individualism touted so enthusiastically in Ayn Rand's objectivism, for instance, has seen its day.

People intellectually aligned with the Enlightenment's revolt against medieval monarchies now see that the great democratic virtues of liberty and choice are won only by coalitions and "middle range" associations not dissimilar from de Tocqueville's vision. How then should persons be understood? Communitarianism provides a synthesis that promotes the relation-between as prior to selfhood, without losing selfhood.

The communitarian vision has been understood here as an emerging synthesis in which liberal individualism and tribalism each share their margins and nurture their overlapping fringes. The liberal takes membership in a wider world to be the project by which conscience is shaped by moral norms. The tribalist recognizes that norms once considered distinctive in fact are shared, that norms celebrated by one's own village—the village identity—are reflected, mirrored, and perhaps even developed among neighbors upstream (Cooper, 1989, 269). In that case, why not trade? Why not marry? Why not share literature, make speeches, inquire, talk?

At the same time, the communitarian vision claims a distinctiveness and therefore an identity apart from liberalism and tribalism, a moral center which depends on neither and cannot be reduced to the best of each. That distinctiveness is communitarianism's assertion concerning the ontological point of departure: the relation between, which generates language and norms.

Communitarianism is centered neither on the individual nor the collective, but inexorably on the integuments everywhere apparent in social institutions of all varieties and sizes. "Why talk?" was a published conversation by communications scholar Walter Ong, who answered his question in communitarian terms before the intellectual movement which employs that name congealed (Altree, 1973, 1).

But communitarianism has yet to reach a "tipping point." It remains a moment of skeptical interest in the West, a forbidden zone of distrust and danger in parts of the world, and the best explanation for political corruption in urban densities from Chicago to Kinshasa.

What climate change must communitarianism experience for its peace-building potential to rise above the distrust, nepotism, and ennui situated for centuries at the very nexus which communitarianism projects as its first-order foundation? Is there an intellectual future beyond a few books, a small movement, an occasional conference or rhetorical appeal to brother/sisterhood? In this essay, communitarianism's trajectory is cast in terms of three concluding claims.

Communitarianism must provide an account of the conscience. When a child asks about the location of the soul, pointing to her head or chest or abdomen, wondering where to probe the organ's contours, adult respondents resort to some version of "none of the above" and "all of the above." Conscience carries the same locational vagaries and sensate certainties. The contemplative person understands that personhood is equivalent to soul-awareness, the maturity of moral judgment, expansion of sympathy, prioritizing of values, exercise of choice and courage, reflective self-sacrifice, the sense that one's life matters, that one cannot resign from moral accountability, that moral choice sets personal direction and creates a profile that one increasingly recognizes to be the self, the "I am."

Communitarianism cannot situate conscience into disembodied space, the relation-between, but it can and must reorient there. Moral judgment moves us toward a future, Aristotle observed. The vegetative soul reproduces, the appetitive soul does that plus transports itself and communicates; the contemplative soul alone uses symbols to grasp the meaning of things. Humans have no other planet-sharing genus quite like themselves: hungry for explanation, restless without Verstehen, searching for shalom among the details and the macrocosms. Communitarianism insists that the orientation of the conscience be the relation of the self to other selves and to the world as it presents in ritual, social organization, literature—all moments of the quest. Communitarianism stands in dialogical contrariness to orientations fixed on the self and protests those which headily despise the other in idol worship of aggrandized self (from Nietzsche to modern consumerists.) Communitarianism insists that moral judgment serve the relation-between, embracing the other and conditioning the happiness of the self to the prosperity of that space-between. The purpose of the quest is enriched mutuality. The proper orientation of the soul—however deeply selfhood is nourished, protected, or educated—is outbound, stewardly, restless, at the other end of the day, at peace.

Second, communitarianism must articulate a persuasive moral claim beyond consensus or tradition. Michael J. Sandel (2005) makes this point in his distinction between the "free speech" claims of Martin Luther King's Selma march and the "free speech" claims of the American Nazi Party's effort to parade their swastikas through Skokie, Illinois. Sandel notes that liberals (who concede no discrimination to conceptions of the good in the judgment of rights) and communitarians (who concede the good to majoritarian will) cannot distinguish between these two events. But "common sense" makes the first proper and the second improper, because common sense sees the moral purpose of each and comes to moral judgment before rights are assigned. (Sandel, 2005, 258)

The Enlightenment insisted that moral trust is accessible to all persons of rational temper. Sociologists or poll-takers might discern majoritarian trends, but no one (children and the mentally handicapped excepted) was absent the capacity to apprehend the fixed truths which sovereignly guide moral judgment. Post-modernity abandons fixed truths. Contemporary tribalism has polarized fixed truths into dichotomies which now justify torture, genocide, strategic ruination, political favoritism, and a world order festering with rhetorical stake-planting and wall-building. The public square is now a kill-zone; the public debate a rant. Accessible moral truth a hand-me-down from leader to follower accompanied by requisite goods bearing the value sufficient to sustain life another day. Between relativism and fundamentalism, moral foundations quiver, truth evaporates, consensus declines.

Communitarianism insists that the wisdom accumulated from centuries of reflection, and the orientation of conscience toward mutuality, are grand moral claims in a sustaining pattern of norms that offer the best middle-range account of moral obligation and accountability. That claim must be situated in an appeal to human dignity and directed toward life. Life must be prized, violence must be loss.

At this point the argument warrants a word concerning religious claims, lest the vast majority of theists in our world conclude, wrongly, that their commitments are out-of-step with a communitarian convergence. Comparing the claims and histories of world religions is well beyond the scope of this chapter, and the casual assertion that all faiths converge around a few ineluctable moral verities is naïve. Nonetheless, from major faith to upstart cult, morality and spirituality are cousins of the first order. One cannot conceive a religious movement shorn of moral teaching, nor a valued moral doctrine not also embedded in a world faith. What is the communitarian to do with such a potpourri: sample it, transcend it, avoid it?

Commonly, the communitarian secularist prefers the rhetoric of public policy (justice, fairness, equity) over the religious counterpart (divine command, agape, sharia). There appears a rising volume among secularists concerning the negative impact of religion on community-building, especially as Europe and the United States stumble at exporting democracy to the Middle East and tensions rise with violence. The secularist has precious little language in common with Muslim culture, and increasingly a language intolerant of the theology and ethics of the Christian West. Dialogue requires that the religiously committed move decisively toward the rhetoric of equity if any talk will occur.

In Christian intellectual circles, the communitarian vision enjoys a developed theological apparatus and a common language. The trinitarian basis of Christian theology is itself an appeal to communitarian mutuality as explanation of the character of the godhead. This plays out in the Old and New Testament as dialogical ethics which reaches beyond the Trinity in covenantal communication with humankind. Divine commands so eminent in Christian ethics (the Ten Commandments) are famously interpreted by communities of faith operating within wider cultures. Moral accountability is situated in community norms considered under the guidance of the living presence of deity. In this context, the communitarian vision flourishes. The same happens, no doubt, in other faith contexts.

Third, communitarianism must offer hope. In his remarkable essay on hope, political scientist Glenn Tinder (1963) notes the common human "ability and desire to reach out to the remote past and the remote future" in order to understand the potential of one's life. It would seem a limitless task, nearly impossible. Yet we persist, because at the end of the journey, there lies the promise of universal peace. Historians, poets, and neuroscientists describe a similar human bent: the practice of universal norms discovered through stories re-enacted and told through time and across space (Gazzaniga, 2005, 161). We must speak to and about each other to discover the quite common moral convictions which sustain and enrich life. James Q. Wilson (1993, 234) observes:

> The idea of autonomous individuals choosing everything—their beliefs and values, their history and traditions, their social forms and family structures—is a vainglorious idea, one that could be invented only by thinkers who felt compelled to construct society out of theories.

We build culture with words primarily, but also in architecture, public policy, sculpture, film—all means of symbolic constructions wanting to connect, and the reason is hope, or as Kierkegaard put it, "a passion for what is possible." (Moltmann, 1967, 20)

Communitarianism is robust with hope, if delicately humble on past performance. History and daily journalism focus on the terrible breakdowns in the relation-between: personal disregard, institutional corruption, state-guided violence against faceless populations. The history of communitarian shalom would take fewer pages indeed. But no one thinking about people and values believes the last chapter is yet written. Hope carries each of us past "the existing situation and seeks for opportunities of bringing history into ever better correspondence to the promised future." (Moltmann, `967, 330)

We need to take the argument much further here. Each reader will reflect on texts, conversations, or meetings where present circumstance shifted toward a promise unrealized but tangible. Like a magnet pulling ions, hope lifts the line of sight from London's fog to Norway's crisp fjordic vistas. Hope breeds passion. Scholars rarely weep while reading their work publicly, but those gathered at the James Carey symposium at the University of Illinois in October 2006 did, remembering a generative presence and rehearsing key communicational concepts about which, when he died, Carey had not yet said the last word. It was a festival of hope and a celebration of intellectual community. Readers will each have their stories.

Communitarians are those who will trudge through the history of race to find a moment of mutuality between human stock of differing hues. They will tremble at the grotesque failures of mutuality, even in the last century, but insist that the future is not written by the past, even to the point of believing that mutual regard will be the flower that brings a point of color to the weed bed of human failure. Hope leads forward, overriding vengeance and pressing for peace.

On the 50th anniversary of Japan's entering the Bretton Woods accords, linking that nation's economic future to the rest of the world, ending its isolation and making it a member nation, Mieko Nishimizu (2002, quoted in Senger, 2006, 32) acknowledged the change of era that his national history represented:

> The future...differs from the past most notably in that the Earth itself is the relevant unit with which to frame and measure that future. Discriminating issues that shape the future are all fundamentally global. We belong to one inescapable network of mutuality: mutuality of ecosystems: mutuality of freer movement of information, ideas, people, capital, goods and services; and mutuality of peace and security. We are tied indeed in a single fabric of destiny on Planet Earth.

Communitarianism provides ontological footing to claims such as this; and moral direction, albeit largely experimental and frequently flawed, for how such claims may play out.

## REFERENCES

Altree, Wayne. *Why Talk? A Conversation About Language with Walter J. Ong.* San Francisco: Chandler and Sharp, 1973.

Appiah, Kwame Anthony. *Cosmopolitan: Ethics in a World of Strangers.* New York: W.W. Norton, 2006.

Bellah, Robert. *Habits of the Heart: Individualism and Commitment in American Life.* Berkeley: University of California Press, 1996.

Brown, Lee. "Understanding and Ontology in Traditional African Thought," in *African Philosophy,* edited by Lee M. Brown. New York: Oxford, 2004.

Bujo, Benezet. *Foundation of an African Ethic: Beyond the Universal Claims of Western Morality.* Nairobi: Paulines, 2001.

Chang, June and Jon Halliday. *Mao*. New York: Knopf, 2005.

Christians, Clifford G., "The Social Ethics of Agnew Heller," in *Moral Engagement in Public Life*, edited by Sharon L. Bracci and Clifford G. Christians. New York: Peter Lang, 2002.

Christians, Clifford, John Ferré, and Mark Fackler. *Good News: Social Ethics and the Press*. New York: Oxford University Press, 1993.

Cooper, Thomas W. *Communication Ethics and Global Change*. New York: Longman, 1989.

Ehlstain, Jean Bethke. "Democracy and the Politics od Difference," in *The Essentail Communitarian Reader*, edited by Amitai Etzoni. Lanham, MD: Rowman & Littlefield, 1998.

Ellul, Jacques. *The Technological Society*. Trans. by John Wilkinson. New York: Knopf, 1964.

Fergusson, David. *Community, Liberalism, and Christian Ethics*. New York: Cambridge University Press, 1998.

Fried, Charles. *Modern Liberty and the Limits of Government*. New York: Norton, 2007.

Gazzaniga, Michael S. *The Ethical Brain*. New York: Dana Press, 2005.

Hausman, Carl. *Crisis of Conscience: Perspectives on Journalism Ethics*. New York: HarperCollins, 1992.

Hocking, William Ernest. *Man and the State*. New Haven, CT: Yale University Press, 1926.

Hutchins, Robert M. *Great Books: The Foundation of a Liberal Education*. New York: Simon and Shuster, 1954.

Kirkpatrick, Frank G. *Community: A Trinity of Models*. Washington, D.C.: Georgetown University Press, 1986.

Leigh, Robert D. ed. *A Free and Responsible Press*. Chicago: University of Chicago Press, 1947.

Lewis, Tom. *Empire of the Air*. New York: HarperCollins, 1991.

MacLeish, Archibald. *Poetry and Journalism*. Minneapolis: University of Minnesota Press, 1958.

Mayor, Federico. *The World Ahead: Our Future in the Making*. New York: Palgrave, 2001.

Merrill, John C. *The Dialectic of Journalism*. Baton Rouge: Louisiana State University Press, 1989.

Merrill, John C. *The Princely Press*. Lanham, MD: University Press of America, 1998.

Moltmann, Jurgen. *Theology of Hope*. Trans by James W. Leitch. New York: Harper and Row, 1967.

Niebuhr, Reinhold. "Introduction" in *Responsibility in Mass Communication*, edited by Wilbur Schramm. New York: Harper and Row, 1957.

Nishimizu, Mieko. "Looking Back, Leaping Forward," keynote address, The 50th Anniversary of Japan's Bretton Woods Membership symposium, Tokyo, September 10, 2002.

Nussbaum, Martha C. *Sex and Social Justice*. New York: Oxford, 1999.

Percy, Walker. *Lost in the Cosmos*. New York: Washington Square Press, 1984.

Putnam, Robert D. *Bowling Alone*. New York: Simon and Shuster, 2000.

Rosen, Jay. *What Are Journalists For?* New Haven, CT: Yale University Press, 1999.

Sandel, Michael J. "The Limits of Communitarianism," in *Public Philosophy: Essays on Morality in Politics*. Cambridge, MA: Harvard University Press, 2005.

Schultze, Quentin. *Habits of the High-Tech Heart*. Grand Rapids, MI: Baker Academic, 2002.

Peter Senger, "Systems Citizenship," in *The Leader of the Future* 2, edited by Frances Hesselbein and Marshall Goldsmith. San Francisco: Jossey-Bass, 2006.

Siebert, Fred, Theodore Peterson, and Wilbur Schramm. *Four Theories of the Press*. Urbana: University of Illinois Press, 1956.

Taylor, Charles. *Sources of the Self: The Making of the Modern Identity*. Cambridge, MA: Harvard University Press, 1989.

Tinder, Glenn. *The Fabric of Hope*. Grand Rapids, MI: Eerdmans, 1999.

Tönnies, Ferdinand. *Community and Society*. Trans. by Charles P Loomis. New York: Harper Torchbooks, 1963.

Weatherford, Jack. *Genghis Khan and the Making of the Modern World*. New York: Three Rivers Press, 2004.

Wilson, James Q. *The Moral Sense*. New York: Free Press, 1993.

Wiredu, Kwasi. *Cultural Universals and Particulars*. Bloomington: Indiana University Press, 1996.

# 23

# Freedom of Expression and the Liberal Democratic Tradition

## G. Stuart Adam

Although modern democracies come in many forms and varieties, each is a complex human system that reflects the constitutive power of certain basic principles. Beneath the layers and accretions of procedure and purpose, the principles that guide their various practices include guarantees in law or convention,

- that legislatures will be responsible for making and modifying the law;
- that elections for determining the composition of legislatures and the executive will be held regularly;
- that all adult citizens are enfranchised;
- that the law (rather than the arbitrary will of officials) is supreme and enforced by an independent judiciary;
- that citizens are free to form associations; and
- that speech and expression are free.

Each of these principles is foundational, so it doesn't make a lot of sense to say one is more important than the other. However, it does make sense to say that the other principles would not operate properly if speech were not free—if the operations of government, social institutions, and the state were not subject to scrutiny and criticism. So for a long time—at least since the early 18th century—democratic theory has pointed to free expression as the lubricant that allows the machinery of democracy to function. It was said as early as 1704, for example, when British writers were pressing for the reform of the law of seditious libel, that "...there's no Freedom either civil or ecclesiastical, but where the liberty of the Press is maintained" (Tindal, 1704, 14). A parallel view was expressed by an anonymous writer in the mid-18th century who said the press's freedom is the "most valuable branch of our constitution; to which we owe being a free people" (Anon, *Old England*, 1747) To some writers the freedom of the press "was the "palladium of the English Constitution" (Anon, *The English Review*, 1787, 313) and to others it was "the only necessary law to the Constitution" (Carlile, 1823, cited in Wickwar, 1928).

In due course, the beliefs sponsoring such commentary would be inscribed formally on democratic constitutions. To take two familiar examples—an early and a late one—the First Amendment of the Constitution of the United States (1791) says that Congress shall make no law abridging "freedom of speech or of the press" and section 2(b) of the Canadian Charter of Rights and Freedoms (1982) declares that the fundamental freedoms include "freedom of thought, belief, opinion and expression, including freedom of the press and other media of communication."

In what follows I will attempt to elucidate the idea behind such constitutional provisions. First, I explore in some detail the arguments John Milton published in his pamphlet Aeropagitica in 1644. It continues to be the most influential meditation on the subject in the English language as it provides the inspirational basis for what I call the liberal part of the argument. I will then describe the way in which the idea later evolved so that it connected personal freedom forcefully to the broader project of democratic life and governance. I conclude with observations on the moral and legal context within which the concept applies and a further reflection on its current meaning. Along the way I assume that journalists have a special responsibility for understanding and reflecting in their work the effects of a vigorously understood principle of free expression.

A final note by way of introduction: Although I do not distinguish carefully in this text between forms of democracy—between populist and liberal democracy, for example —liberal democracy is the model I have in mind. In this respect, I follow political theorist Amy Gutman's view that liberal democracies not only encourage "the self-determination of individuals under conditions of interdependence," but also "qualify the value of popular rule by recognizing a set of basic liberties that take priority over popular rule" (Gutman; 411, 413).

## THE INTELLECTUAL ARGUMENT

It was the renewal of licensing in June 1643, after two years of Puritan control of Parliament, which led Milton to write the *Areopagitica*. Published as a pamphlet, it was in some respects an essay in Reformation theology. It contains vivid echoes of the divisions within the Christian church between Roman Catholics and Protestant reformers and, within the Church of England itself, between traditionalists and Puritan dissenters. It also contains the direct echoes of the political divisions that were at issue in the period of the English Civil Wars and the later disposal of the King. Oliver Cromwell, who was the political leader of the dissenters and who, in due course, would become Lord Protector, was first elected to Parliament in 1640. Such was the religious and political context in which Milton's essay was published.

The treatise was ostensibly addressed to Parliament, which Milton compared, tendentiously, to the mythic Greek court of Areopagus where perfect justice was supposed to have prevailed. The many references to classical and Biblical texts testify to Milton's erudition: and the power and scope of the argument testify to his ingenuity and intellect, although it may be added, it was not without the stain of prejudice. In a text in which toleration was identified strongly as a virtue, Milton seemed to exclude Roman Catholics, his religious adversaries, from the benefits of liberty when he wrote:

> ...if all cannot be of one mind—as who looks they should be?—this doubtless is more wholesome, more prudent, and more Christian, that many be tolerated, rather than all compelled. I mean not tolerated popery, and open superstition, which, as it extirpates all religious and civil supremacies, so itself should be extirpate, provided first that all charitable and compassionate means be used to win and regain the weak and the misled..." (Milton, 747)

Despite his evident hostility toward Roman Catholic doctrines and principles of religious organization, Milton was not suggesting a special licensing system for Catholics. He was only commenting on how the laws of sedition and blasphemy might be applied in the wake of free publication. It was licensing—the pre-censorship or what moderns would call the prior restraint of books and papers—to which he was objecting in the *Areopagitica*, but it is important to note that his arguments could well have challenged contemporary notions of sedition and blasphemy.

However, it was no accident that Milton singled out his religious adversaries. He was avowedly Protestant and the first part of *Areopagitica* is devoted to showing that the philosophy of the Church of Rome was the inspiration for the practice of licensing that the Protestant parliamentarians had just re-established. In the classical world of the Greeks and Romans, he said, blasphemous works were prosecuted after they had been published, not before. It was the influence of the Church that led to indexing and licensing. He wrote:

> …primitive councils and bishops were wont only to declare what books were not commendable, passing no further, but leaving it to each one's conscience to read or lay by, till after the year 800…when the Popes of Rome, engrossing what they pleased of political rule into their own hands, extended their dominion over men's eyes as they had before over their judgments, burning and prohibiting to be read what they fancied not. (Milton, 724)

According to Milton, the culminating event in the process of aggrandizement and irrationality was the Inquisition, a point which would not have been lost on the Protestants of the day. Thus, he concluded the first part of his presentation with the claim:

> We have it not that can be heard of, from any ancient state, or polity or church, nor by an statue left us by our ancestors elder or later, nor from the modern custom of any reformed city or church abroad; but from the most antichristian council The Council of Trent and the most tyrannous inquisition that ever inquired. Till then books were ever as freely admitted into the world as any other birth; the issue of the brain was no more stifled than the issue of the womb. (Milton, 725)

Despite the obvious energy Milton put into the part of the presentation dealing with the history of licensing—it occupied one-third of the text—he was wise enough to admit that the fact the Church of Rome invented it was not itself sufficient reason for rejecting it. As he wrote, "…some will say, what though the inventors were bad, the thing for all that may be good" (Milton, 725). The sense of his position was simply that it would be wise to look skeptically upon any "fruit" of the Church of Rome. He was suggesting a prudential skepticism and suggesting, further, that the return to licensing, which was the occasion for his pamphlet, was probably a betrayal of the Reformation. But at the same time he admitted that the constraints of good argument forced him to make the case on its merits alone. Accordingly, Milton concentrated in the balance of his presentation on three interwoven, but nevertheless distinctive, sets of claims. The first concerned some essentially practical questions bearing on the utility of licensing. The second and third concerned the evil effects of licensing measured against Reformation notions of rationality and virtue. It is the formulation of these arguments for which *Areopagitica* is remembered.

On a practical level, Milton said that licensing "conduces nothing to the end for which it was framed" (Milton, 731). For one thing, it did not put a stop to seditious or blasphemous writing. Those who want to take the risks and circulate their material will do so regardless of the licenser, he said. "Do we not see, not once or oftener, but weekly —that continued Court libel against the Parliament and City…dispersed among us, for all licensing can do?" (Milton, 733). Besides, he said, dissenting or schism-producing ideas need not be circulated through the press. They may be passed on mouth-to-mouth and a licenser is impotent to stop them.

Furthermore, licensing actually leads to a result that is the opposite to the one intended. Milton argued that the act of forbidding certain ideas from being circulated gives them a significance they would not otherwise possess. In this vein, he wrote that "instead of suppressing sects and schism, it raises them and invests them with a reputation" (Milton, 739). He added, parenthetically, that if the act was intended to cultivate manners and virtue in English society, it would only be consistent to regulate other activities in the same manner. In a mocking tone, he wrote: "If we think to regulate printing, thereby to rectify manners, we must regulate all recreations and pastimes, all that is delightful to man. No music must be heard, no song be set or sung, but what is grave and Doric…Who shall be the rectors of daily rioting? And what shall be done to inhibit the multitude that frequent those houses where drunkenness is old and harbored?" (Milton, 732).

Finally, in a tone, which could well have suited the 20th century, Milton said that if the licensing system was to be effective—that is, to cultivate manners and improve thought—such effectiveness would be dependant on the quality of the licenser. He put the case this way: If a licensing system is to be used to improve society, then it is important that the licenser be "above the common measure, both studious, learned and judicious" (Milton, 733). But how could it be so? Milton asked. The work is tedious, "an unpleasing journey-work" which could have only one result—namely, that the licenser would be "either ignorant, imperious and remiss, or largely pecuniary" (Milton, 733). To give his argument a modern twist, he was saying that the leveling hand of bureaucracy would likely kill the very improvements its sponsors sought to foster.

In short, there was a compelling case, based primarily on practical considerations, for putting licensing aside. But the real force of Milton's case was dependent on his exposition of the conditions that ought to circumscribe moral and rational life. In this respect, he put aside arguments that focused on the impotence of the act to achieve its goals and brought into view the positive evils it would cause. The sense of his argument was that licensing is destructive of reason and virtue, the two things men of God and justice should be interested in cultivating.

At the core of this and several collateral claims were images of man and mind which were utterly Protestant—that is to say, individualistic and rationalistic. In making his case Milton was pushing, as his contemporary Thomas Hobbes would push, the individual rather than the community into the foreground of consciousness. Milton said that individual men are capable of investigating and arriving at the nature of truth unaided by priests or politicians and an enlightened society is one that takes the faculty of reason and gives it a life—in individuals. Not to do so is "undervaluing and vilifying the whole nation" (Milton, 735). He went on to say that "…to distrust the judgment and the honesty of one who hath but a common repute in learning and never yet offended, as not to count him fit to print his mind without a tutor and examiner, lest he should drop a schism, or something of corruption, is the greatest displeasure and indignity to a free and knowing spirit that can be put upon him" (Milton, 735).

But granting freedom to such individuals was not merely a matter of recognizing and allowing for the conditions of human dignity. There was a theological and, one could say, utilitarian justification as well. According to Milton, the intellectual power possessed by an individual, however modest, was almost literally a fragment of the divine. The God of Milton's imagination was a God of Reason and the venue of this reason was man's mind. Thus to discourage independent thought through licensing was to deprive society of *reason* itself. He wrote,"…who kills a man kills a reasonable creature, God's image; but he who destroys a good book, kills reason itself, kills the image of God, as it were, in the eye….a good book is the precious lifeblood of a master spirit, embalmed and treasured up on purpose to a life beyond" (Milton, 730).

Although he enshrined reason in the minds of independent men, Milton did not at the same time exclude evil and irrationality from the picture. Falsehood and vice were in man's mind just as truth and virtue were. But his faith was such that the growth of rationality and virtue could only occur in the face of falsehood and evil. He did not believe, for example, that a "cloistered virtue," or a virtue proceeding from obedience, were virtues at all. Virtue could only come into being when it was enacted independently by individuals who could also choose to do evil. Thus, the dominion of rationality and virtue—a dominion that was guaranteed in faith—would only come about through the interplay of opposing forces in a marketplace of ideas.

The idea of this marketplace is implied in a passage that occurred early in the text when he wrote that "all opinions, yea errors, know, read and collated, are of main service and assistance toward the speedy attainment of what is truest" (Milton, 727). Much later in the text, it received fuller treatment. He wrote:

> And though all the winds of doctrine were let loose to play upon the earth, so Truth be in the field, we do injuriously by licensing and prohibiting to misdoubt her strength. Let her and Falsehood grapple; who ever knew Truth put to the worse, in a free and open encounter. Her confuting is the best and surest suppressing. (746)

It made no difference to the principle at stake that reason and virtue were measurably distinct concepts. Where good and evil (as opposed to truth and falsehood) were the entangled elements, the marketplace operated in much the same way. "Good and evil we know in the field of this world grow up together almost inseparably; and the knowledge of good is so involved and inter-woven with the knowledge of evil; and in so many cunning resemblances hardly to be discerned, that those confused seeds which were imposed on Psyche as an incessant labor to cull out and sort asunder" (Milton, 728).

He concluded this last passage with the question "what wisdom can there be to choose what continence to forbear without the knowledge of evil?" (Milton, 728).

Milton went further in the substance of the argument and the rhetoric of persuasion. He wrote prophetically, convinced that he possessed direct knowledge of God's will. He claimed, for example, "god is decreeing to begin some new and great period in his church, even to the reforming of the reformation itself" (Milton, 747). But all the arguments, based on the theology and philosophy of his brand of low-church Protestantism, led inevitably to the claim he laid out in the opening passages of the text, namely, that licensing "could be primely to the discouragement of all learning and the stop of truth, not only by disexercising and blunting our abilities in what we know already, but by hindering and cropping the discovery that might be yet further made in both religious and civil wisdom" (Milton, 720).

The cadence to the argument resonates in the mind of every good liberal as it was Milton who said, "Give me liberty to know, to utter and to argue freely according to conscience, above all liberties" (Milton, 746).

## CONNECTIONS TO LIBERAL DEMOCRACY

John Milton made the first and most influential case for the individual right of freedom of expression. But he wasn't the only one. He had argued for the removal of the restraints of licensing and constructed a case that would in later centuries demolish others, particularly those associated with the law of seditious libel. In making such a case, he offered as its dividend an inspirational vision of material, philosophical, spiritual, and moral progress. He did this, as we have seen, within the frame of his version of Christian belief. Later writers would in due course argue in a more secular voice and tie the theory of free expression more directly to a vision of democratic process and governance. Individual freedom would not only be an essential condition of social life; it would also be an essential condition for the operation of a democratic government.

In my view there are two grounds on which rights of free expression are justified. The first is the ground of natural right. In this tradition it is asserted simply that there are certain rights that are inviolable and the state has no positive right to deprive a citizen of them. It is assumed simply that individual rights are cosmic, located in nature and, if denied, are deformed by the authority of the state. A natural rights position promotes the view that the record of human thought and expression stands on its own as a starting point for social and political life. There is a sense in which Milton expressed a natural rights view.

If one is uncomfortable with the implications of a natural rights philosophy and contemplates the construction of a system of free expression, one can slip into a utilitarian position. It is the dominant line among those who have argued historically for a democratic system of free expression. The American legal scholar, Thomas Emerson who has written thoughtfully on this subject, is among those who propose a utilitarian understanding of what he calls the affirmative theory. He formulates four functions or, to use the more classical language, utilities, which the system of free expression ought to serve. He says: "Maintenance of a system of free expression is necessary (1) as a method of assuring individual self fulfillment, (2) as a means of attaining the truth, (3) as a method of securing participation by the members of society in social, including political decision making, and (4) as a means of maintaining the balance between stability and change in the society" (Emerson, 1966, 3).

The philosopher of individuality and self-development is pre-eminently John Stuart Mill. He followed the example set by Milton, but his view of the individual was purely secular. He did not invoke a deity to forecast virtue and rationality. But he did believe that freedom, rationality, and virtue were companions. In his essay, *On Liberty* (1859), he said that "the source of everything respectable in man either as an intellectual or moral being [is that] his errors are corrigible. He is capable of rectifying his mistakes, by discussion and experience. Not by experience alone. There must be discussion, to show how experience is to be interpreted" (J. S. Mill, 1859/2006, 26–27).

John Stuart Mill's aim was to convince his fellow Britons that they should encourage, on a society-wide scale, opportunities for all individuals to grow intellectually. He went on to say: "It really is of importance, not only what men do, but also what manner of men they are that do it. Among the works of man, which human life is rightly employed in perfecting and beautifying, is man himself" (J. S. Mill, 68).

So for Mill and for others the right to know, to contemplate, to reflect and to choose and express oneself was justified by the promise that any individual would become more accomplished, more thoughtful and more wise than he or she might have been if the field of information and truth was not unduly restricted. For John Stuart Mill the cultivation of the individual and of individuality was a primary cultural goal that was obviously connected to the project of truth, Emerson's second function.

As noted, Milton created the foundations for a trust in individual reason as the medium for the pursuit of truth. Milton had said in the seventeenth century that, "...our faith and knowledge thrives by exercise.... Truth is a streaming fountain; if her waters flow not in perpetual progression, they sicken into a muddy pool of conformity and tradition" (Milton, 745). Milton believed that the removal of a censoring power and the emancipation of the intellect would produce wisdom and insight in all fields. The promise was that individual insight would become collective knowledge. Ideas originating in individuals would in due course be incorporated into society and in due course shape its development.

John Stuart Mill added memorable words to this belief when he provided his four-part strategy for promoting truth through the device of free speech. He said, first that

> if any opinion is compelled to silence, that opinion may, for aught we can certainly know, be true.
> To deny this is to assume our own fallibility. Secondly, though the silenced opinion be an error,

it may…contain a portion of truth; and since the general or prevailing opinion on any subject is rarely or never the whole truth, it is only by the collision of adverse opinions that the remainder of the truth has any chance of being supplied. Thirdly, even if the received opinion be not only true, but the whole truth; unless it is suffered to be, and actually is, vigorously and earnestly contested, it will, by most of those who receive it, be held in the manner of a prejudice, with little comprehension or feeling of its rational grounds. And not only this, but, fourthly, the meaning of the doctrine itself will be in danger of being lost, or enfeebled, and deprived of its vital effect on the character and conduct: the dogma becoming a mere formal profession, inefficacious for good, but cumbering the ground and preventing the growth of any real and heartfelt conviction…. (J. S. Mill, 60, 61)

So John Stuart Mill, writing in the mid-19th century, put a cap on the belief Milton promoted in the mid-17th century that individual freedom was the best guarantor of intellectual progress.

The philosophers of participatory decision making, Emerson's third function, connected such individual freedom directly to democratic life and amongst them in the English-speaking world none is more important than John Stuart Mill's father, James. He wrote a major essay on the subject titled "Liberty of the Press" (1825) for an early edition of the *Encyclopedia Britannica* in which he said that "[t]he point of greatest importance to [government] is, to keep the people at large from complaining, or from knowing or thinking that they have any ground of complaint. If this object is fully attained, they may then, without anxiety, and without trouble, riot in the pleasures of misrule" (J. Mill, 1825/1967, 18).

In James Mill's view the method of preventing governors from rioting in the pleasures of misrule would be to install a system of reporting and commentary on the activities of government. In his view, these rights of reporting and commentary would be subject only to very limited notions of seditious libel and by the law of civil defamation. The rest would be free territory. He wrote:

The end which is sought…by allowing anything to be said in censure of the government, is, to ensure the goodness of government…. If the goodness of government could be ensured by any preferable means, it is evident that all censure of the government ought to be prohibited. All discontent with the government is only good, in so far as it is a means of removing real cause of discontent. (J. Mill, 18)

Accordingly, he said, "the only means of removing the defects of vicious governments [is through] the freedom of the press" or, as he put it later in this passage, the freedom of the press "is the greatest safeguard of the interests of mankind" (J. Mill, 18).

Many democratic theorists, including James Mill, argued the case for freedom in the name of Emerson's fourth function, the maintenance of a balance between stability and change. The position is part and parcel of a simple theory of democracy that says nothing more profound than if people have the freedom to know, to utter, and to argue, as Milton had asked, they will be heard and their grievances will be redressed. In other words, a recourse to violence would be unnecessary. It is such an understanding that governs a liberal and very limited interpretation of the law of seditious libel. Historically, that law or the laws it has inspired has been used conservatively on occasion against opponents of the social and political order. I am refering not only to the Alien and Sedition Acts, but later attempts to silence communists. The current discontents involving Islamic fundamentalists in Britain calling for jihad may tempt politicians similarly to reassess liberal standards, which do include limits on free speech by notions of incitement. A way of putting it is to say that the liberal view is speech that starts an argument is free; speech that incites a riot or a violent act is not: more on this below.

In sum, Emerson's functions can be used to explore and justify the sources and justifications for the right of freedom of expression. But there is more to the concept than that. Democratic theory incorporates an operational principle of majority rule—in elections, in votes in the legislatures and even on judicial panels. So the principle of majority rule is a defining feature of democratic governance.

But John Stuart Mill argued that such a principle, important though it may be, should itself be limited. He said that majorities should not deprive individuals of their rights of free expression. He said the notion that "the people have no need to limit their power over themselves might seem axiomatic when popular government was a thing only dreamed about...." But in light of the serious aim of promoting individual human growth and the attendant benefits to all society he said it is necessary to protect individuals from the majority. He went on to say:

> The limitation...of the power over individuals loses none of its importance when the holders of power are regularly accountable to the community.... Protection...against the tyranny of the magistrate is not enough. There needs protection also against the tyranny of the prevailing opinion and feeling; against the tendency of society to impose...its own ideas and practices as rules of conduct on those who dissent from them. (J. S. Mill, 10–11)

In other words, the system would not be democratic if a democratic principle could be used to usurp the individual rights on which the system was dependent. Moreover, the protections, while certainly necessary to protect individuals from the power of legislatures, were also necessary to protect individuals from the tyranny of convention and consensus in society at large.

In summary, what liberal philosophers had in common, although they expressed it differently and with different goals in mind, is the belief that certain liberties or rights must be secure for a recognizably democratic system to occur. For example, there cannot be a democracy if the right to oppose is not secure; nor can there be a democracy if governments possess the power to define the meaning of events and values; nor can there be democracy if governments are not themselves governed by rules. Accordingly, a fundamental rule out of which democracies are constructed is the rule that says speech will be free. No government possesses the right to abrogate this fundamental freedom. Put a little differently the act of governance in democracies is circumscribed by the notion of free expression. The limit on the power of governments is established by an understanding that the majorities they represent can, without violating other democratic rules, destroy the very rights on which the whole system turns. To give full license to the idea of majority rule without providing a limit to it would in the end be a denial of democracy itself.

The image or analogy that best suits this line of thinking comes as much from architecture as from philosophy. This is not to deny that philosophical questions are important in the resolution of the puzzles of democratic theory, but rather to acknowledge that we build systems of politics and governance just as we build buildings. As a consequence, the fundamental freedoms may be seen as the architectural foundations on which the democratic edifice rests. In the meantime, the steps that make it possible for liberal democrats to advocate freedom of expression with such determination includes the reasons we have already reviewed. Most importantly and directly, they include: (1) a prudential concern that politicians and officials may be tempted to turn the machinery of the state to narrow and self-serving purposes; (2) a belief that virtue and progress are more likely to come from acts of individual choice rather than acts of compulsion; (3) a belief that activities of the state, conceived in the broadest political as well as in a narrow governmental sense, are the public's business; and (4) a belief that individuals summed up into a public can be trusted. With respect to this last point, it does not follow that no judgment or sanction should ever be imposed on speech. Rather, it is believed that in order for the benefits of freedom to occur, the court of public opinion should normally be used to censure and condemn evil or injurious speech and that the law and regulatory powers of the state should be used only for the narrowest and rarest of reasons.

The point that the law might be used to limit occasions of speech, calls for a postscript of sorts. The statement that the regulatory powers of the state might be used at all, however rarely and however minimally, seems to contradict the letter and spirit of the ideas we have been considering. But in practice, freedom, like pretty well everything else, is circumscribed. For example, James Mill recognized, in his powerful defense of the press's freedom, that as a practical matter the law of civil defamation should be used to protect individuals from unjustified injuries to their reputations. He also defended a carefully and narrowly defined concept of seditious libel that could legitimately be used to protect democratic institutions from disruptions that would prevent them from operating. Similarly, John Stuart Mill's *On Liberty* contains a justification for limits on speech that might incite rioting or put an individual or group at risk. In this vein, he said an

> opinion that corn-dealers are starvers of the poor, or that private property is robbery, ought to be unmolested when simply circulated through the press, but may justly incur punishment when delivered orally to an excited mob assembled before the house of a corn-dealer, or when handed about the same mob in the form of a placard. (J. S. Mill, 64)

Mill's corn-dealers' example foreshadows the rule Oliver Wendell Holmes enunciated in the Schenk case (1919) in which he commented that it would be a crime to falsely shout fire in a crowded theater and thereby cause panic.

Thomas Emerson notes more broadly that certain goals of society, particularly those associated with the administration of justice, can come into conflict with the exercise of free speech. He is thinking of the prohibition that forbids the circulation of testimony adduced in a grand jury in the United States (or a preliminary hearing in Canada) or the requirement that a judge under the law of contempt can require a journalist to reveal the name of a source when the fact it might yield is crucial to the resolution of a criminal case. He says thoughtfully that in "constructing and maintaining a system of freedom of expression, the principal problems and major controversies have arisen when the attempt is made to fit the affirmative theory—that is the affirmative functions served by the system—into a more comprehensive scheme of social values and social goals." (Emerson, 1966, 15) Emerson is saying that certain limitations on freedom of expression may be justified, but it is inadvisable to enact them until an affirmative theory justifying freedom is firmly established and incorporated. He notes that

> the theory of freedom of expression involves more than a technique for arriving at better social judgments through democratic procedures. It comprehends a vision of society, a faith and a whole way of life.... It contemplates a mode of life that, through encouraging toleration, skepticism, reason and initiative, will allow man to realize his full potentialities. It spurns the alternative of a society that is tyrannical, conformist, irrational and stagnant. It is this concept of society that was embodied in the first amendment. (Emerson, 1966, 14)

So the affirmative theory is a comprehensive doctrine of the sources and expectations associated with freedom of expression. The challenge has been to justify freedom resolutely and in a manner that will prevent erosions. In other words, Emerson invites us to consider a powerful doctrine of freedom expression of the press and then to assimilate it—one could say almost reluctantly and only out of necessity—into other social, and particularly legal, goals of society.

Perhaps a second and brief postscript should be added. Milton asked in the *Areopagitica* to be given liberty "to know, to utter and to argue freely according to conscience, above all liberties." His words are remembered for the freedom they proclaimed—less so, I imagine, for the solemn obligation that conditioned his declaration. So it is important to stress that he included the words "according to conscience" in his cadence. Thus, the tradition of freedom calls on those who claim it not to deceive or to lie and, more positively, to act in good faith.

## APPLICATIONS TO JOURNALISM

Journalistic activity has always been looked upon by some individuals or groups with suspicion and fear. In the 19th century, when James Mill wrote his essay on the press, the social and political elites wanted to limit and control the press, no doubt because they could then "riot in the pleasures of misrule." That James Mill thought so is no surprise. Nor is it a surprise that democrats such as James and John Stuart Mill and many who wrote in the century before them would identify with the career and welfare of the press, an upstart institution that was challenging those very elites. The faith in the press as an instrument for achieving good works began when the democratic spirit took hold and challenged established power.

But now, that phase of the democratic revolution is over. To some degree the press is an established institution or even part of an establishment and it has become, accordingly, harder to believe that it possesses and acquits the democratic mandate it once did. Members of the left—those committed to political correctness particularly—are sometimes tempted to suspect that the press is not a genuinely democratic institution. So they join other groups speaking a conservative language in discrediting it and the journalists who man it.

Another reason that complicates the application of the "liberal" blueprint to journalists is the word "media." That word directs attention to institutions in which most journalists work rather than to journalists themselves. Such institutions may be very large and, notwithstanding profound differences in function, they have some of the characteristics of major commercial, entertainment and industrial enterprises. In this vein, Russell Baker has noted, as current newspapers fall under the control of corporations attuned to profit rather than public service, that some of what we once called the press and journalism has become entangled in the "squalor" of a "vague organism called 'media'" (Baker, 2007, 12).

Yet another reason is that journalists have agendas for covering society's stories and issues that don't always square obviously with their democratic obligations. The operations and practices of the news media sometimes confuse members of the public and seem to them sometimes to be remotely connected to the difficult chore of supporting the democratic edifice. The agenda might embrace, for example, the for-sale sign on Paris Hilton's LA mansion as well as the Supreme Court's deliberations on matters related to *Roe vs. Wade*. Finally, journalists are not able to camouflage their errors in judgment and behavior. Like the politicians whose work they so carefully monitor, their limitations and errors—and their courage and acumen—are public events.

Still, it is important to continue to recognize that there is much to be gained by conferring a wide measure of freedom on journalists to practice their craft as they see fit. First, the right or liberty is conferred on citizens. It is they who have the right to know what is going on about them and what the government is doing on their behalf. Equally, they have the right or liberty as citizens to "utter and to argue freely." Second, if citizens have these liberties, then journalists possess them as well. It is hard to imagine it being otherwise. That some citizens exercise these rights and freedoms more vigorously than others is consistent with the division of labor in complex societies. This is not to make a virtue of the size and complexity of our society, bur rather to recognize, perhaps even tragically, that such divisions of labor and specialization are inevitable.

Put a little differently, the division of labor in a complex society makes it inevitable that specialists will emerge in the areas of communication and culture. In this respect, society's writers, including all who make a living as journalists, are on the receiving end of an act of delegation. Fundamental rights of freedom or expression are handled by journalists on behalf of the members of the public who are more distant from the centers of political and public action. The exercise of these rights by writers, broadcasters, and journalists in a complex society is what brings the democratic process into being. Journalists and writers start the process of discussion and judgment by conveying and commenting on the news. They flood the air with stories and opinions covering an enormous range of political and social events. In a rough way, the notion that guides their work is that there is a public that is interested in what they say. That the law permits them a wide territory within which to practice their craft is consistent with the aims of democracy: the more freedom, the more discussion, the more democracy.

But to say the process begins with journalist and journalism is obviously different from saying it ends with them. The public discussion begins in part where journalists sign off. Political, religious, and moral discussion in society at large, along with gossip and trivia, take some of what is contained in journalism as points of reference. But for political and governmental discussion considered on its own, the relation between the journalists and the public is both vital and profound.

To say that it could be arranged and done better and with better effects is obvious. To say that it is never done well is to fail to examine carefully what the best of our journalists are able to achieve under difficult circumstances. To say that journalists carry the full burden of responsibility for democracy is to miss the point. The key point is to recognize that in a developed society, we give a life to the notion of freedom of expression and democracy by conferring rights on citizens and by encouraging journalists especially to enact those rights. This is how we do it.

Accordingly, the journalist's perspective on freedom of expression and the body of reasoning it implies is that democracy is the issue. The ability of journalists to practice their craft turns on the manner in which the rights of freedom are secured in law and tradition. Put differently, citizens need these rights to be citizens of a democracy; creative people such as journalists need these rights in order to be genuinely and safely creative. These are not differences in kind so much as they are differences in degree. But they explain why journalists see themselves as being specially associated with the defense of these rights.

## REFERENCES

Anon. *Old England*, no. 187, Nov. 28, 1747.

Anon. *The English Review*, Vol. 9, (1787), p. 313.

Russell Baker. "Goodbye to Newspapers?" *New York Review of Books*, Vol. 54, no. 13, 2007.

Richard Carlile. Article in *The Republican*, July 11, 1823.

Thomas I. Emerson. *Toward a General Theory of the First Amendment*. New York, 1966.

Amy Gutman. "Democracy" in Robert Goodwin and Philip Petit, eds. *A Companion to Contemporary Political Philosophy*. Oxford, 1933.

James Mill. *Essays on Government, Jurisprudence, Liberty of the Press, and the Law of Nations*. New York, 1967. (Original work published 1825)

John Stuart Mill. *On Liberty and the Subjection of Women* (Alan Ryan ed.), London, 2006. (Original work published 1859)

John Milton. *Aeropagitica* in *John Milton: Complete Poems and Major Prose* (Merritt Y. Hughes ed.). New York, 1957. (Original work published 1644)

Mathew Tindal. *Reasons against retraining the Press*. London, 1704.

William Wickwar. *The Struggle for Freedom of the Press, 1819–1832*. London, 1928.

# 24

# Media Ownership in a Corporate Age[1]

## Matthew P. McAllister and Jennifer M. Proffitt

Summer 2007 was big for News Corp., owner of various Fox subsidiaries and one of the largest media conglomerates in the world. One celebrated event for the corporation was the global premiere of *The Simpsons Movie*, a theatrical film based on the very long-running Fox network television series. As part of the massive publicity campaign for the movie, Matt Groening, the creator of *The Simpsons*, appeared on a late July installment of the U.S. cable television program *The Daily Show*, hosted by Jon Stewart. At one point during the interview, they had this exchange:

*Groening:* We love biting the hand that feeds us [on *The Simpsons*]. We love attacking Fox. It's really good. But let me clarify. There are many suction cups on the tentacles of the News Corp octopus.
*Stewart:* I believe they've just added a whole other arm.
*Groening:* Yes, We're a little suction cup at *The Simpsons*. But we've gotten in trouble for attacking Fox News, for instance.
*Stewart:* Is that true?
*Groening:* Yes. We had an episode in which we had Fox News, and we had the little news crawl. And that was one of our favorite moments.
*Stewart:* That was wonderful.
*Groening:* "Albert Einstein plus Brad Pitt equals Dick Cheney." That was one. "Rupert Murdoch, terrific dancer." That was another. We have been forbidden from doing that again. Because the Fox viewer might confuse our cartoon with actual news.

This impish exchange raises several issues about media ownership in a corporate age. Media corporations are indeed "multi-armed" entities that may consider a billion dollar-plus brand like *The Simpsons* to be "little," even as a multi-media blitz for it is in full force. Ownership potentially affects the viewpoint and tone of both journalism (à la the Fox News cable channel; see Proffitt, 2007a) and non-journalistic entertainment (hand slapping of *The Simpsons*). Media creators may feel pressure to fit in with corporate agendas, either by promoting agenda items/ worldviews or by not criticizing them (true even if in this specific case Groening was joking— and it is unclear if he completely was). And giant media octopi are constantly looking to add useful tentacles, such as News Corp's acquisition of the Dow Jones Corporation during that same summer, alluded to by Stewart.

Such characteristics of corporate media ownership have implications for the media's role in democracy, for diversity, for policy, and for ethics—on a variety of levels. This chapter will discuss basic trends and implications of large media ownership in a corporate age by engaging much of the increasingly sizable literature on mega-media corporations. The first section will briefly review the nature of large-media ownership today, including reasons for why it has taken the form that it has. Following this, the chapter will explore concerns about how large corporate media ownership may undermine democracy. The chapter will conclude with a discussion of ownership and media ethics.

## THE NATURE OF CORPORATE MEDIA OWNERSHIP

Concerns about who owns the media have existed at least since the adolescence of industrial-age media: Max Weber, one of the founders of sociology, argued in a 1910 speech about the need to be wary of the dangers of newspaper "trusts," among other economic forces upon media (Weber, 1910/1976). Although not analyses of specific media ownership patterns per se, the work of certain Frankfurt School theorists assumed monolithic ownership structures and foreshadowed modern criticisms of media ownership, such as standardization of content (Horkheimer & Adorno, 1948/2001). Concentration and conglomeratization of media became an object of study by journalistic and media studies scholars with the 1983 publication of *The Media Monopoly* by Ben H. Bagdikian and subsequent updates (such as Bagdikian, 2004). Robert McChesney is also a key scholar in foregrounding, from a critical media studies perspective, large media ownership (especially 1999, 2004). Other scholars have also looked critically at general media ownership patterns (e.g., Alger, 1998; Baker, 2007; Barnouw et al., 1997; Bettig & Hall, 2003; Croteau & Hoynes, 2006; Hesmondhalgh, 2002; Schiller, 1989; in addition to the medium-specific work discussed below).

Not all scholars believe media ownership is sufficiently concentrated to warrant concern. Compaine argues in one of his authored chapters in the often-cited work *Who Owns the Media*, that the number of "leading firms" in the media industries is increasing (Compaine & Gomery, 2000, Chapter 8). In another work, he calls the idea of a media monopoly a "myth," citing as evidence his own industry data and previous quantitative studies about ownership and content diversity/quality (Compaine, 2005).

However, Baker (2007) specifically answers Compaine's claim of a plethora of media owners with several counter-arguments, including these four: (1) concentration may be more apparent if one considers media separately, rather than as one large entity that sums all companies regardless of medium; (2) media organizations may serve different, but essential functions in a given industry such as production, distribution and exhibition, and can therefore leverage industrial power through such ownership strategies as vertical and horizontal integration; (3) specific markets, especially in local areas, may belie what seems to be a more open market nationally in some circumstances; and (4) quantitative studies that correlate ownership with content are often problematic measures of ownership dangers, given the general philosophy of checks and balances of ownership in democracy (more on this in a later section) and the difficulty of operationalizing and measuring nebulous concepts like "diversity." About this latter point, Einstein has argued that her own quantitative data has been narrowly interpreted by pro-industry forces to justify self-interested deregulation policies (see her trade journal piece, Einstein, 2004, commenting on data found in Einstein, 2003; see also Kunz, 2007, p. vii). Others have also argued that while smaller media producers still exist, they are increasingly intertwined with larger media firms, a partnership which offers some advantages, but also erodes the concept of "alternative" (Hesmondhalgh, 2002).

Other critics highlight concentration of ownership in different industries and different sectors in the same media industry, a direct link to the first three points noted above. The local monopoly enjoyed by many newspapers and their vertical integration of production, distribution and exhibition give them an influence that exceeds the number of companies nationally. Vertical integration of production and distribution in both the motion picture and television industries exacerbate the influence that a few significant companies (Time Warner, Disney, Viacom, News Corp.) have over those industries (Kunz, 2007; Meehan, 2005; Wasko, 2003). For example, despite being called a "no show in the major segments of newspapers and broadcasting" by Compaine (Compaine & Gomery, 2000, p. 485)—perhaps because it does not solely own one of the Big Four U.S. television networks—Time Warner nevertheless owns significant television program production companies with inroads into syndication. "Never in the history of TV has one broadcast entity dominated programming like the CBS Television Distribution Group" (Berman, 2006, p. 38); the company resulted from a merger in 2006. In radio, Clear Channel owns more than twice as many U.S. radio stations—well over 800—as its number two competitor, and this *after* selling off hundreds of its smallest, least profitable stations in 2007 and 2008. The recorded music industry is concentrated at many different levels, including production—via the "loose integration" with multi-media conglomerates of the Big Four music companies (Burkart, 2005)—and exhibition, shown by the influence of Wal-Mart as a music distributor both nationally and in many communities (Fox, 2005). The comic book industry features a near duopoly at the production level via Marvel and DC Comics, and a near monopoly at distribution (to comic bookshops) through a company named Diamond (McAllister, 2001). Scholars have also argued that concentration of media ownership is also a problem in many other countries besides the United States (Thomas & Nain, 2004).

And although the number of media owners increases when one looks at the entire media system rather than players in individual industries, it is also true that several of the largest media conglomerates are cross-media owners, meaning that they are major forces in several media industries. As noted above, concentration of ownership in particular media industries has been a concern for several decades. However, McChesney (1999) contends that one difference between the past and the current situation is that in the past different companies controlled each medium: the broadcast networks in television, the "Majors" in film. But now often the same companies dominate in different industries. Time Warner, for example, is a significant or dominant player in film and broadcast television production; film and broadcast television distribution; cable television production, distribution and exhibition; Internet exhibition; and comic book production.

At least four major factors have influenced the creation of modern media ownership. Although decried by some industry press accounts as out-of-date—but reinforced by News Corp's acquisition of Dow Jones right before the creation of a Fox financial cable channel—the concept of "synergy" still guides many large media corporations as they look to maximize revenue and publicity by moving branded licenses through owned subsidiaries (Meehan, 1991). Newer forms of synergy may be more focused on reaching target markets through multiple means, such as Disney's multi-media kids strategies using Disney-branded films and videos, Disney radio, The Disney Channel, Disney theme parks, and Saturday morning programming on ABC (see Budd & Kirsch, 2005; Wasko 2001).

New media technologies and digitization have also encouraged media growth, as corporations look to be "converged" economically/structurally to match predicted technological convergence. In addition to websites based upon traditional media brands (cnn.com; espn.com), Time Warner's (financially disastrous) acquisition by AOL in 2000, News Corp's ownership of MySpace.com, Viacom's purchase of IFILM and Neopets, Inc., and Disney's grab of Club Penguin, a kids social networking site, are examples of big media's eagerness to digitally converge.

Globalization has also encouraged large media growth, as media empires peddle their own worldwide branded products such as Superman (Time Warner), *The Simpsons* (News Corp), and

*Dora the Explorer* (Viacom). In addition, non-media global advertisers desire media corporations with large-scale distribution for global campaigns. This trend is encouraged not just by brands like McDonalds and Coca-Cola, but also by global advertising organizations such as Omnicom (more on this below), and thus facilitated by such media outlets as MTV, operating more than 120 channels throughout the world.

Finally, large media corporations have gotten bigger because they have been allowed to. Policies which favor privatization of media resources as well as the elimination of regulations, such as the Financial Interest and Syndication Rules and caps on broadcast ownership, have both influenced growth and been influenced *by* growth through the lobbying and legal clout of big media (Proffitt, 2007b; Ramey, 2007).

It should also be noted that a factor accentuating the power of a few very large media corporations is the uniformity of structure that many of them share, as well as those in the lower tiers of influence. Baker (2007) argues that, in addition to a diversity of owners, a diversity of ownership structures—publicly traded corporations, non-profit corporations, non-stock corporations, government owned, sole proprietorships, partnerships, cooperatives—would be democratically healthy. But the corporate structure dominates. In fact, the publicly traded corporation may be especially problematic as an ownership structure for media. The profit expectation emphasized not just by dividend payments but by publicly known, changing and traded stock values and the scrutiny of quarterly earnings reports, places pressure on short-term growth and profit maximization, not just a reasonable return, all of which increase the salience of the below factors.

Also exacerbating the emphasis on profits are private equity firms which, since at least 2005, have been making bids for and buying up media corporations such as Clear Channel, Cumulus, record company EMI, Univision, and the Tribune Company. Private equity firms are not held to the same regulations and standards as publicly held corporations, which results in a lack of transparency, undermining the ideal of the media as watchdog. While private equity firms tend to break up concentrated corporations, such as the case of Clear Channel selling off hundreds of its radio stations and its television station group, the goals of such firms are short-term and include quick returns on their investments, improved efficiencies (including cutting labor and wages), higher profit margins, and the tendency to within a few years sell the company or go public. Such incentives accentuate the tensions between the economic goals of media-as-businesses and the democratic goals of media-as-valued-communication resources

## HOW OWNERSHIP MAY UNDERMINE DEMOCRACY

Owners of media operations may exert influence over content and distribution in a variety of ways, including the allocation of particular resources over other possibilities; the hiring and firing of key personnel and the perceived work autonomy by these personnel; the general climate of the operation shaped through private and public statements; and even direct intervention in day-to-day operations, although this may be rare in large corporations.

Of course, in the larger system of the political economy of the media, media ownership is one of several systems that may affect the structure, availability and range of messages in the media. Other systems include the profit motive generally, different media funding systems (including advertising), and content sources, such as public relations activities. And many of the criticisms below would apply to these other economic pressures. As will be seen, some of the dangers concern how ownership trends partner with these additional pressures to create a less-than-ideal democratic system. The discussion of these dangers will begin with an umbrella explanation, and from there become more specific about media ownership influences.

## UNDERMINING ASSURANCES OF DISTRIBUTIVE DEMOCRACY AND MORAL AUTONOMY

Baker (2007) posits that a sufficient argument for a diversity of ownership is the "Democratic Distribution Principle": "a claim that democracy implies as wide as practical a dispersal of power within the public sphere" (p. 7). This principle helps to prevent controlling forces throughout the wider society, since, to use a Habermasian concept, the public sphere can influence political support, and, when abused by a few controlling forces (including media ownership), can undermine democracy. However, measures of content diversity in media, even if done without bias and with subtlety (rarely accomplished, in Baker's view), are insufficient safeguards. Sometimes, a complete diversity of views and opinions will not be found in media/the public sphere, but this limited scope may not result from powerful, controlling forces, but instead may be legitimate if democracy, through authentic deliberation, has decided on the parameters of reasonable ideas. For example, most of us can agree that cable TV systems are under no democratic obligation to carry The Pro-Nazi Channel; content analyses that find no Nazi representation should not conclude a lack of democratic process as a reason for this exclusion.

This is complicated by the assurance of some degree of moral autonomy that democracy requires of citizens in evaluating the range of information as legitimate or manipulated. Christman (2003) offers a basic definition of autonomy as "to be one's own person, to be directed by considerations, desires, conditions, and characteristics that are not simply imposed externally upon one, but are part of what can somehow be considered one's authentic self," including freedom from the manipulation of external forces. Autonomy can be consensus oriented, as an autonomous person may choose, upon reflection, to adapt the values of a larger social group, such as a community. Although admittedly an ideal, true moral autonomy requires not just the adoption of values true to oneself, but also "second-order" reflection/values that allow authentic awareness and (re-)evaluation of one's values and desires (Christman, 2003).

If the public sphere and the wider culture are limited in terms of information, perspectives and even broader values, then this limitation may corrupt not just first-order values, but also second-order values; our ability to evaluate our value system. If we assume that the larger culture has the ability to enculturate/socialize members of that culture, from an ideological perspective this would lead to hegemony, where the key definitions of life and society—including our moral evaluation of ourselves and others—would be influenced by power structures in a society that also influence culture. Both our values, and our ability to evaluate our values, would be degraded in such a situation.

Combining then an unmeasurable democratically distributive range of ideas with the need for autonomous second-order reflection provides a justification for diverse media ownership. If one may not know when the range of ideas in media may be the result of a democratic deliberation, or the result of limited (and therefore potentially limiting) media ownership, and if there is a danger of ideologically slanted or narcotizing media content undermining our ability to assess reflection of our own values, then the dangers of media ownership need to be minimized as much as possible. The best way to ensure that media ownership does not negatively affect democratic distribution and moral autonomy is to expand the number and categories of owners.

But if media ownership can limit the range of ideas—or expand them in less-than-useful ways—how is this likely to occur, especially given the dominance of the profit-obsessed corporate structure? What specific content dangers have critics of concentrated media ownership raised?

## EMPHASIZING STANDARDIZATION: DEEMPHASIZING LOCALISM

Many critics have argued that large media owners encourage standardized content across various holdings, both to exploit economies of scale and to develop consistent brand images (Croteau & Hoynes, 2006; McChesney, 2004). This clearly affects local communities, especially in its reduction of media content specifically for that community.

Localism has long been a fundamental aspect of broadcasting and its regulation (see for example Napoli, 2001). As early as the 1920s, broadcasters were viewed as public trustees, a concept solidified in the Radio Act of 1927 and the allocation of broadcast licenses. Broadcasters were give free licenses (and a monopoly) with the agreement that they would serve the interests and needs of the community in which they were located, as the airwaves were considered public property rather than private property. The Federal Communications Commission (n.d.) has defined broadcast television and radio as "distinctly local media" and has enacted requirements to ensure the needs of the community are served. Indeed, broadcasting is crucial for local communities as evidenced by the September 11, 2001, attacks and Hurricane Katrina in 2005. Broadcasters have argued that economic realities, particularly competition from other media, suggest that multiple ownership and the financial efficiencies that accompany it are necessary in order for free over-the-air broadcasting to survive. With concentration of ownership, broadcasters are able to benefit from standardization and centralization of production, but localism requires decentralization (Proffitt, 2007b). As can be seen in radio since the Telecommunications Act of 1996 lifted national ownership caps, the promise of localism often takes a backseat to the benefits of economies of scale.

The rise of large radio group owners such as Clear Channel, which formats playlists and news from headquarters, has led to the systematic replacement of local radio programming by nationally distributed canned programming and news. Technology such as Voice Tracking has also allowed large radio group owners to cut labor because the same disc jockeys can be heard across the United States. Syndicated national radio programming is also cheaper to produce and distribute among radio stations than it is to have a local news team or local public affairs programming for each radio station one owns. Additionally, radio news broadcasts are often distributed by services such as CBS Corp.'s Metro Networks/Shadows. As of 2007, its website boasts that it provides traffic, weather, news, and sports reports for over 2,200 radio and television stations, reaching over 100 million adult listeners. Metro often supplies the same news coverage, including to multiple stations within the same market, and employs the same announcers who use different names to complement the station's format (Schwartzman, 2000).

This trend is evident in broadcast television as well, as it is cheaper to recycle network news and to use video news releases created by the public relations industry to be distributed free to news stations than it is to pay additional journalists. To reduce costs and increase revenue, Sinclair Broadcasting, one of the largest television groups, has cut local news from several of its stations, replacing news with syndicated entertainment programming. In other markets, Sinclair has sought opportunities for "news partnerships" to share resources with non-Sinclair stations in the same markets. Its News Central program, among other things, serves a wire service function by providing news feeds to its stations that still produce news (Bachman, 2006). Centralized and standardized news is quite problematic from a democratic standpoint considering that many people still receive their information about the community in which they live from their local television news. But for the horizontally integrated company, centralization and standardization benefits the bottom line.

## EMPHASIS ON PROMOTION AND MULTI-MEDIA REVENUE STREAMS

Large media corporations emphasize the promotion of their products to an outlandish degree. The average cost of marketing a major U.S. studio film in 2007 was more than $35 million (Motion Picture Association, 2008). Time Warner and Disney are among the largest advertisers in the world. Network television sacrifices millions in advertising revenue each year to air promotional spots for their own programs. Significant "below the line" marketing and promotional activity is added to traditional advertising spending. Both why they do this, and how they do this, speak to their characteristics as corporate media and the damage these characteristics may impose upon cultural vibrancy.

Why media corporations emphasize marketing includes such medium specific reasons as the importance of a big box office during opening weekend (film) and the increased competition among broadcast and cable networks (TV) (McAllister, 2000). But another reason has to do with the nature of promotion among synergy-oriented companies. Modern media conglomerates not only have multiple licenses to promote, but also multiple subsidiaries in which to promote them. This brings us to the "how" question, because media conglomerates do not just promote brands through advertising, but also through general promotional activities that fully exploit their media subsidiaries.

A major way this is done is through "plugola," defined in this context as the appearance of one media brand in another media branded text owned by the same corporation, for promotional purposes (McAllister, 2002). If characters in one television program appear in another television program owned by the same production company, then this would be plugola. When actors from a Fox television program are shown in the audience of a televised sporting event with the announcers commenting, this also would be plugola.

One particularly disturbing characteristic is the use of journalism to promote corporate holdings. In this case, "fluff" news stories are created around a corporately owned media license. Certainly the emphasis on ratings and profit has increased big media's tendency to cover celebrity and "lifestyle" over more issue-oriented news, but so has the number of brands the corporation wants to promote with corporately owned news. This is especially an issue when news operations are owned by larger conglomerates which are primarily entertainment oriented (such as Disney's ownership of ABC News). Synergistic plugola news stories are common in corporate news, including dozens or even hundreds of stories about specific programs such as NBC's *Seinfeld* (McAllister, 2002) and CBS's *Survivor* (McAllister, 2003); plugola stories in local markets (Higgins & Sussman, 2007); and news stories about a sport (NASCAR), which had an incentive not just to plug the sport, or the broadcast of the sport on a particular network (such as NBC), but also to narratively construct a particular type of viewer-consumer (the "NASCAR dad") for the sport (Vavrus, 2007). Such stories not only absorb valuable news time/space that could be devoted to other stories, but also typically infuse the story with a consumption orientation, in this case the desirability of consuming media brands.

Perhaps even more significant is the expansive nature of the mediated "text" in cross-media corporate ownership. Meehan (1991) argued that a media brand such as Batman could be conceptualized as a "commodity inter-text," in which the various manifestations of the brand—Batman in film, comics, TV, novelizations, video games, soundtracks, amusement park rides—become a giant self-referential promotion for the brand. Sandler (2003) contended that one reason animation has become such a cultural force is the corporate flexibility that this form offers for branding, merchandising and cross-media synergy. Meehan (2005) notes how a brand can be reused throughout a media empire in its original form through a variety of techniques she labels "recirculation" (such as syndication), "repackaging" (DVD versions), "reversioning" (Director's Cuts), "recycling" (tribute specials/clip shows) and "redeployment" (spin-off series). Proffitt, Tchoi, and McAllister (2007) observed that the promotional incentives in corporate texts were enhanced in The Matrix franchise, as the various licensed texts created an "intertextual flow" in which a grand, linked narrative was touted: to not buy the video game or promotional DVD meant that fans missed a piece of the plot or character development. Such expansive corporate texts push off the cultural agenda other potential aesthetic or political offerings.

Many works have also noted how the movement of texts through different media outlets may ultimately dilute potentially resistant or counter-hegemonic messages in the text. In terms of fantasy characters, for example, scholars have pointed to the textual "sanitization" of Batman in Warner Brothers films in the 1990s (Terrill, 2000) and of X-Men's Wolverine in Fox films (Johnson, 2007), the downplaying of class issues in the translation of Harry Potter from books to film (Waetjen & Gibson, 2007), and the removal of some of the most subversive elements in Powerpuff Girls merchandise when compared to the original cartoons (Van Fuqua, 2003).

## VULNERABILITY TO BIG ADVERTISING

Despite the title, the first six editions of Bagdikian's *Media Monopoly* explored two dangers of modern media empires, not just one: ownership influence (the monopoly part) and advertiser influence. One chapter explicitly dealt with the interaction between the two: Chapter 7, simply titled "Monopoly" (regrettably, this chapter was absent from the 2004 edition). Among his arguments is that large-scale advertising encourages large-media growth, as mega-media organizations can offer more cost efficiencies and conveniences to advertisers and thus exploit a competitive advantage compared to smaller firms. Smaller media firms, then, are less attractive to large-scale advertisers and have a tougher time surviving. In addition, advertising wants to reach as many consumers as possible (even when targeting relatively narrow demographics), thus increasing uniformity across media holdings, as advertisers look for media content that is non-controversial, non-threatening and consumption-oriented. One study found that Advertising Directors at chain newspapers were more likely to report the intrusion of advertising influences upon news content than non-chain papers (An & Bergen, 2007).

Besides encouraging growth and uniformity, advertising may also be especially influential with large media owners. As corporate media look to sell their own brands and break out of the "clutter," they often partner with product advertisers to develop cross-promotional campaigns to increase publicity: to make sure the promotional volume, in the words of *This is Spinal Tap*, "Goes to 11." Such cross-promotional deals come with a price, often in the form of product placement (product appears in a media text), the more intrusive product integration (product becomes central to a media text), and other forms of advertising's appropriation of media symbols (McAllister, 2000). Big advertising, then, can further emphasize the promotional thrust of large-media corporations.

The global nature of media corporations and advertising organizations also has increased the power of advertising over media. Although consumers know the names of large-media corporations and large advertisers, much less known are large-scale advertising agencies and companies that own these agencies. In fact, ownership concentration is not just a concern with media companies, but also with advertising agencies. The top four global advertising organizations (Omnicom, WPP Group, Interpublic, and Publicis) accounted for nearly 55% of advertising revenue from U.S. media in 2007 (Agency Report, 2008). Global advertising/marketing organizations such as Omnicom, the largest in the world, own several global agencies and, among other activities, advertising agencies directly engage in buying advertising time/space from media companies.

Since, when dealing the global media corporations, a global advertising agency such as BBDO does not just represent one client, but several clients, and does not even just represent its own clients, but potentially all of the clients of its corporate owner (in this case, Omnicom) representing literally billions of dollars in billings, this gives corporately owned agencies a tremendous amount of clout with media corporations.

A last advertising-oriented consideration of ownership is that the more advertising-funded subsidiaries that a multi-media corporation has, the more vulnerable that corporation becomes to advertising-induced pressure, even when non-advertising subsidiaries are involved (Baker, 2007). Thus, if an advertiser is satirized in a Warner Brothers movie, the advertiser may retaliate by threatening to withdraw advertising from Time Warner magazines and cable television networks. Even more generally, pressure groups may boycott advertisers of a corporation's holdings if they object to media content in any subsidiary of that corporation. If at all successful, such boycotts reinforce advertising's influence over media content—in this case even media content not directly supported by advertising, but nevertheless connected to a cross-media owner.

## ETHICS AND MEDIA OWNERSHIP IN A CORPORATE AGE

The issue of corporate media ownership and its effects upon content and culture is ultimately a structural issue. As such, this issue is addressed, at best, by changes in the incentives of the larger economic system or, second best, by the implementation of policies about media structure that mitigate the destructive growth and character of media owners and its effect upon culture (such policy recommendations are offered by Bagdikian, 2004; Baker, 2007; Ramey, 2007, among others). But ethical considerations can play a role in sparking such legislation and larger changes, and in negotiating through the current media landscape until such changes occur.

Government legislators can embrace democratic principles both in terms of what policies are best to maintain democratic vibrancy (including ownership policies), and what democratic process is best to decide on such polices (keeping powerful media lobbies at bay). The earlier section on democratic distribution and moral autonomy argued that the desire for diverse ownership is a democratic investment that can help philosophically ensure a vibrant system. As such, Baker (2007) and others note that concern about media ownership is not a clear cut "right versus left" political issue, and as such bi-partisan pressure may help keep politicians on target. In addition, citizens groups such as Free Press (www.freepress.org) can help focus policy makers on their ethical and democratic obligations.

Media owners, in turn, can maintain an ethical stance in distinguishing between maximized profits and reasonable profits, especially as the drive to maximize profits may lead to many if not most of the typical dangers of large corporate media ownership (standardization, promotion, advertising influence, etc.). Owners should, in other words, embrace a "Public Sphere" model of media in addition a "Market" model (Croteau & Hoynes, 2006). Again, the corporate structure is more likely to reward maximization versus reasonableness, but perhaps media-specific policies that create democratic incentives—and disincentives—for owners and create more diversity in ownership structures can help remind media owners that, because they are in the media, they have other socio-cultural obligations to fulfill besides those to the shareholders.

Media workers, when working in a larger corporate context, may feel concerned about the effects of this context upon their job and the conflicts this context can create with their journalistic, aesthetic and ideological standards (Turow, 1994). When teaching classes to future media workers that address issues of owner and advertiser influences, frequently students will wonder how they may negotiate such structures with their own values. One way is to look for contradictions in this complex system that can allow for creative autonomy (Hesmondhalgh, 2002), and exploit those contradictions when they are presented. As noted at the beginning of this chapter, although the media creators of *The Simpsons* may feel heat when ridiculing the right-wing stance of Fox News, they still "love" to do it.

Media studies scholars and teachers can be active in raising issues of media ownership. Besides scholars' roles in classroom and outreach issues involving ownership, Napoli and Gillis (2006) argued that government policy makers may be increasingly open to communications scholars, not just economists, as resources for decision making.

Finally, media users/citizens can apply personal ethics by both keeping informed of how media ownership may influence the media choices they have (who owns whom, for example), supporting alternative forms and funding of media, and letting their governmental representatives know when they believe media policies should be changed or enforced. Citizens who believe they are most informed about media ownership also tend to be more troubled by media ownership trends and policies (cited in Baker, 2007). The ethics of using media in an age of corporate ownership involves not just being informed, but being informed about that particular issue and looking for opportunities to contribute as active media citizens.

## NOTE

1. The authors thank John Christman for his helpful advice on sections of this chapter.

## REFERENCES

Agency Report. (2008, May 5). *Advertising Age*, pp. S1–S15.

Alger, Dean (1998). *Megamedia: How Giant Corporations Dominate Mass Media, Distort Competition, and Endanger Democracy*. Lanham, MD: Rowman & Littlefield.

An, Soontae & Bergen, Lori (2007). Advertiser Pressure on Daily Newspapers: A Survey of Advertising Sales Executives. *Journal of Advertising, 36*(2), 111–121.

Bachman, Katy (2006, March 20). Sinclair Scales Back News Central. *Mediaweek*. Accessed August 6, 2007 at http://www.mediaweek.com/mw/news/recent_display.jsp?vnu_content_id=1002198225

Bagdikian, Ben H. (1983). *The Media Monopoly*. Boston: Beacon Press.

Bagdikian, Ben H. (2004). *The New Media Monopoly*. Boston: Beacon Press.

Baker, C. Edwin (2007). *Media Concentration and Democracy: Why Ownership Matters*. New York: Cambridge University Press.

Barnouw, Erik et al. (1997). *Conglomerates and the Media*. New York: New Press.

Berman, Marc (2006, October 9). Small(er) World. *Mediaweek*, p. 38.

Bettig, Ronald, & Hall, Jeanne (2003). *Big Media, Big Money: Cultural Texts and Political Economy*. Lanham, MD: Rowman & Littlefield.

Budd, Mike, & Kirsch, Max H. (Eds.). (2005). *Rethinking Disney: Private Control, Public Dimensions*. Middletown, CT: Wesleyan University Press.

Burkart, Patrick (2005). Loose Integration in the Popular Music Industry. *Popular Music and Society, 28*(4), 489–500.

Christman, John (2003). Autonomy in Moral and Political Philosophy. In E. N. Zalta (Ed.), *The Stanford Encyclopedia of Philosophy*. Accessed August 3, 2007 at http://plato.stanford.edu/entries/autonomy-moral/

Compaine, Benjamin (2005). *The Media Monopoly Myth—How New Competition Is Expanding Our Sources of Information and Entertainment*. Accessed August 2, 2007 at http://www.newmillenniumresearch.org/archive/Final_Compaine_Paper_050205.pdf

Compaine, Benjamin, M., & Gomery, Douglas (2000). *Who Owns the Media? Competition and Concentration in the Mass Media Industry* (3rd ed.). Mahwah, NJ: Erlbaum.

Croteau, David, & Hoynes, William (2006). *The Business of Media: Corporate Media and the Public Interest* (2nd ed.). Thousand Oaks, CA: Sage.

Einstein, Mara (2003, April 28). Dereg? We Should Talk Re-Reg. *Broadcasting & Cable*, p. 50.

Einstein, Mara (2004). *Media Diversity: Economics, Ownership, and the FCC.* Mahwah, NJ: Erlbaum.

Federal Communications Commission. (n.d.). *Broadcasting and Localism: FCC Consumer Facts.* Washington, D.C.: Federal Communications Commission. Accessed August 4, 2007 at http://www.fcc.gov/localism/Localism_Fact_Sheet.pdf

Fox, Mark A. (2005). Market Power in Music Retailing: The Case of Wal-Mart. *Popular Music and Society*, 28(4), 501–519.

Hesmondhalgh, David (2002). *The Cultural Industries.* Thousand Oaks, CA: Sage.

Higgins, Carey L., & Sussman, Gerald (2007). Plugola: News for Profit, Entertainment, and Network Consolidation. In T. A. Gibson & M. Lowes (Eds.), *Urban Communication: Production, Text, Context* (pp. 141–162). Lanham, MD: Rowman & Littlefield.

Horkheimer, Max, & Adorno, Theodor W. (2001). The Culture Industry: Enlightenment as Mass Deception. In D. M. Kellner & M. G. Durham (Eds.), *Media and Cultural Studies: Key Works* (pp. 71–101). Malden, MA: Blackwell.

Johnson, Derek (2007). Will the Real Wolverine Please Stand Up? Marvel's Mutation from Monthlies to Movies. In I. Gordon, M. Jancovich, & M. P. McAllister (Eds.), *Film and Comic Books* (pp. 64–85). Jackson, MS: University Press of Mississippi.

McAllister, Matthew P. (2000). From Flick to Flack: The Increased Emphasis on Marketing by Media Entertainment Corporations. In R. Andersen & L. A. Strate (Eds.), *Critical Studies in Media Commercialism* (pp. 101–122). New York: Oxford University Press.

McAllister, Matthew P. (2001). Ownership Concentration in the U.S. Comic Book Industry. In M. P. McAllister, E. H. Sewell, Jr., & I. Gordon, (Eds.), *Comics and Ideology* (pp. 15–38). New York: Peter Lang.

McAllister, Matthew P. (2002). Television News Plugola and the Last Episode of *Seinfeld. Journal of Communication*, 52(2), 383–401.

McAllister, Matthew P. (2003). Selling *Survivor*: The Use of TV News to Promote Commercial Entertainment. In A. N. Valdivia (Ed.), *A Companion to Media Studies* (pp. 209–226). Oxford, UK: Blackwell.

McChesney, Robert W. (1999). *Rich Media, Poor Democracy: Communication Politics in Dubious Times.* Urbana, IL: University of Illinois Press.

McChesney, Robert W. (2004). *The Problem of the Media: U.S. Communication Politics in the 21st Century.* New York: Monthly Review Press.

Meehan, Eileen R. (1991). "Holy Commodity Fetish, Batman!": The Political Economy of a Commercial Intertext. In R. E. Pearson & W. Uricchio (Eds.), *The Many Lives of the Batman: Critical Approaches to a Superhero and His Media* (pp. 47–65). New York: Routledge.

Meehan, Eileen, R. (2005). *Why TV Is Not Our Fault: Television Programming, Viewers, and Who's Really in Charge.* Lanham, MD: Rowman & Littlefield.

Motion Picture Association. (2008). *2007 U.S. Theatrical Market Statistics.* Accessed May 12, 2008 at http://www.mpaa.org/researchStatistics.asp.

Napoli, Phillip M. (2001). *Foundations of Communications Policy: Principles and Process in the Regulation of Electronic Media.* Cresskill, NJ: Hampton Press.

Napoli, Phillip M., & Gillis, Nancy. (2006).Reassessing the Potential Contribution of Communications Research to Communications Policy: The Case of Media Ownership. *Journal of Broadcasting and Electronic Media, 50*(4), 671–691.

Proffitt, Jennifer M. (2007a). Challenges to democratic discourse: Media concentration and the marginalization of dissent. *Review of Education, Pedagogy, and Cultural Studies*, 29(1), 65–84.

Proffitt, Jennifer M. (2007b). Juggling justifications: Modifications to the National Television Station Ownership Rule. *Journal of Broadcasting & Electronic Media, 51*(4), 575–595.

Proffitt, Jennifer M., Tchoi, Djung Y., & McAllister, Matthew P. (2007). Plugging Back into *The Matrix*:

The Intertextual Flow of Corporate Media Commodities. *Journal of Communication Inquiry, 31*(3), 239–254.

Ramey, Carl R. (2007). *Mass Media Unleashed: How Washington Policymakers Shortchanged the American Public*. Lanham, MD: Rowman & Littlefield.

Sandler, Kevin S. (2003). Synergy Nirvana: Brand Equity, Television Animation, and Cartoon Network. In C. A. Stabile & M. Harrison (Eds.), *Prime Time Animation: Television Animation and American Culture* (pp. 89–109). New York: Routledge.

Schiller, Herbert I. (1989). *Culture Inc: The Corporate Takeover of Public Expression*. New York: Oxford University Press.

Schwartzman, Andrew Jay (2000). Viacom-CBS Merger: Media Competition and Consolidation in the New Millennium. *Federal Communications Law Journal, 52*(3), 513–518.

Terrill, Robert E. (2000). Spectacular Repression: Sanitizing the Batman. *Critical Studies in Media Communication, 17*(4), 493–509.

Thomas, Pradip N., & Nain, Zaharom (2004). *Who Owns the Media? Global Trends and Local Resistances*. New York: Zed Books.

Turow, Joseph (1994). Hidden Conflicts and Journalistic Norms: The Case of Self-Coverage. *Journal of Communication, 44*(2), 29–46.

Van Fuqua, Joy (2003). "What Are Those Little Girls Made of?" The Powerpuff Girls and Consumer Culture. In C. A. Stabile & M. Harrison (Eds.) *Prime Time Animation: Television Animation and American Culture* (pp. 205–219). New York: Routledge.

Vavrus, Mary (2007). The Politics of NASCAR Dads: Branded Media Paternity. *Critical Studies in Media Communication, 24*(3), 245–261.

Waetjen, Jarrod, & Gibson, Timothy A. (2007). Harry Potter and the Commodity Fetish: Activating Corporate Readings in the Journey from Text to Commercial Intertext. *Communication and Critical/Cultural Studies, 4*(1), 3–26.

Wasko, Janet (2001). *Understanding Disney: The Manufacture of Fantasy*. Boston: Polity Press.

Wasko, Janet (2003). *How Hollywood Works*. Thousand Oaks, CA: Sage.

Weber, Max (1976). Towards a Sociology of the Press. *Journal of Communication, 26*(3), 96–101.

# 25

# The Media in Evil Circumstances

## Robert S. Fortner

Although the question of what constitutes "evil" has engaged philosophers for more than 2000 years, the issue of how media should behave, or what their role is, in circumstances that we might all agree are evil, is much more recent. Arguably the concern is less than seventy-five years old, arising initially when the Nazis came to power in Germany and began to use propaganda to prepare the population for war and the Holocaust. Some might argue that the concern should be extended backward further, perhaps to the war-mongering of William Randolph Hearst near the end of the 19th century, or the exposés of the muckrakers in the early 20th century. Others might suggest the use of photography by Jacob Riis as a medium to expose the depredations of New York's slums or even Matthew Brady's photography of the carnage of the American Civil War. But the most sustained scholarly concern with the role of media in circumstances where people have been slaughtered—whether by serial killers, rapist-murderers, terrorists, or rebel movements, in wars or through state-sponsored genocide and ethnic cleansing—has occurred since the end of the Second World War, and especially in the last two decades.

Scholars have taken several positions on how the media have operated in evil circumstances. By far the most scholarship has been directed to analysis of the role of media in war—and, more recently, how domestic media have been used or have eagerly participated in the justification for going to war, or how media have become tools of warring powers through propaganda and "public diplomacy." Some research has concentrated, too, on how the media have been mobilized by totalitarian or absolutist regimes to justify their policies and how they have propagandized their own people through media use. This has occurred sometimes by state control of the media themselves, or through strictly enforced censorship, or direct or implied threats for non-compliance with state directives. At other times it has been the result of the media's voluntary compliance, or endorsement, of the state's policies. Still other scholars have been more concerned with how independent media have reported about violence, whether individual or collective in nature. Still others have concentrated on specific aspects of the media–evil nexus, such as the manipulation of media by terrorists, or the clash of ideals in covering violence of various kinds.

This essay will examine some of the most significant scholarship on the relationship between media and evil—or how the media have functioned in evil circumstances—as participants, dupes, signalers, critics, legitimizers, or sensationalists of evil. Then it will provide a perspective on media in evil circumstances that is still to be fully explored.

Kevin G. Barnhurst (1991, p. 75) argues that authorities who study terrorism and the media take one of two perspectives. The first perspective is that "the media play an essential role [in terrorism] and that news coverage spreads terrorism like a disease." The second is that "the media are victims of terrorists," responding initially to violence and then reducing coverage as it becomes routine. The first of these perspectives suggests that the media are either participants in evil itself or merely signalers of evil, while the second sees the media as dupes or sensationalists—even when they are critics. Each of these perspectives requires some elaboration.

## MEDIA AS PARTICIPANTS IN EVIL

Media can be forced into participation in evil using a variety of methods, or they can voluntarily participate. In Rwanda, for instance, members of the Hutu elite invested in the creation of radio station RTML and it, in turn, incited the genocide. "Do not kill these inyenzi (cockroaches) with a bullet, cut them to pieces with a machete," broadcaster Valerie Bemerki counseled her listeners (Mirzoeff, 2004). And listeners also heard Simon Birkindi's song, "I Hate These Hutus," "a long delineation of all the different Hutu who were held to be insufficiently loyal" (Gourevitch, 1998, p. 100). Although some Rwandans, especially in the northern half of the country, could hear the Rwandan Patriotic Front station, Radio Muhabura, "it did little to contribute to the free flow of information. Instead, as its name suggests, Radio Muhabura [Leading the Way] continued the culture of propaganda and counter-propaganda, providing little concrete information about events and spending a lot of air time presenting and promoting the RPF to the Rwandan population." (Article 19, 1996, pp. 23–24) Kellow and Steeves (1998) also reported, based on Reporters Sans Frontières' documents, that newspapers in Burundi were operating similarly, fanning the flames of hatred there just as RTML was doing in Rwanda. In Ivory Coast in 2002 the media were owned by political leaders who used them to spread hate messages targeting different political parties, ethnic groups and religions (Alexis and Mpambara, 2003, p. 3). (These efforts were paltry, however, compared to the total use of media by the Nazi regime in the 1930s and 40s (see Gupta, 2001, p. 123). And the Serbs used similar means, with Warren Zimmermann, the American Ambassador to Yugoslavia saying, "It was TV that promoted the hatreds. It gave people myths and called them history" (quoted by Gupta, 2001, p. 123). "Accounts of the wars in the Balkans and the Rwandan Genocide which reject the 'ancient hatreds' interpretation have emphasized the role played by the media in creating killers from one-time neighbours who had managed to co-exist peaceably for lengthy periods, if not perpetually," Susan L. Carruthers wrote (2000, p. 46). In Yugoslavia, the main agent of the "alien virus" was Srpski Radio Knin, "a Serb-run radio station pouring out anti-Croat propaganda" and Serbian Radio-Television. "As one Sarajevo-based journalist put it, 'Every person killed in this war was first killed in the newsrooms" (Carruthers, 2000, p. 47). Gupta likewise discusses the use of media by the Pol Pot regime in Cambodia and the Habyarimana regime in Rwanda (p. 159). As Mark Frohardt and Jonathan Temin put it (2003, p. 2), "media can be extremely powerful tools used to promote violence...." And, as Dusan Reljic concludes about Europe: "the media plays a significant part in whipping up nationalist feelings of xenophobia, racism or ethnic chauvinism," even when conflict is not imminent. They do so by reinforcing "existing differences and thus accelerat[ing] a disintegrating effect on the homogeneity of the population" (n.d., p. 2).

On a more voluntary level was the "collaboration" of the American press with the Bush administration in conceptualizing and justifying the war to force Saddam Hussein from Kuwait (Kelman, 1995, p. 121). And, in another variant, Eytan Gilboa (2000, p. 295) wrote that "sometimes during severe international crises, the media provide the only channel for communication and negotiation between rival actors.... Officials more frequently use global television rather than traditional diplomatic channels to deliver messages." Gilboa cites instances of the

Iran hostage crisis, the 1985 hijacking of a TWA jet to Beirut, the 1990–1991 Gulf conflict, and a 1998 communiqué of conciliation from Iranian President Khatami as examples of state use of media to deliver messages during crises (see also O'Heffernan, 2001, p. 3 on TV's "global crisis communication role"). Finally, Lee Artz (2004, p. 80), calls the photographs and drawings run by the *New York Times* during the second Iraq war "perhaps the most revealing instances of media's complicity with U. S. propaganda…" (see also Solomon, 2004, p. 57).

## MEDIA AS DUPES IN EVIL CIRCUMSTANCE

Media become the dupes of evil when they, as a result of their own commitments or principles, unwittingly become tools of evil. Terry Anderson, a journalist who was held captive by terrorists in Lebanon for over five years put it this way (1993, p. 129): "In my opinion, the very reporting of a political kidnapping, an assassination or a deadly bombing is a first victory for the terrorist. Without the world's attention, these acts of viciousness are pointless." Anderson goes on to argue that even when the media run long analyses about terrorist organizations, they legitimize them. Susan Carruthers (2000) has argued that the media have become more willing accomplices in wartime propaganda, but Danny Schechter (2004, pp. 30–31) outlines a variety of techniques used by U.S. administrations to "seduce and co-opt" the media).

## MEDIA AS SIGNALERS OF EVIL

Media sometimes are the first to indicate that evil is about to break out, or they signal the beginning of a campaign of evil. Often, such as the cases in Rwanda, Yugoslavia, and Georgia, this signaling actually occurred via obfuscation. The media in these societies "signaled" "imminent" threats against the majority populations of Hutus, Georgians, and Serbs, "though there was only flimsy evidence provided to support them," and thus constructed fear and the "foundation for taking violent action through 'self-defense'" (Frohardt and Temin, 2003, p. 6). An analysis by Piers Robinson of the role of news media in provoking humanitarian interventions (2000, p. 8), suggested that media coverage of humanitarian crises did "trigger the use of air power but not the deployment of troops" in Bosnia, and that in other cases, including Somalia and Kosovo, claims made that media are influential in driving foreign policy are "not without substance." And Morand Fachot (2001, p. 53) argues that "An indisputable consequence of the 'CNN effect' is the shortening of the news cycle, which forces politicians and the military to react swiftly to events, often in the absence of an appropriate context or background: they now have to operate in a round-the-clock, real-time, global news environment." And former Secretary of State James Baker III wrote in 1995, "In Iraq, Bosnia, Somalia, Rwanda, and Chechnya, among others, the real-time coverage of conflict by the electronic media has served to create a powerful new imperative for prompt action that was not present in less frenetic [times]" (quoted in Gilboa, 2005, p. 28; see also Albright, 2001, p. 105).

### Media as Critics of Evil

Media can sometimes bring pressure to bear in evil circumstances by rallying world opinion to occurrences of evil or encouraging condemnation by nation-states. Unfortunately, there has been little scholarly attention to this potential aspect of media behavior, largely because the media have become increasingly reactive in reportage as a result of reducing their foreign bureaus and depending more on stringers who are paid to report "events" rather than to signal possibilities or to bring moral probity to the instances of evil that they witness. Some individual reporters, such as Thomas Friedman for the *New York Times*, have responsibly criticized evil, but most such criticism evaporated with the collapse of the Soviet Union as "evil empire." President Bush's characterization of Iraq, Iran, and North Korea as an "axis of evil" never really caught on with the media beyond its panache as a catch-phrase, and reporting of conflicts between the U. S. and each of these three societies has been treated within traditional categories of political gamesmanship rather than as a confrontation with "evil."

The criticism that does emerge, too, does not always follow the same pattern. For instance, after the attacks on the World Trade Center and the Pentagon in 2001, Michael Wolff wrote that the U.S. media's response was one of what he called "notionlessness." "A retreat, over a period of years, from consistent, in-depth coverage of world affairs left journalists, readers and audiences to identify the villain as some pure spasm of all-powerful, far-reaching apocalyptic irrationality" (quoted by Lynch, 2002, p. 10).

## MEDIA LEGITIMIZING EVIL

Chris Hedges (2003, p. 6) writes that war

> dominates culture, distorts memory, corrupts language, and infects everything around it, even humor, which becomes preoccupied with the grim realities of smut and death. Fundamental questions about the meaning, or meaninglessness, of our place on the planet are laid bare when we watch those around us sink to the lowest depths. War exposes the capacity for evil that lurks not far below the surface within all of us.

And the media's role in providing access to alternative viewpoints about going to war in Iraq was, as John F. Stacks puts it (2003–2004, p. 20), "abysmally thin. The full texture and shape of the internal government debate (and one assumes there was some debate) was not known to the public. Without knowing much about the stakes and reasons for the war, the public supported the president." This is legitimation by omission. Similarly, when the Bush administration claimed that videos issued by Osama bin Laden might contained coded messages and called on American television networks not to air them unedited, the "networks took the request one step further and declined to air virtually any video of bin Laden" (Bamford, 2001, p. 20).

## MEDIA AS SENSATIONALISTS

Media can, and sometimes do, exploit evil for their own purposes, principally to increase circulation or ratings. During the Gulf War, when the British press was actively debating what levels of carnage were appropriate to show to viewers, the *Sun* newspaper, which was an avid supporter of Prime Minister Tony Blair's policies, "opportunistically latched on" to

> extremely brief, and heavily pixellated, footage of the dead bodies of Staff Sergeant Simon Cullingworth and Sapper Luke Allsopp, who were killed in an ambush during the war, footage which the BBC, along with other UK broadcasters and the press, had refused to show at the time of its original release.... The *Sun* referred to the footage variously as an "atrocity", "sickening" and "beyond comprehension", although in fact the only thing that was truly sickening about this episode was the *Sun's* entirely cynical exploitation of the grief of the dead men's relatives for its proprietor's commercial ends. (Petley, 2003, p. 78)

## ANALYZING THE ROLE OF MEDIA IN EVIL CIRCUMSTANCES

What all of this suggests is that the media have a variety of impacts, sometimes even contradictory impacts, within evil circumstances. While the media may signal atrocities, violence, and conflict through the so-called CNN effect, they can also easily be co-opted by adroit application of media relations strategies by governments, essentially becoming cheerleaders for policies that might, themselves, cause such circumstances. They can both dampen evil by exposing it to the world and heighten it by sensationalizing it. They can legitimize it by giving perpetrators the publicity they seek and, at the same time, horrify the world with the brutality of these perpetrators. These descriptive analyses of the role of media indicate both a complex set of roles, and a tendency toward irresponsibility seen through the lens of ethics.

It could be argued that the complexity of the media's response to evil circumstances is the result of their independence—and that this confirms the value of a free press. But there are two responses that must be made to such an assertion. First, the role of the press within domestic contexts to support the policies of their governments—however disreputable—casts significant doubt on their independence. This is true even within democracies with guarantees of a free press (such as the United States), and those with a long tradition of a free press (such as Canada and Great Britain). So it is questionable whether complexity is necessarily indicative of independence. Second is the ease with which governments are able to enlist, or co-opt, the press to do its bidding. Although the media complained bitterly in the aftermath of the first Gulf War that the military had exerted undue interference and control on their reporting (with the criticism being "swift, high-powered, and damning" (Skoco and Woodger, 2000, p. 79), by the time of the second Gulf War the military had become even more adept at controlling the press. But the agreements that had been reached in 1992 between the press and the military (9 principles of combat coverage) were largely abandoned by the Bush administration's adoption of new rules for embedded journalists during Operation Iraqi Freedom. The result of the decision to "embed" reporters in Iraq resulted in very narrow "soda straw" views of the war as it progressed, made the reporters dependent on the military for protection in ways that the press had not experienced before, and made it difficult to report independently—both for policy reasons that reporters bought into (such as limitations on the use of electronic equipment and specific information that should not be reported) and for interpersonal reasons, since some reporters apparently participated in identifying targets and "passing ammunition" and thus became part of the military's mission, rather than just observers of it (see Artz, 2004, pp. 82–83; Bernhard, 2003, pp. 86–87; Calabrese, 2005, p. 157; Larson, 2004; Tehranian, 2004, pp. 238–239). Whatever the difficulties were, however, a RAND report on the experience concluded that, "Overall, there were far fewer press complaints during this war than seen in previous major conventional operations… (Paul and Kim, 2004, p. 81). Once the push into Baghdad was complete, journalists abandoned their "embeds" in droves, dropping from an estimated 570 to 750 to "roughly 100" within six months, to under 50 in another six months, and to under 10 by October 2006. All of this was occurring, of course, while the "evil" of civilian deaths, insurgency and political gridlock gripped Iraq and American and allied forces absorbed more casualties than they had during the brief war itself. It appears to be a lack of realistic perspective on the part of the press (see Vaina, 2006; Al-Marashi, 2006, pp. 1–2).

The various behaviors of the press in evil circumstances, when examined independently, provide but thin descriptions. But when they are seen in their entirety, in their complexity, and in their contradictions, a thicker description is possible. This thicker description—whether the focus is on genocide, war, ethnic conflict, domestic or international media—suggests that the most accurate descriptor of their collective behavior is opportunism. By and large the media have been willing to abandon their independence and shelve their skepticism for short term gains—either to support or ingratiate themselves to the powerful, or to "get the story" for their audiences.

This is perhaps no surprise, as "getting the story" is what journalism is all about. But most journalists would agree that this goal should not be met by becoming too cozy with those in power. The Poynter Institute, for instance, calls for journalists to "hold the powerful account-able" (Steele, 2000), and many journalists objected to the term "embed" to describe their deploy-ment with U.S. forces in Iraq for what it suggested. In cases where the media clearly supported genocidal policies (in the breakup of Yugoslavia and the subsequent military actions in Bosnia and Kosovo, in Rwanda and Burundi), of course, "getting the story" essentially meant toeing the party line, abandoning any pretense to independence.

What this attention to media ecology may raise as an issue is whether the actions of indi-vidual journalists have in any way ameliorated or exacerbated the actions of the media as an institution. Certainly there are instances in which reporters have adopted a stance that was not in accordance with the desires of their governments. Anne Garrels' reporting from Baghdad dur-ing the second Gulf war, which often discovered that events were not as being reported by other U.S. media outlets or as the Bush administration or military spokespersons claimed, is a case in point (see Garrels, 2004). Anna Politkovskaya's reporting on the Chechen War (which apparently cost her her life) comes in this category, as does Willem Marx's exposé (2006) of the U.S. mili-tary's propaganda activities in Iraq. Perhaps the most poignant and powerful treatments of the consequences of evil have come from feature-length films (*Hotel Rwanda, Sometimes in April, Osama, Turtles Can Fly, Blood Diamond, The Last King of Scotland, Lord of War,* for instance), documentaries such as those produced by Democracy Now or the Media Education Foundation criticizing media practices in response to evil, or accounts of the effects of evil on those who have been its victims (see Neuffer, 2002, on the conflicts in Bosnia and Rwanda;  Mertus, Tesanovic, Metikos, and Roric, 1997, on Bosnia and Croatia; Gourevitch, 1998, on Rwanda; Seierstad, 2003, on Afghanistan; or Shadid, 2006, on Iraq). Although collectively these may suggest that signifi-cant attention has been given to evil by media practitioners, in reality, they are too little, too late. Most of these accounts are published after the consequences of evil have become apparent, even in the mainstream press, and together these treatments cover 30 years of history, thus providing but a glimpse into the consequences of evil.

## REQUIREMENTS OF THE MEDIA IN EVIL CIRCUMSTANCES

The media cannot control the political, social, cultural, or military context within which they may be called to operate. Sometimes circumstances may call on the media to function outside their "comfort zone." Clearly in some cases there is little that can be done to demand a different standard of behavior. For instance, if the media are controlled by the state, dominant political parties, kinship, tribal identity-politics or military force, it is naïve to expect the press to function independently. In such cases, it is more likely that the media will become instruments of evil than signalers or critics. Even condemnation or successful prosecution of media owners for being part of a genocidal regime (as happened with two Hutus associated with RTML in Kigali) only occurs after the fact, so it has no immediate impact on the atrocities as they are taking place.

Nevertheless, there are standards to which the media should be held—even if only rhetori-cally. For instance, as Roy Peter Clark puts it (2006), "In politics, each term carries ideological meaning, even as it appears to the world in the sheep's clothing of impartiality."  Clark refers in his essay to George Orwell's diatribe against the abuse of language. Orwell (1946) argued that "All issues are political issues, and politics itself is a mass of lies, evasions, folly, hatred, and schizophrenia. When the general atmosphere is bad, language must suffer." This, of course, is a conclusion that it behooves all journalists to recognize. Orwell goes on to explain his objections to toeing the party line.

Orthodoxy, of whatever colour, seems to demand a lifeless, imitative style.... When one watches some tired hack on the platform mechanically repeating the familiar phrases—*bestial, atrocities, iron heel, bloodstained tyranny, free peoples of the world, stand shoulder to shoulder*—one often has a curious feeling that one is not watching a live human being but some kind of dummy: a feeling which suddenly becomes stronger at moments when the light catches the speaker's spectacles and turns them into blank discs which seem to have no eyes behind them. And this is not altogether fanciful. A speaker who uses that kind of phraseology has gone some distance toward turning himself into a machine. The appropriate noises are coming out of his larynx, but his brain is not involved, as it would be if he were choosing his words for himself. If the speech he is making is one that he is accustomed to make over and over again, he may be almost unconscious of what he is saying, as one is when one utters the responses in church. And this reduced state of consciousness, if not indispensable, is at any rate favourable to political conformity.

In our time, political speech and writing are largely the defence of the indefensible. Things like the continuance of British rule in India, the Russian purges and deportations, the dropping of the atom bombs on Japan, can indeed be defended, but only by arguments which are too brutal for most people to face, and which do not square with the professed aims of the political parties. Thus political language has to consist largely of euphemism, question-begging and sheer cloudy vagueness. Defenceless villages are bombarded from the air, the inhabitants driven out into the countryside, the cattle machine-gunned, the huts set on fire with incendiary bullets: this is called *pacification*. Millions of peasants are robbed of their farms and sent trudging along the roads with no more than they can carry: this is called *transfer of population* or *rectification of frontiers*. People are imprisoned for years without trial, or shot in the back of the neck or sent to die of scurvy in Arctic lumber camps: this is called *elimination of unreliable elements*. Such phraseology is needed if one wants to name things without calling up mental pictures of them.

Clark's example, picking up on Orwell's argument, is that,

Today, the debate is framed by simple phrases, repeated so often to stay "on message," that they turn into slogans, another substitute for critical thinking. So one side wants to "stay the course" without settling for the "status quo," and condemns political opponents who want to "cut and run." It is one job of the journalist to avoid the trap of repeating catch phrases, such as "the war on terror," disguised as arguments, and to help the public navigate the great distances between "stay the course" and "cut and run." Surely, they are not the only options.

And Karim H. Karim argues that

even though the events of September 11, 2001 were extraordinary, their reporting was routinely placed within the cultural frames that have long been in place to cover violence, terrorism, and Islam. The focus was on the immediate reaction rather than the broader causes of the attacks or the existence of structural violence in global society. As the hunt began for the "Islamic terrorists," the media failed to provide a nuanced and contextual understanding of Muslims or the nature of the "Islamic peril." Journalists generally echoed the Bush administration's polarized narrative frame of good versus evil. (cited by Zelizer and Allan, 2003)

"By reporting, however neutral they try to be" Eknes and Endresen say (1999, p. 11), "journalists take on a role that makes them distinct from passive observers of an event or situation. By putting some stories on the front page and ignoring others, journalists and media influence the setting of agendas and thereby the evolution of conflicts or political processes.
When conflicts loom, the political discourse becomes conflict-oriented, as do local media." In other words, for journalists to provide an "objective" account of evil, it is necessary that they

be circumspect in their choice of language. They cannot allow those in power—elites, politicians, propagandists, spin doctors, military authorities, and so on—to determine the nature of their stories by providing the vocabulary they should use to write those stories. They should be skeptical of words that are condemnatory, or absolutist, or obscure, because such words hide more than they reveal. Neither should they hide behind the notion of "objectivity" by quoting those who use such language without pointing out its demonizing, dehumanizing, obfuscating, or absolutist qualities. These qualities stifle debate, suggest the existence of an irreconcilable antipodal condition that is unlikely to represent the true conditions of a conflict, and obscure the common humanity of the participants.

None of these are acceptable for journalists who are seeking the truth of a matter, or who are attempting to put the day's events in a context that gives them meaning. Once the meaning of words is left to those with policies to pursue, strategies to execute, or evil to consummate, the press has lost its independence and its ability to tell an accurate story. Related to this issue of language use is that of mythic framing (or archetypal framing) of stories (see Lynch, 2001). The outbreak of violence against the "other" is often preceded by characterizing a dispute in some mythic frame: "axis of evil," "greater Serbia," the "hamitic hypotheses" (Rwanda), "betrayal" (Cambodia), the "Jewish conspiracy" (the Third Reich), etc. In Yugoslavia, for instance, "Well before any fighting began in Bosnia, Croatian television, like Serbian, was airing nationalist broadcasts discussing how the Serbs intended to exterminate the Croat population in order to form a 'Greater Serbia.' These incendiary programmes suggested to Croats that they were in mortal danger from the Serbs and that they should arm themselves before it was too late" (Price, 2000, p. 5). Melone, Terzis, and Beleli (2002, p. 1) conclude: "Instead of reflecting pluralism in the social and political structures and thereby contributing to the creation of an informed critical citizenry within a country, the media often act as a mouthpiece for ethnic power circles. Thus a deliberate distortion of news coverage for particular interests easily exacerbates the tension between opposed factions and becomes a main trigger of violent conflict."

Since conflict, by definition, pits one against the "other," people are asked to identify with one or another side. And since putting an historical or mythic spin on events has appeal to people who wish to think of themselves not as perpetrators of evil, but as victims of it, such myths, or the archetypes of victimhood (such as the Jews to whom the Serbs compared themselves as victims), have tremendous power in mobilizing support for murderous regimes. In Yugoslavia both Serbs and Croats used a "covenantal cycle" teleology as the core of their nationalism. This allowed the use of images suggesting "the constant battle between good and evil throughout history—the 'chosen' nation versus its many enemies" (MacDonald, 2002, p. 5). In the portrayals used by Croats, Serbs were "an evil, expansionary, annihilatory other, seeking first to invade, then to enslave, and then to exterminate the Croat people.... Other important myths include the *Antemurale Christianitatis*, the belief that Croatia represented the easternmost outpost of European civilisation" (p. 8). But Serbs, too, were dependent on the same teleology as the basis of their myths to undergird nationalist aspirations (MacDonald, 2002, pp. 15-16).

These conflicts are then what are referred to as "identity conflicts" in which "the mobilisation of people in identity groups [is] based on race, religion, culture, language, and so on" (Hieber, 2001, p. 10). In such conflicts it is crucial that parties, histories, religions, ethnic demographics, and traditions be treated both respectfully and equally. Otherwise, by using the framing adopted by one or the other of the conflicting groups, the media unwittingly becomes both a legitimizing force and an unwitting participant in whatever follows. Although adopting an independent frame and discussing conflict in neutral language will not necessarily prevent conflict, it will both maintain the credibility of the media and prevent media incitement of violence.

Not all journalists will agree with this stance, of course. The Institute of War and Peace

Reporting, for instance, contrasts the "beaten track of objectivity" with the "polemical and the partisan." It highlights the debate between those who remain "clinically neutral" with those who practice a "journalism of attachment" (Davis, 2001, p. 7). But this is a mischaracterization of the issue. The conflict is not between neutrality and attachment. It is between true neutrality, socially-constructed "neutrality," and attachment. What IWPR discusses is the latter two aspects of this issue. A socially-constructed neutrality is one that reports conflict on the basis of the language, images, and socially-constructed or resurrected myths and archetypes of identity politics as defined by the conflicting parties. This must be contrasted with a true neutrality that seeks the truth without resorting to such demonizing language and images, and mythic constructs provided to the media by those in conflict. This is a truer or purer form of neutrality than can be achieved using pre-constructed ideas.

Is this naïve? Perhaps. But it is in accord with a recognition that the "construction of 'otherness' plays a key role in the formation and transformation of political boundaries constructed in terms of moral superiority/inferiority as well as in the conflict generated by such formation and transformation" (Wilmer, 1998). If journalists use the terminology and concepts of either of the warring factions in reporting the events occurring within the context of conflict, it contributes to the construction of "otherness," becomes entangled in the moral boundaries being constructed, and not only compromises its neutrality but helps concretize the boundaries that make atrocity possible. Refusing to participate in such boundary construction by careful choice of words, images, and archetypes of understanding makes neutrality real and avoids passive participation in morally reprehensible acts. It is to recognize that "It is the social actors who use the conceptual systems of their culture and the linguistic and other representational systems to construct meaning, to make the world meaningful, to communicate about the world meaningfully to others" (Michel Foucault, quoted by Reich, 2003, p. 11; see also Murray and Cowden, 1999).

Such expectations, of course, although they might apply to media that have thrown in with political factions that engage in evil, are unlikely to have much traction in a more general context. So much of the abuse people suffer at the hands of the media is unlikely to be solved by such reportorial tactics. But using such tactics will at least reduce the involvement of the external press in such evil. As Loretta Hieber puts it (1998), traditional journalism that "seeks to report conflicts for a general audience in a manner aimed at promoting peace rather than inflaming existing tensions" is one means of media intervention.

Such changes in practice are no small matter. Robert Karl Manoff (1998) argues that the scale of human slaughter in the twentieth century was "something new in human history." Whereas a "mere 19 million people died in the 211 major conflicts of the Nineteenth Century" and only seven million in the eighteenth, the twentieth century saw 110 million people killed in 250 significant armed conflicts, with

> many times that number wounded, crippled, and mutilated..... Mass violence on a previously unimaginable scale has become universalized, industrialized, and routinized. By now there are 233 politically active communal groups in 93 countries, representing fully one-sixth of humanity, at present engaged in political or military struggles from which more than 20 million refugees are currently in flight.

The industrialization of mass violence began with the Third Reich (Bauman, 1989), and has continued with the increasing distribution and use of cheap weaponry—from Kalashnikovs to machetes, tanks to heavy machine guns, helicopter gunships to "smart bombs" and "bunker busters." And if Benjamin Barber (1995) and Thomas Friedman (1999) are correct in their assessment of the oppositional tendencies of the current age—where grasping for modernity goes hand in hand with tribalism—then the likelihood that such conflicts will diminish over time seems dim indeed.

Such tribal identities and the hatred that often accompanies them suggest that the media must see both parties (or all parties in multi-party conflict) as the "other," and not use definitions of the "other" as supplied by any of the conflicting parties themselves. There is some foundational justification for such a perspective. Most of the world's major religions, for instance, do have expectations that those defined as the "other" will not be subject to degradation or violence. But, at the same time, while any of them might serve as a foundation for journalists to justify refusal to accept characterizations that are the result of military or political expediency, or even to protect people so identified as enemies, several of these religious traditions have been compromised by world conflicts. Different factions are fighting for the soul of Islam as those with more moderate views—the majority of Muslims by all accounts—find their faith debased by those who equate it with terrorism, or ridiculed by those with more radical leanings. Judaism, both as historical "enemy" of Arabs in its Zionist form and as aggressor in the guise of Israeli anti-terror policies, is currently a frail reed to support the weight of the media. And Christianity, too, has seen its moral authority weakened in conflict situations by the willingness of those who share a faith to slaughter one another (Protestants vs. Catholics in Northern Ireland, Orthodox vs. Catholic in Croatia, Catholics and Adventists indicted for crimes against humanity in Rwanda) and by controversies apparently inadvertently initiated by Pope Benedict. So while the foundation for an independent ethical stance for the media may be present in these traditions, all find their moral authority weakened by circumstances.

The dominance of the Western media is being challenged as never before around the world. New satellite channels, new independent media outlets, new applications on the Internet (including blogs, vlogs, Youtube, Google video) and citizen journalism via cell phone, have all developed using different understandings of the role of communication media in conflict situations. The uploading of bomb damage from Israeli warplanes in Beirut via cell phone cameras and the Internet to Google Earth so that the world could see the results within hours of the nighttime raids challenges the notion of "big media" as gatekeepers, as those who construct the meaning for the world's peoples, and contribute to the global understanding of history. But the Western media are still the *sine qua non* of ethics in the world of media—whether deserved or not. In the long run, this is the truly significant aspect of practice that media professionals should cherish. As Fred H. Cate puts it (1996, p. 19), "the power of public communications...poses important issues about the capacity of such communications to misinform, distort, and misfocus attention." This is where the Western media must concentrate its attention—on preventing such results. But it is also easy to lose this quality to other media systems, especially if all that characterizes Western media is increasing attention to sensationalism, decreasing attention to investigation, and continuing use of the words, images, myths, archetypes and socially-constructed frames of understanding that are promoted by groups perpetrating evil—whether those are domestic or foreign.

## REFERENCES

Albright, Madeleine K. (2001). "Around-the-Clock News Cycle a Double-Edged Sword." Interviewed by Nicholas Kralev. *Press/Politics.* 6. (1). 105–108.

Alexis, Monique, and Mpambara, Ines. (2002, March). *IMS Assessment Mission: The Rwanda Media Experience from the Genocide.* International Media Support.

Al-Marashi, Ibrahim. (2006). "The Dynamics of Iraq's Media: Ethno-Sectarian Violence, Political Islam, Public Advocacy, and Globalization." http://www.policy.hu/almarashi/policypaperdecember2006. html. Accessed January 11, 2007.

Anderson, Terry. (1993). "Terrorism and Censorship: The Media in Chains." *Journal of International Affairs.* 47. (1). 127–136.

Article 19. (1996). *Broadcasting Genocide: Censorship, Propaganda & State-Sponsored Violence in Rwanda 1990–1994.*

Artz, Lee. (2004). "War as Promotional 'Photo Op': The *New York Times*'s Visual Coverage of the U. S. Invasion of Iraq." *War, Media, and Propaganda: A Global Perspective.* Yahya R. Kamalipour and Nancy Snow, Eds. Lanham, MD: Rowman and Littlefield. 79–92.

Bamford, James. (2001, Winter). "Is the Press Up to the Task of Reporting These Stories?" *Nieman Reports.* 19–22.

Barber, Benjamin R. (1995). *Jihad vs. McWorld.* New York: Random House.

Barnhurst, Kevin G. (1991). "Contemporary Terrorism in Peru: Senderoso and the Media." *Journal of Communication.* 41. (4). 75–89.

Bauman, Zygmunt. (1989). *Modernity and the Holocaust.* Ithaca, NY: Cornell University Press.

Bernhard, Nancy. (2003, Summer). "Embedding Reporters on the Frontline." *Nieman Reports.* 86–88.

Calabrese, Andrew. (2005). "Casus Belli: U.S. Media and the Justification of the Iraq War." *Television and New Media.* 6 (2). 153–175.

Carruthers, Susan L. (2000). *The Media at War.* New York: Palgrave.

Cate, Fred H. (1996). "Communications, Policy-Making, and Humanitarian Crises." *From Massacres to Genocide: The Media, Public Policy, and Humanitarian Crises.* Robert I. Rotberg and Thomas G. Weiss, Eds. Washington, D.C.: The Brookings Institution. 15–44.

Clark, Roy Peter. (2006). "Civil War and Civil Language: Word Choice and the Newsroom." PoynterOnline. Accessed January 10, 2007, http://www.poynteronline.org

Davis, Alan. "Introduction: Regional Media in Conflict." Institute for War and Peace Reporting. (2001). *Regional Media in Conflict: Case Studies in Local War Reporting.* (June). 4–11. www.iwpr.net. Accessed January 11, 2007.

Eknes, Åge, and Endresen, Lena C. (1999). *Local Media Support.* Fafo-report 320. Oslo, Norway: Fafo Institute for Applied Social Science.

Fachot, Morand. (2001, January-February). "The Media Dimension in Foreign Interventions." *Options Politiques.* 50–55.

Friedman, Thomas L. (1999). *The Lexus and the Olive Tree: Understanding Globalization.* New York: Farrar, Straus and Giroux.

Frohardt, Mark, and Temin, Jonathan. (2003). *Use and Abuse of Media in Vulnerable Societies.* Special Report 110. Washington, D.C.: United States Institute of Peace.

Garrels, Anne. (2004). *Naked in Baghdad: The Iraq War and the Aftermath as Seen by NPR's Correspondent.* New York: Picador.

Gilboa, Eytan. (2000). "Mass Communication and Diplomacy: A Theoretical Framework." *Communication Theory.* 10. (3). 275–310.

Gilboa, Eytan. (2005). "The CNN Effect: The Search for a Communication Theory of International Relations." *Political Communication.* 22. 27–49.

Gourevitch, Philip. (1998). *We Wish to Inform You that Tomorrow We Will be Killed with Our Children.* New York: Picador.

Gupta, Dipak K. (2001). *Path to Collective Madness: A Study in Social Order and Political Pathology.* Westport, CT: Praeger.

Hedges, Chris. (2003). *War Is a Force That Gives Us Meaning.* New York: Random House. Accessed on www.coldtype.net January 7, 2007.

Hieber, Loretta. (1998). "Media as Intervention: A Report from the Field." *Track Two.* 7. (4). www.ccr.uct.ac.za. Accessed January 11, 2007.

Hieber, Loretta. (2001). *Lifeline Media: Reaching Populations in Crisis.* Washington, D.C.: Post-Conflict Unit, The World Bank.

Kellow, Christine L., and Steeves, H. Leslie. (1998). "The Role of Radio in the Rwandan Genocide." *Journal of Communication.* 48. (3). 107–128.

Kelman, Herbert C. (1995). "Decision Making and Public Discourse in the Gulf War: An Assessment of Underlying Psychological and Moral Assumptions." *Peace and Conflict.* 1. (2). 117–130.

Larson, Ronald Paul. (2004). "Anatomy of a Bonding: An Embedded Reporter's Account of the Bonding Process with Soldiers." *War, Media, and Propaganda: A Global Perspective*. Yahya R. Kamalipour and Nancy Snow, Eds. Lanham, MD: Rowman and Littlefield. 125–130.

Lynch, Jake. (2001). "Iraq, Peace Journalism and the Construction of Truth." www.wacc.org.uk. Accessed January 9, 2007.

Lynch, Jake. (2002, March–April). "Journalist Ethics and Reporting Terrorism." *The Conflict, Security & Development Group Bulletin*. 9–11.

MacDonald, David Bruce. (2002). *Balkan Holocausts? Serbian and Croatian Victim-Centered Propaganda and the War in Yugoslavia*. New York: Manchester University Press.

Manoff, Robert Karl. (1998). "Telling the Truth to Peoples at Risk: Some Introductory Thoughts on Media & Conflict." www.bu.edu/globalbeat/pubs/manoff0798.html. Accessed January 11, 2007.

Marx, Willem. (2006, September). "Misinformation Intern: My Summer as a Military Propagandist in Iraq." *Harper's Magazine*. 51–59.

Melone, Sandra D., Terzis, Georgios, and Beleli, Ozsel. (2002). "Using the Media for Conflict Transformation: The Common Ground Experience." *Berghof Handbook for Conflict Transformation*. www.berghof-center.org. Accessed January 11, 2007.

Mertus, Julie, Tesanovic, Jasmina, Metikos, Habiba, and Boric, Rada, Eds. (1997). *The Suitcase: Refugee Voices from Bosnia and Croatia*. Berkeley, CA: University of California Press.

Mirzoeff, Nicholas. (2004, April 10). "Invisible Again: Rwanda and Representation after Genocide." BBC News. Accessed on www.questia.com January 1, 2007.

Murray, Shoon Kathleen, and Cowden, Jonathan A. (1999). "The Role of 'Enemy Images' and Ideology in Elite Belief Systems." *International Studies Quarterly*. 43. 455–481.

Neuffer, Elizabeth. (2002). *The Keys to My Neighbor's House: Seeking Justice in Bosnia and Rwanda*. New York: Picador.

O'Heffernan, Patrick. (1993). "Sobering Thoughts on Sound Bites Seen 'Round the World.'" In *Desert Storm and the Mass Media*. Bradley S. Greenberg and Walter Gantz, Eds. Hampton Press. Reproduced on July 2, 2001. Accessed at http://ics.leeds.ac.uk/papers/vf01.cfm?folder=193&outfit=pmt, January 7, 2007.

Orwell, George. (1946). "Politics and the English Language." http://www.orwell.ru/library/essays/politics/english/e_polit. Accessed January 10, 2007.

Paul, Christopher, and Kim, James J. (2004). "Reporters on the Battlefield: The Embedded Press System in Historical Context." Santa Monica, CA: RAND Corporation.

Petley, Julian. (2003). "War Without Death: Responses to Distant Suffering." *Journal for Crime, Conflict and the Media*. 1. (1). 72–85.

Price, Monroe E. (2000). "Part II: The Case Studies—Bosnia-Herzegovina. "Restructuring the Media in Post-Conflict Societies: Four Perspectives." Monroe E. Price, Ed. *Cardozo Online Journal of Conflict Resolution*. 2. (1). 1–56. http://www.cojcr.org/vol2no1/article01.html. Accessed January 11, 2007.

Reich, Hannah. (2003). "Constructive Discourse Transformation: Media Work in Asymmetrical, Intercultural Conflicts—The Case of the Middle East." Berghof Occasional Paper No. 22. Berghof Research Center for Constructive Conflict Management. www.berghof-center.org. Accessed January 9, 2007.

Reljic, Dusan. (n.d.) *The News Media and the Transformation of Ethnopolitical Conflicts*. Berghof Research Center for Constructive Conflict Management. Accessed at www.berghof-handbook.net on January 9, 2007.

Robinson, Piers. (2000, April 10–13). "The News Media and Intervention: Critical Media Coverage, Policy Uncertainty and Air Power Intervention during Humanitarian Crisis." Paper for the Political Studies Association—UK Annual Conference. London.

Schechter, Danny. (2004). "Selling the Iraq War: The Media Management Strategies We Never Saw." *War, Media, and Propaganda: A Global Perspective*. Yahya R. Kamalipour and Nancy Snow, Eds. Lanham, MD: Rowman and Littlefield. 25–32.

Seierstad, Åsne. (2003). *The Bookseller of Kabul*. Ingrid Christopherson, Trans. New York: Little, Brown.

Shadid, Anthony. (2006). *Night Draws Near: Iraq's People in the Shadow of America's War*. New York: Picador.

Skoko, Mirjana and Woodger, William. (2000). "The Military and the Media." *Degraded Capability: The Media and the Kosovo Crisis.* Philip Hammond and Edward S. Herman, Eds. Sterling, VA: Pluto Press. 79–87.

Solomon, Norman. (2004). "Spinning War and Blotting Out Memory." *War, Media, and Propaganda: A Global Perspective.* Yahya R. Kamalipour and Nancy Snow, Eds. Lanham, MD: Rowman and Littlefield. 47–58.

Stacks, John F. (2003–2004, Winter). "Hard Times for Hard News: A Clinical Look at U. S. Foreign Coverage." *World Policy Journal.* 12–21.

Steele, Bob. (2000). "Guiding Principles for the Journalist." PoynterOnline. Accessed January 10, 2007, http://www.poynteronline.org

Tehranian, Majid. (2004). "War, Media, and Propaganda: An Epilogue." *War, Media, and Propaganda: A Global Perspective.* Yahya R. Kamalipour and Nancy Snow, Eds. Lanham, MD: Rowman and Littlefield. 237–242.

Vaina, David. (2006). "The Vanishing Embedded Reporter in Iraq." October 26. Accessed on www.journalism.org on January 9, 2007.

Wilmer, Franke. (1998). "The Social Construction of Conflict and Reconciliation in Former Yugoslavia." *Social Justice.* 25. (4). 90+. Accessed on www.questia.com on January 1, 2007.

Zelizer, Barbie, and Allan, Stuart. (2003). "Introduction: When Trauma Shapes the News." *Journalism after September 11.* Barbie Zelizer and Stuart Allan, Eds. New York: Routledge. 1–24.

# 26

# Ethical Tensions in News Making: What Journalism Has In Common with Other Professions

## Sandra L. Borden and Peggy Bowers

There has been increasing recognition of the commonalities between journalism and other professions. At the Applied Media Ethics Colloquium sponsored by the *Journal of Mass Media Ethics* in 2003, teams composed of media ethicists and ethicists who study other professions compared ethical concerns across fields, suggesting places where journalism and other professions converged morally and places where they went their separate ways. This chapter continues that work by situating the study of comparative ethical concerns within previous research on professionalism in journalism and by drawing parallels with other professions to illustrate key ethical tensions that cut across domains. This analysis centralizes ethical concerns regarding epistemology and identity to derive the following ethical tensions: the tension between attachment and disinterest; the tension between authority and fallibility; the tension between autonomy and accountability; the tension between individual and community; and the tension between procedure and substance. In discussing these tensions, we suggest parallels with medicine, the academy, engineering, public administration, and law. Underlying all these tensions is the peculiar nature of professional power, its uses and abuses.

## WHO IS A PROFESSIONAL?

Noting the lack of a common literature and common associations among mainstream journalists, Weaver, Beam, Brownlee, Voakes, & Wilhoit (2007) conclude: "There is a professional mindset among U.S. journalists, but its influence is found mainly in individual news organizations rather than in the larger institutions of journalism" (p. 243). This assessment illustrates the attribute approach to studying professions. Basically, an occupation qualifies as a profession if it possesses certain idealized attributes. These attributes include: mastery of a complex body of knowledge, considerable discretion in how members define and perform their work; organization along collegial lines of authority; and a commitment to public service and common standards of excellence. Journalists usually get left off the list of professions based on the attribute approach. Although journalists are committed to public service, their ethical views are quite diverse, their expertise is disputed, and their prerogatives are severely limited by the hierarchical organizations that employ them.

Some professionalism scholars dismiss idealized attributes as irrelevant and focus on professional identity from the perspective of the workers themselves. This phenomenological approach focuses on what professionalism means when workers use the term. Studies that focus on journalists' perception of objectivity as an ethical norm are an example of this approach (Beam, 1990). Of course, many workers aspire to the prestige and purposefulness that professionalism implies and invoke the term as nothing more than a way of expressing their own personal commitment to competence and service. However, the professional label is problematic for journalists because of its implications for controlling member entry. Many journalists think that any barriers to entry—especially legal ones, such as licensing—pose intolerable dangers to press freedoms under the First Amendment. Therefore, the term "professional" is contested among journalists themselves. Some embrace and promote it; others reject it on principle. The fact that many journalists see themselves as professionals, however, has moral significance insofar as they make promises and other commitments related to this identity. Journalists' fidelity to these commitments can be evaluated in moral terms.

## POWER AND PROFESSIONALISM

American journalism also enjoys enough status and legitimacy to wield considerable influence, whether or not it possesses enough traditional attributes to qualify as a full-fledged profession. To the degree that their influence translates into dependency and vulnerability on the part of others, we can scrutinize journalists' responsible exercise of power (Elliott, 1986). Professional ethics, with its assumption of power asymmetries in professional relationships, provides a useful starting point for such an examination. May (2001) suggested that professional authority is essentially adversarial because it is based on the ability of professionals to protect clients from negatives such as diseases, lawsuits, and despots. Clients are forced to accept diminished autonomy in their relationships with professionals in exchange for their protection. "Structurally, the professional's relationship to the client resembles the relationship of the Lockean state to the citizen. Both the state and the professional owe their original authority to a threat" (pp. 61–62).

In journalism, this feature of professionalism is captured in the image of the press as watchdog: You need us to be on the lookout for corrupt officials, business scams, tornadoes, and crime waves while you go on with your busy lives. If something important comes up, we'll let you know. Journalism's clients become monitorial citizens (Schudson, 1998) whose only role is to scan the news for immediate threats to their well-being and who, by definition, must rely on journalists to tell them what they ought to care about. Sometimes, clients resent their diminished autonomy enough to walk away from the professional relationship altogether. In fact, the migration of news audiences to non-professional bloggers and other "content providers" may be partly motivated by a desire for more egalitarian transactions.

Journalism's agenda-setting function has been highlighted by critics of the media's power at least since Vice President Spiro Agnew's public critiques in 1969 (Altschull, 1990). In fact, Bowers, Meyers, and Babbili (2004) defined power as "the ability to achieve one's agenda, usually by manipulating others" (p. 227). Using this definition, they concluded that the institutional procedures used to define news control more than just what gets on the radar of public opinion; they also control the agenda in journalists' interactions with subjects and sources, with the public, and with other nations. Power in journalism is also problematic because the profession lacks a proximate relationship with its clients, the "public." Journalism's clientele exists as a diffuse entity often conceptualized in self-serving terms. There is no opportunity for journalists to personally invest themselves in the well-being of their clients or to sympathize with their vulnerability.

Although other professionals face the temptation of stereotyping their clients, there is a reality check built into their interactions with individuals seeking their services. Journalists, by contrast, have their most personal interactions with sources and subjects; that is, third parties in the professional–client relationship. As third parties, sources and subjects cannot count on being the intended beneficiaries in their interactions with journalists. There is, in other words, no concrete basis for trusting that journalists will refrain from exploiting the vulnerability of either the public or the individuals who provide the raw material for news stories.

## PROFESSIONALISM AND JOURNALISM ETHICS

### Professionalism as a Source of Individual Autonomy

Individual autonomy is an important presumption of those who train for and enter the professions, and it is no different in journalism. Journalism ethics scholars, too, have privileged autonomy. In one of his earlier and best-known works (1974), Merrill famously championed radical freedom for journalists. He wrote, "The authentic journalist—the truly moral one—would not act to please somebody or to gain some advantage or to secure some reward....The act should be done because the journalist is convinced that it is right" (p. 186). Merrill's unflinching call for radical autonomy propelled him to oppose most reform movements of the 20th century, including public journalism, and to worry about the waning of press autonomy in the face of increasing public participation in journalism. His position on autonomy did not mean he embraced professionalism as others have. In fact, he called professions a "narrow, monolithic, self-centered fellowship of true believers" (1986, p. 56) who posed a threat to press freedom. His students and colleagues have not shared this view of professions, but have supported his emphasis on autonomy as central to the journalistic mission (e.g. Barger & Barney, 2004) and under siege in the contemporary environment of new media (Singer, 2007).

Indeed, journalists have a "visceral attachment to autonomy" (Glasser & Gunther, 2005, p. 389). They want to choose which stories to cover, how to cover them, and how to report or illustrate them. They also expect, more generally, to be independent from other individuals within and without the profession, an expectation reinforced by the competitive ethos of American newsrooms and the liberal tradition of interpreting freedom of expression as a negative right. Weaver et al. (2007) found that perceived autonomy is a major predictor of job satisfaction and intention to continue working as a journalist. Ironically, rather than being a paragon of journalistic practice, autonomy itself may make it difficult to ask normative questions and to promote a democratically useful press (Kunelius, 2006). Finally, as Glasser and Gunther noted, journalists' reluctance to participate directly in allocative decisions at their organizations has had the unintended consequence of limiting their actual influence on the conditions and quality of their work.

### Professionalism as an Instrument of Organizational Control

It is true that professionalism does afford practitioners some measure of discretion (Soloski, 1989), but the high level of autonomy implied by many professional ethics codes does not exist—if it ever did. Far from enjoying total control over their work, most professionals labor within bureaucratic structures that organize work along hierarchical lines of authority. These professionals have used various strategies to insulate themselves from organizational influences—for example, newspapers until recently enforced an imaginary "wall" between their editorial and advertising departments.

However, the reality of organizational life is that professionals are as susceptible as other employees to organizational socialization processes and reward systems. Indeed, research on the sociology of news work suggests that news organizations have successfully co-opted professional values by equating them with efficient routines that unobtrusively control news workers even while affording them some freedom from direct supervision (e.g., Gans, 1980; Soloski; Tuchman, 1977). Journalists' level of autonomy is, in fact, so inadequate relative to professional expectations that some authors have suggested that journalists are effectively excused from meeting the stringent moral obligations of truthfulness and independence espoused by their profession (Birkhead, 1986; McManus, 1997). In other words, they cannot be held fully accountable after all.

## Professionalism as a Source of Accountability and Ethical Norms

Professionals are to avoid abusing the inherent power inequality in the professional–client relationship by acting as trustees of their clients' best interests. To earn the trust of their clients and of society, professionals voluntarily adopt codes of ethics that spell out their aspirations and minimal moral expectations. That is, they make themselves answerable, or accountable, to others. In journalism, there are a number of professional societies that have made public statements about ethical standards that apply to journalists generally (e.g., the code of the Society for Professional Journalists) and to particular subsets of the profession (e.g., the code of the National Press Photographers Association). These statements tend to focus on the principles of truthfulness, independence, and non-maleficence.

Nevertheless, journalists do not appeal regularly to their own ethics codes when making ethical decisions (Boeyink, 1994). And, although the ethics code for the Society of Professional Journalists embraces accountability as one of its four guiding principles, journalists (like other professionals) are better at preventing interference from outsiders than they are at inviting scrutiny from outsiders. This stance has become more and more of a losing proposition as "transparency" becomes the new motto of public communicators who are no longer willing to simply trust journalists' motives and expertise.

## Professionalism as a Source of Individual Identity

When professionals become socialized into a profession, they acquire a new identity. That identity includes expectations of collegiality and autonomy, as well as commitments to a common purpose and common standards of excellence. Social scientists studying professionalism have tried to measure such dimensions of professional identity via individual indicators, such as membership in professional organizations. Embedded in these inquiries are questions about the central role of professionalism and professionalization in how journalists construct their identities and embody journalistic values (McLeod & Hawley, 1964). Longitudinal studies exploring the demographics of newsrooms in the United States and globally have illuminated the changing face of journalism and suggested roles that journalists feel most comfortable playing—for example, as information disseminators, interpreters, or adversaries (Weaver et al., 2007). They also reflect roles that are more surprising or less comfortable for journalists—for example, cultural elite and corporate creatures (Overholser, 1998).

The latter term is itself a subject of special scrutiny in the literature on professionalism and identity. Such studies are a kind of contemporary and journalistic development of Whyte's (1956) classic treatise, *Organization Man*, in which he argued that a social ethic is at work in society, morally legitimating "pressures of society against the individual" and exploiting our belief that belongingness is the "ultimate need of the individual" (p. 7). What that means is that organizational identity impinges on journalists' constructions of their own professional identities. Nevertheless, professionalism also provides a strong alternative target of identification within news organizations. Professional journalists, in effect, have access to independent external standards for evaluating journalistic work and news management (Soloski, 1989). With the right amount of solidarity, the profession can function as a moral community that can provide a frame of reference for feeling both professional shame and professional pride (Borden, 2007). Unfortunately, an emphasis on professionalism as an individual characteristic rather than one that is held in common with other colleagues has impeded the development of professional organizations and unions that could address journalists' work conditions (Fedler, 2006; Glasser & Gunther, 2005; Weaver et al., 2007) and could offer concrete support for individuals who take courageous action in behalf of the profession's shared values (Borden, 2000). In fact, Weaver and Wilhoit (1996) wrote, "contrary to many of the critics, journalism's major problems may stem from too little professionalization, not too much" (p. 127).

## Professionalism as a Source of Cultural Authority

Professionalism gives journalism, like other occupations that claim to produce specialized knowledge, a measure of *cultural authority*; that is, authority to interpret reality (Winch, 1997). Other professions have the authority to announce medical breakthroughs or offer legal interpretations; journalism's niche is sifting through events and issues and declaring some of these to be "news." This determination is made by applying specialized gate keeping, reporting, and writing techniques.

According to Winch (1997), cultural authority has three dimensions: collegial (based on the regard of peers), cognitive (based on recognized intellectual standards), and moral (based on an altruistic orientation). All three dimensions are significantly enhanced by professional status: Self-regulation serves as quality control. Expertise guarantees need for services. A vocational orientation limits the pursuit of self-interest. The more professionalized an occupation is, the more convincing are its claims of legitimacy and the more power it enjoys in society. Journalism's rather weak claims to professional status partly explain its relative lack of occupational power within organizations and within the market. Journalism's cultural authority has also suffered because "laypersons" now have easy access to information on the Internet and can fact-check stories and personally examine the raw materials on which news accounts are based.

That being said, journalists will take what they can get. When journalism's cultural authority is threatened, its practitioners move to rhetorically draw boundaries that will solidify their standing with the public, whether the threat comes from purveyors of entertainment (Bishop, 2004; Winch, 1997) or the information slingers on the Internet (Singer, 2003). For example, journalists in the 1980s denounced the tabloids as unreliable purveyors of gossip. In the 1990s, they criticized cable TV pundits who mixed fact with opinion. Today, they point out that most bloggers do not do their own reporting.

## Professionalism and the Production of Knowledge

Knowledge is a "core generating trait" of professionalism (as cited in Macdonald 1995, p. 185). Journalists do not necessarily lay claim to the auspicious task of creating knowledge, though they would readily accede their part in reporting the knowledge that others create or discover. Still, journalists' participation in producing that unique animal known as news reflects a larger epistemological battle between an impartial account of an objective reality on the one hand and a socially and culturally constructed narrative of society's goals and values on the other.

Sociologists in the 1970s called into question objectivity's ability to effect what its practitioners intended:

> Bringing to the forefront issues like values, roles, and ethics, what emerged from (the sociological) literature was a growing recognition that journalists crafted standards of action collectively with others and that those standards in turn structured journalists' approaches to news. (Zelizer, 2004, p. 58)

Tuchman (1972) portrayed objectivity as a strategic ritual whose uses were both pragmatic and procedural. Schudson's (1978) historical study of the rise of objectivity further exposed its less-than-sanctimonious origins. Thus began the questioning of whether and to what extent newspeople would be able to execute their mission of reporting the truth with dispassionate exactitude. Tumber and Prentoulis (2005) remarked that, "the problems of basing a professional practice on such an illusive concept have never ceased to challenge" (p. 65).

Critiques of objectivity flung open the door of postmodern questioning (Hallin, 1992), as did scandals in newsgathering (Eason, 1986). At the center of the debate was the very nature of language itself. According to Taylor (1985), language can never be neutral and by its very nature constitutes rather than merely describes. This process of articulation means that journalists will not be able to portray some sort of truth with a capital T regardless of their use (or omission) of adjectives and adverbs. Some scholars suggest that objectivity can be refurbished by incorporating contemporary insights into the nature of knowledge and inquiry (Ryan, 2001; Ward, 2005). However, if knowledge is contingent rather than pre-existent, epistemologically constructed rather than objective, constituted rather than depicted by language, professionalism arguably functions as an impediment to media morality by occluding the journalist's role in creating news. Scraps of information replace the holistic cloth of knowledge. In T.S. Eliot's (1962) astute formulation, "Where is the wisdom we have lost in knowledge? Where is the knowledge we have lost in information?" (pp. 96–97).

## FUNDAMENTAL ETHICAL TENSIONS IN JOURNALISM AND OTHER PROFESSIONS

One of the most difficult ethical tensions in the work of professionals, and especially those who come face-to-face with human affliction and suffering, is to establish the appropriate relationship between attachment and disinterest.

### The Tension between Attachment and Disinterest: Parallels with Medicine

To what degree should a professional be interested only in the problem posed (diagnosis or treatment, gathering of information), removed from the actual person whom it affects? In 2006, *Quill* magazine highlighted the "unique dilemma" of whether Western journalists should help the subjects of their stories in developing countries (Reporters in Africa, 2006). Dilemma, with its Greek etymology, is a well-suited word, because it implies that both choices seem good, but exact a high price.

Although medicine is more self-consciously, directly, and unabashedly a helping profession than journalism, it too faces this enigma of negotiating the relationship between professional disinterest and attachment. Although a physician must display enough disinterest to approach diagnostic problems impartially and to maintain adequate interpersonal distance with patients, it does not seem ethically optimal to regard the persons under one's care exclusively in terms of clinical interest. Journalists likewise must see the persons about whom they report, take some responsibility for the consequences of their words and images, and yet avoid an emotional investment so deep that it precludes the ability to complexly describe multiple perspectives. It is the age-old tension implicit in journalism and in professionalism generally—the often forced dichotomy between being professional and being human (Bowers, 1998). One of the most poignant examples is that of South African photojournalist Kevin Carter, who committed suicide three months after accepting the 1994 Pulitzer Prize for his dramatic image of a vulture awaiting the demise of a starving Sudanese child.[1] Carter said after taking photographs for a half-hour, he left the toddler alone, sat under a tree to smoke a cigarette and cried. Reporters covering Hurricane Katrina faced the same predicament, some of them ultimately wading into chest-high water to pull a driver out of his sinking car, crying on air, giving food to those who were ill.

Another important issue is the power difference between professionals and the persons with whom they deal. Both journalists and doctors are in the dominant position. Many people involved in newsworthy events have had no experience with journalism, cannot imagine how they could appear in a story, and are notably unskilled at protecting their own interests. On the other hand, third parties often share an adversarial role, or at least one of disinterest, as shown by the common use of the term "source" to describe such persons. If the source is media savvy, the adversarial relationship is less morally problematic. In contrast, the equivalent in medicine is rarely the case. Many patients today come in much better informed than in the past, but they admittedly have no expertise in medicine and have much more willingness to trust the medical profession as a whole to protect their health interests. Both doctors and journalists must walk with ethical care in the life-and-death dramas of those whom they encounter. Bird (2005) has contended that journalists could profit by incorporating ethnography into their writing, a sentiment other scholars have echoed. Although she admits this would lead to greater ethical dilemmas, she maintains it would also lead to journalists becoming "aware of their sources as people" and "critical of the kind of easy answers that claim the story comes first" (p. 307). In other words, they might exercise authentic empathy, rather than the strategic empathy they routinely enact in their interactions with sources and subjects (Borden, 1993).

## The Tension between Authority and Fallibility: Parallels with the Academy

All professions can be morally evaluated in part on their exercise of what Code (1987) calls *epistemic responsibility*—that is, whether they use "good enough" standards to know what they claim to know. To demonstrate their reliability, professionals often vouch for the claims they make on the basis of expertise, which can be grounded in scientific study, objective reporting procedures, and so on. However, they risk looking naïve or self-serving if they do not acknowledge that they make mistakes or even that non-professionals may sometimes have the answers. This situation creates a tension between invoking authority and acknowledging fallibility. In this regard, journalists have much in common with academics. Scholars are more comfortable than journalists about stating the limitations of their research methods and even acknowledging the underlying assumptions of their work. That being said, they still have a stake in conferring authoritative status on their findings to distinguish scholarship from common-sense intuitions. Nowhere is this more evident than in the classroom, where the unequal status between teacher and student is predicated primarily on the professor's superior (and credentialed) knowledge of the field.

Certainly, raising questions is as useful as answering them when it comes to learning. Professors as well as journalists would be professing their expertise more responsibly and more credibly if they acknowledged the constructed and tentative nature of knowledge. For journalists, this would mean being more transparent about how they determine what is news and framing news in more tentative terms (Borden, 2007). They might network with citizen journalists and bloggers to provide citizens with a more complex view of the world while not relinquishing their special status as knowers who rely on independent reporting and other epistemological disciplines drawn from journalism's unique professional tradition.

## The Tension between Autonomy and Accountability: Parallels with Engineering

By making themselves answerable to those who depend on them, professionals voluntarily place limits on their discretion and get into the messy business of weighing the moral claims of diverse stakeholders. Professionals traditionally have addressed this tension between autonomy and accountability by ordering their obligations to moral claimants. Clients come first, then colleagues, then society, then third parties. In practice, however, the organizational context of professional work often defeats this strategy. Organizations typically mediate the relationships between professionals and their clients. Clients don't pay professionals directly, nor do they seek their services as individuals. Rather, they go through the organizations that employ professionals (Newton, Hodges, & Keith, 2004). This structure makes professionals directly accountable to their employers and only indirectly accountable to their clients. In this regard, journalists and engineers find themselves facing similar challenges.

Both journalistic and engineering clients are thus vulnerable to organizational professionals who may elect to pursue the interests of their employer over their interests. The best-known engineering example is the 1986 *Challenger* disaster. Robert Lund—an engineer who also was a vice president in the company that manufactured the space shuttle's defective rocket booster—was pressured to downplay the safety concerns he had as an engineer and to prioritize instead the efficiency and publicity concerns he had as a manager. The results, as we know, were tragic. Journalists likewise face situations in which the public's interest and the corporation's interest may be at odds. A well-known example is the decision by corporate officers at CBS News to initially prevent *60 Minutes* from airing a segment in 1995 that exposed wrongdoing by a major tobacco company. The story showed that Brown & Williamson deliberately manipulated the chemical content of its cigarettes to make them more addictive. CBS said it nixed the story for fear of being sued. Eventually, *60 Minutes* aired a shorter version of the story without identifying the whistleblower.

The organizational context of professional work is not the only complication. What about the moral claims of entities such as democracy or the environment? How is an engineer supposed to weigh the interests of an endangered owl against the interests of a client whose project will damage the owls' habitat? How is a journalist supposed to figure out the right approach to covering a referendum that effectively diminishes the rights of some citizens while enjoying strong support from the majority of voters in her state? Engineers are broadly accountable for being good stewards of the environment, just as journalists are broadly accountable for being good stewards of democracy. But the best way of resolving the kinds of conflicts illustrated by these examples is far from clear.

## The Tension between Individual and Community: Parallels with Public Administration

Community is another abstraction that tests the moral imagination of professionals. Professions may be collectives, but they are collectives that vouch for certain capacities of mind and heart belonging to *individual* practitioners (Larson, 1977). The tension between individual and communal identities is especially problematic for professions such as journalism, which have a prominent civic dimension. Excessive individualism threatens to impoverish conceptions of professionals as well as conceptions of citizens. In this regard, journalists have much in common with public administrators.

Christians, Schultze, and Sims (1978) note that early American newspaper editors used to train young apprentices with the idea that "reporting for a newspaper prepared one adequately to understand life" (p. 38). The way that a journalist inhabited the various roles involved in newspapering was inseparable from his understanding of his place in the local community. In contrast, the university-based system emphasized training to prepare one for specialized roles that were transferable from one community to another. This interchangeability made journalists at once more marketable and more scientific. It also made them resident aliens in the communities they covered. The resulting mindset of technical rationality, as Adams and Balfour (1998) call it in the public administration context, narrowed the moral concerns of professionals by removing any necessary reference to social goods. Indeed, any attempt to assert community claims as such is construed as interference or bullying.

This limitation makes interpreting the "public interest" difficult for both journalists and public administrators. What can the "public interest" mean in the modern sense if not an aggregation of individual interests? And so journalists report on opinion polls, and public administrators trust that the votes tallied on Election Day authoritatively express the will of the people. As Jos and Tompkins (1995) note, expanding public participation and dialogue means that public administrators may sometimes have to confront citizens with hard truths about the effects of public policy and the limits of government action. Likewise, journalists may need to do more than explain how much the latest government program is going to cost; they may need to help citizens make sense of the bill's underlying philosophy and whether it is likely to promote goals that sustain communities. They also need to resist equating "public" with the "majority"; in fact, there are a number of "publics" that may need help in articulating their separate interests and being heard—and heeded—in the larger public sphere (Haas & Steiner, 2001).

## The Tension between Procedure and Substance: Parallels with Law

In the tension between the Right and the Good, law as a profession is predisposed to favor the Right, which can lead to a valueless orientation. There is no substantive notion of the Good because of the assumption that values are not based in reason. While some scholars argue that values *can* be based in reason (Taylor, 1997), the concern here is what we will call proceduralism. Proceduralism is most closely identified with the political philosophy of liberalism, which is rights-based, rule-driven, and atomistic, and favors justice to the exclusion of compassion and other social values. The justice system embodies such a philosophy by emphasizing trust in the procedure to produce an ethical outcome (e.g., the jury system in which the mechanism for evidence examination and debate supposedly produces justice). In the case of journalism, this can be illustrated by the willingness of reporters to answer for the procedure used in newsgathering and writing, but not for the outcome of a story. It is a case of what Pech and Leibel (2006) call a "purely epistemic" (p. 146) practice disconnected from any ontological goal. In other words, journalists often make decisions based on what a procedure says they can do rather than determining what is good to do. The 2005 controversy over the Danish cartoons depicting the prophet Mohammed is one example. Journalists justified publishing the cartoons despite their offensiveness to many Muslims by saying it was their right, rather than by articulating why it was a *good* thing to do.

When journalists and other professionals make moral decisions based exclusively on rights, procedures, or autonomy, they forfeit opportunities to foster political discourse and to situate themselves in community; they ultimately risk making themselves meaningless in a global environment (Bowers, 2007; Glendon, 1991; Sandel, 1982). Freidson (2001) explained, "Transcendent values add moral substance to the technical content of disciplines" (p. 222). Yet this implies resisting "economic and political restrictions that arbitrarily limit (the profession's) benefits to others." May (2001) recommended that professionals engage in teaching and persuasion aimed at cultivating good habits, not just skillful technique aimed at neutralizing looming threats. In this way, clients would be actively involved in promoting shared goods, such as justice and knowledge.

## SUGGESTIONS FOR FURTHER RESEARCH

Ethical concerns regarding epistemology and identity manifest themselves in a series of tensions especially pronounced in professionals, including journalists. These tensions, of attachment and disinterest, authority and fallibility, autonomy and accountability, individual and community, procedure and substance, serve as one rubric for understanding the normative claims on professional life. They are only a beginning, but they also offer fruitful guidance for future research that can more broadly expand and complicate our thinking on professional ethics and its relationship to the practice of journalism.

Most fundamentally, journalism ethics scholarship and pedagogy must closely address the lived experiences of practicing journalists—past, present, and future—in a meaningful way (Pottker, 2005). This may mean searching for new problems, framing traditional problems in a new way, or being mindful of the changing cast of actors on the media landscape (Whitehouse & McPherson, 2002). The urgent need for more professional/academic dialogue clearly shone in the Media Ethics Summit II of 2007. For the first time in 20 years, media practitioners from a diverse set of professional organizations and senior ethics scholars met to discuss the state of media ethics. Many important concerns emerged from the discussions as practitioners shared the contemporary conditions under which they work as well as problems they foresaw. Such conversations need to be more frequent and the formal thoughts of the respective groups more accessible to one another.

Comparisons to the staid and often slowly adaptive professions such as medicine and law should function as tacit reminders that, for journalism ethics to be fecund, it must seek fresh soil and new horizons. On the other hand, well-established professions provide a roadmap for guild power (Larson, 1977) and collective consciousness, which could help improve journalists' working conditions and provide direction to technological innovation in journalistic practice. Without vision journalism ethics will perish—that is true, but so is the fact that ethics must be practical enough to realize the ideal. Toward that end, Harcup's (2002) call for academics to address the role of journalists as workers is timely. He wrote, "Seemingly oblivious to such mundane matters as the working conditions of practitioners, many academics continue to debate the ethics of journalism while ignoring the conditions under which such journalism is produced" (p. 112). Future research must consider how technology is changing the role and the identity of professionals (Starck, 2001). Here the work of Carey (1969, 1989) is worth re-examination, as he so astutely worried about the implications of the professional communicator privileging the descriptive while subsuming the interpretive. Cultural approaches (e.g., Zelizer, 1993), meanwhile, have the potential to move the field beyond a conception of professional identity as a static personal trait to a richer conception of professional identity as a dynamic construction that is negotiated in the context of professional interactions with colleagues, bosses, publics, and third parties.

It may be time to acknowledge the limited professional autonomy that journalists enjoy in practice and start devoting sustained effort to articulating the ethical responsibilities of news executives, media owners, and citizens (e.g., Adam, Craft, & Cohen, 2004; Barger & Barney, 2004). Journalism ethics scholars, meanwhile, can draw on the resources of journalism's own tradition to articulate and promote a more sophisticated professional epistemology that retains the best of objectivity while shedding its worst liabilities, along the lines suggested by Ward (2005). Finally, researchers must engage in thoughtful analysis of key political concepts as they relate to journalism's purpose and practices, including democracy, citizenship, and community. The professional journalist, after all, works in the public interest. Any useful system of ethical thought must accommodate that goal.

## NOTE

1. The incident has re-emerged in professional memory with the 2007 release of the documentary, *The Live and Death of Kevin Carter*.

## REFERENCES

Adam, G. S., Craft, S., & Cohen, E. D. (2004). Three essays on journalism and virtue. *Journal of Mass Media Ethics, 19* (3–4), 247–275.

Adams, G. B., & Balfour, D. L. (2004). *Unmasking administrative evil* (rev. ed.). Armonk, NY: M. E. Sharpe.

Altschull, H. (1990). *From Milton to McLuhan: The ideas behind American journalism*. New York: Longman.

Barger, W., & Barney, R. (2004). Media-citizen reciprocity as a moral mandate. *Journal of Mass Media Ethics, 19*(3&4), 191–206.

Beam, R. A. (1990). Journalism professionalism as an organizational-level concept. *Journalism Monographs*, No. 121, 1–43.

Bird, S. E. (2005). The journalist as ethnographer? How anthropology can enrich journalistic practice. In E. W. Rothenbuhler & M. Coman (Eds.), *Media anthropology* (pp. 301–308). Thousand Oaks, CA: Sage.

Birkhead, D. (1986). News media ethics and the management of professionals. *Journal of Mass Media Ethics, 1*(2), 37–46.

Bishop, R. (2004). The accidental journalist: Shifting professional boundaries in the wake of Leonardo DiCaprio's interview with former President Clinton. *Journalism Studies, 5*(1), 31–43.

Boeyink, D. E. (1994). How effective are codes of ethics? A look at three newsrooms. *Journalism Quarterly, 71*, 893–904.

Borden, S. L. (1993). Empathic listening: The journalist's betrayal. *Journal of Mass Media Ethics, 8*(4), 219–226.

Borden, S. L. (2000). A model for evaluating journalist resistance to business constraints. *Journal of Mass Media Ethics, 15*(3), 149–166.

Borden, S. L. (2007). *Journalism-as-practice: MacIntyre, virtue ethics and the press*. Aldershot, UK: Ashgate.

Bowers, P. J. (1998). *Taylor's practical reason and moral decision making among journalists*. Unpublished dissertation.

Bowers, P. J. (2007). Journalism's missed opportunities. *International Journal of Media and Cultural Politics, 3*(1), 89–93.

Bowers, P. J., Meyers, C., & Babbili, A. (2004). Power, ethics, and journalism: Toward an integrative approach. *Journal of Mass Media Ethics, 19*(3&4), 223–246.

Carey, J. (1969, January). The communications revolution and the professional communicator. *Sociological Review*, No. 13, 23–38.

Carey, J. (1989). *Communication as culture: Essays on media and society*. Boston: Unwin Hyman.

Christians, C. G., Schultze, Q. J., & Sims, N. H. (1978). Community, epistemology and mass media ethics, *Journalism History, 5*(2), 38–41, 65–67.

Code, L. (1987). *Epistemic responsibility*. Hanover, NH: University Press of New England.

Eason, D. (1986). On journalistic authority: The Janet Cooke scandal. *Critical Studies in Mass Communication, 3*, 429–447.

Eliot, T. S. (1962). Choruses from "The Rock." In *The complete poems and plays 1909–1950* (pp. 96–97). New York: Harcourt, Brace & World.

Elliott, D. (1986). Foundations for news media responsibility. In D. Elliott (Ed.), *Responsible journalism* (pp. 32–44). Beverly Hills, CA: Sage.

Fedler, F. (2006, August). *Reporters' conflicting attitudes and struggle to unionize*. Paper presented to the Association for Education in Journalism and Mass Communication, San Francisco.

Freidson, E. (2001). *Professionalism: The third logic*. Chicago: University of Chicago Press.

Gans, H. J. (1980). *Deciding what's news: A study of CBS Evening News, NBC Nightly News, Newsweek and Time*. New York: Vintage.

Glasser, T. L., & Gunther, M. (2005). The legacy of autonomy in American journalism. In G. Overholser & K. H. Jamieson (Eds.), *The press* (pp. 384–399). Oxford: Oxford University Press.

Glendon, M. A. (1991). *Rights talk: The impoverishment of political discourse*. New York: Free Press.

Haas, T., & Steiner, L. (2001). Public journalism as a journalism of publics: Implications of the Habermas-Fraser debate for public journalism. *Journalism, 2*(2), 123–147.

Hallin, D. (1992). The passing of the "high modernism" of American journalism. *Journal of Communication, 42*(3), 14–26.

Harcup, T. (2002). Journalists and ethics: The quest for a collective voice. *Journalism Studies, 3*(1), 101–114.

Jos, P. H., & Tompkins, M. E. (1995). Administrative practice and the waning promise of professionalism for public administration. *American Review of Public Administration, 25*(3), 207–273.

Kunelius, R. (2006). Good journalism: On the evaluation criteria of some interested and experienced actors. *Journalism Studies, 7*(5), 71–690.

Larson, M.S. (1977). *The rise of professionalism: A sociological analysis*. Berkeley: University of California Press.

MacDonald, K. M. (1995). *The sociology of the professions*. Thousand Oaks, CA: Sage.

May, W. (2001). *Beleaguered rulers: The public obligation of the professional*. Louisville, KY: Westminster John Knox Press.

McLeod, J. M., & Hawley, S. E., Jr. (1964). Professionalization among newsmen. *Journalism Quarterly, 41*, 529–538, 577.

McManus, J. H. (1997). Who's responsible for journalism? *Journal of Mass Media Ethics, 12*(1), 5–17.

Merrill, J. C. (1974). *The imperative of freedom: A philosophy of journalistic autonomy*. New York: Hastings House.

Merrill, J. C. (1986). Professionalization: Danger to press freedom and pluralism. *Journal of Mass Media Ethics, 1*(2), 56–60.

Newton, L. H., Hodges, L., & Keith, S. (2004). Accountability in the professions: Accountability in journalism. *Journal of Mass Media Ethics, 19*(3–4), 166–190.

Overholser, G. (1998, December). Editor Inc. *American Journalism Review*, pp. 48–62, 65.

Pech, G., & Leibel, R. (2006). Writing in solidarity: Steps toward an ethic of care for journalism. *Journal of Mass Media Ethics, 21* (2&3), 141–155.

Pottker, H. (2005). What is journalism for? Professional ethics between philosophy and practice. *Communications, 30*, 109–116.

Reporters in Africa struggle over when to help. (2006, June/July). *Quill Magazine*, p. 6.

Ryan, M. (2001). Journalistic ethics, objectivity, existential journalism, standpoint epistemology, and public journalism. *Journal of Mass Media Ethics, 16*(1), 3–22.

Sandel, M. (1982). *Liberalism and the limits of justice.* Cambridge, UK: Cambridge University Press.

Schudson, M. (1978). *Discovering the news: A social history of American newspapers.* New York: Basic Books.

Schudson, M. (1998). *The good citizen: A history of American civic life.* New York: Free Press.

Singer, J. B. (2003). Who are these guys? The online challenge to the notion of journalistic professionalism. *Journalism, 4*(2), 139–163.

Singer, J. B. (2007). Contested autonomy: Professional and popular claims on journalistic norms. *Journalism Studies, 8*(1), 79–95.

Soloski, J. (1989). News reporting and professionalism: Some constraints on the reporting of the news. *Media, Culture and Society, 11,* 207–228.

Starck, K. (2001). What's right/wrong with journalism ethics research? *Journalism Studies, 2*(1), 133–152.

Taylor, C. (1985). *Philosophical papers, vol. 1.* Cambridge, UK: Cambridge University Press.

Taylor, C. (1997). *Philosophical arguments.* Cambridge, MA: Harvard University Press.

Tuchman, G. (1972). Objectivity as strategic ritual: An examination of newsmen's notion of objectivity. *American Journal of Sociology, 77,* 660–679.

Tuchman, G. (1977). The exception proves the rule: The study of routine news practices. In P. M. Hirsch, P. V. Miller, & F. G. Kline (Eds.), *Strategies for communication research* (pp. 43–62). Beverly Hills, CA: Sage.

Tumber, H., & Prentoulis, M. (2005). Journalism and the making of a profession. In H. deBurgh (Ed.), *Making journalists: Diverse models, global issues* (pp. 58–74). London: Routledge.

Ward, S. J. A. (2005). *The invention of journalism ethics: The path to objectivity and beyond.* Montreal, Quebec: McGill-Queen's University Press.

Weaver, D. H., Beam, R. A., Brownlee, B. J., Voakes, P. S., & Wilhoit, G. C. (2007). *The American journalist in the 21st century: U.S. news people at the dawn of a new millennium.* Mahwah, NJ: Erlbaum.

Weaver, D. H., & Wilhoit, G. C. (1996). *The American journalist in the 1990s: U.S. news people at the end of an era.* Mahwah, NJ: Erlbaum.

Whitehouse, V., & McPherson, J. B. (2002). Media ethics textbook case studies need new actors and new issues. *Journal of Mass Media Ethics, 17*(3), 226–234.

Whyte, W. H, Jr. (1956). *The organization man.* New York: Simon & Schuster.

Winch, S. P. (1997). *Mapping the cultural space of journalism: How journalists distinguish news from entertainment.* Westport, CT: Praeger.

Zelizer, B. (1993). Journalists as interpretive communities. *Critical Studies in Mass Communication, 10,* 219–237.

Zelizer, B. (2004). *Taking journalism seriously: News and the academy.* Thousand Oaks, CA: Sage.

# 27

# Feminist Media Ethics

## Linda Steiner

## INTRODUCTION

Feminism and feminist ethics address how people can live together in healthy, productive, mutually satisfying ways and can alter social or political obstacles to a healthy, productive mutually satisfying life. Since media are integral to contemporary culture, feminism's commitment to ways of thinking and acting that are transformative and interventionist explains feminisms' concerns with media practices and content. Feminist theorizing, however, may seem a vague resource for helping to resolve ethical dilemmas in media and communication in part because feminists insist on contextualization. Most reject claims that ethical codes can be deduced from a set of timeless, logical, hierarchically-arranged rights; they resist universalizing, abstract, and disembodied conceptions. Furthermore, multiple approaches to ethics have emerged from feminism's differing accounts of how social relationships emerge in the first place: "Feminist ethics comprises a complex and theoretically *dis*unified body of work" (Calhoun, 2004, p. 8). Feminists repudiate philosophies that deauthorize women as moral agents or exclude women's experiences as a source of moral reflection. But, among other issues, they debate whether women and men engage in the same modes of ethical reasoning.

More to the point, feminist philosophers rarely focus explicit attention on media, and media scholars are rarely at the forefront of feminist ethics.[1] Perhaps the low status within philosophy's pecking order of feminist theory, of normative ethics and of moral psychology (Meyers, 2005), discourages a turn to professional ethics. Nonetheless, a feminist approach to professional ethics may be derived from four strands of work. First, and discussed below in the greatest detail, are the key concepts in feminist ethics. For example, the proposal of an ethics of care, while it is contested, applies to a range of journalism issues. Second, feminist epistemology applies not only to academic research in media and journalism but also to ethical dilemmas in professional practice. Embedded in feminist theories of ethical knowledge-seeking are concerns with researcher-subject relationships and critiques of objectivity relevant to journalism. Third, feminism's normative concerns with issues of verbal and visual representation and language per se highlight ethical dimensions of news and entertainment. Fourth, activists' complaints about various forms of workplace discrimination challenge media institutions to design workplaces that enable and encourage ethical sensitivity. Feminist ethics, then, applies to news and entertainment, and can help analyze and resolve problems that emerge in media research, content, and the workplace.

## THE EMERGENCE AND DEVELOPMENT OF FEMINIST ETHICS

Although second-wave feminists understood and practiced feminism as explicitly normative, scholars paid relatively little attention to developing a feminist ethics until the 1982 publication of *In a Different Voice: Psychological Theory and Women's Development*, widely regarded as a ground-breaking study of women's ways of analyzing and resolving dilemmas. Trained as a developmental psychologist, Carol Gilligan accused her former mentor Lawrence Kohlberg of missing women's distinctive ways of thinking, since his conception of morality as based in formal, abstract notions of rights, rules, and justice was based on interviews with males. This methodological failure accounted for why women apparently rarely attained the highest stage of moral development, as Kohlberg defined it. Gilligan's interviews with women (all white, middle-class North Americans) showed their moral development beginning selfishly and then maturing through a conventional stage based in relationships and responsibility to a post-conventional stage grounded in universal care.

> A morality of rights and abstract reason begins with an amoral agent who is separate from others and who independently elects moral principles to obey. In contrast, a morality of responsibility and care begins with a self who is enmeshed in a network of relations to others, and whose moral deliberation aims to maintain these relations. (Kittay & Meyers, 1987, p. 10)

For the next two decades, feminists debated the extent to which women's ethical decision-making differed from men's. Noddings (1984), for example, identified an intimate ethic of care that privileged maternal caring as a model for/of ethical decision making. Human interaction and dyadic caring relationships are ontologically fundamental. Noddings claimed that genuine caring—directed at people in definite relationships—involves "engrossment" (thoroughly attending to the cared-for, ignoring one's own concerns) and "motivational displacement" (setting aside one's goals to focus on the cared-for) and thus involves no judging or evaluating. Meanwhile, in adopting the goals of the cared-for, care-givers are transformed. Emphasizing that all humans depend on non-reciprocal caring by others, first as infants and children, and likely later as well, Kittay (1999) likewise saw this relationship of dependency as paradigmatic.

Others celebrated feminine traits and virtues that are popularly (and by so-called "maternal" thinkers) associated with women. Ruddick (1989) emphasized how mothers work hard to socialize children and cultivate their virtues while sometimes encouraging them to eschew values and traits that otherwise seem necessary for social success, but that they deem unethical. Mothering is a learned way of thinking, so if men spent as much time attending to children as women do, presumably men would also think maternally. Similarly, Manning (1992) took women's nurturing relationships as a model for care, adding that everyone has special responsibilities and is obligated to act on a disposition to care.

Although these scholars largely eschewed biological explanations, their works were widely criticized for essentializing sex/gender and conflating female/feminine/feminist. Gilligan (1982) ignored the impact of a history of sex stereotyping and subordination and falsely universalized women, ignoring differences in experiences interstructured with race, ethnicity, class, sexual orientation, as well as historical and material circumstances (Steiner, 1989). The debate shifted, however, once Gilligan (1987) explicitly denied that care/justice are opposites or that one is superior to the other. Care and justice cannot be "readily integrated" (p. 30), she conceded, and, practically speaking, only one can be deployed at a single moment; yet, one may be aware of both. More to the point, all relationships, public and private, can be characterized both in terms of equality and attachment. Both inequality and detachment are grounds for moral concern. Everyone is vulnerable both to oppression and abandonment.

Connected as it was to the "spontaneous" caring of children, Noddings's version of women's maternal role was even more controversial. Nonetheless, Noddings's 2002 book *Starting at Home* acknowledged, "Even theories, like children, can grow up and move into the public world" (p. 2). While the home is where people learn how to care, direct personal "caring-for" (or being cared-for) teaches "caring-about." So now, instead of rejecting rights-based approaches, she sees justice ethics as extensions of caring: "justice itself is dependent on caring-about, and caring-about is in turn dependent on caring-for" (p. 6).

This review of the initial emergence of an ethic of care, then, raises two main issues. First is the question of the term "feminist ethics" itself. By 1995 Gilligan distinguished between a "feminine" ethic of care, emphasizing special obligations and interpersonal relationships, and a "feminist" ethic of care, emphasizing connection. Indeed, she noted that the latter exposes disconnections in a feminine selflessness and self-sacrifice premised on a faulty, patriarchal opposition between relationships and autonomy. Koehn (1998) argues that feminine and feminist ethics share some problems but are not distinct categories. Koehn labels her approach "female ethics" because she opposed ethical traditions dominated by men/males and because canonical male philosophers have historically ignored women's interests.

Meanwhile, African-American women draw from Christian theology, black history, and feminist theory (but repudiating feminism's ethnocentrism) to generate "womanist" ethics.[2] But, many women moral philosophers are not feminist (Calhoun, 2004). Some men are. Notably, conceding that one could conceptualize the ethics of care without attaching an adjective, Sevenhuijsen (1998) refers to the "feminist ethics of care" both for the sake of historical accuracy and to show how care and ethics are interwoven with gender in ways requiring feminist interpretation. (Feminist ethicists rarely ignore care altogether.) Most importantly, the relevant perspectives cannot apply only to women or women's interests. All major problems and ethical dilemmas have impact for both women and men, although the consequences may be different and unequal. So I treat "feminist ethics" as acknowledging women's historical experiences and grounded in feminist theory, but understanding—and wanting to correct—the problems "engendered" by a host of power inequities.

More important than nomenclature is how care itself has developed. Some ethicists remain highly sympathetic, commending the ethic of care for highlighting, if not mitigating, important defects in justice theory, including its impersonality and potential for arbitrariness.

Caring is understood as including "everything we do directly to help others to meet their basic needs, develop or sustain their basic capabilities, and alleviate or avoid pain or suffering, *in an attentive, responsive and respectful matter*" (Engster, 2005, p. 55, italics in the original). Moreover, instead of deriving our duty to care from others' dependency on us, Engster grounds the obligation to care for others on our (common) dependency on others. Because we demand care from others for the reproduction of society, we should care for others in need. Drawing on Augustine and Emmanuel Levinas, and also sacredness, for her claim that caring is basic to flourishing as a human being, Grouenhout (2004) asserts that humans naturally tend to offer care, accept care, and to be caring—defined as the emotion involved in "tending to the physical needs of others" (p. 24).

Some ethicists are hostile. Maternal care may be extreme, oppressive, or at least distorted. Caring, or excessive caring, not only can hurt women (they can be exploited, for example) but also maims their capacity for moral autonomy and thus moral action (as when they protect people who are exploitive). For Bartky (1990), doing the family's emotional work and bolstering men's egos disempowers women, even if they demur on this point or are paid to care. Mendus (2000) says "domestic virtues are deformed when they are translated to a public world" (p. 114); meanwhile, political problems are characteristically large-scale and do not emerge at the level of individual relationships. In proposing lesbian ethics, Hoagland (1988) sees the "heterosexual" model of femininity as ultimately offering an ethics of dependence that amounts to a masculine model of the feminine; manipulation becomes the primary mode of female agency. Hoagland accuses Noddings of proposing an ethics of agape. Koehn (1998) suggests that maternal care approaches are politically naïve, over-privilege the earth mother, and too easily dismiss autonomy. The ethics of care is "insufficiently suspicious of the classically feminine moral failing of self-sacrifice" and open to invidious partiality (Jaggar 2000, p. 456).[3] And, of course, regardless of how care works as an ideal, it does not necessarily describe women's actual behavior, even with respect to other women.

The following sections outline and assess attempts to modify, extend, or challenge caring. I then show applications to questions of journalism practice, media research, news and entertainment content, and media workplaces. Articulating a practicable, productive ethic of care for journalism requires at a minimum extending the world of the moral beyond the family and even beyond friendship relationships.[4]

In my view, an ethical schema that works only for one sex or only in one domain will not suffice. Feminist theorizing emphasizes context but also the connection of the personal and political, so feminist ethics must serve media professionals at work and at home. Moreover, feminist ethics must be able to evaluate care, and criticize harmful, excessive, and other forms of unethical caring. Caring must be politicized and reconstructed to include caring for (some) strangers and distant communities if it is to be useful to media professionals—who are in relationships not only with known and "seen" sources and subjects, but also audiences not known to media professionals personally (Steiner & Okrusch, 2006). It is not that everyone and all issues must be treated equally. As Bell (2005) notes, ethical intersubjectivity cannot alone answer the question of ethics: "How far—across how much space and time, encompassing how many people—should I care?" (p. 502). Indeed, "Socializing care has the potential of infusing care values into political decisions and accepted ideas that underlie social values" (Hamington & Miller, 2006, p. xiv). A social ethic of care would simultaneously embrace human particularity and honor "the obligation to uphold that particularity in a social context of rights and fairness" (p. xv).

## REVISIONS OF THE ETHICS OF CARE

For Noddings (1984), care is not a virtue but a source of virtues, while Held (2006) sees care as both practice (in terms of caring relations) and value, but not as a virtue. Others propose a virtue ethics featuring both justice and care, usually with care put first, or as one among several feminist virtues. Justice and care, as values, invoke different moral considerations; but as practices, caring may also need values such as justice. Held defends the ethic of care as a distinct normative theory that emphasizes respecting and meeting the needs of particular others we take responsibility for. She calls for developing frameworks of caring about and for one another at both community and global levels. Sevenhuijsen (1998) and Sander-Staudt (2006) each note the risks in marrying care and justice. Sander-Staudt eventually prefers a freestanding feminist care ethic, albeit working collaboratively with virtue ethics; at best, even an open marriage between care and virtue ethics would require a prenuptial agreement and marital therapy. Worried that a hasty marriage will exclude politics, Sevenhuijsen (1998) sees care broadly, as a source of moral and political judgment, and thus treats care as a form of practice and human agency, and ethics as a political virtue.

Koehn (1998) proposes dialogic female ethics, on the grounds that if an ethic of care or empathy provides no incentive to self-reflection, caregivers may indulge in self-righteous anger, manipulation, or even violence. While care is intrinsically good, it cannot provide for the complete good; indeed, each of us is prone to error. Her solution is to structure opportunities for receivers of care to contest caregivers' expectations. Such a space requires principles (not rules), she says. Her dialogic female ethics thus incorporates the principles of male ethics into the consultative ethos of female ethics. It stresses human interdependence; requires empathy for the vulnerable; treats the domestic realm as having public significance; respects difference and individuality; emphasizes imaginative discourse and listening; and is transformative. But the "critical conversations" Koehn offers as crucial correctives are literal and interpersonal, without apparent application to professionals.

Many feminist theorists resist walling off the personal from the political, unwilling to regard justice as appropriate only to the public/political sphere while reserving care for the domains of family and charitable organizations. Care is relevant to the political domain, although it is needed most clearly in family and friendship contexts (Held, 2006). Care alone cannot handle all issues of justice and rights, but may be a broad framework for individual rights; it points to ways for radical restructuring of social, economic, and political policies. Commending the ethic of care for moral and political judgments, Tronto (1995) distinguished four phrases of care, each of which has a concomitant value: caring about, attentiveness; taking care of, responsibility; care giving, competence; and care receiving, responsiveness. Although many criticize her version of care as overly broad (for a review, see Sander-Staudt, 2006), Tronto insists: "[C]are is not solely private or parochial; it can concern institutions, societies, even global levels of thinking" (p. 145). She concedes that material imbalances in the amount of care that people receive, when integrated with justice, raise political questions: Determining who needs or deserves which kinds of care requires knowledge and thus public deliberation.

Denzin (1997) and Christians (2002, 2003) propose "feminist communitarian ethics," which is aimed at ennobling human experience, facilitating civic transformation, and promoting universal solidarity. Their point, following Benhabib, is that communitarianism takes as fundamental the social nature of the self, the connection of personal dignity and communal well-being, as well as the importance of care, justice, and interpersonal respect. Feminist communitarianism presumes that the community is ontologically and morally prior to persons; values, moral commitments and existential meanings are negotiated dialogically. How feminist communitarianism is different from communitarianism is not precisely clear, and using the terms interchangeably may be misleading. Denzin (1997) both embraces and rejects the universal, both embraces and rejects justice (see pp. 274–277).

Moreover, communitarian-minded philosophers do not necessarily ally themselves with feminism. Some of them ignore the effects of patriarchy and sex discrimination, as well as race, sexuality, or class, thus leaving in place a family in which sexual difference is deeply entrenched. Weiss (1995) explains why feminists and communitarians "have not been, are not, and perhaps cannot or should not be more consistent allies" (p. 161): With their more formal and even universalized notion of community, communitarians ignore feminists' concerns both with the profound impact of social context and the potential repression of specific communities. Communitarians worry about the loss of community boundaries whereas feminists worry about the costs of traditional boundaries (p. 167). Friedman (1993), for example, warns against communitarians, given their warm invocation of the norms and traditions of families, neighborhoods, and nations. That said, feminists might yet develop a distinctive version of communitarian ethic that usefully and significantly extends caring. More recently, Christians (2004) treats feminist communitarianism as an intermediary step to dialogic communitarianism, which, in embodying both communitarian political philosophy and feminist social ethics, is the most mature version of communal normative theory.

Finally, Fraser (1986) helpfully indicates how dominant groups (by gender, class, race) control the means of interpretation and communication, including by controlling official vocabularies, rhetorical devices, idioms for communicating one's needs, and the paradigms of argumentation accepted as authoritative in adjudicating conflicting claims. Rejecting a "universalist-formal" ethic, she advocates a dialogical ethic that "permits the thematization and critique of interpretations of needs, of definitions of situations and of the social conditions of dialogue, instead of establishing a privileged model of moral deliberation which effectively shields such matters from scrutiny" (p. 426). But instead of endorsing Gilligan's relational-interactive model of identity or highlighting emotions like love (although some feminists have recently rediscovered love), Fraser emphasizes a contextual, collective dimension in order to advocate the standpoint of the collective concrete other, a perspective focusing on that intermediate zone of group identity. The space between unique individuality and universal humanity leads Fraser to an ethic of solidarity governed by "norms of collective solidarities as expressed in shared but non-universal social practices" (p. 428).

Thus, to suggest caring as appropriate for journalists, who otherwise are committed to a formalist, rights-based insistence on neutrality, distance, and objectivity, requires first a politicized care that potentially embraces needy strangers and deserving communities. Importantly for media work, this notion of care requires thought, evaluation, deliberation, informed debate; even this radicalized notion of care cannot alone undergird an entire moral theory. Not all intimate caring relationships and contexts are moral; not all political "causes" are inherently moral and progressive.

## APPLYING THE ETHICS OF CARE TO RESEARCH

Sketching even an outline of feminist epistemology is impossible here, but feminist theories of researchers' ethical obligations to subjects, to social science, and to society have multiple implications for journalism/media research in both academic and applied "industrial" contexts. As both "a way of knowing and a coherent moral perspective" (Gilligan, 1987, p. 29), the ethic of care requires researchers as a voluntary community to be highly self-reflective and self-conscious about their ethical and scientific responsibilities. Feminist research takes seriously choice of topic: important problems, with potential for having a transformative impact, that help publics assess policies and provide good (valid, practical) reasons for acting (Koehn, 1998). Ethical researchers make research accessible to communities who need it, sharing it with subjects themselves, not merely at the end, but as the research proceeds. Agents of knowledge are not fundamentally different from objects of knowledge; both are socially located in space and time (Harding, 1993). Researchers humbly acknowledge their positioning and partiality, and do not claim to have all or "the" knowledge about others. Jaggar (2000) optimistically adds that "feminism's views about the processes, methods, and conclusions of good moral thinking are sufficiently varied, contested, and negotiable that each can provide a useful check on others" (p. 465).

Rouse (2004) specifically denies that feminist science is an epistemological analogue to an ethics of care. Nevertheless, he contrasts feminist scientists' "caring" attitude to androcentric aspirations to detachment. Feminist reconstructions of objectivity are, he says, attempts to hold knowers accountable for what they do (and for the effects of what they do) and to determine to whom and to what they need to be held accountable. These attempts take place with the recognition that inquiry and representation are inevitably partial and based in a particular perspective.

Feminists are concerned with the following ethical issues in research: who gets to speak, who is heard as authoritative and how knowledge claims become authoritative, whose concerns or potential responses must be considered when constructing knowledge accounts, who has access to the material and social resources needed for research, and how the resulting authorization of knowers/knowledge changes people's lives (Rouse, 2004).

Feminist moral epistemology thus offers a prescription for ethical research, including about media. Such ethics guide choice of topic, for example, including genres such as soap operas and romance novels, otherwise discredited by being associated with women and women's pleasure. Lotz (2000) suggests "studying up" audiences (e.g., industry executives and media policy makers) and introspective "native study," in contrast to the colonizing anthropologist who gazes upon exotic Others. Feminist epistemology also urges qualitative methods, despite the enormous investment of energy, emotion, time, and labor they require. When media scholars undertake ethnography, feminist principles again advise reflexivity, exposing power relations between researcher and participants, sharing conclusions or initial drafts with research participants, and attending to their feedback.

Denzin (1997) likewise sees a feminist communitarian ethic as building collaborative, reciprocal, friendly, trusting relations with ethnographic subjects, which includes giving them a voice in research design. It rejects positivism's ethical principles (beneficence, anonymity, and justice) and norms (validity and random selection). Instead, this ethic is grounded in community, so that research serves the community, reflects a community's multiple voices, and enables participants to act to transform their social world. Christians (2002) takes feminist communitarians to assume humans can "articulate situated moral rules that are grounded in local community and group understanding" (p. 169). Research so guided will represent multiple voices, enhance moral discernment, and promote transformation. Some researchers show its application, for example, to online communication. This approach requires researchers to: understand that members of newsgroups need to consent to research and accept the identity and purpose of the researcher, respect each participant and encourage the mission of the group; let participants have a say in the research questions, and use the research to benefit the group and its participants (Hall, Frederick, & Johns 2004).

## FEMINIST ETHICS FOR JOURNALISTS

The apparent fact that Noddings's caregivers can, ethically-speaking, care in private relationships and for relatively few people would seem by definition to exclude professional relationships. Perhaps journalists' resistance to such ethical approaches reflects not only their sense that this does not describe their work but that it cannot, given their ongoing struggle to maintain strategic routines. Associations with feminism would not appear to help much. More cynically, one might suspect that journalists and other media professionals prefer ethical codes that short-circuit external criticism by automatically forbidding risky and time-consuming processes of considering context and particularity. A former BBC correspondent ventures a "journalism of attachment"— "a journalism that cares as well as knows; that is aware of its responsibilities; that will not stand neutrally between good and evil, right and wrong" (Bell, 1998, p. 19). Otherwise, "caring" has little resonance among journalists. A duty to care is but rarely referenced at the Poynter Center, although one Center reporter who had covered religion and ethics mentions Gilligan's ethic of caring (McBride, 2002).

While not dispositive it is worth noting that the evidence that women journalists "do" ethics differently than men is mixed, at best. Journalism training and medium (print, broadcast, etc.), as well as socio-economic background and political values predict journalists' values and approaches to ethical decision making far better than gender (Weaver, 1997; Weaver & Wilhoit, 1996). Many women journalists adamantly deny that they report "like" or "as" women, although women may cover different topics, even covering them slightly differently—for example, more about the problems of women, more female sources, more human context (see Chambers, Steiner, & Fleming, 2004). Certainly the moral epistemology of media professionals deserves study—not descriptive surveys but careful analysis of the conditions and contexts that allow for or constrain ethical practices among advertisers, film producers, television programmers, photojournalists, and so on.

Principles of extended or politicized caring and the ethics at the heart of feminist epistemology, then, can be embedded in journalism practice. Journalists so inspired will report on important problems, with potential for having a transformative impact; and will want to make their work accessible to the disenfranchised. Christians (2003) properly notes that the promise-based nature of communal obligation provides a richer ethics for research than does the thin, truncated, extrinsic code of contractualism. His point applies equally to journalism, and this is fundamentally an issue of caring. Properly linking research and practice, Denzin calls on ethnographers to function as public journalists and advocates a "communitarian journalism that treats communication and newsmaking as value-laden activities and as forms of social narrative rooted in the community" (p. 157). Guzenhauser (2006) analogously posits a relational ethic that depends on caring researchers, with contact requiring subjectivity, and researcher and researched both contributing knowledge to the relation.

Unlike Guzenhauser, who calls for researchers to reflect Noddings's motivational displacement and engrossment, however, I take feminism to tolerate, and even urge, criticism and evaluation. Thus, a "caring" epistemology does not require reporters to believe all subjects equally, much less to treat them as co-equals in the processes of gathering or interpreting news. Rather, it requires reporters to bracket their assumptions about sources and hear sources out in their particularity. It requires reporters to see themselves as on the same plane as others (or to acknowledge their privilege) and not to deceive subjects.

At a minimum, caring journalists, no less than philosophers and educational psychologists, will listen attentively. The voices of some news sources who speak in the vocabulary of care and connection may be silenced or marginalized by journalists' assumptions about rule-based logic. Just as important, caring journalists would avoid the sexism and sex stereotypes that otherwise lead to hearing only women's caring voices but remaining deaf to men speaking in this idiom. In some cases, allowing caring voices to emerge requires listening more closely. In other cases, it requires asking new questions, additional questions. Christians (2002) rightly urges journalism "toward critique, multivocal representation of the marginalized, and social transformation" (p. 170). It may suggest altogether new formats. Public journalism, for example, is most directly consistent with communitarian ethics per se. Both begin with concern for how citizens are engaged in local communities; both address the problems of individualism.

Using "spectacular" live fund-raisers shown on television as examples, Silk (1998) suggests that media audiences can "care at a distance." His distinction between benevolence (caring about others) and beneficence (caring for others) echoes Noddings's distinction between caring about and caring for. But Silk's point is that media content can inspire responsive actions in distant contexts (third party beneficence); acting at a distance to produce mass media information that inspires self-help support groups is itself a form of beneficence. He concludes that the quasi-interaction facilitated by print and broadcast news content may relieve suffering and reduce people's sense of isolation, without the embarrassment of face-to-face interaction. Such empirical claims about caring themselves are contested. Certainly what may be intended as a caring performance can turn out to be patronizing or worse. Some raise the specter of compassion fatigue: "The more suffering that people see on their TV screens, the less concerned they feel. Current events demobilize them; images kill the feeling of obligation within them" (quoted in Tester, 2001, p. 5). Thus, journalists are ethically obligated not only to be sensitive to the voice of care, but also to evaluate and help readers evaluate claims to caring and suffering and to evaluate policies and proposals to ameliorate suffering (including problems in the structures and processes of care-giving). This politicized version of care calls on media to privilege the problems, stories, and counter-stories of marginalized or subordinated peoples and others who deserve care and compassion.

## STANDPOINT THEORY AND JOURNALISM

Other streams in feminist epistemology do not address care specifically but connect to ethics and are relevant to journalism ethics. Despite their disagreements, Western feminist ethicists share a distinctively feminist naturalism, which Jaggar (2000) defines as rooted in concerns about contingent inequalities and advocating multidisciplinary approaches to understanding human knowledge. That is, feminist moral philosophy does not appeal to reason alone, and distrusts totally rationalist approaches. Naturalized epistemology inevitably must "operate within a circle of what its practitioners take to be their best methods and conclusions" (Jaggar, 2000, p. 456).

Feminist standpoint theory emphasizes attention to how all knowledge is socially situated; that is, the historical and cultural contexts of knowledge are important and meaningful. Standpoint feminists challenge the ideological practices and procedures of androcentric science, whose claim to perform "the god-trick of seeing everything from nowhere" (Haraway, 1991, p. 189) conceals, rather than reveals, the working of power.[5] Standpoint feminists rely on critical evaluation to determine which social locations tend to promote better knowledge claims, including the locations of those conducting the research. Moreover, communities are the primary makers of meaning, "the primary loci—the primary generators, repositories, holders, and acquirers—of knowledge (Nelson, 1993, p.124). Reconceptualizing knowers as "individuals-in-communities," avoids atomism and incorporates "the social and communal elements of knowing without the difficulties associated with the community model" (Grasswick, 2004, p. 98). Moral dialogue among a community of interlocutors will correct biases that individuals cannot detect in themselves (Friedman, 1993). Feminists suggest subordinated people are compelled to understand those who dominate them, but that dominant groups do not need to understand those they subordinate and hence do not.[6] Grounding research in the perspectives of those most marginalized will generate less partial, less distorted accounts. Beginning with the standpoint of women as a subordinated class, then, incorporates bias into the method of knowledge-seeking.

Journalists would need to acknowledge how, as journalists, they are not exempt from these dynamics. Media professionals—like other people--would state their positions openly and offer mutual critiques, not as a matter of competition, but for transparency and to correct the overall value of their work. Standpoint epistemology requires journalists "to rethink themselves and their craft from the position of marginalized Others, thus uncovering unconscious ethnocentric, sexist, racist, and heterosexist biases that distort news production" (Durham, 1998, p. 132). Becoming engaged in the consequences of stories for the disenfranchised would "subvert from within the hegemonies in current news practice" (p. 135). Arguably, standpoint theory not only requires news accounts that include the powerless as sources, but also that women are hired for their distinctive standpoints.

That said, in the same way that the enforced maternal giving may be distorting, so may the experience of subordination and oppression. Harding's assertion that people can achieve a "traitorous" identity, betraying their privileged positions so as to understand others, is vigorously challenged. In an essay itself hotly contested, Hekman (1997) takes postmodernism and poststructuralism to undermine not only the presumption of "a" better view, but also standpoint theory's presupposition that women share a privileged vantage point.

There are other ways to acknowledge how "particular social relations and their power dynamics have shaped the form and content of knowledge production" (Grasswick, 2004, p. 88). Fine, Weis, Weseen, and Wong (2003) suggest that researchers ask themselves, among other questions: "Have I connected the 'voices' and 'stories' of individuals back to the set of historic, structural, and economic relations in which they are situated," "Have I described the mundane" (rather than surfing through transcripts to find what is exotic or sensational), "Have I considered how these data could be used for progressive, conservative, repressive social politics," and "Where have I backed into the passive voice and decoupled my responsibility for my interpretations."

Similarly, hooks (1989) asserts: "When we write about the experiences of a group to which we do not belong, we should think about the ethics of our actions, considering whether or not our work will be used to reinforce and perpetuate domination" (p. 43). Complaining that the overvaluation of scholarship by whites about blacks maintains racism, hooks suggests that whites, including white feminists, overestimate their insights into other people (Valdivia, 2002), a position that applies to both academic and media worlds. These scholars understand such questions have no single right or fixed answer. Granted, conventional ethics bars journalists from considering the implications or potential consequences of stories. Yet, these are questions we could also ask of ourselves and journalism practice. Scholarship would be quite different if we did.

## REPRESENTATION AS AN ETHICAL ISSUE

Feminist scholars and activists have condemned news and entertainment content that traffics in commodification and objectification. Much of the second wave feminist attention was provoked by fears that sexist content, especially pornography, had "real" effects on the actions, attitudes, and short- and even long-term potential of all. At the heart of the critique is the realization that to be represented in media signifies social existence, while "absence means symbolic annihilation" (Gerbner & Gross, 1976, p.182). Tuchman (1978) drew greater attention to how media images symbolically annihilate women by excluding, trivializing, or demonizing them. It is in this context that feminists advocate—and produce—distinctive representations in mainstream commercial and alternative media, both news and entertainment, including employing gender-neutral language. This logic also makes the issue of who is able to represent whom. Fraser (1986) calls for groups to achieve "a degree of collective control over the means of interpretation and communication sufficient to enable one to participate on a par with members of other groups in moral and political deliberation; that is, to speak and be heard, to tell one's own life-story, to press one's claims and point of view in one's own voice" (p. 428).

These efforts imply normative standards for evaluating how people, relations, power, and behaviors are represented in journalism, advertising, music lyrics and music videos, and in other media, including television, cable, and film. It is uncaring and unfair to trivialize women candidates for political office, or to demonize lesbians. To sexually exploit, objectify, and trivialize a group—simply by virtue of group identification—violates feminist ethics.[7] Fairness is not a matter of equality, even equality between men and women. Magazines that sell subscriptions and products by making men deeply unhappy with their bodies are not fair simply as a counterpart to a history of magazine content and advertising depicting an impossible "ideal" woman. Music videos that subvert the typical pattern by objectifying men, ostensibly for the pleasure of women audiences, remain unethical. Sports news that sexualizes the bodies of African-American men, to take one more prominent and not accidental example, is likewise problematic. Again, the issue is ethics; no observable ill effects need to be alleged, much less proven, for distorted representations to be seen as unethical. The flip side is that since behavior is not involved, government censorship or other legal action is not the solution. The logic of feminist ethics suggests that ethical dilemmas should be resolved through conversation and debate.

## FEMINIST ETHICS AND THE WORKPLACE

The feminist critique of a distorting polarity between the public arena as the legitimate and valued site of work (and masculinity) and a private arena devalued because of its association with emotion, domestic, and reproductive processes (and women) (Ashcraft, 2000) can be applied to media organizations. Feminists propose alternative forms of workplace organization and organizing: horizontal rather than hierarchical, flexible and rotating rather than bureaucratic and rigid, granting agency and humanity to employees rather than objectifying or subordinating them, and blurring conventional boundaries between the personal and political. For example, many second and third wave feminist newspapers, cable collectives, and other kinds of media organizations are committed, as a matter of feminist principle, to experimenting with collaborative structures and rotating leadership (or no leadership at all) as well as family-friendly and collectivist policies (Endres & Lueck,1996; Riano,1994; Steiner, 1992). The pattern holds, by the way, internationally. For example, in Korea, feminist collectives have produced feminist webzines according to feminist principles; by organizing themselves in non-hierarchical, participatory ways, they sustain an egalitarian women's community in both the real and virtual worlds (Choi, Steiner, & Kim, 2006).

Such organizations do not support a claim that women are more ethical in actual practice. The issues are structural, with ideas about ethics enforced by university training, workplace socialization, and professional organizations. Moreover, feminist ways of working and organizing do not consistently succeed in merging personal and emotional dimensions with rational, political, and professional dimensions. *Ms.*, the magazine that tried to bring feminism to the mainstream, wanted to be egalitarian and collective, in the spirit of the women's movement. Efforts to include everyone in decision making resulted in an unclear chaotic chain of command and a "tyranny of structurelessness, however; submissions were sometimes overedited and sometimes lost (Farrell, 1998). Arguably there is a trade-off between efficient production of content and experimentation with egalitarian organization; while some feminist collectives privilege participation in feminist-inspired processes, others care more about feminist information.

Indeed, feminism's openness to struggle, to contradiction (or at least to provisional, experimental, emergent processes), and to aspirational ethics explains failures to achieve ethical purity. Ashcraft (2000), for example, describes a feminist organization that explicitly institutionalized principles of "ethical communication." In the name of empowerment and "bounded emotionality" members were required to express themselves authentically to the group, disclose emotions and feelings, and expose conflict. But tensions resulted from such tenets. Nonetheless, feminist ethics would urge active opposition to sexism and sexual harassment. It endorses policies that support active parenting and fair wages. Media organizations did not invent untenable double standards and double binds for women (i.e., requiring women to adopt behaviors and styles associated with men, yet condemning them when they do so, and simultaneously, mandating that women do women's work and act, even dress, like women, but then condemning them for doing so). But they need not amplify and reproduce sexism.

## THE FUTURE OF FEMINIST ETHICS IN MEDIA

Feminist approaches to ethics challenge women's subordination, prescribe morally justifiable ways of resisting oppressive practices, and envision morally desirable alternatives that promote emancipation. Indeed, although inverting male values and privileging women's interests does not suffice for feminist ethics, Jaggar (1992) asserts that a model not committed to challenging perceived male bias is non-feminist. Fully feminist ethics, far more than their feminine and maternal counterparts, are distinctively political: They are committed "to the elimination of women's subordination—and that of other oppressed persons—in all of its manifestations (Tong, 2003). A feminist approach to ethics asks questions about *power* even before it asks questions about *good* and *evil*, *care* and *justice*, or maternal and paternal thinking."

Could an ethics, including one useful for media, be feminist without relying on gender or on ideas about sex differences? After all, gender oppression is always woven with domination by sexual orientation, class, race, ethnicity, and religion. Gender itself is a social construct, albeit a consistently powerful one. So, feminism as a way of studying and thinking about social and political relationships offers ethical and epistemological principles that correct misogynist biases without forever reifying women's experience. Meanwhile, even if feminism is not credited with transforming ethics, "[u]niversal ethical theory, with its attendant universal ethical subject…is now regarded suspiciously not just by feminists, but by most contributors to debates on ethics" (Bell, 2005, p. 498).

The suggestion of an "ethics from the margins" of bell hooks is notable here. Valdivia (2002) finds in hooks a "politics of ethics," albeit not a highly systematic one. From a different perspective (in appealing to social contracts that parties voluntarily commit to), Baehr (2004) likewise calls for feminist politics not based on gender, "or at least one that makes extremely minimal ontological claims about gender" (p. 414), thereby avoiding an unhelpful sameness–difference debate. Bell (2005) notes, "Some feminists are now highly skeptical of the possibility of 'an ethical [way of] being'" (p. 497). Perhaps the reluctance to study feminist ethics reflects a tendency within feminism to associate "morality" with repressive moralizing. Eschewing the term "ethics," Walker (1998) proposes an "expressive-collaborative" model of morality. For Walker, negotiation of moral knowledge involves "socially situated and socially sustained practices of responsibility" (p. 201), modified during reflection and interaction; what matters is not theory, but how we actually live and judge.[8]

But, with feminism's persuasive critique of the abstract disembodied ethical subject generating a healthy respect for difference, a multiculturalist feminism may yet construct a non-sexist theory that respects difference of all sorts. A multiculturalist feminist ethics can incorporate values (such as community) and responsibilities (such as caring) that historically are associated with women, without assuming that all women around the globe are permanently, much less equally, subordinated and pressed into patriarchal domestic, reproductive, and sexual arrangements.. If ethics is about what we ought to do, whether or not this comes naturally, we can tilt toward care of those who need it most, globally, rather than those we love or give birth to. Indeed, a context-sensitive notion of gender is consistent with feminism and feminist ethics, even as these incorporate into community, connection, and caring, at local and distant levels—or wherever community, connection, and caring are most required.

In practice feminist ethicists and rights-based ethicists are unlikely to resolve ethical dilemmas in polar ways. After all, again as a practical matter, both practitioners and audiences probably (investigation is necessary at both theoretical and empirical levels) already listen to, if not heed, the voices of both justice and connection. Nonetheless, at a minimum, what amounts to a politicized feminist ethics would provide a coherent and enriched account of why media are important and why ethical media practices are important.

Media both symbolize and celebrate structures of human life and thinking. So, media content, production, and consumption are implicated in two highly networked ways. First, news and entertainment are integral to modeling how processes of feminist ethics operate in daily life. The development and incorporation of feminist ethics, among other "channels," requires deploying these understandings both in the media content and in the structure of media organizations themselves.

## NOTES

1. The rare exception is Sevenhuijsen (1998), who discusses a Dutch newspaper article about nursing home care that, without mentioning ethics, highlights several moral questions; her point is that the article invites "judging with care," and includes addressing the audience in terms of attitudes of caring, by viewing care as a form of social agency, and by attending to a site in the community where care goes on.
2. I have ignored Black "womanist" as well as lesbian ethics here, but see Hoagland (1988).
3. Sevenhuijsen (1998) reconceptualizes care in political terms but mentions her own mothering as important to her evaluation of the genealogy of care; she defends the articulation of the mother–child bond as an ideal type and model of reasoning; that is, not as about actual mothers and children. Ultimately, she regards the "motherly metaphor" as relying too heavily on a mythical and inadequate image of "Woman."
4. Friedman (1993) says friendships are more equal and reciprocal than mother–child relationships.
5. For discussion of standpoint theory, see Harding (1986, 1991, 1993); and especially essays in Harding (2004); as well as Collins (1990), Haraway (1988), Hartsock (1983), and Smith (1974).
6. Letherby (2003) takes the apparent similarity between values and ideas identified as characteristically "black" and those characteristically "female" to suggest that subordinate groups think in similar ways.
7. This is not a "moralistic" judgment about which sexual behaviors are immoral; feminist ethics favors protecting more frank discussion of sex and sexuality, not burying it.
8. Conversely, the theoretical-juridical models that conventionally form the template for utilitarian, contract, neo-Kantian or rights-based theories represent morality as "a compact, propositionally codifiable, impersonally action-guiding code within an agent, or as a compact set of law-like propositions" (Walker, 1998, p. 7).

## REFERENCES

Ashcraft, K. L. (2000). Empowering "professional" relationships: Organizational communication meets feminist practice. *Management Communication Quarterly, 13*(4), 347–392.

Baehr, A. R. (2004). Feminist politics and feminist pluralism: Can we do feminist political theory without theories of gender? *The Journal of Political Philosophy, 12*(4), 411–436.

Bartky, S. L. (Ed.). (1990). *Femininity and domination.* New York: Routledge.

Bell, M. (1998). The journalism of attachment. In M. Kieran (Ed), *Media ethics* (pp. 15–22). London: Routledge.

Bell, V. (2005). Ethics. In P. Essed, D. T. Goldberg, & A. Kobayashi (Eds.), *A companion to gender studies* (pp. 497–508). Malden, MA: Blackwell.

Calhoun, C. (2004). Introduction. In C. Cheshire (Ed.), *Setting the moral compass: Essays by women philosophers* (pp. 3–19). New York: Oxford University Press.

Chambers, D., L. Steiner, & C. Fleming (2004). *Women and journalism.* New York: Routledge.

Choi, Y., L. Steiner, & S. Kim (2006). Claiming feminist space in Korean cyberterritory, *Javnost—The Public, 13,* 65–84.

Christians, C. G. (2002). Norman Denzin's feminist communitarian ethics. *Studies in Symbolic Interaction, 25*,167–177.

Christians, C. G. (2003). Ethics and politics in qualitative research. In N. K. Denzin & Y. S. Lincoln (Eds.), *The Landscape of qualitative research: Theories and* issues (pp. 208–244). Thousand Oaks, CA: Sage.

Christians, C. G. (2004). Ubuntu and communitarianism in media ethics. *Ecquid Novi, 25*(2), 235–256.

Collins, P. (1990). *Black feminist thought: Knowledge, consciousness, and the politics of empowerment.* New York: Routledge.

Denzin, N. K. (1997). *Interpretive ethnography: Ethnographic practices for the 21st century.* Thousand Oaks, CA: Sage.

Durham, M. G. (1998). On the relevance of standpoint epistemology to the practice of journalism: The case for "strong objectivity." *Communication Theory, 8*(2), 117–140.

Endres, K., & T. Lueck (Eds.). (1996). *Women's periodicals in the United States: Social and political issues.* Westport, CT: Greenwood Press.

Engster, D. (2005). Rethinking care theory: The practice of caring and the obligation to care. *Hypatia, 20*(3), 50–74.

Farrell, A. Erdman (1998). *Yours in sisterhood: Ms. Magazine and the promise of popular feminism.* Chapel Hill: University of North Carolina Press.

Fine, M., L. Weis, S. Weseen, & L. Wong (2003). For whom? Qualitative research, representations, and social responsibilities. In N. K. Denzin & Y.S. Lincoln. *The landscape of qualitative research: Theories and issues* (pp. 167–207). Thousand Oaks, CA: Sage.

Fraser, N. (1986). Toward a discourse ethic of solidarity. *Praxis International, 5*(4), 425–429.

Friedman, M. (1993). *What are friends for? Feminist perspectives on personal relationships and moral theory.* Ithaca, NY: Cornell University Press.

Gerbner, G., & Gross, L. (1976). Living with television: The violence profile. *Journal of Communication, 26*, 172–199.

Gilligan, C. (1982). *In a different voice: Psychological theory and women's development.* Cambridge, MA: Harvard University Press.

Gilligan, C. (1987). Moral orientation and moral development" In E. F. Kittay & D. T. Meyers (Eds.), *Women and moral theory* (pp. 19–33). Totowa, NJ: Rowman & Littlefield.

Gilligan, C. (1995). Hearing the difference: Theorizing connection. *Hypatia, 10*(2), 120–127.

Grasswick, H. E. (2004). Individuals-in-communities: The search for a feminist model of epistemic subjects. *Hypatia: A Journal of Feminist Philosophy, 19*(3), 85–120.

Grouenhout, R. E. (2004). *Connected lives: Human nature and an ethics of care.* Lanham, MD: Rowman & Littlefield.

Gunzenhauser, M. G. (2006). A moral epistemology of knowing subjects: Theorizing a relational turn for qualitative research. *Qualitative Inquiry, 12*(3), 621–647.

Hamington, M., & D. C. Miller (Eds.). (2006). *Socializing care: Feminist ethics and public issues.* Oxford: Rowman & Littlefield.

Haraway, D. (1988). Situated knowledges: The science question in feminism and the privilege of partial perspective. *Feminist Studies, 14*, 575–599.

Haraway, D. (1991). *Simians, cyborgs and women: The reinvention of women.* London: Free Association.

Harding, S. (1986). *The science question in feminism.* Ithaca, NY: Cornell University Press.

Harding, S. (1991). *Whose science? Whose knowledge? Thinking from women's lives.* Ithaca, NY: Cornell University Press.

Harding, S. (1993). Rethinking standpoint epistemology: What is strong objectivity? In L. Alcoff & E. Potter (Eds.), *Feminist epistemologies* (pp. 49–82). New York: Routledge.

Harding, S. (Ed). (2004). *The feminist standpoint theory reader: Intellectual and political controversies.* New York: Routledge.

Hartsock, N. (1983). The feminist standpoint: Developing the ground for a specifically feminist historical materialism. In S. Harding & M. Hintikka (Eds.), *Discovering reality: Feminist perspectives on epistemology, metaphysics, methodology, and the philosophy of science (pp.* 283–310). Dordrecht: D. Reidel.

Hekman, S. (1997). Truth and method: Feminist standpoint theory revisited. *Signs: Journal of Women in Culture and Society, 22*(2), 342–365.

Held, V. (2006). *The ethics of care: Personal, political, and global.* Oxford: Oxford University Press.

Hoagland, S. (1988). *Lesbian ethics: Toward new value.* Palo Alto, CA: Institute of Lesbian Studies.

hooks, b. (1989). *Talking back: Thinking feminist, thinking Black.* Boston: South End.

Jaggar, A. (1992). Feminist ethics. In L. Becker & C. Becker (Eds.), *Encyclopedia of ethics (pp.* 361–369). New York: Garland.

Jaggar, A. (2000). Ethics naturalized: Feminism's contribution to moral epistemology. *Metaphilosophy, 31,* 452–467.

Kittay, E. F. (1999). *Love's labor: Essays on women, equality, and dependency.* New York: Routledge.

Kittay, E. F., & D. T. Meyers (Eds.). (1987). *Women and moral theory.* Totowa, NJ: Rowman & Littlefield.

Koehn, D. (1998). *Rethinking feminist ethics: Care, trust and empathy.* New York: Routledge.

Letherby, G. (2003). *Feminist research in theory and practice.* Philadelphia: Open University Press.

Lotz, A. D. (2000). Assessing qualitative television audience research: Incorporating feminist and anthropological theoretical innovation. *Communication Theory, 10*(4), 447–467.

Manning, R. C. (1992). *Speaking from the heart: A feminist perspective on ethics.* Lanham, MD: Rowman & Littlefield.

McBride, K. (2002). The ethics of justice and care in the American media: A tale of two reporters. http://poynteronline.org/content/content_view.asp?id=4688. posted Jan. 9. Accessed January 25, 2007

Mendus, S. (2000). *Feminism and emotion: Readings in moral and political philosophy.* New York: St. Martin's Press.

Meyers, D. Tietjens (2005). Women philosophers, sidelined challenges, and professional philosophy. *Hypatia, 20*(3), 149–152,

Nelson, L. Hankinson (1993). Epistemological communities. In Linda Alcoff & Elizabeth Potter (Eds.), *Feminist epistemologies.* New York: Routledge.

Noddings, N. (1984). *Caring: A feminine approach to ethics and moral education.* Berkeley: University of California Press.

Noddings, N. (2002). *Starting at home: Caring and social policy.* Berkeley: University of California Press.

Riano, P. (Ed.). (1994). *Women in grassroots communication.* Thousand Oaks, CA: Sage.

Rouse, J. (2004). Feminism and the social construction of scientific knowledge. In S. Harding (Ed.), *The feminist standpoint theory reader: Intellectual and political controversies* (pp. 353–374). New York: Routledge.

Ruddick, S. (1989). *Maternal thinking: Toward a politics of peace.* New York: Beacon.

Sander-Staudt, M. (2006). The unhappy marriage of care ethics and virtue ethics. *Hypatia, 21*(4), 21–39.

Sevenhuijsen, S. (1998). *Citizenship and the ethics of care.* New York: Routledge.

Silk, J. (1998). Caring at a distance. *Ethics, Place and Environment, 1*(2), 165–182.

Smith, D. (1974). Women's perspective as a radical critique of sociology. *Sociological Inquiry, 44,* 7–13.

Steiner, L. (1989). Feminist theorizing and communication ethics. *Communication, 12*(3), 157–173.

Steiner, L. (1992). The history and structure of women's alternative media. In L. Rakow (Ed.), *Women making meaning: New feminist directions in communication* (pp. 121–143). New York: Routledge.

Steiner, L., & C. M. Okrusch (2006). Care as a virtue for journalists. *Journal of Mass Media Ethics, 21*(2&3), 102–122.

Tester, K. (2001). *Compassion, morality and the media.* Philadelphia: Open University Press.

Tong, R. (2003, Winter). Feminist ethics. In E. N. Zalta (Ed.), *The Stanford encyclopedia of philosophy.* http://plato.stanford.edu/archives/win2003/entries/feminism-ethics/ Accessed January 3, 2006.

Tronto, J. C. (1995). Care as a basis for radical political judgments. *Hypatia, 10*(2), 141–149.

Tronto, J. C. (2006). Vicious circles of privatized caring. In M. Hamington & D. C. Miller (Eds.), *Socializing care: Feminist ethics and public issues* (pp. 3–26). Lanham, MD: Rowman & Littlefield.

Tuchman, G. (1978). Introduction: The symbolic annihilation of women by the mass media. In G. Tuchman, A. K. Daniels, & J. Benet (Eds.), *Hearth and home: Images of women in the mass media* (pp. 3–38). New York: Oxford University Press.

Valdivia, A. N. (2002). bell hooks: Ethics from the margins. In S. L. Bracci & C. G. Christians (Eds.), *Moral engagement in public life: Theorists for contemporary ethics* (pp. 238–256). New York: Peter Lang.

Walker, M. U. (1998). *Moral understandings: A feminist study in ethics.* New York: Routledge.

Weaver, D. (1997). Women as journalists. In P. Norris (Ed.), *Women, media, and politics* (pp. 21–40). New York: Oxford University Press.

Weaver, D. H., & Wilhoit, G. C. (1996). *The American journalist in the 1990s: U.S. news people at the end of an era.* Mahwah, NJ: Erlbaum.

Weiss, P. A. (1995). Feminism and communitarianism: Comparing critiques of liberalism. In P. A. Weiss & M. Friedman (Eds.), *Feminism and Community* (pp. 161–186). Philadelphia: Temple University Press.

# 28

# Global Media Ecology: Why There Is No Global Media Ethics Standard

## Mark D. Alleyne

## INTRODUCTION

It was the decade 1978 to 1988 that saw an explosion of academic writing on global media ethics (Righter 1978; Smith 1980; Fenby 1986; Nordenstreng, González Manet et al. 1986). However, the 20th century ended and the new century started with relatively little to show for such activity (Christians, Ferré et al. 1993; Rao & Lee 2005). This futility was the result of at least six factors. First, ethics codes are other means by which individuals and groups (as large as nation-states and international organizations) engage in subjectivity: they are declaring who they are, and so assertions of rights, obligations and prohibitions must be seen as more than mere professional practice and training guidelines. Second, mass media is an especially difficult area in which to establish universals because all the key themes of human primordialism—such as race, ethnicity, nationalism, ideology, and gender—depend on mass media to pursue the tasks of social and identity construction, recruitment, indoctrination and fixing cultural meaning. Third media institutions became a key dimension of the changed nature of international conflict, making the media more of a strategic tool than ever before and making media ethics less likely to be left unaffected by those waging armed conflict. Fourth, the industrialization of media organizations had profound implications for the conceptualization of media ethics. And fifth and sixth are two factors related to the international political system: the tarnished reputation of the United Nations system and the resulting subordination of media ethics discourses to wider discussions on the nature of the international system. This chapter is a critical analysis of these six points in turn.

## BACKGROUND

What inspired the considerable writings about international media ethics during the 1978–1988 period was the transnational debate that was then raging over the proposal at UNESCO and at the UN General Assembly for a "New World Information and Communication Order" (NWICO), referred to here as the new information order. A coalition of less powerful states first proposed a "New International Economic Order," a proposal for global economic justice. They were emboldened by the success of the Organization of Petroleum Exporting Countries (OPEC) in extracting higher prices for oil from the industrialized states. The new information order was then advanced as a necessary corollary because it would also attack global inequality at the ideological level. The new information order attracted considerable worldwide attention because it was the first attempt to promulgate media principles and norms that would be global in scope. This happened because never before had there been an international political structure—the United Nations system—that enveloped so much of humanity. Not only did the United Nations have a membership that was much larger than that of the League of Nations that it succeeded, but also it was designed to maintain peace in an international system in which formal colonialism was declining and "national self-determination" was being promoted. So when the new information order was floated there was the UN's international public information structure in place to promote it globally in a way that was never possible before (Lehmann 1999; Alleyne 2003). It also attracted attention because it had consequences for the media. Some information order proposals for government regulation attracted alarm, especially from media owners. However, other media workers participated in drafting the proposals and supported them.

This United Nations context is as important to understanding the ecology of discourse about universal media ethics as it is for other topics on the international agenda, such as the ethics of nuclear disarmament, racial equality, anti-terrorism or child labor. Discussion of media ethics was framed mainly by UN-system priorities rather than by professional associations, media entrepreneurs or workers. For example, professional associations have been preoccupied by concerns at the national and regional levels, such as censorship, government secrecy, working conditions and state legislation aimed at the press. In contrast, the kernel of the UN project—the maintenance of international peace —was the most prominent of the new information order principles and placed them within the framework of the UN's promotion of human rights and racial quality. This framing makes it easier to understand why the complete name of a highlight of the new information order movement—UNESCO's 1978 Mass Media Declaration—was the "Declaration on Fundamental Principles Concerning the Contribution of the Mass Media to Strengthening Peace and International Understanding, to the Promotion of Human Rights and to Countering Racialism, Apartheid and Incitement to War." The Declaration's Preamble said it was based on a number of the significant UN resolutions, but it did not make reference to any of the professional codes adopted by professional bodies. The text was also a testament to the rhetorical power of the so-called "global south", especially the assertion in Article II that:

> With the view of the strengthening of peace and international understanding to promoting human rights and to countering racialism, apartheid and incitement to war, the mass media throughout the world, by reason of their role, contribute to promoting human rights, in particular by giving expression to oppressed peoples who struggle against colonialism, neo-colonialism, foreign occupation and all forms of racial discrimination and oppression and who are unable to make their voices heard within their own territories. (UNESCO 1979)

In North America and Europe professional associations have avoided declaring such an activist mission for the media. However, scholars suggest the media institutionally and collectively have been complicit in maintaining systems of oppression; for example, racism in the American South and South African apartheid (UNESCO 1979; Mills 2004). Libertarian and social responsibility advocates for the press argue that their systems hold out possibilities of redemption in ways that authoritarian and communist systems do not—there are examples of courageous reporters and editors challenging authority to expose "the truth" just as there are examples of the opposite (Siebert 1956).

But it is important to understand that the "media debate" of 1978–1988 was essentially an exchange at cross-purposes. The UN framework was designed for sovereign states, the entities with primary legal standing in the international system. Resolutions, declarations and conventions reflected the interests of states. However, professional bodies of media owners and workers generally do not trust governments, especially when governments propose codes of ethics to govern their enterprises and work. So although another highlight of the new information order debate, the 1980 MacBride Report, contained a list of recommendations much wider than the UN-oriented frame, the bulk of its recommendations were organized according to the themes of UN internationalism, such as "independence and self-reliance", "cultural identity", "international cooperation", "international understanding", and "development" (International Commission for the Study of Communication Problems and MacBride 1980, 253–275).

A decade later, the reason why UNESCO's 1991 "Declaration of Windhoek on Promoting an Independent and Pluralistic African Press" came to be regarded as a watershed document is because it directly named governments, not transnational corporations, as the main obstacle to press freedom. This was a radical assertion from a document emanating from the state-run UN system. The Declaration said an independent, pluralistic and free press was "essential to the development and maintenance of democracy in a nation, and for economic development." And it defined an independent press as one "independent from governmental, political or economic control or from control of materials and infrastructure essential for the production and dissemination of newspapers, magazines and periodicals." Its specific indictment of government activity in relation to the press was the statement that

> In Africa today, despite the positive developments in some countries, in many countries journalists, editors, and publishers are victims of repression—they are murdered, arrested, detained and censored, and are restricted by economical (sic) and political pressures such as restrictions on newsprint, licensing systems which restrict the opportunity to publish, visa restrictions which prevent the free movement of journalists, restrictions on the exchange of news and information, and limitations on the circulation of newspapers within countries and across national borders. In some countries, one-party States control the totality of information. (Alleyne 1997, Appendix 7)

The 1991 Declaration signaled not only a victory for the information order's detractors but also the lesson that the acceptance of debates about international media ethics was closely linked to the ecology of the global political economy. We cannot understand progress or retreat from a global normative standard of media ethics; rather, the issues must be considered within an understanding of changes in state power, the relationship between the market and the state, and modifications in the ideological assumptions about the optimum form of world order needed to ensure peace and prosperity.

This shift in frames about media ethics from the priorities of states to those of markets and other non-state actors happened as a consequence of key historical events: the demise of the Communist Bloc and the consequent end of the Cold War simultaneous with world debt crisis and the resulting World Bank and International Monetary Fund's "structural adjustment" policies that forced indebted states to adopt a range of neo-liberal economic policies that had dire consequences for their national political systems. Government control of the economy was circumscribed and this also meant more liberal approaches to the organization of civil society, especially freer press systems. This triumph of liberalism also appeared at the level of international organization, most notably the 1994 creation of the World Trade Organization. The WTO would soon become the major mechanism by which adherence to neo-liberalism ideology would be policed because states wishing to benefit fully from the perks of the global trading system would have no choice but to join the body and obey its rules.

International telecommunications institutions were the first to illustrate the deep challenges to state power that resulted from these historic changes. The monopoly that state-run bodies had in the provision of international satellite service had been broken in 1984 with the establishment of PanAmSat, but in 1998 the International Telecommunication Union (ITU) went a step further in giving private companies membership in this regulatory body that previously had only recognized only states as members. The dominant international satellite service provider, INTELSAT, was privatized in 2001.

Although there was a resurgence of state power after "911", under the guise of the national security imperatives of the "war on terror", there was never a return to the heady days of the new information order when even the idea that the UN system could be an arbiter of media ethics was entertained. This background and context is critical to the analysis of the six points explored in this chapter.

## INTERNATIONAL IDENTITY POLITICS

For professional associations of journalists the professed goals of ethics codes—such as securing journalists' safety, promoting the public's right to know and enhancing civic participation—are often ends in themselves. However, in transnational debates between many state and non-state actors, seldom is the acceptance of media ethics the central point of the arguments. Debates about press freedom actually become merely new ways of fighting old conflicts.

A clear example of this dynamic at work was when the United States, the United Kingdom and Singapore withdrew from UNESCO in 1984 and 1985. The agency's detractors complained that its work had become "politicized", that it was mismanaged and corrupt, and that it threatened press freedom. In reality the news debate at UNESCO was the Cold War being fought by other means. When the United States and the United Kingdom in particular ceased membership of UNESCO they had regular diplomatic ties with apartheid South Africa, a state not known for press freedom or many other human rights. And, similarly, while the United States maintained a trade embargo and isolationist policy against Cuba, on the grounds that Cuba was anti-democratic, it contradictorily had diplomatic ties with several Latin American dictatorships. This political context suggests the new information order proposal was controversial for many more reasons than its supposed threat to press freedom. The proposal provided an opportunity for states to define who they were and to embark on a process of redefining what institutions of the UN system should be. This struggle is evident in the language of the Mass Media Declaration and the MacBride Report quoted above. The Communist Bloc and the Non-Aligned Movement in particular attempted to redirect the project's focus to a more direct attack on capitalism and racialism.

More than 20 years later, in the midst of the "War on Terror", another transnational debate would be sparked when the largest Danish newspaper, *Jyllands-Posten*, published 12 cartoon depictions of the Prophet Mohammad as a means of testing whether fear of Muslim retaliation had constricted press freedom (Caldwell 2006; Sheikh 2006). Mass demonstrations in countries with large Muslim populations and violent protests in several locations left dozens dead. At the core of the dispute was the conflict between the Islamic prohibition of representations of the Prophet Mohammad on the grounds that such a practice encourages idolatry, and the liberal value of free speech rights cherished as fundamental to political identities in North American and Europe. It was a clash between religious and liberal-democratic values.

If there was any belief that the transnational discourse on a single universal ethical media standard could be conducted only among media managers and journalists the "Prophet cartoons" controversy dispelled it. In the context of an international environment where the "War on Terror" had seemed to many a war on Islam, many Muslims felt that the central issue was respect for their religious identities. For this definitional reason they attempted to retaliate by the only means at their disposals: formal written protests to the Danish government, mass protest, boycotts of Danish companies and products. The actions of a few Danish media workers had set in motion a series of events with profound consequences for the Danish economy and the Danish diplomatic service. Although the protesters sought and got an apology from the editor of *Jyllands-Posten*, the major responsibility for responding to the complaints was the domain of the country's diplomats—the primary representatives of a nation-state's national identity in an international order where governments have established for themselves the role of chief official transnational actors.

However, media actors and their representatives stubbornly stuck to the idea that such incidents could be reduced to a matter of free speech. For example, one American editorial opined that "[U]nder the principle of freedom of expression, blasphemy can be vulgar, in execrable taste, offensive in the extreme, but never prohibited." It also observed that "[T]he most violent element of Islam now feels it has a right and a duty to censor the Western press while tolerating vile caricatures of Judaism and Christianity in its own"(2006).

## UNIVERSALITY VERSUS PRIMORDIALISM

The "Prophet cartoons" storm also raises the question of whether universality is the best means for international norm-setting given the critical role of the media in primordiality. Universality and primordiality sit at opposite ends of the spectrum. In essence universality puts its faith in the assumption that there are commonalities in the human experience that facilitate the adoption of universal standards. Primordiality eschews that position in favor of cultural relativism (Van Liedekerke 2004).

Significantly, proponents of the new information order were seeking change through mechanisms of the status quo. The UN system they used was established after World War II on the assumption that a functional network of international organizations would promote universality as the preferred version of internationalism. Media ethics was merely one dimension of social life in which the UN sought to develop universal codes.

It is important to interrogate the logic of universality and explore alternatives to it. While in some areas of international interaction universality has practical utility, it might not be necessary in others. For example, safe international transport logically requires universal air traffic control norms and aircraft safety standards. Conversely, while it is not impossible to make the argument for the necessity of having universal media standards, it does demand more persuasion. There are also a number of areas of social life where universal standards were not established. In the areas of technology, no universal standards were achieved for television transmission, measurements, electric voltage, or motor vehicle driving practice concerning whether to use the right or left side of the road.

It is in the area of social values that the failures to attain universality are most pertinent to our evaluation of the international media ethics discourse. Furor of the type sparked by the Prophet cartoons suggests that media ethics is best regarded in a manner similar to social values—in other words, wide variation about issues as is reflected in international disagreement about the state's role in capital punishment or statutory rape. A universal standard in this area is unlikely in the foreseeable future due to the deep primordial investment of different social systems in values very affected by the media. (For a different view, see Elliott's chapter in Part I of this volume.)

## MEDIA AND WAR

Although the increased use of terrorism against civilian targets as a means of waging war would become the major matter on the agenda of media advocates at the start of the twenty-first century, a number of changes in the way international conflict was waged had been taking place for some time before that profoundly affected the discourse on media ethics (Tehranian 2002). In the 20th century war evolved from being organized violence between military forces to include the technological perfection of the science of killing: weapons of mass destruction. Increasingly the majority of victims of armed conflict were civilians, not soldiers. Concurrently, the nature of international diplomacy changed, giving the mass public an even greater interest in international politics when, beginning with Article 18 of the League of Nations Covenant, the practice of secret diplomacy was ended and the value of "public opinion" promoted (Alleyne 2003).

The 20th century was to a large extent the century when the propaganda war was invented. Such a tool was needed to massage public opinion to accept the sacrifices needed to wage war and as another front on which the enemy could be fought. After World War II propaganda agencies went from being ad hoc enterprises set up temporarily during wartime to standing "public diplomacy" bodies, the function of which was to "win hearts and minds" by maintaining a good image of the states that sponsored them. The work of such organizations as the Italian Cultural Institute, the United States Information Agency, the Goëthe Foundation (of Germany) and the Alliance Française included such activities as language training, outreach to opinion leaders such as journalists and academics, production of audio-visual media to promote their countries, and sponsorship of student exchanges. From its founding the United Nations had a department dedicated to image and issue promotion—the Department of Public Information—that deployed many of the same techniques.

The coming of permanent, organized propaganda bodies to international relations had profound implications for the practice of journalism specifically and the media work in general. Often it has been difficult to distinguish between international reporting as disinterested, professional work and propaganda on the behalf of home countries (Goss 2002). This results not only from conscious or unconscious coverage decisions by journalists and media organizations, but also from bribery and other forms of direct intervention of intelligence and public diplomacy agencies to influence media content (Kumar 2006).

While some state-run or state-supported international media—such as the British Broadcasting Corporation (BBC) and the Voice of America—claim to protect journalistic professionalism via their charters, in other countries, such as North Korea, Cuba and the People's Republic of China, ruling political philosophies did not make distinctions between an idealized notion of impartial journalism and state or party propaganda. During the Cold War this political variance extended to the level of transnational professional bodies, with the International Organization of Journalists (IOJ) representing journalists from socialist countries and organizations such as the Inter-American Press Association (IAPA), advocating the media ethics of the "free world".

In the United States the impact of permanent propaganda agencies on international media ethics was illustrated again when it was revealed in 2006 that journalists for the sister newspaper of the *Miami Herald*, *El Nuevo Herald*, had been paid to appear in U.S. public diplomacy programs against the Cuban government. The scandal forced the newspapers' publisher to resign (Merzer 2006; Olson 2006). However, this kind of propaganda work by the U.S. government in a cold war against Cuba was matched by similar programs to expedite the hot war in Iraq. In 2005 the George W. Bush administration employed a public relations firm to plant stories in Iraqi news media and pay money to compliant Iraqi journalists (Goodnough 2006).

## INDUSTRIALIZATION OF THE MEDIA

Since the new information order debate one of the most under-studied phenomena has been the divergence in the perspectives on media ethics between two very different types of professional associations advocating international press freedom. Because UNESCO's media initiatives were so threatening, a plethora of organizations were created, mainly in North America and Europe, with the expressed goal of defending freedom of the press. However, at the same time the media became increasingly industrialized. Newspapers especially evolved in the latter half of the 20th century from being small-scale enterprises, often family businesses, to being components of multi-million dollar corporations. So at the very time more voices developed to lobby for protection of the media from government threats, an even sharper distinction between two discrete, and often competing, logics of press freedom emerged. The most widely disseminated of these logics is what I call the "modernist" logic of the international press freedom lobby dominated by groups comprised largely of media owners and executives. The other is the "populist" logic of the much smaller number of organizations advocating on the behalf of reporters and other media workers.

By the early 21st century declining profitability had made it almost standard business practice to place newspapers and magazines into large conglomerates where individual outlets could benefit from synergies with other media, and where losses for the corporation in those sectors could be cushioned by gains in its other businesses. The Internet clearly speeded up the demise of traditional newspapers and magazines. However, the tendency for mass media to be part of big business was evident 20 years earlier. Cees J. Hamelink, in his classic *Finance and Information: A Study of Converging Interests*, observed that

> Conglomeration, integration, interlocking and concentration all point to the conclusion that the transnational information-industrial complex knows no free market or open competition. This is very large business for very large corporations only. (Hamelink 1983, 37)

Hamelink believed that the interlocking directorships of media corporations, banks and key firms of the military-industrial complex compromised journalistic integrity. He wondered, "Are the media capable of criticizing the power elites and society's differential access to its basic resources, or do the interlocks limit their role to maintaining and legitimizing social inequality" (Hamelink 1983, 102).

The steady concentration of media ownership into fewer and fewer hands had a profound effect on intellectual rumination about the international political economy of the media as an institution. Scholars documented the trend and its consequences (McChesney 1999; Herman & Chomsky 2002). So, in contrast to the new information order years, there was less focus on the power of an elite group of states and more attention to a small group of transnational firms, not allied necessarily to the political ideology of a particular state but more committed to a neo-liberal international political economy. Critics argued that under neo-liberalism information and culture were treated no differently than commodities and manufactured goods. The World Summit on the Information Society (WSIS) process was meant to give a hearing to these concerns and to find alternative strategies that would be more equitable and sustainable for the world (Servaes, Carpentier et al. 2006).

The concerns about conglomeration and concentration notwithstanding, it can be argued that the most intellectually challenging result of these trends has been the impact on the very conception of press freedom. The modernist press freedom logic of the proprietors and media executives argues that: media independent of government control are preferable in order to sustain democracies; mass media are representatives of the people; repression of mass media is repression of public expression; the health of independent media is a key gauge of the welfare of liberal democracies. This discursive construction of press freedom is evident in a long list of lobbyist groups, many of which were founded in the wake of the new information order. They include: the World Press Freedom Committee (WPFC), Freedom House, The Freedom Forum, the Commonwealth Press Union (CPU), Article 19, the Inter-American Press Association (IAPA), Canadian Journalists for Free Expression (formerly the Canadian Committee to Protect Journalists), the International Freedom of Expression Exchange, the International Press Institute (IPI), the Committee to Protect Journalists (CPJ), Human Rights Watch, and the World Association of Newspapers (WAN).

The WPFC's 1981 Declaration of Talloires and 1987 Charter for a Free Press, and the IAPA's 1994 Declaration of Chapultepec all had three features in common. They conflated freedom of the press with individual freedom. They asserted that there were no acceptable grounds for censorship of any kind. And they had a singular focus of attack on government restrictions on press freedom.

The populist logic of Reporters Sans Frontières, Index on Censorship, and the International Federation of Journalists provide a very different take on press freedom. They isolate the interests of media owners for scrutiny and assert that the interests of media owners are not necessarily the same as those of media workers and the general public. They believe that there must be public scrutiny of media organizations, just like other capitalist institutions. This position also tolerates some restrictions on the press in the interest of fostering democracy.

Of the three bodies the IFJ is the most strident in advocating a critique of media industrialization and concentration. For example, at its twenty-fifth Congress in 2004 it approved a resolution that said

> International organizations through the United Nations should respect the principle of freedom of information and apply rigorous anti-trust policies to regulate the world media market, to limit media concentration and to prevent the growth of ubiquitous monopolies. In order to ensure real conditions of pluralism in the various national, regional and linguistic sectors, there should be international rules governing media cross ownership and respect for national agreements and charters of social, cultural and professional rights of employees. (IFJ 2004)

The same resolution also called for a "fight against laws or regulations that strengthen media concentration, or weaken existing antitrust rules, or damage public broadcasting, or subordinate information to commercial and advertising interests."

This ideological divide between the populist and modernist approaches to press freedom is significant because it structures the relations of divergent sectors of the international press freedom lobby with the international political system. For example, while some groups like the WPFC remain skeptical of the entire UN project and its internationalism, the IFJ promotes itself as the voice for journalists at the UN and even commits itself to promoting UN projects, such as the UN's global media initiative to combat AIDS (IFJ 2004, Resolution 26, HIV-AIDS). Similarly, the implications of media concentration for democracy go largely uninterrogated by groups such as the IAPA in favor of a libertarian ideology that fails to even interrogate class, racial and other biases of the media. Libertarian media lobby groups have also shown a much greater willingness to criticize socialist governments than administrations on the right of the political spectrum. So while Index on Censorship focused attention on the compromise of civil liberties by the Bush and Blair administrations' "war on terror" through the publication of critiques by such left intellectuals as Noam Chomsky and John Pilger, international libertarian press freedom groups paid more attention to such administrations as Cuba, Venezuela and North Korea. In other words, there are competing visions of press freedom as a component of democracy-building (Plaisance 2005).

## THE QUESTIONABLE UN PROJECT

Of course, the very fact that there became a plethora of non-governmental organizations (NGOs) devoted to press freedom was as much a consequence of lack of confidence in the UN as it was a manifestation of the UN's success in propagating internationally the idea of human rights. In the 1970s and 1980s the UN's proposed NWICO had literally sent shock waves through media elite circles around the world. The WPFC was founded to challenge it, and its Declaration of Talloires was the product of a "Voices of Freedom" conference of several media groups from around the world that was convened by the WPFC to demonstrate a united front against UNESCO's supposed threat to press freedom.

In 2007, several years after the demise of the NWICO at UNESCO, the WPFC still declared on its website that it was unique among press freedom groups because its major objective was to monitor "threats that develop at UNESCO, the UN and other leading intergovernmental organizations." The Committee also described itself as a "watchdog for free news media at UNESCO, the UN, OSCE, Council of Europe, European Union, UN Commission on Human Rights and other international meetings considering free-press issues"(WPFC 2007).

This suspicion of international institutions, and the UN in particular, is based on the particular conundrum that confronts activists for the implementation of binding international laws and norms to guarantee freedom of the press. A fundamental principle of the post-World War II international order that gave the world the Universal Declaration of Human Rights and the two covenants that it spawned was state sovereignty. Only states have had the privilege of being able to form and join the international organizations that create international law. However, as was argued in the previous section, the vast majority of international press freedom NGOs focus on the state as the major threat to press freedom. So when the international press freedom lobby merely mentions the concept of "human rights" it is ironically deploying a construct of the states system to argue against the abuse of state power.

Of course, there is more to this dynamic than a mere suspicion of states and the international institutions they produced. A lasting contribution of the NWICO debate has been its inspiration of intellectual reflection on the evolution of the international organization in the post-World War II period. When the UN Secretariat, UNESCO and most of the other parts of the UN system were established the political configuration of the world was vastly different from what it would become even 30 years later. The Allied Powers, which conceived of UNESCO as a vehicle for the propagation of the ideas of the French Enlightenment around the world as the best intellectual basis for peace and social progress, rapidly became numerical minorities in the UN system when decolonization took off in the 1950s and 1960s. Although they were outnumbered by coalitions of former colonies, such as the Non-Aligned Movement and the Group of 77, they still held power and privilege through permanent membership of the UN Security Council and the veto power that came with it. However, the UN and UNESCO were far different creatures from what they were conceived to be in the late 1940s. These states found themselves on the defensive against demands from the expanded membership of the international system that argued for such ideas as "national self determination", a New International Economic Order, and the NWICO. The promotion of the value of the Enlightenment seemed hypocritical when compared to support for apartheid. One UN General Assembly resolution labeled Zionism a form of racism.

Therefore, when the WPFC cast a weary eye on the UN and invested heavily in journalism training programs in many of the countries that had supported the NWICO it was being suspicious not so much of what the UN project was but what it had become. To many in the United States in particular the UN had become an unruly entity, beyond the control of the powers that set it up, no longer reliable to pursue the ideological agenda they envisioned for it (Preston, Herman et al. 1989).

This problem leaves the larger dilemma of how to create international law and norms for press freedom when there is no trust in the sole mechanism in place to do such work in the world political order.

## MEDIA ETHICS AND WORLD ORDER

In his analysis of right-wing Venezuelan media complicity in the brief overthrow of the democratically elected administration of Hugo Chávez, American political scientist Dan Hellinger noted consideration of media ethics at the domestic level should not be divorced from its context within an evolving global political economy. The globalization of neo-liberal ideology had consequences for the way certain media and particular journalists did their work.

> The chavista agenda of change inevitably places him in conflict with the highly globalized media. Chávez has proclaimed himself an opponent of economic globalization and the uncontested hegemony of the United States. Venezuela's media barons preside over enterprises linked in many ways to national and global economic forces and communications. So, the media responds in kind, almost welcoming indiscreet condemnations as evidence that they are merely defending democracy. (Hellinger 2003)

The situation in Venezuela that Hellinger described was a case study in the evolution of the political economy of the mass media about which Hamelink had warned 20 years earlier. However, the difference between 2003 and 1983 was that Hamelink's analysis had been somewhat limited to a discrete analysis of what had happened to information industries, especially the media. However, Hellinger widened the study of media ethics to argue that scholars cannot achieve a comprehensive understanding of how the media does its work (especially ideologically) without understanding media as a key element in a wider transnational discourse on the nature of the international system. When Hamelink completed his study in the early 1980s the global debt crisis was already in motion, but its full consequences had not yet been seen. The severely indebted countries had to be bailed out by the World Bank and International Monetary Fund (IMF). But these two powerful international institutions insisted that the indebted countries had to implement "structural adjustment" policies that were in effect guidelines for how to make capitalism the preferred economic model. Structural adjustment advocated an end to large state enterprises and monopolies, especially in telecommunications. They promoted the "free market" as the best means of allocating resources, thereby enhancing the power of private firms and investment capital (George and Sabelli 1994). The creation of the World Trade Organization (WTO) in 1994 accelerated this process because it increased pressure on all states to embrace free trade, if they wished to participate fully in the international economy.

Because media corporations were increasingly part of larger and larger transnational corporations and conglomerates, neo-liberalism directly affected their fortunes. Indeed, the American intellectual property industries (especially in film, music and computer software) were among the most strident advocates for the WTO and the envisioned increased protection the WTO would provide against piracy because the WTO could make enforcement of copyright protection a condition for getting "Most Favored Nation" status and easier access to foreign markets (International Intellectual Property Alliance 1997).

Neo-liberalism also raised the level of participation by private firms in the international organizations that regulate the international political economy. For example, the exclusion of private firms from membership in international organizations (because they did not have standing as sovereign states) was ended in 1998 when the ITU extended membership to firms.

At the turn of the century the electoral popularity of populist, socialistic politicians in Latin America, such as Chávez and Evo Morales of Bolivia, put these governments on a collision course not only with the forces of neo-liberalism but also their domestic capitalist oligarchies. These classes had traditionally owned or controlled the press.

The logic that the press is synonymous with "the people", so popular with the majority of international press freedom NGOs, is difficult to sustain, especially in reference to Latin America. The Venezuelan coup made this evident. However, anti-Chávez media, independent of the government but not independent of oligarchic interest, were able to indulge in biased reporting and later shield themselves behind the banner of press freedom. Restrictions on press freedom or attempts to respond to powerful media bias by the Chávez government were quickly identified as government clamp-downs and ominous signs for the press everywhere by international press freedom groups, especially the IAPA (Hellinger 2003, 25).

## CONCLUSION

The analysis presented here has been an attempt to enhance the literature on international media ethics by putting the problem of transnational norm-setting in wider historical and theoretical context. What can be described as an international press freedom lobby is by no means a monolithic entity. Contrary to one popular belief, the transnational discourse on freedom of expression and civil liberties became more diverse at the dawn of the new century rather than more unilinear in favor of liberal or libertarian ideology. The central point of the position set out here is that media ethics as an international problem should not be seen as a matter of special interests, but as central to the very way international politics is conducted. This approach does not foster optimism that the much-desired international standard will be found any time soon, or that it will ever be achieved.

## REFERENCES

Alleyne, M. D. (1997). *News revolution: political and economic decisions about global information*. New York: St. Martin's Press.

Alleyne, M. D. (2003). *Global lies? Propaganda, the UN, and world order*. Houndmills, Basingstoke, UK: Palgrave Macmillan.

Caldwell, C. (2006). The reality of cartoon violence. *Financial Times*: 11.

Christians, C. G., J. P. Ferré et al. (1993). *Good news: Social ethics and the press*. New York, Oxford University Press.

Editorial. (2006). "Hateful hypocrisy over cartoons." *Knight Ridder Tribune Business News: 1.*

Fenby, J. (1986). *The international news services*. New York: Schocken Books.

George, S. and F. Sabelli (1994). *Faith and credit: The World Bank's secular empire*. Boulder, CO: Westview Press.

Goodnough, A. (2006). U.S. Paid 10 Journalists for Anti-Castro Reports. *New York Times*: A.9.

Goss, B. M. (2002). "Deeply concerned about the welfare of the Iraqi people": The sanctions regime against Iraq in the New York Times (1996–1998). *Journalism Studies* 3(1): 83–99.

Hamelink, C. J. (1983). *Finance and information: A study of converging interests*. Norwood, NJ: Ablex.

Hellinger, D. (2003). Media mayhem: Violence in Venezuela sparked by press. *St. Louis Journalism Review* 33(253): 24.

Herman, E. S. and N. Chomsky (2002). *Manufacturing consent: The political economy of the mass media*. New York: Pantheon Books.

International Commission for the Study of Communication Problems and S. MacBride (1980). *Many voices, one world: towards a new more just and more efficient world information and communication order.* London: Kogan Page; New York: Unipub.

International Federation of Journalists (IFJ). (2004). Resolutions adopted by IFJ World Congress 2004. Retrieved March 21, 2007, from http://www.ifj.org/default.asp?index=2554&Language=EN.

International Intellectual Property Alliance. (1997). *Estimates of 1995 U.S. trade losses due to foreign piracy and levels of piracy.* Washington, D.C.: The Alliance.

Kumar, D. (2006). Media, war, and propaganda: Strategies of information management during the 2003 Iraq War. *Communication & Critical/Cultural Studies* 3(1): 48–69.

Lehmann, I. A. (1999). *Peacekeeping and public information: Caught in the crossfire.* London; Portland, OR: F. Cass.

McChesney, R. W. (1999). *Rich media, poor democracy: Communication politics in dubious times.* Urbana: University of Illinois Press.

Merzer, M. (2006). Herald publisher resigns: The publisher of The Miami Herald and El Nuevo Herald stepped down today and reversed recent firings of writers at El Nuevo Herald. *Knight Ridder Tribune Business News*: 1.

Mills, K. (2004). *Changing channels: The civil rights case that transformed television.* Jackson, MS: University Press of Mississippi.

Nordenstreng, K., E. González Manet, et al. (1986). *New international information and communication order: Sourcebook.* Prague: International Organization of Journalists.

Olson, K. D. (2006). "Cuba controversy." *News Media and the Law* 30(4): 24.

Plaisance, P. L. (2005). The mass media as discursive network: Building on the implications of libertarian and communitarian claims for news media ethics theory. *Communication Theory* 15(3): 292–313.

Preston, W., E. S. Herman et al. (1989). *Hope and folly: The United States and UNESCO, 1945–1985.* Minneapolis: University of Minnesota Press.

Rao, S. and L. Seow Ting (2005). Globalizing media ethics? An assessment of universal ethics among international political journalists." *Journal of Mass Media Ethics* 20(2/3): 99–120.

Righter, R. (1978). *Whose news? : Politics, the press, and the Third World.* New York, Times Books.

Servaes, J., N. Carpentier et al. (2006). *Towards a sustainable information society: Deconstructing WSIS.* Bristol, UK; Portland, OR: Intellect.

Sheikh, F. (2006). Mideast: Western-style freedoms on trial in cartoon furor. *Global Information Network*: 1.

Siebert, F. S. (1956). *Four theories of the press: the authoritarian, libertarian, social responsibility, and Soviet communist concepts of what the press should be and do.* Urbana: University of Illinois Press.

Smith, A. (1980). *The geopolitics of information: How Western culture dominates the world.* New York: Oxford University Press.

Tehranian, M. (2002). Peace journalism: Negotiating global media ethics. *Harvard International Journal of Press/Politics* 7(2): 58.

UNESCO. (1979). *Declaration on fundamental principles concerning the contribution of the mass media to strengthening peace and international understanding, to the promotion of human rights, and to countering racialism, apartheid and incitement to war.* Paris: UNESCO.

Van Liedekerke, L. (2004). Media ethics: From corporate governance to governance, to corporate social responsibility. *Communications: The European Journal of Communication Research* 29(1): 27–42.

World Press Freedom Committee (WPFC). (2007). Welcome to the World Press Freedom Committee.

# Index